BEST CUSTOMERS

DEMOGRAPHICS OF CONSUMER DEMAND

T0642672

BEST
CUSTOMERS

DEMOGRAPHICS OF CONSUMER DEMAND

LAS POSITAS COLLEGE LIBRARY
3000 CAMPUS HILL DRIVE
LIVERMORE, CA 94551

WITHDRAWN

New Strategist Press, LLC
Amityville, New York

117.46

Ref.
HC
100
C6
B47
2014

New Strategist Press, LLC.
P.O. Box 635, Amityville, New York 11701
800/848-0842; 631/608-8795
www.newstrategist.com

© 2014. NEW STRATEGIST PRESS, LLC.

All rights reserved.

No part of this book may be reproduced, stored in a retrieval system, or transmitted in any form or by any means, electronic, mechanical, photocopying, microfilming, recording, or otherwise without written permission from the Publisher.

Printed in the United States of America.

ISBN 978-1-940308-41-8 (hardcover)
ISBN 978-1-940308-42-5 (paper)
ISBN 978-1-940308-43-2 (ebook)

√

Table of Contents

Introduction

Welcome to the 10th edition of *Best Customers: Demographics of Consumer Demand*, a unique examination of how changing demographics are reshaping the consumer marketplace. *Best Customers* reveals who the best and biggest customers are for hundreds of individual products and services, alerting marketers to potential booms and busts in the years ahead.

Based on data from the Bureau of Labor Statistics' 2012 Consumer Expenditure Survey, *Best Customers* examines spending patterns by the demographic characteristics of households. For most consumer products and services, demographics drive demand. *Best Customers* analyzes household spending on more than 300 products and services by age of householder, household income, household type, race and Hispanic origin of householder, region of residence, and educational attainment of householder. It identifies which households spend the most on a product or service (the best customers) and which control the largest share of spending (the biggest customers).

Household demographics are not static, but ever changing, influencing the consumer market during good times and bad. Today, the aging of the population is one of the most important factors in determining consumer demand. The rapid growth of the Asian, black, and Hispanic populations makes their spending ever more important to business success. Education, living arrangements, and geography also determine who spends what—critical information as the consumer marketplace becomes increasingly competitive. *Best Customers* reveals the demographic trends behind spending, allowing marketers to prepare for what lies ahead.

Demographic Trends

Two demographic trends are key to today's consumer markets: the aging of the baby-boom generation and the rise of Asian, black, and Hispanic consumers.

Born between 1946 and 1964, the baby-boom generation spanned the ages of 48 through 66 in 2012. As boomers filled the 55-to-64 age group during the past decade, the percentage of households headed by empty-nesters grew each year. Having children leave home is one of life's major transitions, and spending patterns change accordingly. Empty-nesters spend less on groceries, for example, and more on meals in full-service restaurants. Spending on alcoholic beverages increases after the teetotaler years of child rearing. Empty-nesters are the biggest spenders on travel. And instead of buying children's clothes, they devote more to men's and women's apparel. Although boomers were severely affected by the Great Recession, their financial problems are going to make them even more important consumers in the years ahead. Millions of two-earner baby-boom couples in their peak earning years will remain in the labor force longer than they had expected. This should boost the incomes and spending power of older Americans, delaying the shift to a reduced standard of living after retirement. An understanding of the spending patterns of these older Americans is vital to staying afloat during the coming years.

Asians, blacks, Hispanics, and other minorities account for a growing share of the nation's population. In 2012, the 5.4 million Asian, 15.6 million black, and 15.6 million Hispanic consumer units accounted for 29 percent of the national total and for 25 percent of household spending. The average Asian household has a higher income and spends more money than the average non-Hispanic white household. Although the incomes and spending of blacks and Hispanics are below average, both groups spend much more than average on many individual products and services. The distinct spending patterns of Asians, blacks, and Hispanics make them a major force in many consumer markets. As competition for customers becomes ever more heated, effective wooing of Asians, blacks, and Hispanics has never been more important.

How to Use This Book

Best Customers is divided into 21 chapters, arranged alphabetically, each focusing on a major spending category as defined by the Bureau of Labor Statistics—such as entertainment, groceries (or what the bureau calls "food at home"), transportation, and so on. Within each chapter, individual products and services are arranged alphabetically. Three chapters of *Best Customers*—computers, telephone, and travel—are unique groupings produced by New Strategist to highlight important spending patterns. The Bureau of Labor Statistics includes computer and telephone spending in its housing category, and it groups the various travel items into the entertainment, food, housing, and transportation categories.

Most individual products and services included in the Consumer Expenditure Survey are analyzed in *Best Customers*. Two types of items are excluded from the book: "other" categories, such as "other food at home," for which an analysis of spending patterns cannot provide meaningful conclusions; and products and services with spending data considered unreliable by New Strategist because of small sample sizes.

Each table in *Best Customers* analyzes household spending on a particular product or service, showing average spending, indexed spending, and market share of spending by age of householder, household income, household type, race and Hispanic origin of householder, region of residence, and educational attainment of householder. New Strategist has calculated the indexes and market shares to reveal the trends. Text accompanies each table that identifies the best and biggest customers, analyzes spending patterns, describes spending trends for the product over the past few years, and predicts future trends based on the nation's changing demographics.

Spending Data

Best Customers is based on unpublished, detailed data collected by the Bureau of Labor Statistics' Consumer Expenditure Survey, an ongoing, nationwide survey of household spending. A complete accounting of household expenditures, the Consumer Expenditure Survey includes everything from big-ticket items such as homes and cars to small purchases like laundry detergent and video games. The survey does not include expenditures by government, business, or nonprofit institutions.

The Consumer Expenditure Survey uses consumer unit rather than household as its sampling unit. In this book, the terms "consumer unit" and "household" are used interchangeably. The Bureau of Labor Statistics defines "consumer unit" as "a single person or group of persons in a sample household related by blood, marriage, adoption or other legal arrangement or who share responsibility for at least two out of three major types of expenses—food, housing, and other expenses." For more information about the Consumer Expenditure Survey and consumer units, see Appendix A.

• **Average Spending.** The average spending figures in *Best Customers* are unpublished data from the Bureau of Labor Statistics' 2012 Consumer Expenditure Survey. The Bureau of Labor Statistics calculates average spending for all households in a segment, not just for those who bought an item. When examining the averages, it is important to remember that by including both purchasers and nonpurchasers in the calculation, the average spending amount is often greatly reduced—especially for infrequently purchased items. For example, the average household spent $237 on day care centers, nursery schools, and preschools in 2012. Since only a small percentage of households spends money on day care, this figure greatly underestimates the amount spent on day care centers by those who use them. To get a more realistic picture of how much buyers spend on an item, Appendix B shows the percentage of households that purchased individual products and services during the average quarter of 2012, and the amount purchasers spent per quarter. According to Appendix B, only 4.4 percent of households spent on day care centers during the average quarter of 2012. The purchasers spent an average of $1,335 per quarter, for an estimated annual cost of $5,340—a much more realistic figure than the average of $237 for all households. For frequently purchased items—such as bread—the average spending figures give a fairly accurate account of actual spending. But for most of the products and services examined in *Best Customers*, average spending figures are less revealing than indexes and market shares.

Average spending figures are useful for determining the market potential of a product or service in a local area. By multiplying the average amount married couples spend on children's clothing by the number of married couple households in the San Diego metropolitan area, for example, marketers can estimate the size of the market for children's clothing in San Diego. The San Diego media could show those figures to potential advertisers to prove the demand for children's clothing in the area. (Note: Because of sampling errors, average values can vary—especially for infrequently purchased items.)

• **Indexed Spending (Best Customers).** Indexed spending figures compare the spending of demographic segments with that of the average household. To compute the indexes, New Strategist's statisticians divide the amount a household segment spends on a particular item by how much the average household spends on the item, and then multiply the resulting figure by 100. An index of 100 is the average for all households. An index of 125 means average spending by households in a segment is 25 percent above average (100 plus 25). An index of 80 means average spending by households in a segment is 20 percent below average (100 minus 20).

Spending indexes can reveal hidden markets—household segments with a high propensity to buy a particular product or service but which are overshadowed by larger household segments that account for a bigger share of the total market. Householders aged 65 to 74, for example, account for 15 percent of the market for full-service breakfasts, less than the 18 percent share accounted for by householders aged 35 to 44. But a look at the indexed spending figures reveals that, in fact, the older householders are the better customers. Householders aged 65 to 74 spend 25 percent more than the average household on full-service breakfasts, while householders aged 35 to 44 spend just 3 percent more than the average household on this item. Using the index column in the spending tables, marketers can see that older householders are in fact their better customers and adjust their business strategy accordingly. (Note: Because of sampling errors, small differences in index values are usually insignificant. But the broader patterns revealed by indexes can guide marketers to the best customers.)

• **Market Share (Biggest Customers).** To calculate market share figures, New Strategist first determines the total amount all households spend on an item by multiplying average household spending on that item by the total number of consumer units (124,416,000). New Strategist then calculates total household spending for each demographic segment by multiplying the segment's average spending on an item by the number of households in the segment. To calculate the percentage of total spending on the item controlled by a demographic segment—i.e., its market share—New Strategist divides each segment's spending on the item by total household spending on the item.

In 2012, for example, college graduates accounted for 60 percent of total household spending on ship fares. The cruise industry could reach most of its customers if it targeted only this demographic segment. Of course, by single-mindedly targeting the biggest customers, businesses cannot nurture potential growth markets. An additional danger of focusing only on the biggest customers is that businesses may end up ignoring their best customers. This is especially problematic because market shares are unstable, thanks to baby booms and busts over the past half-century. In 2012, for example, householders aged 45 to 54 were one of the biggest customers of housekeeping services, controlling 23 percent of the market—but only because the age group was filled with the younger members of the large baby-boom generation. In fact, the best customers of housekeeping services are the oldest householders. Those aged 75 or older spend 92 percent more than the average household on housekeeping services, whereas the 45-to-54 age group spends only 15 percent more than average on this item. Although the older age group controls only 19 percent of the housekeeping services market today, the share will expand greatly as boomers age into their seventies. The best customers of housekeeping services will become the biggest customers as well. Marketers who ignore their best customers in favor of the biggest customers may end up with no customers.

• **Age of Householder.** Age is one of the best predictors of spending because lifestage determines most consumer wants and needs. Ongoing changes in the age structure of the population will have a profound effect on consumer spending. This is why *Best Customers* explores spending by age in so much detail, using it as the primary guide to consumer trends in the years ahead.

Changes in the size of age groups will dramatically affect spending in many categories over the next few years. The number of adults aged 35 to 44 will expand as millennials enter the age group, replacing the small generation X. Millennials have been postponing marriage and childbearing, suppressing spending on products and services for infants and young children. As millennials begin to play catch-up, look for spending on these items to rise. The small generation X is now filling the 45-to-54 age group, reducing the share of the consumer market controlled by the nation's most affluent households and biggest spenders. This could dampen average household spending overall. The large baby-boom generation has completely filled the 55-to-64 age group and the oldest boomers are approaching age 70. Millions are transitioning out of the workforce, which should boost spending on full-service restaurants, alcoholic beverages, and travel.

Not only will the sizes of age groups change but, as younger generations replace older ones, attitudes and behavior will also change. New Strategist takes into account not only the changing numbers, but also changing attitudes and lifestyles.

• **Household Income.** It is no surprise that the most affluent households spend the most. For most of the products and services examined in *Best Customers*, households with the highest incomes appear to be the best and biggest customers. Yet the story behind spending is more complex than income alone. Most spending is driven by lifestage (age) or lifestyle (household type), and secondarily by income. For that reason *Best Customers* identifies high-income households as the best and biggest customers only when income has an extraordinary effect on spending or when an item is a purely discretionary expense—such as spending on wine at restaurants and bars. While most businesses would do well to target the affluent, they will find it difficult to design a product or craft a message if they ignore the lifestage and lifestyle reasons for spending.

• **Household Type.** Household type is one of the most important determinants of spending for several reasons. The presence of children requires families to spend on products and services for children. Not only that, but households with children tend to include more people than those without children, and household size is an important determinant of spending. Because married couples head most of the nation's households, they account for the majority of spending in most categories. But single parents are important in some markets, and single-person households account for a large share of spending on many items. (Note: Market shares by household type do not sum to 100 percent because not all household types are shown.)

• **Race and Hispanic Origin of Householder.** The Bureau of Labor Statistics classifies households by the self-identified race and Hispanic origin of the householder. The bureau classifies households into three racial groups: Asian, black, and "white and other," where "other" includes Alaska Natives, American Indians, and Native Hawaiians and other Pacific Islanders as well as those who report more than one race. Because Hispanics may be of any race, the bureau separately classifies all households into one of two Hispanic origin categories: Hispanic or non-Hispanic. Within the non-Hispanic origin group there are blacks and "whites and all other races," which in this classification include non-Hispanic Alaska Natives, American Indians, Asians, and Native Hawaiians and other Pacific Islanders as well as non-Hispanics reporting more than one race.

To simplify things for *Best Customers*, we narrowed the race and Hispanic origin categories to four: Asians (including Hispanic Asians), blacks (including Hispanic blacks), Hispanics (a group that also includes Hispanic Asians and blacks), and non-Hispanic whites and others (a group that also includes non-Hispanic Asians). Because there is overlap among the four race and Hispanic origin groups, numbers by race and Hispanic origin do not sum to the total.

On average, Asian households spend more than non-Hispanic white households, whereas black and Hispanic households spend less. But there is great variation by individual product and service category. Asians do not spend much on pets, for example. Blacks and Hispanics spend disproportionately on children's clothes.

The spending of Asians, blacks, and Hispanics differs from that of non-Hispanic whites for a variety of reasons. Asians are, on average, younger and better educated than non-Hispanic whites. Hispanic households are more likely to include children. Food preferences differ by race and Hispanic origin as well. Geographic location can influence purchasing patterns, and Asians and Hispanics are concentrated in the West, while most blacks live in the South. As the numbers of Asians, blacks, and Hispanics grow, their spending is becoming increasingly important to the nation's economy. Consequently it is important to understand spending patterns by race and Hispanic origin.

• **Region of Residence.** For many products and services, regional differences in spending are small. But for some items, spending differences by region are pronounced. There are several reasons for this, including differences in regional economies, climate, physical infrastructure, racial and ethnic composition, and access to resources. Differences in regional population growth rates also affect household spending patterns.

• **Educational Attainment of Householder.** The population is becoming increasingly educated, and the spending of educated consumers differs from that of those with less education. College graduates headed 32 percent of the nation's households in 2012. Because income rises directly with education, households headed by college graduates tend to spend more on most discretionary items than those headed by people who went no further than high school. Because older generations are less educated than younger ones, older Americans are overrepresented among householders with a high school diploma or less education. Consequently, the spending of less-educated householders reflects their older age. As well-educated boomers enter the older age groups in the years ahead, the spending of older Americans is going to change. This is one of the most important spending trends of the coming decade.

Appendices

Best Customers includes four appendices and a glossary of terms.

• **Appendix A** describes the Consumer Expenditure Survey in more detail and tells readers how to contact the Bureau of Labor Statistics.

• **Appendix B** shows the percentage of households that purchased the products and services examined in the Consumer Expenditure Survey during the average quarter of 2012. It also shows how much purchasers spent on items during the average quarter. In some cases, the quarterly spending figure alone is a good estimate of how much a typical purchaser spends. Take new cars, for example, which is a one-time rather than an ongoing expense. In the average quarter of 2012, 0.8 percent of households bought a new car, spending on average $22,767. (The Consumer Expenditure Survey counts the net cost of an item at the time of purchase, whether households pay for it at once or over time.) For ongoing expenses, however, the quarterly spending figure must be multiplied by four to get an estimate of how much households spend annually on the product or service. Forty-two percent of households bought women's clothes during the average quarter of 2012, for example, and spent $204 during the quarter. The annual spending of households that buy women's clothes can reasonably be estimated at four times $204, or $816. Appendix B not only supplies readers with invaluable insight into the propensity of households to buy individual products and services, but also provides a more realistic view of how much purchasers spend.

• **Appendix C** ranks products and services by the amount the average household spends on them, from highest to lowest. It shows which categories are most important to the household budget. The relative standing of products and services is often surprising. To know that gasoline is the fifth-biggest expense of the average household puts the media's focus on gasoline prices into perspective. The fact that out-of-pocket health insurance cost is the seventh-biggest household expense, ahead of property taxes and electricity, for example, explains why many households feel strapped by health care costs.

• **Appendix D** shows trends in household spending by major category between 2000 and 2012. During those years, spending by the average household rose a tiny 1 percent, after adjusting for inflation. But this small gain between 2000 and 2012 masks the spending ups and downs that took place during those years. Average household spending increased 9 percent between 2000 and 2006 (the year overall household spending peaked), then fell 8 percent between 2006 and 2010 (the year overall household spending bottomed out) as the Great Recession took hold, and rose again, by 2 percent, between 2010 and 2012. Households cut their spending deeply on many items during the past few years, revealing American households to be cautious spenders. This caution can be seen in the spending trends for many of the individual products and services analyzed in *Best Customers*.

For More Information

The 10th edition of *Best Customers* examines the demographics of spending on individual products and services and describes how changing demographics will boost or reduce average household spending in the future. To compare and contrast spending patterns on the entire range of goods and services included in the Consumer Expenditure Survey, see the companion volume, the 19th edition of *Household Spending: Who Spends How Much on What*. For analysis of household spending trends by single product category, see New Strategist's Who's Buying reports.

To find out more about these books and reports and to view tables of contents and sample pages, visit New Strategist's web site at http://www.newstrategist.com. All New Strategist books and reports are available in print or as downloads with links to the Excel version of each table.

Chapter 1.
Alcoholic Beverages

Household Spending on Alcoholic Beverages, 2000 to 2012

The average household spent $451 on alcoholic beverages in 2012, 9 percent less than in 2000 after adjusting for inflation. Spending on alcoholic beverages climbed by a substantial 14 percent between 2000 and 2006 (the year when household spending peaked), and then fell 23 percent between 2006 and 2010 as the recession took hold. In the two years since the overall household spending trough year of 2010, spending on alcohol grew by 4 percent. (See Appendix D for overall household spending trends.) Behind the earlier increase was the aging of the baby-boom generation into the empty-nest lifestage, when spending on alcoholic beverages rises.

Alcoholic beverage spending is changing. While the largest share of the alcoholic beverage dollar is still devoted to beer (42 percent), the figure is lower than the 47 percent of 2000. Wine accounted for 30 percent of the alcoholic beverage budget in 2012, up from 26 percent in 2000. Whiskey and other alcoholic beverages accounted for 18 percent of the budget in 2012, about the same as in 2000.

Spending on alcoholic beverages

(average annual spending of households on alcoholic beverages, 2000, 2006, 2010, and 2012; in 2012 dollars)

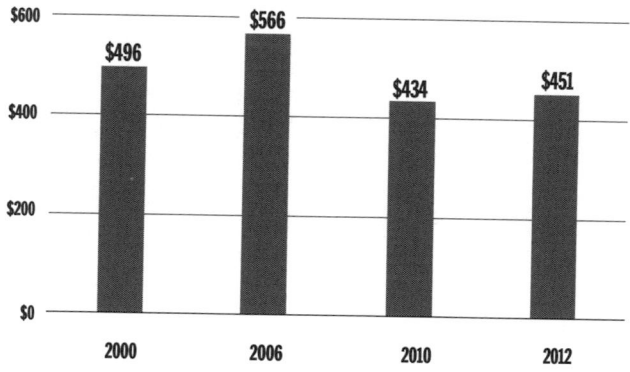

Table 1.1 Alcoholic beverage spending, 2000 to 2012

(average annual and percent distribution of household spending on alcoholic beverages by category, 2000 to 2012; percent change and percentage point change in spending, 2000–06, 2006–12, and 2010–12; in 2012 dollars; ranked by amount spent)

	average annual household spending (in 2012$)				percent change		
	2012	2010	2006	2000	2010–12	2006–12	2000–06
Average household spending on alcoholic beverages	$451.16	$433.77	$566.08	$495.73	4.0%	−20.3%	14.2%
Beer and ale	188.43	174.56	237.62	232.62	7.9	−20.7	2.2
Beer and ale at home	112.49	108.27	141.04	149.34	3.9	−20.2	−5.6
Beer and ale at restaurants, bars	75.94	66.29	96.59	83.28	14.6	−21.4	16.0
Wine	137.16	127.39	164.44	130.44	7.7	−16.6	26.1
Wine at home	102.62	92.33	117.04	106.72	11.1	−12.3	9.7
Wine at restaurants, bars	34.54	35.06	47.40	23.72	−1.5	−27.1	99.8
Whiskey and other alcohol	81.76	86.84	114.63	87.02	−5.9	−28.7	31.7
Whiskey and other alcohol at restaurants, bars	47.43	54.02	73.91	40.91	−12.2	−35.8	80.7
Whiskey and other alcohol at home	34.33	32.82	40.71	46.12	4.6	−15.7	−11.7
Alcoholic beverages on trips	43.80	44.97	49.38	45.65	−2.6	−11.3	8.2

					percentage point change		
PERCENT DISTRIBUTION OF SPENDING	2012	2010	2006	2000	2010–12	2006–12	2000–06
Average household spending on alcoholic beverages	100.0%	100.0%	100.0%	100.0%	–	–	–
Beer and ale	41.8	40.2	42.0	46.9	1.5	−0.2	−4.9
Beer and ale at home	24.9	25.0	24.9	30.1	0.0	0.0	−5.2
Beer and ale at restaurants, bars	16.8	15.3	17.1	16.8	1.5	−0.2	0.3
Wine	30.4	29.4	29.0	26.3	1.0	1.4	2.7
Wine at home	22.7	21.3	20.7	21.5	1.5	2.1	−0.9
Wine at restaurants, bars	7.7	8.1	8.4	4.8	−0.4	−0.7	3.6
Whiskey and other alcohol	18.1	20.0	20.2	17.6	−1.9	−2.1	2.7
Whiskey and other alcohol at restaurants, bars	10.5	12.5	13.1	8.3	−1.9	−2.5	4.8
Whiskey and other alcohol at home	7.6	7.6	7.2	9.3	0.0	0.4	−2.1
Alcoholic beverages on trips	9.7	10.4	8.7	9.2	−0.7	1.0	−0.5

Note: Percentage point change calculations are based on unrounded figures. "–" means not applicable.
Source: Bureau of Labor Statistics, 2000, 2006, 2010. and 2012 Consumer Expenditure Surveys; calculations by New Strategist

Alcoholic Beverages Purchased on Trips

Best customers: Householders aged 55 to 64
                   Married couples without children at home
                   Non-Hispanic whites
                   Households in the West
                   College graduates

Customer trends: Average household spending on alcoholic beverages purchased on trips should begin to grow again
                   as boomers retire and spend more time and money traveling.

The biggest spenders on alcoholic beverages purchased on trips can be found in a variety of demographic categories. Householders aged 55 to 64 spend 20 percent more than average on this item. Married couples without children at home (most of them older) spend 77 percent more than average on alcoholic beverages while on trips. These empty-nesters spend more than other household types on alcoholic beverages while traveling because they no longer need to devote their time and money to children's wants and needs. Non-Hispanic whites spend 19 percent more than average on alcoholic beverages while traveling and constitute 90 percent of the market. Households in the West spend 19 percent more than average on alcohol while traveling. College graduates spend twice the average on this item.

Average household spending on alcoholic beverages purchased on trips grew by 8 percent between 2000 and 2006, after adjusting for inflation, then fell 11 percent between 2006 and 2012. Behind the decline was the Great Recession, which reduced spending on travel. In the years ahead, spending on this item should rise again as boomers retire and spend more time and money traveling.

Table 1.2 Alcoholic beverages purchased on trips

Total household spending $5,449,420,800.00
Average household spends   43.80

AGE OF HOUSEHOLDER	AVERAGE HOUSEHOLD SPENDING	BEST CUSTOMERS (index)	BIGGEST CUSTOMERS (market share)
Average household	$43.80	100	100.0%
Under age 25	22.58	52	3.4
Aged 25 to 34	49.77	114	18.4
Aged 35 to 44	44.83	102	17.8
Aged 45 to 54	48.53	111	21.9
Aged 55 to 64	52.39	120	21.9
Aged 65 to 74	43.50	99	12.0
Aged 75 or older	21.08	48	4.7

	AVERAGE HOUSEHOLD SPENDING	BEST CUSTOMERS (index)	BIGGEST CUSTOMERS (market share)
HOUSEHOLD INCOME			
Average household	**$43.80**	**100**	**100.0%**
Under $20,000	10.62	24	5.1
$20,000 to $39,999	14.22	32	7.3
$40,000 to $49,999	27.11	62	5.5
$50,000 to $69,999	36.90	84	12.2
$70,000 to $79,999	42.62	97	5.4
$80,000 to $99,999	68.80	157	13.9
$100,000 or more	118.51	271	50.7
HOUSEHOLD TYPE			
Average household	**43.80**	**100**	**100.0**
Married couples	59.60	136	66.1
Married couples, no children	77.66	177	37.0
Married couples with children	48.43	111	26.0
Oldest child under age 6	49.77	114	5.2
Oldest child aged 6 to 17	49.47	113	13.4
Oldest child aged 18 or older	45.79	105	7.4
Single parent with child under age 18	14.50	33	1.7
Single person	29.67	68	20.1
RACE AND HISPANIC ORIGIN			
Average household	**43.80**	**100**	**100.0**
Asian	37.59	86	3.7
Black	14.51	33	4.2
Hispanic	21.94	50	6.3
Non-Hispanic white and other	52.29	119	89.6
REGION			
Average household	**43.80**	**100**	**100.0**
Northeast	47.75	109	19.7
Midwest	44.25	101	22.4
South	36.64	84	31.2
West	52.05	119	26.8
EDUCATION			
Average household	**43.80**	**100**	**100.0**
Less than high school graduate	8.20	19	2.4
High school graduate	17.72	40	10.1
Some college	35.62	81	16.7
Associate's degree	32.09	73	7.2
Bachelor's degree or more	88.17	201	63.5
Bachelor's degree	80.37	183	36.6
Master's, professional, doctoral degree	101.58	232	26.9

Note: Market shares may not sum to 100.0 because of rounding and missing categories by household type. "Asian" and "black" include Hispanics and non-Hispanics who identify themselves as being of the respective race alone. "Hispanic" includes people of any race who identify themselves as Hispanic. "Other" includes people who identify themselves as non-Hispanic and as Alaska Native, American Indian, Asian (who are also included in the "Asian" row), or Native Hawaiian or other Pacific Islander, as well as non-Hispanics reporting more than one race.
Source: Calculations by New Strategist based on the Bureau of Labor Statistics' 2012 Consumer Expenditure Survey

Beer and Ale at Home

Best customers: Householders aged 25 to 34
Married couples with preschoolers
Hispanics
Households in the Midwest

Customer trends: Average household spending on beer and ale consumed at home should grow in the years ahead
as the millennial generation marries, has children, and spends more time at home.

Because beer and ale consumed at home is such a common purchase, average household spending on this item does not vary all that much by demographic segment. Householders aged 25 to 34 spend 38 percent more than the average household on beer and ale for home consumption. Married couples with preschoolers outspend the average by one-quarter, and Hispanics spend 12 percent more than average on beer and ale at home despite their lower incomes. Spending by households in the Midwest surpasses the average by 12 percent.

Average household spending on beer and ale consumed at home was falling before the Great Recession, and the economic downturn accelerated the decline. But spending on this item grew 4 percent between 2010 and 2012 as recovery began. Spending on beer and ale consumed at home should grow in the years ahead as the millennial generation marries, has children, and spends more time at home.

Table 1.3 Beer and ale at home

Total household spending	$13,995,555,840.00
Average household spends	112.49

	AVERAGE HOUSEHOLD SPENDING	BEST CUSTOMERS (index)	BIGGEST CUSTOMERS (market share)
AGE OF HOUSEHOLDER			
Average household	**$112.49**	**100**	**100.0%**
Under age 25	118.71	106	6.9
Aged 25 to 34	155.10	138	22.3
Aged 35 to 44	120.78	107	18.6
Aged 45 to 54	125.06	111	22.0
Aged 55 to 64	113.35	101	18.4
Aged 65 to 74	74.26	66	8.0
Aged 75 or older	38.53	34	3.3

	AVERAGE HOUSEHOLD SPENDING	BEST CUSTOMERS (index)	BIGGEST CUSTOMERS (market share)
HOUSEHOLD INCOME			
Average household	**$112.49**	**100**	**100.0%**
Under $20,000	54.40	48	10.2
$20,000 to $39,999	95.25	85	19.1
$40,000 to $49,999	97.92	87	7.7
$50,000 to $69,999	123.75	110	15.9
$70,000 to $79,999	129.01	115	6.4
$80,000 to $99,999	187.62	167	14.7
$100,000 or more	156.11	139	26.0
HOUSEHOLD TYPE			
Average household	**112.49**	**100**	**100.0**
Married couples	129.09	115	55.7
Married couples, no children	131.44	117	24.4
Married couples with children	119.37	106	24.9
Oldest child under age 6	140.40	125	5.7
Oldest child aged 6 to 17	116.56	104	12.3
Oldest child aged 18 or older	110.95	99	7.0
Single parent with child under age 18	59.83	53	2.8
Single person	85.39	76	22.5
RACE AND HISPANIC ORIGIN			
Average household	**112.49**	**100**	**100.0**
Asian	97.00	86	3.7
Black	69.90	62	7.8
Hispanic	126.17	112	14.1
Non-Hispanic white and other	117.25	104	78.2
REGION			
Average household	**112.49**	**100**	**100.0**
Northeast	106.02	94	17.0
Midwest	125.54	112	24.7
South	102.41	91	33.9
West	121.44	108	24.3
EDUCATION			
Average household	**112.49**	**100**	**100.0**
Less than high school graduate	85.84	76	10.0
High school graduate	115.05	102	25.5
Some college	121.00	108	22.2
Associate's degree	129.41	115	11.4
Bachelor's degree or more	109.50	97	30.7
Bachelor's degree	118.45	105	21.0
Master's, professional, doctoral degree	94.37	84	9.7

Note: Market shares may not sum to 100.0 because of rounding and missing categories by household type. "Asian" and "black" include Hispanics and non-Hispanics who identify themselves as being of the respective race alone. "Hispanic" includes people of any race who identify themselves as Hispanic. "Other" includes people who identify themselves as non-Hispanic and as Alaska Native, American Indian, Asian (who are also included in the "Asian" row), or Native Hawaiian or other Pacific Islander, as well as non-Hispanics reporting more than one race.
Source: Calculations by New Strategist based on the Bureau of Labor Statistics' 2012 Consumer Expenditure Survey

Beer and Ale at Restaurants and Bars

Best customers: Householders under age 35
Married couples with preschoolers
People who live alone
Non-Hispanic whites
Households in the Northeast and Midwest

Customer trends: Average household spending on beer and ale at restaurants and bars may rise in the years ahead
as the recession loosens its grip—but only if discretionary income grows.

Householders under age 35 are the best customers of beer and ale at restaurants and bars, spending 19 to 80 percent more than the average household on this item. Married couples with preschoolers spend 27 percent more than average on beer at bars. People who live alone, whose spending surpasses average on only a few items, spend 5 percent more than average on beer at bars. Non-Hispanic whites spend 15 percent more than average on this item and account for 87 percent of the market. Households in the Northeast and Midwest spend 20 to 21 percent more than the average on beer and ale at restaurants and bars.

Average household spending on beer and ale consumed at restaurants and bars has been on a seesaw ride. It grew 16 percent between 2000 and 2006, after adjusting for inflation, then fell 31 percent through 2010, but rebounded strongly with a 15 percent rise in spending from 2010 to 2012. Behind the spending decline was the Great Recession and consequent belt tightening, as well as a shift in the preferences of young adults for whiskey and other alcohol when out at restaurants and bars. With the spending trough year of 2010 behind us, spending on beer and ale at restaurants and bars may rise in the years ahead as the recession loosens its grip—but only if discretionary income grows.

Table 1.4 Beer and ale at restaurants and bars

Total household spending $9,448,151,040.00
Average household spends 75.94

AGE OF HOUSEHOLDER	AVERAGE HOUSEHOLD SPENDING	BEST CUSTOMERS (index)	BIGGEST CUSTOMERS (market share)
Average household	$75.94	100	100.0%
Under age 25	90.46	119	7.8
Aged 25 to 34	137.04	180	29.2
Aged 35 to 44	81.23	107	18.6
Aged 45 to 54	79.50	105	20.7
Aged 55 to 64	63.63	84	15.3
Aged 65 to 74	33.24	44	5.3
Aged 75 or older	18.47	24	2.4

	AVERAGE HOUSEHOLD SPENDING	BEST CUSTOMERS (index)	BIGGEST CUSTOMERS (market share)
HOUSEHOLD INCOME			
Average household	$75.94	100	100.0%
Under $20,000	25.91	34	7.2
$20,000 to $39,999	48.25	64	14.3
$40,000 to $49,999	67.97	90	7.9
$50,000 to $69,999	82.45	109	15.7
$70,000 to $79,999	108.08	142	7.9
$80,000 to $99,999	87.60	115	10.2
$100,000 or more	149.94	197	37.0
HOUSEHOLD TYPE			
Average household	75.94	100	100.0
Married couples	77.93	103	49.8
Married couples, no children	89.32	118	24.5
Married couples with children	73.99	97	22.9
Oldest child under age 6	96.73	127	5.8
Oldest child aged 6 to 17	70.82	93	11.1
Oldest child aged 18 or older	65.10	86	6.0
Single parent with child under age 18	20.24	27	1.4
Single person	79.56	105	31.1
RACE AND HISPANIC ORIGIN			
Average household	75.94	100	100.0
Asian	44.84	59	2.6
Black	26.19	34	4.3
Hispanic	55.96	74	9.2
Non-Hispanic white and other	87.70	115	86.7
REGION			
Average household	75.94	100	100.0
Northeast	91.44	120	21.7
Midwest	91.53	121	26.7
South	57.80	76	28.3
West	77.87	103	23.1
EDUCATION			
Average household	75.94	100	100.0
Less than high school graduate	18.09	24	3.1
High school graduate	47.19	62	15.5
Some college	72.20	95	19.6
Associate's degree	76.15	100	9.9
Bachelor's degree or more	122.35	161	50.8
Bachelor's degree	124.16	163	32.6
Master's, professional, doctoral degree	119.27	157	18.2

Note: Market shares may not sum to 100.0 because of rounding and missing categories by household type. "Asian" and "black" include Hispanics and non-Hispanics who identify themselves as being of the respective race alone. "Hispanic" includes people of any race who identify themselves as Hispanic. "Other" includes people who identify themselves as non-Hispanic and as Alaska Native, American Indian, Asian (who are also included in the "Asian" row), or Native Hawaiian or other Pacific Islander, as well as non-Hispanics reporting more than one race.
Source: Calculations by New Strategist based on the Bureau of Labor Statistics' 2012 Consumer Expenditure Survey

Whiskey and Other Alcohol (except Beer and Wine) at Home

Best customers: Householders aged 55 to 74
Married couples without children at home
Households in the Northeast

Customer trends: Average household spending on whiskey and other alcohol consumed at home may continue to grow
if the millennial generation, which outspends others on whiskey and other alcohol in bars and restaurants,
boosts its home consumption of this item.

Traditionally, older couples are the best customers of whiskey and other alcohol (except beer and wine) consumed at home. Married couples without children at home (most of them empty-nesters) spend 95 percent more than average on this item. Householders aged 65 to 74 spend 36 percent more than average on whiskey and other alcohol at home, and those aged 55 to 64 spend an even greater 52 percent more than average. All other age groups spend (considerably) less than average on this item. Households in the Northeast outspend the average by 28 percent. Non-Hispanic whites represent 86 percent of the market.

Average household spending trends on whiskey and other alcohol consumed at home show a different pattern from other types of alcoholic beverages. Spending on this item fell 12 percent between 2000 and 2006, while spending on most other alcohol categories grew. Spending fell by another 19 percent between 2006 and 2010, in part because of the aging of the category's traditional best customers. But spending on this item rose again, 5 percent from 2010 to 2012. Average household spending on whiskey and other alcohol consumed at home may continue to grow if the millennial generation, which outspends others on whiskey and other alcohol in bars and restaurants, boosts its home consumption of this item.

Table 1.5 Whiskey and other alcohol (except beer and wine) at home

Total household spending $4,271,201,280.00
Average household spends   34.33

	AVERAGE HOUSEHOLD SPENDING	BEST CUSTOMERS (index)	BIGGEST CUSTOMERS (market share)
AGE OF HOUSEHOLDER			
Average household	**$34.33**	**100**	**100.0%**
Under age 25	31.30	91	6.0
Aged 25 to 34	22.81	66	10.7
Aged 35 to 44	32.87	96	16.6
Aged 45 to 54	27.66	81	15.9
Aged 55 to 64	52.29	152	27.9
Aged 65 to 74	46.75	136	16.4
Aged 75 or older	23.97	70	6.8

	AVERAGE HOUSEHOLD SPENDING	BEST CUSTOMERS (index)	BIGGEST CUSTOMERS (market share)
HOUSEHOLD INCOME			
Average household	$34.33	100	100.0%
Under $20,000	19.03	55	11.7
$20,000 to $39,999	21.12	62	13.9
$40,000 to $49,999	17.22	50	4.4
$50,000 to $69,999	26.57	77	11.2
$70,000 to $79,999	78.96	230	12.8
$80,000 to $99,999	32.75	95	8.4
$100,000 or more	70.47	205	38.4
HOUSEHOLD TYPE			
Average household	34.33	100	100.0
Married couples	47.61	139	67.4
Married couples, no children	66.88	195	40.6
Married couples with children	32.64	95	22.4
Oldest child under age 6	24.46	71	3.3
Oldest child aged 6 to 17	34.76	101	12.0
Oldest child aged 18 or older	34.23	100	7.0
Single parent with child under age 18	11.87	35	1.8
Single person	22.51	66	19.5
RACE AND HISPANIC ORIGIN			
Average household	34.33	100	100.0
Asian	28.65	83	3.6
Black	17.12	50	6.3
Hispanic	22.97	67	8.4
Non-Hispanic white and other	39.11	114	85.5
REGION			
Average household	34.33	100	100.0
Northeast	43.89	128	23.1
Midwest	24.25	71	15.7
South	35.87	104	38.9
West	34.11	99	22.4
EDUCATION			
Average household	34.33	100	100.0
Less than high school graduate	10.23	30	3.9
High school graduate	25.58	75	18.6
Some college	31.46	92	18.9
Associate's degree	25.88	75	7.4
Bachelor's degree or more	54.72	159	50.3
Bachelor's degree	38.01	111	22.1
Master's, professional, doctoral degree	82.94	242	28.0

Note: Market shares may not sum to 100.0 because of rounding and missing categories by household type. "Asian" and "black" include Hispanics and non-Hispanics who identify themselves as being of the respective race alone. "Hispanic" includes people of any race who identify themselves as Hispanic. "Other" includes people who identify themselves as non-Hispanic and as Alaska Native, American Indian, Asian (who are also included in the "Asian" row), or Native Hawaiian or other Pacific Islander, as well as non-Hispanics reporting more than one race.
Source: Calculations by New Strategist based on the Bureau of Labor Statistics' 2012 Consumer Expenditure Survey

Whiskey and Other Alcohol (except Beer and Wine) at Restaurants and Bars

Best customers: Householders aged 25 to 44
Married couples without children at home
Asians
Households in the West

Customer trends: Average household spending on whiskey and other alcohol at restaurants and bars may stabilize because the millennial generation appears to be an emerging best customer—but only if discretionary income grows.

Householders aged 25 to 44 spend 21 to 82 percent more than average on whiskey and other alcohol at restaurants and bars. Married couples without children at home, some of them young adults, spend 27 percent more than average on cocktails and shots at bars. Asians outspend the average by 22 percent. Households in the West spend 44 percent more than average on whiskey and other alcohol at restaurants and bars.

Average household spending on whiskey and other alcohol at restaurants and bars grew by an enormous 81 percent between 2000 and 2006, then declined 36 percent over the next six years. Spending on whiskey and other alcohol at restaurants and bars may stabilize in the years ahead because the large millennial generation appears to be an emerging best customer—but only if discretionary income grows.

Table 1.6 Whiskey and other alcohol (except beer and wine) at restaurants and bars

Total household spending $5,901,050,880.00
Average household spends   47.43

	AVERAGE HOUSEHOLD SPENDING	BEST CUSTOMERS (index)	BIGGEST CUSTOMERS (market share)
AGE OF HOUSEHOLDER			
Average household	$47.43	100	100.0%
Under age 25	33.63	71	4.6
Aged 25 to 34	86.44	182	29.5
Aged 35 to 44	57.36	121	21.0
Aged 45 to 54	44.48	94	18.6
Aged 55 to 64	38.83	82	15.0
Aged 65 to 74	27.71	58	7.0
Aged 75 or older	18.01	38	3.7

	AVERAGE HOUSEHOLD SPENDING	BEST CUSTOMERS (index)	BIGGEST CUSTOMERS (market share)
HOUSEHOLD INCOME			
Average household	$47.43	100	100.0%
Under $20,000	16.31	34	7.2
$20,000 to $39,999	32.86	69	15.6
$40,000 to $49,999	39.47	83	7.4
$50,000 to $69,999	46.64	98	14.2
$70,000 to $79,999	62.10	131	7.3
$80,000 to $99,999	64.45	136	12.0
$100,000 or more	92.63	195	36.6
HOUSEHOLD TYPE			
Average household	47.43	100	100.0
Married couples	50.27	106	51.5
Married couples, no children	60.15	127	26.4
Married couples with children	44.97	95	22.3
Oldest child under age 6	41.48	87	4.0
Oldest child aged 6 to 17	51.62	109	12.9
Oldest child aged 18 or older	36.04	76	5.4
Single parent with child under age 18	28.83	61	3.2
Single person	40.86	86	25.6
RACE AND HISPANIC ORIGIN			
Average household	47.43	100	100.0
Asian	57.66	122	5.3
Black	20.88	44	5.5
Hispanic	45.19	95	11.9
Non-Hispanic white and other	52.20	110	82.6
REGION			
Average household	47.43	100	100.0
Northeast	50.50	106	19.2
Midwest	47.93	101	22.4
South	33.12	70	26.0
West	68.22	144	32.4
EDUCATION			
Average household	47.43	100	100.0
Less than high school graduate	12.84	27	3.5
High school graduate	30.36	64	16.0
Some college	44.61	94	19.4
Associate's degree	41.66	88	8.7
Bachelor's degree or more	77.33	163	51.4
Bachelor's degree	75.91	160	31.9
Master's, professional, doctoral degree	79.74	168	19.5

Note: Market shares may not sum to 100.0 because of rounding and missing categories by household type. "Asian" and "black" include Hispanics and non-Hispanics who identify themselves as being of the respective race alone. "Hispanic" includes people of any race who identify themselves as Hispanic. "Other" includes people who identify themselves as non-Hispanic and as Alaska Native, American Indian, Asian (who are also included in the "Asian" row), or Native Hawaiian or other Pacific Islander, as well as non-Hispanics reporting more than one race.
Source: Calculations by New Strategist based on the Bureau of Labor Statistics' 2012 Consumer Expenditure Survey

Wine at Home

Best customers: Householders aged 55 to 74
Married couples without children at home
Married couples with school-aged children
Non-Hispanic whites
Households in the Northeast and West

Customer trends: Average household spending on wine consumed at home should continue to rise as boomers age.

The best customers of wine consumed at home are older non-Hispanic white married couples without children at home (empty-nesters). Couples without children at home spend 75 percent more than average on this item, and householders aged 55 to 74 spend 31 to 44 percent more than average on wine consumed at home. Married couples with school-aged children outspend the average by 36 percent. Non-Hispanic whites spend 17 percent more than average on wine at home and control 88 percent of the market. Households in the Northeast spend 38 percent more than average on wine consumed at home, and those in the West spend 27 percent more.

Average household spending on wine consumed at home has been on a rollercoaster ride. It increased 10 percent between 2000 and 2006, after adjusting for inflation, then fell 21 percent from 2006 to 2010 because of the Great Recession. Between 2010 and 2012, however, average household spending on this item climbed by a substantial 11 percent. Spending on wine consumed at home should continue to rise as boomers age.

Table 1.7 Wine at home

Total household spending $12,767,569,920.00
Average household spends   102.62

AGE OF HOUSEHOLDER	AVERAGE HOUSEHOLD SPENDING	BEST CUSTOMERS (index)	BIGGEST CUSTOMERS (market share)
Average household	$102.62	100	100.0%
Under age 25	49.09	48	3.1
Aged 25 to 34	74.60	73	11.8
Aged 35 to 44	117.96	115	20.0
Aged 45 to 54	95.71	93	18.5
Aged 55 to 64	133.99	131	23.9
Aged 65 to 74	148.23	144	17.4
Aged 75 or older	59.86	58	5.7

	AVERAGE HOUSEHOLD SPENDING	BEST CUSTOMERS (index)	BIGGEST CUSTOMERS (market share)
HOUSEHOLD INCOME			
Average household	$102.62	100	100.0%
Under $20,000	21.71	21	4.5
$20,000 to $39,999	49.83	49	10.9
$40,000 to $49,999	83.94	82	7.2
$50,000 to $69,999	77.57	76	10.9
$70,000 to $79,999	128.87	126	7.0
$80,000 to $99,999	157.28	153	13.5
$100,000 or more	252.67	246	46.1
HOUSEHOLD TYPE			
Average household	102.62	100	100.0
Married couples	139.73	136	66.1
Married couples, no children	179.09	175	36.4
Married couples with children	116.35	113	26.7
Oldest child under age 6	75.97	74	3.4
Oldest child aged 6 to 17	139.36	136	16.2
Oldest child aged 18 or older	103.12	100	7.1
Single parent with child under age 18	33.18	32	1.7
Single person	67.06	65	19.4
RACE AND HISPANIC ORIGIN			
Average household	102.62	100	100.0
Asian	74.76	73	3.2
Black	53.00	52	6.5
Hispanic	47.96	47	5.9
Non-Hispanic white and other	119.89	117	87.7
REGION			
Average household	102.62	100	100.0
Northeast	141.87	138	25.0
Midwest	76.35	74	16.5
South	82.89	81	30.1
West	129.84	127	28.5
EDUCATION			
Average household	102.62	100	100.0
Less than high school graduate	18.40	18	2.3
High school graduate	47.16	46	11.5
Some college	71.88	70	14.4
Associate's degree	109.24	106	10.5
Bachelor's degree or more	195.78	191	60.2
Bachelor's degree	165.22	161	32.1
Master's, professional, doctoral degree	247.45	241	28.0

Note: Market shares may not sum to 100.0 because of rounding and missing categories by household type. "Asian" and "black" include Hispanics and non-Hispanics who identify themselves as being of the respective race alone. "Hispanic" includes people of any race who identify themselves as Hispanic. "Other" includes people who identify themselves as non-Hispanic and as Alaska Native, American Indian, Asian (who are also included in the "Asian" row), or Native Hawaiian or other Pacific Islander, as well as non-Hispanics reporting more than one race.
Source: Calculations by New Strategist based on the Bureau of Labor Statistics' 2012 Consumer Expenditure Survey

Wine at Restaurants and Bars

Best customers: Householders aged 35 to 44
Married couples without children at home
Married couples with preschoolers
Non-Hispanic whites
Households in the Northeast
College graduates

Customer trends: Average household spending on wine at restaurants and bars should begin to grow again as boomers retire—but only if discretionary income grows.

The best customers of wine at restaurants and bars are householders with the time and money to relax with a glass of wine, perhaps over a meal. Married couples without children at home (most of them empty-nesters) spend 89 percent more than average on this item. Householders aged 35 to 44 outspend the average by 34 percent. Married couples with preschoolers spend more than twice the average on wine at restaurants and bars. Non-Hispanic whites spend 20 percent more than average and control 90 percent of the market. Households in the Northeast spend 55 percent more than average on this item. Households headed by college graduates spend twice the average and control 63 percent of the market.

Average household spending on wine at restaurants and bars doubled between 2000 and 2006, after adjusting for inflation, but spending fell 27 percent between 2006 and 2012. Behind the increase in the first part of the decade was the entry of the baby-boom generation into the best-customer lifestage. The Great Recession is largely responsible for the drop in the past few years. Spending on this item should begin to grow again as boomers retire—but only if discretionary income grows.

Table 1.8 Wine at restaurants and bars

Total household spending $4,297,328,640.00
Average household spends   34.54

AGE OF HOUSEHOLDER	AVERAGE HOUSEHOLD SPENDING	BEST CUSTOMERS (index)	BIGGEST CUSTOMERS (market share)
Average household	$34.54	100	100.0%
Under age 25	8.01	23	1.5
Aged 25 to 34	38.48	111	18.0
Aged 35 to 44	46.29	134	23.3
Aged 45 to 54	33.49	97	19.2
Aged 55 to 64	38.93	113	20.6
Aged 65 to 74	32.89	95	11.5
Aged 75 or older	20.89	60	5.9

	AVERAGE HOUSEHOLD SPENDING	BEST CUSTOMERS (index)	BIGGEST CUSTOMERS (market share)
HOUSEHOLD INCOME			
Average household	$34.54	100	100.0%
Under $20,000	5.28	15	3.2
$20,000 to $39,999	13.35	39	8.7
$40,000 to $49,999	18.09	52	4.6
$50,000 to $69,999	25.88	75	10.8
$70,000 to $79,999	33.16	96	5.4
$80,000 to $99,999	60.53	175	15.5
$100,000 or more	97.06	281	52.6
HOUSEHOLD TYPE			
Average household	34.54	100	100.0
Married couples	49.05	142	69.0
Married couples, no children	65.29	189	39.4
Married couples with children	38.79	112	26.4
Oldest child under age 6	73.83	214	9.8
Oldest child aged 6 to 17	39.25	114	13.5
Oldest child aged 18 or older	16.18	47	3.3
Single parent with child under age 18	6.65	19	1.0
Single person	18.74	54	16.1
RACE AND HISPANIC ORIGIN			
Average household	34.54	100	100.0
Asian	19.57	57	2.5
Black	10.17	29	3.7
Hispanic	17.95	52	6.5
Non-Hispanic white and other	41.34	120	89.8
REGION			
Average household	34.54	100	100.0
Northeast	53.44	155	27.9
Midwest	27.63	80	17.7
South	25.77	75	27.8
West	40.67	118	26.5
EDUCATION			
Average household	34.54	100	100.0
Less than high school graduate	4.71	14	1.8
High school graduate	11.17	32	8.1
Some college	20.39	59	12.2
Associate's degree	47.46	137	13.6
Bachelor's degree or more	69.31	201	63.3
Bachelor's degree	57.88	168	33.4
Master's, professional, doctoral degree	88.63	257	29.8

Note: Market shares may not sum to 100.0 because of rounding and missing categories by household type. "Asian" and "black" include Hispanics and non-Hispanics who identify themselves as being of the respective race alone. "Hispanic" includes people of any race who identify themselves as Hispanic. "Other" includes people who identify themselves as non-Hispanic and as Alaska Native, American Indian, Asian (who are also included in the "Asian" row), or Native Hawaiian or other Pacific Islander, as well as non-Hispanics reporting more than one race.
Source: Calculations by New Strategist based on the Bureau of Labor Statistics' 2012 Consumer Expenditure Survey

Chapter 2.
Apparel

Household Spending on Apparel, 2000 to 2012

Average household spending on apparel has been falling for years, dropping from $2,475 in 2000, after adjusting for inflation, to just $1,736 in 2012—a 30 percent decline. The apparel category includes men's, women's, and children's clothes as well as shoes, jewelry, watches, dry cleaning, and coin-operated laundry. Falling prices are one factor behind the decline in spending on this category as cheaper imports allow people to buy more for less. Another factor is the shift toward casual dress in the workplace and at social functions.

Average household spending on women's clothes—which account for the largest share of apparel spending (33 percent in 2012)—fell by 29 percent between 2000 and 2012, after adjusting for inflation. Spending on men's clothes fell by an almost equal 30 percent. Spending on women's shoes declined by 24 percent, and men's shoe spending was 29 percent lower. Spending on children's clothing has fared poorly as well, with 26 and 31 percent declines in average household spending on girls' and boys' clothes, respectively. Average household spending on infants' clothes dropped by a stark 42 percent in part because of the ongoing baby bust. Jewelry spending declined 34 percent as households slashed discretionary spending in these financially turbulent times. Spending on professional laundry and dry cleaning declined by a large 46 percent.

Average household spending on apparel may continue to slip as boomers approach retirement and no longer need even business casual attire. At some point, however, apparel spending will bottom out and then stabilize.

Spending on apparel

(average annual spending of households on apparel, 2000, 2006, 2010 and 2012; in 2012 dollars)

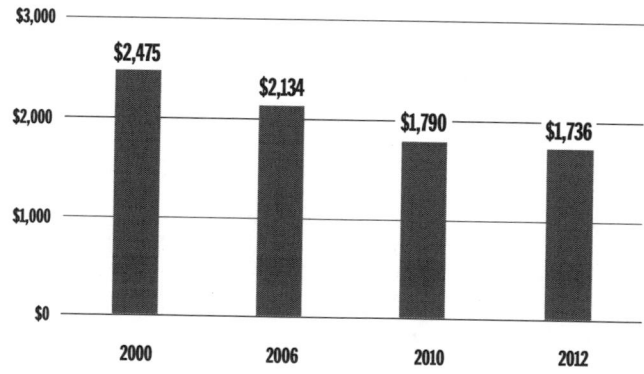

Table 2.1 Apparel spending, 2000 to 2012

(average annual household spending on apparel and percent distribution, by category, 2000 to 2012; percent change in spending and percentage point change in distribution, 2000–06, 2006-12, and 2010–12; in 2012 dollars; ranked by amount spent)

	average annual household spending (in 2012$)				percent change		
	2012	2010	2006	2000	2010–12	2006–12	2000–06
Average household spending on apparel	$1,735.80	$1,789.74	$2,134.10	$2,474.81	–3.0%	–18.7%	–13.8%
Women's apparel	572.53	591.21	715.88	809.46	–3.2	–20.0	–11.6
Men's apparel	319.73	320.14	401.54	459.04	–0.1	–20.4	–12.5
Women's shoes	158.87	154.04	163.59	207.93	3.1	–2.9	–21.3
Girls' apparel	115.92	106.45	139.44	157.45	8.9	–16.9	–11.4
Men's shoes	111.75	106.49	112.53	156.73	4.9	–0.7	–28.2
Jewelry	94.38	101.59	142.80	143.09	–7.1	–33.9	–0.2
Boys' apparel	87.96	81.89	103.57	127.68	7.4	–15.1	–18.9
Children's shoes	76.21	58.90	69.99	92.78	29.4	8.9	–24.6
Infants' apparel	63.31	95.37	109.02	109.22	–33.6	–41.9	–0.2
Professional apparel laundry and dry cleaning	52.24	52.15	70.55	96.53	0.2	–26.0	–26.9
Coin-operated apparel laundry and dry cleaning	40.21	41.14	44.24	50.57	–2.3	–9.1	–12.5
Sewing material, patterns, and notions	12.94	10.69	21.07	12.59	21.1	–38.6	67.4
Shoe and apparel repair and alteration	7.55	8.15	8.31	10.04	–7.4	–9.2	–17.2

					percentage point change		
PERCENT DISTRIBUTION OF SPENDING	2012	2010	2006	2000	2010–12	2006–12	2000–06
Average household spending on apparel	100.0%	100.0%	100.0%	100.0%	–	–	–
Women's apparel	33.0	33.0	33.5	32.7	0.0	–0.6	0.8
Men's apparel	18.4	17.9	18.8	18.5	0.5	–0.4	0.3
Women's shoes	9.2	8.6	7.7	8.4	0.5	1.5	–0.7
Girls' apparel	6.7	5.9	6.5	6.4	0.7	0.1	0.2
Men's shoes	6.4	6.0	5.3	6.3	0.5	1.2	–1.1
Jewelry	5.4	5.7	6.7	5.8	–0.2	–1.3	0.9
Boys' apparel	5.1	4.6	4.9	5.2	0.5	0.2	–0.3
Children's shoes	4.4	3.3	3.3	3.7	1.1	1.1	–0.5
Infants' apparel	3.6	5.3	5.1	4.4	–1.7	–1.5	0.7
Professional apparel laundry and dry cleaning	3.0	2.9	3.3	3.9	0.1	–0.3	–0.6
Coin-operated apparel laundry and dry cleaning	2.3	2.3	2.1	2.0	0.0	0.2	0.0
Sewing material, patterns, and notions	0.7	0.6	1.0	0.5	0.1	–0.2	0.5
Shoe and apparel repair and alteration	0.4	0.5	0.4	0.4	0.0	0.0	0.0

Note: Numbers do not add to total because not all categories are shown. Percentage point change calculations are based on unrounded figures.
"–" means not applicable.
Source: Bureau of Labor Statistics, 2000, 2006, 2010, and 2012 Consumer Expenditure Surveys; calculations by New Strategist

Boys' Apparel

Best customers: Married couples with children under age 18
Single parents
Householders aged 25 to 44
Asians and Hispanics

Customer trends: Average household spending on boys' apparel may increase as the large millennial generation has children.

Not surprisingly, the best customers of boys' apparel are households with children, driven especially by those with school-aged children. Married couples with children at home spend two-and-one-half times the average on this category, while the subgroup with school-aged children spends nearly four times the average. Single parents spend more than twice the average on boys' clothes. Householders aged 35 to 44 spend over double the average on boys' clothes because most are parents, and those aged 25 to 34 spend 43 percent more than average on this item. Asian householders spend 63 percent more than average, and Hispanic householders 51 percent more than average on this category. Behind the higher spending of Hispanics are their larger families.

Average household spending on boys' clothes fell 21 percent between 2006 and 2010, the peak and trough years for household spending. But spending on this item rebounded with a 7 percent increase between 2010 and 2012, after adjusting for inflation. As the large millennial generation has children, average household spending on boys' clothes may continue to increase—especially if the downward spiral in clothing prices comes to an end.

Table 2.2 Boys' apparel

Total household spending $10,943,631,360.00
Average household spends 87.96

AGE OF HOUSEHOLDER	AVERAGE HOUSEHOLD SPENDING	BEST CUSTOMERS (index)	BIGGEST CUSTOMERS (market share)
Average household	$87.96	100	100.0%
Under age 25	27.03	31	2.0
Aged 25 to 34	125.93	143	23.1
Aged 35 to 44	192.92	219	38.1
Aged 45 to 54	93.02	106	20.9
Aged 55 to 64	50.37	57	10.5
Aged 65 to 74	28.25	32	3.9
Aged 75 or older	9.32	11	1.0

	AVERAGE HOUSEHOLD SPENDING	BEST CUSTOMERS (index)	BIGGEST CUSTOMERS (market share)
HOUSEHOLD INCOME			
Average household	**$87.96**	**100**	**100.0%**
Under $20,000	38.62	44	9.2
$20,000 to $39,999	66.22	75	17.0
$40,000 to $49,999	61.98	70	6.2
$50,000 to $69,999	91.30	104	15.0
$70,000 to $79,999	104.58	119	6.6
$80,000 to $99,999	104.34	119	10.5
$100,000 or more	166.20	189	35.4
HOUSEHOLD TYPE			
Average household	**87.96**	**100**	**100.0**
Married couples	129.35	147	71.4
Married couples, no children	29.05	33	6.9
Married couples with children	217.37	247	58.1
Oldest child under age 6	125.14	142	6.5
Oldest child aged 6 to 17	332.18	378	44.9
Oldest child aged 18 or older	83.38	95	6.7
Single parent with child under age 18	201.99	230	12.0
Single person	13.11	15	4.4
RACE AND HISPANIC ORIGIN			
Average household	**87.96**	**100**	**100.0**
Asian	143.04	163	7.0
Black	93.87	107	13.4
Hispanic	133.09	151	19.0
Non-Hispanic white and other	79.50	90	67.8
REGION			
Average household	**87.96**	**100**	**100.0**
Northeast	102.35	116	21.0
Midwest	72.47	82	18.3
South	85.23	97	36.1
West	96.30	109	24.7
EDUCATION			
Average household	**87.96**	**100**	**100.0**
Less than high school graduate	70.33	80	10.4
High school graduate	82.75	94	23.5
Some college	87.38	99	20.5
Associate's degree	84.33	96	9.5
Bachelor's degree or more	100.34	114	36.0
Bachelor's degree	104.72	119	23.7
Master's, professional, doctoral degree	92.95	106	12.3

Note: Market shares may not sum to 100.0 because of rounding and missing categories by household type. "Asian" and "black" include Hispanics and non-Hispanics who identify themselves as being of the respective race alone. "Hispanic" includes people of any race who identify themselves as Hispanic. "Other" includes people who identify themselves as non-Hispanic and as Alaska Native, American Indian, Asian (who are also included in the "Asian" row), or Native Hawaiian or other Pacific Islander, as well as non-Hispanics reporting more than one race.
Source: Calculations by New Strategist based on the Bureau of Labor Statistics' 2012 Consumer Expenditure Survey

Children's Shoes

Best customers: Married couples with school-aged children
Single parents
Householders aged 35 to 44
Hispanics, blacks, and Asians

Customer trends: Average household spending on shoes for children may increase as the large millennial generation enters parenthood.

Married couples with school-aged children spend more than three-and-one-half times the average on children's shoes and account for 43 percent of the market. Single parents spend more than three times the average on this item and account for another 17 percent of the market. Hispanics spend close to twice the average on shoes for children. Blacks and Asians spend about one-third more than average. Because householders aged 35 to 44 are likely to have children at home, their spending on children's shoes is over twice the average.

Average household spending on children's shoes fell 25 percent between 2000 and 2006, after adjusting for inflation, as less expensive imports allowed consumers to buy more for less. Spending on children's shoes then began to rise and showed a solid 29 percent increase between 2010 and 2012. Spending on children's shoes should continue to rise as the large millennial generation has children and the Hispanic population grows.

Table 2.3 **Children's shoes**

Total household spending $9,481,743,360.00
Average household spends 76.21

AGE OF HOUSEHOLDER	AVERAGE HOUSEHOLD SPENDING	BEST CUSTOMERS (index)	BIGGEST CUSTOMERS (market share)
Average household	$76.21	100	100.0%
Under age 25	19.90	26	1.7
Aged 25 to 34	98.65	129	20.9
Aged 35 to 44	175.70	231	40.0
Aged 45 to 54	96.01	126	24.9
Aged 55 to 64	30.59	40	7.3
Aged 65 to 74	25.21	33	4.0
Aged 75 or older	0.74	1	0.1

	AVERAGE HOUSEHOLD SPENDING	BEST CUSTOMERS (index)	BIGGEST CUSTOMERS (market share)
HOUSEHOLD INCOME			
Average household	$76.21	100	100.0%
Under $20,000	45.89	60	12.7
$20,000 to $39,999	60.22	79	17.8
$40,000 to $49,999	59.99	79	7.0
$50,000 to $69,999	64.98	85	12.3
$70,000 to $79,999	95.19	125	7.0
$80,000 to $99,999	82.95	109	9.6
$100,000 or more	138.79	182	34.1
HOUSEHOLD TYPE			
Average household	76.21	100	100.0
Married couples	104.98	138	66.9
Married couples, no children	19.44	26	5.3
Married couples with children	185.99	244	57.4
Oldest child under age 6	92.91	122	5.6
Oldest child aged 6 to 17	277.71	364	43.3
Oldest child aged 18 or older	90.99	119	8.4
Single parent with child under age 18	246.08	323	16.9
Single person	4.45	6	1.7
RACE AND HISPANIC ORIGIN			
Average household	76.21	100	100.0
Asian	100.24	132	5.7
Black	103.09	135	17.0
Hispanic	142.53	187	23.4
Non-Hispanic white and other	61.05	80	60.1
REGION			
Average household	76.21	100	100.0
Northeast	82.52	108	19.5
Midwest	71.49	94	20.8
South	71.21	93	34.8
West	84.13	110	24.9
EDUCATION			
Average household	76.21	100	100.0
Less than high school graduate	80.33	105	13.8
High school graduate	64.94	85	21.2
Some college	74.31	98	20.1
Associate's degree	39.36	52	5.1
Bachelor's degree or more	96.20	126	39.8
Bachelor's degree	99.33	130	26.0
Master's, professional, doctoral degree	90.91	119	13.8

Note: Market shares may not sum to 100.0 because of rounding and missing categories by household type. "Asian" and "black" include Hispanics and non-Hispanics who identify themselves as being of the respective race alone. "Hispanic" includes people of any race who identify themselves as Hispanic. "Other" includes people who identify themselves as non-Hispanic and as Alaska Native, American Indian, Asian (who are also included in the "Asian" row), or Native Hawaiian or other Pacific Islander, as well as non-Hispanics reporting more than one race.
Source: Calculations by New Strategist based on the Bureau of Labor Statistics' 2012 Consumer Expenditure Survey

Coin-Operated Apparel Laundry and Dry Cleaning

Best customers: Householders under age 35
Low-income households
Single parents
Hispanics, blacks, and Asians
Households in the Northeast
Least-educated householders

Customer trends: Average household spending on coin-operated apparel laundry and dry cleaning may continue to decline as the rental market moves upscale and laundry equipment is installed in more rental units.

The biggest spenders at coin-operated laundries are householders under age 35, who spend 69 to 78 percent more than average on this item. Not surprisingly, low-income households also spend more than average on this category. Many low-income householders are single parents, and the latter spend 68 percent more than average at laundromats. Asian and black householders spend, respectively, 42 and 77 percent more than average at coin-operated laundries, while Hispanic households spend almost three times the average. Many of these householders are renters and do not have a washer or dryer at home. Spending at laundromats by households in the Northeast is 67 percent above average. Householders without a high school diploma spend twice the average on this item.

Average household spending on coin-operated laundry and dry cleaning fell both before and after the Great Recession. These declines occurred despite the increase in the young-adult and Hispanic populations. Spending on coin-operated apparel laundry and dry cleaning may continue to decline as the rental market moves upscale and laundry equipment is installed in more rental units.

Table 2.4 Coin-operated apparel laundry and dry cleaning

Total household spending $5,002,767,360.00
Average household spends   40.21

AGE OF HOUSEHOLDER	AVERAGE HOUSEHOLD SPENDING	BEST CUSTOMERS (index)	BIGGEST CUSTOMERS (market share)
Average household	**$40.21**	**100**	**100.0%**
Under age 25	71.51	178	11.7
Aged 25 to 34	68.13	169	27.4
Aged 35 to 44	46.04	114	19.9
Aged 45 to 54	36.72	91	18.1
Aged 55 to 64	26.33	65	12.0
Aged 65 to 74	23.01	57	6.9
Aged 75 or older	16.98	42	4.1

	AVERAGE HOUSEHOLD SPENDING	BEST CUSTOMERS (index)	BIGGEST CUSTOMERS (market share)
HOUSEHOLD INCOME			
Average household	$40.21	100	100.0%
Under $20,000	58.47	145	30.6
$20,000 to $39,999	53.31	133	29.9
$40,000 to $49,999	50.62	126	11.1
$50,000 to $69,999	35.82	89	12.9
$70,000 to $79,999	30.43	76	4.2
$80,000 to $99,999	22.48	56	4.9
$100,000 or more	13.68	34	6.4
HOUSEHOLD TYPE			
Average household	40.21	100	100.0
Married couples	29.44	73	35.6
Married couples, no children	18.36	46	9.5
Married couples with children	34.50	86	20.2
Oldest child under age 6	44.04	110	5.0
Oldest child aged 6 to 17	38.74	96	11.5
Oldest child aged 18 or older	21.18	53	3.7
Single parent with child under age 18	67.67	168	8.8
Single person	39.53	98	29.2
RACE AND HISPANIC ORIGIN			
Average household	40.21	100	100.0
Asian	57.22	142	6.2
Black	70.98	177	22.2
Hispanic	110.43	275	34.4
Non-Hispanic white and other	23.78	59	44.4
REGION			
Average household	40.21	100	100.0
Northeast	67.34	167	30.2
Midwest	31.34	78	17.3
South	27.83	69	25.8
West	47.68	119	26.7
EDUCATION			
Average household	40.21	100	100.0
Less than high school graduate	79.45	198	25.8
High school graduate	42.51	106	26.4
Some college	37.28	93	19.1
Associate's degree	31.14	77	7.6
Bachelor's degree or more	26.92	67	21.1
Bachelor's degree	29.20	73	14.5
Master's, professional, doctoral degree	22.99	57	6.6

Note: Market shares may not sum to 100.0 because of rounding and missing categories by household type. "Asian" and "black" include Hispanics and non-Hispanics who identify themselves as being of the respective race alone. "Hispanic" includes people of any race who identify themselves as Hispanic. "Other" includes people who identify themselves as non-Hispanic and as Alaska Native, American Indian, Asian (who are also included in the "Asian" row), or Native Hawaiian or other Pacific Islander, as well as non-Hispanics reporting more than one race.
Source: Calculations by New Strategist based on the Bureau of Labor Statistics' 2012 Consumer Expenditure Survey

Girls' Apparel

Best customers:
Married couples with children under age 18
Single parents
Householders aged 35 to 44
Hispanics, Asians, and blacks

Customer trends:
Average household spending on children's apparel may increase as the large millennial generation has children.

The average household spends more on clothes for girls than for boys—an average of $116 for girls' clothes versus $88 for boys' clothes in 2012. The big spenders on girls' clothes are, not surprisingly, the same households that spend the most on boys' clothes. Married couples with school-aged children at home spend nearly three-and-one-half times the average on girls' clothes, and single parents spend almost three times the average. Couples with preschoolers spend 41 percent more than average on girls' clothes. Householders aged 35 to 44 spend over twice the average because most are parents. Hispanic, Asian, and black householders spend between 31 and 46 percent more than average on girls' clothes.

As less expensive imports drove clothing prices down and the Great Recession reduced overall spending, average household spending on girls' clothes fell 32 percent between 2000 and 2010, after adjusting for inflation. Spending on this category recovered with a solid 9 percent rise between 2010 and 2012, however. As the large millennial generation has children, spending on girls' clothes may continue to increase—especially if the downward spiral in clothing prices comes to a halt.

Table 2.5 Girls' apparel

Total household spending $14,422,302,720.00
Average household spends   115.92

	AVERAGE HOUSEHOLD SPENDING	BEST CUSTOMERS (index)	BIGGEST CUSTOMERS (market share)
AGE OF HOUSEHOLDER			
Average household	**$115.92**	**100**	**100.0%**
Under age 25	22.32	19	1.3
Aged 25 to 34	151.53	131	21.1
Aged 35 to 44	242.50	209	36.3
Aged 45 to 54	132.73	115	22.7
Aged 55 to 64	63.74	55	10.1
Aged 65 to 74	68.99	60	7.2
Aged 75 or older	10.81	9	0.9

	AVERAGE HOUSEHOLD SPENDING	BEST CUSTOMERS (index)	BIGGEST CUSTOMERS (market share)
HOUSEHOLD INCOME			
Average household	$115.92	100	100.0%
Under $20,000	62.12	54	11.3
$20,000 to $39,999	84.73	73	16.5
$40,000 to $49,999	97.33	84	7.4
$50,000 to $69,999	101.47	88	12.6
$70,000 to $79,999	124.56	107	6.0
$80,000 to $99,999	154.61	133	11.8
$100,000 or more	215.85	186	34.9
HOUSEHOLD TYPE			
Average household	115.92	100	100.0
Married couples	164.22	142	68.8
Married couples, no children	59.21	51	10.6
Married couples with children	263.17	227	53.4
Oldest child under age 6	163.53	141	6.4
Oldest child aged 6 to 17	396.22	342	40.7
Oldest child aged 18 or older	103.38	89	6.3
Single parent with child under age 18	334.83	289	15.1
Single person	14.02	12	3.6
RACE AND HISPANIC ORIGIN			
Average household	115.92	100	100.0
Asian	164.99	142	6.2
Black	152.25	131	16.5
Hispanic	168.75	146	18.2
Non-Hispanic white and other	100.98	87	65.4
REGION			
Average household	115.92	100	100.0
Northeast	117.57	101	18.3
Midwest	115.92	100	22.2
South	120.08	104	38.6
West	107.72	93	20.9
EDUCATION			
Average household	115.92	100	100.0
Less than high school graduate	102.43	88	11.5
High school graduate	97.54	84	21.0
Some college	103.65	89	18.4
Associate's degree	112.68	97	9.6
Bachelor's degree or more	144.88	125	39.4
Bachelor's degree	137.11	118	23.6
Master's, professional, doctoral degree	158.06	136	15.8

Note: Market shares may not sum to 100.0 because of rounding and missing categories by household type. "Asian" and "black" include Hispanics and non-Hispanics who identify themselves as being of the respective race alone. "Hispanic" includes people of any race who identify themselves as Hispanic. "Other" includes people who identify themselves as non-Hispanic and as Alaska Native, American Indian, Asian (who are also included in the "Asian" row), or Native Hawaiian or other Pacific Islander, as well as non-Hispanics reporting more than one race.
Source: Calculations by New Strategist based on the Bureau of Labor Statistics' 2012 Consumer Expenditure Survey

Infants' Apparel

Best customers: Married couples with preschoolers
Single parents
Householders under age 45
Asians and Hispanics

Customer trends: Average household spending on infants' apparel will begin to grow only when the ongoing baby bust comes to an end.

The average household spent $63 on clothes for infants in 2012. By far the biggest spenders on infants' clothes are married couples with preschoolers. This household type spends nearly eight times the average on baby clothes. Spending on infants' apparel by single parents is more than double the average. Householders aged 25 to 34 also spend more than twice the average because many have newborns and toddlers. Those under age 25 spend 78 percent more on infants' clothes, and those aged 35 to 44 spend 49 percent more. Hispanic householders spend 54 percent more than average on infants' clothes because of their larger families, and Asians outspend the average by a similar 56 percent.

Average household spending on infants' apparel fell by a stunning 34 percent between 2010 and 2012, after adjusting for inflation. During this time period, spending on many other categories was beginning to grow again after the Great Recession. Behind the plunge in spending on infants' clothes is the ongoing baby bust, with the nation's fertility rate falling to a record low. Average household spending on infants' clothes will begin to grow only when the ongoing baby bust comes to an end.

Table 2.6 Infants' apparel

Total household spending $7,876,776,960.00
Average household spends   63.31

AGE OF HOUSEHOLDER	AVERAGE HOUSEHOLD SPENDING	BEST CUSTOMERS (index)	BIGGEST CUSTOMERS (market share)
Average household	$63.31	100	100.0%
Under age 25	112.42	178	11.6
Aged 25 to 34	141.09	223	36.0
Aged 35 to 44	94.52	149	25.9
Aged 45 to 54	31.66	50	9.9
Aged 55 to 64	34.41	54	9.9
Aged 65 to 74	25.20	40	4.8
Aged 75 or older	3.98	6	0.6

	AVERAGE HOUSEHOLD SPENDING	BEST CUSTOMERS (index)	BIGGEST CUSTOMERS (market share)
HOUSEHOLD INCOME			
Average household	**$63.31**	**100**	**100.0%**
Under $20,000	41.94	66	13.9
$20,000 to $39,999	46.35	73	16.5
$40,000 to $49,999	69.96	111	9.8
$50,000 to $69,999	60.18	95	13.7
$70,000 to $79,999	65.45	103	5.8
$80,000 to $99,999	95.85	151	13.4
$100,000 or more	91.86	145	27.2
HOUSEHOLD TYPE			
Average household	**63.31**	**100**	**100.0**
Married couples	88.32	140	67.8
Married couples, no children	23.99	38	7.9
Married couples with children	143.61	227	53.3
Oldest child under age 6	487.83	771	35.2
Oldest child aged 6 to 17	81.94	129	15.4
Oldest child aged 18 or older	30.66	48	3.4
Single parent with child under age 18	132.82	210	11.0
Single person	8.26	13	3.9
RACE AND HISPANIC ORIGIN			
Average household	**63.31**	**100**	**100.0**
Asian	98.84	156	6.8
Black	60.12	95	11.9
Hispanic	97.34	154	19.3
Non-Hispanic white and other	58.21	92	69.0
REGION			
Average household	**63.31**	**100**	**100.0**
Northeast	71.66	113	20.4
Midwest	59.65	94	20.9
South	66.84	106	39.3
West	54.34	86	19.3
EDUCATION			
Average household	**63.31**	**100**	**100.0**
Less than high school graduate	67.14	106	13.8
High school graduate	50.02	79	19.7
Some college	59.46	94	19.3
Associate's degree	69.46	110	10.8
Bachelor's degree or more	72.93	115	36.3
Bachelor's degree	69.66	110	21.9
Master's, professional, doctoral degree	78.45	124	14.4

Note: Market shares may not sum to 100.0 because of rounding and missing categories by household type. "Asian" and "black" include Hispanics and non-Hispanics who identify themselves as being of the respective race alone. "Hispanic" includes people of any race who identify themselves as Hispanic. "Other" includes people who identify themselves as non-Hispanic and as Alaska Native, American Indian, Asian (who are also included in the "Asian" row), or Native Hawaiian or other Pacific Islander, as well as non-Hispanics reporting more than one race.
Source: Calculations by New Strategist based on the Bureau of Labor Statistics' 2012 Consumer Expenditure Survey

Jewelry

Best customers: **Householders aged 25 to 44**
Married couples without children at home
Married couples with school-aged or older children at home
Asians
Households in the West

Customer trends: **Average household spending on jewelry may continue to decline in the years ahead as tighter budgets limit discretionary spending.**

Householders aged 25 to 34 spend 45 percent more than average on jewelry, and those aged 35 to 44 spend 24 percent more. Married couples without children at home (most of them empty-nesters) spend 29 percent more than average on jewelry. Those with school-aged or older children at home spend 27 to 38 percent more than average on this item. Asian householders spend double the average on jewelry, and householders in the West, where many Asians reside, outspend the average by 22 percent.

Average household spending on jewelry fell 34 percent between 2006 and 2012, after adjusting for inflation. Behind the decline was belt tightening due to the Great Recession. One factor behind the decline in spending on jewelry is the postponement of marriage by young adults, with fewer buying engagement and wedding rings. Spending on jewelry may continue to fall in the years ahead as tighter budgets limit discretionary spending, especially among young adults.

Table 2.7 Jewelry

Total household spending $11,742,382,080.00
Average household spends   94.38

AGE OF HOUSEHOLDER	AVERAGE HOUSEHOLD SPENDING	BEST CUSTOMERS (index)	BIGGEST CUSTOMERS (market share)
Average household	$94.38	100	100.0%
Under age 25	67.62	72	4.7
Aged 25 to 34	136.86	145	23.4
Aged 35 to 44	116.77	124	21.5
Aged 45 to 54	95.52	101	20.0
Aged 55 to 64	96.16	102	18.6
Aged 65 to 74	74.30	79	9.5
Aged 75 or older	21.41	23	2.2

	AVERAGE HOUSEHOLD SPENDING	BEST CUSTOMERS (index)	BIGGEST CUSTOMERS (market share)
HOUSEHOLD INCOME			
Average household	**$94.38**	**100**	**100.0%**
Under $20,000	29.14	31	6.5
$20,000 to $39,999	30.96	33	7.4
$40,000 to $49,999	44.13	47	4.1
$50,000 to $69,999	49.43	52	7.6
$70,000 to $79,999	118.01	125	7.0
$80,000 to $99,999	146.35	155	13.7
$100,000 or more	270.94	287	53.7
HOUSEHOLD TYPE			
Average household	**94.38**	**100**	**100.0**
Married couples	126.47	134	65.1
Married couples, no children	122.13	129	27.0
Married couples with children	114.80	122	28.6
Oldest child under age 6	68.26	72	3.3
Oldest child aged 6 to 17	129.80	138	16.4
Oldest child aged 18 or older	119.63	127	8.9
Single parent with child under age 18	23.51	25	1.3
Single person	63.16	67	19.9
RACE AND HISPANIC ORIGIN			
Average household	**94.38**	**100**	**100.0**
Asian	187.80	199	8.6
Black	35.04	37	4.7
Hispanic	48.49	51	6.4
Non-Hispanic white and other	111.80	118	88.9
REGION			
Average household	**94.38**	**100**	**100.0**
Northeast	92.53	98	17.7
Midwest	75.10	80	17.6
South	94.23	100	37.2
West	115.09	122	27.5
EDUCATION			
Average household	**94.38**	**100**	**100.0**
Less than high school graduate	18.59	20	2.6
High school graduate	49.34	52	13.0
Some college	62.88	67	13.7
Associate's degree	120.52	128	12.6
Bachelor's degree or more	173.76	184	58.1
Bachelor's degree	157.78	167	33.3
Master's, professional, doctoral degree	201.20	213	24.7

Note: Market shares may not sum to 100.0 because of rounding and missing categories by household type. "Asian" and "black" include Hispanics and non-Hispanics who identify themselves as being of the respective race alone. "Hispanic" includes people of any race who identify themselves as Hispanic. "Other" includes people who identify themselves as non-Hispanic and as Alaska Native, American Indian, Asian (who are also included in the "Asian" row), or Native Hawaiian or other Pacific Islander, as well as non-Hispanics reporting more than one race.
Source: Calculations by New Strategist based on the Bureau of Labor Statistics' 2012 Consumer Expenditure Survey

Men's Apparel

Best customers: Householders aged 35 to 54
Married couples with school-aged or older children at home
Asians
Households in the West

Customer trends: Average household spending on men's clothes will continue to decline as the large baby-boom generation retires.

In 2012, the average household spent $320 on men's clothes versus the larger $573 spent on women's clothes. Both figures are more than 20 percent below what they were in 2006, after adjusting for inflation. Falling prices are one reason for the long-term decline in spending on men's and women's clothes, as cheaper imports allow consumers to buy more for less. Also behind the long-term decline is the trend toward more casual attire in the workplace and at social functions. A third factor is the Great Recession, which worsened the ongoing decline in spending on clothes.

The biggest spenders on men's clothes are households with working men. This explains why married couples with adult children at home spend 93 percent more than average on this item, since many of these households include more than one working man. Couples with school-aged children outspend the average by 28 percent. Householders aged 35 to 54 spend 31 to 32 percent more than average on men's clothes. Asians outspend the average by 44 percent. Households in the West spend 22 percent more than average on men's apparel.

Average household spending on men's clothes fell 20 percent between 2006 and 2012 as the Great Recession cut household budgets. Spending on men's clothes will continue to decline as the large baby-boom generation retires and no longer requires business attire.

Table 2.8 Men's apparel

Total household spending $39,779,527,680.00
Average household spends   319.73

	AVERAGE HOUSEHOLD SPENDING	BEST CUSTOMERS (index)	BIGGEST CUSTOMERS (market share)
AGE OF HOUSEHOLDER			
Average household	**$319.73**	**100**	**100.0%**
Under age 25	278.81	87	5.7
Aged 25 to 34	294.63	92	14.9
Aged 35 to 44	423.30	132	23.0
Aged 45 to 54	419.23	131	26.0
Aged 55 to 64	314.74	98	18.0
Aged 65 to 74	229.75	72	8.7
Aged 75 or older	114.99	36	3.5

	AVERAGE HOUSEHOLD SPENDING	BEST CUSTOMERS (index)	BIGGEST CUSTOMERS (market share)
HOUSEHOLD INCOME			
Average household	**$319.73**	**100**	**100.0%**
Under $20,000	132.42	41	8.7
$20,000 to $39,999	166.29	52	11.7
$40,000 to $49,999	202.03	63	5.6
$50,000 to $69,999	279.84	88	12.6
$70,000 to $79,999	438.06	137	7.6
$80,000 to $99,999	529.67	166	14.6
$100,000 or more	677.55	212	39.7
HOUSEHOLD TYPE			
Average household	**319.73**	**100**	**100.0**
Married couples	396.56	124	60.2
Married couples, no children	352.75	110	23.0
Married couples with children	450.85	141	33.2
Oldest child under age 6	298.98	94	4.3
Oldest child aged 6 to 17	407.74	128	15.2
Oldest child aged 18 or older	618.12	193	13.6
Single parent with child under age 18	264.98	83	4.3
Single person	198.46	62	18.4
RACE AND HISPANIC ORIGIN			
Average household	**319.73**	**100**	**100.0**
Asian	461.56	144	6.3
Black	305.55	96	12.0
Hispanic	345.17	108	13.5
Non-Hispanic white and other	317.76	99	74.6
REGION			
Average household	**319.73**	**100**	**100.0**
Northeast	352.16	110	19.9
Midwest	282.12	88	19.6
South	283.32	89	33.0
West	391.48	122	27.6
EDUCATION			
Average household	**319.73**	**100**	**100.0**
Less than high school graduate	243.13	76	9.9
High school graduate	237.06	74	18.5
Some college	272.29	85	17.5
Associate's degree	291.08	91	9.0
Bachelor's degree or more	454.49	142	44.8
Bachelor's degree	455.24	142	28.4
Master's, professional, doctoral degree	453.27	142	16.5

Note: Market shares may not sum to 100.0 because of rounding and missing categories by household type. "Asian" and "black" include Hispanics and non-Hispanics who identify themselves as being of the respective race alone. "Hispanic" includes people of any race who identify themselves as Hispanic. "Other" includes people who identify themselves as non-Hispanic and as Alaska Native, American Indian, Asian (who are also included in the "Asian" row), or Native Hawaiian or other Pacific Islander, as well as non-Hispanics reporting more than one race.
Source: Calculations by New Strategist based on the Bureau of Labor Statistics' 2012 Consumer Expenditure Survey

Men's Shoes

Best customers: Householders aged 35 to 44
                            Married couples with children at home
                            Asians, blacks, and Hispanics

Customer trends: Average household spending on men's shoes will decline as the large baby-boom
                            generation retires.

The best customers of men's shoes are married couples with adult children at home. These households spend 76 percent more than the average on men's shoes because there are more men in the household. Couples with preschoolers outspend the average by 44 percent. Householders ranging in age from 25 to 54 spend 19 to 40 percent more than average on men's shoes. Blacks and Hispanics spend, respectively, 23 and 20 percent more than average on this item, and the spending of Asian householders is nearly twice the average.

Spending on men's shoes recently reversed its former steep decline. Low-cost imports were behind the 28 percent drop in spending from 2000 to 2006, but spending held steady in the six years since, even showing a 5 percent increase from 2010 to 2012, after adjusting for inflation. As the growing Asian and Hispanic populations boost spending on men's shoes, the bigger trend may be the aging of the baby-boom generation, however, which is likely to dampen spending on this item.

Table 2.9 Men's shoes

Total household spending $13,903,488,000.00
Average household spends   111.75

AGE OF HOUSEHOLDER	AVERAGE HOUSEHOLD SPENDING	BEST CUSTOMERS (index)	BIGGEST CUSTOMERS (market share)
Average household	$111.75	100	100.0%
Under age 25	92.96	83	5.5
Aged 25 to 34	136.24	122	19.7
Aged 35 to 44	156.20	140	24.3
Aged 45 to 54	133.49	119	23.6
Aged 55 to 64	100.51	90	16.5
Aged 65 to 74	74.03	66	8.0
Aged 75 or older	22.86	20	2.0

	AVERAGE HOUSEHOLD SPENDING	BEST CUSTOMERS (index)	BIGGEST CUSTOMERS (market share)
HOUSEHOLD INCOME			
Average household	**$111.75**	**100**	**100.0%**
Under $20,000	65.48	59	12.3
$20,000 to $39,999	71.74	64	14.5
$40,000 to $49,999	98.03	88	7.8
$50,000 to $69,999	98.18	88	12.7
$70,000 to $79,999	142.25	127	7.1
$80,000 to $99,999	165.25	148	13.0
$100,000 or more	195.01	175	32.7
HOUSEHOLD TYPE			
Average household	**111.75**	**100**	**100.0**
Married couples	145.37	130	63.2
Married couples, no children	124.25	111	23.2
Married couples with children	164.36	147	34.6
Oldest child under age 6	160.42	144	6.5
Oldest child aged 6 to 17	146.35	131	15.6
Oldest child aged 18 or older	196.87	176	12.4
Single parent with child under age 18	81.64	73	3.8
Single person	70.00	63	18.6
RACE AND HISPANIC ORIGIN			
Average household	**111.75**	**100**	**100.0**
Asian	218.67	196	8.5
Black	137.85	123	15.5
Hispanic	134.59	120	15.1
Non-Hispanic white and other	103.27	92	69.4
REGION			
Average household	**111.75**	**100**	**100.0**
Northeast	122.09	109	19.7
Midwest	92.52	83	18.4
South	114.65	103	38.2
West	117.78	105	23.7
EDUCATION			
Average household	**111.75**	**100**	**100.0**
Less than high school graduate	137.93	123	16.1
High school graduate	92.81	83	20.7
Some college	98.52	88	18.2
Associate's degree	88.24	79	7.8
Bachelor's degree or more	132.84	119	37.5
Bachelor's degree	131.70	118	23.5
Master's, professional, doctoral degree	134.76	121	14.0

Note: Market shares may not sum to 100.0 because of rounding and missing categories by household type. "Asian" and "black" include Hispanics and non-Hispanics who identify themselves as being of the respective race alone. "Hispanic" includes people of any race who identify themselves as Hispanic. "Other" includes people who identify themselves as non-Hispanic and as Alaska Native, American Indian, Asian (who are also included in the "Asian" row), or Native Hawaiian or other Pacific Islander, as well as non-Hispanics reporting more than one race.
Source: Calculations by New Strategist based on the Bureau of Labor Statistics' 2012 Consumer Expenditure Survey

Professional Apparel Laundry and Dry Cleaning

Best customers: Householders aged 45 to 64
High-income households
Married couples
Blacks
Households in the Northeast
College graduates

Customer trends: Average household spending on professional apparel laundry and dry cleaning is likely to fall as boomers retire and their need for this service declines.

The biggest spenders on professional laundry and dry cleaning are affluent, educated older householders. Households with incomes of $100,000 or more spend three-and-one-third times the average on professional laundry and dry cleaning. College graduates spend more than twice the average. Married couples spend 41 percent more than average on this item, the figure peaking at 69 percent among those with school-aged children. Householders ranging in age from 45 to 64 spend 20 to 55 percent more than average on professional laundry and dry cleaning. Black householders spend 18 percent more. Spending on this item by households in the Northeast is 36 percent higher than average.

Average household spending on professional apparel laundry and dry cleaning declined both before and after the Great Recession, after adjusting for inflation. After plunging for so many years, spending on this item stabilized between 2010 and 2012. This period of stability may be short lived. Spending on professional laundry and dry cleaning may continue to decline as boomers retire and fewer dress in business clothes.

Table 2.10 Professional apparel laundry and dry cleaning

Total household spending $6,499,491,840.00
Average household spends   52.24

AGE OF HOUSEHOLDER	AVERAGE HOUSEHOLD SPENDING	BEST CUSTOMERS (index)	BIGGEST CUSTOMERS (market share)
Average household	$52.24	100	100.0%
Under age 25	16.49	32	2.1
Aged 25 to 34	42.22	81	13.1
Aged 35 to 44	58.45	112	19.4
Aged 45 to 54	80.74	155	30.6
Aged 55 to 64	62.59	120	21.9
Aged 65 to 74	40.41	77	9.3
Aged 75 or older	19.29	37	3.6

	AVERAGE HOUSEHOLD SPENDING	BEST CUSTOMERS (index)	BIGGEST CUSTOMERS (market share)
HOUSEHOLD INCOME			
Average household	$52.24	100	100.0%
Under $20,000	8.99	17	3.6
$20,000 to $39,999	14.02	27	6.1
$40,000 to $49,999	24.93	48	4.2
$50,000 to $69,999	32.73	63	9.1
$70,000 to $79,999	44.81	86	4.8
$80,000 to $99,999	61.48	118	10.4
$100,000 or more	172.70	331	61.9
HOUSEHOLD TYPE			
Average household	52.24	100	100.0
Married couples	73.49	141	68.3
Married couples, no children	67.83	130	27.1
Married couples with children	81.84	157	36.8
Oldest child under age 6	71.41	137	6.2
Oldest child aged 6 to 17	88.09	169	20.1
Oldest child aged 18 or older	78.05	149	10.5
Single parent with child under age 18	16.93	32	1.7
Single person	34.11	65	19.4
RACE AND HISPANIC ORIGIN			
Average household	52.24	100	100.0
Asian	58.13	111	4.8
Black	61.42	118	14.8
Hispanic	31.60	60	7.6
Non-Hispanic white and other	54.16	104	77.8
REGION			
Average household	52.24	100	100.0
Northeast	71.27	136	24.6
Midwest	30.44	58	12.9
South	53.88	103	38.4
West	55.75	107	24.0
EDUCATION			
Average household	52.24	100	100.0
Less than high school graduate	13.13	25	3.3
High school graduate	17.42	33	8.3
Some college	34.07	65	13.4
Associate's degree	35.17	67	6.6
Bachelor's degree or more	113.19	217	68.3
Bachelor's degree	94.47	181	36.0
Master's, professional, doctoral degree	145.32	278	32.3

Note: Market shares may not sum to 100.0 because of rounding and missing categories by household type. "Asian" and "black" include Hispanics and non-Hispanics who identify themselves as being of the respective race alone. "Hispanic" includes people of any race who identify themselves as Hispanic. "Other" includes people who identify themselves as non-Hispanic and as Alaska Native, American Indian, Asian (who are also included in the "Asian" row), or Native Hawaiian or other Pacific Islander, as well as non-Hispanics reporting more than one race.
Source: Calculations by New Strategist based on the Bureau of Labor Statistics' 2012 Consumer Expenditure Survey

Sewing Materials, Patterns, and Notions

Best customers: Householders aged 55 to 74
                       Married couples
                       Households in the West and Midwest

Customer trends: Average household spending on sewing materials, patterns, and notions is likely to fall in the years ahead
                       as younger generations with little sewing experience fill the best-customer age groups.

The biggest spenders on sewing materials for clothing are older, married householders. Householders aged 55 to 74 spend 41 to 49 percent more than average on sewing materials. Married couples spend 35 percent more than average overall, with spending peaking at more than three times the average among those with preschoolers. Households in the West and Midwest spend, respectively, 52 and 34 percent more than average on this item.

Average household spending on sewing materials, patterns, and notions fell by 15 percent between 2000 and the overall spending trough year of 2010, after adjusting for inflation. But spending on this item more than recovered—with a 21 percent gain—between 2010 and 2012. Average household spending on sewing materials, patterns, and notions is likely to fall in the years ahead as younger generations with little sewing experience fill the best-customer age groups.

Table 2.11 Sewing materials, patterns, and notions

Total household spending $1,609,943,040.00
Average household spends   12.94

	AVERAGE HOUSEHOLD SPENDING	BEST CUSTOMERS (index)	BIGGEST CUSTOMERS (market share)
AGE OF HOUSEHOLDER			
Average household	**$12.94**	**100**	**100.0%**
Under age 25	3.72	29	1.9
Aged 25 to 34	10.79	83	13.5
Aged 35 to 44	10.94	85	14.7
Aged 45 to 54	11.96	92	18.3
Aged 55 to 64	18.29	141	25.9
Aged 65 to 74	19.33	149	18.0
Aged 75 or older	11.04	85	8.3

	AVERAGE HOUSEHOLD SPENDING	BEST CUSTOMERS (index)	BIGGEST CUSTOMERS (market share)
HOUSEHOLD INCOME			
Average household	**$12.94**	**100**	**100.0%**
Under $20,000	6.50	50	10.6
$20,000 to $39,999	10.81	84	18.8
$40,000 to $49,999	10.87	84	7.4
$50,000 to $69,999	17.31	134	19.3
$70,000 to $79,999	11.52	89	5.0
$80,000 to $99,999	16.63	129	11.3
$100,000 or more	19.44	150	28.1
HOUSEHOLD TYPE			
Average household	**12.94**	**100**	**100.0**
Married couples	17.48	135	65.6
Married couples, no children	15.53	120	25.0
Married couples with children	20.40	158	37.1
Oldest child under age 6	39.94	309	14.1
Oldest child aged 6 to 17	14.35	111	13.2
Oldest child aged 18 or older	18.32	142	10.0
Single parent with child under age 18	2.09	16	0.8
Single person	7.04	54	16.2
RACE AND HISPANIC ORIGIN			
Average household	**12.94**	**100**	**100.0**
Asian	13.06	101	4.4
Black	5.50	43	5.3
Hispanic	5.84	45	5.7
Non-Hispanic white and other	15.34	119	89.0
REGION			
Average household	**12.94**	**100**	**100.0**
Northeast	6.92	53	9.7
Midwest	17.37	134	29.8
South	9.20	71	26.5
West	19.61	152	34.1
EDUCATION			
Average household	**12.94**	**100**	**100.0**
Less than high school graduate	18.93	146	19.1
High school graduate	11.99	93	23.1
Some college	13.08	101	20.8
Associate's degree	10.54	81	8.0
Bachelor's degree or more	12.08	93	29.4
Bachelor's degree	9.22	71	14.2
Master's, professional, doctoral degree	16.90	131	15.2

Note: Market shares may not sum to 100.0 because of rounding and missing categories by household type. "Asian" and "black" include Hispanics and non-Hispanics who identify themselves as being of the respective race alone. "Hispanic" includes people of any race who identify themselves as Hispanic. "Other" includes people who identify themselves as non-Hispanic and as Alaska Native, American Indian, Asian (who are also included in the "Asian" row), or Native Hawaiian or other Pacific Islander, as well as non-Hispanics reporting more than one race.
Source: Calculations by New Strategist based on the Bureau of Labor Statistics' 2012 Consumer Expenditure Survey

Shoe and Apparel Repair and Alteration

Best customers: Householders aged 45 to 54
                         Married couples without children at home
                         Married couples with school-aged or older children at home
                         Households in the West

Customer trends: Average household spending on shoe and apparel repair and alteration should continue
                         to decline as boomers retire and have less need for maintaining professional clothes.

The biggest spenders on shoe and apparel repair and alteration are householders aged 45 to 54, who spend 21 percent more than average on this item. Married couples without children at home spend 42 percent more than average on shoe and apparel repair and alteration. Those with school-aged or older children at home spend 37 to 39 percent more than average on this item. Households in the West outspend the average by 26 percent.

Average household spending on shoe and apparel repair and alteration fell 17 percent between 2000 and 2006, after adjusting for inflation, and was down by another 9 percent between 2006 and 2012. Spending on this item is likely to continue to decline as boomers retire and have less need for maintaining professional clothes.

Table 2.12 Shoe and apparel repair and alteration

Total household spending $939,340,800.00
Average household spends   7.55

AGE OF HOUSEHOLDER	AVERAGE HOUSEHOLD SPENDING	BEST CUSTOMERS (index)	BIGGEST CUSTOMERS (market share)
Average household	$7.55	100	100.0%
Under age 25	5.18	69	4.5
Aged 25 to 34	7.25	96	15.5
Aged 35 to 44	5.88	78	13.5
Aged 45 to 54	9.12	121	23.9
Aged 55 to 64	8.13	108	19.7
Aged 65 to 74	8.44	112	13.5
Aged 75 or older	7.19	95	9.3

	AVERAGE HOUSEHOLD SPENDING	BEST CUSTOMERS (index)	BIGGEST CUSTOMERS (market share)
HOUSEHOLD INCOME			
Average household	**$7.55**	**100**	**100.0%**
Under $20,000	2.55	34	7.1
$20,000 to $39,999	4.03	53	12.0
$40,000 to $49,999	4.75	63	5.6
$50,000 to $69,999	7.01	93	13.4
$70,000 to $79,999	8.07	107	6.0
$80,000 to $99,999	10.25	136	12.0
$100,000 or more	17.70	234	43.9
HOUSEHOLD TYPE			
Average household	**7.55**	**100**	**100.0**
Married couples	9.62	127	61.9
Married couples, no children	10.72	142	29.6
Married couples with children	9.41	125	29.3
Oldest child under age 6	5.15	68	3.1
Oldest child aged 6 to 17	10.47	139	16.5
Oldest child aged 18 or older	10.35	137	9.7
Single parent with child under age 18	2.94	39	2.0
Single person	5.43	72	21.4
RACE AND HISPANIC ORIGIN			
Average household	**7.55**	**100**	**100.0**
Asian	6.16	82	3.5
Black	5.78	77	9.6
Hispanic	5.10	68	8.5
Non-Hispanic white and other	8.25	109	82.0
REGION			
Average household	**7.55**	**100**	**100.0**
Northeast	8.17	108	19.5
Midwest	6.64	88	19.5
South	6.56	87	32.4
West	9.55	126	28.5
EDUCATION			
Average household	**7.55**	**100**	**100.0**
Less than high school graduate	1.40	19	2.4
High school graduate	3.66	48	12.1
Some college	6.54	87	17.8
Associate's degree	6.59	87	8.6
Bachelor's degree or more	14.12	187	59.0
Bachelor's degree	11.94	158	31.5
Master's, professional, doctoral degree	17.86	237	27.5

Note: Market shares may not sum to 100.0 because of rounding and missing categories by household type. "Asian" and "black" include Hispanics and non-Hispanics who identify themselves as being of the respective race alone. "Hispanic" includes people of any race who identify themselves as Hispanic. "Other" includes people who identify themselves as non-Hispanic and as Alaska Native, American Indian, Asian (who are also included in the "Asian" row), or Native Hawaiian or other Pacific Islander, as well as non-Hispanics reporting more than one race.
Source: Calculations by New Strategist based on the Bureau of Labor Statistics' 2012 Consumer Expenditure Survey

Women's Apparel

Best customers: **Householders aged 45 to 54**
Married couples
Asians
Households in the West

Customer trends: **Average household spending on women's clothes is likely to continue to decline as boomer women retire from the workforce and have fewer reasons to shop for clothes.**

The average household spends more on women's clothes than on any other apparel category—$573 in 2012, or one-third of the apparel dollar. The biggest spenders on women's clothes are householders aged 45 to 54, who spend 18 percent more than the average household on this item. Married couples with children at home spend 32 percent more than average on women's clothes, the figure peaking among those with adult children at home, who outspend the average by 45 percent because there are more women in the household. Married couples without children at home (most of them older empty-nesters) spend 23 percent more than average on women's clothes. Asians spend 17 percent more than average on women's clothes. Households in the West, where many Asians reside, outspend the average by 15 percent.

Average household spending on women's clothes declined by 27 percent between 2000 and 2010, after adjusting for inflation, and fell another 3 percent between 2010 and 2012. Falling prices are one reason for the decline in spending, as cheaper imports allow consumers to buy more for less. Spending on women's clothes is likely to continue to decline as aging boomer women retire from the workforce and have fewer reasons to shop for clothes.

Table 2.13 Women's apparel

Total household spending $71,231,892,480.00
Average household spends   572.53

AGE OF HOUSEHOLDER	AVERAGE HOUSEHOLD SPENDING	BEST CUSTOMERS (index)	BIGGEST CUSTOMERS (market share)
Average household	**$572.53**	**100**	**100.0%**
Under age 25	398.76	70	4.6
Aged 25 to 34	649.19	113	18.3
Aged 35 to 44	557.71	97	16.9
Aged 45 to 54	676.34	118	23.4
Aged 55 to 64	629.00	110	20.1
Aged 65 to 74	521.80	91	11.0
Aged 75 or older	331.93	58	5.7

	AVERAGE HOUSEHOLD SPENDING	BEST CUSTOMERS (index)	BIGGEST CUSTOMERS (market share)
HOUSEHOLD INCOME			
Average household	**$572.53**	100	100.0%
Under $20,000	223.87	39	8.2
$20,000 to $39,999	370.75	65	14.6
$40,000 to $49,999	482.35	84	7.5
$50,000 to $69,999	556.11	97	14.0
$70,000 to $79,999	779.89	136	7.6
$80,000 to $99,999	794.56	139	12.2
$100,000 or more	1,097.38	192	35.9
HOUSEHOLD TYPE			
Average household	**572.53**	100	100.0
Married couples	729.50	127	61.9
Married couples, no children	706.95	123	25.7
Married couples with children	758.21	132	31.1
Oldest child under age 6	695.69	122	5.5
Oldest child aged 6 to 17	740.00	129	15.4
Oldest child aged 18 or older	827.76	145	10.2
Single parent with child under age 18	501.69	88	4.6
Single person	322.18	56	16.7
RACE AND HISPANIC ORIGIN			
Average household	**572.53**	100	100.0
Asian	672.33	117	5.1
Black	468.18	82	10.3
Hispanic	600.84	105	13.2
Non-Hispanic white and other	585.41	102	76.7
REGION			
Average household	**572.53**	100	100.0
Northeast	555.00	97	17.5
Midwest	549.52	96	21.3
South	544.17	95	35.4
West	656.93	115	25.9
EDUCATION			
Average household	**572.53**	100	100.0
Less than high school graduate	357.51	62	8.2
High school graduate	393.31	69	17.1
Some college	530.52	93	19.1
Associate's degree	629.21	110	10.9
Bachelor's degree or more	803.01	140	44.2
Bachelor's degree	761.49	133	26.5
Master's, professional, doctoral degree	873.25	153	17.7

Note: Market shares may not sum to 100.0 because of rounding and missing categories by household type. "Asian" and "black" include Hispanics and non-Hispanics who identify themselves as being of the respective race alone. "Hispanic" includes people of any race who identify themselves as Hispanic. "Other" includes people who identify themselves as non-Hispanic and as Alaska Native, American Indian, Asian (who are also included in the "Asian" row), or Native Hawaiian or other Pacific Islander, as well as non-Hispanics reporting more than one race.
Source: Calculations by New Strategist based on the Bureau of Labor Statistics' 2012 Consumer Expenditure Survey

Women's Shoes

Best customers: Householders aged 45 to 54
Married couples with school-aged or older children at home
Single parents
Blacks and Hispanics

Customer trends: Average household spending on women's shoes may continue to decline as boomer
women retire from the workforce and need fewer shoes.

The best customers of women's shoes are married couples with adult children at home. They spend 88 percent more than average on women's shoes. Behind the higher spending are their larger households, many of which include more than one adult female. Couples with school-aged children and single parents spend, respectively, 20 and 26 percent more than average on women's shoes. Householders aged 45 to 54 outspend the average on women's shoes by 29 percent. Black and Hispanic households spend, respectively, 12 and 15 percent more than average on women's shoes.

Average household spending on women's shoes fell 26 percent between 2000 and 2010, after adjusting for inflation, and another 3 percent between 2010 and 2012. Falling prices are one factor behind the decline in spending on women's shoes as cheaper imports allow consumers to buy more for less. Spending on women's shoes may continue to decline as boomer women retire from the workforce and need fewer shoes.

Table 2.14 Women's shoes

Total household spending $19,765,969,920.00
Average household spends   158.87

AGE OF HOUSEHOLDER	AVERAGE HOUSEHOLD SPENDING	BEST CUSTOMERS (index)	BIGGEST CUSTOMERS (market share)
Average household	$158.87	100	100.0%
Under age 25	109.61	69	4.5
Aged 25 to 34	176.32	111	17.9
Aged 35 to 44	161.50	102	17.6
Aged 45 to 54	205.62	129	25.6
Aged 55 to 64	154.04	97	17.7
Aged 65 to 74	127.07	80	9.6
Aged 75 or older	110.07	69	6.8

	AVERAGE HOUSEHOLD SPENDING	BEST CUSTOMERS (index)	BIGGEST CUSTOMERS (market share)
HOUSEHOLD INCOME			
Average household	**$158.87**	**100**	**100.0%**
Under $20,000	74.91	47	9.9
$20,000 to $39,999	111.82	70	15.9
$40,000 to $49,999	171.24	108	9.5
$50,000 to $69,999	148.42	93	13.5
$70,000 to $79,999	216.79	136	7.6
$80,000 to $99,999	187.18	118	10.4
$100,000 or more	277.10	174	32.7
HOUSEHOLD TYPE			
Average household	**158.87**	**100**	**100.0**
Married couples	197.39	124	60.3
Married couples, no children	182.62	115	24.0
Married couples with children	219.83	138	32.5
Oldest child under age 6	171.28	108	4.9
Oldest child aged 6 to 17	190.78	120	14.3
Oldest child aged 18 or older	298.54	188	13.3
Single parent with child under age 18	200.47	126	6.6
Single person	70.16	44	13.1
RACE AND HISPANIC ORIGIN			
Average household	**158.87**	**100**	**100.0**
Asian	153.62	97	4.2
Black	177.71	112	14.1
Hispanic	183.38	115	14.5
Non-Hispanic white and other	151.66	95	71.7
REGION			
Average household	**158.87**	**100**	**100.0**
Northeast	164.88	104	18.7
Midwest	138.86	87	19.4
South	164.96	104	38.7
West	163.90	103	23.2
EDUCATION			
Average household	**158.87**	**100**	**100.0**
Less than high school graduate	117.87	74	9.7
High school graduate	111.39	70	17.5
Some college	195.94	123	25.4
Associate's degree	124.12	78	7.7
Bachelor's degree or more	196.83	124	39.1
Bachelor's degree	209.19	132	26.2
Master's, professional, doctoral degree	175.94	111	12.9

Note: Market shares may not sum to 100.0 because of rounding and missing categories by household type. "Asian" and "black" include Hispanics and non-Hispanics who identify themselves as being of the respective race alone. "Hispanic" includes people of any race who identify themselves as Hispanic. "Other" includes people who identify themselves as non-Hispanic and as Alaska Native, American Indian, Asian (who are also included in the "Asian" row), or Native Hawaiian or other Pacific Islander, as well as non-Hispanics reporting more than one race.
Source: Calculations by New Strategist based on the Bureau of Labor Statistics' 2012 Consumer Expenditure Survey

Chapter 3.
Computers

Household Spending on Computers, 2000 to 2012

Thirty years ago the average household spent nothing on computers. Now computers are a central appliance in most homes and an important expenditure category. Average household spending on computer information services (Internet service) more than quadrupled since 2000, after adjusting for inflation. The average household spends twice as much on computer information services as on computers themselves. In 2000, computer hardware accounted for 70 percent of the average household's computer budget, while computer information services accounted for just 23 percent. By 2012, computer hardware accounted for a much smaller 30 percent of the computer budget, while Internet services accounted for a much larger 61 percent.

The average household spent $548 on computer hardware, software, and information services in 2012—53 percent more than in 2000, after adjusting for inflation. Spending trends differ by category, however. Household spending on computer hardware fell 35 percent between 2000 and 2012, after adjusting for inflation. In contrast, spending on computer software and accessories rose by 32 percent.

Spending on computers

(average annual spending of households on computer hardware, software, and information services, 2000, 2006, 2010, and 2012; in 2012 dollars)

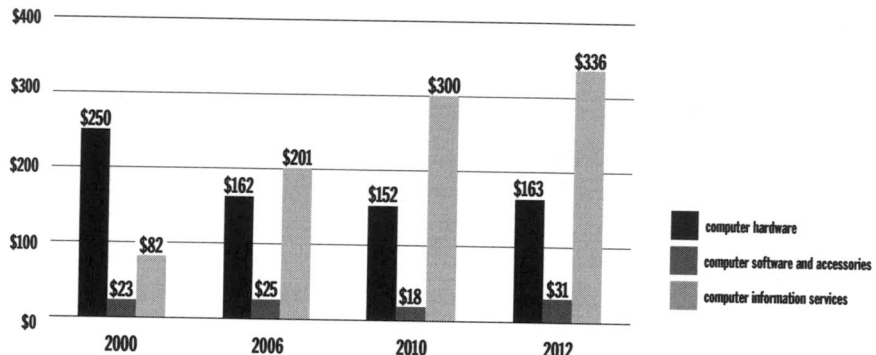

Table 3.1 Computer spending, 2000 to 2012

(average annual household spending on computer hardware, software, and information services for nonbusiness use and percent distribution, by category, 2000 to 2012; percent change in spending, 2000–06, 2006–12, and 2010–12; in 2012 dollars; ranked by amount spent)

	average annual household spending (in 2012$)				percent change		
	2012	2010	2006	2000	2010–12	2006–12	2000–06
Average household spending on computer equipment and services	**$547.87**	**$487.64**	**$397.26**	**$359.23**	**12.4%**	**37.9%**	**10.6%**
Computer information services	336.30	300.23	200.94	81.81	12.0	67.4	145.6
Computers and computer hardware	162.71	152.23	162.39	250.43	6.9	0.2	–35.2
Computer software and accessories	30.89	17.78	24.71	23.32	73.7	25.0	6.0
Internet services away from home	8.25	1.96	1.87	–	321.3	341.7	–
Repair of computer systems	5.52	7.68	7.35	3.67	–28.1	–24.9	100.3
Portable memory	3.76	7.43	–	–	–49.4	–	–
Computer systems installation	0.44	0.33	–	–	34.8	–	–

					percentage point change		
PERCENT DISTRIBUTION OF SPENDING	2012	2010	2006	2000	2010–12	2006–12	2000–06
Average household spending on computer equipment and services	**100.0%**	**100.0%**	**100.0%**	**100.0%**	–	–	–
Computer information services	61.4	61.6	50.6	22.8	–0.2	10.8	27.8
Computers and computer hardware	29.7	31.2	40.9	69.7	–1.5	–11.2	–28.8
Computer software and accessories	5.6	3.6	6.2	6.5	2.0	–0.6	–0.3
Internet services away from home	1.5	0.4	0.5	–	1.1	1.0	–
Repair of computer systems	1.0	1.6	1.8	1.0	–0.6	–0.8	0.8
Portable memory	0.7	1.5	–	–	–0.8	–	–
Computer systems installation	0.1	0.1	–	–	0.0	–	–

Note: Percentage point change calculations are based on unrounded figures. "–" means not applicable or data are unavailable.
Source: Bureau of Labor Statistics, 2000, 2006, 2010, and 2012 Consumer Expenditure Surveys; calculations by New Strategist

Computer Accessories

Best customers: Householders aged 45 to 74
Married couples without children at home
Married couples with school-aged or older children at home
Households in the West

Customer trends: Average household spending on computer accessories is likely to grow as more facets of the average home become computerized.

The best customers of computer accessories are middle-aged or older couples with or without children at home. Householders aged 45 to 74 spend 20 to 34 percent more than the average household on computer accessories and control 62 percent of household spending on this item. Married couples without children at home (most of them older empty-nesters) spend 40 percent more than average on computer accessories. Those with school-aged children outspend the average on this item by 37 percent, and married couples with adult children at home do so by 51 percent. Households in the West spend 43 percent more than average on computer accessories.

Because computer accessories only recently became a separate line item in the Consumer Expenditure Survey, there are no comparative spending data for previous years. Average household spending on computer accessories is likely to grow as more facets of the average home become computerized.

Table 3.2 Computer accessories

Total household spending $1,971,993,600.00
Average household spends   15.85

AGE OF HOUSEHOLDER	AVERAGE HOUSEHOLD SPENDING	BEST CUSTOMERS (index)	BIGGEST CUSTOMERS (market share)
Average household	$15.85	100	100.0%
Under age 25	10.45	66	4.3
Aged 25 to 34	11.16	70	11.4
Aged 35 to 44	13.44	85	14.7
Aged 45 to 54	19.47	123	24.3
Aged 55 to 64	18.98	120	21.9
Aged 65 to 74	21.17	134	16.1
Aged 75 or older	11.80	74	7.3

	AVERAGE HOUSEHOLD SPENDING	BEST CUSTOMERS (index)	BIGGEST CUSTOMERS (market share)
HOUSEHOLD INCOME			
Average household	**$15.85**	**100**	**100.0%**
Under $20,000	7.85	50	10.4
$20,000 to $39,999	11.28	71	16.0
$40,000 to $49,999	12.21	77	6.8
$50,000 to $69,999	15.38	97	14.0
$70,000 to $79,999	19.40	122	6.8
$80,000 to $99,999	15.17	96	8.4
$100,000 or more	31.71	200	37.5
HOUSEHOLD TYPE			
Average household	**15.85**	**100**	**100.0**
Married couples	20.66	130	63.3
Married couples, no children	22.22	140	29.2
Married couples with children	20.28	128	30.1
Oldest child under age 6	11.09	70	3.2
Oldest child aged 6 to 17	21.67	137	16.3
Oldest child aged 18 or older	23.89	151	10.6
Single parent with child under age 18	8.29	52	2.7
Single person	11.09	70	20.8
RACE AND HISPANIC ORIGIN			
Average household	**15.85**	**100**	**100.0**
Asian	17.50	110	4.8
Black	10.69	67	8.5
Hispanic	7.01	44	5.5
Non-Hispanic white and other	18.21	115	86.2
REGION			
Average household	**15.85**	**100**	**100.0**
Northeast	16.37	103	18.6
Midwest	14.05	89	19.7
South	12.57	79	29.5
West	22.65	143	32.2
EDUCATION			
Average household	**15.85**	**100**	**100.0**
Less than high school graduate	3.58	23	2.9
High school graduate	9.63	61	15.1
Some college	16.31	103	21.2
Associate's degree	14.31	90	8.9
Bachelor's degree or more	26.04	164	51.8
Bachelor's degree	24.68	156	31.0
Master's, professional, doctoral degree	28.38	179	20.8

Note: Market shares may not sum to 100.0 because of rounding and missing categories by household type. "Asian" and "black" include Hispanics and non-Hispanics who identify themselves as being of the respective race alone. "Hispanic" includes people of any race who identify themselves as Hispanic. "Other" includes people who identify themselves as non-Hispanic and as Alaska Native, American Indian, Asian (who are also included in the "Asian" row), or Native Hawaiian or other Pacific Islander, as well as non-Hispanics reporting more than one race.
Source: Calculations by New Strategist based on the Bureau of Labor Statistics' 2012 Consumer Expenditure Survey

Computer Information Services

Best customers: Householders aged 25 to 54
Married couples with children at home
Asians

Customer trends: Average household spending on computer information services will grow more slowly now that the majority of households are online, although some growth remains as younger householders replace older generations without Internet access.

Average household spending on computer information services shows relatively little variation by demographic characteristic because the item is so universally purchased. The best customers of Internet access are households with children. Householders ranging in age from 25 to 54 spend 10 to 18 percent more than the average household on Internet service and control 61 percent of the market for this item. Married couples with children at home spend 34 percent more than average on Internet service. Asian households outspend the average by 15 percent.

In the year 2000, computer information services ranked seventh in average household spending among information and consumer electronics categories. It is now poised to pass residential telephone service for third place. Average household spending on computer information services grew 67 percent between 2006 and 2012, after adjusting for inflation. The average household spends eight times as much on computer information services as on newspaper and magazine subscriptions. The growth in spending for online service is likely to slow now that the majority of households are online, although some growth remains as younger householders replace older generations without Internet access.

Table 3.3 Computer information services

Total household spending $41,841,100,800.00
Average household spends   336.30

AGE OF HOUSEHOLDER	AVERAGE HOUSEHOLD SPENDING	BEST CUSTOMERS (index)	BIGGEST CUSTOMERS (market share)
Average household	$336.30	100	100.0%
Under age 25	235.56	70	4.6
Aged 25 to 34	368.29	110	17.7
Aged 35 to 44	388.84	116	20.1
Aged 45 to 54	396.23	118	23.3
Aged 55 to 64	357.98	106	19.5
Aged 65 to 74	291.12	87	10.4
Aged 75 or older	151.49	45	4.4

	AVERAGE HOUSEHOLD SPENDING	BEST CUSTOMERS (index)	BIGGEST CUSTOMERS (market share)
HOUSEHOLD INCOME			
Average household	$336.30	100	100.0%
Under $20,000	147.77	44	9.2
$20,000 to $39,999	252.48	75	16.9
$40,000 to $49,999	331.09	98	8.7
$50,000 to $69,999	387.19	115	16.6
$70,000 to $79,999	417.88	124	6.9
$80,000 to $99,999	454.51	135	11.9
$100,000 or more	532.26	158	29.6
HOUSEHOLD TYPE			
Average household	336.30	100	100.0
Married couples	414.33	123	59.8
Married couples, no children	375.78	112	23.3
Married couples with children	449.29	134	31.4
Oldest child under age 6	404.10	120	5.5
Oldest child aged 6 to 17	447.72	133	15.8
Oldest child aged 18 or older	481.17	143	10.1
Single parent with child under age 18	298.25	89	4.7
Single person	211.43	63	18.7
RACE AND HISPANIC ORIGIN			
Average household	336.30	100	100.0
Asian	385.70	115	5.0
Black	261.11	78	9.8
Hispanic	268.44	80	10.0
Non-Hispanic white and other	360.14	107	80.4
REGION			
Average household	336.30	100	100.0
Northeast	362.26	108	19.4
Midwest	329.94	98	21.8
South	303.87	90	33.7
West	375.39	112	25.2
EDUCATION			
Average household	336.30	100	100.0
Less than high school graduate	172.29	51	6.7
High school graduate	275.41	82	20.4
Some college	344.72	103	21.1
Associate's degree	377.92	112	11.1
Bachelor's degree or more	433.83	129	40.7
Bachelor's degree	427.44	127	25.3
Master's, professional, doctoral degree	444.79	132	15.4

Note: Market shares may not sum to 100.0 because of rounding and missing categories by household type. "Asian" and "black" include Hispanics and non-Hispanics who identify themselves as being of the respective race alone. "Hispanic" includes people of any race who identify themselves as Hispanic. "Other" includes people who identify themselves as non-Hispanic and as Alaska Native, American Indian, Asian (who are also included in the "Asian" row), or Native Hawaiian or other Pacific Islander, as well as non-Hispanics reporting more than one race.
Source: Calculations by New Strategist based on the Bureau of Labor Statistics' 2012 Consumer Expenditure Survey

Computer Software

Best customers: Householders under age 25 and aged 35 to 54
Married couples with children at home
Asians
Households in the West

Customer trends: Average household spending on computer software is unlikely to grow much in the years ahead as desktop computers become less popular and spending shifts toward apps for handheld devices.

The best customers of computer software are young and middle-aged householders with children at home. Householders aged 35 to 54 spend 14 to 20 percent more than the average household on computer software. Householders under age 25 spend 76 percent more than average on software. Married couples with children at home spend 35 percent more than average on this item, the figure peaking at 90 percent among those with preschoolers. Spending on this item by Asians is 96 percent higher than average. Households in the West, where many Asians reside, spend 90 percent more than average on software.

Because computer software only recently became a separate line item (separate from computer accessories) in the Consumer Expenditure Survey, there are no comparative spending data for previous years. Average household spending on computer software is unlikely to grow much in the years ahead as desktop computers become less popular and spending shifts toward apps for handheld devices.

Table 3.4 Computer software

Total household spending $1,871,216,640.00
Average household spends   15.04

AGE OF HOUSEHOLDER	AVERAGE HOUSEHOLD SPENDING	BEST CUSTOMERS (index)	BIGGEST CUSTOMERS (market share)
Average household	$15.04	100	100.0%
Under age 25	26.43	176	11.5
Aged 25 to 34	14.60	97	15.7
Aged 35 to 44	17.08	114	19.7
Aged 45 to 54	18.09	120	23.8
Aged 55 to 64	15.73	105	19.1
Aged 65 to 74	9.24	61	7.4
Aged 75 or older	4.22	28	2.7

	AVERAGE HOUSEHOLD SPENDING	BEST CUSTOMERS (index)	BIGGEST CUSTOMERS (market share)
HOUSEHOLD INCOME			
Average household	**$15.04**	**100**	**100.0%**
Under $20,000	7.57	50	10.6
$20,000 to $39,999	8.65	58	13.0
$40,000 to $49,999	6.98	46	4.1
$50,000 to $69,999	13.69	91	13.1
$70,000 to $79,999	20.35	135	7.6
$80,000 to $99,999	18.24	121	10.7
$100,000 or more	32.90	219	41.0
HOUSEHOLD TYPE			
Average household	**15.04**	**100**	**100.0**
Married couples	18.72	124	60.5
Married couples, no children	16.64	111	23.1
Married couples with children	20.33	135	31.8
Oldest child under age 6	28.59	190	8.7
Oldest child aged 6 to 17	18.06	120	14.3
Oldest child aged 18 or older	18.81	125	8.8
Single parent with child under age 18	9.81	65	3.4
Single person	8.90	59	17.6
RACE AND HISPANIC ORIGIN			
Average household	**15.04**	**100**	**100.0**
Asian	29.52	196	8.5
Black	8.18	54	6.8
Hispanic	10.80	72	9.0
Non-Hispanic white and other	16.87	112	84.2
REGION			
Average household	**15.04**	**100**	**100.0**
Northeast	13.15	87	15.8
Midwest	10.91	73	16.1
South	10.23	68	25.3
West	28.58	190	42.8
EDUCATION			
Average household	**15.04**	**100**	**100.0**
Less than high school graduate	4.50	30	3.9
High school graduate	8.79	58	14.6
Some college	13.03	87	17.8
Associate's degree	22.05	147	14.5
Bachelor's degree or more	23.47	156	49.2
Bachelor's degree	24.97	166	33.1
Master's, professional, doctoral degree	20.88	139	16.1

Note: Market shares may not sum to 100.0 because of rounding and missing categories by household type. "Asian" and "black" include Hispanics and non-Hispanics who identify themselves as being of the respective race alone. "Hispanic" includes people of any race who identify themselves as Hispanic. "Other" includes people who identify themselves as non-Hispanic and as Alaska Native, American Indian, Asian (who are also included in the "Asian" row), or Native Hawaiian or other Pacific Islander, as well as non-Hispanics reporting more than one race.
Source: Calculations by New Strategist based on the Bureau of Labor Statistics' 2012 Consumer Expenditure Survey

Computers and Computer Hardware for Nonbusiness Use

Best customers: Householders aged 35 to 64
Married couples with school-aged or older children at home
Asians
Households in the West

Customer trends: Average household spending on computers and computer hardware for nonbusiness use may rise over the next few years as a growing share of households purchase tablet computers.

The best customers of computers and computer hardware for nonbusiness use are households with children, especially children of college age. Householders aged 35 to 64—many with college-aged kids—spend 11 to 20 percent more than the average household on computers. Married couples with school-aged children spend 56 percent more than the average household on this item, and those with adult children at home spend 77 percent more. Asians spend 61 percent more than average on computers. Households in the West, where many Asians reside, spend 16 percent more than average on computers.

Average household spending on computers and computer hardware for nonbusiness use fell by 35 percent between 2000 and 2006, after adjusting for inflation, and stayed level over the next six-year period. Between the overall spending trough year of 2010 and 2012, however, spending on computers grew 7 percent. Spending on computer hardware may rise in the next few years as an increasing share of households purchase tablet computers.

Table 3.5 **Computers and computer hardware for nonbusiness use**

Total household spending $20,243,727,360.00
Average household spends   162.71

AGE OF HOUSEHOLDER	AVERAGE HOUSEHOLD SPENDING	BEST CUSTOMERS (index)	BIGGEST CUSTOMERS (market share)
Average household	**$162.71**	**100**	**100.0%**
Under age 25	153.10	94	6.2
Aged 25 to 34	166.70	102	16.6
Aged 35 to 44	194.70	120	20.8
Aged 45 to 54	184.61	113	22.5
Aged 55 to 64	180.45	111	20.3
Aged 65 to 74	145.25	89	10.8
Aged 75 or older	49.65	31	3.0

	AVERAGE HOUSEHOLD SPENDING	BEST CUSTOMERS (index)	BIGGEST CUSTOMERS (market share)
HOUSEHOLD INCOME			
Average household	$162.71	100	100.0%
Under $20,000	62.43	38	8.1
$20,000 to $39,999	89.89	55	12.5
$40,000 to $49,999	125.84	77	6.8
$50,000 to $69,999	163.51	100	14.5
$70,000 to $79,999	191.70	118	6.6
$80,000 to $99,999	207.80	128	11.3
$100,000 or more	349.95	215	40.3
HOUSEHOLD TYPE			
Average household	162.71	100	100.0
Married couples	214.48	132	64.0
Married couples, no children	181.67	112	23.3
Married couples with children	250.93	154	36.3
Oldest child under age 6	186.75	115	5.2
Oldest child aged 6 to 17	253.58	156	18.5
Oldest child aged 18 or older	287.97	177	12.5
Single parent with child under age 18	113.62	70	3.7
Single person	85.59	53	15.6
RACE AND HISPANIC ORIGIN			
Average household	162.71	100	100.0
Asian	261.95	161	7.0
Black	107.41	66	8.3
Hispanic	115.89	71	8.9
Non-Hispanic white and other	179.90	111	83.0
REGION			
Average household	162.71	100	100.0
Northeast	169.39	104	18.8
Midwest	157.47	97	21.5
South	147.15	90	33.7
West	188.21	116	26.1
EDUCATION			
Average household	162.71	100	100.0
Less than high school graduate	62.38	38	5.0
High school graduate	97.65	60	15.0
Some college	153.24	94	19.4
Associate's degree	164.44	101	10.0
Bachelor's degree or more	261.31	161	50.6
Bachelor's degree	262.85	162	32.2
Master's, professional, doctoral degree	258.67	159	18.5

Note: Market shares may not sum to 100.0 because of rounding and missing categories by household type. "Asian" and "black" include Hispanics and non-Hispanics who identify themselves as being of the respective race alone. "Hispanic" includes people of any race who identify themselves as Hispanic. "Other" includes people who identify themselves as non-Hispanic and as Alaska Native, American Indian, Asian (who are also included in the "Asian" row), or Native Hawaiian or other Pacific Islander, as well as non-Hispanics reporting more than one race.
Source: Calculations by New Strategist based on the Bureau of Labor Statistics' 2012 Consumer Expenditure Survey

Internet Services Away from Home

Best customers: Householders aged 35 to 44
Married couples with children under age 18
Single parents
Asians
Households in the Northeast

Customer trends: Average household spending on Internet services away from home is likely to be constrained in the years ahead by free wifi connections offered by hotels and coffee shops.

The best customers for Internet services away from home are younger householders with children. Married couples with preschoolers spend 31 percent more than average on Internet services away from home, and those with school-aged children spend 45 percent more. Householders aged 35 to 44, most with children, spend 51 percent more than average on this item. Single parents, whose spending approaches average on only a few items, spend 17 percent more than average on Internet services away from home. Spending on this item is 50 percent above average among Asians. Households in the Northeast spend 54 percent more than average on Internet services away from home.

Average household spending on Internet services away from home (a category added to the Consumer Expenditure Survey in 2005) grew by a slow 5 percent between 2006 and 2010, then surged between 2010 and 2012. This recent increase may be an anomaly in the expenditure data. Average household spending on Internet services away from home is likely to be constrained in the years ahead by free wifi connections offered by hotels and coffee shops.

Table 3.6 Internet services away from home

Total household spending	$1,026,432,000.00
Average household spends	8.25

AGE OF HOUSEHOLDER	AVERAGE HOUSEHOLD SPENDING	BEST CUSTOMERS (index)	BIGGEST CUSTOMERS (market share)
Average household	$8.25	100	100.0%
Under age 25	6.16	75	4.9
Aged 25 to 34	9.34	113	18.3
Aged 35 to 44	12.46	151	26.2
Aged 45 to 54	8.26	100	19.8
Aged 55 to 64	7.08	86	15.7
Aged 65 to 74	7.40	90	10.8
Aged 75 or older	3.63	44	4.3

	AVERAGE HOUSEHOLD SPENDING	BEST CUSTOMERS (index)	BIGGEST CUSTOMERS (market share)
HOUSEHOLD INCOME			
Average household	**$8.25**	**100**	**100.0%**
Under $20,000	4.52	55	11.5
$20,000 to $39,999	7.07	86	19.3
$40,000 to $49,999	7.28	88	7.8
$50,000 to $69,999	9.86	120	17.3
$70,000 to $79,999	7.76	94	5.3
$80,000 to $99,999	9.52	115	10.2
$100,000 or more	12.64	153	28.7
HOUSEHOLD TYPE			
Average household	**8.25**	**100**	**100.0**
Married couples	9.18	111	54.0
Married couples, no children	7.63	92	19.3
Married couples with children	10.86	132	30.9
Oldest child under age 6	10.83	131	6.0
Oldest child aged 6 to 17	11.99	145	17.3
Oldest child aged 18 or older	8.97	109	7.7
Single parent with child under age 18	9.67	117	6.1
Single person	6.53	79	23.5
RACE AND HISPANIC ORIGIN			
Average household	**8.25**	**100**	**100.0**
Asian	12.38	150	6.5
Black	7.07	86	10.8
Hispanic	9.20	112	14.0
Non-Hispanic white and other	8.32	101	75.7
REGION			
Average household	**8.25**	**100**	**100.0**
Northeast	10.43	126	22.8
Midwest	7.21	87	19.4
South	7.28	88	32.9
West	9.16	111	25.0
EDUCATION			
Average household	**8.25**	**100**	**100.0**
Less than high school graduate	5.34	65	8.5
High school graduate	6.41	78	19.4
Some college	7.99	97	19.9
Associate's degree	9.28	112	11.1
Bachelor's degree or more	10.77	131	41.2
Bachelor's degree	9.51	115	23.0
Master's, professional, doctoral degree	12.94	157	18.2

Note: Market shares may not sum to 100.0 because of rounding and missing categories by household type. "Asian" and "black" include Hispanics and non-Hispanics who identify themselves as being of the respective race alone. "Hispanic" includes people of any race who identify themselves as Hispanic. "Other" includes people who identify themselves as non-Hispanic and as Alaska Native, American Indian, Asian (who are also included in the "Asian" row), or Native Hawaiian or other Pacific Islander, as well as non-Hispanics reporting more than one race.
Source: Calculations by New Strategist based on the Bureau of Labor Statistics' 2012 Consumer Expenditure Survey

Portable Memory

Best customers: Householders aged 35 to 54
Married couples with children at home
Asians
Households in the Northeast and West

Customer trends: Average household spending on portable memory may have peaked as the growing use of cloud computing allows people to secure their documents and access them from multiple devices.

The biggest spenders on portable memory are middle-aged householders with children at home. Householders ranging in age from 35 to 54 spend 28 to 44 percent more than the average household on USB sticks and other memory devices. Married couples with children at home spend 58 percent more than average on portable memory. Asian households spend 77 percent more than average on this item. Households in the Northeast and West outspend the average by 21 and 24 percent, respectively.

Portable memory was not included in the Consumer Expenditure Survey until recently, which limits the analysis of spending trends. Average household spending on portable memory fell 49 percent between 2010 and 2012, after adjusting for inflation. It may fade even more as the growing use of cloud computing allows people to secure their documents and access them from multiple devices.

Table 3.7 **Portable memory**

Total household spending $467,804,160.00
Average household spends   3.76

	AVERAGE HOUSEHOLD SPENDING	BEST CUSTOMERS (index)	BIGGEST CUSTOMERS (market share)
AGE OF HOUSEHOLDER			
Average household	$3.76	100	100.0%
Under age 25	2.45	65	4.3
Aged 25 to 34	3.35	89	14.4
Aged 35 to 44	5.42	144	25.0
Aged 45 to 54	4.80	128	25.3
Aged 55 to 64	3.95	105	19.2
Aged 65 to 74	3.29	88	10.5
Aged 75 or older	0.49	13	1.3

	AVERAGE HOUSEHOLD SPENDING	BEST CUSTOMERS (index)	BIGGEST CUSTOMERS (market share)
HOUSEHOLD INCOME			
Average household	$3.76	100	100.0%
Under $20,000	1.31	35	7.3
$20,000 to $39,999	2.77	74	16.6
$40,000 to $49,999	2.63	70	6.2
$50,000 to $69,999	4.26	113	16.4
$70,000 to $79,999	3.81	101	5.7
$80,000 to $99,999	3.44	91	8.1
$100,000 or more	7.99	213	39.8
HOUSEHOLD TYPE			
Average household	3.76	100	100.0
Married couples	4.68	124	60.5
Married couples, no children	3.50	93	19.4
Married couples with children	5.94	158	37.1
Oldest child under age 6	5.53	147	6.7
Oldest child aged 6 to 17	6.11	163	19.3
Oldest child aged 18 or older	5.92	157	11.1
Single parent with child under age 18	3.06	81	4.3
Single person	2.48	66	19.6
RACE AND HISPANIC ORIGIN			
Average household	3.76	100	100.0
Asian	6.64	177	7.7
Black	3.24	86	10.8
Hispanic	2.92	78	9.7
Non-Hispanic white and other	4.02	107	80.2
REGION			
Average household	3.76	100	100.0
Northeast	4.55	121	21.8
Midwest	3.70	98	21.8
South	2.88	77	28.5
West	4.66	124	27.9
EDUCATION			
Average household	3.76	100	100.0
Less than high school graduate	1.15	31	4.0
High school graduate	1.97	52	13.1
Some college	3.40	90	18.6
Associate's degree	4.40	117	11.6
Bachelor's degree or more	6.30	168	52.8
Bachelor's degree	5.46	145	28.9
Master's, professional, doctoral degree	7.73	206	23.9

Note: Market shares may not sum to 100.0 because of rounding and missing categories by household type. "Asian" and "black" include Hispanics and non-Hispanics who identify themselves as being of the respective race alone. "Hispanic" includes people of any race who identify themselves as Hispanic. "Other" includes people who identify themselves as non-Hispanic and as Alaska Native, American Indian, Asian (who are also included in the "Asian" row), or Native Hawaiian or other Pacific Islander, as well as non-Hispanics reporting more than one race.
Source: Calculations by New Strategist based on the Bureau of Labor Statistics' 2012 Consumer Expenditure Survey

Repair of Computer Systems for Nonbusiness Use

Best customers: Householders aged 55 to 74
Married couples without children at home
Married couples with adult children at home
Single parents
Asians
Households in the West

Customer trends: Average household spending on repair of computer systems for nonbusiness use is likely
to continue to decline as desktop computer systems become less popular.

The best customers of repair of computer systems for nonbusiness use are older householders and households that include adult children. Householders aged 55 to 74 spend 29 to 48 percent more than the average household on computer repairs. Married couples without children at home, most older, spend 30 percent more than average on computer repair. Couples with adult children at home spend 53 percent above average on this item. Single parents, whose spending approaches average on only a few items, spend a surprising 27 percent above average on computer repair. Asian households spend one-half more than average on this item. Spending on computer repair by households in the West is 33 percent above average.

Average household spending on repair of computer systems for nonbusiness use doubled between 2000 and 2006, after adjusting for inflation, and then fell by one-quarter since then. Behind the decline is the substitution of smartphones and tablets for desktop computer systems, reducing the need for repair. Average household spending on repair of computer systems for nonbusiness use is likely to continue to decline as this substitution continues.

Table 3.8 Repair of computer systems for nonbusiness use

Total household spending $686,776,320.00
Average household spends   5.52

AGE OF HOUSEHOLDER	AVERAGE HOUSEHOLD SPENDING	BEST CUSTOMERS (index)	BIGGEST CUSTOMERS (market share)
Average household	$5.52	100	100.0%
Under age 25	1.83	33	2.2
Aged 25 to 34	6.56	119	19.2
Aged 35 to 44	4.35	79	13.7
Aged 45 to 54	4.52	82	16.2
Aged 55 to 64	7.10	129	23.5
Aged 65 to 74	8.15	148	17.8
Aged 75 or older	4.18	76	7.4

	AVERAGE HOUSEHOLD SPENDING	BEST CUSTOMERS (index)	BIGGEST CUSTOMERS (market share)
HOUSEHOLD INCOME			
Average household	$5.52	100	100.0%
Under $20,000	2.23	40	8.5
$20,000 to $39,999	6.29	114	25.7
$40,000 to $49,999	4.27	77	6.8
$50,000 to $69,999	6.45	117	16.9
$70,000 to $79,999	3.58	65	3.6
$80,000 to $99,999	6.94	126	11.1
$100,000 or more	8.07	146	27.4
HOUSEHOLD TYPE			
Average household	5.52	100	100.0
Married couples	6.43	116	56.6
Married couples, no children	7.19	130	27.2
Married couples with children	6.39	116	27.2
Oldest child under age 6	4.05	73	3.3
Oldest child aged 6 to 17	6.07	110	13.1
Oldest child aged 18 or older	8.42	153	10.8
Single parent with child under age 18	7.01	127	6.7
Single person	3.89	70	20.9
RACE AND HISPANIC ORIGIN			
Average household	5.52	100	100.0
Asian	8.26	150	6.5
Black	2.10	38	4.8
Hispanic	4.30	78	9.8
Non-Hispanic white and other	6.29	114	85.5
REGION			
Average household	5.52	100	100.0
Northeast	5.31	96	17.4
Midwest	4.90	89	19.7
South	4.88	88	32.9
West	7.35	133	30.0
EDUCATION			
Average household	5.52	100	100.0
Less than high school graduate	3.53	64	8.4
High school graduate	4.90	89	22.1
Some college	5.52	100	20.6
Associate's degree	4.61	84	8.2
Bachelor's degree or more	7.12	129	40.7
Bachelor's degree	6.26	113	22.6
Master's, professional, doctoral degree	8.60	156	18.1

Note: Market shares may not sum to 100.0 because of rounding and missing categories by household type. "Asian" and "black" include Hispanics and non-Hispanics who identify themselves as being of the respective race alone. "Hispanic" includes people of any race who identify themselves as Hispanic. "Other" includes people who identify themselves as non-Hispanic and as Alaska Native, American Indian, Asian (who are also included in the "Asian" row), or Native Hawaiian or other Pacific Islander, as well as non-Hispanics reporting more than one race.
Source: Calculations by New Strategist based on the Bureau of Labor Statistics' 2012 Consumer Expenditure Survey

Chapter 4.
Education

Household Spending on Education, 2000 to 2012

The average household spent $1,207 on education in 2012, including $825 for college tuition. Although public colleges cost thousands of dollars a year, and private colleges tens of thousands, the averages reported here are low because relatively few households have education expenses. A more realistic spending figure for college tuition can be found in Appendix B, which shows the spending of purchasers only. During the average quarter of 2012, just 5.7 percent of households spent on college tuition, but those who did spent $3,599 per quarter out-of-pocket. Between 2000 and 2012, average household spending on college tuition increased 70 percent, after adjusting for inflation.

More important than average spending figures are the patterns of spending by demographic characteristic. Householders under age 25 and those aged 45 to 54 are the biggest spenders on college tuition. The younger householders are paying for their own college education, while the older ones are paying for their children's education. Because of volatility in the financial markets and tighter lending standards, average household spending on education may stabilize or even decline in the years ahead.

Spending on college tuition

(average household spending on college tuition, 2000, 2006, 2010, and 2012; in 2012 dollars)

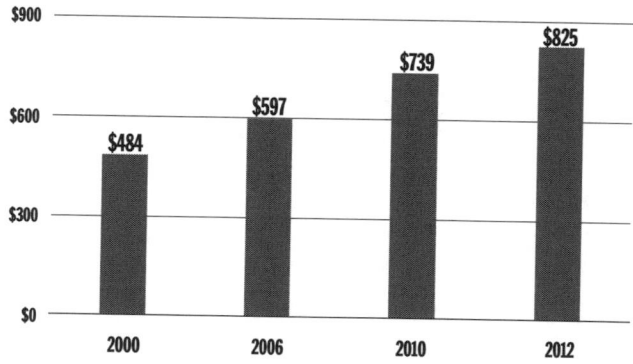

Table 4.1 Education spending, 2000 to 2012

(average annual household spending on education and percent distribution, by category, 2000 to 2012; percent change and percentage point change in spending, 2000–06, 2006–12, and 2000–12; in 2012 dollars; ranked by amount spent)

	average annual household spending (in 2012$)				percent change		
	2012	2010	2006	2000	2010–12	2006–12	2000–06
Average annual household spending on education	$1,207.35	$1,131.31	$1,011.06	$842.55	6.7%	19.4%	20.0%
Tuition, college	824.99	738.74	596.61	484.37	11.7	38.3	23.2
Tuition, elementary and high school	169.04	164.28	178.19	135.22	2.9	−5.1	31.8
Books and supplies, college	65.30	67.17	68.64	70.21	−2.8	−4.9	−2.2
Miscellaneous school supplies	51.86	66.90	62.31	65.50	−22.5	−16.8	−4.9
Other school expenses including rentals	42.82	36.60	54.29	32.00	17.0	−21.1	69.7
Books and supplies, elementary and high school	16.25	13.84	19.00	18.56	17.5	−14.5	2.4
Test preparation, tutoring services	15.86	10.74	–	–	47.7	–	–
Tuition, other schools	10.70	20.58	27.99	32.56	−48.0	−61.8	−14.0
Tuition, vocational and technical schools	7.66	9.68	–	–	−20.8	–	–
Books and supplies, other schools	1.78	1.25	–	–	42.1	–	–
Books and supplies, vocational and technical schools	0.71	1.03	–	–	−31.2	–	–
Books and supplies, day care and nursery	0.38	0.52	4.02	4.12	−26.3	−90.5	−2.4

					percentage point change		
PERCENT DISTRIBUTION OF SPENDING	2012	2010	2006	2000	2010–12	2006–12	2000–06
Average annual household spending on education	100.0%	100.0%	100.0%	100.0%	–	–	–
Tuition, college	68.3	65.3	59.0	57.5	3.0	9.3	1.5
Tuition, elementary and high school	14.0	14.5	17.6	16.0	−0.5	−3.6	1.6
Books and supplies, college	5.4	5.9	6.8	8.3	−0.5	−1.4	−1.5
Miscellaneous school supplies	4.3	5.9	6.2	7.8	−1.6	−1.9	−1.6
Other school expenses including rentals	3.5	3.2	5.4	3.8	0.3	−1.8	1.6
Books and supplies, elementary and high school	1.3	1.2	1.9	2.2	0.1	−0.5	−0.3
Test preparation, tutoring services	1.3	0.9	–	–	0.4	–	–
Tuition, other schools	0.9	1.8	2.8	3.9	−0.9	−1.9	−1.1
Tuition, vocational and technical schools	0.6	0.9	–	–	−0.2	–	–
Books and supplies, other schools	0.1	0.1	–	–	0.0	–	–
Books and supplies, vocational and technical schools	0.1	0.1	–	–	0.0	–	–
Books and supplies, day care and nursery	0.0	0.0	0.4	0.5	0.0	−0.4	−0.1

Note: Percentage point change calculations are based on unrounded figures. "–" means not applicable or data are unavailable.
Source: Bureau of Labor Statistics, 2000, 2006, 2010, and 2012 Consumer Expenditure Surveys; calculations by New Strategist

Books and Supplies, College

Best customers: Householders under age 25 and aged 45 to 54
Married couples with adult children at home
Asians

Customer trends: Average household spending on books and supplies for college will decline as college students search for less-expensive alternatives such as renting or downloading texts.

Not surprisingly, college students are the best customers of college books and supplies. Householders under age 25 spend three-and-one-third times the average on this item and account for 22 percent of the market. Married couples with children aged 18 or older at home spend nearly three times the average on college books and supplies. Asian households spend almost twice the average.

Average household spending on college books and supplies fell 7 percent between 2000 and 2012, after adjusting for inflation. Behind the decline is the valiant attempt by students and parents to cut costs as tuition soars. Spending on books and supplies for college is likely to decline further in the years ahead as students search for less-expensive books via the Internet.

Table 4.2 Books and supplies, college

Total household spending $8,124,364,800.00
Average household spends 65.30

AGE OF HOUSEHOLDER	AVERAGE HOUSEHOLD SPENDING	BEST CUSTOMERS (index)	BIGGEST CUSTOMERS (market share)
Average household	$65.30	100	100.0%
Under age 25	218.87	335	22.0
Aged 25 to 34	59.60	91	14.8
Aged 35 to 44	49.16	75	13.1
Aged 45 to 54	98.54	151	29.9
Aged 55 to 64	57.69	88	16.2
Aged 65 to 74	14.02	21	2.6
Aged 75 or older	10.52	16	1.6

	AVERAGE HOUSEHOLD SPENDING	BEST CUSTOMERS (index)	BIGGEST CUSTOMERS (market share)
HOUSEHOLD INCOME			
Average household	**$65.30**	**100**	**100.0%**
Under $20,000	62.57	96	20.2
$20,000 to $39,999	34.84	53	12.0
$40,000 to $49,999	34.72	53	4.7
$50,000 to $69,999	38.32	59	8.5
$70,000 to $79,999	53.51	82	4.6
$80,000 to $99,999	77.74	119	10.5
$100,000 or more	137.96	211	39.6
HOUSEHOLD TYPE			
Average household	**65.30**	**100**	**100.0**
Married couples	75.90	116	56.5
Married couples, no children	52.98	81	16.9
Married couples with children	98.49	151	35.5
Oldest child under age 6	51.58	79	3.6
Oldest child aged 6 to 17	60.55	93	11.0
Oldest child aged 18 or older	192.77	295	20.8
Single parent with child under age 18	48.54	74	3.9
Single person	52.81	81	24.0
RACE AND HISPANIC ORIGIN			
Average household	**65.30**	**100**	**100.0**
Asian	124.59	191	8.3
Black	53.49	82	10.3
Hispanic	50.93	78	9.8
Non-Hispanic white and other	69.63	107	80.0
REGION			
Average household	**65.30**	**100**	**100.0**
Northeast	76.64	117	21.2
Midwest	65.42	100	22.2
South	51.29	79	29.3
West	79.25	121	27.3
EDUCATION			
Average household	**65.30**	**100**	**100.0**
Less than high school graduate	18.51	28	3.7
High school graduate	30.25	46	11.6
Some college	81.06	124	25.6
Associate's degree	68.84	105	10.4
Bachelor's degree or more	100.98	155	48.8
Bachelor's degree	100.59	154	30.7
Master's, professional, doctoral degree	101.66	156	18.1

Note: Market shares may not sum to 100.0 because of rounding and missing categories by household type. "Asian" and "black" include Hispanics and non-Hispanics who identify themselves as being of the respective race alone. "Hispanic" includes people of any race who identify themselves as Hispanic. "Other" includes people who identify themselves as non-Hispanic and as Alaska Native, American Indian, Asian (who are also included in the "Asian" row), or Native Hawaiian or other Pacific Islander, as well as non-Hispanics reporting more than one race.
Source: Calculations by New Strategist based on the Bureau of Labor Statistics' 2012 Consumer Expenditure Survey

Books and Supplies, Elementary and High School

Best customers: Householders aged 35 to 54
                        Married couples with school-aged or older children at home
                        Single parents
                        Asians and Hispanics

Customer trends: Average household spending on books and supplies for elementary and high school may continue to grow
                        in the years ahead as schools become increasingly dependent on parents to provide books and supplies.

The best customers of books and supplies for elementary and high school are parents with school-aged children. Married couples with children aged 6 to 17 spend over four times the average on this item. Single parents spend over twice the average on books and supplies for elementary and high school. Together these groups control 63 percent of the market. Householders aged 35 to 54 spend much more than average on this item because many have school-aged children. Asian households spend 88 percent more than average on elementary and high school books and supplies, and Hispanics spend 19 percent more.

Average household spending on books and supplies for elementary and high school grew 2 percent between 2000 and 2006 (the year overall household spending peaked), and then fell by a sharp 27 percent between 2006 and 2010 as the Great Recession set in and parents cut back on their spending. In the two years since the overall household spending trough year of 2010 spending on this item began to rise again, growing by 14 percent. With schools cutting budgets and becoming increasingly dependent on parents to provide books and supplies, this category may continue to grow in the years ahead.

Table 4.3 Books and supplies, elementary and high school

Total household spending $2,021,760,000.00
Average household spends   16.25

	AVERAGE HOUSEHOLD SPENDING	BEST CUSTOMERS (index)	BIGGEST CUSTOMERS (market share)
AGE OF HOUSEHOLDER			
Average household	$16.25	100	100.0%
Under age 25	3.52	22	1.4
Aged 25 to 34	13.69	84	13.6
Aged 35 to 44	36.78	226	39.3
Aged 45 to 54	26.47	163	32.2
Aged 55 to 64	9.38	58	10.6
Aged 65 to 74	3.00	18	2.2
Aged 75 or older	1.04	6	0.6

	AVERAGE HOUSEHOLD SPENDING	BEST CUSTOMERS (index)	BIGGEST CUSTOMERS (market share)
HOUSEHOLD INCOME			
Average household	**$16.25**	**100**	**100.0%**
Under $20,000	4.51	28	5.8
$20,000 to $39,999	10.48	64	14.5
$40,000 to $49,999	13.66	84	7.4
$50,000 to $69,999	21.86	135	19.4
$70,000 to $79,999	12.00	74	4.1
$80,000 to $99,999	16.23	100	8.8
$100,000 or more	34.54	213	39.8
HOUSEHOLD TYPE			
Average household	**16.25**	**100**	**100.0**
Married couples	25.11	155	75.1
Married couples, no children	3.63	22	4.7
Married couples with children	42.81	263	61.9
Oldest child under age 6	3.54	22	1.0
Oldest child aged 6 to 17	70.49	434	51.6
Oldest child aged 18 or older	21.55	133	9.4
Single parent with child under age 18	35.51	219	11.5
Single person	1.26	8	2.3
RACE AND HISPANIC ORIGIN			
Average household	**16.25**	**100**	**100.0**
Asian	30.59	188	8.2
Black	15.98	98	12.4
Hispanic	19.38	119	15.0
Non-Hispanic white and other	15.79	97	72.9
REGION			
Average household	**16.25**	**100**	**100.0**
Northeast	16.14	99	17.9
Midwest	13.03	80	17.8
South	18.01	111	41.3
West	16.59	102	23.0
EDUCATION			
Average household	**16.25**	**100**	**100.0**
Less than high school graduate	9.78	60	7.9
High school graduate	11.76	72	18.0
Some college	13.42	83	17.0
Associate's degree	20.88	128	12.7
Bachelor's degree or more	22.87	141	44.4
Bachelor's degree	17.28	106	21.2
Master's, professional, doctoral degree	32.47	200	23.2

Note: Market shares may not sum to 100.0 because of rounding and missing categories by household type. "Asian" and "black" include Hispanics and non-Hispanics who identify themselves as being of the respective race alone. "Hispanic" includes people of any race who identify themselves as Hispanic. "Other" includes people who identify themselves as non-Hispanic and as Alaska Native, American Indian, Asian (who are also included in the "Asian" row), or Native Hawaiian or other Pacific Islander, as well as non-Hispanics reporting more than one race.
Source: Calculations by New Strategist based on the Bureau of Labor Statistics' 2012 Consumer Expenditure Survey

Test Preparation and Tutoring Services

Best customers: Householders aged 45 to 54
High-income households
Married couples with school-aged or older children at home
Asians
Householders with a graduate degree

Customer trends: Average household spending on test preparation is likely to continue to rise as parents try
to boost their child's college opportunities.

The biggest spenders on test preparation and tutoring services are affluent, educated parents with children in high school who are hoping higher test scores will lead to more college choices and larger financial aid packages. Householders aged 45 to 54, many with school-aged children, spend more than twice the average on test prep and tutoring services. Households with incomes of $100,000 or more spend more than three times the average on this item, as do married couples with school-aged children. Asian households spend nearly three times the average on test preparation and tutoring services. Householders with a graduate degree spend more than three times the average on test preparation and tutoring services.

Test preparation and tutoring services is a relatively new item on the Consumer Expenditure Survey, permitting only a few years of spending trend analysis. Average household spending on test prep and tutoring services climbed by a substantial 48 percent between 2010 and 2012, after adjusting for inflation. Behind this increase is the parental frenzy to buff up children's college applications with higher test scores. Average household spending on test preparation is likely to continue to rise as parents try to boost their child's college opportunities.

Table 4.4 Test preparation and tutoring services

Total household spending $1,973,237.76
Average household spends   15.86

AGE OF HOUSEHOLDER	AVERAGE HOUSEHOLD SPENDING	BEST CUSTOMERS (index)	BIGGEST CUSTOMERS (market share)
Average household	$15.86	100	100.0%
Under age 25	9.41	59	3.9
Aged 25 to 34	16.07	101	16.4
Aged 35 to 44	16.74	106	18.3
Aged 45 to 54	39.71	250	49.6
Aged 55 to 64	7.92	50	9.1
Aged 65 to 74	2.58	16	2.0
Aged 75 or older	1.24	8	0.8

	AVERAGE HOUSEHOLD SPENDING	BEST CUSTOMERS (index)	BIGGEST CUSTOMERS (market share)
HOUSEHOLD INCOME			
Average household	**$15.86**	**100**	**100.0%**
Under $20,000	9.06	57	12.0
$20,000 to $39,999	2.23	14	3.2
$40,000 to $49,999	3.78	24	2.1
$50,000 to $69,999	18.97	120	17.3
$70,000 to $79,999	6.25	39	2.2
$80,000 to $99,999	9.72	61	5.4
$100,000 or more	48.99	309	57.8
HOUSEHOLD TYPE			
Average household	**15.86**	**100**	**100.0**
Married couples	24.18	152	74.0
Married couples, no children	3.14	20	4.1
Married couples with children	43.18	272	64.0
Oldest child under age 6	4.33	27	1.2
Oldest child aged 6 to 17	58.54	369	43.9
Oldest child aged 18 or older	42.42	267	18.9
Single parent with child under age 18	6.02	38	2.0
Single person	6.64	42	12.4
RACE AND HISPANIC ORIGIN			
Average household	**15.86**	**100**	**100.0**
Asian	44.13	278	12.1
Black	4.60	29	3.6
Hispanic	6.96	44	5.5
Non-Hispanic white and other	19.23	121	91.0
REGION			
Average household	**15.86**	**100**	**100.0**
Northeast	21.59	136	24.6
Midwest	12.23	77	17.1
South	14.59	92	34.3
West	16.95	107	24.1
EDUCATION			
Average household	**15.86**	**100**	**100.0**
Less than high school graduate	1.50	9	1.2
High school graduate	8.38	53	13.2
Some college	7.89	50	10.2
Associate's degree	18.15	114	11.3
Bachelor's degree or more	32.21	203	64.0
Bachelor's degree	21.99	139	27.6
Master's, professional, doctoral degree	49.75	314	36.4

Note: Market shares may not sum to 100.0 because of rounding and missing categories by household type. "Asian" and "black" include Hispanics and non-Hispanics who identify themselves as being of the respective race alone. "Hispanic" includes people of any race who identify themselves as Hispanic. "Other" includes people who identify themselves as non-Hispanic and as Alaska Native, American Indian, Asian (who are also included in the "Asian" row), or Native Hawaiian or other Pacific Islander, as well as non-Hispanics reporting more than one race.
Source: Calculations by New Strategist based on the Bureau of Labor Statistics' 2012 Consumer Expenditure Survey

Tuition, College

Best customers: Householders under age 25 and aged 45 to 54
High-income households
Married couples with adult children at home
Asians
Households in the Northeast

Customer trends: Average household spending on college tuition may stabilize or even decline in the years ahead as the nation's economic problems make college unaffordable for a growing share of families.

The biggest spenders on college tuition are, not surprisingly, young adults who attend college and the parents who pay for those expenses. This explains why householders under age 25 and householders aged 45 to 54 spend about twice the average amount on college tuition. Married couples with adult children at home spend three-and-three-quarter times the average on college tuition since many have children in school. Asian households spend three times the average, and households in the Northeast spend 66 percent more than average on this item. Households with incomes of $100,000 or more spend three times the average on college tuition.

Average household spending on college tuition soared 70 percent between 2000 and 2012, after adjusting for inflation. Behind the increase was the growing proportion of households with children in college as boomers sent their children to school. Also behind the increase is the rise in the cost of college. Average household spending on college tuition may stabilize or even decline in the years ahead as the nation's economic problems make college unaffordable for a growing share of families.

Table 4.5 **Tuition, college**

Total household spending $102,641,955,840.00
Average household spends   824.99

AGE OF HOUSEHOLDER	AVERAGE HOUSEHOLD SPENDING	BEST CUSTOMERS (index)	BIGGEST CUSTOMERS (market share)
Average household	$824.99	100	100.0%
Under age 25	1,586.57	192	12.6
Aged 25 to 34	733.38	89	14.4
Aged 35 to 44	442.88	54	9.3
Aged 45 to 54	1,702.94	206	40.9
Aged 55 to 64	873.62	106	19.4
Aged 65 to 74	142.73	17	2.1
Aged 75 or older	116.51	14	1.4

	AVERAGE HOUSEHOLD SPENDING	BEST CUSTOMERS (index)	BIGGEST CUSTOMERS (market share)
HOUSEHOLD INCOME			
Average household	**$824.99**	**100**	**100.0%**
Under $20,000	474.32	57	12.1
$20,000 to $39,999	322.08	39	8.8
$40,000 to $49,999	346.11	42	3.7
$50,000 to $69,999	362.48	44	6.3
$70,000 to $79,999	590.46	72	4.0
$80,000 to $99,999	831.25	101	8.9
$100,000 or more	2,474.67	300	56.2
HOUSEHOLD TYPE			
Average household	**824.99**	**100**	**100.0**
Married couples	1,140.60	138	67.2
Married couples, no children	821.36	100	20.8
Married couples with children	1,482.68	180	42.3
Oldest child under age 6	504.95	61	2.8
Oldest child aged 6 to 17	911.48	110	13.1
Oldest child aged 18 or older	3,077.82	373	26.3
Single parent with child under age 18	354.64	43	2.3
Single person	522.55	63	18.8
RACE AND HISPANIC ORIGIN			
Average household	**824.99**	**100**	**100.0**
Asian	2,505.43	304	13.2
Black	407.24	49	6.2
Hispanic	265.31	32	4.0
Non-Hispanic white and other	988.06	120	89.9
REGION			
Average household	**824.99**	**100**	**100.0**
Northeast	1,366.67	166	29.9
Midwest	872.47	106	23.4
South	495.63	60	22.4
West	888.72	108	24.3
EDUCATION			
Average household	**824.99**	**100**	**100.0**
Less than high school graduate	99.29	12	1.6
High school graduate	273.79	33	8.3
Some college	771.30	93	19.3
Associate's degree	811.88	98	9.7
Bachelor's degree or more	1,600.40	194	61.2
Bachelor's degree	1,409.42	171	34.1
Master's, professional, doctoral degree	1,928.36	234	27.1

Note: Market shares may not sum to 100.0 because of rounding and missing categories by household type. "Asian" and "black" include Hispanics and non-Hispanics who identify themselves as being of the respective race alone. "Hispanic" includes people of any race who identify themselves as Hispanic. "Other" includes people who identify themselves as non-Hispanic and as Alaska Native, American Indian, Asian (who are also included in the "Asian" row), or Native Hawaiian or other Pacific Islander, as well as non-Hispanics reporting more than one race.
Source: Calculations by New Strategist based on the Bureau of Labor Statistics' 2012 Consumer Expenditure Survey

Tuition, Elementary and High School

Best customers: Householders aged 35 to 54
High-income households
Married couples with school-aged or older children at home
Single parents
Asians
College graduates

Customer trends: Average household spending on elementary and high school tuition may continue to decline as the nation's economic problems make private school unaffordable for a growing share of families.

The biggest spenders on elementary and high school tuition are affluent parents with school-aged children. Householders aged 35 to 54 spend about twice the average on private school tuition because many are parents. Married couples with school-aged children spend five times the average on this item. Households with incomes of $100,000 or more spend three-and-one-half times the average on elementary and high school tuition. Asians spend more than twice the average amount on elementary and high school tuition. College graduates, who rank among the most affluent households, also spend over twice the average on this item.

Average household spending on private school tuition rose 32 percent between 2000 and 2006, after adjusting for inflation. Spending on this item then declined 8 percent between 2006 and the overall household spending trough year of 2010. Spending recovered slightly over the ensuing two years, rising 3 percent. Behind the earlier increase was the burgeoning number of parents searching for alternatives to public school as well as the rapid rise in private school tuition. The Great Recession curtailed spending on private school education. Average household spending on elementary and high school tuition may decline in the years ahead as the nation's economic problems make private school unaffordable for a growing share of families.

Table 4.6 Tuition, elementary and high school

Total household spending $21,031,280,640.00
Average household spends   169.04

AGE OF HOUSEHOLDER	AVERAGE HOUSEHOLD SPENDING	BEST CUSTOMERS (index)	BIGGEST CUSTOMERS (market share)
Average household	$169.04	100	100.0%
Under age 25	3.77	2	0.1
Aged 25 to 34	88.24	52	8.4
Aged 35 to 44	330.64	196	34.0
Aged 45 to 54	384.76	228	45.0
Aged 55 to 64	59.94	35	6.5
Aged 65 to 74	27.98	17	2.0
Aged 75 or older	67.94	40	3.9

	AVERAGE HOUSEHOLD SPENDING	BEST CUSTOMERS (index)	BIGGEST CUSTOMERS (market share)
HOUSEHOLD INCOME			
Average household	$169.04	100	100.0%
Under $20,000	31.36	19	3.9
$20,000 to $39,999	22.47	13	3.0
$40,000 to $49,999	62.88	37	3.3
$50,000 to $69,999	76.83	45	6.6
$70,000 to $79,999	219.82	130	7.3
$80,000 to $99,999	181.10	107	9.5
$100,000 or more	600.71	355	66.5
HOUSEHOLD TYPE			
Average household	169.04	100	100.0
Married couples	285.52	169	82.0
Married couples, no children	9.38	6	1.2
Married couples with children	542.71	321	75.5
Oldest child under age 6	120.19	71	3.2
Oldest child aged 6 to 17	869.11	514	61.1
Oldest child aged 18 or older	265.72	157	11.1
Single parent with child under age 18	279.01	165	8.7
Single person	30.42	18	5.3
RACE AND HISPANIC ORIGIN			
Average household	169.04	100	100.0
Asian	381.83	226	9.8
Black	84.50	50	6.3
Hispanic	58.79	35	4.4
Non-Hispanic white and other	202.64	120	90.0
REGION			
Average household	169.04	100	100.0
Northeast	213.56	126	22.8
Midwest	113.19	67	14.8
South	158.82	94	35.0
West	205.21	121	27.4
EDUCATION			
Average household	169.04	100	100.0
Less than high school graduate	26.48	16	2.0
High school graduate	49.31	29	7.3
Some college	72.68	43	8.9
Associate's degree	185.30	110	10.8
Bachelor's degree or more	380.55	225	71.0
Bachelor's degree	291.73	173	34.4
Master's, professional, doctoral degree	533.07	315	36.6

Note: Market shares may not sum to 100.0 because of rounding and missing categories by household type. "Asian" and "black" include Hispanics and non-Hispanics who identify themselves as being of the respective race alone. "Hispanic" includes people of any race who identify themselves as Hispanic. "Other" includes people who identify themselves as non-Hispanic and as Alaska Native, American Indian, Asian (who are also included in the "Asian" row), or Native Hawaiian or other Pacific Islander, as well as non-Hispanics reporting more than one race.
Source: Calculations by New Strategist based on the Bureau of Labor Statistics' 2012 Consumer Expenditure Survey

Tuition, Vocational and Technical Schools

Best customers: Householders aged 25 to 44
                   Asians and blacks
                   Households in the West

Customer trends: Average household spending on vocational and technical school tuition may rise in the years ahead
                   as parents search for lower-cost alternatives to college.

The biggest spenders on vocational and technical school tuition are adults aged 25 to 44 who are attending these schools. These householders spend 78 to 89 percent more than average on vocational and technical school tuition. Asians and blacks spend, respectively, 72 and 47 percent above average on this item and represent 26 percent of the market. Households in the West spend over twice the average on vocational and technical school tuition.

Spending on vocational and technical schools tuition became part of the Consumer Expenditure Survey only in 2007, and data from earlier years are nonexistent. Average household spending on this item declined 21 percent between 2010 and 2012. Spending on vocational and technical school tuition may rise in the years ahead as parents search for lower-cost alternatives to college.

Table 4.7 Tuition, vocational and technical schools

Total household spending $953,026,560.00
Average household spends   7.66

AGE OF HOUSEHOLDER	AVERAGE HOUSEHOLD SPENDING	BEST CUSTOMERS (index)	BIGGEST CUSTOMERS (market share)
Average household	$7.66	100	100.0%
Under age 25	1.38	18	1.2
Aged 25 to 34	13.67	178	28.8
Aged 35 to 44	14.48	189	32.8
Aged 45 to 54	5.26	69	13.6
Aged 55 to 64	7.73	101	18.5
Aged 65 to 74	1.53	20	2.4
Aged 75 or older	2.09	27	2.7

	AVERAGE HOUSEHOLD SPENDING	BEST CUSTOMERS (index)	BIGGEST CUSTOMERS (market share)
HOUSEHOLD INCOME			
Average household	$7.66	100	100.0%
Under $20,000	1.30	17	3.6
$20,000 to $39,999	5.53	72	16.3
$40,000 to $49,999	15.03	196	17.4
$50,000 to $69,999	3.15	41	5.9
$70,000 to $79,999	14.55	190	10.6
$80,000 to $99,999	7.38	96	8.5
$100,000 or more	15.43	201	37.7
HOUSEHOLD TYPE			
Average household	7.66	100	100.0
Married couples	6.71	88	42.5
Married couples, no children	6.53	85	17.8
Married couples with children	4.92	64	15.1
Oldest child under age 6	3.39	44	2.0
Oldest child aged 6 to 17	7.56	99	11.7
Oldest child aged 18 or older	1.45	19	1.3
Single parent with child under age 18	4.03	53	2.8
Single person	4.99	65	19.3
RACE AND HISPANIC ORIGIN			
Average household	7.66	100	100.0
Asian	13.20	172	7.5
Black	11.28	147	18.5
Hispanic	2.79	36	4.6
Non-Hispanic white and other	7.86	103	77.0
REGION			
Average household	7.66	100	100.0
Northeast	2.99	39	7.0
Midwest	4.33	57	12.5
South	6.27	82	30.5
West	16.96	221	49.9
EDUCATION			
Average household	7.66	100	100.0
Less than high school graduate	4.93	64	8.4
High school graduate	5.77	75	18.8
Some college	7.00	91	18.8
Associate's degree	11.29	147	14.6
Bachelor's degree or more	9.57	125	39.4
Bachelor's degree	11.60	151	30.2
Master's, professional, doctoral degree	6.09	80	9.2

Note: Market shares may not sum to 100.0 because of rounding and missing categories by household type. "Asian" and "black" include Hispanics and non-Hispanics who identify themselves as being of the respective race alone. "Hispanic" includes people of any race who identify themselves as Hispanic. "Other" includes people who identify themselves as non-Hispanic and as Alaska Native, American Indian, Asian (who are also included in the "Asian" row), or Native Hawaiian or other Pacific Islander, as well as non-Hispanics reporting more than one race.
Source: Calculations by New Strategist based on the Bureau of Labor Statistics' 2012 Consumer Expenditure Survey

Chapter 5.
Entertainment

Household Spending on Entertainment, 2000 to 2012

Average household spending on entertainment grew 5 percent between 2000 and 2012, after adjusting for inflation. Behind this increase, however, were big gains in a few categories and big losses in many others. Between 2000 and 2006, the year when overall household spending peaked, average household spending on entertainment climbed 9 percent. Spending then dropped 4 percent between 2006 and 2012 as the Great Recession took hold. These relatively small changes mask the volatility of individual categories within the entertainment category.

Household spending on pet purchase, supplies, and medicines, for example, almost tripled between 2000 and 2012 and spending on pet food rose 70 percent, after adjusting for inflation. In contrast, spending on compact discs, records, and audio tapes dropped 78 percent, as did spending on photo processing. Video game hardware and software spending rose 114 percent from 2000 to 2010, the year when overall household spending was at its lowest, then declined 25 percent over the ensuing two years. Spending on cable television, the entertainment bundle's largest component in terms of dollars spent, increased 53 percent between 2000 and 2010, then remained flat over the next two years. Spending on (high-definition) television sets rose 71 percent between 2000 and 2006, then fell 31 percent from 2006 to 2012.

Cable and satellite television services now account for 25 percent of the average household's entertainment spending, up from 17 percent in 2000. Americans appear to be devoting more dollars to observing rather than participating in events. Between 2000 and 2012, average household spending fell on fees for participant sports, fees for recreational lessons, and recreational expenses on trips.

Spending on entertainment

*(average annual spending of households on entertainment,
2000, 2006, 2010, and 2012; in 2012 dollars)*

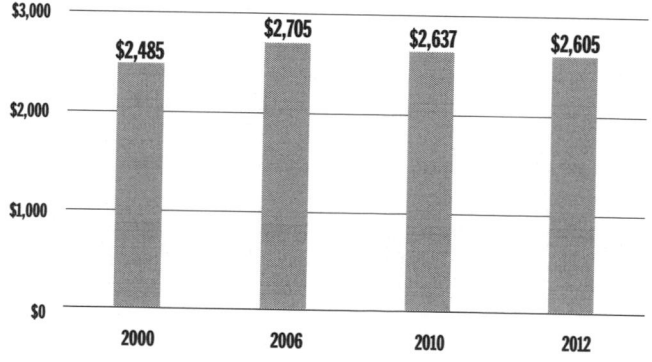

Table 5.1 Entertainment spending, 2000 to 2012

(average annual household spending on entertainment and percent distribution, by category, 2000 to 2012; percent change and percentage point change in spending, 2000–06, 2006–12, and 2010–12; in 2012 dollars; ranked by amount spent)

	average annual household spending (in 2012$)				percent change		
	2012	2010	2006	2000	2010–12	2006–12	2000–06
Average household spending on entertainment	$2,605.15	$2,636.96	$2,705.39	$2,484.60	–1.2%	–3.7%	8.9%
Cable and satellite television services	661.76	654.37	613.89	428.23	1.1	7.8	43.4
Pet food	194.70	173.94	151.48	114.62	11.9	28.5	32.2
Movie, theater, amusement park, and other admissions (including on trips)	168.75	163.20	182.92	178.80	3.4	–7.7	2.3
Veterinarian services	149.95	119.53	106.79	88.00	25.5	40.4	21.4
Pet purchase, supplies, and medicines	135.69	171.11	62.88	50.80	–20.7	115.8	23.8
Club memberships (civic, recreational, health)	127.44	127.11	140.63	130.90	0.3	–9.4	7.4
Fees for participant sports (including on trips)	118.19	113.98	123.91	142.05	3.7	–4.6	–12.8
Toys, games, hobbies, and tricycles	114.59	124.01	98.31	161.28	–7.6	16.6	–39.0
Recreational vehicles (boats, campers, trailers), including rentals	113.89	146.69	247.34	177.08	–22.4	–54.0	39.7
Television sets	102.24	125.01	148.50	87.08	–18.2	–31.1	70.5
Fees for recreational lessons	92.55	99.41	115.67	99.65	–6.9	–20.0	16.1
Admission to sports events (including on trips)	65.45	62.77	62.77	67.08	4.3	4.3	–6.4
Athletic gear, game tables, exercise equipment	60.99	49.78	66.18	78.18	22.5	–7.8	–15.4
Recreational expenses on trips	41.98	45.44	64.35	67.97	–7.6	–34.8	–5.3
Pet services	41.70	40.93	38.73	25.81	1.9	7.7	50.1
Video game hardware and software	40.29	53.49	38.84	24.96	–24.7	3.7	55.6
Sound components, equipment, and accessories	32.07	29.13	38.62	56.60	10.1	–17.0	–31.8
Photographic equipment	31.17	25.53	37.08	26.95	22.1	–15.9	37.6
Video cassettes, tapes, and discs	29.70	28.83	46.92	27.73	3.0	–36.7	69.2
Hunting and fishing equipment	29.06	27.55	32.66	34.47	5.5	–11.0	–5.2
Bicycles	21.69	16.25	14.86	15.64	33.5	45.9	–5.0
Photographer's fees	21.12	17.50	25.56	26.89	20.7	–17.4	–5.0
Musical instruments and accessories, including rental and repair	18.50	17.56	19.17	44.05	5.3	–3.5	–56.5
Rental of video cassettes, tapes, discs, films	15.72	22.65	35.81	55.41	–30.6	–56.1	–35.4
Satellite radio service	14.83	15.34	–	–	–3.3	–	–
Rental of party supplies for catered affairs	12.63	13.40	–	–	–5.8	–	–
Compact discs, records, and audio tapes	11.78	14.52	38.76	52.61	–18.9	–69.6	–26.3
Camping equipment	11.06	14.12	11.84	22.69	–21.7	–6.6	–47.8
Streamed and downloaded audio	10.39	7.05	4.12	–	47.3	152.0	–
Photo processing	9.15	12.02	20.36	41.91	–23.9	–55.1	–51.4
Stamp and coin collecting	8.80	2.92	6.40	–	201.7	37.5	–
Personal digital audio players	7.41	12.02	19.83	–	–38.4	–62.6	–
Video cassette recorders and video disc players	7.35	10.63	18.36	31.73	–30.9	–60.0	–42.1
Live entertainment for catered affairs	6.48	10.89	–	–	–40.5	–	–
Global positioning system devices	5.66	5.48	–	–	3.4	–	–
Streamed and downloaded video	5.35	2.04	1.17	–	161.9	356.1	–
Applications, games, ringtones for handheld devices	3.86	–	–	–	–	–	–
Online gaming services	3.51	2.68	–	–	30.7	–	–
Repair of TV, radio, and sound equipment	3.09	2.83	6.30	4.31	9.1	–50.9	46.2

PERCENT DISTRIBUTION OF SPENDING	average annual household spending (in 2012$)				percentage point change		
	2012	2010	2006	2000	2010–12	2006–12	2000–06
Average household spending on entertainment	**100.0%**	**100.0%**	**100.0%**	**100.0%**	–	–	–
Cable and satellite television services	25.4	24.8	22.7	17.2	0.6	2.7	5.5
Pet food	7.5	6.6	5.6	4.6	0.9	1.9	1.0
Movie, theater, amusement park, and other admissions (including on trips)	6.5	6.2	6.8	7.2	0.3	–0.3	–0.4
Veterinarian services	5.8	4.5	3.9	3.5	1.2	1.8	0.4
Pet purchase, supplies, and medicines	5.2	6.5	2.3	2.0	–1.3	2.9	0.3
Club memberships (civic, recreational, health)	4.9	4.8	5.2	5.3	0.1	–0.3	–0.1
Fees for participant sports (including on trips)	4.5	4.3	4.6	5.7	0.2	0.0	–1.1
Toys, games, hobbies, and tricycles	4.4	4.7	3.6	6.5	–0.3	0.8	–2.9
Recreational vehicles (boats, campers, trailers), including rentals	4.4	5.6	9.1	7.1	–1.2	–4.8	2.0
Television sets	3.9	4.7	5.5	3.5	–0.8	–1.6	2.0
Fees for recreational lessons	3.6	3.8	4.3	4.0	–0.2	–0.7	0.3
Admission to sports events (including on trips)	2.5	2.4	2.3	2.7	0.1	0.2	–0.4
Athletic gear, game tables, exercise equipment	2.3	1.9	2.4	3.1	0.5	–0.1	–0.7
Recreational expenses on trips	1.6	1.7	2.4	2.7	–0.1	–0.8	–0.4
Pet services	1.6	1.6	1.4	1.0	0.0	0.2	0.4
Video game hardware and software	1.5	2.0	1.4	1.0	–0.5	0.1	0.4
Sound components, equipment, and accessories	1.2	1.1	1.4	2.3	0.1	–0.2	–0.9
Photographic equipment	1.2	1.0	1.4	1.1	0.2	–0.2	0.3
Video cassettes, tapes, and discs	1.1	1.1	1.7	1.1	0.0	–0.6	0.6
Hunting and fishing equipment	1.1	1.0	1.2	1.4	0.1	–0.1	–0.2
Bicycles	0.8	0.6	0.5	0.6	0.2	0.3	–0.1
Photographer's fees	0.8	0.7	0.9	1.1	0.1	–0.1	–0.1
Musical instruments and accessories, including rental and repair	0.7	0.7	0.7	1.8	0.0	0.0	–1.1
Rental of video cassettes, tapes, discs, films	0.6	0.9	1.3	2.2	–0.3	–0.7	–0.9
Satellite radio service	0.6	0.6	–	–	0.0	–	–
Rental of party supplies for catered affairs	0.5	0.5	–	–	0.0	–	–
Compact discs, records, and audio tapes	0.5	0.6	1.4	2.1	–0.1	–1.0	–0.7
Camping equipment	0.4	0.5	0.4	0.9	–0.1	0.0	–0.5
Streamed and downloaded audio	0.4	0.3	0.2	–	0.1	0.2	–
Photo processing	0.4	0.5	0.8	1.7	–0.1	–0.4	–0.9
Stamp and coin collecting	0.3	0.1	0.2	–	0.2	0.1	–
Personal digital audio players	0.3	0.5	0.7	–	–0.2	–0.4	–
Video cassette recorders and video disc players	0.3	0.4	0.7	1.3	–0.1	–0.4	–0.6
Live entertainment for catered affairs	0.2	0.4	–	–	–0.2	–	–
Global positioning system devices	0.2	0.2	–	–	0.0	–	–
Streamed and downloaded video	0.2	0.1	0.0	–	0.1	0.2	–
Applications, games, ringtones for handheld devices	0.1	–	–	–	–	–	–
Online gaming services	0.1	0.1	–	–	0.0	–	–
Repair of TV, radio, and sound equipment	0.1	0.1	0.2	0.2	0.0	–0.1	0.1

Note: Numbers do not add to total because not all categories are shown. Percentage point change calculations are based on unrounded figures. "–" means not applicable or data are unavailable.
Source: Bureau of Labor Statistics, 2000, 2006, 2010, and 2012 Consumer Expenditure Surveys; calculations by New Strategist

Admission to Sports Events (Including on Trips)

Best customers: Householders aged 45 to 64
High-income households
Married couples without children at home
Married couples with school-aged or older children at home
Non-Hispanic whites
Households in the Midwest

Customer trends: Average household spending on admissions to sports events may resume its decline in the years ahead as high-definition television and online streaming of sports events substitute for the real thing.

The best customers of sports events are affluent, middle-aged and older married couples. Householders aged 45 to 64 spend 46 to 49 percent more than average on admissions to sports events and control 56 percent of the market. Married couples without children at home (mostly older empty-nesters) spend 61 percent more than average. Households with incomes of $100,000 or more spend over three times the average on sports events and control 60 percent of the market. Households with school-aged children spend twice the average on this item, while those with adult children at home spend 53 percent more. Non-Hispanic whites spend 20 percent more than average on this item, and households in the Midwest spend 29 percent more.

Average household spending on admissions to sports events declined 6 percent between 2000 and 2006, after adjusting for inflation, then remained flat between 2006 and 2010 (the year overall household spending bottomed out). Spending on sports event admissions rose 4 percent between 2010 and 2012, a possible sign of economic recovery. Spending on sports events may resume its decline in the years ahead, however, as high-definition television and online streaming of events substitute for the real thing.

Table 5.2 Admission to sports events (including on trips)

Total household spending $8,143,027,200.00
Average household spends   65.45

	AVERAGE HOUSEHOLD SPENDING	BEST CUSTOMERS (index)	BIGGEST CUSTOMERS (market share)
AGE OF HOUSEHOLDER			
Average household	**$65.45**	**100**	**100.0%**
Under age 25	29.33	45	2.9
Aged 25 to 34	50.61	77	12.5
Aged 35 to 44	71.41	109	18.9
Aged 45 to 54	97.71	149	29.5
Aged 55 to 64	95.45	146	26.7
Aged 65 to 74	36.92	56	6.8
Aged 75 or older	17.31	26	2.6

	AVERAGE HOUSEHOLD SPENDING	BEST CUSTOMERS (index)	BIGGEST CUSTOMERS (market share)
HOUSEHOLD INCOME			
Average household	$65.45	100	100.0%
Under $20,000	11.98	18	3.9
$20,000 to $39,999	19.83	30	6.8
$40,000 to $49,999	24.76	38	3.3
$50,000 to $69,999	36.90	56	8.1
$70,000 to $79,999	67.52	103	5.8
$80,000 to $99,999	87.62	134	11.8
$100,000 or more	210.66	322	60.3
HOUSEHOLD TYPE			
Average household	65.45	100	100.0
Married couples	100.23	153	74.4
Married couples, no children	105.63	161	33.6
Married couples with children	107.37	164	38.6
Oldest child under age 6	53.10	81	3.7
Oldest child aged 6 to 17	132.61	203	24.1
Oldest child aged 18 or older	99.92	153	10.8
Single parent with child under age 18	43.09	66	3.5
Single person	30.07	46	13.6
RACE AND HISPANIC ORIGIN			
Average household	65.45	100	100.0
Asian	58.22	89	3.9
Black	24.88	38	4.8
Hispanic	25.31	39	4.8
Non-Hispanic white and other	78.81	120	90.4
REGION			
Average household	65.45	100	100.0
Northeast	68.90	105	19.0
Midwest	84.35	129	28.6
South	50.07	77	28.5
West	69.51	106	23.9
EDUCATION			
Average household	65.45	100	100.0
Less than high school graduate	7.45	11	1.5
High school graduate	25.29	39	9.6
Some college	58.31	89	18.3
Associate's degree	53.30	81	8.0
Bachelor's degree or more	129.69	198	62.5
Bachelor's degree	101.95	156	31.0
Master's, professional, doctoral degree	177.34	271	31.4

Note: Market shares may not sum to 100.0 because of rounding and missing categories by household type. "Asian" and "black" include Hispanics and non-Hispanics who identify themselves as being of the respective race alone. "Hispanic" includes people of any race who identify themselves as Hispanic. "Other" includes people who identify themselves as non-Hispanic and as Alaska Native, American Indian, Asian (who are also included in the "Asian" row), or Native Hawaiian or other Pacific Islander, as well as non-Hispanics reporting more than one race.
Source: Calculations by New Strategist based on the Bureau of Labor Statistics' 2012 Consumer Expenditure Survey

Applications, Games, and Ringtones for Handheld Devices

Best customers: Householders aged 25 to 44
                      Married couples with children at home
                      Single parents
                      Households in the West

Customer trends: Average household spending on applications, games, and ringtones for handheld devices
                      will rise as ownership of smartphones grows.

The best customers of applications, games, and ringtones for handheld devices are younger adults with children at home. Householders ranging in age from 25 to 44 spend 45 to 51 percent more than average on apps, games, and ringtones and control 50 percent of the market. Married couples with children at home spend 83 percent more than average on this item, the figure peaking at more than twice the average among couples with school-aged children. Single parents, whose spending approaches average on only a few items, spend 2 percent more than average on applications, games, and ringtones for handheld devices. The spending on this item by households in the West is 40 percent above average.

Because applications, games, and ringtones for handheld devices are a recently added category in the Consumer Expenditure Survey, there are no comparative spending data for previous years. Average household spending on apps and games will increase as smartphone ownership grows.

Table 5.3 Applications, games, and ringtones for handheld devices

Total household spending $480,245,760.00
Average household spends   3.86

	AVERAGE HOUSEHOLD SPENDING	BEST CUSTOMERS (index)	BIGGEST CUSTOMERS (market share)
AGE OF HOUSEHOLDER			
Average household	**$3.86**	**100**	**100.0%**
Under age 25	3.03	78	5.1
Aged 25 to 34	5.58	145	23.4
Aged 35 to 44	5.83	151	26.2
Aged 45 to 54	4.48	116	23.0
Aged 55 to 64	3.55	92	16.8
Aged 65 to 74	0.98	25	3.1
Aged 75 or older	0.94	24	2.4

	AVERAGE HOUSEHOLD SPENDING	BEST CUSTOMERS (index)	BIGGEST CUSTOMERS (market share)
HOUSEHOLD INCOME			
Average household	$3.86	100	100.0%
Under $20,000	1.29	33	7.0
$20,000 to $39,999	2.13	55	12.4
$40,000 to $49,999	2.88	75	6.6
$50,000 to $69,999	4.87	126	18.2
$70,000 to $79,999	5.74	149	8.3
$80,000 to $99,999	5.81	151	13.3
$100,000 or more	7.04	182	34.1
HOUSEHOLD TYPE			
Average household	3.86	100	100.0
Married couples	4.87	126	61.3
Married couples, no children	2.70	70	14.6
Married couples with children	7.05	183	42.9
Oldest child under age 6	5.08	132	6.0
Oldest child aged 6 to 17	7.98	207	24.6
Oldest child aged 18 or older	6.77	175	12.4
Single parent with child under age 18	3.94	102	5.4
Single person	2.23	58	17.2
RACE AND HISPANIC ORIGIN			
Average household	3.86	100	100.0
Asian	3.72	96	4.2
Black	3.81	99	12.4
Hispanic	4.12	107	13.4
Non-Hispanic white and other	3.82	99	74.3
REGION			
Average household	3.86	100	100.0
Northeast	3.69	96	17.3
Midwest	3.13	81	18.0
South	3.45	89	33.3
West	5.39	140	31.5
EDUCATION			
Average household	3.86	100	100.0
Less than high school graduate	1.96	51	6.6
High school graduate	1.91	49	12.3
Some college	4.81	125	25.7
Associate's degree	4.47	116	11.4
Bachelor's degree or more	5.37	139	43.9
Bachelor's degree	5.55	144	28.7
Master's, professional, doctoral degree	5.06	131	15.2

Note: Market shares may not sum to 100.0 because of rounding and missing categories by household type. "Asian" and "black" include Hispanics and non-Hispanics who identify themselves as being of the respective race alone. "Hispanic" includes people of any race who identify themselves as Hispanic. "Other" includes people who identify themselves as non-Hispanic and as Alaska Native, American Indian, Asian (who are also included in the "Asian" row), or Native Hawaiian or other Pacific Islander, as well as non-Hispanics reporting more than one race.
Source: Calculations by New Strategist based on the Bureau of Labor Statistics' 2012 Consumer Expenditure Survey

Athletic Gear, Game Tables, and Exercise Equipment

Best customers: Householders aged 35 to 54
                       Married couples without children at home
                       Married couples with school-aged or older children at home
                       Single parents
                       Asians
                       Households in the South

Customer trends: Average household spending on athletic gear, game tables, and exercise equipment may resume
                       its decline as the small generation X passes through the best-customer age groups.

The best customers of athletic gear, game tables, and exercise equipment are parents. Householders aged 35 to 54, most with children, spend 37 to 44 percent more than average on athletic equipment. Married couples with school-aged or older children at home spend much more than average on these items. Single parents, whose spending is below average on most items, devote 7 percent more than the average household to athletic gear. Married couples without children at home spend 48 percent more than average on this category, Asians spend 61 percent more, and households in the South spend 38 percent more and control over half the market.

Average household spending on athletic gear, game tables, and exercise equipment fell 22 percent between 2000 and 2012, after adjusting for inflation. Although spending recovered between 2010 (the year overall household spending bottomed out) and 2012, the increase may be a temporary burst due to pent-up demand. Average household spending on athletic gear, game tables, and exercise equipment may resume its decline as the small generation X passes through the best-customer age groups.

Table 5.4 Athletic gear, game tables, and exercise equipment

Total household spending $7,588,131,840.00
Average household spends 60.99

AGE OF HOUSEHOLDER	AVERAGE HOUSEHOLD SPENDING	BEST CUSTOMERS (index)	BIGGEST CUSTOMERS (market share)
Average household	$60.99	100	100.0%
Under age 25	31.33	51	3.4
Aged 25 to 34	52.98	87	14.0
Aged 35 to 44	87.62	144	24.9
Aged 45 to 54	83.43	137	27.1
Aged 55 to 64	69.02	113	20.7
Aged 65 to 74	43.60	71	8.6
Aged 75 or older	6.54	11	1.0

	AVERAGE HOUSEHOLD SPENDING	BEST CUSTOMERS (index)	BIGGEST CUSTOMERS (market share)
HOUSEHOLD INCOME			
Average household	**$60.99**	**100**	**100.0%**
Under $20,000	15.29	25	5.3
$20,000 to $39,999	30.76	50	11.4
$40,000 to $49,999	27.31	45	4.0
$50,000 to $69,999	53.20	87	12.6
$70,000 to $79,999	135.40	222	12.4
$80,000 to $99,999	101.10	166	14.6
$100,000 or more	128.97	211	39.6
HOUSEHOLD TYPE			
Average household	**60.99**	**100**	**100.0**
Married couples	90.13	148	71.8
Married couples, no children	90.06	148	30.8
Married couples with children	96.57	158	37.2
Oldest child under age 6	39.92	65	3.0
Oldest child aged 6 to 17	127.56	209	24.9
Oldest child aged 18 or older	80.16	131	9.3
Single parent with child under age 18	65.25	107	5.6
Single person	24.05	39	11.7
RACE AND HISPANIC ORIGIN			
Average household	**60.99**	**100**	**100.0**
Asian	98.08	161	7.0
Black	12.61	21	2.6
Hispanic	48.43	79	10.0
Non-Hispanic white and other	71.13	117	87.5
REGION			
Average household	**60.99**	**100**	**100.0**
Northeast	31.89	52	9.4
Midwest	44.25	73	16.1
South	84.34	138	51.5
West	62.57	103	23.1
EDUCATION			
Average household	**60.99**	**100**	**100.0**
Less than high school graduate	23.66	39	5.1
High school graduate	46.18	76	18.9
Some college	49.68	81	16.8
Associate's degree	53.97	88	8.7
Bachelor's degree or more	96.27	158	49.8
Bachelor's degree	67.35	110	22.0
Master's, professional, doctoral degree	145.15	238	27.6

Note: Market shares may not sum to 100.0 because of rounding and missing categories by household type. "Asian" and "black" include Hispanics and non-Hispanics who identify themselves as being of the respective race alone. "Hispanic" includes people of any race who identify themselves as Hispanic. "Other" includes people who identify themselves as non-Hispanic and as Alaska Native, American Indian, Asian (who are also included in the "Asian" row), or Native Hawaiian or other Pacific Islander, as well as non-Hispanics reporting more than one race.
Source: Calculations by New Strategist based on the Bureau of Labor Statistics' 2012 Consumer Expenditure Survey

Bicycles

Best customers: Householders aged 25 to 44

High-income households

Married couples without children at home

Married couples with school-aged or older children at home

Asians

Households in the West

College graduates

Customer trends: Average household spending on bicycles may continue to rise as younger adults seek alternatives to the automobile and bike-friendly urban populations grow.

Younger adults are the best customers of bicycles, buying bikes for their children, commuting, and exercise. Householders aged 25 to 44—most of them parents—spend 29 to 83 percent more than average on bicycles. Married couples with school-aged or older children at home spend 23 to 50 percent more. Households with incomes of $100,000 or more spend three times the average on bicycles and control well over half the market. Asian households outspend the average by 30 percent. Spending on bicycles by households in the West is 89 percent above average. College graduates spend a bit more than twice the average on this item.

Average household spending on bicycles fell 5 percent between 2000 and 2006, after adjusting for inflation, then increased by an impressive 46 percent between 2006 and 2012. The lion's share of the increase occurred between 2010 (the year when overall household spending bottomed out) and 2012. One factor behind the increased spending on bicycles is the Great Recession, which not only boosted urban populations but also reduced automobile use. Spending on bicycles may continue to rise as younger adults seek alternatives to the automobile and bike-friendly urban populations grow.

Table 5.5 Bicycles

Total household spending $2,698,583,040.00

Average household spends   21.69

	AVERAGE HOUSEHOLD SPENDING	BEST CUSTOMERS (index)	BIGGEST CUSTOMERS (market share)
AGE OF HOUSEHOLDER			
Average household	$21.69	100	100.0%
Under age 25	20.14	93	6.1
Aged 25 to 34	28.02	129	20.9
Aged 35 to 44	39.61	183	31.7
Aged 45 to 54	19.14	88	17.5
Aged 55 to 64	24.49	113	20.7
Aged 65 to 74	4.83	22	2.7
Aged 75 or older	1.17	5	0.5

	AVERAGE HOUSEHOLD SPENDING	BEST CUSTOMERS (index)	BIGGEST CUSTOMERS (market share)
HOUSEHOLD INCOME			
Average household	$21.69	100	100.0%
Under $20,000	5.74	26	5.6
$20,000 to $39,999	8.23	38	8.6
$40,000 to $49,999	14.39	66	5.9
$50,000 to $69,999	17.83	82	11.9
$70,000 to $79,999	10.55	49	2.7
$80,000 to $99,999	21.20	98	8.6
$100,000 or more	65.82	303	56.8
HOUSEHOLD TYPE			
Average household	21.69	100	100.0
Married couples	31.56	146	70.7
Married couples, no children	38.74	179	37.2
Married couples with children	27.79	128	30.1
Oldest child under age 6	16.75	77	3.5
Oldest child aged 6 to 17	32.64	150	17.9
Oldest child aged 18 or older	26.75	123	8.7
Single parent with child under age 18	13.40	62	3.2
Single person	9.32	43	12.8
RACE AND HISPANIC ORIGIN			
Average household	21.69	100	100.0
Asian	28.24	130	5.6
Black	8.57	40	5.0
Hispanic	9.41	43	5.4
Non-Hispanic white and other	25.91	119	89.7
REGION			
Average household	21.69	100	100.0
Northeast	16.02	74	13.3
Midwest	18.31	84	18.7
South	14.84	68	25.5
West	40.90	189	42.5
EDUCATION			
Average household	21.69	100	100.0
Less than high school graduate	6.50	30	3.9
High school graduate	9.13	42	10.5
Some college	13.90	64	13.2
Associate's degree	11.14	51	5.1
Bachelor's degree or more	46.31	214	67.3
Bachelor's degree	57.32	264	52.7
Master's, professional, doctoral degree	27.40	126	14.7

Note: Market shares may not sum to 100.0 because of rounding and missing categories by household type. "Asian" and "black" include Hispanics and non-Hispanics who identify themselves as being of the respective race alone. "Hispanic" includes people of any race who identify themselves as Hispanic. "Other" includes people who identify themselves as non-Hispanic and as Alaska Native, American Indian, Asian (who are also included in the "Asian" row), or Native Hawaiian or other Pacific Islander, as well as non-Hispanics reporting more than one race.
Source: Calculations by New Strategist based on the Bureau of Labor Statistics' 2012 Consumer Expenditure Survey

Cable and Satellite Television Services

Best customers: Householders aged 45 to 74
Married couples

Customer trends: Average household spending on cable and satellite television services may be at a peak
as younger adults turn to Internet streaming services.

Cable and satellite television service is the number-one entertainment expenditure of the average household. Because cable service is nearly universal, average household spending on the service does not vary much by demographic characteristic. By age, the best customers are householders ranging in age from 45 to 74, who spend 10 to 11 percent more than average on this item. Married couples without children at home (most of them empty-nesters) spend 17 percent more than average on cable television, while couples with children at home spend 14 percent more.

Spending on cable and satellite television services grew by an anemic 1 percent from 2010 to 2012 (or just 0.6 percent per year), a far cry from the 5.4 percent average annual growth between 2000 and 2010, after adjusting for inflation. Behind the slowing growth are Netflix, Apple TV, Hulu, and other competitors offering less expensive television alternatives. Expect to see average household spending on cable and satellite television service begin to decline in the years ahead.

Table 5.6 Cable and satellite television services

Total household spending $82,333,532,160.00
Average household spends 661.76

AGE OF HOUSEHOLDER	AVERAGE HOUSEHOLD SPENDING	BEST CUSTOMERS (index)	BIGGEST CUSTOMERS (market share)
Average household	$661.76	100	100.0%
Under age 25	331.36	50	3.3
Aged 25 to 34	578.89	87	14.1
Aged 35 to 44	683.50	103	17.9
Aged 45 to 54	727.60	110	21.8
Aged 55 to 64	734.43	111	20.3
Aged 65 to 74	729.73	110	13.3
Aged 75 or older	628.67	95	9.3

	AVERAGE HOUSEHOLD SPENDING	BEST CUSTOMERS (index)	BIGGEST CUSTOMERS (market share)
HOUSEHOLD INCOME			
Average household	**$661.76**	**100**	**100.0%**
Under $20,000	415.67	63	13.2
$20,000 to $39,999	571.07	86	19.4
$40,000 to $49,999	649.48	98	8.7
$50,000 to $69,999	692.65	105	15.1
$70,000 to $79,999	793.80	120	6.7
$80,000 to $99,999	794.46	120	10.6
$100,000 or more	927.54	140	26.2
HOUSEHOLD TYPE			
Average household	**661.76**	**100**	**100.0**
Married couples	767.30	116	56.3
Married couples, no children	771.87	117	24.3
Married couples with children	755.02	114	26.8
Oldest child under age 6	660.74	100	4.6
Oldest child aged 6 to 17	756.99	114	13.6
Oldest child aged 18 or older	812.66	123	8.7
Single parent with child under age 18	570.14	86	4.5
Single person	501.71	76	22.5
RACE AND HISPANIC ORIGIN			
Average household	**661.76**	**100**	**100.0**
Asian	503.29	76	3.3
Black	670.52	101	12.7
Hispanic	517.08	78	9.8
Non-Hispanic white and other	684.32	103	77.6
REGION			
Average household	**661.76**	**100**	**100.0**
Northeast	733.23	111	20.0
Midwest	624.32	94	20.9
South	687.42	104	38.7
West	598.93	91	20.4
EDUCATION			
Average household	**661.76**	**100**	**100.0**
Less than high school graduate	509.22	77	10.0
High school graduate	654.14	99	24.6
Some college	638.42	96	19.9
Associate's degree	713.47	108	10.6
Bachelor's degree or more	729.98	110	34.8
Bachelor's degree	713.18	108	21.5
Master's, professional, doctoral degree	758.84	115	13.3

Note: Market shares may not sum to 100.0 because of rounding and missing categories by household type. "Asian" and "black" include Hispanics and non-Hispanics who identify themselves as being of the respective race alone. "Hispanic" includes people of any race who identify themselves as Hispanic. "Other" includes people who identify themselves as non-Hispanic and as Alaska Native, American Indian, Asian (who are also included in the "Asian" row), or Native Hawaiian or other Pacific Islander, as well as non-Hispanics reporting more than one race.
Source: Calculations by New Strategist based on the Bureau of Labor Statistics' 2012 Consumer Expenditure Survey

Camping Equipment

Best customers: Householders aged 25 to 44
Married couples with children at home
Hispanics
Households in the West

Customer trends: Average household spending on camping equipment may rise in the years ahead as the large millennial generation fills the best-customer lifestage.

The best customers of camping equipment are parents with children. Couples with children at home spend nearly two-and-one-half times the average on camping equipment and control 55 percent of the camping equipment market. Householders aged 35 to 44, most with children, spend almost twice the average on this item, and those aged 25 to 34 spend 29 percent more. Hispanics outspend the average on this item by 26 percent. Households in the West spend twice the average on camping equipment and control 45 percent of the market.

Average household spending on camping equipment dropped by more than half between 2000 and 2012, after adjusting for inflation. One factor behind the decline, which was particularly steep between 2000 and 2006, was the exit of the baby-boom generation from the best-customer lifestage. Spending on camping equipment may stabilize or even rise in the years ahead as the large millennial generation fills the best-customer lifestage.

Table 5.7 Camping equipment

Total household spending	$1,376,040,960.00
Average household spends	11.06

AGE OF HOUSEHOLDER	AVERAGE HOUSEHOLD SPENDING	BEST CUSTOMERS (index)	BIGGEST CUSTOMERS (market share)
Average household	$11.06	100	100.0%
Under age 25	0.26	2	0.2
Aged 25 to 34	14.31	129	20.9
Aged 35 to 44	21.41	194	33.6
Aged 45 to 54	12.25	111	21.9
Aged 55 to 64	11.87	107	19.6
Aged 65 to 74	1.49	13	1.6
Aged 75 or older	1.88	17	1.7

	AVERAGE HOUSEHOLD SPENDING	BEST CUSTOMERS (index)	BIGGEST CUSTOMERS (market share)
HOUSEHOLD INCOME			
Average household	**$11.06**	**100**	**100.0%**
Under $20,000	3.75	34	7.1
$20,000 to $39,999	5.52	50	11.3
$40,000 to $49,999	11.57	105	9.3
$50,000 to $69,999	12.18	110	15.9
$70,000 to $79,999	14.12	128	7.1
$80,000 to $99,999	8.87	80	7.1
$100,000 or more	27.23	246	46.1
HOUSEHOLD TYPE			
Average household	**11.06**	**100**	**100.0**
Married couples	17.27	156	75.8
Married couples, no children	7.25	66	13.7
Married couples with children	25.94	235	55.1
Oldest child under age 6	15.08	136	6.2
Oldest child aged 6 to 17	31.88	288	34.3
Oldest child aged 18 or older	22.80	206	14.5
Single parent with child under age 18	10.96	99	5.2
Single person	4.26	39	11.4
RACE AND HISPANIC ORIGIN			
Average household	**11.06**	**100**	**100.0**
Asian	6.61	60	2.6
Black	5.20	47	5.9
Hispanic	13.89	126	15.7
Non-Hispanic white and other	11.56	105	78.5
REGION			
Average household	**11.06**	**100**	**100.0**
Northeast	3.44	31	5.6
Midwest	4.24	38	8.5
South	12.15	110	40.9
West	22.26	201	45.4
EDUCATION			
Average household	**11.06**	**100**	**100.0**
Less than high school graduate	3.78	34	4.5
High school graduate	8.89	80	20.0
Some college	7.60	69	14.2
Associate's degree	6.94	63	6.2
Bachelor's degree or more	19.08	173	54.4
Bachelor's degree	20.19	183	36.4
Master's, professional, doctoral degree	17.22	156	18.1

Note: Market shares may not sum to 100.0 because of rounding and missing categories by household type. "Asian" and "black" include Hispanics and non-Hispanics who identify themselves as being of the respective race alone. "Hispanic" includes people of any race who identify themselves as Hispanic. "Other" includes people who identify themselves as non-Hispanic and as Alaska Native, American Indian, Asian (who are also included in the "Asian" row), or Native Hawaiian or other Pacific Islander, as well as non-Hispanics reporting more than one race.
Source: Calculations by New Strategist based on the Bureau of Labor Statistics' 2012 Consumer Expenditure Survey

Club Memberships (Social, Recreational, Health)

Best customers: Householders aged 35 to 74
High-income households
Married couples without children at home
Married couples with school-aged or older children at home
Non-Hispanic whites
Households in the Midwest and West
College graduates

Customer trends: Average household spending on club memberships should begin to grow again as aging boomers gain more free time and look for ways to plug into their community.

Club memberships are the sixth-most important entertainment expenditure. Affluent, educated, middle-aged and older married couples are the best customers of clubs. These households are the glue of every community, funding and supporting a variety of organizations ranging from civic groups to the YMCA to country clubs. Householders aged 35 to 44 spend 35 percent more than the average household on memberships, and householders ranging in age from 45 to 74 spend at least an average amount on this item. Married couples without children at home (most of them empty-nesters) spend 40 percent more than average on club memberships. Couples with school-aged children spend over twice the average, and those with adult children at home spend 22 percent more. Non-Hispanic whites outspend minorities by a wide margin. Households with incomes of $100,000 or more spend over three times the average on club memberships, and college graduates spend more than twice the average. Households in the Midwest and West outspend the average by 29 and 23 percent, respectively.

Average household spending on club memberships rose 7 percent between 2000 and 2006, the year in which overall household spending peaked. Spending then dropped 10 percent between 2006 and 2010, the year in which overall household spending bottomed out, and remained flat in the ensuing two years to 2012. Spending on club memberships should grow again as aging boomers gain more free time and look for ways to plug into their community.

Table 5.8 Club memberships (social, recreational, health)

Total household spending $15,855,575,040.00
Average household spends   127.44

	AVERAGE HOUSEHOLD SPENDING	BEST CUSTOMERS (index)	BIGGEST CUSTOMERS (market share)
AGE OF HOUSEHOLDER			
Average household	$127.44	100	100.0%
Under age 25	47.07	37	2.4
Aged 25 to 34	110.07	86	14.0
Aged 35 to 44	171.49	135	23.4
Aged 45 to 54	134.30	105	20.9
Aged 55 to 64	127.91	100	18.4
Aged 65 to 74	138.64	109	13.1
Aged 75 or older	103.32	81	7.9

	AVERAGE HOUSEHOLD SPENDING	BEST CUSTOMERS (index)	BIGGEST CUSTOMERS (market share)
HOUSEHOLD INCOME			
Average household	$127.44	100	100.0%
Under $20,000	17.63	14	2.9
$20,000 to $39,999	40.29	32	7.1
$40,000 to $49,999	77.33	61	5.4
$50,000 to $69,999	76.25	60	8.6
$70,000 to $79,999	143.61	113	6.3
$80,000 to $99,999	153.23	120	10.6
$100,000 or more	401.98	315	59.1
HOUSEHOLD TYPE			
Average household	127.44	100	100.0
Married couples	187.39	147	71.4
Married couples, no children	178.49	140	29.2
Married couples with children	209.44	164	38.6
Oldest child under age 6	131.94	104	4.7
Oldest child aged 6 to 17	271.29	213	25.3
Oldest child aged 18 or older	155.29	122	8.6
Single parent with child under age 18	47.03	37	1.9
Single person	75.80	59	17.7
RACE AND HISPANIC ORIGIN			
Average household	127.44	100	100.0
Asian	137.96	108	4.7
Black	47.03	37	4.6
Hispanic	42.73	34	4.2
Non-Hispanic white and other	154.78	121	91.2
REGION			
Average household	127.44	100	100.0
Northeast	117.68	92	16.7
Midwest	163.99	129	28.5
South	92.44	73	27.0
West	157.16	123	27.8
EDUCATION			
Average household	127.44	100	100.0
Less than high school graduate	10.68	8	1.1
High school graduate	40.39	32	7.9
Some college	73.68	58	11.9
Associate's degree	86.26	68	6.7
Bachelor's degree or more	292.61	230	72.4
Bachelor's degree	268.67	211	42.0
Master's, professional, doctoral degree	333.73	262	30.4

Note: Market shares may not sum to 100.0 because of rounding and missing categories by household type. "Asian" and "black" include Hispanics and non-Hispanics who identify themselves as being of the respective race alone. "Hispanic" includes people of any race who identify themselves as Hispanic. "Other" includes people who identify themselves as non-Hispanic and as Alaska Native, American Indian, Asian (who are also included in the "Asian" row), or Native Hawaiian or other Pacific Islander, as well as non-Hispanics reporting more than one race.
Source: Calculations by New Strategist based on the Bureau of Labor Statistics' 2012 Consumer Expenditure Survey

Compact Disks, Audio Tapes, and Records

Best customers: Householders aged 45 to 54
Married couples
Households in the West

Customer trends: Average household spending on compact disks, audio tapes, and records will continue to decline as online downloads dominate music purchases.

Married couples spend 11 percent more than average on compact disks, audio tapes, and records, the figure peaking among those with adult children at home at 36 percent more than average. Householders aged 45 to 54 outspend the average by 30 percent on this item. Households in the West spend 31 percent more than average on recordings.

Average household spending on CDs, audio tapes, and records fell by an enormous 78 percent between 2000 and 2010, after adjusting for inflation, and spending was down by 19 percent in the following two years. The decline in spending will continue as downloads replace compact disks as the preferred way to purchase music.

Table 5.9 Compact disks, audio tapes, and records

Total household spending $1,465,620,480.00
Average household spends   11.78

	AVERAGE HOUSEHOLD SPENDING	BEST CUSTOMERS (index)	BIGGEST CUSTOMERS (market share)
AGE OF HOUSEHOLDER			
Average household	**$11.78**	**100**	**100.0%**
Under age 25	11.16	95	6.2
Aged 25 to 34	11.03	94	15.1
Aged 35 to 44	10.92	93	16.1
Aged 45 to 54	15.31	130	25.7
Aged 55 to 64	11.41	97	17.7
Aged 65 to 74	10.60	90	10.8
Aged 75 or older	9.93	84	8.2

	AVERAGE HOUSEHOLD SPENDING	BEST CUSTOMERS (index)	BIGGEST CUSTOMERS (market share)
HOUSEHOLD INCOME			
Average household	**$11.78**	**100**	**100.0%**
Under $20,000	5.85	50	10.4
$20,000 to $39,999	8.78	75	16.8
$40,000 to $49,999	10.78	92	8.1
$50,000 to $69,999	15.12	128	18.5
$70,000 to $79,999	14.02	119	6.6
$80,000 to $99,999	11.30	96	8.5
$100,000 or more	19.49	165	31.0
HOUSEHOLD TYPE			
Average household	**11.78**	**100**	**100.0**
Married couples	13.03	111	53.7
Married couples, no children	13.13	111	23.2
Married couples with children	13.35	113	26.6
Oldest child under age 6	11.45	97	4.4
Oldest child aged 6 to 17	12.53	106	12.7
Oldest child aged 18 or older	15.98	136	9.6
Single parent with child under age 18	5.83	49	2.6
Single person	10.51	89	26.5
RACE AND HISPANIC ORIGIN			
Average household	**11.78**	**100**	**100.0**
Asian	9.84	84	3.6
Black	10.33	88	11.0
Hispanic	7.73	66	8.2
Non-Hispanic white and other	12.67	108	80.7
REGION			
Average household	**11.78**	**100**	**100.0**
Northeast	12.79	109	19.6
Midwest	12.07	102	22.7
South	8.89	75	28.1
West	15.46	131	29.6
EDUCATION			
Average household	**11.78**	**100**	**100.0**
Less than high school graduate	6.26	53	6.9
High school graduate	7.60	65	16.1
Some college	12.28	104	21.5
Associate's degree	8.30	70	7.0
Bachelor's degree or more	18.12	154	48.5
Bachelor's degree	17.11	145	28.9
Master's, professional, doctoral degree	19.85	169	19.6

Note: Market shares may not sum to 100.0 because of rounding and missing categories by household type. "Asian" and "black" include Hispanics and non-Hispanics who identify themselves as being of the respective race alone. "Hispanic" includes people of any race who identify themselves as Hispanic. "Other" includes people who identify themselves as non-Hispanic and as Alaska Native, American Indian, Asian (who are also included in the "Asian" row), or Native Hawaiian or other Pacific Islander, as well as non-Hispanics reporting more than one race.
Source: Calculations by New Strategist based on the Bureau of Labor Statistics' 2012 Consumer Expenditure Survey

Fees for Participant Sports (Including on Trips)

Best customers: Householders aged 35 to 44
Married couples with children at home
Single parents
Asians

Customer trends: Average household spending on fees for participant sports may continue to grow as the large millennial generation begins to replace the small generation X in the best-customer lifestage.

Fees for participant sports include a broad range of recreational charges from greens fees for golfers to fees for children's sports leagues. Those who spend the most on fees for participant sports are parents. Married couples with children at home spend over twice the average on this item. Single parents, whose spending is well below average on most items, spend slightly more than average on fees for participant sports. Householders aged 35 to 44, most of them parents, spend 50 percent more than average on fees for participant sports. Asians spend 46 percent more than average on this item.

Average household spending on fees for participant sports declined 20 percent between 2000 and 2010, after adjusting for inflation, followed by a 4 percent increase over the ensuing two years. Spending on this category may continue to grow as the large millennial generation begins to replace the small generation X in the best-customer lifestage.

Table 5.10 Fees for participant sports (including on trips)

Total household spending	$14,704,727,040.00
Average household spends	118.19

	AVERAGE HOUSEHOLD SPENDING	BEST CUSTOMERS (index)	BIGGEST CUSTOMERS (market share)
AGE OF HOUSEHOLDER			
Average household	**$118.19**	**100**	**100.0%**
Under age 25	21.45	18	1.2
Aged 25 to 34	109.51	93	15.0
Aged 35 to 44	177.87	150	26.1
Aged 45 to 54	128.29	109	21.5
Aged 55 to 64	119.60	101	18.5
Aged 65 to 74	140.97	119	14.4
Aged 75 or older	39.18	33	3.2

	AVERAGE HOUSEHOLD SPENDING	BEST CUSTOMERS (index)	BIGGEST CUSTOMERS (market share)
HOUSEHOLD INCOME			
Average household	$118.19	100	100.0%
Under $20,000	11.70	10	2.1
$20,000 to $39,999	47.38	40	9.0
$40,000 to $49,999	105.23	89	7.9
$50,000 to $69,999	111.81	95	13.7
$70,000 to $79,999	135.27	114	6.4
$80,000 to $99,999	107.63	91	8.0
$100,000 or more	330.35	280	52.3
HOUSEHOLD TYPE			
Average household	118.19	100	100.0
Married couples	185.56	157	76.3
Married couples, no children	136.50	115	24.1
Married couples with children	246.70	209	49.1
Oldest child under age 6	156.34	132	6.0
Oldest child aged 6 to 17	315.62	267	31.8
Oldest child aged 18 or older	188.31	159	11.2
Single parent with child under age 18	120.93	102	5.4
Single person	37.91	32	9.5
RACE AND HISPANIC ORIGIN			
Average household	118.19	100	100.0
Asian	172.76	146	6.3
Black	48.84	41	5.2
Hispanic	54.88	46	5.8
Non-Hispanic white and other	140.15	119	89.0
REGION			
Average household	118.19	100	100.0
Northeast	149.69	127	22.9
Midwest	137.18	116	25.7
South	72.01	61	22.7
West	150.21	127	28.6
EDUCATION			
Average household	118.19	100	100.0
Less than high school graduate	36.72	31	4.1
High school graduate	50.23	42	10.6
Some college	82.38	70	14.4
Associate's degree	97.82	83	8.2
Bachelor's degree or more	232.76	197	62.1
Bachelor's degree	198.31	168	33.4
Master's, professional, doctoral degree	291.13	246	28.6

Note: Market shares may not sum to 100.0 because of rounding and missing categories by household type. "Asian" and "black" include Hispanics and non-Hispanics who identify themselves as being of the respective race alone. "Hispanic" includes people of any race who identify themselves as Hispanic. "Other" includes people who identify themselves as non-Hispanic and as Alaska Native, American Indian, Asian (who are also included in the "Asian" row), or Native Hawaiian or other Pacific Islander, as well as non-Hispanics reporting more than one race.
Source: Calculations by New Strategist based on the Bureau of Labor Statistics' 2012 Consumer Expenditure Survey

Fees for Recreational Lessons

Best customers: Householders aged 35 to 54
High-income households
Married couples with school-aged children
Asians
Households in the Northeast and West
College graduates

Customer trends: Average household spending on fees for recreational lessons may continue to decline in the years ahead because the small generation X is in the best-customer age groups.

The best customers of fees for recreational lessons are parents. Married couples with school-aged children spend more than four times the average on fees for recreational lessons and control 56 percent of the market. Householders aged 35 to 54, who are likely to be parents, spend from 52 percent more to well over twice the average on this category. Households with incomes of $100,000 or more spend three-and-one-third times the average on recreational lessons and control 62 percent of the market. Asians and college graduates, two affluent demographic segments, spend well over twice the average on fees for recreational lessons. Households in the Northeast spend 59 percent more than average on fees for recreational lessons, and those in the West spend 29 percent more.

Average household spending on fees for recreational lessons climbed 16 percent between 2000 and 2006, after adjusting for inflation. Behind the rise was the parental frenzy to ensure that children are well rounded. The Great Recession disrupted those dreams, however, and in the 2006-to-2012 time period spending on this item fell by 20 percent. Spending on fees for recreational lessons may continue to decline in the years ahead because the small generation X is in the best-customer age groups.

Table 5.11 Fees for recreational lessons

Total household spending $11,514,700,800.00
Average household spends 92.55

AGE OF HOUSEHOLDER	AVERAGE HOUSEHOLD SPENDING	BEST CUSTOMERS (index)	BIGGEST CUSTOMERS (market share)
Average household	$92.55	100	100.0%
Under age 25	22.15	24	1.6
Aged 25 to 34	69.66	75	12.2
Aged 35 to 44	203.72	220	38.2
Aged 45 to 54	140.43	152	30.0
Aged 55 to 64	66.01	71	13.1
Aged 65 to 74	33.24	36	4.3
Aged 75 or older	6.09	7	0.6

	AVERAGE HOUSEHOLD SPENDING	BEST CUSTOMERS (index)	BIGGEST CUSTOMERS (market share)
HOUSEHOLD INCOME			
Average household	$92.55	100	100.0%
Under $20,000	13.48	15	3.1
$20,000 to $39,999	21.06	23	5.1
$40,000 to $49,999	47.96	52	4.6
$50,000 to $69,999	63.09	68	9.8
$70,000 to $79,999	101.99	110	6.2
$80,000 to $99,999	98.70	107	9.4
$100,000 or more	305.59	330	61.8
HOUSEHOLD TYPE			
Average household	92.55	100	100.0
Married couples	150.98	163	79.2
Married couples, no children	40.91	44	9.2
Married couples with children	262.70	284	66.7
Oldest child under age 6	100.91	109	5.0
Oldest child aged 6 to 17	432.32	467	55.6
Oldest child aged 18 or older	81.40	88	6.2
Single parent with child under age 18	81.02	88	4.6
Single person	25.07	27	8.0
RACE AND HISPANIC ORIGIN			
Average household	92.55	100	100.0
Asian	220.79	239	10.3
Black	37.80	41	5.1
Hispanic	46.77	51	6.3
Non-Hispanic white and other	109.26	118	88.6
REGION			
Average household	92.55	100	100.0
Northeast	147.04	159	28.7
Midwest	93.43	101	22.4
South	49.34	53	19.9
West	119.47	129	29.1
EDUCATION			
Average household	92.55	100	100.0
Less than high school graduate	13.57	15	1.9
High school graduate	24.08	26	6.5
Some college	59.47	64	13.2
Associate's degree	104.26	113	11.1
Bachelor's degree or more	197.33	213	67.2
Bachelor's degree	159.23	172	34.3
Master's, professional, doctoral degree	262.77	284	33.0

Note: Market shares may not sum to 100.0 because of rounding and missing categories by household type. "Asian" and "black" include Hispanics and non-Hispanics who identify themselves as being of the respective race alone. "Hispanic" includes people of any race who identify themselves as Hispanic. "Other" includes people who identify themselves as non-Hispanic and as Alaska Native, American Indian, Asian (who are also included in the "Asian" row), or Native Hawaiian or other Pacific Islander, as well as non-Hispanics reporting more than one race.
Source: Calculations by New Strategist based on the Bureau of Labor Statistics' 2012 Consumer Expenditure Survey

Hunting and Fishing Equipment

Best customers: Householders aged 25 to 34 and 45 to 54
                             Married couples without children at home
                             Married couples with school-aged or older children at home
                             Non-Hispanic whites
                             Households in the Midwest

Customer trends: Average household spending on hunting and fishing equipment is likely to continue to decline
                             as a growing share of the American population lives in metropolitan areas.

Non-Hispanic whites in the Midwest are the best customers of hunting and fishing equipment. Households headed by non-Hispanic whites spend 20 percent more than the average household on hunting and fishing equipment, and households in the Midwest spend 62 percent more. By age, the young and the middle aged spend more than average on hunting and fishing equipment. Householders aged 25 to 34 spend 48 percent more than average, and householders aged 45 to 54 spend 26 percent more. Married couples without children at home spend two-and-one-quarter times the average on hunting and fishing equipment. Couples with school-aged or older children at home spend 43 to 61 percent more than average.

Average household spending on hunting and fishing equipment, which had fallen 20 percent between 2000 and 2010, after adjusting for inflation, increased by 5 percent from 2010 to 2012. Behind the spending decline is the growing urbanization of the American population, with more than 80 percent of the population now living in a metropolitan area. Spending on hunting and fishing equipment is likely to continue to decline as the urbanization trend continues.

Table 5.12 Hunting and fishing equipment

Total household spending $3,615,528,960.00
Average household spends   29.06

AGE OF HOUSEHOLDER	AVERAGE HOUSEHOLD SPENDING	BEST CUSTOMERS (index)	BIGGEST CUSTOMERS (market share)
Average household	$29.06	100	100.0%
Under age 25	5.95	20	1.3
Aged 25 to 34	42.91	148	23.9
Aged 35 to 44	29.81	103	17.8
Aged 45 to 54	36.64	126	25.0
Aged 55 to 64	30.81	106	19.4
Aged 65 to 74	22.50	77	9.3
Aged 75 or older	9.30	32	3.1

	AVERAGE HOUSEHOLD SPENDING	BEST CUSTOMERS (index)	BIGGEST CUSTOMERS (market share)
HOUSEHOLD INCOME			
Average household	**$29.06**	**100**	**100.0%**
Under $20,000	5.08	17	3.7
$20,000 to $39,999	13.87	48	10.8
$40,000 to $49,999	31.00	107	9.4
$50,000 to $69,999	17.55	60	8.7
$70,000 to $79,999	19.63	68	3.8
$80,000 to $99,999	49.30	170	15.0
$100,000 or more	75.32	259	48.5
HOUSEHOLD TYPE			
Average household	**29.06**	**100**	**100.0**
Married couples	48.67	167	81.3
Married couples, no children	65.81	226	47.2
Married couples with children	37.15	128	30.1
Oldest child under age 6	9.79	34	1.5
Oldest child aged 6 to 17	41.63	143	17.0
Oldest child aged 18 or older	46.72	161	11.3
Single parent with child under age 18	15.49	53	2.8
Single person	7.26	25	7.4
RACE AND HISPANIC ORIGIN			
Average household	**29.06**	**100**	**100.0**
Asian	8.52	29	1.3
Black	11.05	38	4.8
Hispanic	12.38	43	5.3
Non-Hispanic white and other	34.82	120	89.9
REGION			
Average household	**29.06**	**100**	**100.0**
Northeast	12.17	42	7.6
Midwest	46.99	162	35.9
South	29.37	101	37.6
West	24.33	84	18.9
EDUCATION			
Average household	**29.06**	**100**	**100.0**
Less than high school graduate	19.26	66	8.7
High school graduate	35.60	123	30.5
Some college	26.39	91	18.7
Associate's degree	18.59	64	6.3
Bachelor's degree or more	32.77	113	35.6
Bachelor's degree	41.02	141	28.1
Master's, professional, doctoral degree	18.83	65	7.5

Note: Market shares may not sum to 100.0 because of rounding and missing categories by household type. "Asian" and "black" include Hispanics and non-Hispanics who identify themselves as being of the respective race alone. "Hispanic" includes people of any race who identify themselves as Hispanic. "Other" includes people who identify themselves as non-Hispanic and as Alaska Native, American Indian, Asian (who are also included in the "Asian" row), or Native Hawaiian or other Pacific Islander, as well as non-Hispanics reporting more than one race.
Source: Calculations by New Strategist based on the Bureau of Labor Statistics' 2012 Consumer Expenditure Survey

Live Entertainment for Catered Affairs

Best customers: Householders aged 25 to 34 and 45 to 54
High-income households
Married couples without children at home
Married couples with adult children at home
Asians
College graduates

Customer trends: Average household spending on live entertainment for catered affairs is likely to decline in the years ahead as households tighten their belts.

The best customers of live entertainment for catered affairs are affluent households whose children are marrying. Households with incomes of $100,000 or more spend almost four times the average on live entertainment. College graduates and Asians, two relatively well-to-do demographics, spend nearly two-and-one-half to over three times the average on live entertainment for catered affairs. Householders aged 25 to 34 outspend the average by two-thirds and those aged 45 to 54 do so by one-half. Married couples without children at home spend one-third more than average on live entertainment, whereas couples with adult children at home spend well over twice the average on this item.

Live entertainment for catered affairs is a relatively new item in the Consumer Expenditure Survey, and comparable data from 2000 or 2006 do not exist. Average household spending on this item fell 40 percent between 2010 and 2012 and is likely to decline further in the years ahead as households tighten their belts.

Table 5.13 **Live entertainment for catered affairs**

Total household spending $806,215,680.00
Average household spends   6.48

	AVERAGE HOUSEHOLD SPENDING	BEST CUSTOMERS (index)	BIGGEST CUSTOMERS (market share)
AGE OF HOUSEHOLDER			
Average household	**$6.48**	**100**	**100.0%**
Under age 25	2.22	34	2.2
Aged 25 to 34	10.95	169	27.3
Aged 35 to 44	4.56	70	12.2
Aged 45 to 54	9.97	154	30.5
Aged 55 to 64	5.82	90	16.4
Aged 65 to 74	5.89	91	11.0
Aged 75 or older	0.30	5	0.5

	AVERAGE HOUSEHOLD SPENDING	BEST CUSTOMERS (index)	BIGGEST CUSTOMERS (market share)
HOUSEHOLD INCOME			
Average household	**$6.48**	**100**	**100.0%**
Under $20,000	0.49	8	1.6
$20,000 to $39,999	1.46	23	5.1
$40,000 to $49,999	3.29	51	4.5
$50,000 to $69,999	3.83	59	8.5
$70,000 to $79,999	3.85	59	3.3
$80,000 to $99,999	3.02	47	4.1
$100,000 or more	25.25	390	73.0
HOUSEHOLD TYPE			
Average household	**6.48**	**100**	**100.0**
Married couples	8.54	132	64.0
Married couples, no children	8.70	134	28.0
Married couples with children	8.07	125	29.3
Oldest child under age 6	1.00	15	0.7
Oldest child aged 6 to 17	6.96	107	12.8
Oldest child aged 18 or older	14.51	224	15.8
Single parent with child under age 18	2.98	46	2.4
Single person	1.74	27	8.0
RACE AND HISPANIC ORIGIN			
Average household	**6.48**	**100**	**100.0**
Asian	20.52	317	13.7
Black	0.63	10	1.2
Hispanic	5.02	77	9.7
Non-Hispanic white and other	7.69	119	89.1
REGION			
Average household	**6.48**	**100**	**100.0**
Northeast	6.62	102	18.4
Midwest	8.60	133	29.4
South	3.72	57	21.4
West	8.87	137	30.8
EDUCATION			
Average household	**6.48**	**100**	**100.0**
Less than high school graduate	2.27	35	4.6
High school graduate	1.48	23	5.7
Some college	3.47	54	11.0
Associate's degree	1.34	21	2.0
Bachelor's degree or more	15.76	243	76.7
Bachelor's degree	15.07	233	46.4
Master's, professional, doctoral degree	16.95	262	30.4

Note: Market shares may not sum to 100.0 because of rounding and missing categories by household type. "Asian" and "black" include Hispanics and non-Hispanics who identify themselves as being of the respective race alone. "Hispanic" includes people of any race who identify themselves as Hispanic. "Other" includes people who identify themselves as non-Hispanic and as Alaska Native, American Indian, Asian (who are also included in the "Asian" row), or Native Hawaiian or other Pacific Islander, as well as non-Hispanics reporting more than one race.
Source: Calculations by New Strategist based on the Bureau of Labor Statistics' 2012 Consumer Expenditure Survey

Movie, Theater, Amusement Park, and Other Admissions (Including on Trips)

Best customers: Householders aged 35 to 64
Married couples without children at home
Married couples with school-aged or older children at home
Asians
Households in the West

Customer trends: Average household spending on movie, theater, and amusement park tickets is likely to decline
in the years ahead as streaming movies at home becomes the norm.

Spending on movie tickets dominates this item, which is the third-largest entertainment spending category. The best customers of movie, theater, amusement park, and other admissions are teens and young adults, which explains why householders ranging in age from 35 to 64, many with teenage and older children at home, spend 15 to 19 percent more than average on this item. Married couples with school-aged children spend 83 percent more than average on movie and other tickets. Those with adult children at home spend 51 percent more. Married couples without children at home spend 21 percent more than average on movie, theater, amusement park, and other admissions. Asian households spend 38 percent more than average on this item and households in the West, where many Asians reside, spend 32 percent more.

Average household spending on movie, theater, amusement park, and other admissions fell 8 percent between 2006 and 2012, after adjusting for inflation. Behind the decline in spending was changing technology, as DVDs and pay-per-view streaming allowed consumers to see movies at home rather than in a theater. Spending on this category is likely to decline in the years ahead as streaming movies at home becomes the norm.

Table 5.14 Movie, theater, amusement park, and other admissions (including on trips)

Total household spending $20,995,200,000.00
Average household spends   168.75

AGE OF HOUSEHOLDER	AVERAGE HOUSEHOLD SPENDING	BEST CUSTOMERS (index)	BIGGEST CUSTOMERS (market share)
Average household	$168.75	100	100.0%
Under age 25	113.06	67	4.4
Aged 25 to 34	172.48	102	16.5
Aged 35 to 44	200.59	119	20.6
Aged 45 to 54	194.24	115	22.8
Aged 55 to 64	197.64	117	21.4
Aged 65 to 74	136.23	81	9.7
Aged 75 or older	77.77	46	4.5

	AVERAGE HOUSEHOLD SPENDING	BEST CUSTOMERS (index)	BIGGEST CUSTOMERS (market share)
HOUSEHOLD INCOME			
Average household	**$168.75**	**100**	**100.0%**
Under $20,000	51.23	30	6.4
$20,000 to $39,999	77.56	46	10.4
$40,000 to $49,999	101.45	60	5.3
$50,000 to $69,999	149.10	88	12.8
$70,000 to $79,999	196.25	116	6.5
$80,000 to $99,999	226.81	134	11.9
$100,000 or more	422.00	250	46.8
HOUSEHOLD TYPE			
Average household	**168.75**	**100**	**100.0**
Married couples	230.04	136	66.2
Married couples, no children	203.76	121	25.2
Married couples with children	265.16	157	36.9
Oldest child under age 6	168.77	100	4.6
Oldest child aged 6 to 17	308.12	183	21.7
Oldest child aged 18 or older	255.08	151	10.7
Single parent with child under age 18	110.62	66	3.4
Single person	106.10	63	18.7
RACE AND HISPANIC ORIGIN			
Average household	**168.75**	**100**	**100.0**
Asian	232.22	138	6.0
Black	87.31	52	6.5
Hispanic	110.80	66	8.2
Non-Hispanic white and other	191.89	114	85.4
REGION			
Average household	**168.75**	**100**	**100.0**
Northeast	193.34	115	20.7
Midwest	147.20	87	19.3
South	136.86	81	30.2
West	222.96	132	29.8
EDUCATION			
Average household	**168.75**	**100**	**100.0**
Less than high school graduate	45.94	27	3.6
High school graduate	83.18	49	12.3
Some college	131.48	78	16.0
Associate's degree	164.06	97	9.6
Bachelor's degree or more	313.05	186	58.5
Bachelor's degree	272.12	161	32.1
Master's, professional, doctoral degree	383.34	227	26.4

Note: Market shares may not sum to 100.0 because of rounding and missing categories by household type. "Asian" and "black" include Hispanics and non-Hispanics who identify themselves as being of the respective race alone. "Hispanic" includes people of any race who identify themselves as Hispanic. "Other" includes people who identify themselves as non-Hispanic and as Alaska Native, American Indian, Asian (who are also included in the "Asian" row), or Native Hawaiian or other Pacific Islander, as well as non-Hispanics reporting more than one race.
Source: Calculations by New Strategist based on the Bureau of Labor Statistics' 2012 Consumer Expenditure Survey

Musical Instruments and Accessories Purchase, Rental, and Repair

Best customers: Householders 45 to 54
High-income households
Married couples with school-aged children
Asians
Households in the West

Customer trends: Average household spending on the purchase, rental, and repair of musical instruments and accessories is likely to decline further in the years ahead as households and school districts tighten their belts.

The best customers of purchase, rental, and repair of musical instruments and accessories are well-to-do families with children. Married couples with school-aged children spend over three times the average on this item, as do households with incomes of $100,000 or more. Householders aged 45 to 54, many with school-aged children, spend 83 percent more than average on musical instruments. Asians spend twice the average, and households in the West spend 56 percent more on musical instruments.

Average household spending on the purchase, rental, and repair of musical instruments and accessories fell by a steep 60 percent between 2000 and 2010, the year overall household spending bottomed out, and then posted a small 5 percent gain in the ensuing two years, after adjusting for inflation. Behind the decline are school budget woes, which make fewer music programs available to schoolchildren. Spending on this item is likely to decline further in the years ahead as households and school districts tighten their belts.

Table 5.15 Musical instruments and accessories purchase, rental, and repair

Total household spending $2,301,696,000.00
Average household spends   18.50

	AVERAGE HOUSEHOLD SPENDING	BEST CUSTOMERS (index)	BIGGEST CUSTOMERS (market share)
AGE OF HOUSEHOLDER			
Average household	$18.50	100	100.0%
Under age 25	16.88	91	6.0
Aged 25 to 34	17.57	95	15.4
Aged 35 to 44	20.31	110	19.1
Aged 45 to 54	33.85	183	36.2
Aged 55 to 64	17.65	95	17.5
Aged 65 to 74	7.40	40	4.8
Aged 75 or older	2.09	11	1.1

	AVERAGE HOUSEHOLD SPENDING	BEST CUSTOMERS (index)	BIGGEST CUSTOMERS (market share)
HOUSEHOLD INCOME			
Average household	**$18.50**	**100**	**100.0%**
Under $20,000	4.19	23	4.8
$20,000 to $39,999	5.96	32	7.3
$40,000 to $49,999	10.55	57	5.0
$50,000 to $69,999	14.45	78	11.3
$70,000 to $79,999	12.93	70	3.9
$80,000 to $99,999	12.68	69	6.0
$100,000 or more	59.42	321	60.1
HOUSEHOLD TYPE			
Average household	**18.50**	**100**	**100.0**
Married couples	24.88	134	65.3
Married couples, no children	14.63	79	16.5
Married couples with children	35.38	191	45.0
Oldest child under age 6	3.13	17	0.8
Oldest child aged 6 to 17	57.47	311	36.9
Oldest child aged 18 or older	19.00	103	7.2
Single parent with child under age 18	14.77	80	4.2
Single person	11.72	63	18.8
RACE AND HISPANIC ORIGIN			
Average household	**18.50**	**100**	**100.0**
Asian	37.50	203	8.8
Black	6.39	35	4.3
Hispanic	11.92	64	8.1
Non-Hispanic white and other	21.58	117	87.6
REGION			
Average household	**18.50**	**100**	**100.0**
Northeast	11.84	64	11.6
Midwest	19.69	106	23.6
South	14.71	80	29.6
West	28.91	156	35.2
EDUCATION			
Average household	**18.50**	**100**	**100.0**
Less than high school graduate	3.56	19	2.5
High school graduate	6.89	37	9.3
Some college	15.80	85	17.6
Associate's degree	21.37	116	11.4
Bachelor's degree or more	34.72	188	59.2
Bachelor's degree	27.63	149	29.8
Master's, professional, doctoral degree	46.89	253	29.4

Note: Market shares may not sum to 100.0 because of rounding and missing categories by household type. "Asian" and "black" include Hispanics and non-Hispanics who identify themselves as being of the respective race alone. "Hispanic" includes people of any race who identify themselves as Hispanic. "Other" includes people who identify themselves as non-Hispanic and as Alaska Native, American Indian, Asian (who are also included in the "Asian" row), or Native Hawaiian or other Pacific Islander, as well as non-Hispanics reporting more than one race.
Source: Calculations by New Strategist based on the Bureau of Labor Statistics' 2012 Consumer Expenditure Survey

Online Gaming Services

Best customers: Householders under age 35
Married couples with school-aged or older children at home
Non-Hispanic whites

Customer trends: Average household spending on online gaming services will grow as younger generations replace older ones.

The best customers of online gaming services are adolescents and young adults. Householders under age 35 spend 34 to 58 percent more than average on online gaming services. Married couples with school-aged or older children at home spend 38 to 62 percent more than average on this item. Non-Hispanic whites and others dominate spending on online gaming services and account for 89 percent of the market.

Because online gaming services is a recently added category in the Consumer Expenditure Survey, there are no comparative spending data for 2000 or 2006. Between 2010 and 2012 average household spending on online gaming services grew 31 percent. Average household spending on online gaming services will grow as younger generations replace older ones.

Table 5.16 Online gaming services

Total household spending $436,700,160.00
Average household spends   3.51

	AVERAGE HOUSEHOLD SPENDING	BEST CUSTOMERS (index)	BIGGEST CUSTOMERS (market share)
AGE OF HOUSEHOLDER			
Average household	**$3.51**	**100**	**100.0%**
Under age 25	4.69	134	8.8
Aged 25 to 34	5.54	158	25.5
Aged 35 to 44	4.19	119	20.7
Aged 45 to 54	4.14	118	23.3
Aged 55 to 64	2.86	81	14.9
Aged 65 to 74	1.50	43	5.1
Aged 75 or older	0.56	16	1.6

	AVERAGE HOUSEHOLD SPENDING	BEST CUSTOMERS (index)	BIGGEST CUSTOMERS (market share)
HOUSEHOLD INCOME			
Average household	$3.51	100	100.0%
Under $20,000	1.68	48	10.1
$20,000 to $39,999	2.38	68	15.3
$40,000 to $49,999	2.14	61	5.4
$50,000 to $69,999	3.40	97	14.0
$70,000 to $79,999	3.62	103	5.8
$80,000 to $99,999	6.01	171	15.1
$100,000 or more	6.43	183	34.3
HOUSEHOLD TYPE			
Average household	3.51	100	100.0
Married couples	4.17	119	57.7
Married couples, no children	2.86	81	17.0
Married couples with children	5.06	144	33.9
Oldest child under age 6	3.76	107	4.9
Oldest child aged 6 to 17	5.68	162	19.2
Oldest child aged 18 or older	4.86	138	9.8
Single parent with child under age 18	2.40	68	3.6
Single person	2.44	70	20.6
RACE AND HISPANIC ORIGIN			
Average household	3.51	100	100.0
Asian	2.79	79	3.4
Black	1.37	39	4.9
Hispanic	1.67	48	6.0
Non-Hispanic white and other	4.18	119	89.4
REGION			
Average household	3.51	100	100.0
Northeast	3.72	106	19.1
Midwest	3.13	89	19.8
South	3.33	95	35.3
West	4.01	114	25.7
EDUCATION			
Average household	3.51	100	100.0
Less than high school graduate	1.44	41	5.4
High school graduate	2.62	75	18.6
Some college	4.55	130	26.7
Associate's degree	2.19	62	6.2
Bachelor's degree or more	4.80	137	43.1
Bachelor's degree	4.63	132	26.3
Master's, professional, doctoral degree	5.10	145	16.9

Note: Market shares may not sum to 100.0 because of rounding and missing categories by household type. "Asian" and "black" include Hispanics and non-Hispanics who identify themselves as being of the respective race alone. "Hispanic" includes people of any race who identify themselves as Hispanic. "Other" includes people who identify themselves as non-Hispanic and as Alaska Native, American Indian, Asian (who are also included in the "Asian" row), or Native Hawaiian or other Pacific Islander, as well as non-Hispanics reporting more than one race.
Source: Calculations by New Strategist based on the Bureau of Labor Statistics' 2012 Consumer Expenditure Survey

Personal Digital Audio Players

Best customers: Householders aged 25 to 54
Married couples with school-aged or older children at home
Single parents
Asians
Households in the Northeast and West

Customer trends: Average household spending on personal digital audio players may continue to decline in the years ahead as they wither in the competition with smartphones that offer music functions.

Apple's sleek iPods have created such a demand for personal digital audio players that the Bureau of Labor Statistics added them as a new expenditure category in 2005. The best customers of these devices are married couples with children. Married couples with school-aged children spend almost three times the average on this item, while those with adult children at home spend two-thirds more than average. Householders aged 35 to 44, many of them with children at home, spend twice the average on this item, while the adjacent younger and older 10-year age groups spend, respectively, 26 and 53 percent more than average on personal digital audio players. Single parents, whose spending approaches average on only a few items, spend 19 percent more than average on audio players. Asians outspend the average by 42 percent. Households in the Northeast spend 28 percent more than average, and those in the West spend 20 percent more.

There are no decade-long spending trends for this new product category. Between 2006 and 2012, spending on personal digital audio players declined by a stunning 63 percent. Behind the decline was price discounting as less expensive products entered the market as well as the shift toward listening to music on smartphones. Average household spending on personal digital audio players may continue to decline in the years ahead as this product competes with smartphones that offer music functions.

Table 5.17 Personal digital audio players

Total household spending $921,922,560.00
Average household spends   7.41

AGE OF HOUSEHOLDER	AVERAGE HOUSEHOLD SPENDING	BEST CUSTOMERS (index)	BIGGEST CUSTOMERS (market share)
Average household	$7.41	100	100.0%
Under age 25	3.22	43	2.8
Aged 25 to 34	9.33	126	20.4
Aged 35 to 44	15.43	208	36.1
Aged 45 to 54	11.34	153	30.3
Aged 55 to 64	3.30	45	8.2
Aged 65 to 74	1.21	16	2.0
Aged 75 or older	0.19	3	0.3

	AVERAGE HOUSEHOLD SPENDING	BEST CUSTOMERS (index)	BIGGEST CUSTOMERS (market share)
HOUSEHOLD INCOME			
Average household	**$7.41**	**100**	**100.0%**
Under $20,000	2.15	29	6.1
$20,000 to $39,999	4.66	63	14.2
$40,000 to $49,999	4.82	65	5.8
$50,000 to $69,999	5.69	77	11.1
$70,000 to $79,999	9.89	133	7.5
$80,000 to $99,999	15.04	203	17.9
$100,000 or more	14.85	200	37.5
HOUSEHOLD TYPE			
Average household	**7.41**	**100**	**100.0**
Married couples	10.67	144	69.9
Married couples, no children	4.88	66	13.7
Married couples with children	15.67	211	49.7
Oldest child under age 6	5.90	80	3.6
Oldest child aged 6 to 17	21.41	289	34.4
Oldest child aged 18 or older	12.30	166	11.7
Single parent with child under age 18	8.83	119	6.2
Single person	3.23	44	12.9
RACE AND HISPANIC ORIGIN			
Average household	**7.41**	**100**	**100.0**
Asian	10.49	142	6.1
Black	7.31	99	12.4
Hispanic	7.95	107	13.4
Non-Hispanic white and other	7.32	99	74.1
REGION			
Average household	**7.41**	**100**	**100.0**
Northeast	9.50	128	23.1
Midwest	7.85	106	23.5
South	5.23	71	26.3
West	8.91	120	27.1
EDUCATION			
Average household	**7.41**	**100**	**100.0**
Less than high school graduate	3.46	47	6.1
High school graduate	3.86	52	13.0
Some college	5.17	70	14.4
Associate's degree	11.69	158	15.6
Bachelor's degree or more	11.98	162	51.0
Bachelor's degree	10.83	146	29.1
Master's, professional, doctoral degree	13.95	188	21.8

Note: Market shares may not sum to 100.0 because of rounding and missing categories by household type. "Asian" and "black" include Hispanics and non-Hispanics who identify themselves as being of the respective race alone. "Hispanic" includes people of any race who identify themselves as Hispanic. "Other" includes people who identify themselves as non-Hispanic and as Alaska Native, American Indian, Asian (who are also included in the "Asian" row), or Native Hawaiian or other Pacific Islander, as well as non-Hispanics reporting more than one race.
Source: Calculations by New Strategist based on the Bureau of Labor Statistics' 2012 Consumer Expenditure Survey

Pet Food

Best customers:
Householders aged 45 to 74
Married couples without children at home
Married couples with school-aged or older children at home
Non-Hispanic whites
Households in the West

Customer trends:
Average household spending on pet food may continue to grow because the large baby-boom generation is solidly in the best-customer age groups.

While some may disagree, the Consumer Expenditure Survey categorizes pets as an entertainment expense. Pet food accounts for the largest share of pet expenses and ranks second in overall entertainment spending. Householders aged 45 to 74 spend 12 to 61 percent more than the average household on pet food. Married couples without children at home spend 38 percent more than average on pet food, and those with school-aged or older children at home spend 29 to 56 percent more. Non-Hispanic whites spend 18 percent more than average on pet food and control 89 percent of the market. Households in the West spend 22 percent more than average on pet food.

Average household spending on pet food rose by a steep 70 percent between 2000 and 2012, after adjusting for inflation. Spending on pet food may continue to grow because the large baby-boom generation is solidly in the best-customer age groups.

Table 5.18 Pet food

Total household spending	$24,223,795,200.00
Average household spends	194.70

AGE OF HOUSEHOLDER	AVERAGE HOUSEHOLD SPENDING	BEST CUSTOMERS (index)	BIGGEST CUSTOMERS (market share)
Average household	$194.70	100	100.0%
Under age 25	90.76	47	3.1
Aged 25 to 34	145.13	75	12.0
Aged 35 to 44	170.82	88	15.2
Aged 45 to 54	218.24	112	22.2
Aged 55 to 64	312.50	161	29.4
Aged 65 to 74	221.08	114	13.7
Aged 75 or older	96.97	50	4.9

	AVERAGE HOUSEHOLD SPENDING	BEST CUSTOMERS (index)	BIGGEST CUSTOMERS (market share)
HOUSEHOLD INCOME			
Average household	$194.70	100	100.0%
Under $20,000	85.39	44	9.2
$20,000 to $39,999	148.98	77	17.2
$40,000 to $49,999	172.68	89	7.8
$50,000 to $69,999	192.28	99	14.3
$70,000 to $79,999	273.89	141	7.9
$80,000 to $99,999	249.11	128	11.3
$100,000 or more	333.99	172	32.1
HOUSEHOLD TYPE			
Average household	194.70	100	100.0
Married couples	262.85	135	65.6
Married couples, no children	269.46	138	28.9
Married couples with children	267.39	137	32.3
Oldest child under age 6	196.26	101	4.6
Oldest child aged 6 to 17	303.34	156	18.5
Oldest child aged 18 or older	251.76	129	9.1
Single parent with child under age 18	100.71	52	2.7
Single person	124.04	64	18.9
RACE AND HISPANIC ORIGIN			
Average household	194.70	100	100.0
Asian	76.44	39	1.7
Black	59.90	31	3.9
Hispanic	116.46	60	7.5
Non-Hispanic white and other	230.12	118	88.7
REGION			
Average household	194.70	100	100.0
Northeast	175.51	90	16.3
Midwest	202.04	104	23.0
South	173.54	89	33.2
West	238.09	122	27.6
EDUCATION			
Average household	194.70	100	100.0
Less than high school graduate	157.31	81	10.6
High school graduate	177.68	91	22.8
Some college	197.10	101	20.8
Associate's degree	321.85	165	16.3
Bachelor's degree or more	180.52	93	29.2
Bachelor's degree	172.22	88	17.6
Master's, professional, doctoral degree	194.55	100	11.6

Note: Market shares may not sum to 100.0 because of rounding and missing categories by household type. "Asian" and "black" include Hispanics and non-Hispanics who identify themselves as being of the respective race alone. "Hispanic" includes people of any race who identify themselves as Hispanic. "Other" includes people who identify themselves as non-Hispanic and as Alaska Native, American Indian, Asian (who are also included in the "Asian" row), or Native Hawaiian or other Pacific Islander, as well as non-Hispanics reporting more than one race.
Source: Calculations by New Strategist based on the Bureau of Labor Statistics' 2012 Consumer Expenditure Survey

Pet Purchase, Supplies, and Medicines

Best customers: Householders aged 35 to 64
Married couples without children at home
Married couples with school-aged or older children at home
Non-Hispanic whites

Customer trends: Average household spending on pet purchases, supplies, and medicines may stabilize in the years ahead along with the cost of pet medications.

Pets are so popular in the United States that spending on pet purchase, supplies, and medicines does not vary much by demographic characteristic, except by race and Hispanic origin. Householders ranging in age from 35 to 64 spend 14 to 36 percent more than average on pet purchase, supplies, and medicines. Married couples spend 25 percent more, the figure peaking at 40 percent among couples with school-aged children. To understand the market, it is almost more helpful to know who is least likely to spend on pets—single parents, people who live alone, low-income households, the youngest and the oldest householders, and minority householders all spend considerably less than average on pet purchase, supplies, and medicines.

Average household spending on pet purchase, supplies, and medicines more than tripled between 2000 and 2010, after adjusting for inflation, as pharmaceutical companies offered a growing variety of pricey medications. Between 2010 and 2012, however, spending on this category fell 21 percent as consumers reacted to the shock of higher pet costs by searching for substitutes and greater competition reduced the price of medications. Average household spending on pet purchase, supplies, and medicines may stabilize in the years ahead along with the cost of pet medications.

Table 5.19 Pet purchase, supplies, and medicines

| Total household spending | $16,882,007,040.00 |
| Average household spends | 135.69 |

AGE OF HOUSEHOLDER	AVERAGE HOUSEHOLD SPENDING	BEST CUSTOMERS (index)	BIGGEST CUSTOMERS (market share)
Average household	$135.69	100	100.0%
Under age 25	73.78	54	3.6
Aged 25 to 34	124.11	91	14.8
Aged 35 to 44	161.02	119	20.6
Aged 45 to 54	184.48	136	26.9
Aged 55 to 64	154.95	114	20.9
Aged 65 to 74	108.26	80	9.6
Aged 75 or older	50.35	37	3.6

	AVERAGE HOUSEHOLD SPENDING	BEST CUSTOMERS (index)	BIGGEST CUSTOMERS (market share)
HOUSEHOLD INCOME			
Average household	**$135.69**	**100**	**100.0%**
Under $20,000	60.34	44	9.4
$20,000 to $39,999	99.82	74	16.6
$40,000 to $49,999	120.97	89	7.9
$50,000 to $69,999	133.64	98	14.2
$70,000 to $79,999	167.33	123	6.9
$80,000 to $99,999	219.65	162	14.3
$100,000 or more	223.08	164	30.8
HOUSEHOLD TYPE			
Average household	**135.69**	**100**	**100.0**
Married couples	169.31	125	60.6
Married couples, no children	161.47	119	24.8
Married couples with children	172.05	127	29.8
Oldest child under age 6	117.47	87	3.9
Oldest child aged 6 to 17	189.29	140	16.6
Oldest child aged 18 or older	178.29	131	9.3
Single parent with child under age 18	107.18	79	4.1
Single person	80.99	60	17.7
RACE AND HISPANIC ORIGIN			
Average household	**135.69**	**100**	**100.0**
Asian	51.84	38	1.7
Black	46.12	34	4.3
Hispanic	82.95	61	7.7
Non-Hispanic white and other	159.29	117	88.1
REGION			
Average household	**135.69**	**100**	**100.0**
Northeast	133.56	98	17.8
Midwest	137.71	101	22.5
South	142.20	105	39.0
West	124.65	92	20.7
EDUCATION			
Average household	**135.69**	**100**	**100.0**
Less than high school graduate	101.02	74	9.7
High school graduate	111.29	82	20.5
Some college	139.04	102	21.1
Associate's degree	165.80	122	12.1
Bachelor's degree or more	157.72	116	36.7
Bachelor's degree	149.43	110	21.9
Master's, professional, doctoral degree	171.95	127	14.7

Note: Market shares may not sum to 100.0 because of rounding and missing categories by household type. "Asian" and "black" include Hispanics and non-Hispanics who identify themselves as being of the respective race alone. "Hispanic" includes people of any race who identify themselves as Hispanic. "Other" includes people who identify themselves as non-Hispanic and as Alaska Native, American Indian, Asian (who are also included in the "Asian" row), or Native Hawaiian or other Pacific Islander, as well as non-Hispanics reporting more than one race.
Source: Calculations by New Strategist based on the Bureau of Labor Statistics' 2012 Consumer Expenditure Survey

Pet Services

Best customers:
Householders aged 45 to 64
Married couples without children at home
Married couples with children under age 18
Non-Hispanic whites
Households in the West

Customer trends:
Average household spending on pet services is likely to stabilize or even decline in the years ahead as the large baby-boom generation retires.

The best customers of pet services—such as dog walking and day care—are busy, working adults. Householders ranging in age from 45 to 64 spend 50 to 51 percent more than average on this item. Married couples without children at home (most of them empty-nesters) spend two-thirds more than average on pet services, while those with school-aged or younger children spend 28 to 45 percent more than average. Non-Hispanic whites outspend minorities by a large margin and account for 91 percent of the market. Households in the West spend 20 percent more than average on pet services.

Average household spending on pet services rose 62 percent between 2000 and 2012, after adjusting for inflation, as the baby-boom generation filled the best-customer life stage and day care services for dogs became more popular. Spending on pet services is likely to stabilize or even decline in the years ahead as the large baby-boom generation retires.

Table 5.20 Pet services

Total household spending $5,188,147,200.00
Average household spends 41.70

AGE OF HOUSEHOLDER	AVERAGE HOUSEHOLD SPENDING	BEST CUSTOMERS (index)	BIGGEST CUSTOMERS (market share)
Average household	$41.70	100	100.0%
Under age 25	8.24	20	1.3
Aged 25 to 34	31.70	76	12.3
Aged 35 to 44	39.42	95	16.4
Aged 45 to 54	62.54	150	29.7
Aged 55 to 64	62.97	151	27.6
Aged 65 to 74	32.10	77	9.3
Aged 75 or older	14.55	35	3.4

	AVERAGE HOUSEHOLD SPENDING	BEST CUSTOMERS (index)	BIGGEST CUSTOMERS (market share)
HOUSEHOLD INCOME			
Average household	**$41.70**	**100**	**100.0%**
Under $20,000	11.69	28	5.9
$20,000 to $39,999	17.66	42	9.5
$40,000 to $49,999	20.35	49	4.3
$50,000 to $69,999	40.99	98	14.2
$70,000 to $79,999	36.13	87	4.8
$80,000 to $99,999	69.29	166	14.7
$100,000 or more	103.66	249	46.5
HOUSEHOLD TYPE			
Average household	**41.70**	**100**	**100.0**
Married couples	59.21	142	69.0
Married couples, no children	69.22	166	34.6
Married couples with children	55.05	132	31.0
Oldest child under age 6	53.29	128	5.8
Oldest child aged 6 to 17	60.31	145	17.2
Oldest child aged 18 or older	47.31	113	8.0
Single parent with child under age 18	27.61	66	3.5
Single person	26.09	63	18.6
RACE AND HISPANIC ORIGIN			
Average household	**41.70**	**100**	**100.0**
Asian	12.07	29	1.3
Black	9.14	22	2.8
Hispanic	19.48	47	5.9
Non-Hispanic white and other	50.82	122	91.5
REGION			
Average household	**41.70**	**100**	**100.0**
Northeast	40.19	96	17.4
Midwest	42.29	101	22.5
South	36.98	89	33.0
West	50.13	120	27.1
EDUCATION			
Average household	**41.70**	**100**	**100.0**
Less than high school graduate	12.54	30	3.9
High school graduate	23.10	55	13.8
Some college	39.53	95	19.5
Associate's degree	36.85	88	8.7
Bachelor's degree or more	71.41	171	54.0
Bachelor's degree	63.85	153	30.5
Master's, professional, doctoral degree	84.39	202	23.5

Note: Market shares may not sum to 100.0 because of rounding and missing categories by household type. "Asian" and "black" include Hispanics and non-Hispanics who identify themselves as being of the respective race alone. "Hispanic" includes people of any race who identify themselves as Hispanic. "Other" includes people who identify themselves as non-Hispanic and as Alaska Native, American Indian, Asian (who are also included in the "Asian" row), or Native Hawaiian or other Pacific Islander, as well as non-Hispanics reporting more than one race.
Source: Calculations by New Strategist based on the Bureau of Labor Statistics' 2012 Consumer Expenditure Survey

Photo Processing

Best customers: Householders aged 25 to 54
                  Married couples
                  Asians
                  Households in the Midwest

Customer trends: Average household spending on photo processing will continue to slip as home printers reduce
                  processing needs.

The best customers of photo processing are married couples with children. Couples with preschoolers spend two-and-one-half times the average on photo processing as they get digital pictures of their children processed into prints. Couples with school-aged or older children at home spend 33 to 82 percent more than average on this item. Householders aged 25 to 54, many of them parents, spend 17 to 37 percent more than average on photo processing, and married couples without children at home (most of them older empty-nesters) spend 27 percent more than average. Households in the Midwest spend 21 percent more on photo processing than the average household. Asians spend 85 percent more than average on this item.

Average household spending on photo processing fell by an enormous 78 percent between 2000 and 2012, after adjusting for inflation. Behind the decline was the shift to digital photography, which allows families to process pictures on their computers and printers at home. Spending on photo processing will continue to decline as this trend continues.

Table 5.21 Photo processing

Total household spending $1,138,406,400.00
Average household spends   9.15

	AVERAGE HOUSEHOLD SPENDING	BEST CUSTOMERS (index)	BIGGEST CUSTOMERS (market share)
AGE OF HOUSEHOLDER			
Average household	$9.15	100	100.0%
Under age 25	3.30	36	2.4
Aged 25 to 34	11.60	127	20.5
Aged 35 to 44	12.57	137	23.8
Aged 45 to 54	10.68	117	23.1
Aged 55 to 64	8.53	93	17.1
Aged 65 to 74	7.21	79	9.5
Aged 75 or older	3.39	37	3.6

	AVERAGE HOUSEHOLD SPENDING	BEST CUSTOMERS (index)	BIGGEST CUSTOMERS (market share)
HOUSEHOLD INCOME			
Average household	**$9.15**	**100**	**100.0%**
Under $20,000	1.89	21	4.3
$20,000 to $39,999	3.61	39	8.9
$40,000 to $49,999	6.00	66	5.8
$50,000 to $69,999	10.60	116	16.7
$70,000 to $79,999	16.08	176	9.8
$80,000 to $99,999	14.55	159	14.0
$100,000 or more	19.73	216	40.4
HOUSEHOLD TYPE			
Average household	**9.15**	**100**	**100.0**
Married couples	14.43	158	76.6
Married couples, no children	11.62	127	26.5
Married couples with children	16.54	181	42.5
Oldest child under age 6	23.01	251	11.5
Oldest child aged 6 to 17	16.67	182	21.7
Oldest child aged 18 or older	12.13	133	9.4
Single parent with child under age 18	7.54	82	4.3
Single person	3.16	35	10.3
RACE AND HISPANIC ORIGIN			
Average household	**9.15**	**100**	**100.0**
Asian	16.94	185	8.0
Black	4.09	45	5.6
Hispanic	3.58	39	4.9
Non-Hispanic white and other	10.92	119	89.6
REGION			
Average household	**9.15**	**100**	**100.0**
Northeast	9.30	102	18.3
Midwest	11.03	121	26.7
South	7.34	80	29.9
West	10.16	111	25.0
EDUCATION			
Average household	**9.15**	**100**	**100.0**
Less than high school graduate	3.19	35	4.6
High school graduate	4.23	46	11.5
Some college	7.54	82	17.0
Associate's degree	10.17	111	11.0
Bachelor's degree or more	16.24	177	56.0
Bachelor's degree	13.94	152	30.4
Master's, professional, doctoral degree	20.19	221	25.6

Note: Market shares may not sum to 100.0 because of rounding and missing categories by household type. "Asian" and "black" include Hispanics and non-Hispanics who identify themselves as being of the respective race alone. "Hispanic" includes people of any race who identify themselves as Hispanic. "Other" includes people who identify themselves as non-Hispanic and as Alaska Native, American Indian, Asian (who are also included in the "Asian" row), or Native Hawaiian or other Pacific Islander, as well as non-Hispanics reporting more than one race.
Source: Calculations by New Strategist based on the Bureau of Labor Statistics' 2012 Consumer Expenditure Survey

Photographer's Fees

Best customers: Householders aged 25 to 34
Married couples with children at home
Asians

Customer trends: Average household spending on photographer's fees is likely to decline in the years ahead
as professional photographers lose ground in the competition with digital technology.

Average household spending on photographer's fees is all about children, and the best customers of this item are married couples with children. Married couples with preschoolers spend two-and-one-half times the average on photographer's fees, and those with school-aged or older children at home spend 42 to 68 percent more than average on this item. Householders aged 25 to 34 spend 61 percent more than average on this item because most are parents. Asians spend well over twice the average on photographer's fees, and average spending on this item by households in the West, where many Asians reside, tops the average by 16 percent.

Average household spending on photographer's fees dropped by a substantial 35 percent between 2000 and 2010, after adjusting for inflation. Between 2010 and 2012 spending on photographer's fees grew by 21 percent, a sign of economic recovery. Spending on this category is likely to resume its decline in the years ahead as professional photographers lose ground in the competition with digital technology.

Table 5.22 Photographer's fees

Total household spending $2,627,665,920.00
Average household spends   21.12

	AVERAGE HOUSEHOLD SPENDING	BEST CUSTOMERS (index)	BIGGEST CUSTOMERS (market share)
AGE OF HOUSEHOLDER			
Average household	$21.12	100	100.0%
Under age 25	26.39	125	8.2
Aged 25 to 34	34.10	161	26.1
Aged 35 to 44	20.21	96	16.6
Aged 45 to 54	25.94	123	24.3
Aged 55 to 64	24.04	114	20.8
Aged 65 to 74	6.76	32	3.9
Aged 75 or older	0.23	1	0.1

	AVERAGE HOUSEHOLD SPENDING	BEST CUSTOMERS (index)	BIGGEST CUSTOMERS (market share)
HOUSEHOLD INCOME			
Average household	**$21.12**	**100**	**100.0%**
Under $20,000	3.00	14	3.0
$20,000 to $39,999	4.44	21	4.7
$40,000 to $49,999	17.24	82	7.2
$50,000 to $69,999	20.88	99	14.3
$70,000 to $79,999	16.96	80	4.5
$80,000 to $99,999	33.94	161	14.2
$100,000 or more	58.81	278	52.1
HOUSEHOLD TYPE			
Average household	**21.12**	**100**	**100.0**
Married couples	31.66	150	72.8
Married couples, no children	27.85	132	27.5
Married couples with children	37.23	176	41.4
Oldest child under age 6	53.06	251	11.5
Oldest child aged 6 to 17	35.46	168	20.0
Oldest child aged 18 or older	29.98	142	10.0
Single parent with child under age 18	16.14	76	4.0
Single person	4.02	19	5.7
RACE AND HISPANIC ORIGIN			
Average household	**21.12**	**100**	**100.0**
Asian	50.14	237	10.3
Black	6.71	32	4.0
Hispanic	7.33	35	4.4
Non-Hispanic white and other	25.79	122	91.7
REGION			
Average household	**21.12**	**100**	**100.0**
Northeast	17.92	85	15.3
Midwest	20.84	99	21.9
South	20.80	98	36.7
West	24.50	116	26.1
EDUCATION			
Average household	**21.12**	**100**	**100.0**
Less than high school graduate	3.27	15	2.0
High school graduate	9.32	44	11.0
Some college	15.92	75	15.5
Associate's degree	25.14	119	11.8
Bachelor's degree or more	39.99	189	59.7
Bachelor's degree	38.42	182	36.3
Master's, professional, doctoral degree	42.68	202	23.5

Note: Market shares may not sum to 100.0 because of rounding and missing categories by household type. "Asian" and "black" include Hispanics and non-Hispanics who identify themselves as being of the respective race alone. "Hispanic" includes people of any race who identify themselves as Hispanic. "Other" includes people who identify themselves as non-Hispanic and as Alaska Native, American Indian, Asian (who are also included in the "Asian" row), or Native Hawaiian or other Pacific Islander, as well as non-Hispanics reporting more than one race.
Source: Calculations by New Strategist based on the Bureau of Labor Statistics' 2012 Consumer Expenditure Survey

Photographic Equipment

Best customers:
Householders aged 35 to 44
Married couples without children at home
Married couples with school-aged or older children at home
Asians and non-Hispanic whites
Households in the West
College graduates

Customer trends:
Average household spending on photographic equipment is likely to continue to decline now that digital cameras have replaced film cameras in most homes and smartphones with cameras are dampening demand for stand-alone equipment.

Household spending on digital cameras is the driving force in this category. The best customers of photographic equipment are middle-aged married couples with school-aged or older children at home. Householders aged 35 to 44 (many with children) spend a surprising two-and-one-half times the average on photographic equipment and are the only age group to exceed the spending average on this item. The parents of school-aged children spend 67 percent more than average on photographic equipment, and couples with adult children at home spend 21 percent more than average. The spending on this item by Asian householders is 79 percent above average, and households in the West, where many Asians reside, spend twice the average on photographic equipment. College graduates outspend the average by a factor of 2.2.

Between 2000 and 2006 (the year household spending peaked), average household spending on photographic equipment grew 38 percent, after adjusting for inflation, but between 2006 and 2012 spending fell 16 percent. The replacement of film cameras with digital cameras was behind the increase earlier in the decade—a substitution that is largely complete. Behind the more recent decline is the substitution of smartphone cameras for digital cameras. Spending on photographic equipment is likely to continue this decline in the years ahead as smartphone cameras dampen demand for stand-alone equipment.

Table 5.23 Photographic equipment

Total household spending $3,878,046,720.00
Average household spends 31.17

AGE OF HOUSEHOLDER	AVERAGE HOUSEHOLD SPENDING	BEST CUSTOMERS (index)	BIGGEST CUSTOMERS (market share)
Average household	$31.17	100	100.0%
Under age 25	17.41	56	3.7
Aged 25 to 34	25.50	82	13.2
Aged 35 to 44	78.32	251	43.6
Aged 45 to 54	28.97	93	18.4
Aged 55 to 64	24.17	78	14.2
Aged 65 to 74	12.66	41	4.9
Aged 75 or older	6.42	21	2.0

	AVERAGE HOUSEHOLD SPENDING	BEST CUSTOMERS (index)	BIGGEST CUSTOMERS (market share)
HOUSEHOLD INCOME			
Average household	$31.17	100	100.0%
Under $20,000	6.56	21	4.4
$20,000 to $39,999	10.52	34	7.6
$40,000 to $49,999	14.36	46	4.1
$50,000 to $69,999	22.36	72	10.4
$70,000 to $79,999	122.40	393	21.9
$80,000 to $99,999	38.89	125	11.0
$100,000 or more	67.58	217	40.6
HOUSEHOLD TYPE			
Average household	31.17	100	100.0
Married couples	48.41	155	75.4
Married couples, no children	59.65	191	39.9
Married couples with children	42.19	135	31.8
Oldest child under age 6	23.75	76	3.5
Oldest child aged 6 to 17	52.01	167	19.8
Oldest child aged 18 or older	37.56	121	8.5
Single parent with child under age 18	12.46	40	2.1
Single person	13.80	44	13.1
RACE AND HISPANIC ORIGIN			
Average household	31.17	100	100.0
Asian	55.66	179	7.7
Black	9.42	30	3.8
Hispanic	10.82	35	4.4
Non-Hispanic white and other	38.14	122	91.8
REGION			
Average household	31.17	100	100.0
Northeast	22.79	73	13.2
Midwest	22.88	73	16.3
South	21.07	68	25.2
West	62.74	201	45.4
EDUCATION			
Average household	31.17	100	100.0
Less than high school graduate	5.95	19	2.5
High school graduate	11.89	38	9.5
Some college	18.67	60	12.3
Associate's degree	19.53	63	6.2
Bachelor's degree or more	68.66	220	69.5
Bachelor's degree	76.91	247	49.2
Master's, professional, doctoral degree	54.50	175	20.3

Note: Market shares may not sum to 100.0 because of rounding and missing categories by household type. "Asian" and "black" include Hispanics and non-Hispanics who identify themselves as being of the respective race alone. "Hispanic" includes people of any race who identify themselves as Hispanic. "Other" includes people who identify themselves as non-Hispanic and as Alaska Native, American Indian, Asian (who are also included in the "Asian" row), or Native Hawaiian or other Pacific Islander, as well as non-Hispanics reporting more than one race.
Source: Calculations by New Strategist based on the Bureau of Labor Statistics' 2012 Consumer Expenditure Survey

Recreational Vehicles (Boats, Campers, Trailers) Purchase and Rental

Best customers: Householders aged 35 to 54
Married couples with children at home
Non-Hispanic whites

Customer trends: Average household spending on the purchase and rental of recreational vehicles is likely to continue its decline as households curtail their discretionary spending and early retirement becomes less common.

Middle-aged non-Hispanic white couples with children are the best customers of the purchase and rental of recreational vehicles—such as boats, trailers, and campers. Married couples with children at home spend twice the average on recreational vehicles, and householders aged 35 to 54 spend 33 to 74 percent more than average. Non-Hispanic whites completely dominate the recreational vehicle market and account for 98 percent of spending in this category.

Average household spending on the purchase and rental of recreational vehicles declined 54 percent between 2006 and 2012, after adjusting for inflation, dropping the category from second to ninth place in the dollar amount devoted to entertainment. Behind the decline is belt tightening in the face of the Great Recession. Spending on recreational vehicles is likely to continue its decline in the years ahead as households further curtail discretionary spending and early retirement becomes less common.

Table 5.24 Recreational vehicles (boats, campers, trailers) purchase and rental

Total household spending $14,169,738,240.00
Average household spends 113.89

AGE OF HOUSEHOLDER	AVERAGE HOUSEHOLD SPENDING	BEST CUSTOMERS (index)	BIGGEST CUSTOMERS (market share)
Average household	$113.89	100	100.0%
Under age 25	36.33	32	2.1
Aged 25 to 34	42.59	37	6.0
Aged 35 to 44	198.09	174	30.2
Aged 45 to 54	151.44	133	26.3
Aged 55 to 64	96.28	85	15.5
Aged 65 to 74	87.66	77	9.3
Aged 75 or older	123.57	108	10.6

	AVERAGE HOUSEHOLD SPENDING	BEST CUSTOMERS (index)	BIGGEST CUSTOMERS (market share)
HOUSEHOLD INCOME			
Average household	**$113.89**	**100**	**100.0%**
Under $20,000	1.90	2	0.4
$20,000 to $39,999	23.21	20	4.6
$40,000 to $49,999	16.69	15	1.3
$50,000 to $69,999	154.70	136	19.6
$70,000 to $79,999	30.11	26	1.5
$80,000 to $99,999	97.67	86	7.6
$100,000 or more	338.86	298	55.7
HOUSEHOLD TYPE			
Average household	**113.89**	**100**	**100.0**
Married couples	191.14	168	81.5
Married couples, no children	143.27	126	26.2
Married couples with children	228.53	201	47.2
Oldest child under age 6	303.86	267	12.2
Oldest child aged 6 to 17	162.62	143	17.0
Oldest child aged 18 or older	290.91	255	18.0
Single parent with child under age 18	13.64	12	0.6
Single person	46.81	41	12.2
RACE AND HISPANIC ORIGIN			
Average household	**113.89**	**100**	**100.0**
Asian	7.09	6	0.3
Black	14.11	12	1.6
Hispanic	4.50	4	0.5
Non-Hispanic white and other	148.67	131	98.0
REGION			
Average household	**113.89**	**100**	**100.0**
Northeast	91.56	80	14.5
Midwest	110.82	97	21.6
South	122.52	108	40.1
West	120.54	106	23.8
EDUCATION			
Average household	**113.89**	**100**	**100.0**
Less than high school graduate	87.50	77	10.0
High school graduate	36.18	32	7.9
Some college	121.62	107	22.0
Associate's degree	233.88	205	20.3
Bachelor's degree or more	143.62	126	39.8
Bachelor's degree	88.37	78	15.5
Master's, professional, doctoral degree	238.53	209	24.3

Note: Market shares may not sum to 100.0 because of rounding and missing categories by household type. "Asian" and "black" include Hispanics and non-Hispanics who identify themselves as being of the respective race alone. "Hispanic" includes people of any race who identify themselves as Hispanic. "Other" includes people who identify themselves as non-Hispanic and as Alaska Native, American Indian, Asian (who are also included in the "Asian" row), or Native Hawaiian or other Pacific Islander, as well as non-Hispanics reporting more than one race.
Source: Calculations by New Strategist based on the Bureau of Labor Statistics' 2012 Consumer Expenditure Survey

Rental of Party Supplies for Catered Affairs

Best customers:
Householders aged 45 to 64
High-income households
Married couples
Asians and Hispanics
Households in the West
College graduates

Customer trends:
Average household spending on the rental of party supplies for catered affairs is likely to decline in the years ahead as households tighten their belts.

The best customers of rental of party supplies for catered affairs are the affluent. Households with incomes of $100,000 or more spend three-and-one-third times the average on the rental of party supplies. College graduates, a relatively well-off demographic, spend over twice the average on rental of party supplies for catered affairs. Asian and Hispanic households also spend twice the average on this item, and households in the West, where many Asians and Hispanics reside, spend 80 percent more than average on party supply rental. Householders aged 45 to 54 spend twice the average and those aged 55 to 64 spend one-third more than average on this item. Married couples outspend the average by two-thirds, the figure peaking among couples with adult children at home at close to four times the average.

Rental of party supplies for catered affairs is a relatively new item in the Consumer Expenditure Survey, and comparable data from 2000 or 2006 do not exist. Average household spending on this item declined 6 percent between 2010 and 2012. Average household spending on rental of party supplies for catered affairs is likely to decline further in the years ahead as households tighten their belts.

Table 5.25 Rental of party supplies for catered affairs

Total household spending $1,571,374,080.00
Average household spends 12.63

AGE OF HOUSEHOLDER	AVERAGE HOUSEHOLD SPENDING	BEST CUSTOMERS (index)	BIGGEST CUSTOMERS (market share)
Average household	$12.63	100	100.0%
Under age 25	4.29	34	2.2
Aged 25 to 34	9.29	74	11.9
Aged 35 to 44	11.51	91	15.8
Aged 45 to 54	26.76	212	41.9
Aged 55 to 64	16.58	131	24.0
Aged 65 to 74	3.60	29	3.4
Aged 75 or older	0.83	7	0.6

	AVERAGE HOUSEHOLD SPENDING	BEST CUSTOMERS (index)	BIGGEST CUSTOMERS (market share)
HOUSEHOLD INCOME			
Average household	**$12.63**	**100**	**100.0%**
Under $20,000	1.23	10	2.1
$20,000 to $39,999	4.50	36	8.0
$40,000 to $49,999	6.54	52	4.6
$50,000 to $69,999	8.37	66	9.6
$70,000 to $79,999	18.72	148	8.3
$80,000 to $99,999	8.07	64	5.6
$100,000 or more	41.70	330	61.8
HOUSEHOLD TYPE			
Average household	**12.63**	**100**	**100.0**
Married couples	20.95	166	80.6
Married couples, no children	18.38	146	30.3
Married couples with children	26.39	209	49.1
Oldest child under age 6	15.46	122	5.6
Oldest child aged 6 to 17	18.02	143	17.0
Oldest child aged 18 or older	47.57	377	26.6
Single parent with child under age 18	8.43	67	3.5
Single person	1.82	14	4.3
RACE AND HISPANIC ORIGIN			
Average household	**12.63**	**100**	**100.0**
Asian	28.20	223	9.7
Black	7.06	56	7.0
Hispanic	25.97	206	25.8
Non-Hispanic white and other	11.30	89	67.2
REGION			
Average household	**12.63**	**100**	**100.0**
Northeast	9.59	76	13.7
Midwest	10.36	82	18.2
South	9.33	74	27.5
West	22.73	180	40.6
EDUCATION			
Average household	**12.63**	**100**	**100.0**
Less than high school graduate	5.85	46	6.0
High school graduate	4.84	38	9.6
Some college	6.37	50	10.4
Associate's degree	8.45	67	6.6
Bachelor's degree or more	26.98	214	67.4
Bachelor's degree	30.91	245	48.8
Master's, professional, doctoral degree	20.23	160	18.6

Note: Market shares may not sum to 100.0 because of rounding and missing categories by household type. "Asian" and "black" include Hispanics and non-Hispanics who identify themselves as being of the respective race alone. "Hispanic" includes people of any race who identify themselves as Hispanic. "Other" includes people who identify themselves as non-Hispanic and as Alaska Native, American Indian, Asian (who are also included in the "Asian" row), or Native Hawaiian or other Pacific Islander, as well as non-Hispanics reporting more than one race.
Source: Calculations by New Strategist based on the Bureau of Labor Statistics' 2012 Consumer Expenditure Survey

Repair of Television, Radio, and Sound Equipment

Best customers: Householders aged 35 to 44 and 55 or older
Married couples with adult children at home
Hispanics
Households in the West

Customer trends: Average household spending on repair of television, radio, and sound equipment may stabilize
or even grow in the years ahead because it is more economical to repair than to replace
expensive high-definition television sets.

The best customers of television, radio, and sound equipment repair are the oldest householders. Householders aged 65 to 74 spend 57 percent more than the average household on television, radio, and sound equipment repairs. The adjacent younger and older age groups spend 14 to 19 percent more. Householders aged 35 to 44 outspend the average on this item by 22 percent. Married couples with adult children at home spend 91 percent more than average on TV and audio repair. Hispanics spend 18 percent more than average on the repair of television sets. Households in the West spend nearly twice the average on such repairs.

Average household spending on repair of television, radio, and sound equipment grew 46 percent between 2000 and 2006 after adjusting for inflation, then fell 51 percent between 2006 and 2012. One factor behind the recent decline is the relatively new inventory of television sets in the nation's households. Average household spending on this category may stabilize or even grow in the years ahead because it is more economical to repair than to replace expensive high-definition television sets.

Table 5.26 Repair of television, radio, and sound equipment

Total household spending $384,445,440.00
Average household spends   3.09

AGE OF HOUSEHOLDER	AVERAGE HOUSEHOLD SPENDING	BEST CUSTOMERS (index)	BIGGEST CUSTOMERS (market share)
Average household	$3.09	100	100.0%
Under age 25	1.09	35	2.3
Aged 25 to 34	2.52	82	13.2
Aged 35 to 44	3.76	122	21.1
Aged 45 to 54	1.88	61	12.0
Aged 55 to 64	3.53	114	20.9
Aged 65 to 74	4.86	157	19.0
Aged 75 or older	3.68	119	11.6

	AVERAGE HOUSEHOLD SPENDING	BEST CUSTOMERS (index)	BIGGEST CUSTOMERS (market share)
HOUSEHOLD INCOME			
Average household	**$3.09**	**100**	**100.0%**
Under $20,000	1.25	40	8.5
$20,000 to $39,999	2.07	67	15.1
$40,000 to $49,999	1.63	53	4.7
$50,000 to $69,999	2.08	67	9.7
$70,000 to $79,999	0.66	21	1.2
$80,000 to $99,999	4.89	158	14.0
$100,000 or more	7.75	251	47.0
HOUSEHOLD TYPE			
Average household	**3.09**	**100**	**100.0**
Married couples	4.30	139	67.6
Married couples, no children	3.25	105	21.9
Married couples with children	3.11	101	23.7
Oldest child under age 6	2.53	82	3.7
Oldest child aged 6 to 17	1.68	54	6.5
Oldest child aged 18 or older	5.90	191	13.5
Single parent with child under age 18	0.50	16	0.8
Single person	2.16	70	20.8
RACE AND HISPANIC ORIGIN			
Average household	**3.09**	**100**	**100.0**
Asian	1.39	45	1.9
Black	1.90	61	7.7
Hispanic	3.65	118	14.8
Non-Hispanic white and other	3.21	104	78.0
REGION			
Average household	**3.09**	**100**	**100.0**
Northeast	3.06	99	17.9
Midwest	2.64	85	18.9
South	1.65	53	19.9
West	5.94	192	43.3
EDUCATION			
Average household	**3.09**	**100**	**100.0**
Less than high school graduate	1.25	40	5.3
High school graduate	2.55	83	20.6
Some college	3.10	100	20.7
Associate's degree	5.94	192	19.0
Bachelor's degree or more	3.39	110	34.6
Bachelor's degree	3.34	108	21.5
Master's, professional, doctoral degree	3.48	113	13.1

Note: Market shares may not sum to 100.0 because of rounding and missing categories by household type. "Asian" and "black" include Hispanics and non-Hispanics who identify themselves as being of the respective race alone. "Hispanic" includes people of any race who identify themselves as Hispanic. "Other" includes people who identify themselves as non-Hispanic and as Alaska Native, American Indian, Asian (who are also included in the "Asian" row), or Native Hawaiian or other Pacific Islander, as well as non-Hispanics reporting more than one race.
Source: Calculations by New Strategist based on the Bureau of Labor Statistics' 2012 Consumer Expenditure Survey

Satellite Radio Service

Best customers: Householders aged 35 to 74
Married couples without children at home
Married couples with school-aged or older children at home

Customer trends: Average household spending on satellite radio service will depend more on trends in technology
than on demographic change in the years ahead.

Householders aged 35 to 74 spend 12 to 27 percent more than average on satellite radio service and control 80 percent of the market. Married couples without children at home, most of them empty-nesters, spend 34 percent more than average on this item. Couples with school-aged or older children at home spend 40 to 66 percent more than average on satellite radio service.

Satellite radio service is a relatively new item in the Consumer Expenditure Survey, which limits the analysis of spending trends. Between 2010 and 2012 average household spending on satellite radio service declined by a modest 3 percent. Spending on satellite radio will in the years ahead depend more on trends in technology than on demographic change.

Table 5.27 Satellite radio service

Total household spending $1,845,089,280.00
Average household spends   14.83

AGE OF HOUSEHOLDER	AVERAGE HOUSEHOLD SPENDING	BEST CUSTOMERS (index)	BIGGEST CUSTOMERS (market share)
Average household	**$14.83**	**100**	**100.0%**
Under age 25	6.39	43	2.8
Aged 25 to 34	12.29	83	13.4
Aged 35 to 44	16.63	112	19.5
Aged 45 to 54	18.81	127	25.1
Aged 55 to 64	16.83	113	20.8
Aged 65 to 74	18.10	122	14.7
Aged 75 or older	5.70	38	3.8

	AVERAGE HOUSEHOLD SPENDING	BEST CUSTOMERS (index)	BIGGEST CUSTOMERS (market share)
HOUSEHOLD INCOME			
Average household	**$14.83**	**100**	**100.0%**
Under $20,000	6.22	42	8.8
$20,000 to $39,999	10.60	72	16.1
$40,000 to $49,999	9.59	65	5.7
$50,000 to $69,999	12.51	84	12.2
$70,000 to $79,999	13.48	91	5.1
$80,000 to $99,999	19.33	130	11.5
$100,000 or more	32.16	217	40.6
HOUSEHOLD TYPE			
Average household	**14.83**	**100**	**100.0**
Married couples	19.87	134	65.1
Married couples, no children	19.92	134	28.0
Married couples with children	21.00	142	33.3
Oldest child under age 6	15.92	107	4.9
Oldest child aged 6 to 17	20.79	140	16.7
Oldest child aged 18 or older	24.63	166	11.7
Single parent with child under age 18	13.36	90	4.7
Single person	8.24	56	16.5
RACE AND HISPANIC ORIGIN			
Average household	**14.83**	**100**	**100.0**
Asian	14.45	97	4.2
Black	9.39	63	8.0
Hispanic	9.24	62	7.8
Non-Hispanic white and other	16.65	112	84.3
REGION			
Average household	**14.83**	**100**	**100.0**
Northeast	16.93	114	20.6
Midwest	12.39	84	18.5
South	16.78	113	42.1
West	12.34	83	18.7
EDUCATION			
Average household	**14.83**	**100**	**100.0**
Less than high school graduate	9.20	62	8.1
High school graduate	12.47	84	21.0
Some college	13.07	88	18.2
Associate's degree	13.85	93	9.2
Bachelor's degree or more	20.49	138	43.6
Bachelor's degree	17.06	115	22.9
Master's, professional, doctoral degree	26.39	178	20.7

Note: Market shares may not sum to 100.0 because of rounding and missing categories by household type. "Asian" and "black" include Hispanics and non-Hispanics who identify themselves as being of the respective race alone. "Hispanic" includes people of any race who identify themselves as Hispanic. "Other" includes people who identify themselves as non-Hispanic and as Alaska Native, American Indian, Asian (who are also included in the "Asian" row), or Native Hawaiian or other Pacific Islander, as well as non-Hispanics reporting more than one race.
Source: Calculations by New Strategist based on the Bureau of Labor Statistics' 2012 Consumer Expenditure Survey

Sound Components, Equipment, and Accessories (Includes Radios and Tape Recorders)

Best customers:
Householders aged 35 to 44 and 55 to 64
High-income households
Married couples without children at home
Married couples with children under age 18
Households in the Northeast
College graduates

Customer trends:
Average household spending on sound components, equipment, and accessories is unlikely to rise in the years ahead because of continued price discounting and product substitution.

The best customers of sound components, equipment, and accessories are affluent, educated couples living in the Northeast. Households with incomes of $100,000 or more spend three times the average on sound equipment and accessories. College graduates, an affluent demographic, spend nearly twice the average on this item, as do married couples without children at home. Married couples with children under age 18 spend 32 to 63 percent more than average on audio equipment. Householders aged 35 to 44 spend 23 percent more than average on this item, but those aged 55 to 64 outspend the average by 90 percent.

Average household spending on sound components, equipment, and accessories fell by 49 percent between 2000 and 2010, the trough year of overall spending. From then to 2012 spending on this item improved by 10 percent, after adjusting for inflation. Behind the decline was the substitution of personal digital audio equipment (such as iPods) for larger systems. Average household spending on this category is unlikely to rise much in the years ahead because of continued price discounting and product substitution.

Table 5.28 Sound components, equipment, and accessories (includes radios and tape recorders)

Total household spending $3,990,021,120.00
Average household spends 32.07

	AVERAGE HOUSEHOLD SPENDING	BEST CUSTOMERS (index)	BIGGEST CUSTOMERS (market share)
AGE OF HOUSEHOLDER			
Average household	**$32.07**	**100**	**100.0%**
Under age 25	15.07	47	3.1
Aged 25 to 34	18.71	58	9.4
Aged 35 to 44	39.51	123	21.4
Aged 45 to 54	28.57	89	17.6
Aged 55 to 64	61.08	190	34.9
Aged 65 to 74	26.72	83	10.0
Aged 75 or older	11.66	36	3.6

	AVERAGE HOUSEHOLD SPENDING	BEST CUSTOMERS (index)	BIGGEST CUSTOMERS (market share)
HOUSEHOLD INCOME			
Average household	**$32.07**	**100**	**100.0%**
Under $20,000	9.96	31	6.5
$20,000 to $39,999	19.67	61	13.8
$40,000 to $49,999	21.55	67	5.9
$50,000 to $69,999	14.85	46	6.7
$70,000 to $79,999	25.14	78	4.4
$80,000 to $99,999	19.41	61	5.3
$100,000 or more	97.28	303	56.8
HOUSEHOLD TYPE			
Average household	**32.07**	**100**	**100.0**
Married couples	51.99	162	78.7
Married couples, no children	65.93	206	42.9
Married couples with children	45.28	141	33.2
Oldest child under age 6	42.21	132	6.0
Oldest child aged 6 to 17	52.42	163	19.4
Oldest child aged 18 or older	35.42	110	7.8
Single parent with child under age 18	21.85	68	3.6
Single person	11.06	34	10.2
RACE AND HISPANIC ORIGIN			
Average household	**32.07**	**100**	**100.0**
Asian	21.25	66	2.9
Black	25.82	81	10.1
Hispanic	15.61	49	6.1
Non-Hispanic white and other	35.81	112	83.8
REGION			
Average household	**32.07**	**100**	**100.0**
Northeast	70.62	220	39.8
Midwest	17.74	55	12.3
South	24.04	75	27.9
West	28.52	89	20.0
EDUCATION			
Average household	**32.07**	**100**	**100.0**
Less than high school graduate	15.46	48	6.3
High school graduate	15.81	49	12.3
Some college	16.82	52	10.8
Associate's degree	26.34	82	8.1
Bachelor's degree or more	63.54	198	62.5
Bachelor's degree	33.61	105	20.9
Master's, professional, doctoral degree	114.89	358	41.6

Note: Market shares may not sum to 100.0 because of rounding and missing categories by household type. "Asian" and "black" include Hispanics and non-Hispanics who identify themselves as being of the respective race alone. "Hispanic" includes people of any race who identify themselves as Hispanic. "Other" includes people who identify themselves as non-Hispanic and as Alaska Native, American Indian, Asian (who are also included in the "Asian" row), or Native Hawaiian or other Pacific Islander, as well as non-Hispanics reporting more than one race.
Source: Calculations by New Strategist based on the Bureau of Labor Statistics' 2012 Consumer Expenditure Survey

Streamed and Downloaded Audio

Best customers: Householders aged 25 to 54
                   Married couples with children at home
                   Households in the West and Northeast

Customer trends: Average household spending on streamed and downloaded audio should rise in the years ahead
                   as downloads become the norm for buying music.

Streamed and downloaded audio is a spending category newly added to the Consumer Expenditure Survey in 2005. It captures spending on music downloads from sites such as iTunes and pay-per-listen programming. The best customers of audio downloads are households with school-aged children, which spend two-and-one-quarter times the average on this item. Those with preschoolers spend 39 percent more than average on streamed and downloaded audio, and those with adult children at home spend 58 percent more. Householders ranging in age from 25 to 54, many with children, spend 41 to 57 percent more than average on this item. Households in the West and Northeast spend, respectively, 34 and 24 percent more than average on streamed and downloaded audio.

Spending on streamed and downloaded audio more than doubled between 2006 and 2012, after adjusting for inflation. Average household spending on music downloads should increase greatly in the years ahead.

Table 5.29 Streamed and downloaded audio

Total household spending $1,292,682,240.00
Average household spends   10.39

AGE OF HOUSEHOLDER	AVERAGE HOUSEHOLD SPENDING	BEST CUSTOMERS (index)	BIGGEST CUSTOMERS (market share)
Average household	$10.39	100	100.0%
Under age 25	8.65	83	5.5
Aged 25 to 34	14.97	144	23.3
Aged 35 to 44	16.36	157	27.3
Aged 45 to 54	14.65	141	27.9
Aged 55 to 64	7.65	74	13.5
Aged 65 to 74	1.94	19	2.3
Aged 75 or older	0.27	3	0.3

	AVERAGE HOUSEHOLD SPENDING	BEST CUSTOMERS (index)	BIGGEST CUSTOMERS (market share)
HOUSEHOLD INCOME			
Average household	**$10.39**	**100**	**100.0%**
Under $20,000	2.11	20	4.3
$20,000 to $39,999	3.77	36	8.2
$40,000 to $49,999	5.81	56	4.9
$50,000 to $69,999	8.32	80	11.6
$70,000 to $79,999	11.01	106	5.9
$80,000 to $99,999	13.78	133	11.7
$100,000 or more	29.63	285	53.4
HOUSEHOLD TYPE			
Average household	**10.39**	**100**	**100.0**
Married couples	14.62	141	68.3
Married couples, no children	9.51	92	19.1
Married couples with children	19.74	190	44.7
Oldest child under age 6	14.49	139	6.4
Oldest child aged 6 to 17	23.73	228	27.2
Oldest child aged 18 or older	16.41	158	11.1
Single parent with child under age 18	9.52	92	4.8
Single person	5.49	53	15.7
RACE AND HISPANIC ORIGIN			
Average household	**10.39**	**100**	**100.0**
Asian	8.76	84	3.7
Black	4.08	39	4.9
Hispanic	5.45	52	6.6
Non-Hispanic white and other	12.25	118	88.5
REGION			
Average household	**10.39**	**100**	**100.0**
Northeast	12.84	124	22.3
Midwest	8.68	84	18.5
South	8.08	78	29.0
West	13.92	134	30.2
EDUCATION			
Average household	**10.39**	**100**	**100.0**
Less than high school graduate	1.49	14	1.9
High school graduate	4.48	43	10.8
Some college	9.93	96	19.7
Associate's degree	10.77	104	10.2
Bachelor's degree or more	18.92	182	57.4
Bachelor's degree	16.78	162	32.2
Master's, professional, doctoral degree	22.60	218	25.2

Note: Market shares may not sum to 100.0 because of rounding and missing categories by household type. "Asian" and "black" include Hispanics and non-Hispanics who identify themselves as being of the respective race alone. "Hispanic" includes people of any race who identify themselves as Hispanic. "Other" includes people who identify themselves as non-Hispanic and as Alaska Native, American Indian, Asian (who are also included in the "Asian" row), or Native Hawaiian or other Pacific Islander, as well as non-Hispanics reporting more than one race.
Source: Calculations by New Strategist based on the Bureau of Labor Statistics' 2012 Consumer Expenditure Survey

Streamed and Downloaded Video

Best customers: **Householders aged 25 to 44**
                       Married couples with children at home
                       Households in the West

Customer trends: **Average household spending on streamed and downloaded video should rise in the years ahead**
                       as Internet equipped television sets become the norm.

Streamed and downloaded video is a spending category newly added to the Consumer Expenditure Survey in 2005. It captures spending on streaming services such as Netflix as well as pay-per-view programming for computers and Internet equipped television sets. The best customers of video downloads are households with school-aged children, which spend 86 percent more than average on this item. Couples with preschoolers outspend the average by 54 percent, and those with adult children at home by 39 percent. Householders aged 25 to 44, many with children, spend 40 to 51 percent more than average on streamed and downloaded video. Households in the West spend fully twice the average on this item.

Streamed and downloaded video is a relatively new item in the Consumer Expenditure Survey and comparable data from 2000 do not exist. Between 2006 and 2012 average household spending in this category nearly quadrupled, after adjusting for inflation. Average household spending on streamed and downloaded video should continue to increase greatly in the years ahead.

Table 5.30 Streamed and downloaded video

Total household spending $665,625,600.00
Average household spends   5.35

AGE OF HOUSEHOLDER	AVERAGE HOUSEHOLD SPENDING	BEST CUSTOMERS (index)	BIGGEST CUSTOMERS (market share)
Average household	$5.35	100	100.0%
Under age 25	3.48	65	4.3
Aged 25 to 34	8.10	151	24.5
Aged 35 to 44	7.48	140	24.3
Aged 45 to 54	6.40	120	23.7
Aged 55 to 64	4.58	86	15.7
Aged 65 to 74	2.51	47	5.7
Aged 75 or older	1.04	19	1.9

	AVERAGE HOUSEHOLD SPENDING	BEST CUSTOMERS (index)	BIGGEST CUSTOMERS (market share)
HOUSEHOLD INCOME			
Average household	**$5.35**	**100**	**100.0%**
Under $20,000	1.42	27	5.6
$20,000 to $39,999	2.19	41	9.2
$40,000 to $49,999	3.63	68	6.0
$50,000 to $69,999	5.59	104	15.1
$70,000 to $79,999	7.24	135	7.6
$80,000 to $99,999	7.29	136	12.0
$100,000 or more	12.69	237	44.4
HOUSEHOLD TYPE			
Average household	**5.35**	**100**	**100.0**
Married couples	7.30	136	66.3
Married couples, no children	5.95	111	23.2
Married couples with children	8.87	166	39.0
Oldest child under age 6	8.24	154	7.0
Oldest child aged 6 to 17	9.97	186	22.2
Oldest child aged 18 or older	7.42	139	9.8
Single parent with child under age 18	3.21	60	3.1
Single person	3.00	56	16.6
RACE AND HISPANIC ORIGIN			
Average household	**5.35**	**100**	**100.0**
Asian	5.76	108	4.7
Black	1.93	36	4.5
Hispanic	2.59	48	6.1
Non-Hispanic white and other	6.37	119	89.4
REGION			
Average household	**5.35**	**100**	**100.0**
Northeast	3.57	67	12.0
Midwest	4.19	78	17.4
South	3.65	68	25.4
West	10.70	200	45.1
EDUCATION			
Average household	**5.35**	**100**	**100.0**
Less than high school graduate	0.75	14	1.8
High school graduate	2.10	39	9.8
Some college	5.06	95	19.5
Associate's degree	4.56	85	8.4
Bachelor's degree or more	10.25	192	60.4
Bachelor's degree	8.87	166	33.0
Master's, professional, doctoral degree	12.62	236	27.4

Note: Market shares may not sum to 100.0 because of rounding and missing categories by household type. "Asian" and "black" include Hispanics and non-Hispanics who identify themselves as being of the respective race alone. "Hispanic" includes people of any race who identify themselves as Hispanic. "Other" includes people who identify themselves as non-Hispanic and as Alaska Native, American Indian, Asian (who are also included in the "Asian" row), or Native Hawaiian or other Pacific Islander, as well as non-Hispanics reporting more than one race.
Source: Calculations by New Strategist based on the Bureau of Labor Statistics' 2012 Consumer Expenditure Survey

Television Sets

Best customers: **Householders aged 25 to 54**
Married couples with children at home

Customer trends: **Average household spending on television sets is likely to continue to decline because most households have replaced their old sets with high-definition versions.**

The best customers of television sets are married couples with school-aged children. They spend 52 percent more than average on television sets, and those with adult children at home spend 34 percent more. Householders aged 25 to 54, many with children at home, spend 11 to 13 percent more than average on this item and control 60 percent of the market for television sets.

Average household spending on television sets grew 71 percent between 2000 and 2006 (the year overall household spending peaked) as high-definition sets became de rigueur. Then growth turned to decline and average household spending on television sets fell 31 percent between 2006 and 2012, after adjusting for inflation. Average household spending on television sets is likely to continue to decline now that most households have replaced their old sets with HD versions.

Table 5.31 Television sets

Total household spending	$12,720,291,840.00
Average household spends	102.24

AGE OF HOUSEHOLDER	AVERAGE HOUSEHOLD SPENDING	BEST CUSTOMERS (index)	BIGGEST CUSTOMERS (market share)
Average household	$102.24	100	100.0%
Under age 25	108.65	106	7.0
Aged 25 to 34	113.88	111	18.0
Aged 35 to 44	115.80	113	19.7
Aged 45 to 54	115.01	112	22.3
Aged 55 to 64	101.32	99	18.1
Aged 65 to 74	77.95	76	9.2
Aged 75 or older	60.47	59	5.8

	AVERAGE HOUSEHOLD SPENDING	BEST CUSTOMERS (index)	BIGGEST CUSTOMERS (market share)
HOUSEHOLD INCOME			
Average household	**$102.24**	**100**	**100.0%**
Under $20,000	43.49	43	8.9
$20,000 to $39,999	71.35	70	15.7
$40,000 to $49,999	111.66	109	9.7
$50,000 to $69,999	80.77	79	11.4
$70,000 to $79,999	103.77	101	5.7
$80,000 to $99,999	147.51	144	12.7
$100,000 or more	195.79	192	35.9
HOUSEHOLD TYPE			
Average household	**102.24**	**100**	**100.0**
Married couples	127.93	125	60.8
Married couples, no children	112.14	110	22.9
Married couples with children	143.10	140	32.9
Oldest child under age 6	122.02	119	5.4
Oldest child aged 6 to 17	154.94	152	18.0
Oldest child aged 18 or older	136.77	134	9.4
Single parent with child under age 18	77.15	75	4.0
Single person	62.70	61	18.2
RACE AND HISPANIC ORIGIN			
Average household	**102.24**	**100**	**100.0**
Asian	62.63	61	2.7
Black	105.53	103	13.0
Hispanic	87.42	86	10.7
Non-Hispanic white and other	104.25	102	76.5
REGION			
Average household	**102.24**	**100**	**100.0**
Northeast	103.43	101	18.3
Midwest	103.62	101	22.5
South	94.18	92	34.3
West	113.27	111	25.0
EDUCATION			
Average household	**102.24**	**100**	**100.0**
Less than high school graduate	80.64	79	10.3
High school graduate	76.94	75	18.8
Some college	116.95	114	23.6
Associate's degree	91.45	89	8.8
Bachelor's degree or more	124.97	122	38.5
Bachelor's degree	128.33	126	25.0
Master's, professional, doctoral degree	119.20	117	13.5

Note: Market shares may not sum to 100.0 because of rounding and missing categories by household type. "Asian" and "black" include Hispanics and non-Hispanics who identify themselves as being of the respective race alone. "Hispanic" includes people of any race who identify themselves as Hispanic. "Other" includes people who identify themselves as non-Hispanic and as Alaska Native, American Indian, Asian (who are also included in the "Asian" row), or Native Hawaiian or other Pacific Islander, as well as non-Hispanics reporting more than one race.
Source: Calculations by New Strategist based on the Bureau of Labor Statistics' 2012 Consumer Expenditure Survey

Toys, Games, Hobbies, and Tricycles

Best customers: Householders aged 25 to 44
Married couples with children under age 18

Customer trends: Average household spending on toys, games, hobbies, and tricycles should rise in the years ahead as the large millennial generation fills the best-customer lifestage.

The best customers of toys, games, hobbies, and tricycles are parents with children under age 18. This explains why householders aged 25 to 44, many of them parents, spend 37 to 47 percent more than average on this item. Married couples with children under age 18 spend more than twice the average on toys, games, hobbies, and tricycles.

Average household spending on toys, games, hobbies, and tricycles has been on a rollercoaster ride. Spending on this item fell by 39 percent between 2000 and 2006, after adjusting for inflation, then climbed between 2006 and 2010 before falling again between 2010 and 2012. Behind the earlier decline was price discounting, with parents able to buy more for less. Behind the 2010-to-2012 decline was the ongoing baby bust as young adults postponed marriage and childbearing. Spending on toys, games, hobbies, and tricycles should rise in the years ahead as the large millennial generation fills the best-customer lifestage.

Table 5.32 Toys, games, hobbies, and tricycles

Total household spending	$14,256,829,440.00		
Average household spends	114.59		

AGE OF HOUSEHOLDER	AVERAGE HOUSEHOLD SPENDING	BEST CUSTOMERS (index)	BIGGEST CUSTOMERS (market share)
Average household	$114.59	100	100.0%
Under age 25	74.69	65	4.3
Aged 25 to 34	156.57	137	22.1
Aged 35 to 44	168.75	147	25.6
Aged 45 to 54	107.79	94	18.6
Aged 55 to 64	96.08	84	15.3
Aged 65 to 74	97.17	85	10.2
Aged 75 or older	40.30	35	3.4

	AVERAGE HOUSEHOLD SPENDING	BEST CUSTOMERS (index)	BIGGEST CUSTOMERS (market share)
HOUSEHOLD INCOME			
Average household	**$114.59**	**100**	**100.0%**
Under $20,000	35.50	31	6.5
$20,000 to $39,999	81.39	71	16.0
$40,000 to $49,999	97.53	85	7.5
$50,000 to $69,999	102.68	90	12.9
$70,000 to $79,999	160.82	140	7.8
$80,000 to $99,999	148.56	130	11.4
$100,000 or more	230.15	201	37.6
HOUSEHOLD TYPE			
Average household	**114.59**	**100**	**100.0**
Married couples	163.41	143	69.3
Married couples, no children	106.69	93	19.4
Married couples with children	221.08	193	45.4
Oldest child under age 6	288.65	252	11.5
Oldest child aged 6 to 17	256.93	224	26.7
Oldest child aged 18 or older	119.18	104	7.3
Single parent with child under age 18	92.44	81	4.2
Single person	35.14	31	9.1
RACE AND HISPANIC ORIGIN			
Average household	**114.59**	**100**	**100.0**
Asian	95.33	83	3.6
Black	47.08	41	5.2
Hispanic	120.43	105	13.2
Non-Hispanic white and other	125.02	109	81.9
REGION			
Average household	**114.59**	**100**	**100.0**
Northeast	129.74	113	20.4
Midwest	104.65	91	20.2
South	94.57	83	30.7
West	145.54	127	28.6
EDUCATION			
Average household	**114.59**	**100**	**100.0**
Less than high school graduate	58.64	51	6.7
High school graduate	78.96	69	17.2
Some college	109.82	96	19.7
Associate's degree	116.92	102	10.1
Bachelor's degree or more	165.65	145	45.6
Bachelor's degree	153.60	134	26.7
Master's, professional, doctoral degree	186.03	162	18.8

Note: Market shares may not sum to 100.0 because of rounding and missing categories by household type. "Asian" and "black" include Hispanics and non-Hispanics who identify themselves as being of the respective race alone. "Hispanic" includes people of any race who identify themselves as Hispanic. "Other" includes people who identify themselves as non-Hispanic and as Alaska Native, American Indian, Asian (who are also included in the "Asian" row), or Native Hawaiian or other Pacific Islander, as well as non-Hispanics reporting more than one race.
Source: Calculations by New Strategist based on the Bureau of Labor Statistics' 2012 Consumer Expenditure Survey

Veterinary Services

Best customers: Householders aged 55 to 74
Married couples without children at home
Married couples with school-aged or older children at home
Non-Hispanic whites

Customer trends: Average household spending on veterinary services should continue to grow in the years ahead
as the large baby-boom generation fills the best-customer age groups.

The best customers of veterinary services are older married couples, many of whom have older pets that require extensive veterinary care. Householders aged 55 to 74 spend 35 to 40 percent more than average on veterinary services. Married couples with school-aged or older children at home spend 45 to 48 percent more than average on veterinary services, and those without children at home (many of them older empty nesters) spend 49 percent more. Non-Hispanic whites dominate this category, spending 26 percent more than average.

Average household spending on veterinary services grew by an enormous 70 percent between 2000 and 2012, after adjusting for inflation. In 2012, veterinary services ranked fourth in entertainment spending, up from ninth in 2000. Spending on veterinary services should continue to grow in the years ahead as the large baby-boom generation fills the best-customer age groups.

Table 5.33 Veterinary services

Total household spending $18,656,179,200.00
Average household spends 149.95

AGE OF HOUSEHOLDER	AVERAGE HOUSEHOLD SPENDING	BEST CUSTOMERS (index)	BIGGEST CUSTOMERS (market share)
Average household	$149.95	100	100.0%
Under age 25	12.07	8	0.5
Aged 25 to 34	102.42	68	11.0
Aged 35 to 44	142.36	95	16.5
Aged 45 to 54	155.13	103	20.5
Aged 55 to 64	209.47	140	25.6
Aged 65 to 74	202.80	135	16.3
Aged 75 or older	157.23	105	10.2

	AVERAGE HOUSEHOLD SPENDING	BEST CUSTOMERS (index)	BIGGEST CUSTOMERS (market share)
HOUSEHOLD INCOME			
Average household	**$149.95**	**100**	**100.0%**
Under $20,000	49.89	33	7.0
$20,000 to $39,999	146.99	98	22.1
$40,000 to $49,999	24.25	16	1.4
$50,000 to $69,999	153.07	102	14.7
$70,000 to $79,999	176.46	118	6.6
$80,000 to $99,999	173.64	116	10.2
$100,000 or more	308.45	206	38.5
HOUSEHOLD TYPE			
Average household	**149.95**	**100**	**100.0**
Married couples	210.93	141	68.3
Married couples, no children	223.36	149	31.1
Married couples with children	195.57	130	30.7
Oldest child under age 6	89.50	60	2.7
Oldest child aged 6 to 17	222.35	148	17.6
Oldest child aged 18 or older	216.99	145	10.2
Single parent with child under age 18	44.00	29	1.5
Single person	85.56	57	16.9
RACE AND HISPANIC ORIGIN			
Average household	**149.95**	**100**	**100.0**
Asian	21.13	14	0.6
Black	30.84	21	2.6
Hispanic	34.20	23	2.9
Non-Hispanic white and other	188.98	126	94.6
REGION			
Average household	**149.95**	**100**	**100.0**
Northeast	142.67	95	17.2
Midwest	136.58	91	20.2
South	169.79	113	42.2
West	136.29	91	20.5
EDUCATION			
Average household	**149.95**	**100**	**100.0**
Less than high school graduate	31.69	21	2.8
High school graduate	115.52	77	19.2
Some college	155.78	104	21.4
Associate's degree	230.71	154	15.2
Bachelor's degree or more	191.79	128	40.3
Bachelor's degree	159.18	106	21.2
Master's, professional, doctoral degree	246.90	165	19.1

Note: Market shares may not sum to 100.0 because of rounding and missing categories by household type. "Asian" and "black" include Hispanics and non-Hispanics who identify themselves as being of the respective race alone. "Hispanic" includes people of any race who identify themselves as Hispanic. "Other" includes people who identify themselves as non-Hispanic and as Alaska Native, American Indian, Asian (who are also included in the "Asian" row), or Native Hawaiian or other Pacific Islander, as well as non-Hispanics reporting more than one race.
Source: Calculations by New Strategist based on the Bureau of Labor Statistics' 2012 Consumer Expenditure Survey

Video Cassette Recorders and Video Disc Players

Best customers: Householders aged 25 to 54
                   Married couples with children under age 18
                   Households in the Northeast

Customer trends: Average household spending on video cassette recorders and video disc players will continue
                   to decline because of technological change.

The best customers of video cassette recorders and video disc players are parents with children buying equipment for their family's enjoyment. Householders ranging in age from 25 to 54 spend 27 to 35 percent more than average on video players and control 69 percent of the market. Married couples with school-aged children spend 86 percent more than average on video players. Households in the Northeast outspend the average on this item by 37 percent.

Average household spending on video cassette recorders and video disc players fell 77 percent between 2000 and 2012, after adjusting for inflation. Changing technology and falling prices were behind the decline as VCRs became obsolete, cheaper imports reduced costs, and high-definition television sets allowed users to download movies. Average household spending on this item will continue to decline because of technological change.

Table 5.34 **Video cassette recorders and video disc players**

Total household spending $914,457,600.00
Average household spends   7.35

AGE OF HOUSEHOLDER	AVERAGE HOUSEHOLD SPENDING	BEST CUSTOMERS (index)	BIGGEST CUSTOMERS (market share)
Average household	$7.35	100	100.0%
Under age 25	4.49	61	4.0
Aged 25 to 34	9.34	127	20.5
Aged 35 to 44	9.92	135	23.4
Aged 45 to 54	9.39	128	25.3
Aged 55 to 64	6.36	87	15.8
Aged 65 to 74	5.31	72	8.7
Aged 75 or older	1.65	22	2.2

	AVERAGE HOUSEHOLD SPENDING	BEST CUSTOMERS (index)	BIGGEST CUSTOMERS (market share)
HOUSEHOLD INCOME			
Average household	$7.35	100	100.0%
Under $20,000	3.86	53	11.1
$20,000 to $39,999	5.60	76	17.2
$40,000 to $49,999	6.50	88	7.8
$50,000 to $69,999	8.80	120	17.3
$70,000 to $79,999	7.96	108	6.0
$80,000 to $99,999	11.83	161	14.2
$100,000 or more	10.36	141	26.4
HOUSEHOLD TYPE			
Average household	7.35	100	100.0
Married couples	9.18	125	60.7
Married couples, no children	6.86	93	19.5
Married couples with children	10.82	147	34.6
Oldest child under age 6	8.65	118	5.4
Oldest child aged 6 to 17	13.69	186	22.2
Oldest child aged 18 or older	7.39	101	7.1
Single parent with child under age 18	5.97	81	4.3
Single person	5.44	74	22.0
RACE AND HISPANIC ORIGIN			
Average household	7.35	100	100.0
Asian	8.13	111	4.8
Black	7.14	97	12.2
Hispanic	5.01	68	8.5
Non-Hispanic white and other	7.76	106	79.2
REGION			
Average household	7.35	100	100.0
Northeast	10.10	137	24.8
Midwest	7.00	95	21.1
South	5.53	75	28.0
West	8.49	116	26.0
EDUCATION			
Average household	7.35	100	100.0
Less than high school graduate	4.89	67	8.7
High school graduate	6.08	83	20.6
Some college	7.51	102	21.0
Associate's degree	10.28	140	13.8
Bachelor's degree or more	8.35	114	35.8
Bachelor's degree	7.21	98	19.6
Master's, professional, doctoral degree	10.30	140	16.3

Note: Market shares may not sum to 100.0 because of rounding and missing categories by household type. "Asian" and "black" include Hispanics and non-Hispanics who identify themselves as being of the respective race alone. "Hispanic" includes people of any race who identify themselves as Hispanic. "Other" includes people who identify themselves as non-Hispanic and as Alaska Native, American Indian, Asian (who are also included in the "Asian" row), or Native Hawaiian or other Pacific Islander, as well as non-Hispanics reporting more than one race.
Source: Calculations by New Strategist based on the Bureau of Labor Statistics' 2012 Consumer Expenditure Survey

Video Cassettes, Tapes, and Discs

Best customers: Householders aged 25 to 34
                    Married couples with children at home
                    Asians
                    Households in the West

Customer trends: Average household spending on video cassettes, tapes, and discs is likely to continue to fall
                    as these items are replaced by streamed video.

The best customers of video cassettes, tapes, and discs are married couples with children, many of them buying children's programming to keep the kids entertained. Married couples with children at home spend 72 percent more than average on this item, The figure peaks among those with preschoolers, who spend twice the average. Householders aged 25 to 34, many with young children, spend 24 percent more than average on videos and DVDs. Asian householders spend 51 percent more than average on this item, and households in the West, where many Asians reside, outspend the average by 26 percent.

Average household spending on video cassettes, tapes, and discs grew 69 percent between 2000 and 2006, after adjusting for inflation. Between 2006 and 2012, spending fell by 37 percent. Behind the earlier increase was the substitution of DVDs for videos as DVD players replaced VCRs. Average household spending on video cassettes, tapes, and discs is likely to continue to fall as these items are replaced by streamed video.

Table 5.35 Video cassettes, tapes, and discs

Total household spending $3,695,155,200.00
Average household spends   29.70

	AVERAGE HOUSEHOLD SPENDING	BEST CUSTOMERS (index)	BIGGEST CUSTOMERS (market share)
AGE OF HOUSEHOLDER			
Average household	$29.70	100	100.0%
Under age 25	27.78	94	6.1
Aged 25 to 34	36.83	124	20.0
Aged 35 to 44	31.68	107	18.5
Aged 45 to 54	33.08	111	22.0
Aged 55 to 64	30.69	103	18.9
Aged 65 to 74	29.30	99	11.9
Aged 75 or older	6.56	22	2.2

	AVERAGE HOUSEHOLD SPENDING	BEST CUSTOMERS (index)	BIGGEST CUSTOMERS (market share)
HOUSEHOLD INCOME			
Average household	**$29.70**	**100**	**100.0%**
Under $20,000	12.41	42	8.8
$20,000 to $39,999	16.07	54	12.2
$40,000 to $49,999	32.26	109	9.6
$50,000 to $69,999	40.10	135	19.5
$70,000 to $79,999	27.53	93	5.2
$80,000 to $99,999	35.48	119	10.5
$100,000 or more	53.70	181	33.9
HOUSEHOLD TYPE			
Average household	**29.70**	**100**	**100.0**
Married couples	37.87	128	61.9
Married couples, no children	26.73	90	18.8
Married couples with children	50.95	172	40.3
Oldest child under age 6	59.49	200	9.1
Oldest child aged 6 to 17	54.48	183	21.8
Oldest child aged 18 or older	39.71	134	9.4
Single parent with child under age 18	24.51	83	4.3
Single person	16.45	55	16.4
RACE AND HISPANIC ORIGIN			
Average household	**29.70**	**100**	**100.0**
Asian	44.99	151	6.6
Black	29.62	100	12.5
Hispanic	19.26	65	8.1
Non-Hispanic white and other	31.41	106	79.4
REGION			
Average household	**29.70**	**100**	**100.0**
Northeast	22.58	76	13.7
Midwest	28.05	94	20.9
South	29.57	100	37.1
West	37.33	126	28.3
EDUCATION			
Average household	**29.70**	**100**	**100.0**
Less than high school graduate	10.48	35	4.6
High school graduate	22.79	77	19.1
Some college	33.67	113	23.3
Associate's degree	39.48	133	13.1
Bachelor's degree or more	36.52	123	38.8
Bachelor's degree	34.66	117	23.3
Master's, professional, doctoral degree	39.65	134	15.5

Note: Market shares may not sum to 100.0 because of rounding and missing categories by household type. "Asian" and "black" include Hispanics and non-Hispanics who identify themselves as being of the respective race alone. "Hispanic" includes people of any race who identify themselves as Hispanic. "Other" includes people who identify themselves as non-Hispanic and as Alaska Native, American Indian, Asian (who are also included in the "Asian" row), or Native Hawaiian or other Pacific Islander, as well as non-Hispanics reporting more than one race.
Source: Calculations by New Strategist based on the Bureau of Labor Statistics' 2012 Consumer Expenditure Survey

Video Game Hardware and Accessories

Best customers: Householders aged 25 to 44
Married couples with school-aged children
Single parents
Blacks and Asians

Customer trends: Average household spending on video game hardware and accessories will continue to rise as younger generations, raised on video games, become a larger share of the overall population.

Children and teenagers are the best customers of video game hardware and accessories. That explains why householders aged 25 to 44—most with children at home—spend much more than others on this item. Together the 25-to-44 age groups control 63 percent of household spending in this market. Married couples with school-aged children spend over two-and-one-half times the average on video game hardware and accessories. Single parents, whose spending approaches average on only a few items, spend nearly twice the average on video game hardware. Blacks and Asians are some of the best customers of video game hardware and accessories, respectively spending 87 and 68 percent more than the average household on this item.

Video game hardware has only recently become a category separate from video game software in the Consumer Expenditure Survey. Average household spending on the combined category climbed 56 percent between 2000 and 2006, after adjusting for inflation. Spending then slowed, increasing by only 4 percent between 2006 and 2012 and actually fell between 2010 and 2012. Average household spending on video game hardware may resume its rise in the years ahead as younger generations, raised on video games, become a larger share of the overall population.

Table 5.36 Video game hardware and accessories

Total household spending $4,607,124,480.00
Average household spends   37.03

	AVERAGE HOUSEHOLD SPENDING	BEST CUSTOMERS (index)	BIGGEST CUSTOMERS (market share)
AGE OF HOUSEHOLDER			
Average household	$37.03	100	100.0%
Under age 25	16.08	43	2.8
Aged 25 to 34	60.61	164	26.5
Aged 35 to 44	77.40	209	36.3
Aged 45 to 54	44.03	119	23.5
Aged 55 to 64	13.73	37	6.8
Aged 65 to 74	9.14	25	3.0
Aged 75 or older	–	–	–

	AVERAGE HOUSEHOLD SPENDING	BEST CUSTOMERS (index)	BIGGEST CUSTOMERS (market share)
HOUSEHOLD INCOME			
Average household	$37.03	100	100.0%
Under $20,000	14.89	40	8.5
$20,000 to $39,999	31.79	86	19.3
$40,000 to $49,999	24.00	65	5.7
$50,000 to $69,999	36.87	100	14.4
$70,000 to $79,999	80.36	217	12.1
$80,000 to $99,999	43.10	116	10.3
$100,000 or more	62.08	168	31.4
HOUSEHOLD TYPE			
Average household	37.03	100	100.0
Married couples	53.19	144	69.8
Married couples, no children	39.50	107	22.2
Married couples with children	64.90	175	41.2
Oldest child under age 6	37.51	101	4.6
Oldest child aged 6 to 17	96.19	260	30.9
Oldest child aged 18 or older	29.76	80	5.7
Single parent with child under age 18	72.56	196	10.3
Single person	10.74	29	8.6
RACE AND HISPANIC ORIGIN			
Average household	37.03	100	100.0
Asian	62.29	168	7.3
Black	69.18	187	23.5
Hispanic	32.41	88	11.0
Non-Hispanic white and other	32.26	87	65.4
REGION			
Average household	37.03	100	100.0
Northeast	48.54	131	23.7
Midwest	22.59	61	13.5
South	46.61	126	46.9
West	26.25	71	16.0
EDUCATION			
Average household	37.03	100	100.0
Less than high school graduate	61.70	167	21.8
High school graduate	21.83	59	14.7
Some college	35.94	97	20.0
Associate's degree	39.30	106	10.5
Bachelor's degree or more	39.57	107	33.7
Bachelor's degree	54.86	148	29.5
Master's, professional, doctoral degree	13.72	37	4.3

Note: Market shares may not sum to 100.0 because of rounding and missing categories by household type. "Asian" and "black" include Hispanics and non-Hispanics who identify themselves as being of the respective race alone. "Hispanic" includes people of any race who identify themselves as Hispanic. "Other" includes people who identify themselves as non-Hispanic and as Alaska Native, American Indian, Asian (who are also included in the "Asian" row), or Native Hawaiian or other Pacific Islander, as well as non-Hispanics reporting more than one race. "–" means sample is too small to make a reliable estimate.
Source: Calculations by New Strategist based on the Bureau of Labor Statistics' 2012 Consumer Expenditure Survey

Video Game Software

Best customers: Householders under age 45
Married couples with children under age 18
Asians and blacks
Households in the Northeast

Customer trends: Average household spending on video game software is certain to grow in the years ahead as younger generations, raised on video games, become a larger share of the overall population.

Children and teenagers are the best customers of video game software. Householders under age 45 spend more than twice the average on this item, while older householders spend virtually nothing at all. Married couples with school-aged children spend 59 percent more than average, while couples with preschoolers spend over four times the average on video game software. Asians and blacks are some of the best customers of video game software, spending between two-and-one-half and three times the average on this item. Households in the Northeast spend nearly two-and-one-half times the average on video game software.

Video game software has only recently become a category separate from video game hardware in the Consumer Expenditure Survey. Average household spending on the combined category climbed 56 percent between 2000 and 2006, after adjusting for inflation. Spending then slowed, increasing by only 4 percent between 2006 and 2012 and actually fell between 2010 and 2012. Average household spending on video game software is certain to grow in the years ahead as younger generations, raised on video games, become a larger share of the overall population.

Table 5.37 Video game software

Total household spending	$405,596,160.00
Average household spends	3.26

AGE OF HOUSEHOLDER	AVERAGE HOUSEHOLD SPENDING	BEST CUSTOMERS (index)	BIGGEST CUSTOMERS (market share)
Average household	$3.26	100	100.0%
Under age 25	7.93	243	16.0
Aged 25 to 34	7.99	245	39.6
Aged 35 to 44	7.32	225	39.0
Aged 45 to 54	0.52	16	3.2
Aged 55 to 64	–	–	–
Aged 65 to 74	–	–	–
Aged 75 or older	–	–	–

	AVERAGE HOUSEHOLD SPENDING	BEST CUSTOMERS (index)	BIGGEST CUSTOMERS (market share)
HOUSEHOLD INCOME			
Average household	**$3.26**	**100**	**100.0**
Under $20,000	–	–	–
$20,000 to $39,999	2.45	75	16.9
$40,000 to $49,999	1.27	39	3.4
$50,000 to $69,999	5.75	176	25.5
$70,000 to $79,999	3.50	107	6.0
$80,000 to $99,999	2.38	73	6.4
$100,000 or more	5.17	159	29.7
HOUSEHOLD TYPE			
Average household	**3.26**	**100**	**100.0**
Married couples	3.38	104	50.4
Married couples, no children	2.03	62	13.0
Married couples with children	5.20	160	37.5
Oldest child under age 6	13.56	416	19.0
Oldest child aged 6 to 17	5.19	159	18.9
Oldest child aged 18 or older	–	–	–
Single parent with child under age 18	2.43	75	3.9
Single person	3.04	93	27.7
RACE AND HISPANIC ORIGIN			
Average household	**3.26**	**100**	**100.0**
Asian	9.97	306	13.3
Black	7.97	244	30.7
Hispanic	3.19	98	12.3
Non-Hispanic white and other	2.46	75	56.6
REGION			
Average household	**3.26**	**100**	**100.0**
Northeast	7.92	243	43.9
Midwest	3.22	99	21.9
South	1.21	37	13.8
West	2.91	89	20.1
EDUCATION			
Average household	**3.26**	**100**	**100.0**
Less than high school graduate	1.59	49	6.4
High school graduate	2.96	91	22.6
Some college	4.76	146	30.1
Associate's degree	5.31	163	16.1
Bachelor's degree or more	2.45	75	23.7
Bachelor's degree	2.80	86	17.1
Master's, professional, doctoral degree	1.85	57	6.6

Note: Market shares may not sum to 100.0 because of rounding and missing categories by household type. "Asian" and "black" include Hispanics and non-Hispanics who identify themselves as being of the respective race alone. "Hispanic" includes people of any race who identify themselves as Hispanic. "Other" includes people who identify themselves as non-Hispanic and as Alaska Native, American Indian, Asian (who are also included in the "Asian" row), or Native Hawaiian or other Pacific Islander, as well as non-Hispanics reporting more than one race. "–" means sample is too small to make a reliable estimate.
Source: Calculations by New Strategist based on the Bureau of Labor Statistics' 2012 Consumer Expenditure Survey

Video Tape, Disc, and Film Rental

Best customers: Householders aged 25 to 44
                           Married couples with children at home
                           Single parents
                           Households in the West

Customer trends: Average household spending on video rentals will continue to decline as streamed video
                           becomes more popular.

Parents are the best customers of video rentals. This explains why householders aged 25 to 44—many of whom are parents—spend 47 to 54 percent more than the average household on this item. Married couples with children at home spend 70 percent more than average on video rentals, the figure peaking at 99 percent among those with school-aged children. Single parents, whose spending approaches average on only a few items, spend 6 percent more than average on video rentals. Households in the West spend 39 percent more than average on this item.

Average household spending on video and DVD rentals fell by 72 percent between 2000 and 2012, after adjusting for inflation. Falling prices and changing technology are behind the steep decline. Competition reduced rental fees in the earlier part of the time period, and in the latter part households have been opting for downloads or streaming video. Average household spending is likely to continue to decline as streamed video becomes more popular.

Table 5.38 Video tape, disc, and film rental

Total household spending $1,955,819,520.00
Average household spends   15.72

AGE OF HOUSEHOLDER	AVERAGE HOUSEHOLD SPENDING	BEST CUSTOMERS (index)	BIGGEST CUSTOMERS (market share)
Average household	$15.72	100	100.0%
Under age 25	16.46	105	6.9
Aged 25 to 34	23.04	147	23.7
Aged 35 to 44	24.23	154	26.8
Aged 45 to 54	16.48	105	20.7
Aged 55 to 64	11.62	74	13.5
Aged 65 to 74	8.53	54	6.5
Aged 75 or older	3.01	19	1.9

	AVERAGE HOUSEHOLD SPENDING	BEST CUSTOMERS (index)	BIGGEST CUSTOMERS (market share)
HOUSEHOLD INCOME			
Average household	**$15.72**	**100**	**100.0%**
Under $20,000	6.06	39	8.1
$20,000 to $39,999	11.52	73	16.5
$40,000 to $49,999	13.45	86	7.6
$50,000 to $69,999	19.15	122	17.6
$70,000 to $79,999	22.24	141	7.9
$80,000 to $99,999	23.13	147	13.0
$100,000 or more	24.63	157	29.3
HOUSEHOLD TYPE			
Average household	**15.72**	**100**	**100.0**
Married couples	20.46	130	63.2
Married couples, no children	13.35	85	17.7
Married couples with children	26.68	170	39.9
Oldest child under age 6	21.52	137	6.2
Oldest child aged 6 to 17	31.36	199	23.7
Oldest child aged 18 or older	22.13	141	9.9
Single parent with child under age 18	16.72	106	5.6
Single person	8.06	51	15.2
RACE AND HISPANIC ORIGIN			
Average household	**15.72**	**100**	**100.0**
Asian	13.45	86	3.7
Black	7.56	48	6.0
Hispanic	15.96	102	12.7
Non-Hispanic white and other	17.04	108	81.4
REGION			
Average household	**15.72**	**100**	**100.0**
Northeast	11.87	76	13.6
Midwest	15.82	101	22.3
South	13.82	88	32.7
West	21.86	139	31.3
EDUCATION			
Average household	**15.72**	**100**	**100.0**
Less than high school graduate	9.12	58	7.6
High school graduate	11.72	75	18.6
Some college	16.21	103	21.2
Associate's degree	18.42	117	11.6
Bachelor's degree or more	20.45	130	41.0
Bachelor's degree	19.90	127	25.2
Master's, professional, doctoral degree	21.40	136	15.8

Note: Market shares may not sum to 100.0 because of rounding and missing categories by household type. "Asian" and "black" include Hispanics and non-Hispanics who identify themselves as being of the respective race alone. "Hispanic" includes people of any race who identify themselves as Hispanic. "Other" includes people who identify themselves as non-Hispanic and as Alaska Native, American Indian, Asian (who are also included in the "Asian" row), or Native Hawaiian or other Pacific Islander, as well as non-Hispanics reporting more than one race.
Source: Calculations by New Strategist based on the Bureau of Labor Statistics' 2012 Consumer Expenditure Survey

Chapter 6.
Financial Services

Household Spending on Financial Services, 2000 to 2012

Average household spending on financial products and services and cash contributions rose 9 percent between 2000 and 2006, the year when overall household spending peaked, after adjusting for inflation. Spending on this broad category then fell 10 percent in the ensuing six-year period for a cumulative 3 percent loss from 2000 to 2012. Mixed trends, including less spending on taxes and more spending on charitable contributions, were behind the small overall drop in spending.

Average household spending on federal income tax declined by a substantial 51 percent between 2000 and 2012, after adjusting for inflation, because of tax cuts and layoffs. Spending on state and local income taxes fell 30 percent. Other losing categories during the 2000-to-2012 time period include gifts of stocks, bonds, and mutual funds to people in other households (down 95 percent from 2000 to 2012), occupational expenses (down 62 percent), credit card membership fees (down 54 percent), finance charges except for mortgages and vehicles (down 46 percent), and safe deposit box rental (down 45 percent) among others.

Average household spending on cash contributions increased strongly between 2000 and 2006 (the year household spending peaked), climbing by 34 percent after adjusting for inflation (see Appendix D for this figure), but from 2006 to 2010 overall cash contribution spending fell 19 percent as households tightened their belts. From 2010 to 2012 cash contribution spending rose again, by 11 percent, for a cumulative gain of 20 percent over the 12-year period. Among cash contributions, those to political organizations showed the strongest percentage gain (181 percent), but contributions to religious organizations are the largest by far in terms of dollars spent. The average household's lottery and gambling losses were 4 percent larger in 2012 than 2000, after adjusting for inflation, but the small overall increase masks tremendous swings as losses grew 46 percent between 2000 and 2006, and then fell 28 percent over the ensuing six-year period.

Cash contributions to religious organizations

(average annual spending of households on cash contributions to religious organizations, 2000, 2006, 2010, and 2012; in 2012 dollars)

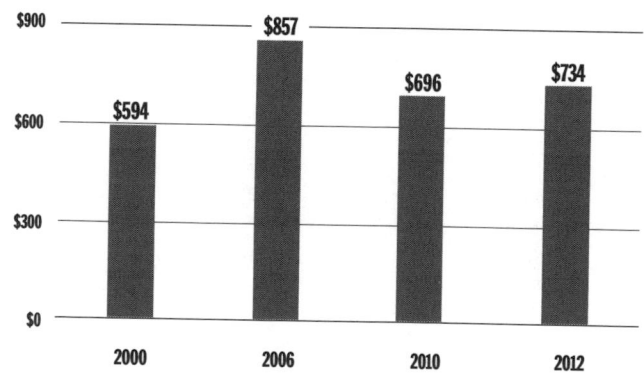

Table 6.1 Financial spending, 2000 to 2012

(average annual household spending on financial products and services and cash contributions, and percent distribution, by category, 2000 to 2012; percent change in spending and percentage point change in distribution, 2000–06, 2006–12, and 2010–12; in 2012 dollars; ranked by amount spent)

	average annual household spending (in 2012$)				percent change		
	2012	2010	2006	2000	2010–12	2006–12	2000–06
Average household spending on financial products and services	**$10,229.35**	**$9,755.63**	**$11,406.20**	**$10,501.11**	**4.9%**	**−10.3%**	**8.6%**
Deductions for Social Security*	4,040.62	4,109.02	4,339.74	2,853.80	−1.7	−6.9	*
Tax, federal income (net, after refund)	1,568.33	1,195.76	1,948.84	3,212.35	31.2	−19.5	−39.3
Cash contributions to religious organizations	734.30	696.01	857.38	594.16	5.5	−14.4	44.3
Contributions to retirement accounts (nonpayroll deposits)	582.46	493.91	509.94	519.52	17.9	14.2	−1.8
Tax, state and local income (net, after refund)	526.08	507.98	591.17	749.05	3.6	−11.0	−21.1
Deductions for private pensions (payroll deductions)*	511.80	619.91	691.77	483.51	−17.4	−26.0	*
Cash gifts	464.50	419.12	465.45	–	10.8	−0.2	–
Insurance, life and other personal except health	352.61	334.95	366.87	531.47	5.3	−3.9	−31.0
Cash contributions to charitable organizations	233.63	167.95	218.89	186.49	39.1	6.7	17.4
Child support	208.46	231.74	245.75	–	−10.0	−15.2	–
Finance charges, except mortgage and vehicle	181.53	195.82	230.80	337.82	−7.3	−21.3	−31.7
Legal fees	138.71	135.54	181.04	138.61	2.3	−23.4	30.6
Support for college students	104.82	102.95	107.45	–	1.8	−2.4	–
Deductions for government retirement	100.54	95.18	87.67	93.76	5.6	14.7	−6.5
Alimony expenses	86.01	39.51	52.57	–	117.7	63.6	–
Accounting fees	75.03	68.99	71.01	73.57	8.8	5.7	−3.5
Funeral expenses	72.17	83.56	65.45	94.25	−13.6	10.3	−30.6
Lottery and gambling losses	57.93	82.89	80.85	55.47	−30.1	−28.3	45.8
Occupational expenses	48.41	54.37	50.71	128.32	−11.0	−4.5	−60.5
Cash contributions to educational institutions	38.77	37.76	127.91	26.61	2.7	−69.7	380.6
Cash contributions to political organizations	24.90	13.48	25.27	8.87	84.8	−1.5	185.0
Bank service charges	23.10	23.63	24.09	26.52	−2.2	−4.1	−9.2
Gifts to members of other households of stocks, bonds, and mutual funds	17.16	11.15	27.67	356.63	53.9	−38.0	−92.2
Cemetery lots, vaults, maintenance fees	13.16	15.92	22.07	17.96	−17.3	−40.4	22.9
Shopping club membership fees	10.16	8.95	8.62	–	13.5	17.8	–
Vacation clubs	7.38	3.59	–	–	105.5	–	–
Safe deposit box rental	3.36	3.84	4.25	6.11	−12.6	−20.9	−30.4
Credit card membership fees	2.92	1.81	2.15	6.28	61.2	35.7	−65.7
Dating services	0.50	0.34	0.82	–	48.4	−39.0	–

PERCENT DISTRIBUTION OF SPENDING	average annual household spending (in 2012$)				percentage point change		
	2012	2010	2006	2000	2010–12	2006–12	2000–06
Average household spending on financial products and services	**100.0%**	**100.0%**	**100.0%**	**100.0%**	–	–	–
Deductions for Social Security*	39.5	42.1	38.0	27.2	–2.6	1.5	*
Tax, federal income (net, after refund)	15.3	12.3	17.1	30.6	3.1	–1.8	–13.5
Cash contributions to religious organizations	7.2	7.1	7.5	5.7	0.0	–0.3	1.9
Contributions to retirement accounts (nonpayroll deposits)	5.7	5.1	4.5	4.9	0.6	1.2	–0.5
Tax, state and local income (net, after refund)	5.1	5.2	5.2	7.1	–0.1	0.0	–2.0
Deductions for private pensions (payroll deductions)*	5.0	6.4	6.1	4.6	–1.4	–1.1	*
Cash gifts	4.5	4.3	4.1	–	0.2	0.5	–
Insurance, life and other personal except health	3.4	3.4	3.2	5.1	0.0	0.2	–1.8
Cash contributions to charitable organizations	2.3	1.7	1.9	1.8	0.6	0.4	0.1
Child support	2.0	2.4	2.2	–	–0.3	–0.1	–
Finance charges, except mortgage and vehicle	1.8	2.0	2.0	3.2	–0.2	–0.2	–1.2
Legal fees	1.4	1.4	1.6	1.3	0.0	–0.2	0.3
Support for college students	1.0	1.1	0.9	–	0.0	0.1	–
Deductions for government retirement	1.0	1.0	0.8	0.9	0.0	0.2	–0.1
Alimony expenses	0.8	0.4	0.5	–	0.4	0.4	–
Accounting fees	0.7	0.7	0.6	0.7	0.0	0.1	–0.1
Funeral expenses	0.7	0.9	0.6	0.9	–0.2	0.1	–0.3
Lottery and gambling losses	0.6	0.8	0.7	0.5	–0.3	–0.1	0.2
Occupational expenses	0.5	0.6	0.4	1.2	–0.1	0.0	–0.8
Cash contributions to educational institutions	0.4	0.4	1.1	0.3	0.0	–0.7	0.9
Cash contributions to political organizations	0.2	0.1	0.2	0.1	0.1	0.0	0.1
Bank service charges	0.2	0.2	0.2	0.3	0.0	0.0	0.0
Gifts to members of other households of stocks, bonds, and mutual funds	0.2	0.1	0.2	3.4	0.1	–0.1	–3.2
Cemetery lots, vaults, maintenance fees	0.1	0.2	0.2	0.2	0.0	–0.1	0.0
Shopping club membership fees	0.1	0.1	0.1	–	0.0	0.0	–
Vacation clubs	0.1	0.0	–	–	0.0	–	–
Safe deposit box rental	0.0	0.0	0.0	0.1	0.0	0.0	0.0
Credit card membership fees	0.0	0.0	0.0	0.1	0.0	0.0	0.0
Dating services	0.0	0.0	0.0	–	0.0	0.0	–

*Recent spending on pensions and Social Security is not comparable with 2000 because of changes in methodology.
Note: Percentage point change calculations are based on unrounded figures. "–" means not applicable or data are unavailable.
Source: Bureau of Labor Statistics, 2000, 2006, 2010, and 2012 Consumer Expenditure Surveys; calculations by New Strategist

Accounting Fees

Best customers: Householders aged 45 to 74
                        Married couples without children at home
                        Married couples with school-aged or older children at home
                        Non-Hispanic whites
                        Households in the West

Customer trends: Average household spending on accounting fees may stabilize in the years ahead as better tax and estate planning software programs allow boomers to handle their finances without the help of a professional.

The best customers of accountants are households with the most complex financial matters. Householders with the highest incomes (aged 45 to 54) and those newly retired (aged 65 to 74) spend 41 and 45 percent, respectively, more than average on accounting fees. Married couples without children at home (most of them older empty-nesters) spend 44 percent more than average. Not only are these households less likely to be computer savvy, but they often have complex financial circumstances as they settle their parents' estates and attempt to simplify their own. Married couples with school-aged or older children at home outspend the average by 37 to 48 percent. Non-Hispanic whites dominate spending on this category and account for 90 percent of the accounting fees market. Households in the West outspend the average on this item by 51 percent.

Average household spending on accounting fees fell 6 percent between 2000 and 2010 (when overall household spending bottomed out), after adjusting for inflation. Behind the decline was the recession, which forced some households to tighten their belts and buy software rather than services to handle their finances. In the two years after 2010, spending on accounting fees grew 9 percent, more than recovering the earlier loss. Spending on accounting fees may stabilize in the years ahead as better tax and estate planning software programs allow boomers to handle their finances without the help of a professional.

Table 6.2 Accounting fees

Total household spending $9,334,932,480.00
Average household spends   75.03

AGE OF HOUSEHOLDER	AVERAGE HOUSEHOLD SPENDING	BEST CUSTOMERS (index)	BIGGEST CUSTOMERS (market share)
Average household	$75.03	100	100.0%
Under age 25	13.21	18	1.2
Aged 25 to 34	31.96	43	6.9
Aged 35 to 44	60.20	80	13.9
Aged 45 to 54	106.03	141	28.0
Aged 55 to 64	89.46	119	21.8
Aged 65 to 74	109.16	145	17.5
Aged 75 or older	82.23	110	10.7

	AVERAGE HOUSEHOLD SPENDING	BEST CUSTOMERS (index)	BIGGEST CUSTOMERS (market share)
HOUSEHOLD INCOME			
Average household	**$75.03**	**100**	**100.0%**
Under $20,000	15.17	20	4.3
$20,000 to $39,999	36.16	48	10.9
$40,000 to $49,999	64.17	86	7.6
$50,000 to $69,999	61.54	82	11.8
$70,000 to $79,999	93.27	124	6.9
$80,000 to $99,999	86.61	115	10.2
$100,000 or more	193.74	258	48.3
HOUSEHOLD TYPE			
Average household	**75.03**	**100**	**100.0**
Married couples	102.51	137	66.4
Married couples, no children	107.67	144	29.9
Married couples with children	100.84	134	31.6
Oldest child under age 6	70.86	94	4.3
Oldest child aged 6 to 17	110.96	148	17.6
Oldest child aged 18 or older	103.16	137	9.7
Single parent with child under age 18	24.49	33	1.7
Single person	53.22	71	21.1
RACE AND HISPANIC ORIGIN			
Average household	**75.03**	**100**	**100.0**
Asian	78.18	104	4.5
Black	27.10	36	4.5
Hispanic	34.35	46	5.7
Non-Hispanic white and other	89.73	120	89.8
REGION			
Average household	**75.03**	**100**	**100.0**
Northeast	82.65	110	19.9
Midwest	63.13	84	18.7
South	55.19	74	27.4
West	113.43	151	34.1
EDUCATION			
Average household	**75.03**	**100**	**100.0**
Less than high school graduate	21.71	29	3.8
High school graduate	53.76	72	17.9
Some college	66.27	88	18.2
Associate's degree	77.04	103	10.1
Bachelor's degree or more	119.01	159	50.0
Bachelor's degree	96.62	129	25.7
Master's, professional, doctoral degree	157.48	210	24.4

Note: Market shares may not sum to 100.0 because of rounding and missing categories by household type. "Asian" and "black" include Hispanics and non-Hispanics who identify themselves as being of the respective race alone. "Hispanic" includes people of any race who identify themselves as Hispanic. "Other" includes people who identify themselves as non-Hispanic and as Alaska Native, American Indian, Asian (who are also included in the "Asian" row), or Native Hawaiian or other Pacific Islander, as well as non-Hispanics reporting more than one race.
Source: Calculations by New Strategist based on the Bureau of Labor Statistics' 2012 Consumer Expenditure Survey

Bank Service Charges

Best customers: Householders aged 25 to 64
Married couples with school-aged children
Single parents
Blacks
Households in the West

Customer trends: Average household spending on bank service charges may rise in the years ahead if federal regulations tighten standards and force banks to make money the old-fashioned way.

The biggest spenders on bank service charges are householders who cannot maintain the larger bank balances necessary to receive free checking and other services. Households headed by working-age adults, ranging in age from 25 to 64, spend well more than average on bank service charges. Married couples with school-aged children, many of them struggling to make ends meet, spend 53 percent more than average on this item. Single parents, whose spending on most items is well below average, spend 15 percent more than average on bank fees. Another group whose spending on most items is well below average, blacks, outspend the average on bank fees by 15 percent. Households in the West spend 25 percent more than average on this item.

Average household spending on bank service charges has been steadily declining. From 2000 to 2012, average household spending on bank service charges fell 13 percent, after adjusting for inflation. Behind the decline is the elimination of fees as banks compete for customers. Average household spending on bank service charges may rise in the years ahead if federal regulations tighten standards and force banks to make money the old-fashioned way.

Table 6.3 Bank service charges

Total household spending $2,874,009,600.00
Average household spends   23.10

AGE OF HOUSEHOLDER	AVERAGE HOUSEHOLD SPENDING	BEST CUSTOMERS (index)	BIGGEST CUSTOMERS (market share)
Average household	$23.10	100	100.0%
Under age 25	22.00	95	6.2
Aged 25 to 34	26.31	114	18.4
Aged 35 to 44	26.76	116	20.1
Aged 45 to 54	28.18	122	24.1
Aged 55 to 64	25.54	111	20.2
Aged 65 to 74	15.38	67	8.0
Aged 75 or older	6.66	29	2.8

	AVERAGE HOUSEHOLD SPENDING	BEST CUSTOMERS (index)	BIGGEST CUSTOMERS (market share)
HOUSEHOLD INCOME			
Average household	$23.10	100	100.0%
Under $20,000	12.39	54	11.3
$20,000 to $39,999	20.26	88	19.8
$40,000 to $49,999	23.92	104	9.2
$50,000 to $69,999	23.18	100	14.5
$70,000 to $79,999	24.35	105	5.9
$80,000 to $99,999	28.34	123	10.8
$100,000 or more	35.26	153	28.6
HOUSEHOLD TYPE			
Average household	23.10	100	100.0
Married couples	26.18	113	55.0
Married couples, no children	21.73	94	19.6
Married couples with children	30.14	130	30.7
Oldest child under age 6	22.32	97	4.4
Oldest child aged 6 to 17	35.27	153	18.2
Oldest child aged 18 or older	26.56	115	8.1
Single parent with child under age 18	26.67	115	6.1
Single person	17.23	75	22.1
RACE AND HISPANIC ORIGIN			
Average household	23.10	100	100.0
Asian	12.18	53	2.3
Black	26.77	116	14.6
Hispanic	19.38	84	10.5
Non-Hispanic white and other	23.18	100	75.3
REGION			
Average household	23.10	100	100.0
Northeast	24.59	106	19.2
Midwest	18.38	80	17.6
South	21.74	94	35.1
West	28.78	125	28.1
EDUCATION			
Average household	23.10	100	100.0
Less than high school graduate	15.05	65	8.5
High school graduate	19.97	86	21.6
Some college	23.58	102	21.0
Associate's degree	26.36	114	11.3
Bachelor's degree or more	27.57	119	37.6
Bachelor's degree	29.40	127	25.4
Master's, professional, doctoral degree	24.43	106	12.3

Note: Market shares may not sum to 100.0 because of rounding and missing categories by household type. "Asian" and "black" include Hispanics and non-Hispanics who identify themselves as being of the respective race alone. "Hispanic" includes people of any race who identify themselves as Hispanic. "Other" includes people who identify themselves as non-Hispanic and as Alaska Native, American Indian, Asian (who are also included in the "Asian" row), or Native Hawaiian or other Pacific Islander, as well as non-Hispanics reporting more than one race.
Source: Calculations by New Strategist based on the Bureau of Labor Statistics' 2012 Consumer Expenditure Survey

Cash Contributions to Charitable Organizations

Best customers: Householders aged 55 or older
High-income households
Married couples without children at home
Married couples with adult children at home
Non-Hispanic whites
Households in the Northeast and West
College graduates

Customer trends: Average household spending on charitable donations should continue to rise as baby boomers fill the best-customer age groups.

The biggest cash donors to charitable organizations are households with the greatest amount of discretionary income—older, white, educated married couples. Householders aged 55 to 74 spend 58 to 71 percent more than average on this item, and those aged 75 or older spend one-third more than average. Together households headed by people aged 55 or older account for 62 percent of charitable giving. Households with incomes of $100,000 and more contribute over three times the average amount to charitable organizations and are responsible for 60 percent of giving. Married couples without children at home (most of them empty-nesters) spend twice the average on cash gifts to charities and account for 43 percent of all charitable giving. Non-Hispanic whites give 27 percent more than average. Households in the Northeast outspend the average on this item by 59 percent, and those in the West spend 30 percent more. College graduates (who dominate the affluent) give well more than twice the average to charitable organizations.

Average household giving to charitable organizations grew 17 percent between 2000 and 2006, after adjusting for inflation, then fell 23 percent in the ensuing four years. Behind the decline was household belt tightening during the Great Recession. Between 2010 (the year when overall household spending bottomed out) and 2012 donations to charitable organizations rebounded strongly, growing by 39 percent. Expect to see charitable donations continue to rise because the large baby-boom generation is filling the best-customer age groups.

Table 6.4 Cash contributions to charitable organizations

Total household spending $29,067,310,080.00
Average household spends 233.63

	AVERAGE HOUSEHOLD SPENDING	BEST CUSTOMERS (index)	BIGGEST CUSTOMERS (market share)
AGE OF HOUSEHOLDER			
Average household	**$233.63**	**100**	**100.0%**
Under age 25	54.75	23	1.5
Aged 25 to 34	81.53	35	5.6
Aged 35 to 44	105.53	45	7.8
Aged 45 to 54	268.11	115	22.7
Aged 55 to 64	368.02	158	28.8
Aged 65 to 74	400.20	171	20.6
Aged 75 or older	305.91	131	12.8

	AVERAGE HOUSEHOLD SPENDING	BEST CUSTOMERS (index)	BIGGEST CUSTOMERS (market share)
HOUSEHOLD INCOME			
Average household	**$233.63**	**100**	**100.0%**
Under $20,000	63.13	27	5.7
$20,000 to $39,999	101.51	43	9.8
$40,000 to $49,999	118.68	51	4.5
$50,000 to $69,999	111.97	48	6.9
$70,000 to $79,999	151.81	65	3.6
$80,000 to $99,999	257.37	110	9.7
$100,000 or more	745.71	319	59.8
HOUSEHOLD TYPE			
Average household	**233.63**	**100**	**100.0**
Married couples	339.19	145	70.5
Married couples, no children	476.42	204	42.5
Married couples with children	258.38	111	26.0
Oldest child under age 6	157.37	67	3.1
Oldest child aged 6 to 17	231.95	99	11.8
Oldest child aged 18 or older	368.26	158	11.1
Single parent with child under age 18	59.14	25	1.3
Single person	143.93	62	18.3
RACE AND HISPANIC ORIGIN			
Average household	**233.63**	**100**	**100.0**
Asian	236.78	101	4.4
Black	58.51	25	3.1
Hispanic	37.70	16	2.0
Non-Hispanic white and other	295.76	127	95.0
REGION			
Average household	**233.63**	**100**	**100.0**
Northeast	371.58	159	28.7
Midwest	215.62	92	20.5
South	135.74	58	21.6
West	302.65	130	29.2
EDUCATION			
Average household	**233.63**	**100**	**100.0**
Less than high school graduate	50.09	21	2.8
High school graduate	95.37	41	10.2
Some college	135.19	58	11.9
Associate's degree	118.05	51	5.0
Bachelor's degree or more	519.42	222	70.1
Bachelor's degree	391.50	168	33.4
Master's, professional, doctoral degree	739.10	316	36.7

Note: Market shares may not sum to 100.0 because of rounding and missing categories by household type. "Asian" and "black" include Hispanics and non-Hispanics who identify themselves as being of the respective race alone. "Hispanic" includes people of any race who identify themselves as Hispanic. "Other" includes people who identify themselves as non-Hispanic and as Alaska Native, American Indian, Asian (who are also included in the "Asian" row), or Native Hawaiian or other Pacific Islander, as well as non-Hispanics reporting more than one race.
Source: Calculations by New Strategist based on the Bureau of Labor Statistics' 2012 Consumer Expenditure Survey

Cash Contributions to Educational Organizations

Best customers: Householders aged 35 to 54 and 75 or older
                   High-income households
                   Married couples without children at home
                   Married couples with adult children at home
                   Non-Hispanic whites
                   Households in the Northeast
                   College graduates

Customer trends: Average household spending on contributions to educational organizations is likely to continue to grow
                   in the years ahead as expanding numbers of college graduates give back to their school.

The biggest spenders on educational contributions are affluent, white, and educated. These are the households with the discretionary income to spend on their alma mater. Householders aged 75 or older spend one-third more than the average on contributions to educational organizations, and those aged 35 to 54 give 29 to 32 percent more than average. Households with incomes of $100,000 and more contribute three-and-three-quarter times the average amount to educational organizations and are responsible for 70 percent of giving. Married couples without children at home, most of them older empty-nesters, give 89 percent more than average to educational organizations, and couples with adult children at home give 39 percent more. Non-Hispanic whites dominate donations to educational organizations, giving 24 percent more than average. Households in the Northeast donate more than twice the average to schools and universities. College graduates spend two-and-three-quarter times the average on this item.

Average household spending on donations to educational organizations, which had increased enormously between 2000 and 2006 (possibly an anomaly in the Consumer Expenditure Survey data) returned to more normal slow growth between 2010 and 2012. Spending on contributions to educational organizations is likely to continue to grow in the years ahead as expanding numbers of college graduates give back to their school.

Table 6.5 Cash contributions to educational institutions

Total household spending $4,823,608,320.00
Average household spends   38.77

AGE OF HOUSEHOLDER	AVERAGE HOUSEHOLD SPENDING	BEST CUSTOMERS (index)	BIGGEST CUSTOMERS (market share)
Average household	$38.77	100	100.0%
Under age 25	1.31	3	0.2
Aged 25 to 34	11.82	30	4.9
Aged 35 to 44	49.84	129	22.3
Aged 45 to 54	51.12	132	26.1
Aged 55 to 64	45.86	118	21.6
Aged 65 to 74	37.66	97	11.7
Aged 75 or older	51.86	134	13.1

	AVERAGE HOUSEHOLD SPENDING	BEST CUSTOMERS (index)	BIGGEST CUSTOMERS (market share)
HOUSEHOLD INCOME			
Average household	**$38.77**	**100**	**100.0%**
Under $20,000	12.09	31	6.6
$20,000 to $39,999	6.93	18	4.0
$40,000 to $49,999	5.19	13	1.2
$50,000 to $69,999	24.06	62	9.0
$70,000 to $79,999	18.82	49	2.7
$80,000 to $99,999	28.51	74	6.5
$100,000 or more	145.07	374	70.1
HOUSEHOLD TYPE			
Average household	**38.77**	**100**	**100.0**
Married couples	53.51	138	67.0
Married couples, no children	73.13	189	39.3
Married couples with children	42.40	109	25.7
Oldest child under age 6	19.33	50	2.3
Oldest child aged 6 to 17	44.51	115	13.7
Oldest child aged 18 or older	53.76	139	9.8
Single parent with child under age 18	17.34	45	2.3
Single person	31.67	82	24.3
RACE AND HISPANIC ORIGIN			
Average household	**38.77**	**100**	**100.0**
Asian	29.93	77	3.3
Black	17.10	44	5.5
Hispanic	5.25	14	1.7
Non-Hispanic white and other	47.91	124	92.8
REGION			
Average household	**38.77**	**100**	**100.0**
Northeast	89.83	232	41.8
Midwest	27.58	71	15.8
South	20.88	54	20.1
West	38.42	99	22.3
EDUCATION			
Average household	**38.77**	**100**	**100.0**
Less than high school graduate	1.39	4	0.5
High school graduate	9.11	23	5.9
Some college	9.44	24	5.0
Associate's degree	11.08	29	2.8
Bachelor's degree or more	105.51	272	85.8
Bachelor's degree	62.67	162	32.2
Master's, professional, doctoral degree	179.07	462	53.6

Note: Market shares may not sum to 100.0 because of rounding and missing categories by household type. "Asian" and "black" include Hispanics and non-Hispanics who identify themselves as being of the respective race alone. "Hispanic" includes people of any race who identify themselves as Hispanic. "Other" includes people who identify themselves as non-Hispanic and as Alaska Native, American Indian, Asian (who are also included in the "Asian" row), or Native Hawaiian or other Pacific Islander, as well as non-Hispanics reporting more than one race.
Source: Calculations by New Strategist based on the Bureau of Labor Statistics' 2012 Consumer Expenditure Survey

Cash Contributions to Political Organizations

Best customers: Householders aged 45 to 74
High-income households
Married couples without children at home
Married couples with school-aged or older children at home
Non-Hispanic whites
Households in the West
College graduates

Customer trends: Average household spending on cash contributions to political organizations will rise now
that the Supreme Court has struck down limits on how much individuals can give.

The biggest spenders on political contributions are older, affluent, white, and educated. These are the households with the discretionary income to devote to political causes. Householders aged 65 to 74 spend two-and-one-half times the average on contributions to political organizations. Householders aged 45 to 64 contribute 21 to 46 percent more than average. Householders with incomes of $100,000 or more give more than three times the average to political causes. Married couples without children at home (most of them empty-nesters) give 86 percent more, and those with school-aged or older children at home give 24 to 49 percent more than average. Non-Hispanic whites donate 23 percent more than average. Households in the West spend three-quarters more than average on this item. College graduates, who dominate the affluent, spend almost two-and-one-half times the average on political donations.

Average household spending on donations to political organizations grew strongly between 2000 and 2006, fell sharply between 2006 and 2010, then expanded by a substantial 84 percent between 2010 and the presidential election year of 2012. With the Supreme Court giving the green light to unlimited campaign donations by individuals, average household spending on political contributions will rise.

Table 6.6 Cash contributions to political organizations

Total household spending $3,097,958,400.00
Average household spends   24.90

AGE OF HOUSEHOLDER	AVERAGE HOUSEHOLD SPENDING	BEST CUSTOMERS (index)	BIGGEST CUSTOMERS (market share)
Average household	$24.90	100	100.0%
Under age 25	1.25	5	0.3
Aged 25 to 34	5.00	20	3.2
Aged 35 to 44	8.78	35	6.1
Aged 45 to 54	36.27	146	28.8
Aged 55 to 64	30.22	121	22.2
Aged 65 to 74	61.22	246	29.6
Aged 75 or older	24.50	98	9.6

	AVERAGE HOUSEHOLD SPENDING	BEST CUSTOMERS (index)	BIGGEST CUSTOMERS (market share)
HOUSEHOLD INCOME			
Average household	**$24.90**	**100**	**100.0%**
Under $20,000	6.95	28	5.9
$20,000 to $39,999	13.43	54	12.2
$40,000 to $49,999	11.88	48	4.2
$50,000 to $69,999	9.57	38	5.6
$70,000 to $79,999	16.64	67	3.7
$80,000 to $99,999	24.58	99	8.7
$100,000 or more	79.45	319	59.7
HOUSEHOLD TYPE			
Average household	**24.90**	**100**	**100.0**
Married couples	34.74	140	67.8
Married couples, no children	46.23	186	38.7
Married couples with children	29.12	117	27.5
Oldest child under age 6	5.75	23	1.1
Oldest child aged 6 to 17	37.09	149	17.7
Oldest child aged 18 or older	30.79	124	8.7
Single parent with child under age 18	0.63	3	0.1
Single person	20.17	81	24.1
RACE AND HISPANIC ORIGIN			
Average household	**24.90**	**100**	**100.0**
Asian	5.01	20	0.9
Black	10.88	44	5.5
Hispanic	3.74	15	1.9
Non-Hispanic white and other	30.72	123	92.6
REGION			
Average household	**24.90**	**100**	**100.0**
Northeast	20.61	83	14.9
Midwest	19.60	79	17.5
South	18.86	76	28.2
West	43.51	175	39.4
EDUCATION			
Average household	**24.90**	**100**	**100.0**
Less than high school graduate	1.82	7	1.0
High school graduate	6.81	27	6.8
Some college	16.99	68	14.1
Associate's degree	7.63	31	3.0
Bachelor's degree or more	59.31	238	75.1
Bachelor's degree	38.08	153	30.5
Master's, professional, doctoral degree	95.78	385	44.6

Note: Market shares may not sum to 100.0 because of rounding and missing categories by household type. "Asian" and "black" include Hispanics and non-Hispanics who identify themselves as being of the respective race alone. "Hispanic" includes people of any race who identify themselves as Hispanic. "Other" includes people who identify themselves as non-Hispanic and as Alaska Native, American Indian, Asian (who are also included in the "Asian" row), or Native Hawaiian or other Pacific Islander, as well as non-Hispanics reporting more than one race.
Source: Calculations by New Strategist based on the Bureau of Labor Statistics' 2012 Consumer Expenditure Survey

Cash Contributions to Religious Organizations

Best customers: Householders aged 55 or older
               Married couples
               Blacks
               Households in the South

Customer trends: Average household spending on cash contributions to religious organizations should continue to grow
               as boomers enter the lifestage of increased giving.

Contributions to religious organizations are one of the most important items in the household budget, ranking 17th among the items on which households spend the most, nestled between lunch at restaurants and cable television service. Those donating the most to religious organizations are older married couples. Householders aged 55 or older spend 22 to 33 percent more than the average household on cash contributions to churches and religious organizations. Married couples without children at home (most of them empty-nesters) spend 75 percent more than average, while couples with children of any age at home spend 46 percent more. Blacks, whose spending is below average on most items, contribute 8 percent more than the average amount to religious institutions, and households in the South, where many blacks reside, donate 16 percent more than average.

Average household giving to religious organizations rose 44 percent between 2000 and 2006, after adjusting for inflation, and then dropped 19 percent in the four ensuing years as the Great Recession reduced discretionary spending. In the two years following the overall household spending trough year of 2010 cash contributions to religious organizations rose 6 percent. The aging of the population into the lifestage when giving is greatest suggests continued growth in this category.

Table 6.7 Cash contributions to religious organizations

Total household spending $91,358,668,800.00
Average household spends   734.30

	AVERAGE HOUSEHOLD SPENDING	BEST CUSTOMERS (index)	BIGGEST CUSTOMERS (market share)
AGE OF HOUSEHOLDER			
Average household	**$734.30**	**100**	**100.0%**
Under age 25	156.24	21	1.4
Aged 25 to 34	475.93	65	10.5
Aged 35 to 44	627.65	85	14.8
Aged 45 to 54	798.37	109	21.5
Aged 55 to 64	978.10	133	24.4
Aged 65 to 74	894.34	122	14.7
Aged 75 or older	955.32	130	12.7

	AVERAGE HOUSEHOLD SPENDING	BEST CUSTOMERS (index)	BIGGEST CUSTOMERS (market share)
HOUSEHOLD INCOME			
Average household	**$734.30**	**100**	**100.0%**
Under $20,000	279.89	38	8.0
$20,000 to $39,999	423.07	58	13.0
$40,000 to $49,999	495.13	67	6.0
$50,000 to $69,999	739.35	101	14.5
$70,000 to $79,999	927.90	126	7.1
$80,000 to $99,999	1,047.68	143	12.6
$100,000 or more	1,523.37	207	38.8
HOUSEHOLD TYPE			
Average household	**734.30**	**100**	**100.0**
Married couples	1,130.97	154	74.8
Married couples, no children	1,281.78	175	36.4
Married couples with children	1,072.67	146	34.3
Oldest child under age 6	844.12	115	5.2
Oldest child aged 6 to 17	1,026.20	140	16.6
Oldest child aged 18 or older	1,298.79	177	12.5
Single parent with child under age 18	260.11	35	1.9
Single person	389.22	53	15.7
RACE AND HISPANIC ORIGIN			
Average household	**734.30**	**100**	**100.0**
Asian	451.26	61	2.7
Black	794.61	108	13.6
Hispanic	217.77	30	3.7
Non-Hispanic white and other	809.40	110	82.7
REGION			
Average household	**734.30**	**100**	**100.0**
Northeast	435.81	59	10.7
Midwest	777.93	106	23.5
South	854.77	116	43.4
West	731.37	100	22.4
EDUCATION			
Average household	**734.30**	**100**	**100.0**
Less than high school graduate	299.34	41	5.3
High school graduate	481.14	66	16.3
Some college	606.03	83	17.0
Associate's degree	771.71	105	10.4
Bachelor's degree or more	1,186.59	162	51.0
Bachelor's degree	1,063.28	145	28.9
Master's, professional, doctoral degree	1,398.34	190	22.1

Note: Market shares may not sum to 100.0 because of rounding and missing categories by household type. "Asian" and "black" include Hispanics and non-Hispanics who identify themselves as being of the respective race alone. "Hispanic" includes people of any race who identify themselves as Hispanic. "Other" includes people who identify themselves as non-Hispanic and as Alaska Native, American Indian, Asian (who are also included in the "Asian" row), or Native Hawaiian or other Pacific Islander, as well as non-Hispanics reporting more than one race.
Source: Calculations by New Strategist based on the Bureau of Labor Statistics' 2012 Consumer Expenditure Survey

Cash Gifts, Other than Charitable, Educational, Political, or Religious

Best customers:　Householders aged 65 or older
　　　　　　　　　Married couples without children at home
　　　　　　　　　Households in the West

Customer trends:　Average household spending on cash gifts is likely to grow in the years ahead as aging boomers
　　　　　　　　　attempt to help their struggling adult children.

Many older parents give money to their adult children to help them make a down payment on a home, to defray a grandchild's college expenses, or to cover necessities like health insurance and day care. Householders aged 75 or older spend two-and-one-third times the average on such cash gifts, and householders aged 65 to 74 give one-half more than the average amount in cash gifts. Married couples without children at home (most of them empty-nesters) give 77 percent more than average in cash gifts. Households in the West outspend the average by 72 percent on this item.

Cash gifts is a relatively new item in the Consumer Expenditure Survey and comparable data for 2000 do not exist. Average household spending on cash gifts was nearly identical in 2006 and 2012, after adjusting for inflation, but there was an 11 percent dip in 2010, the year overall household spending bottomed out. As millions of boomers move into the best-customer lifestage in the years ahead—many with struggling adult children—average household spending on cash gifts may grow.

Table 6.8　Cash gifts, other than charitable, educational, political, or religious

Total household spending　　　　　　$57,791,232,000.00
Average household spends　　　　　　　　464.50

AGE OF HOUSEHOLDER	AVERAGE HOUSEHOLD SPENDING	BEST CUSTOMERS (index)	BIGGEST CUSTOMERS (market share)
Average household	$464.50	100	100.0%
Under age 25	140.80	30	2.0
Aged 25 to 34	197.22	42	6.9
Aged 35 to 44	201.84	43	7.5
Aged 45 to 54	534.71	115	22.8
Aged 55 to 64	500.07	108	19.7
Aged 65 to 74	694.74	150	18.0
Aged 75 or older	1,097.56	236	23.1

	AVERAGE HOUSEHOLD SPENDING	BEST CUSTOMERS (index)	BIGGEST CUSTOMERS (market share)
HOUSEHOLD INCOME			
Average household	**$464.50**	**100**	**100.0%**
Under $20,000	130.19	28	5.9
$20,000 to $39,999	322.54	69	15.6
$40,000 to $49,999	292.91	63	5.6
$50,000 to $69,999	543.58	117	16.9
$70,000 to $79,999	415.06	89	5.0
$80,000 to $99,999	584.21	126	11.1
$100,000 or more	989.51	213	39.9
HOUSEHOLD TYPE			
Average household	**464.50**	**100**	**100.0**
Married couples	583.73	126	61.0
Married couples, no children	821.56	177	36.9
Married couples with children	254.65	55	12.9
Oldest child under age 6	195.31	42	1.9
Oldest child aged 6 to 17	235.19	51	6.0
Oldest child aged 18 or older	325.82	70	4.9
Single parent with child under age 18	100.35	22	1.1
Single person	446.75	96	28.6
RACE AND HISPANIC ORIGIN			
Average household	**464.50**	**100**	**100.0**
Asian	424.33	91	4.0
Black	175.80	38	4.8
Hispanic	260.41	56	7.0
Non-Hispanic white and other	546.29	118	88.3
REGION			
Average household	**464.50**	**100**	**100.0**
Northeast	417.22	90	16.2
Midwest	450.37	97	21.5
South	294.32	63	23.6
West	797.57	172	38.7
EDUCATION			
Average household	**464.50**	**100**	**100.0**
Less than high school graduate	215.08	46	6.0
High school graduate	304.19	65	16.3
Some college	357.88	77	15.9
Associate's degree	295.75	64	6.3
Bachelor's degree or more	816.97	176	55.5
Bachelor's degree	764.97	165	32.8
Master's, professional, doctoral degree	906.28	195	22.6

Note: Market shares may not sum to 100.0 because of rounding and missing categories by household type. "Asian" and "black" include Hispanics and non-Hispanics who identify themselves as being of the respective race alone. "Hispanic" includes people of any race who identify themselves as Hispanic. "Other" includes people who identify themselves as non-Hispanic and as Alaska Native, American Indian, Asian (who are also included in the "Asian" row), or Native Hawaiian or other Pacific Islander, as well as non-Hispanics reporting more than one race.
Source: Calculations by New Strategist based on the Bureau of Labor Statistics' 2012 Consumer Expenditure Survey

Cemetery Lots, Vaults, Maintenance Fees

Best customers: Householders aged 45 to 54 and 75 or older
People who live alone
Asians
Households in the West

Customer trends: Average household spending on cemetery lots, vaults, and maintenance fees should rise
as the population ages unless more choose cremation.

Not surprisingly, the biggest spenders on cemetery lots, vaults, and maintenance fees are the oldest Americans and their children. Householders aged 75 or older spend nearly three times the average on cemetery lots, and those aged 45 to 54 spend 29 percent more than average, as they bury their spouses and parents, respectively. People who live alone, whose spending is well below average on most items, spend 14 percent above average on cemetery lots and maintenance. The spending of Asians on this item is nearly three times the average. Households in the West, where many Asians reside, spend 72 percent more than average on cemetery lots, vaults, and maintenance fees.

Average household spending on cemetery lots, vaults, and maintenance fees rose 23 percent between 2000 and 2006, after adjusting for inflation, and then declined 40 percent between 2006 and 2012 as households were forced to cut costs in the face of the Great Recession. Spending on cemetery lots, vaults, and maintenance fees should rise with the aging of the population unless more choose cremation.

Table 6.9 Cemetery lots, vaults, maintenance fees

Total household spending $1,637,314,560.00
Average household spends 13.16

AGE OF HOUSEHOLDER	AVERAGE HOUSEHOLD SPENDING	BEST CUSTOMERS (index)	BIGGEST CUSTOMERS (market share)
Average household	$13.16	100	100.0%
Under age 25	1.12	9	0.6
Aged 25 to 34	8.51	65	10.5
Aged 35 to 44	9.52	72	12.6
Aged 45 to 54	16.97	129	25.5
Aged 55 to 64	6.25	47	8.7
Aged 65 to 74	15.29	116	14.0
Aged 75 or older	38.00	289	28.2

	AVERAGE HOUSEHOLD SPENDING	BEST CUSTOMERS (index)	BIGGEST CUSTOMERS (market share)
HOUSEHOLD INCOME			
Average household	$13.16	100	100.0%
Under $20,000	12.98	99	20.7
$20,000 to $39,999	10.81	82	18.5
$40,000 to $49,999	2.68	20	1.8
$50,000 to $69,999	6.19	47	6.8
$70,000 to $79,999	2.25	17	1.0
$80,000 to $99,999	5.81	44	3.9
$100,000 or more	33.26	253	47.3
HOUSEHOLD TYPE			
Average household	13.16	100	100.0
Married couples	12.72	97	46.9
Married couples, no children	6.62	50	10.5
Married couples with children	18.44	140	32.9
Oldest child under age 6	8.10	62	2.8
Oldest child aged 6 to 17	26.41	201	23.9
Oldest child aged 18 or older	11.69	89	6.3
Single parent with child under age 18	1.15	9	0.5
Single person	13.95	106	31.5
RACE AND HISPANIC ORIGIN			
Average household	13.16	100	100.0
Asian	38.39	292	12.6
Black	7.65	58	7.3
Hispanic	7.26	55	6.9
Non-Hispanic white and other	15.04	114	85.8
REGION			
Average household	13.16	100	100.0
Northeast	11.48	87	15.7
Midwest	7.82	59	13.2
South	11.39	87	32.2
West	22.70	172	38.9
EDUCATION			
Average household	13.16	100	100.0
Less than high school graduate	5.68	43	5.6
High school graduate	15.36	117	29.1
Some college	10.04	76	15.7
Associate's degree	8.61	65	6.5
Bachelor's degree or more	17.99	137	43.1
Bachelor's degree	20.73	158	31.4
Master's, professional, doctoral degree	13.28	101	11.7

Note: Market shares may not sum to 100.0 because of rounding and missing categories by household type. "Asian" and "black" include Hispanics and non-Hispanics who identify themselves as being of the respective race alone. "Hispanic" includes people of any race who identify themselves as Hispanic. "Other" includes people who identify themselves as non-Hispanic and as Alaska Native, American Indian, Asian (who are also included in the "Asian" row), or Native Hawaiian or other Pacific Islander, as well as non-Hispanics reporting more than one race.
Source: Calculations by New Strategist based on the Bureau of Labor Statistics' 2012 Consumer Expenditure Survey

Child Support

Best customers: Householders aged 25 to 54
Married couples with preschoolers
Single parents
People who live alone

Customer trends: Average household spending on child support is likely to decline as divorce becomes less common and the small generation X fills the most divorce-prone age group.

The biggest spenders on child support are householders aged 35 to 44, who spend 86 percent more than average on this item. The adjacent 10-year age cohorts on either side spend 40 and 65 percent more than average, respectively. Married couples with preschoolers outspend the average by 58 percent, and single parents do so by 14 percent. People who live alone spend one-quarter more than average on child support.

Child support payments are a relatively new item in the Consumer Expenditure Survey and comparable data for 2000 do not exist. Average household spending on child support declined 15 percent between 2006 and 2012, after adjusting for inflation. With the divorce rate declining and the much smaller generation X now in the most divorce-prone 35-to-44 age group, average household spending on child support should continue to decline.

Table 6.10 Child support

Total household spending $25,935,759,360.00
Average household spends   208.46

AGE OF HOUSEHOLDER	AVERAGE HOUSEHOLD SPENDING	BEST CUSTOMERS (index)	BIGGEST CUSTOMERS (market share)
Average household	$208.46	100	100.0%
Under age 25	60.26	29	1.9
Aged 25 to 34	291.38	140	22.6
Aged 35 to 44	387.28	186	32.3
Aged 45 to 54	343.87	165	32.6
Aged 55 to 64	101.31	49	8.9
Aged 65 to 74	25.18	12	1.5
Aged 75 or older	5.61	3	0.3

	AVERAGE HOUSEHOLD SPENDING	BEST CUSTOMERS (index)	BIGGEST CUSTOMERS (market share)
HOUSEHOLD INCOME			
Average household	**$208.46**	**100**	**100.0%**
Under $20,000	75.58	36	7.6
$20,000 to $39,999	142.47	68	15.4
$40,000 to $49,999	203.71	98	8.6
$50,000 to $69,999	290.44	139	20.1
$70,000 to $79,999	240.23	115	6.4
$80,000 to $99,999	269.22	129	11.4
$100,000 or more	338.14	162	30.4
HOUSEHOLD TYPE			
Average household	**208.46**	**100**	**100.0**
Married couples	143.93	69	33.5
Married couples, no children	77.29	37	7.7
Married couples with children	191.94	92	21.6
Oldest child under age 6	328.36	158	7.2
Oldest child aged 6 to 17	199.26	96	11.4
Oldest child aged 18 or older	91.38	44	3.1
Single parent with child under age 18	238.03	114	6.0
Single person	259.91	125	37.0
RACE AND HISPANIC ORIGIN			
Average household	**208.46**	**100**	**100.0**
Asian	66.39	32	1.4
Black	213.91	103	12.9
Hispanic	210.62	101	12.7
Non-Hispanic white and other	207.25	99	74.6
REGION			
Average household	**208.46**	**100**	**100.0**
Northeast	156.85	75	13.6
Midwest	193.54	93	20.6
South	230.38	111	41.2
West	228.27	110	24.7
EDUCATION			
Average household	**208.46**	**100**	**100.0**
Less than high school graduate	136.10	65	8.5
High school graduate	207.57	100	24.8
Some college	198.53	95	19.6
Associate's degree	248.74	119	11.8
Bachelor's degree or more	233.01	112	35.3
Bachelor's degree	183.22	88	17.5
Master's, professional, doctoral degree	318.53	153	17.7

Note: Market shares may not sum to 100.0 because of rounding and missing categories by household type. "Asian" and "black" include Hispanics and non-Hispanics who identify themselves as being of the respective race alone. "Hispanic" includes people of any race who identify themselves as Hispanic. "Other" includes people who identify themselves as non-Hispanic and as Alaska Native, American Indian, Asian (who are also included in the "Asian" row), or Native Hawaiian or other Pacific Islander, as well as non-Hispanics reporting more than one race.
Source: Calculations by New Strategist based on the Bureau of Labor Statistics' 2012 Consumer Expenditure Survey

Contributions to Retirement Accounts (Nonpayroll Deposits)

Best customers: **Householders aged 45 to 64**
High-income households
Married couples
Asians and Non-Hispanic whites
College graduates

Customer trends: **Average household spending on nonpayroll contributions to retirement accounts should grow as aging boomers attempt to save more for retirement—but only if households can afford to save.**

Affluent households approaching retirement make the largest nonpayroll deposits to retirement accounts. Householders aged 45 to 64 spent 36 to 89 percent more than average on such contributions in 2012 and accounted for 62 percent of the total. Households with incomes of $100,000 or more pack away three-and-three-quarter times the average and account for 69 percent of the market. Married couples without children at home (most of them empty-nesters) spend 55 percent more than average on contributions to retirement accounts, while couples with children at home manage to save 68 percent more than average for retirement. Asians spend 44 percent more than average on nonpayroll contributions and non-Hispanic whites 21 percent more. College graduates, who dominate the affluent, contribute over twice the average to their retirement portfolios.

Average household spending on contributions to retirement accounts declined a slight 5 percent between 2000 and 2010, after adjusting for inflation, but grew by a strong 18 percent in the ensuing two years. As aging boomers attempt to save more for retirement, spending on contributions to retirement accounts may rise—but only if households can afford to save.

Table 6.11 **Contributions to retirement accounts (nonpayroll deposits)**

Total household spending $72,467,343,360.00
Average household spends 582.46

AGE OF HOUSEHOLDER	AVERAGE HOUSEHOLD SPENDING	BEST CUSTOMERS (index)	BIGGEST CUSTOMERS (market share)
Average household	$582.46	100	100.0%
Under age 25	74.53	13	0.8
Aged 25 to 34	396.10	68	11.0
Aged 35 to 44	529.31	91	15.8
Aged 45 to 54	1,098.72	189	37.3
Aged 55 to 64	791.03	136	24.9
Aged 65 to 74	424.61	73	8.8
Aged 75 or older	84.63	15	1.4

	AVERAGE HOUSEHOLD SPENDING	BEST CUSTOMERS (index)	BIGGEST CUSTOMERS (market share)
HOUSEHOLD INCOME			
Average household	**$582.46**	**100**	**100.0%**
Under $20,000	68.17	12	2.5
$20,000 to $39,999	93.58	16	3.6
$40,000 to $49,999	285.35	49	4.3
$50,000 to $69,999	313.55	54	7.8
$70,000 to $79,999	368.65	63	3.5
$80,000 to $99,999	597.76	103	9.1
$100,000 or more	2,153.42	370	69.2
HOUSEHOLD TYPE			
Average household	**582.46**	**100**	**100.0**
Married couples	897.69	154	74.9
Married couples, no children	903.24	155	32.3
Married couples with children	978.35	168	39.5
Oldest child under age 6	841.57	144	6.6
Oldest child aged 6 to 17	1,099.61	189	22.5
Oldest child aged 18 or older	862.37	148	10.4
Single parent with child under age 18	69.31	12	0.6
Single person	318.32	55	16.2
RACE AND HISPANIC ORIGIN			
Average household	**582.46**	**100**	**100.0**
Asian	840.46	144	6.3
Black	292.65	50	6.3
Hispanic	131.95	23	2.8
Non-Hispanic white and other	704.98	121	90.8
REGION			
Average household	**582.46**	**100**	**100.0**
Northeast	597.29	103	18.5
Midwest	406.77	70	15.5
South	644.82	111	41.2
West	640.37	110	24.8
EDUCATION			
Average household	**582.46**	**100**	**100.0**
Less than high school graduate	83.18	14	1.9
High school graduate	253.49	44	10.9
Some college	378.06	65	13.4
Associate's degree	294.49	51	5.0
Bachelor's degree or more	1,272.93	219	68.9
Bachelor's degree	954.76	164	32.7
Master's, professional, doctoral degree	1,819.31	312	36.3

Note: Market shares may not sum to 100.0 because of rounding and missing categories by household type. "Asian" and "black" include Hispanics and non-Hispanics who identify themselves as being of the respective race alone. "Hispanic" includes people of any race who identify themselves as Hispanic. "Other" includes people who identify themselves as non-Hispanic and as Alaska Native, American Indian, Asian (who are also included in the "Asian" row), or Native Hawaiian or other Pacific Islander, as well as non-Hispanics reporting more than one race.
Source: Calculations by New Strategist based on the Bureau of Labor Statistics' 2012 Consumer Expenditure Survey

Credit Card Membership Fees

Best customers: Householders aged 45 to 74
Married couples without children at home
Married couples with adult children at home
Asians
Households in the West

Customer trends: Average household spending on credit card membership fees may continue to rise as new financial regulations tighten lending standards.

The biggest spenders on credit card memberships are households that carry the largest number of cards—older married couples. Householders aged 45 to 74 spend 20 to 27 percent more than the average household on credit card membership fees. Married couples without children at home, most empty-nesters, spend 59 percent more than average, and couples with adult children at home spend 23 percent more. Asians spend 56 percent more than average on credit card membership fees. Households in the West spend 54 percent more than average on this item.

As competition among credit cards has grown, fees have fallen or disappeared entirely. Consequently, average household spending on credit card memberships has plummeted—down 71 percent between 2000 and 2010, after adjusting for inflation. In the two years since, however, spending on this minor financial item rose a strong 61 percent. Spending on credit card membership fees may continue to rise as new financial regulations tighten lending standards.

Table 6.12 Credit card membership fees

Total household spending $363,294,720.00
Average household spends   2.92

AGE OF HOUSEHOLDER	AVERAGE HOUSEHOLD SPENDING	BEST CUSTOMERS (index)	BIGGEST CUSTOMERS (market share)
Average household	$2.92	100	100.0%
Under age 25	1.91	65	4.3
Aged 25 to 34	3.47	119	19.2
Aged 35 to 44	1.57	54	9.3
Aged 45 to 54	3.71	127	25.1
Aged 55 to 64	3.61	124	22.6
Aged 65 to 74	3.51	120	14.5
Aged 75 or older	1.53	52	5.1

	AVERAGE HOUSEHOLD SPENDING	BEST CUSTOMERS (index)	BIGGEST CUSTOMERS (market share)
HOUSEHOLD INCOME			
Average household	$2.92	100	100.0%
Under $20,000	0.85	29	6.2
$20,000 to $39,999	1.56	53	12.0
$40,000 to $49,999	0.67	23	2.0
$50,000 to $69,999	2.43	83	12.0
$70,000 to $79,999	1.77	61	3.4
$80,000 to $99,999	3.97	136	12.0
$100,000 or more	8.20	281	52.6
HOUSEHOLD TYPE			
Average household	2.92	100	100.0
Married couples	3.60	123	59.9
Married couples, no children	4.64	159	33.1
Married couples with children	3.03	104	24.4
Oldest child under age 6	3.11	107	4.9
Oldest child aged 6 to 17	2.67	91	10.9
Oldest child aged 18 or older	3.59	123	8.7
Single parent with child under age 18	1.53	52	2.7
Single person	2.27	78	23.1
RACE AND HISPANIC ORIGIN			
Average household	2.92	100	100.0
Asian	4.55	156	6.8
Black	1.88	64	8.1
Hispanic	1.26	43	5.4
Non-Hispanic white and other	3.38	116	86.9
REGION			
Average household	2.92	100	100.0
Northeast	3.02	103	18.7
Midwest	1.70	58	12.9
South	2.66	91	33.9
West	4.49	154	34.6
EDUCATION			
Average household	2.92	100	100.0
Less than high school graduate	0.96	33	4.3
High school graduate	1.28	44	10.9
Some college	2.60	89	18.3
Associate's degree	1.85	63	6.3
Bachelor's degree or more	5.59	191	60.4
Bachelor's degree	4.60	158	31.4
Master's, professional, doctoral degree	7.29	250	29.0

Note: Market shares may not sum to 100.0 because of rounding and missing categories by household type. "Asian" and "black" include Hispanics and non-Hispanics who identify themselves as being of the respective race alone. "Hispanic" includes people of any race who identify themselves as Hispanic. "Other" includes people who identify themselves as non-Hispanic and as Alaska Native, American Indian, Asian (who are also included in the "Asian" row), or Native Hawaiian or other Pacific Islander, as well as non-Hispanics reporting more than one race.
Source: Calculations by New Strategist based on the Bureau of Labor Statistics' 2012 Consumer Expenditure Survey

Deductions for Government Retirement

Best customers: Householders aged 35 to 64
                        High-income households
                        Married couples
                        Asians
                        College graduates

Customer trends: Average household spending on deductions for government retirement may decline in the years ahead
                        if federal, state, and local governments reduce their workforce.

Affluent middle-aged or older married couples spend the most on government retirement plans. Householders aged 35 to 64 spend 31 to 62 percent more than average on deductions for government retirement. Married couples spend 39 percent more than average on this item, the figure peaking among those with school-aged children at 71 percent above average. Households with incomes of $100,000 or more spend more than three times the average on this item. College graduates, an affluent demographic, spend over twice the average. Asians spend nearly two-thirds more than average on government retirement plans.

Average household spending on deductions for government retirement declined 6 percent between 2000 and 2006, after adjusting for inflation, and then rose 15 percent in the ensuing six years for an overall 7 percent gain. Spending on this item may decline in the years ahead if job cuts make government employment less common.

Table 6.13 Deductions for government retirement

Total household spending	$12,508,784,640.00
Average household spends	100.54

	AVERAGE HOUSEHOLD SPENDING	BEST CUSTOMERS (index)	BIGGEST CUSTOMERS (market share)
AGE OF HOUSEHOLDER			
Average household	**$100.54**	**100**	**100.0%**
Under age 25	13.38	13	0.9
Aged 25 to 34	75.69	75	12.2
Aged 35 to 44	132.08	131	22.8
Aged 45 to 54	158.06	157	31.1
Aged 55 to 64	163.01	162	29.7
Aged 65 to 74	25.35	25	3.0
Aged 75 or older	3.40	3	0.3

	AVERAGE HOUSEHOLD SPENDING	BEST CUSTOMERS (index)	BIGGEST CUSTOMERS (market share)
HOUSEHOLD INCOME			
Average household	$100.54	100	100.0%
Under $20,000	0.79	1	0.2
$20,000 to $39,999	15.34	15	3.4
$40,000 to $49,999	27.02	27	2.4
$50,000 to $69,999	92.97	92	13.4
$70,000 to $79,999	147.19	146	8.2
$80,000 to $99,999	137.65	137	12.1
$100,000 or more	324.56	323	60.4
HOUSEHOLD TYPE			
Average household	100.54	100	100.0
Married couples	140.00	139	67.6
Married couples, no children	122.33	122	25.4
Married couples with children	161.32	160	37.7
Oldest child under age 6	136.01	135	6.2
Oldest child aged 6 to 17	171.51	171	20.3
Oldest child aged 18 or older	160.51	160	11.3
Single parent with child under age 18	63.74	63	3.3
Single person	58.56	58	17.3
RACE AND HISPANIC ORIGIN			
Average household	100.54	100	100.0
Asian	165.28	164	7.1
Black	72.64	72	9.1
Hispanic	62.43	62	7.8
Non-Hispanic white and other	111.36	111	83.1
REGION			
Average household	100.54	100	100.0
Northeast	76.73	76	13.8
Midwest	117.44	117	25.9
South	85.31	85	31.6
West	128.17	127	28.7
EDUCATION			
Average household	100.54	100	100.0
Less than high school graduate	7.18	7	0.9
High school graduate	33.93	34	8.4
Some college	69.92	70	14.3
Associate's degree	91.85	91	9.0
Bachelor's degree or more	214.58	213	67.3
Bachelor's degree	157.67	157	31.3
Master's, professional, doctoral degree	312.32	311	36.1

Note: Market shares may not sum to 100.0 because of rounding and missing categories by household type. "Asian" and "black" include Hispanics and non-Hispanics who identify themselves as being of the respective race alone. "Hispanic" includes people of any race who identify themselves as Hispanic. "Other" includes people who identify themselves as non-Hispanic and as Alaska Native, American Indian, Asian (who are also included in the "Asian" row), or Native Hawaiian or other Pacific Islander, as well as non-Hispanics reporting more than one race.
Source: Calculations by New Strategist based on the Bureau of Labor Statistics' 2012 Consumer Expenditure Survey

Deductions for Private Pensions (Payroll Deductions)

Best customers: **Householders aged 45 to 64**
High-income households
Married couples
Asians
College graduates

Customer trends: **Average household spending on payroll deductions for private pensions may grow as aging boomers attempt to save more for retirement, but only if households can afford to save.**

Affluent older married couples are the biggest spenders on deductions for private pensions. Households with incomes of $100,000 or more spend over three-and-one-half times the average on this item and control 68 percent of the market. Householders aged 45 to 64 spend 59 to 69 percent more than average. Married couples—many of them dual earners—spend 55 percent more than average on this item, the figure peaking at 89 percent above average for households that include school-aged children. Asians spend 58 percent more than average on this item. Households headed by college graduates spend more than twice the average on deductions for private pensions.

Average household spending on deductions for private pensions fell 26 percent between 2006 and 2012, after adjusting for inflation. (Because of a change in methodology, the 2000 figure is not directly comparable with the more recent spending figures.) Spending on this item may grow as aging boomers attempt to save more for retirement, but only if households can afford to save.

Table 6.14 Deductions for private pensions (payroll deductions)

Total household spending $63,676,108,800.00
Average household spends   511.80

AGE OF HOUSEHOLDER	AVERAGE HOUSEHOLD SPENDING	BEST CUSTOMERS (index)	BIGGEST CUSTOMERS (market share)
Average household	$511.80	100	100.0%
Under age 25	68.32	13	0.9
Aged 25 to 34	378.43	74	12.0
Aged 35 to 44	598.08	117	20.3
Aged 45 to 54	815.89	159	31.6
Aged 55 to 64	864.81	169	30.9
Aged 65 to 74	176.66	35	4.2
Aged 75 or older	13.16	3	0.3

	AVERAGE HOUSEHOLD SPENDING	BEST CUSTOMERS (index)	BIGGEST CUSTOMERS (market share)
HOUSEHOLD INCOME			
Average household	**$511.80**	100	100.0%
Under $20,000	7.21	1	0.3
$20,000 to $39,999	49.36	10	2.2
$40,000 to $49,999	185.42	36	3.2
$50,000 to $69,999	324.34	63	9.2
$70,000 to $79,999	484.86	95	5.3
$80,000 to $99,999	714.11	140	12.3
$100,000 or more	1,847.15	361	67.6
HOUSEHOLD TYPE			
Average household	**511.80**	100	100.0
Married couples	790.91	155	75.1
Married couples, no children	734.87	144	29.9
Married couples with children	886.25	173	40.7
Oldest child under age 6	856.15	167	7.6
Oldest child aged 6 to 17	969.74	189	22.5
Oldest child aged 18 or older	764.96	149	10.5
Single parent with child under age 18	236.26	46	2.4
Single person	240.14	47	13.9
RACE AND HISPANIC ORIGIN			
Average household	**511.80**	100	100.0
Asian	808.64	158	6.8
Black	258.41	50	6.3
Hispanic	145.79	28	3.6
Non-Hispanic white and other	614.50	120	90.1
REGION			
Average household	**511.80**	100	100.0
Northeast	650.88	127	23.0
Midwest	523.67	102	22.7
South	369.22	72	26.9
West	624.37	122	27.5
EDUCATION			
Average household	**511.80**	100	100.0
Less than high school graduate	57.28	11	1.5
High school graduate	222.68	44	10.8
Some college	250.66	49	10.1
Associate's degree	524.86	103	10.1
Bachelor's degree or more	1,095.01	214	67.5
Bachelor's degree	757.28	148	29.5
Master's, professional, doctoral degree	1,674.98	327	38.0

Note: Market shares may not sum to 100.0 because of rounding and missing categories by household type. "Asian" and "black" include Hispanics and non-Hispanics who identify themselves as being of the respective race alone. "Hispanic" includes people of any race who identify themselves as Hispanic. "Other" includes people who identify themselves as non-Hispanic and as Alaska Native, American Indian, Asian (who are also included in the "Asian" row), or Native Hawaiian or other Pacific Islander, as well as non-Hispanics reporting more than one race.
Source: Calculations by New Strategist based on the Bureau of Labor Statistics' 2012 Consumer Expenditure Survey

Deductions for Social Security

Best customers: Householders aged 35 to 54
Married couples with children at home
Asians

Customer trends: Average household spending on deductions for Social Security should grow until more boomers retire.

Since Social Security deductions are a percentage of earnings up to a cap, households with workers in their peak earning years are the ones that have the most deducted from their paychecks for Social Security. Householders aged 35 to 54, who are in their peak earning years, have 35 to 40 percent more than the average household deducted from their paychecks for Social Security. Married couples with children at home, many of them at the height of their career, spend 67 percent more than the average on this item. Asians, who have the highest income among racial and ethnic groups, spend 39 percent more than the average on Social Security deductions.

For the average household, Social Security deductions are its biggest expense. The average household spends nearly twice as much on Social Security deductions as on federal, state, and local income taxes combined—an average of $4,041 in 2012. Average household spending on Social Security deductions will continue to grow until large numbers of boomers retire.

Table 6.15 Deductions for Social Security

Total household spending $502,717,777,920.00
Average household spends 4,040.62

AGE OF HOUSEHOLDER	AVERAGE HOUSEHOLD SPENDING	BEST CUSTOMERS (index)	BIGGEST CUSTOMERS (market share)
Average household	$4,040.62	100	100.0%
Under age 25	2,132.45	53	3.5
Aged 25 to 34	4,316.32	107	17.3
Aged 35 to 44	5,441.60	135	23.4
Aged 45 to 54	5,673.21	140	27.8
Aged 55 to 64	4,749.15	118	21.5
Aged 65 to 74	1,793.79	44	5.3
Aged 75 or older	514.40	13	1.2

	AVERAGE HOUSEHOLD SPENDING	BEST CUSTOMERS (index)	BIGGEST CUSTOMERS (market share)
HOUSEHOLD INCOME			
Average household	**$4,040.62**	**100**	**100.0%**
Under $20,000	330.08	8	1.7
$20,000 to $39,999	1,473.91	36	8.2
$40,000 to $49,999	2,700.38	67	5.9
$50,000 to $69,999	3,876.66	96	13.9
$70,000 to $79,999	5,100.62	126	7.0
$80,000 to $99,999	6,192.82	153	13.5
$100,000 or more	10,730.06	266	49.7
HOUSEHOLD TYPE			
Average household	**4,040.62**	**100**	**100.0**
Married couples	5,729.36	142	68.9
Married couples, no children	4,528.78	112	23.4
Married couples with children	6,759.35	167	39.3
Oldest child under age 6	6,131.94	152	6.9
Oldest child aged 6 to 17	6,945.11	172	20.4
Oldest child aged 18 or older	6,851.95	170	12.0
Single parent with child under age 18	2,149.06	53	2.8
Single person	1,763.13	44	13.0
RACE AND HISPANIC ORIGIN			
Average household	**4,040.62**	**100**	**100.0**
Asian	5,601.87	139	6.0
Black	2,969.70	73	9.2
Hispanic	3,452.45	85	10.7
Non-Hispanic white and other	4,314.18	107	80.1
REGION			
Average household	**4,040.62**	**100**	**100.0**
Northeast	4,351.61	108	19.4
Midwest	3,956.92	98	21.7
South	3,773.36	93	34.8
West	4,315.60	107	24.1
EDUCATION			
Average household	**4,040.62**	**100**	**100.0**
Less than high school graduate	1,937.58	48	6.3
High school graduate	2,889.46	72	17.8
Some college	3,432.72	85	17.5
Associate's degree	4,372.93	108	10.7
Bachelor's degree or more	6,114.38	151	47.7
Bachelor's degree	5,709.98	141	28.2
Master's, professional, doctoral degree	6,808.87	169	19.6

Note: Market shares may not sum to 100.0 because of rounding and missing categories by household type. "Asian" and "black" include Hispanics and non-Hispanics who identify themselves as being of the respective race alone. "Hispanic" includes people of any race who identify themselves as Hispanic. "Other" includes people who identify themselves as non-Hispanic and as Alaska Native, American Indian, Asian (who are also included in the "Asian" row), or Native Hawaiian or other Pacific Islander, as well as non-Hispanics reporting more than one race.
Source: Calculations by New Strategist based on the Bureau of Labor Statistics' 2012 Consumer Expenditure Survey

Finance Charges, except Mortgage and Vehicle

Best customers: Householders aged 25 to 44
                       Married couples with children at home
                       Single parents
                       Asians
                       Households in the West

Customer trends: Average household spending on finance charges (except mortgage and vehicle) may fall
                       as households cut their debt.

The biggest spenders on finance charges (except mortgage and vehicle) are the households most likely to carry credit card debt. These are families with children—many of them outfitting their homes for expanding families. Householders ranging in age from 25 to 44 spend 25 to 40 percent more than average on finance charges and account for 44 percent of the market. Married couples with children at home spend 38 percent more, the figure peaking at 51 percent above average among couples with school-aged children. Single parents, whose spending approaches average on only a few items, spend 15 percent more than average on finance charges. Asians outspend the average by 30 percent, and households in the West, where many Asians reside, do so by 29 percent.

Average household spending on finance charges is steadily declining, falling 46 percent between 2000 and 2012, after adjusting for inflation. Falling interest rates are one factor behind the decline. As households cut their debt in the years ahead, average household spending on finance charges may continue to decline.

Table 6.16 Finance charges, except mortgage and vehicle

Total household spending $22,585,236,480.00
Average household spends   181.53

	AVERAGE HOUSEHOLD SPENDING	BEST CUSTOMERS (index)	BIGGEST CUSTOMERS (market share)
AGE OF HOUSEHOLDER			
Average household	**$181.53**	**100**	**100.0%**
Under age 25	81.60	45	2.9
Aged 25 to 34	254.69	140	22.7
Aged 35 to 44	227.56	125	21.8
Aged 45 to 54	194.77	107	21.2
Aged 55 to 64	194.37	107	19.6
Aged 65 to 74	136.43	75	9.1
Aged 75 or older	50.60	28	2.7

	AVERAGE HOUSEHOLD SPENDING	BEST CUSTOMERS (index)	BIGGEST CUSTOMERS (market share)
HOUSEHOLD INCOME			
Average household	$181.53	100	100.0%
Under $20,000	92.73	51	10.7
$20,000 to $39,999	128.23	71	15.9
$40,000 to $49,999	180.00	99	8.8
$50,000 to $69,999	169.08	93	13.5
$70,000 to $79,999	300.55	166	9.2
$80,000 to $99,999	284.09	156	13.8
$100,000 or more	272.01	150	28.1
HOUSEHOLD TYPE			
Average household	181.53	100	100.0
Married couples	221.77	122	59.3
Married couples, no children	192.56	106	22.1
Married couples with children	250.72	138	32.5
Oldest child under age 6	266.97	147	6.7
Oldest child aged 6 to 17	273.89	151	17.9
Oldest child aged 18 or older	201.16	111	7.8
Single parent with child under age 18	209.58	115	6.1
Single person	113.56	63	18.6
RACE AND HISPANIC ORIGIN			
Average household	181.53	100	100.0
Asian	236.13	130	5.6
Black	154.94	85	10.7
Hispanic	139.78	77	9.7
Non-Hispanic white and other	192.62	106	79.6
REGION			
Average household	181.53	100	100.0
Northeast	192.48	106	19.1
Midwest	159.48	88	19.5
South	157.97	87	32.4
West	233.41	129	29.0
EDUCATION			
Average household	181.53	100	100.0
Less than high school graduate	63.81	35	4.6
High school graduate	121.59	67	16.7
Some college	208.91	115	23.7
Associate's degree	192.46	106	10.5
Bachelor's degree or more	256.36	141	44.5
Bachelor's degree	242.13	133	26.6
Master's, professional, doctoral degree	280.79	155	18.0

Note: Market shares may not sum to 100.0 because of rounding and missing categories by household type. "Asian" and "black" include Hispanics and non-Hispanics who identify themselves as being of the respective race alone. "Hispanic" includes people of any race who identify themselves as Hispanic. "Other" includes people who identify themselves as non-Hispanic and as Alaska Native, American Indian, Asian (who are also included in the "Asian" row), or Native Hawaiian or other Pacific Islander, as well as non-Hispanics reporting more than one race.
Source: Calculations by New Strategist based on the Bureau of Labor Statistics' 2012 Consumer Expenditure Survey

Funeral Expenses

Best customers: **Householders aged 65 or older**
Married couples with adult children at home
People who live alone
Asians

Customer trends: **Average household spending on funerals should rise as the population ages unless more choose cremation or other less expensive options.**

Not surprisingly, the biggest spenders on funeral expenses are older Americans. Householders aged 65 to 74 spend 82 percent more than average, and those aged 75 or older spend three-and-three-quarter times the average on funeral costs as they bury parents or spouses. Married couples with adult children at home spend 62 percent more than average on funeral costs, whereas people who (now) live alone spend 34 percent more than average on funeral costs. Asian householders spend one-half more than average on funerals.

Average household spending on funeral expenses fell 31 percent between 2000 and 2006, after adjusting for inflation, and then fluctuated in the ensuing six years, for a cumulative drop of 23 percent. This decline occurred despite the aging of the population and may be due to price discounting on caskets and other funeral costs. Spending on funeral expenses should rise with the aging of the population, unless more choose cremation or other less expensive options when laying to rest their loved ones' remains.

Table 6.17 Funeral expenses

Total household spending $8,979,102,720.00
Average household spends   72.17

AGE OF HOUSEHOLDER	AVERAGE HOUSEHOLD SPENDING	BEST CUSTOMERS (index)	BIGGEST CUSTOMERS (market share)
Average household	$72.17	100	100.0%
Under age 25	10.83	15	1.0
Aged 25 to 34	27.60	38	6.2
Aged 35 to 44	25.52	35	6.1
Aged 45 to 54	49.63	69	13.6
Aged 55 to 64	57.77	80	14.6
Aged 65 to 74	131.12	182	21.9
Aged 75 or older	269.82	374	36.5

	AVERAGE HOUSEHOLD SPENDING	BEST CUSTOMERS (index)	BIGGEST CUSTOMERS (market share)
HOUSEHOLD INCOME			
Average household	$72.17	100	100.0%
Under $20,000	57.39	80	16.7
$20,000 to $39,999	87.76	122	27.4
$40,000 to $49,999	50.21	70	6.2
$50,000 to $69,999	38.94	54	7.8
$70,000 to $79,999	46.57	65	3.6
$80,000 to $99,999	27.18	38	3.3
$100,000 or more	134.88	187	35.0
HOUSEHOLD TYPE			
Average household	72.17	100	100.0
Married couples	60.29	84	40.6
Married couples, no children	82.19	114	23.7
Married couples with children	44.19	61	14.4
Oldest child under age 6	19.30	27	1.2
Oldest child aged 6 to 17	10.56	15	1.7
Oldest child aged 18 or older	116.98	162	11.4
Single parent with child under age 18	3.27	5	0.2
Single person	96.59	134	39.7
RACE AND HISPANIC ORIGIN			
Average household	72.17	100	100.0
Asian	108.40	150	6.5
Black	68.92	95	12.0
Hispanic	72.60	101	12.6
Non-Hispanic white and other	72.89	101	75.8
REGION			
Average household	72.17	100	100.0
Northeast	73.86	102	18.5
Midwest	84.91	118	26.1
South	57.08	79	29.5
West	83.24	115	26.0
EDUCATION			
Average household	72.17	100	100.0
Less than high school graduate	42.83	59	7.7
High school graduate	127.24	176	44.0
Some college	73.09	101	20.9
Associate's degree	40.02	55	5.5
Bachelor's degree or more	50.25	70	22.0
Bachelor's degree	47.86	66	13.2
Master's, professional, doctoral degree	54.36	75	8.7

Note: Market shares may not sum to 100.0 because of rounding and missing categories by household type. "Asian" and "black" include Hispanics and non-Hispanics who identify themselves as being of the respective race alone. "Hispanic" includes people of any race who identify themselves as Hispanic. "Other" includes people who identify themselves as non-Hispanic and as Alaska Native, American Indian, Asian (who are also included in the "Asian" row), or Native Hawaiian or other Pacific Islander, as well as non-Hispanics reporting more than one race.
Source: Calculations by New Strategist based on the Bureau of Labor Statistics' 2012 Consumer Expenditure Survey

Insurance, Life and Other Personal except Health

Best customers: Householders aged 45 to 74
                       Married couples

Customer trends: Average household spending on life and other personal insurance (except health) may continue
                       to grow as boomers age.

The biggest spenders on life and other personal insurance are older married couples with assets to protect. Householders ranging in age from 45 to 74 spend 27 to 47 percent more than the average household on life and other personal insurance and control more than two-thirds of the market. Married couples without children at home, most of them empty-nesters, spend 78 percent more than average on such insurance. Those with children at home spend 43 percent more, the figure peaking among couples with adult children at home at 53 percent.

Average household spending on life and other personal insurance fell 37 percent between 2000 and 2010, after adjusting for inflation, and then increased by 5 percent over the ensuing two-year period. The declining popularity of life insurance as an investment vehicle is one factor behind the earlier decline. Average household spending on life and other personal insurance may continue to grow as boomers age.

Table 6.18 Insurance, life and other personal except health

Total household spending $43,870,325,760.00
Average household spends   352.61

AGE OF HOUSEHOLDER	AVERAGE HOUSEHOLD SPENDING	BEST CUSTOMERS (index)	BIGGEST CUSTOMERS (market share)
Average household	$352.61	100	100.0%
Under age 25	49.96	14	0.9
Aged 25 to 34	143.84	41	6.6
Aged 35 to 44	324.59	92	16.0
Aged 45 to 54	446.45	127	25.1
Aged 55 to 64	517.47	147	26.9
Aged 65 to 74	483.66	137	16.5
Aged 75 or older	290.44	82	8.1

	AVERAGE HOUSEHOLD SPENDING	BEST CUSTOMERS (index)	BIGGEST CUSTOMERS (market share)
HOUSEHOLD INCOME			
Average household	**$352.61**	**100**	**100.0%**
Under $20,000	97.42	28	5.8
$20,000 to $39,999	159.86	45	10.2
$40,000 to $49,999	208.97	59	5.2
$50,000 to $69,999	265.91	75	10.9
$70,000 to $79,999	367.78	104	5.8
$80,000 to $99,999	486.83	138	12.2
$100,000 or more	938.46	266	49.8
HOUSEHOLD TYPE			
Average household	**352.61**	**100**	**100.0**
Married couples	554.49	157	76.4
Married couples, no children	627.19	178	37.1
Married couples with children	505.13	143	33.7
Oldest child under age 6	460.41	131	6.0
Oldest child aged 6 to 17	501.44	142	16.9
Oldest child aged 18 or older	540.26	153	10.8
Single parent with child under age 18	141.95	40	2.1
Single person	153.62	44	12.9
RACE AND HISPANIC ORIGIN			
Average household	**352.61**	**100**	**100.0**
Asian	361.03	102	4.4
Black	321.07	91	11.4
Hispanic	112.25	32	4.0
Non-Hispanic white and other	397.54	113	84.6
REGION			
Average household	**352.61**	**100**	**100.0**
Northeast	332.31	94	17.0
Midwest	334.33	95	21.0
South	393.25	112	41.5
West	319.70	91	20.4
EDUCATION			
Average household	**352.61**	**100**	**100.0**
Less than high school graduate	133.29	38	4.9
High school graduate	232.18	66	16.4
Some college	270.78	77	15.8
Associate's degree	283.54	80	7.9
Bachelor's degree or more	613.70	174	54.9
Bachelor's degree	572.96	162	32.4
Master's, professional, doctoral degree	683.66	194	22.5

Note: Market shares may not sum to 100.0 because of rounding and missing categories by household type. "Asian" and "black" include Hispanics and non-Hispanics who identify themselves as being of the respective race alone. "Hispanic" includes people of any race who identify themselves as Hispanic. "Other" includes people who identify themselves as non-Hispanic and as Alaska Native, American Indian, Asian (who are also included in the "Asian" row), or Native Hawaiian or other Pacific Islander, as well as non-Hispanics reporting more than one race.
Source: Calculations by New Strategist based on the Bureau of Labor Statistics' 2012 Consumer Expenditure Survey

Legal Fees

Best customers: Householders aged 35 to 54
Married couples with school-aged children
Single parents

Customer trends: Average household spending on legal fees may decline in the years ahead if a growing share
of households rent rather than own.

People who are divorcing or buying and selling homes are the biggest spenders on legal fees. Householders aged 35 to 54 spend 30 to 45 percent more than average on legal fees as they hire attorneys to negotiate divorce, child custody, and home sales. Married couples with school-aged children spend 27 percent more than average on legal fees, and single parents, whose spending approaches average on only a few items, spend over three times the average on legal fees.

Average household spending on legal fees grew 31 percent between 2000 and 2006, after adjusting for inflation, then fell 23 percent between 2006 and 2012. The slight increase in spending on legal fees between 2010 and 2012 brought average household spending on this item back to what it was in 2000, after adjusting for inflation. Behind the earlier rise in spending on legal fees was the increased number of real estate transactions during the housing boom. Average household spending on legal fees may decline in the years ahead if a growing share of households rent rather than own.

Table 6.19 Legal fees

Total household spending $17,257,743,360.00
Average household spends   138.71

AGE OF HOUSEHOLDER	AVERAGE HOUSEHOLD SPENDING	BEST CUSTOMERS (index)	BIGGEST CUSTOMERS (market share)
Average household	$138.71	100	100.0%
Under age 25	89.37	64	4.2
Aged 25 to 34	107.79	78	12.6
Aged 35 to 44	201.10	145	25.2
Aged 45 to 54	179.89	130	25.7
Aged 55 to 64	127.56	92	16.8
Aged 65 to 74	107.69	78	9.4
Aged 75 or older	87.93	63	6.2

	AVERAGE HOUSEHOLD SPENDING	BEST CUSTOMERS (index)	BIGGEST CUSTOMERS (market share)
HOUSEHOLD INCOME			
Average household	**$138.71**	**100**	**100.0%**
Under $20,000	51.84	37	7.9
$20,000 to $39,999	99.80	72	16.2
$40,000 to $49,999	116.25	84	7.4
$50,000 to $69,999	160.82	116	16.7
$70,000 to $79,999	104.49	75	4.2
$80,000 to $99,999	135.25	98	8.6
$100,000 or more	288.58	208	39.0
HOUSEHOLD TYPE			
Average household	**138.71**	**100**	**100.0**
Married couples	122.80	89	43.0
Married couples, no children	102.74	74	15.4
Married couples with children	148.77	107	25.2
Oldest child under age 6	110.38	80	3.6
Oldest child aged 6 to 17	176.41	127	15.1
Oldest child aged 18 or older	127.00	92	6.5
Single parent with child under age 18	434.93	314	16.4
Single person	123.50	89	26.4
RACE AND HISPANIC ORIGIN			
Average household	**138.71**	**100**	**100.0**
Asian	37.48	27	1.2
Black	59.12	43	5.4
Hispanic	91.15	66	8.2
Non-Hispanic white and other	160.60	116	86.9
REGION			
Average household	**138.71**	**100**	**100.0**
Northeast	201.43	145	26.2
Midwest	92.92	67	14.9
South	119.14	86	32.0
West	165.90	120	27.0
EDUCATION			
Average household	**138.71**	**100**	**100.0**
Less than high school graduate	74.93	54	7.1
High school graduate	100.99	73	18.2
Some college	104.79	76	15.6
Associate's degree	100.06	72	7.1
Bachelor's degree or more	229.21	165	52.1
Bachelor's degree	207.47	150	29.8
Master's, professional, doctoral degree	266.56	192	22.3

Note: Market shares may not sum to 100.0 because of rounding and missing categories by household type. "Asian" and "black" include Hispanics and non-Hispanics who identify themselves as being of the respective race alone. "Hispanic" includes people of any race who identify themselves as Hispanic. "Other" includes people who identify themselves as non-Hispanic and as Alaska Native, American Indian, Asian (who are also included in the "Asian" row), or Native Hawaiian or other Pacific Islander, as well as non-Hispanics reporting more than one race.
Source: Calculations by New Strategist based on the Bureau of Labor Statistics' 2012 Consumer Expenditure Survey

Lottery and Gambling Losses

Best customers:　　Householders aged 35 to 44 and 55 or older
People who live alone
Asians
Households in the Northeast and West

Customer trends:　　Average household spending on lotteries and gambling is likely to rise in the years ahead as casinos become more widespread and more boomers retire.

The biggest spenders (losers) on lotteries and gambling are households with discretionary time and income. Hoping to strike it rich they buy lottery tickets, travel to Las Vegas, or visit Indian reservations to try their luck. Householders aged 55 or older lost 17 to 62 percent more than average and those aged 35 to 44 gambled away 43 percent more than the average household. People who live alone, who generally spend far less than average on most items, lost 37 percent more than the average amount on lotteries and gambling. Households in the West gamble away 58 percent more than the average household, and those in the Northeast 36 percent more.

Average household losses on lotteries and gambling rose by 46 percent between 2000 and 2006, after adjusting or inflation. Spending held essentially steady between 2006 and 2010, then declined by 30 percent from 2010 to 2012. Spending on this item is likely to rise again in the years ahead as casinos become more widespread and more boomers retire.

Table 6.20 **Lottery and gambling losses**

Total household spending　　　　$7,207,418,880.00
Average household spends　　　　57.93

AGE OF HOUSEHOLDER	AVERAGE HOUSEHOLD SPENDING	BEST CUSTOMERS (index)	BIGGEST CUSTOMERS (market share)
Average household	$57.93	100	100.0%
Under age 25	11.54	20	1.3
Aged 25 to 34	32.11	55	9.0
Aged 35 to 44	83.11	143	24.9
Aged 45 to 54	37.53	65	12.8
Aged 55 to 64	67.58	117	21.4
Aged 65 to 74	74.15	128	15.4
Aged 75 or older	93.61	162	15.8

	AVERAGE HOUSEHOLD SPENDING	BEST CUSTOMERS (index)	BIGGEST CUSTOMERS (market share)
HOUSEHOLD INCOME			
Average household	**$57.93**	**100**	**100.0%**
Under $20,000	44.04	76	16.0
$20,000 to $39,999	63.04	109	24.5
$40,000 to $49,999	54.42	94	8.3
$50,000 to $69,999	61.48	106	15.3
$70,000 to $79,999	28.32	49	2.7
$80,000 to $99,999	42.39	73	6.5
$100,000 or more	80.17	138	25.9
HOUSEHOLD TYPE			
Average household	**57.93**	**100**	**100.0**
Married couples	51.16	88	42.9
Married couples, no children	56.26	97	20.2
Married couples with children	37.15	64	15.1
Oldest child under age 6	16.71	29	1.3
Oldest child aged 6 to 17	44.18	76	9.1
Oldest child aged 18 or older	38.14	66	4.6
Single parent with child under age 18	11.83	20	1.1
Single person	79.28	137	40.6
RACE AND HISPANIC ORIGIN			
Average household	**57.93**	**100**	**100.0**
Asian	73.17	126	5.5
Black	35.00	60	7.6
Hispanic	29.09	50	6.3
Non-Hispanic white and other	66.46	115	86.1
REGION			
Average household	**57.93**	**100**	**100.0**
Northeast	78.73	136	24.5
Midwest	44.66	77	17.1
South	35.38	61	22.7
West	91.80	158	35.7
EDUCATION			
Average household	**57.93**	**100**	**100.0**
Less than high school graduate	21.14	36	4.8
High school graduate	68.34	118	29.4
Some college	87.49	151	31.1
Associate's degree	32.69	56	5.6
Bachelor's degree or more	51.64	89	28.1
Bachelor's degree	49.64	86	17.1
Master's, professional, doctoral degree	55.03	95	11.0

Note: Market shares may not sum to 100.0 because of rounding and missing categories by household type. "Asian" and "black" include Hispanics and non-Hispanics who identify themselves as being of the respective race alone. "Hispanic" includes people of any race who identify themselves as Hispanic. "Other" includes people who identify themselves as non-Hispanic and as Alaska Native, American Indian, Asian (who are also included in the "Asian" row), or Native Hawaiian or other Pacific Islander, as well as non-Hispanics reporting more than one race.
Source: Calculations by New Strategist based on the Bureau of Labor Statistics' 2012 Consumer Expenditure Survey

Occupational Expenses

Best customers: Householders aged 45 to 64
Married couples
Asians
Households in the West and Northeast

Customer trends: Average household spending on occupational expenses may continue to decline in the years ahead unless manufacturing employment begins to grow.

The biggest spenders on occupational expenses are households with workers, particularly union members and licensed professionals such as social workers. Householders ranging in age from 45 to 64 spent 25 to 41 percent more than average on this item. Married couples, most of them dual earners, spend 36 percent more than average on occupational expenses, the figure peaking among those with adult children at home—the household type with the most workers—at 91 percent above average. Asians spend 19 percent more than average on this item. Households in the West spend 43 percent more than average on occupational expenses, and those in the Northeast spend 30 percent more.

Average household spending on occupational expenses fell steeply between 2000 and 2012, down 62 percent after adjusting for inflation. Behind the decline is the loss of union jobs as manufacturing employment fell over the years. Spending on occupational expenses may continue to decline in the years ahead unless manufacturing employment begins to grow.

Table 6.21 Occupational expenses

Total household spending $6,022,978,560.00
Average household spends 48.41

AGE OF HOUSEHOLDER	AVERAGE HOUSEHOLD SPENDING	BEST CUSTOMERS (index)	BIGGEST CUSTOMERS (market share)
Average household	**$48.41**	**100**	**100.0%**
Under age 25	23.55	49	3.2
Aged 25 to 34	56.54	117	18.9
Aged 35 to 44	52.87	109	19.0
Aged 45 to 54	68.15	141	27.9
Aged 55 to 64	60.53	125	22.9
Aged 65 to 74	28.47	59	7.1
Aged 75 or older	5.67	12	1.1

	AVERAGE HOUSEHOLD SPENDING	BEST CUSTOMERS (index)	BIGGEST CUSTOMERS (market share)
HOUSEHOLD INCOME			
Average household	$48.41	100	100.0%
Under $20,000	6.04	12	2.6
$20,000 to $39,999	19.47	40	9.1
$40,000 to $49,999	39.03	81	7.1
$50,000 to $69,999	38.46	79	11.5
$70,000 to $79,999	70.19	145	8.1
$80,000 to $99,999	73.95	153	13.5
$100,000 or more	124.46	257	48.1
HOUSEHOLD TYPE			
Average household	48.41	100	100.0
Married couples	65.67	136	65.9
Married couples, no children	61.58	127	26.5
Married couples with children	73.98	153	35.9
Oldest child under age 6	65.45	135	6.2
Oldest child aged 6 to 17	66.20	137	16.3
Oldest child aged 18 or older	92.61	191	13.5
Single parent with child under age 18	36.45	75	3.9
Single person	20.93	43	12.8
RACE AND HISPANIC ORIGIN			
Average household	48.41	100	100.0
Asian	57.53	119	5.2
Black	30.34	63	7.9
Hispanic	32.93	68	8.5
Non-Hispanic white and other	53.95	111	83.6
REGION			
Average household	48.41	100	100.0
Northeast	62.71	130	23.4
Midwest	55.48	115	25.4
South	24.71	51	19.0
West	69.18	143	32.2
EDUCATION			
Average household	48.41	100	100.0
Less than high school graduate	15.51	32	4.2
High school graduate	39.45	81	20.3
Some college	33.94	70	14.4
Associate's degree	54.94	113	11.2
Bachelor's degree or more	76.53	158	49.9
Bachelor's degree	56.28	116	23.2
Master's, professional, doctoral degree	111.30	230	26.7

Note: Market shares may not sum to 100.0 because of rounding and missing categories by household type. "Asian" and "black" include Hispanics and non-Hispanics who identify themselves as being of the respective race alone. "Hispanic" includes people of any race who identify themselves as Hispanic. "Other" includes people who identify themselves as non-Hispanic and as Alaska Native, American Indian, Asian (who are also included in the "Asian" row), or Native Hawaiian or other Pacific Islander, as well as non-Hispanics reporting more than one race.
Source: Calculations by New Strategist based on the Bureau of Labor Statistics' 2012 Consumer Expenditure Survey

Safe Deposit Box Rental

Best customers: Householders aged 55 or older
Married couples without children at home
Asians and non-Hispanic whites

Customer trends: Average household spending on safe deposit box rentals will continue to decline as paper documents give way to electronic records.

Older Americans are the best customers of safe deposit box rentals because they grew up in an era when only a single paper copy of many important documents existed. Householders aged 55 to 64 spend 26 percent more than average on safe deposit boxes, householders aged 65 to 74 spend 76 percent more, and householders aged 75 or older spend more than two times the average. Together, householders aged 55 or older control two-thirds of the market for safe deposit box rentals. Married couples without children at home, many of them empty-nesters, spend 93 percent more than average on this item. Asians spend two-and-one-third times the average and non-Hispanic whites spend 24 percent more.

Average household spending on safe deposit boxes has plummeted since 2000, falling by 45 percent between then and 2012, after adjusting for inflation. Electronic record keeping and high-tech home security systems are reducing the need for safe deposit boxes, which should limit spending on this item in the future.

Table 6.22 **Safe deposit box rental**

Total household spending $418,037,760.00
Average household spends 3.36

AGE OF HOUSEHOLDER	AVERAGE HOUSEHOLD SPENDING	BEST CUSTOMERS (index)	BIGGEST CUSTOMERS (market share)
Average household	$3.36	100	100.0%
Under age 25	0.12	4	0.2
Aged 25 to 34	0.90	27	4.3
Aged 35 to 44	1.39	41	7.2
Aged 45 to 54	3.57	106	21.0
Aged 55 to 64	4.24	126	23.1
Aged 65 to 74	5.91	176	21.2
Aged 75 or older	7.83	233	22.8

	AVERAGE HOUSEHOLD SPENDING	BEST CUSTOMERS (index)	BIGGEST CUSTOMERS (market share)
HOUSEHOLD INCOME			
Average household	**$3.36**	**100**	**100.0%**
Under $20,000	1.36	41	8.5
$20,000 to $39,999	2.26	67	15.2
$40,000 to $49,999	3.32	99	8.7
$50,000 to $69,999	2.65	79	11.4
$70,000 to $79,999	3.91	116	6.5
$80,000 to $99,999	3.92	117	10.3
$100,000 or more	7.04	210	39.2
HOUSEHOLD TYPE			
Average household	**3.36**	**100**	**100.0**
Married couples	4.28	127	61.9
Married couples, no children	6.48	193	40.2
Married couples with children	2.65	79	18.5
Oldest child under age 6	2.08	62	2.8
Oldest child aged 6 to 17	2.67	79	9.5
Oldest child aged 18 or older	2.97	88	6.2
Single parent with child under age 18	0.47	14	0.7
Single person	2.87	85	25.4
RACE AND HISPANIC ORIGIN			
Average household	**3.36**	**100**	**100.0**
Asian	7.89	235	10.2
Black	1.07	32	4.0
Hispanic	0.73	22	2.7
Non-Hispanic white and other	4.17	124	93.2
REGION			
Average household	**3.36**	**100**	**100.0**
Northeast	3.51	104	18.9
Midwest	3.21	96	21.2
South	3.22	96	35.7
West	3.60	107	24.1
EDUCATION			
Average household	**3.36**	**100**	**100.0**
Less than high school graduate	1.00	30	3.9
High school graduate	2.17	65	16.1
Some college	2.75	82	16.9
Associate's degree	2.64	79	7.8
Bachelor's degree or more	5.88	175	55.2
Bachelor's degree	4.76	142	28.2
Master's, professional, doctoral degree	7.80	232	26.9

Note: Market shares may not sum to 100.0 because of rounding and missing categories by household type. "Asian" and "black" include Hispanics and non-Hispanics who identify themselves as being of the respective race alone. "Hispanic" includes people of any race who identify themselves as Hispanic. "Other" includes people who identify themselves as non-Hispanic and as Alaska Native, American Indian, Asian (who are also included in the "Asian" row), or Native Hawaiian or other Pacific Islander, as well as non-Hispanics reporting more than one race.
Source: Calculations by New Strategist based on the Bureau of Labor Statistics' 2012 Consumer Expenditure Survey

Shopping Club Membership Fees

Best customers: Householders aged 35 to 74
Married couples
Asians
Households in the West

Customer trends: Average household spending on shopping club membership fees may decline as competition
among discounters heats up.

Middle-aged and older married couples are the best customers of shopping club memberships. Householders ranging in age from 35 to 74 spend 13 to 19 percent more than average on this item. Married couples spend 44 percent more than average on shopping club memberships, the figure peaking at 68 percent among those with adult children at home. Households in the West spend 76 percent more than average on this item while those in the other regions spend much less than average. Asians, many of whom live in the West, spend three-quarters more than average on shopping club memberships.

Average household spending on shopping club memberships is minimal and may fall in the years ahead as competition among discounters reduces the need to "join the club" for savings.

Table 6.23 Shopping club membership fees

Total household spending $1,264,066,560.00
Average household spends   10.16

	AVERAGE HOUSEHOLD SPENDING	BEST CUSTOMERS (index)	BIGGEST CUSTOMERS (market share)
AGE OF HOUSEHOLDER			
Average household	**$10.16**	**100**	**100.0%**
Under age 25	2.89	28	1.9
Aged 25 to 34	8.07	79	12.8
Aged 35 to 44	11.67	115	19.9
Aged 45 to 54	12.10	119	23.6
Aged 55 to 64	11.97	118	21.6
Aged 65 to 74	11.43	113	13.6
Aged 75 or older	6.93	68	6.7

	AVERAGE HOUSEHOLD SPENDING	BEST CUSTOMERS (index)	BIGGEST CUSTOMERS (market share)
HOUSEHOLD INCOME			
Average household	$10.16	100	100.0%
Under $20,000	2.31	23	4.8
$20,000 to $39,999	6.02	59	13.4
$40,000 to $49,999	9.24	91	8.0
$50,000 to $69,999	11.12	109	15.8
$70,000 to $79,999	12.56	124	6.9
$80,000 to $99,999	15.72	155	13.7
$100,000 or more	20.32	200	37.4
HOUSEHOLD TYPE			
Average household	10.16	100	100.0
Married couples	14.64	144	70.0
Married couples, no children	13.36	131	27.4
Married couples with children	15.35	151	35.5
Oldest child under age 6	12.37	122	5.6
Oldest child aged 6 to 17	15.51	153	18.2
Oldest child aged 18 or older	17.02	168	11.8
Single parent with child under age 18	5.59	55	2.9
Single person	4.69	46	13.7
RACE AND HISPANIC ORIGIN			
Average household	10.16	100	100.0
Asian	18.02	177	7.7
Black	5.61	55	6.9
Hispanic	9.23	91	11.4
Non-Hispanic white and other	11.06	109	81.7
REGION			
Average household	10.16	100	100.0
Northeast	7.87	77	14.0
Midwest	7.59	75	16.6
South	8.11	80	29.7
West	17.90	176	39.7
EDUCATION			
Average household	10.16	100	100.0
Less than high school graduate	5.84	57	7.5
High school graduate	6.57	65	16.1
Some college	8.71	86	17.7
Associate's degree	11.19	110	10.9
Bachelor's degree or more	15.41	152	47.8
Bachelor's degree	14.25	140	28.0
Master's, professional, doctoral degree	17.41	171	19.9

Note: Market shares may not sum to 100.0 because of rounding and missing categories by household type. "Asian" and "black" include Hispanics and non-Hispanics who identify themselves as being of the respective race alone. "Hispanic" includes people of any race who identify themselves as Hispanic. "Other" includes people who identify themselves as non-Hispanic and as Alaska Native, American Indian, Asian (who are also included in the "Asian" row), or Native Hawaiian or other Pacific Islander, as well as non-Hispanics reporting more than one race.
Source: Calculations by New Strategist based on the Bureau of Labor Statistics' 2012 Consumer Expenditure Survey

Support for College Students

Best customers: Householders aged 45 to 64 and aged 75 or older
Married couples without children at home
Married couples with adult children at home
Asians and non-Hispanic whites
Households in the West
College graduates

Customer trends: Average household spending on support for college students may decline in the years ahead as parents search for ways to cut college costs.

Many parents give money to their college-bound children for living expenses and other items. Householders aged 45 to 64 spend 52 to 85 percent more than average on such support and account for nearly two-thirds of spending. Householders aged 75 or older spend 60 percent more, helping their grandchildren with college costs. Married couples without children at home (most of them empty-nesters) spend 56 percent more than average on this item, and those with adult children at home spend three times the average on support for college students. Asians spend 23 percent more than average on student support. Households in the West spend 30 percent more than average on support for college students. College graduates spend over twice the average on this item.

Average household spending on support for college students held steady over the past 12 years. Average household spending on this item may decline in the years ahead as parents search for ways to cut college costs.

Table 6.24 Support for college students

Total household spending $13,041,285,120.00
Average household spends 104.82

AGE OF HOUSEHOLDER	AVERAGE HOUSEHOLD SPENDING	BEST CUSTOMERS (index)	BIGGEST CUSTOMERS (market share)
Average household	$104.82	100	100.0%
Under age 25	6.18	6	0.4
Aged 25 to 34	11.88	11	1.8
Aged 35 to 44	46.72	45	7.7
Aged 45 to 54	193.71	185	36.6
Aged 55 to 64	159.16	152	27.8
Aged 65 to 74	87.35	83	10.0
Aged 75 or older	167.68	160	15.6

	AVERAGE HOUSEHOLD SPENDING	BEST CUSTOMERS (index)	BIGGEST CUSTOMERS (market share)
HOUSEHOLD INCOME			
Average household	**$104.82**	**100**	**100.0%**
Under $20,000	17.28	16	3.5
$20,000 to $39,999	88.80	85	19.1
$40,000 to $49,999	61.52	59	5.2
$50,000 to $69,999	67.45	64	9.3
$70,000 to $79,999	76.22	73	4.1
$80,000 to $99,999	130.88	125	11.0
$100,000 or more	268.02	256	47.9
HOUSEHOLD TYPE			
Average household	**104.82**	**100**	**100.0**
Married couples	155.38	148	72.0
Married couples, no children	163.14	156	32.4
Married couples with children	166.73	159	37.4
Oldest child under age 6	3.24	3	0.1
Oldest child aged 6 to 17	139.24	133	15.8
Oldest child aged 18 or older	318.79	304	21.5
Single parent with child under age 18	31.57	30	1.6
Single person	71.82	69	20.3
RACE AND HISPANIC ORIGIN			
Average household	**104.82**	**100**	**100.0**
Asian	128.92	123	5.3
Black	61.88	59	7.4
Hispanic	40.37	39	4.8
Non-Hispanic white and other	122.54	117	87.7
REGION			
Average household	**104.82**	**100**	**100.0**
Northeast	91.24	87	15.7
Midwest	90.15	86	19.1
South	101.10	96	35.9
West	136.27	130	29.3
EDUCATION			
Average household	**104.82**	**100**	**100.0**
Less than high school graduate	24.48	23	3.0
High school graduate	26.55	25	6.3
Some college	65.20	62	12.8
Associate's degree	97.04	93	9.1
Bachelor's degree or more	228.27	218	68.7
Bachelor's degree	183.33	175	34.9
Master's, professional, doctoral degree	305.44	291	33.8

Note: Market shares may not sum to 100.0 because of rounding and missing categories by household type. "Asian" and "black" include Hispanics and non-Hispanics who identify themselves as being of the respective race alone. "Hispanic" includes people of any race who identify themselves as Hispanic. "Other" includes people who identify themselves as non-Hispanic and as Alaska Native, American Indian, Asian (who are also included in the "Asian" row), or Native Hawaiian or other Pacific Islander, as well as non-Hispanics reporting more than one race.
Source: Calculations by New Strategist based on the Bureau of Labor Statistics' 2012 Consumer Expenditure Survey

Tax, Federal Income (Net, after Refund)

Best customers: **Householders aged 45 to 64**
High-income households
Married couples
Asians and non-Hispanics whites
College graduates

Customer trends: **Average household spending on federal income taxes is likely to climb as tax rates increase**
to pay for services demanded by the middle class.

Not surprisingly, households with the highest incomes pay the most in federal income tax. Households with incomes of $100,000 or more pay 86 percent of federal income taxes. Householders aged 45 to 64, who have the highest incomes, pay 29 to 98 percent more than average in federal taxes. Married couples, the most affluent household type, pay 28 percent more than average in federal income taxes, the figure peaking at 54 percent above average among couples without children at home, most of them empty-nesters. Asians pay 16 percent more than average in federal income taxes, and non-Hispanics whites pay 29 percent more. Households headed by college graduates, who dominate the nation's affluent, spend over twice the average on federal income taxes.

The average household paid $1,568 in federal income taxes in 2012, 31 percent more than in 2010, the year when overall household spending bottomed out. Average household spending on federal income taxes had fallen by a significant 63 percent between 2000 and 2010, after adjusting for inflation. In the years ahead, spending on this item is likely to rise as the aging middle class demands more services.

Table 6.25 Tax, federal income (net, after refund)

Total household spending $195,125,345,280.00
Average household spends   1,568.33

AGE OF HOUSEHOLDER	AVERAGE HOUSEHOLD SPENDING	BEST CUSTOMERS (index)	BIGGEST CUSTOMERS (market share)
Average household	$1,568.33	100	100.0%
Under age 25	2,481.26	158	10.4
Aged 25 to 34	870.84	56	9.0
Aged 35 to 44	1,144.06	73	12.7
Aged 45 to 54	2,026.95	129	25.6
Aged 55 to 64	3,097.94	198	36.2
Aged 65 to 74	662.52	42	5.1
Aged 75 or older	186.84	12	1.2

	AVERAGE HOUSEHOLD SPENDING	BEST CUSTOMERS (index)	BIGGEST CUSTOMERS (market share)
HOUSEHOLD INCOME			
Average household	**$1,568.33**	**100**	**100.0%**
Under $20,000	−242.90	−15	−3.3
$20,000 to $39,999	−283.00	−18	−4.1
$40,000 to $49,999	157.71	10	0.9
$50,000 to $69,999	625.12	40	5.8
$70,000 to $79,999	1,337.45	85	4.8
$80,000 to $99,999	1,795.58	114	10.1
$100,000 or more	7,188.72	458	85.8
HOUSEHOLD TYPE			
Average household	**1,568.33**	**100**	**100.0**
Married couples	2,011.83	128	62.3
Married couples, no children	2,411.03	154	32.0
Married couples with children	1,812.52	116	27.2
Oldest child under age 6	1,752.65	112	5.1
Oldest child aged 6 to 17	1,726.30	110	13.1
Oldest child aged 18 or older	1,996.57	127	9.0
Single parent with child under age 18	−515.57	−33	−1.7
Single person	1,114.12	71	21.1
RACE AND HISPANIC ORIGIN			
Average household	**1,568.33**	**100**	**100.0**
Asian	1,823.72	116	5.0
Black	178.04	11	1.4
Hispanic	242.58	15	1.9
Non-Hispanic white and other	2,019.65	129	96.7
REGION			
Average household	**1,568.33**	**100**	**100.0**
Northeast	1,767.67	113	20.3
Midwest	1,872.05	119	26.5
South	1,250.00	80	29.7
West	1,635.94	104	23.5
EDUCATION			
Average household	**1,568.33**	**100**	**100.0**
Less than high school graduate	41.03	3	0.3
High school graduate	461.52	29	7.3
Some college	1,392.05	89	18.3
Associate's degree	1,225.41	78	7.7
Bachelor's degree or more	3,298.21	210	66.3
Bachelor's degree	2,404.62	153	30.6
Master's, professional, doctoral degree	4,832.79	308	35.8

Note: Market shares may not sum to 100.0 because of rounding and missing categories by household type. "Asian" and "black" include Hispanics and non-Hispanics who identify themselves as being of the respective race alone. "Hispanic" includes people of any race who identify themselves as Hispanic. "Other" includes people who identify themselves as non-Hispanic and as Alaska Native, American Indian, Asian (who are also included in the "Asian" row), or Native Hawaiian or other Pacific Islander, as well as non-Hispanics reporting more than one race.
Source: Calculations by New Strategist based on the Bureau of Labor Statistics' 2012 Consumer Expenditure Survey

Tax, State and Local Income (Net, after Refund)

Best customers: Householders aged 45 to 64
High-income households
Married couples
Asians and non-Hispanic whites
Households in the Northeast

Customer trends: Average household spending on state and local income taxes will rise as states and localities, squeezed for cash, raise taxes to pay for necessary services.

Households with the highest incomes pay the most in state and local income taxes. Households with incomes of $100,000 or more pay 68 percent of state and local income taxes. Householders aged 45 to 64, who have the highest incomes, spend 29 to 73 percent more than average on this item. Married couples, the most affluent household type, pay 31 percent more than average in state and local income taxes, the figure peaking at 48 percent among those with school-aged children. Asians, who as a group are relatively affluent, pay 17 percent more than average in state and local income taxes. Non-Hispanic whites pay 20 percent more. Households in the Northeast pay 39 percent more than average on these taxes.

Average household spending on state and local income taxes fell by a significant 32 percent between 2000 and 2010, after adjusting for inflation. That steep decline squeezed states and localities for cash, and the pendulum is likely to swing the other way. Between 2010 and 2012, spending on state and local income taxes grew 4 percent. Look for average household spending on state and local income taxes to rise further.

Table 6.26 Tax, state and local income (net, after refund)

Total household spending $65,452,769,280.00
Average household spends   526.08

AGE OF HOUSEHOLDER	AVERAGE HOUSEHOLD SPENDING	BEST CUSTOMERS (index)	BIGGEST CUSTOMERS (market share)
Average household	$526.08	100	100.0%
Under age 25	477.71	91	6.0
Aged 25 to 34	459.97	87	14.1
Aged 35 to 44	541.61	103	17.9
Aged 45 to 54	680.34	129	25.6
Aged 55 to 64	910.95	173	31.7
Aged 65 to 74	159.58	30	3.7
Aged 75 or older	59.18	11	1.1

	AVERAGE HOUSEHOLD SPENDING	BEST CUSTOMERS (index)	BIGGEST CUSTOMERS (market share)
HOUSEHOLD INCOME			
Average household	**$526.08**	**100**	**100.0%**
Under $20,000	7.28	1	0.3
$20,000 to $39,999	59.08	11	2.5
$40,000 to $49,999	202.30	38	3.4
$50,000 to $69,999	360.90	69	9.9
$70,000 to $79,999	452.70	86	4.8
$80,000 to $99,999	676.57	129	11.3
$100,000 or more	1,902.75	362	67.7
HOUSEHOLD TYPE			
Average household	**526.08**	**100**	**100.0**
Married couples	691.20	131	63.8
Married couples, no children	668.94	127	26.5
Married couples with children	741.15	141	33.1
Oldest child under age 6	666.55	127	5.8
Oldest child aged 6 to 17	777.63	148	17.6
Oldest child aged 18 or older	727.89	138	9.8
Single parent with child under age 18	153.84	29	1.5
Single person	345.51	66	19.5
RACE AND HISPANIC ORIGIN			
Average household	**526.08**	**100**	**100.0**
Asian	615.57	117	5.1
Black	220.72	42	5.3
Hispanic	204.35	39	4.9
Non-Hispanic white and other	629.72	120	89.8
REGION			
Average household	**526.08**	**100**	**100.0**
Northeast	731.08	139	25.1
Midwest	603.43	115	25.4
South	343.16	65	24.3
West	588.09	112	25.2
EDUCATION			
Average household	**526.08**	**100**	**100.0**
Less than high school graduate	90.31	17	2.2
High school graduate	312.68	59	14.8
Some college	420.73	80	16.5
Associate's degree	412.84	78	7.7
Bachelor's degree or more	979.48	186	58.7
Bachelor's degree	707.42	134	26.8
Master's, professional, doctoral degree	1,446.70	275	31.9

Note: Market shares may not sum to 100.0 because of rounding and missing categories by household type. "Asian" and "black" include Hispanics and non-Hispanics who identify themselves as being of the respective race alone. "Hispanic" includes people of any race who identify themselves as Hispanic. "Other" includes people who identify themselves as non-Hispanic and as Alaska Native, American Indian, Asian (who are also included in the "Asian" row), or Native Hawaiian or other Pacific Islander, as well as non-Hispanics reporting more than one race.
Source: Calculations by New Strategist based on the Bureau of Labor Statistics' 2012 Consumer Expenditure Survey

Chapter 7.
Furnishings and Equipment

Household Spending on Furnishings and Equipment, 2000 to 2012

In 2012 the average household spent $1,239 on home furnishings and equipment. Average household spending on everything from major appliances to indoor plants and outdoor furniture declined 21 percent since the overall peak spending year of 2006, after adjusting for inflation. Household spending on home furnishings had been stable between 2000 and 2006. Behind the considerable recent decline in spending on furnishings was the Great Recession, which brought foreclosures and curtailed discretionary spending.

The largest home furnishings category, major appliances (such as refrigerators and washing machines), accounts for 16 percent of the dollars spent on home furnishings and equipment. Average household spending on major appliances, which had grown by 9 percent between 2000 and 2006, fell 28 percent between 2006 and 2012, after adjusting for inflation. Some categories experienced even larger declines. Average household spending on curtains and draperies fell 65 percent over the latter time period; window coverings dropped 52 percent; wall units, cabinets, and other furniture experienced a 41 percent decline; and kitchen and dining room furniture saw a 40 percent decrease, to name just the four biggest losing categories.

Other categories saw gains, some quite large. Average household spending on power and hand tools rose 41 percent from 2006 to 2012, after adjusting for inflation. Spending on lamps and light fixtures increased by a solid 40 percent, and spending on portable heating and cooling equipment grew 35 percent since 2006. Outdoor furniture, outdoor equipment, bathroom linens, slipcovers and decorative pillows, and mattresses and springs were the only home furnishings and equipment categories on which average household spending changed by less than 10 percent (plus or minus) during the 2000-to-2012 time period.

Average household spending on home furnishings may increase in the years ahead as millions of boomers become empty-nesters and redecorate their homes, but only if discretionary income grows.

Spending on furnishings and equipment

(average annual spending of households on furnishings and equipment, 2000, 2006, 2010 and 2012; in 2012 dollars)

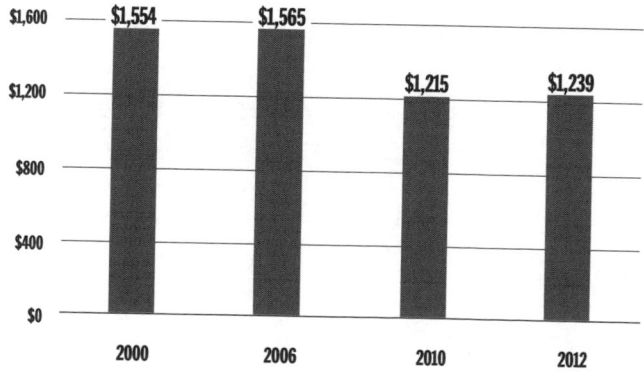

Table 7.1 Household furnishings and equipment spending, 2000 to 2012

(average annual household spending on household furnishings and equipment and percent distribution, by category, 2000 to 2012; percent change and percentage point change in spending, 2000–06, 2006–12, and 2010–12; in 2012 dollars; ranked by amount spent)

	average annual household spending (in 2012$)				percent change		
	2012	2010	2006	2000	2010–12	2006–12	2000–06
Average household spending on household furnishings and equipment	**$1,238.86**	**$1,214.70**	**$1,565.42**	**$1,553.52**	**2.0%**	**–20.9%**	**0.8%**
Appliances, major	197.26	220.26	274.76	251.94	–10.4	–28.2	9.1
Decorative items for the home	126.84	106.73	157.03	236.39	18.8	–19.2	–33.6
Sofas	101.36	88.73	132.16	118.86	14.2	–23.3	11.2
Mattresses and springs	76.43	51.19	74.33	70.52	49.3	2.8	5.4
Lawn and garden equipment	71.11	39.02	56.58	62.43	82.2	25.7	–9.4
Bedroom linens	67.43	48.38	85.92	59.36	39.4	–21.5	44.7
Bedroom furniture, except mattresses and springs	63.24	65.87	96.78	92.14	–4.0	–34.7	5.0
Housewares	63.14	69.41	95.49	86.49	–9.0	–33.9	10.4
Plants and fresh flowers, indoor	53.57	44.85	52.58	76.01	19.4	1.9	–30.8
Power and hand tools	51.13	55.79	36.35	38.11	–8.4	40.7	–4.6
Living room chairs and tables	47.49	55.41	72.64	81.37	–14.3	–34.6	–10.7
Wall units, cabinets, and other furniture	42.39	43.14	72.06	67.48	–1.7	–41.2	6.8
Kitchen and dining room furniture	31.62	33.47	52.89	61.95	–5.5	–40.2	–14.6
Lamps and lighting fixtures	26.83	23.09	19.22	14.40	16.2	39.6	33.5
Appliances, kitchen, small electric	25.90	23.01	21.73	22.72	12.6	19.2	–4.4
Outdoor equipment	24.51	36.58	32.64	24.52	–33.0	–24.9	33.1
Bathroom linens	23.90	19.67	30.49	23.40	21.5	–21.6	30.3
Infants' equipment and furniture	23.01	25.85	27.55	18.97	–11.0	–16.5	45.2
Laundry and cleaning equipment	19.59	18.77	17.45	13.44	4.3	12.3	29.8
Outdoor furniture	19.36	27.79	17.85	20.21	–30.3	8.5	–11.7
Floor coverings, nonpermanent	16.22	18.30	24.85	20.29	–11.4	–34.7	22.5
Window coverings	14.64	24.17	30.37	17.36	–39.4	–51.8	75.0
Closet and storage items	12.60	16.69	20.16	10.71	–24.5	–37.5	88.3
Curtains and draperies	9.88	18.63	27.85	28.08	–47.0	–64.5	–0.8
Portable heating and cooling equipment	8.84	19.72	6.56	7.29	–55.2	34.8	–10.1
Sewing materials for household items	8.48	10.03	13.72	13.00	–15.5	–38.2	5.6
Kitchen and dining room linens	8.15	6.23	9.84	12.41	30.8	–17.2	–20.7
Slipcovers and decorative pillows	3.94	3.91	5.58	3.67	0.9	–29.4	52.2

PERCENT DISTRIBUTION OF SPENDING	average annual household spending (in 2012$)				percentage point change		
	2012	2010	2006	2000	2010–12	2006–12	2000–06
Average household spending on household furnishings and equipment	**100.0%**	**100.0%**	**100.0%**	**100.0%**	–	–	–
Appliances, major	15.9	18.1	17.6	16.2	−2.2	−1.6	1.3
Decorative items for the home	10.2	8.8	10.0	15.2	1.5	0.2	−5.2
Sofas	8.2	7.3	8.4	7.7	0.9	−0.3	0.8
Mattresses and springs	6.2	4.2	4.7	4.5	2.0	1.4	0.2
Lawn and garden equipment	5.7	3.2	3.6	4.0	2.5	2.1	−0.4
Bedroom linens	5.4	4.0	5.5	3.8	1.5	0.0	1.7
Bedroom furniture, except mattresses and springs	5.1	5.4	6.2	5.9	−0.3	−1.1	0.3
Housewares	5.1	5.7	6.1	5.6	−0.6	−1.0	0.5
Plants and fresh flowers, indoor	4.3	3.7	3.4	4.9	0.6	1.0	−1.5
Power and hand tools	4.1	4.6	2.3	2.5	−0.5	1.8	−0.1
Living room chairs and tables	3.8	4.6	4.6	5.2	−0.7	−0.8	−0.6
Wall units, cabinets, and other furniture	3.4	3.6	4.6	4.3	−0.1	−1.2	0.3
Kitchen and dining room furniture	2.6	2.8	3.4	4.0	−0.2	−0.8	−0.6
Lamps and lighting fixtures	2.2	1.9	1.2	0.9	0.3	0.9	0.3
Appliances, kitchen, small electric	2.1	1.9	1.4	1.5	0.2	0.7	−0.1
Outdoor equipment	2.0	3.0	2.1	1.6	−1.0	−0.1	0.5
Bathroom linens	1.9	1.6	1.9	1.5	0.3	0.0	0.4
Infants' equipment and furniture	1.9	2.1	1.8	1.2	−0.3	0.1	0.5
Laundry and cleaning equipment	1.6	1.5	1.1	0.9	0.0	0.5	0.2
Outdoor furniture	1.6	2.3	1.1	1.3	−0.7	0.4	−0.2
Floor coverings, nonpermanent	1.3	1.5	1.6	1.3	−0.2	−0.3	0.3
Window coverings	1.2	2.0	1.9	1.1	−0.8	−0.8	0.8
Closet and storage items	1.0	1.4	1.3	0.7	−0.4	−0.3	0.6
Curtains and draperies	0.8	1.5	1.8	1.8	−0.7	−1.0	0.0
Portable heating and cooling equipment	0.7	1.6	0.4	0.5	−0.9	0.3	−0.1
Sewing materials for household items	0.7	0.8	0.9	0.8	−0.1	−0.2	0.0
Kitchen and dining room linens	0.7	0.5	0.6	0.8	0.1	0.0	−0.2
Slipcovers and decorative pillows	0.3	0.3	0.4	0.2	0.0	0.0	0.1

Note: Percentage point change calculations are based on unrounded figures. "–" means not applicable.
Source: Bureau of Labor Statistics, 2000, 2006, 2010, and 2012 Consumer Expenditure Surveys; calculations by New Strategist

Appliances, Kitchen, Small Electric

Best customers: **Householders aged 35 to 64**
Married couples
Households in the West

Customer trends: **Average household spending on small electric kitchen appliances should continue to grow as boomers buy for their adult children.**

The category "small electric kitchen appliances" includes coffeemakers, food processors, bread makers, and so on. The best customers of small electric kitchen appliances are older married couples. Married couples without children at home (most of them older) spend 34 percent more than average on small electric kitchen appliances, many helping grown children outfit their first homes. Couples with children at home spend 36 percent more than average on small electric kitchen appliances. Householders ranging in age from 35 to 64, many with children, spend 15 to 17 percent more than average on this item and control 64 percent of the market. Households in the West spend nearly one-third more than average on small electric kitchen appliances.

Average household spending on small electric kitchen appliances grew 14 percent between 2000 and 2012, after adjusting for inflation. New single-cup coffee makers accounted for some of this gain (these coffee makers were also behind the surge in spending on coffee from grocery and convenience stores). Also behind the gain was the presence of the large baby-boom generation in the best customer lifestage. Spending on small electric kitchen appliances should continue to grow as boomers buy for their adult children.

Table 7.2 Appliances, kitchen, small electric

Total household spending   **$3,222,374,400.00**
Average household spends   **25.90**

AGE OF HOUSEHOLDER	AVERAGE HOUSEHOLD SPENDING	BEST CUSTOMERS (index)	BIGGEST CUSTOMERS (market share)
Average household	$25.90	100	100.0%
Under age 25	21.58	83	5.5
Aged 25 to 34	23.59	91	14.7
Aged 35 to 44	30.37	117	20.4
Aged 45 to 54	29.69	115	22.7
Aged 55 to 64	30.17	116	21.3
Aged 65 to 74	22.90	88	10.7
Aged 75 or older	12.73	49	4.8

	AVERAGE HOUSEHOLD SPENDING	BEST CUSTOMERS (index)	BIGGEST CUSTOMERS (market share)
HOUSEHOLD INCOME			
Average household	$25.90	100	100.0%
Under $20,000	11.29	44	9.2
$20,000 to $39,999	17.73	68	15.4
$40,000 to $49,999	18.51	71	6.3
$50,000 to $69,999	23.89	92	13.3
$70,000 to $79,999	38.37	148	8.3
$80,000 to $99,999	33.12	128	11.3
$100,000 or more	50.08	193	36.2
HOUSEHOLD TYPE			
Average household	25.90	100	100.0
Married couples	34.11	132	64.0
Married couples, no children	34.71	134	27.9
Married couples with children	35.21	136	32.0
Oldest child under age 6	35.15	136	6.2
Oldest child aged 6 to 17	35.20	136	16.2
Oldest child aged 18 or older	35.27	136	9.6
Single parent with child under age 18	16.14	62	3.3
Single person	16.84	65	19.3
RACE AND HISPANIC ORIGIN			
Average household	25.90	100	100.0
Asian	26.23	101	4.4
Black	16.58	64	8.0
Hispanic	19.36	75	9.4
Non-Hispanic white and other	28.51	110	82.6
REGION			
Average household	25.90	100	100.0
Northeast	24.27	94	16.9
Midwest	23.66	91	20.3
South	23.16	89	33.3
West	33.94	131	29.5
EDUCATION			
Average household	25.90	100	100.0
Less than high school graduate	13.85	53	7.0
High school graduate	19.30	75	18.6
Some college	22.18	86	17.6
Associate's degree	32.01	124	12.2
Bachelor's degree or more	36.63	141	44.6
Bachelor's degree	33.37	129	25.7
Master's, professional, doctoral degree	42.23	163	18.9

Note: Market shares may not sum to 100.0 because of rounding and missing categories by household type. "Asian" and "black" include Hispanics and non-Hispanics who identify themselves as being of the respective race alone. "Hispanic" includes people of any race who identify themselves as Hispanic. "Other" includes people who identify themselves as non-Hispanic and as Alaska Native, American Indian, Asian (who are also included in the "Asian" row), or Native Hawaiian or other Pacific Islander, as well as non-Hispanics reporting more than one race.
Source: Calculations by New Strategist based on the Bureau of Labor Statistics' 2012 Consumer Expenditure Survey

Appliances, Major

Best customers: Householders aged 35 to 54
                            Married couples

Customer trends: Average household spending on major appliances may continue to fall as household formation slows and families tighten their belts.

The biggest spenders on major appliances—the largest expense category among household furnishings and supplies—are married couples who are outfitting their home for expanding families, older couples who are upgrading appliances after their children have left home, and others who are buying them for grown children as they establish their own households. This explains why householders aged 35 to 54 spend 22 to 26 percent more than average on this item. Married couples spend 41 percent more than average on major appliances, the figure peaking at 53 percent among those with school-aged children.

Average household spending on major appliances grew 9 percent between 2000 and the overall peak spending year of 2006, then fell 28 percent from 2006 to 2012, after adjusting for inflation. The Great Recession was behind the decline, as were falling prices. Average household spending on major appliances may continue to decline as household formation slows and families tighten their belts.

Table 7.3 **Appliances, major**

Total household spending $24,542,300,160.00
Average household spends   197.26

	AVERAGE HOUSEHOLD SPENDING	BEST CUSTOMERS (index)	BIGGEST CUSTOMERS (market share)
AGE OF HOUSEHOLDER			
Average household	**$197.26**	**100**	**100.0%**
Under age 25	83.46	42	2.8
Aged 25 to 34	163.64	83	13.4
Aged 35 to 44	249.40	126	21.9
Aged 45 to 54	240.50	122	24.1
Aged 55 to 64	201.89	102	18.7
Aged 65 to 74	224.10	114	13.7
Aged 75 or older	107.56	55	5.3

	AVERAGE HOUSEHOLD SPENDING	BEST CUSTOMERS (index)	BIGGEST CUSTOMERS (market share)
HOUSEHOLD INCOME			
Average household	**$197.26**	**100**	**100.0%**
Under $20,000	76.16	39	8.1
$20,000 to $39,999	120.19	61	13.7
$40,000 to $49,999	153.68	78	6.9
$50,000 to $69,999	201.97	102	14.8
$70,000 to $79,999	244.76	124	6.9
$80,000 to $99,999	284.56	144	12.7
$100,000 or more	387.91	197	36.8
HOUSEHOLD TYPE			
Average household	**197.26**	**100**	**100.0**
Married couples	279.02	141	68.7
Married couples, no children	254.22	129	26.9
Married couples with children	289.92	147	34.6
Oldest child under age 6	248.92	126	5.8
Oldest child aged 6 to 17	301.34	153	18.2
Oldest child aged 18 or older	297.17	151	10.6
Single parent with child under age 18	144.93	73	3.9
Single person	99.99	51	15.1
RACE AND HISPANIC ORIGIN			
Average household	**197.26**	**100**	**100.0**
Asian	192.61	98	4.2
Black	129.08	65	8.2
Hispanic	143.05	73	9.1
Non-Hispanic white and other	217.42	110	82.7
REGION			
Average household	**197.26**	**100**	**100.0**
Northeast	218.75	111	20.0
Midwest	193.95	98	21.8
South	191.63	97	36.2
West	192.62	98	22.0
EDUCATION			
Average household	**197.26**	**100**	**100.0**
Less than high school graduate	119.00	60	7.9
High school graduate	169.80	86	21.5
Some college	181.05	92	18.9
Associate's degree	174.06	88	8.7
Bachelor's degree or more	269.31	137	43.1
Bachelor's degree	276.81	140	28.0
Master's, professional, doctoral degree	256.32	130	15.1

Note: Market shares may not sum to 100.0 because of rounding and missing categories by household type. "Asian" and "black" include Hispanics and non-Hispanics who identify themselves as being of the respective race alone. "Hispanic" includes people of any race who identify themselves as Hispanic. "Other" includes people who identify themselves as non-Hispanic and as Alaska Native, American Indian, Asian (who are also included in the "Asian" row), or Native Hawaiian or other Pacific Islander, as well as non-Hispanics reporting more than one race.
Source: Calculations by New Strategist based on the Bureau of Labor Statistics' 2012 Consumer Expenditure Survey

Bathroom Linens

Best customers: Householders aged 55 to 74
Married couples without children at home
Married couples with school-aged or older children at home
Hispanics
Households in the West

Customer trends: Average household spending on bathroom linens may continue to grow now that boomers are filling the best-customer age groups.

The biggest spenders on bathroom linens are families with children as well as older householders. Married couples with school-aged children spend 65 percent more than the average household on this item, and those with adult children at home spend 50 percent more. Householders aged 55 to 74 spend 30 to 33 percent more than average on bathroom linens. The spending on bathroom linens by married couples without children at home (most older) is 35 percent above average. Hispanics, who tend to have the largest families, outspend the average by 43 percent. Households in the West, where many Hispanics reside, spend 63 percent more.

Average household spending on bathroom linens climbed 30 percent between 2000 and 2006 (the year overall household spending peaked), after adjusting for inflation. Spending on this item fell 35 percent between 2006 and the overall trough-spending year of 2010, but grew by a solid 22 percent between 2010 and 2012. Behind the spending rollercoaster was the Great Recession and recovery. Now that boomers are filling the best-customer age groups, spending on bathroom linens may continue to grow.

Table 7.4 Bathroom linens

| Total household spending | $2,973,542,400.00 |
| Average household spends | 23.90 |

AGE OF HOUSEHOLDER	AVERAGE HOUSEHOLD SPENDING	BEST CUSTOMERS (index)	BIGGEST CUSTOMERS (market share)
Average household	$23.90	100	100.0%
Under age 25	13.30	56	3.6
Aged 25 to 34	19.69	82	13.3
Aged 35 to 44	27.99	117	20.3
Aged 45 to 54	20.27	85	16.8
Aged 55 to 64	31.06	130	23.8
Aged 65 to 74	31.75	133	16.0
Aged 75 or older	15.61	65	6.4

	AVERAGE HOUSEHOLD SPENDING	BEST CUSTOMERS (index)	BIGGEST CUSTOMERS (market share)
HOUSEHOLD INCOME			
Average household	**$23.90**	**100**	**100.0%**
Under $20,000	11.15	47	9.8
$20,000 to $39,999	18.57	78	17.5
$40,000 to $49,999	19.75	83	7.3
$50,000 to $69,999	20.59	86	12.4
$70,000 to $79,999	56.24	235	13.1
$80,000 to $99,999	30.99	130	11.4
$100,000 or more	36.19	151	28.3
HOUSEHOLD TYPE			
Average household	**23.90**	**100**	**100.0**
Married couples	33.79	141	68.7
Married couples, no children	32.37	135	28.2
Married couples with children	34.61	145	34.0
Oldest child under age 6	19.49	82	3.7
Oldest child aged 6 to 17	39.50	165	19.7
Oldest child aged 18 or older	35.88	150	10.6
Single parent with child under age 18	17.42	73	3.8
Single person	11.58	48	14.4
RACE AND HISPANIC ORIGIN			
Average household	**23.90**	**100**	**100.0**
Asian	24.05	101	4.4
Black	16.54	69	8.7
Hispanic	34.22	143	17.9
Non-Hispanic white and other	23.39	98	73.5
REGION			
Average household	**23.90**	**100**	**100.0**
Northeast	19.66	82	14.8
Midwest	17.01	71	15.8
South	21.02	88	32.8
West	39.05	163	36.8
EDUCATION			
Average household	**23.90**	**100**	**100.0**
Less than high school graduate	15.85	66	8.7
High school graduate	25.50	107	26.6
Some college	14.26	60	12.3
Associate's degree	41.52	174	17.2
Bachelor's degree or more	26.69	112	35.2
Bachelor's degree	26.16	109	21.8
Master's, professional, doctoral degree	27.58	115	13.4

Note: Market shares may not sum to 100.0 because of rounding and missing categories by household type. "Asian" and "black" include Hispanics and non-Hispanics who identify themselves as being of the respective race alone. "Hispanic" includes people of any race who identify themselves as Hispanic. "Other" includes people who identify themselves as non-Hispanic and as Alaska Native, American Indian, Asian (who are also included in the "Asian" row), or Native Hawaiian or other Pacific Islander, as well as non-Hispanics reporting more than one race.
Source: Calculations by New Strategist based on the Bureau of Labor Statistics' 2012 Consumer Expenditure Survey

Bedroom Furniture, except Mattresses and Springs

Best customers: Householders aged 25 to 54
Married couples with children at home
Single parents
Blacks

Customer trends: Average household spending on bedroom furniture may rise in the years ahead as more of the large millennial generation enters the best-customer lifestage, but slow household formation may limit any gains in this category.

The best customers of bedroom furniture except mattresses and springs are households with children at home, outfitting their homes for their expanding families. Single parents, whose spending approaches average on only a few items, spend 12 percent more than average on bedroom furniture. Married couples with children spend 64 percent more than average on this item, the figure peaking among those with adult children at home at 83 percent. Householders aged 25 to 54, many with children at home, spend 25 to 48 percent more than average on this item and account for 72 percent of the market. Blacks spend one-third more than average on bedroom furniture.

Average household spending on bedroom furniture except mattresses and springs fell 31 percent between 2000 and 2012, after adjusting for inflation. Behind the decline was the small generation X in the best-customer lifestage as well as the Great Recession. Average household spending on bedroom furniture may rise in the years ahead as more of the large millennial generation enters the best-customer lifestage, but slow household formation may limit any gains in this category.

Table 7.5 Bedroom furniture, except mattresses and springs

Total household spending $7,868,067,840.00
Average household spends   63.24

	AVERAGE HOUSEHOLD SPENDING	BEST CUSTOMERS (index)	BIGGEST CUSTOMERS (market share)
AGE OF HOUSEHOLDER			
Average household	$63.24	100	100.0%
Under age 25	64.62	102	6.7
Aged 25 to 34	82.74	131	21.1
Aged 35 to 44	93.39	148	25.6
Aged 45 to 54	79.36	125	24.8
Aged 55 to 64	51.98	82	15.0
Aged 65 to 74	22.42	35	4.3
Aged 75 or older	15.25	24	2.4

	AVERAGE HOUSEHOLD SPENDING	BEST CUSTOMERS (index)	BIGGEST CUSTOMERS (market share)
HOUSEHOLD INCOME			
Average household	**$63.24**	**100**	**100.0%**
Under $20,000	22.75	36	7.6
$20,000 to $39,999	39.16	62	14.0
$40,000 to $49,999	71.09	112	9.9
$50,000 to $69,999	51.85	82	11.8
$70,000 to $79,999	46.44	73	4.1
$80,000 to $99,999	84.38	133	11.8
$100,000 or more	137.83	218	40.8
HOUSEHOLD TYPE			
Average household	**63.24**	**100**	**100.0**
Married couples	80.88	128	62.1
Married couples, no children	42.29	67	13.9
Married couples with children	103.60	164	38.5
Oldest child under age 6	87.02	138	6.3
Oldest child aged 6 to 17	102.82	163	19.3
Oldest child aged 18 or older	115.63	183	12.9
Single parent with child under age 18	71.00	112	5.9
Single person	34.78	55	16.3
RACE AND HISPANIC ORIGIN			
Average household	**63.24**	**100**	**100.0**
Asian	69.33	110	4.8
Black	85.45	135	17.0
Hispanic	58.43	92	11.6
Non-Hispanic white and other	60.53	96	71.8
REGION			
Average household	**63.24**	**100**	**100.0**
Northeast	54.42	86	15.5
Midwest	59.66	94	20.9
South	73.60	116	43.3
West	56.69	90	20.2
EDUCATION			
Average household	**63.24**	**100**	**100.0**
Less than high school graduate	39.01	62	8.1
High school graduate	39.04	62	15.4
Some college	36.93	58	12.0
Associate's degree	54.05	85	8.4
Bachelor's degree or more	112.45	178	56.1
Bachelor's degree	108.07	171	34.1
Master's, professional, doctoral degree	119.97	190	22.0

Note: Market shares may not sum to 100.0 because of rounding and missing categories by household type. "Asian" and "black" include Hispanics and non-Hispanics who identify themselves as being of the respective race alone. "Hispanic" includes people of any race who identify themselves as Hispanic. "Other" includes people who identify themselves as non-Hispanic and as Alaska Native, American Indian, Asian (who are also included in the "Asian" row), or Native Hawaiian or other Pacific Islander, as well as non-Hispanics reporting more than one race.
Source: Calculations by New Strategist based on the Bureau of Labor Statistics' 2012 Consumer Expenditure Survey

Bedroom Linens

Best customers: **Householders aged 55 to 74**
    Married couples
    Households in the West

Customer trends: **Average household spending on bedroom linens may continue to rise because boomers are filling the best-customer age groups.**

The biggest spenders on bedroom linens are married couples. Those without children at home (most of them older) spend 72 percent more than average on bedroom linens. Those with children at home spend 44 percent more than average on this item. Householders aged 55 to 74 spend 24 to 27 percent more than average on bedroom linens. Householders in the West outspend the average by 26 percent.

Average household spending on bedroom linens, which had grown strongly from 2000 to 2006, fell 44 percent between 2006 and the overall spending trough year of 2010, after adjusting for inflation. In the two ensuing years, however, spending on this item recovered by an astonishing 39 percent as pent-up demand for these items drove spending. Average household spending on bedroom linens may continue to rise because boomers are filling the best-customer age groups.

Table 7.6 Bedroom linens

Total household spending $8,389,370,880.00
Average household spends   67.43

AGE OF HOUSEHOLDER	AVERAGE HOUSEHOLD SPENDING	BEST CUSTOMERS (index)	BIGGEST CUSTOMERS (market share)
Average household	$67.43	100	100.0%
Under age 25	22.10	33	2.1
Aged 25 to 34	58.59	87	14.0
Aged 35 to 44	72.69	108	18.7
Aged 45 to 54	69.92	104	20.5
Aged 55 to 64	85.65	127	23.2
Aged 65 to 74	83.38	124	14.9
Aged 75 or older	46.19	69	6.7

	AVERAGE HOUSEHOLD SPENDING	BEST CUSTOMERS (index)	BIGGEST CUSTOMERS (market share)
HOUSEHOLD INCOME			
Average household	$67.43	100	100.0%
Under $20,000	29.80	44	9.3
$20,000 to $39,999	38.18	57	12.8
$40,000 to $49,999	54.34	81	7.1
$50,000 to $69,999	56.07	83	12.0
$70,000 to $79,999	107.81	160	8.9
$80,000 to $99,999	105.68	157	13.8
$100,000 or more	132.38	196	36.8
HOUSEHOLD TYPE			
Average household	67.43	100	100.0
Married couples	101.98	151	73.5
Married couples, no children	115.72	172	35.8
Married couples with children	96.78	144	33.7
Oldest child under age 6	95.09	141	6.4
Oldest child aged 6 to 17	99.44	147	17.5
Oldest child aged 18 or older	93.39	138	9.8
Single parent with child under age 18	32.76	49	2.5
Single person	39.21	58	17.3
RACE AND HISPANIC ORIGIN			
Average household	67.43	100	100.0
Asian	50.62	75	3.3
Black	52.22	77	9.7
Hispanic	57.65	85	10.7
Non-Hispanic white and other	71.47	106	79.6
REGION			
Average household	67.43	100	100.0
Northeast	53.73	80	14.4
Midwest	49.35	73	16.2
South	74.32	110	41.1
West	85.21	126	28.5
EDUCATION			
Average household	67.43	100	100.0
Less than high school graduate	41.35	61	8.0
High school graduate	51.29	76	19.0
Some college	37.99	56	11.6
Associate's degree	87.29	129	12.8
Bachelor's degree or more	103.33	153	48.3
Bachelor's degree	72.26	107	21.4
Master's, professional, doctoral degree	155.86	231	26.8

Note: Market shares may not sum to 100.0 because of rounding and missing categories by household type. "Asian" and "black" include Hispanics and non-Hispanics who identify themselves as being of the respective race alone. "Hispanic" includes people of any race who identify themselves as Hispanic. "Other" includes people who identify themselves as non-Hispanic and as Alaska Native, American Indian, Asian (who are also included in the "Asian" row), or Native Hawaiian or other Pacific Islander, as well as non-Hispanics reporting more than one race.
Source: Calculations by New Strategist based on the Bureau of Labor Statistics' 2012 Consumer Expenditure Survey

Closet and Storage Items

Best customers: Householders aged 55 to 64
                   Married couples with children under age 18

Customer trends: Average household spending on closet and storage items may rise again as Americans try to
                   organize their burgeoning possessions, but only if discretionary income grows.

Householders aged 55 to 64 are the best customers of closet and storage items, spending 64 percent more than average on this item. Married couples with preschoolers spend four times the average on closet and storage items, and those with school-aged children spend 54 percent more than average on this item.

Average household spending on closet and storage items grew by an enormous 88 percent between 2000 and 2006 (the year overall household spending peaked). Then the pattern reversed and spending on this item fell 37 percent between 2006 and 2012, after adjusting for inflation. Behind the earlier increase was the growing variety of closet and storage items available, while the decline is a result of belt-tightening among financially strapped households. Spending on this item may rise again as Americans try to organize their burgeoning possessions, but only if discretionary income grows.

Table 7.7 Closet and storage items

Total household spending $1,567,641,600.00
Average household spends   12.60

AGE OF HOUSEHOLDER	AVERAGE HOUSEHOLD SPENDING	BEST CUSTOMERS (index)	BIGGEST CUSTOMERS (market share)
Average household	$12.60	100	100.0%
Under age 25	5.27	42	2.7
Aged 25 to 34	14.20	113	18.2
Aged 35 to 44	13.17	105	18.1
Aged 45 to 54	12.64	100	19.9
Aged 55 to 64	20.65	164	30.0
Aged 65 to 74	10.15	81	9.7
Aged 75 or older	1.90	15	1.5

	AVERAGE HOUSEHOLD SPENDING	BEST CUSTOMERS (index)	BIGGEST CUSTOMERS (market share)
HOUSEHOLD INCOME			
Average household	**$12.60**	**100**	**100.0%**
Under $20,000	2.57	20	4.3
$20,000 to $39,999	10.19	81	18.2
$40,000 to $49,999	13.94	111	9.8
$50,000 to $69,999	11.65	92	13.4
$70,000 to $79,999	7.76	62	3.4
$80,000 to $99,999	12.58	100	8.8
$100,000 or more	27.97	222	41.6
HOUSEHOLD TYPE			
Average household	**12.60**	**100**	**100.0**
Married couples	17.20	137	66.3
Married couples, no children	11.37	90	18.8
Married couples with children	24.04	191	44.9
Oldest child under age 6	51.20	406	18.5
Oldest child aged 6 to 17	19.40	154	18.3
Oldest child aged 18 or older	14.84	118	8.3
Single parent with child under age 18	11.44	91	4.8
Single person	4.34	34	10.2
RACE AND HISPANIC ORIGIN			
Average household	**12.60**	**100**	**100.0**
Asian	7.71	61	2.7
Black	7.50	60	7.5
Hispanic	14.03	111	14.0
Non-Hispanic white and other	13.96	111	83.2
REGION			
Average household	**12.60**	**100**	**100.0**
Northeast	14.71	117	21.1
Midwest	11.10	88	19.5
South	11.07	88	32.7
West	14.92	118	26.7
EDUCATION			
Average household	**12.60**	**100**	**100.0**
Less than high school graduate	11.33	90	11.7
High school graduate	6.10	48	12.1
Some college	8.42	67	13.8
Associate's degree	14.96	119	11.7
Bachelor's degree or more	20.18	160	50.5
Bachelor's degree	18.67	148	29.5
Master's, professional, doctoral degree	22.74	180	20.9

Note: Market shares may not sum to 100.0 because of rounding and missing categories by household type. "Asian" and "black" include Hispanics and non-Hispanics who identify themselves as being of the respective race alone. "Hispanic" includes people of any race who identify themselves as Hispanic. "Other" includes people who identify themselves as non-Hispanic and as Alaska Native, American Indian, Asian (who are also included in the "Asian" row), or Native Hawaiian or other Pacific Islander, as well as non-Hispanics reporting more than one race.
Source: Calculations by New Strategist based on the Bureau of Labor Statistics' 2012 Consumer Expenditure Survey

Curtains and Draperies

Best customers: **Householders aged 35 to 44**
                     Married couples
                     Blacks
                     Households in the Northeast

Customer trends: **Average household spending on curtains and draperies is likely to continue to fall as the slow recovery from the Great Recession limits household formation.**

The best customers of curtains and draperies, married couples with school-aged children, spend over twice the average on this item. Householders aged 35 to 44, many with school-aged children, spend 84 percent more than the average household on curtains and draperies. Married couples with preschoolers and those with adult children at home spend, respectively, 47 and 39 percent more than average on this item. Couples without children at home, most older, spend 38 percent more than average on curtains and draperies, perhaps redecorating after their grown children have moved out. Black households, whose spending approaches average on only a few items, spend 38 percent more than average on curtains and draperies. The spending on curtains and drapes by households in the Northeast is 26 percent higher than average.

Average household spending on curtains and draperies was stable between 2000 and 2006 (the year overall household spending peaked), then dropped by a whopping 65 percent between 2006 and 2012, after adjusting for inflation. Behind the decline was reduced homeownership and belt tightening due to the Great Recession. Average household spending on curtains and draperies is likely to continue to fall as the slow recovery from the Great Recession limits household formation.

Table 7.8 Curtains and draperies

Total household spending	$1,229,230,080.00		
Average household spends	9.88		

	AVERAGE HOUSEHOLD SPENDING	BEST CUSTOMERS (index)	BIGGEST CUSTOMERS (market share)
AGE OF HOUSEHOLDER			
Average household	**$9.88**	**100**	**100.0%**
Under age 25	5.11	52	3.4
Aged 25 to 34	9.63	97	15.8
Aged 35 to 44	18.17	184	31.9
Aged 45 to 54	9.76	99	19.6
Aged 55 to 64	7.32	74	13.6
Aged 65 to 74	10.74	109	13.1
Aged 75 or older	2.77	28	2.7

	AVERAGE HOUSEHOLD SPENDING	BEST CUSTOMERS (index)	BIGGEST CUSTOMERS (market share)
HOUSEHOLD INCOME			
Average household	**$9.88**	**100**	**100.0%**
Under $20,000	3.22	33	6.9
$20,000 to $39,999	7.51	76	17.1
$40,000 to $49,999	5.39	55	4.8
$50,000 to $69,999	8.12	82	11.9
$70,000 to $79,999	4.86	49	2.7
$80,000 to $99,999	15.77	160	14.1
$100,000 or more	22.45	227	42.5
HOUSEHOLD TYPE			
Average household	**9.88**	**100**	**100.0**
Married couples	15.08	153	74.1
Married couples, no children	13.60	138	28.7
Married couples with children	17.52	177	41.7
Oldest child under age 6	14.52	147	6.7
Oldest child aged 6 to 17	20.89	211	25.1
Oldest child aged 18 or older	13.78	139	9.8
Single parent with child under age 18	7.83	79	4.2
Single person	3.46	35	10.4
RACE AND HISPANIC ORIGIN			
Average household	**9.88**	**100**	**100.0**
Asian	3.14	32	1.4
Black	13.66	138	17.4
Hispanic	8.64	87	11.0
Non-Hispanic white and other	9.45	96	71.8
REGION			
Average household	**9.88**	**100**	**100.0**
Northeast	12.47	126	22.8
Midwest	7.78	79	17.5
South	10.71	108	40.4
West	8.52	86	19.4
EDUCATION			
Average household	**9.88**	**100**	**100.0**
Less than high school graduate	5.86	59	7.7
High school graduate	6.76	68	17.1
Some college	9.51	96	19.8
Associate's degree	7.54	76	7.5
Bachelor's degree or more	14.99	152	47.8
Bachelor's degree	15.15	153	30.6
Master's, professional, doctoral degree	14.73	149	17.3

Note: Market shares may not sum to 100.0 because of rounding and missing categories by household type. "Asian" and "black" include Hispanics and non-Hispanics who identify themselves as being of the respective race alone. "Hispanic" includes people of any race who identify themselves as Hispanic. "Other" includes people who identify themselves as non-Hispanic and as Alaska Native, American Indian, Asian (who are also included in the "Asian" row), or Native Hawaiian or other Pacific Islander, as well as non-Hispanics reporting more than one race.
Source: Calculations by New Strategist based on the Bureau of Labor Statistics' 2012 Consumer Expenditure Survey

Decorative Items for the Home

Best customers: Householders aged 25 to 34 and 55 to 64
Married couples without children at home
Married couples with preschoolers
Blacks
Households in the South

Customer trends: Average household spending on decorative items for the home may not increase much in the
years ahead unless household formation picks up and discretionary income grows.

Decorative items for the home—a category that includes the many whimsical items of home decor—are the third-largest expense within the home furnishings category, behind major appliances and laundry and cleaning supplies. The biggest spenders on decorative items for the home are young families establishing their home and older empty-nest couples redecorating after grown children have left home. Householders aged 25 to 34 spend twice as much as the average household on decorative items for the home. Married couples with preschoolers spend 68 percent more than average on this item. Married couples without children at home, most of them empty-nesters, spend 86 percent more than average on decorative items, while householders aged 55 to 64 spend 26 percent more. Blacks, whose spending approaches average on only a few items, outspend the average on decorative items for the home by 55 percent. Households in the South, where many blacks reside, spend 23 percent more than average on this item.

Average household spending on decorative household items fell 55 percent between 2000 and 2010, after adjusting for inflation, but then the pattern reversed and spending grew 19 percent over the next two-year period. Behind the decade-long decline was household belt tightening that began well before the Great Recession as consumers stretched their budgets to achieve homeownership. The recent increase in spending is a sign of recovery and a consequence of pent-up demand. Average household spending on decorative items for the home may not increase much in the years ahead unless household formation picks up and discretionary income grows.

Table 7.9 Decorative items for the home

Total household spending $15,780,925,440.00
Average household spends 126.84

AGE OF HOUSEHOLDER	AVERAGE HOUSEHOLD SPENDING	BEST CUSTOMERS (index)	BIGGEST CUSTOMERS (market share)
Average household	$126.84	100	100.0%
Under age 25	46.82	37	2.4
Aged 25 to 34	251.46	198	32.0
Aged 35 to 44	117.97	93	16.1
Aged 45 to 54	72.64	57	11.3
Aged 55 to 64	160.41	126	23.1
Aged 65 to 74	119.40	94	11.3
Aged 75 or older	43.60	34	3.4

	AVERAGE HOUSEHOLD SPENDING	BEST CUSTOMERS (index)	BIGGEST CUSTOMERS (market share)
HOUSEHOLD INCOME			
Average household	$126.84	100	100.0%
Under $20,000	34.88	28	5.8
$20,000 to $39,999	140.17	111	24.9
$40,000 to $49,999	58.00	46	4.0
$50,000 to $69,999	103.84	82	11.8
$70,000 to $79,999	178.35	141	7.9
$80,000 to $99,999	127.69	101	8.9
$100,000 or more	242.06	191	35.7
HOUSEHOLD TYPE			
Average household	126.84	100	100.0
Married couples	183.90	145	70.4
Married couples, no children	235.74	186	38.7
Married couples with children	147.66	116	27.4
Oldest child under age 6	213.65	168	7.7
Oldest child aged 6 to 17	141.71	112	13.3
Oldest child aged 18 or older	116.48	92	6.5
Single parent with child under age 18	61.18	48	2.5
Single person	58.32	46	13.7
RACE AND HISPANIC ORIGIN			
Average household	126.84	100	100.0
Asian	54.06	43	1.8
Black	196.62	155	19.5
Hispanic	85.06	67	8.4
Non-Hispanic white and other	121.86	96	72.1
REGION			
Average household	126.84	100	100.0
Northeast	114.85	91	16.3
Midwest	104.14	82	18.2
South	156.33	123	45.9
West	110.32	87	19.6
EDUCATION			
Average household	126.84	100	100.0
Less than high school graduate	225.40	178	23.2
High school graduate	72.25	57	14.2
Some college	91.08	72	14.8
Associate's degree	114.76	90	8.9
Bachelor's degree or more	159.97	126	39.8
Bachelor's degree	131.01	103	20.6
Master's, professional, doctoral degree	208.93	165	19.1

Note: Market shares may not sum to 100.0 because of rounding and missing categories by household type. "Asian" and "black" include Hispanics and non-Hispanics who identify themselves as being of the respective race alone. "Hispanic" includes people of any race who identify themselves as Hispanic. "Other" includes people who identify themselves as non-Hispanic and as Alaska Native, American Indian, Asian (who are also included in the "Asian" row), or Native Hawaiian or other Pacific Islander, as well as non-Hispanics reporting more than one race.
Source: Calculations by New Strategist based on the Bureau of Labor Statistics' 2012 Consumer Expenditure Survey

Floor Coverings, Nonpermanent

Best customers: Householders aged 45 to 54
High-income households
Married couples
Households in the Midwest and West

Customer trends: Average household spending on nonpermanent floor coverings should stabilize in the years ahead
as the economic recovery proceeds, but slow household formation may limit the gains.

The biggest spenders on nonpermanent floor coverings (rugs) are older well-to-do married couples, as well as those who are outfitting children's rooms. Households with incomes of $100,000 or more spend three times the average on rugs. Married couples without children at home, most of them empty-nesters, spend 26 percent more than average on this item. Householders aged 45 to 54 spend 46 percent more than average on this item because they have the highest incomes. Married couples with children at home spend 81 percent more than average on rugs, the figure peaking among those with preschoolers at nearly three times the average. Households in the Midwest spend 34 percent more than average on this item, and those in the West spend 20 percent more.

Average household spending on nonpermanent floor coverings climbed 22 percent between 2000 and 2006 (the year overall household spending peaked), then fell 35 percent between 2006 and 2012, after adjusting for inflation. Spending on rugs should stabilize in the years ahead as the economic recovery proceeds, but slow household formation may limit the gains.

Table 7.10 Floor coverings, nonpermanent

Total household spending $2,018,027,520.00
Average household spends 16.22

AGE OF HOUSEHOLDER	AVERAGE HOUSEHOLD SPENDING	BEST CUSTOMERS (index)	BIGGEST CUSTOMERS (market share)
Average household	$16.22	100	100.0%
Under age 25	3.58	22	1.4
Aged 25 to 34	12.18	75	12.1
Aged 35 to 44	18.43	114	19.7
Aged 45 to 54	23.66	146	28.9
Aged 55 to 64	17.94	111	20.2
Aged 65 to 74	12.28	76	9.1
Aged 75 or older	14.06	87	8.5

	AVERAGE HOUSEHOLD SPENDING	BEST CUSTOMERS (index)	BIGGEST CUSTOMERS (market share)
HOUSEHOLD INCOME			
Average household	$16.22	100	100.0%
Under $20,000	4.13	25	5.4
$20,000 to $39,999	7.14	44	9.9
$40,000 to $49,999	8.97	55	4.9
$50,000 to $69,999	12.39	76	11.0
$70,000 to $79,999	11.15	69	3.8
$80,000 to $99,999	16.14	100	8.8
$100,000 or more	48.68	300	56.2
HOUSEHOLD TYPE			
Average household	16.22	100	100.0
Married couples	24.68	152	73.9
Married couples, no children	20.51	126	26.4
Married couples with children	29.30	181	42.5
Oldest child under age 6	47.39	292	13.3
Oldest child aged 6 to 17	22.39	138	16.4
Oldest child aged 18 or older	29.25	180	12.7
Single parent with child under age 18	7.28	45	2.4
Single person	7.49	46	13.7
RACE AND HISPANIC ORIGIN			
Average household	16.22	100	100.0
Asian	8.66	53	2.3
Black	6.10	38	4.7
Hispanic	8.50	52	6.6
Non-Hispanic white and other	19.22	118	88.9
REGION			
Average household	16.22	100	100.0
Northeast	17.09	105	19.0
Midwest	21.74	134	29.7
South	10.57	65	24.3
West	19.44	120	27.0
EDUCATION			
Average household	16.22	100	100.0
Less than high school graduate	4.82	30	3.9
High school graduate	9.05	56	13.9
Some college	15.52	96	19.7
Associate's degree	14.33	88	8.7
Bachelor's degree or more	27.66	171	53.8
Bachelor's degree	22.12	136	27.2
Master's, professional, doctoral degree	37.17	229	26.6

Note: Market shares may not sum to 100.0 because of rounding and missing categories by household type. "Asian" and "black" include Hispanics and non-Hispanics who identify themselves as being of the respective race alone. "Hispanic" includes people of any race who identify themselves as Hispanic. "Other" includes people who identify themselves as non-Hispanic and as Alaska Native, American Indian, Asian (who are also included in the "Asian" row), or Native Hawaiian or other Pacific Islander, as well as non-Hispanics reporting more than one race.
Source: Calculations by New Strategist based on the Bureau of Labor Statistics' 2012 Consumer Expenditure Survey

Housewares

Best customers: Householders aged 55 to 64
Married couples without children at home
Married couples with school-aged or older children at home

Customer trends: Average household spending on housewares should rebound as boomers help their adult children outfit their homes, but only if household formation picks up.

Housewares is a category that includes dishes, glassware, flatware, and nonelectric cookware—all the things that fill our kitchen cupboards. The best customers of housewares are older married couples who are redecorating or helping grown children outfit their homes. Householders aged 55 to 64 spend 63 percent more than average on housewares, and married couples without children at home (most of them empty-nesters) spend 56 percent more than average. Married couples with school-aged or older children at home spend 32 to 38 percent more than average on housewares.

After having grown 10 percent between 2000 and 2006 (the year overall household spending peaked), average household spending on housewares fell 34 percent between 2006 and 2012, after adjusting for inflation. Behind the decline was the Great Recession, which limited discretionary spending on many categories. More recently, slow household formation is limiting growth in this category. Average household spending on housewares should rebound as boomers help their adult children outfit their homes, but only if household formation picks up.

Table 7.11 Housewares

Total household spending $7,855,626,240.00
Average household spends   63.14

AGE OF HOUSEHOLDER	AVERAGE HOUSEHOLD SPENDING	BEST CUSTOMERS (index)	BIGGEST CUSTOMERS (market share)
Average household	$63.14	100	100.0%
Under age 25	23.30	37	2.4
Aged 25 to 34	62.98	100	16.1
Aged 35 to 44	52.29	83	14.4
Aged 45 to 54	61.35	97	19.2
Aged 55 to 64	102.83	163	29.8
Aged 65 to 74	69.04	109	13.2
Aged 75 or older	34.30	54	5.3

	AVERAGE HOUSEHOLD SPENDING	BEST CUSTOMERS (index)	BIGGEST CUSTOMERS (market share)
HOUSEHOLD INCOME			
Average household	$63.14	100	100.0%
Under $20,000	23.28	37	7.8
$20,000 to $39,999	32.20	51	11.5
$40,000 to $49,999	50.28	80	7.0
$50,000 to $69,999	62.94	100	14.4
$70,000 to $79,999	127.25	202	11.3
$80,000 to $99,999	90.31	143	12.6
$100,000 or more	118.74	188	35.2
HOUSEHOLD TYPE			
Average household	63.14	100	100.0
Married couples	86.46	137	66.5
Married couples, no children	98.55	156	32.5
Married couples with children	81.56	129	30.4
Oldest child under age 6	67.85	107	4.9
Oldest child aged 6 to 17	83.48	132	15.7
Oldest child aged 18 or older	86.93	138	9.7
Single parent with child under age 18	26.32	42	2.2
Single person	35.20	56	16.6
RACE AND HISPANIC ORIGIN			
Average household	63.14	100	100.0
Asian	63.77	101	4.4
Black	35.43	56	7.1
Hispanic	54.05	86	10.7
Non-Hispanic white and other	69.20	110	82.3
REGION			
Average household	63.14	100	100.0
Northeast	51.39	81	14.7
Midwest	64.27	102	22.6
South	64.18	102	37.9
West	69.79	111	24.9
EDUCATION			
Average household	63.14	100	100.0
Less than high school graduate	35.37	56	7.3
High school graduate	44.39	70	17.5
Some college	51.09	81	16.7
Associate's degree	57.79	92	9.0
Bachelor's degree or more	98.02	155	49.0
Bachelor's degree	86.60	137	27.3
Master's, professional, doctoral degree	117.37	186	21.6

Note: Market shares may not sum to 100.0 because of rounding and missing categories by household type. "Asian" and "black" include Hispanics and non-Hispanics who identify themselves as being of the respective race alone. "Hispanic" includes people of any race who identify themselves as Hispanic. "Other" includes people who identify themselves as non-Hispanic and as Alaska Native, American Indian, Asian (who are also included in the "Asian" row), or Native Hawaiian or other Pacific Islander, as well as non-Hispanics reporting more than one race.
Source: Calculations by New Strategist based on the Bureau of Labor Statistics' 2012 Consumer Expenditure Survey

Infants' Equipment and Furniture

Best customers: Householders aged 25 to 34
Married couples with preschoolers
Single parents
Hispanics
Households in the Northeast and South

Customer trends: Average household spending on infants' equipment and furniture should rebound as the large millennial generation has children.

The best customers of infants' equipment and furniture are young married couples with preschoolers. Married couples with preschoolers spend well over six times the average on this item. Householders aged 25 to 34, many the parents of preschoolers, spend two-and-one-quarter times the average on infants' equipment and furniture and control a sizeable 37 percent of the market. Single parents, whose spending approaches average on only a few items, outspend the average on infants' furniture and equipment by a large 72 percent. Hispanics, who tend to have more children than other racial and ethnic groups, spend 26 percent more than average on infants' equipment and furniture. The spending on this item by households in the Northeast and South is 28 and 23 percent above average, respectively.

Average household spending on infants' equipment and furniture was on an accelerated growth track early in the decade as the number of births in the United States reached a record high. Then came the Great Recession and the trend reversed. After growing 45 percent between 2000 and 2006 (the year overall household spending peaked), spending on infants' equipment and furniture fell 16 percent in the six years from 2006 to 2012, after adjusting for inflation. Behind this decline is the ongoing baby bust, as the slow economic recovery causes young adults to postpone having children. Average household spending on infants' equipment and furniture should rebound as the large millennial generation has children.

Table 7.12 Infants' equipment and furniture

Total household spending $2,862,812,160.00
Average household spends   23.01

AGE OF HOUSEHOLDER	AVERAGE HOUSEHOLD SPENDING	BEST CUSTOMERS (index)	BIGGEST CUSTOMERS (market share)
Average household	$23.01	100	100.0%
Under age 25	23.95	104	6.8
Aged 25 to 34	51.97	226	36.5
Aged 35 to 44	30.46	132	23.0
Aged 45 to 54	13.70	60	11.8
Aged 55 to 64	15.42	67	12.3
Aged 65 to 74	16.19	70	8.5
Aged 75 or older	1.55	7	0.7

	AVERAGE HOUSEHOLD SPENDING	BEST CUSTOMERS (index)	BIGGEST CUSTOMERS (market share)
HOUSEHOLD INCOME			
Average household	$23.01	100	100.0%
Under $20,000	4.59	20	4.2
$20,000 to $39,999	15.03	65	14.7
$40,000 to $49,999	18.39	80	7.1
$50,000 to $69,999	21.92	95	13.8
$70,000 to $79,999	23.27	101	5.6
$80,000 to $99,999	43.11	187	16.5
$100,000 or more	46.59	202	37.9
HOUSEHOLD TYPE			
Average household	23.01	100	100.0
Married couples	32.07	139	67.7
Married couples, no children	25.64	111	23.2
Married couples with children	38.05	165	38.9
Oldest child under age 6	147.51	641	29.2
Oldest child aged 6 to 17	12.21	53	6.3
Oldest child aged 18 or older	12.12	53	3.7
Single parent with child under age 18	39.65	172	9.0
Single person	4.14	18	5.3
RACE AND HISPANIC ORIGIN			
Average household	23.01	100	100.0
Asian	22.61	98	4.3
Black	25.33	110	13.8
Hispanic	29.08	126	15.8
Non-Hispanic white and other	21.62	94	70.5
REGION			
Average household	23.01	100	100.0
Northeast	29.35	128	23.0
Midwest	9.82	43	9.5
South	28.25	123	45.7
West	22.34	97	21.9
EDUCATION			
Average household	23.01	100	100.0
Less than high school graduate	13.79	60	7.8
High school graduate	14.55	63	15.8
Some college	19.58	85	17.5
Associate's degree	18.14	79	7.8
Bachelor's degree or more	37.10	161	50.8
Bachelor's degree	38.31	166	33.2
Master's, professional, doctoral degree	35.09	152	17.7

Note: Market shares may not sum to 100.0 because of rounding and missing categories by household type. "Asian" and "black" include Hispanics and non-Hispanics who identify themselves as being of the respective race alone. "Hispanic" includes people of any race who identify themselves as Hispanic. "Other" includes people who identify themselves as non-Hispanic and as Alaska Native, American Indian, Asian (who are also included in the "Asian" row), or Native Hawaiian or other Pacific Islander, as well as non-Hispanics reporting more than one race.
Source: Calculations by New Strategist based on the Bureau of Labor Statistics' 2012 Consumer Expenditure Survey

Kitchen and Dining Room Furniture

Best customers: Householders aged 25 to 54
Married couples without children at home
Married couples with children under age 18
Single parents
Asians and blacks
Households in the Northeast

Customer trends: Average household spending on kitchen and dining room furniture should stabilize as the large millennial generation marries and has children.

The best customers of kitchen and dining room furniture are young married couples who are outfitting their first homes and empty-nesters redecorating after the children have moved out. Householders aged 25 to 34 spend 55 percent more than average on this item, and those aged 35 to 54 spend 21 to 32 percent more. Married couples without children at home (most of them empty-nesters) spend 19 percent more than average. Couples with preschoolers spend two-and-three-quarter times more than average on kitchen and dining room furniture, and those with school-aged children spend 50 percent more. Single parents, whose spending approaches average on only a few items, spend 21 percent more than average on kitchen and dining room furniture. Asians and blacks spend, respectively, 34 and 30 percent more than average on this item. Spending on kitchen and dining room furniture by households in the Northeast is 44 percent above average.

Average household spending on kitchen and dining room furniture fell by a substantial 49 percent between 2000 and 2012, after adjusting for inflation. Behind the decline is the economic downturn, which not only reduced discretionary spending but slowed household formation to a crawl. Spending on kitchen and dining room furniture should stabilize as the large millennial generation marries and has children.

Table 7.13 Kitchen and dining room furniture

Total household spending	$3,934,033,920.00		
Average household spends	31.62		

AGE OF HOUSEHOLDER	AVERAGE HOUSEHOLD SPENDING	BEST CUSTOMERS (index)	BIGGEST CUSTOMERS (market share)
Average household	$31.62	100	100.0%
Under age 25	18.42	58	3.8
Aged 25 to 34	48.98	155	25.0
Aged 35 to 44	41.74	132	22.9
Aged 45 to 54	38.30	121	24.0
Aged 55 to 64	27.10	86	15.7
Aged 65 to 74	18.44	58	7.0
Aged 75 or older	5.02	16	1.6

	AVERAGE HOUSEHOLD SPENDING	BEST CUSTOMERS (index)	BIGGEST CUSTOMERS (market share)
HOUSEHOLD INCOME			
Average household	$31.62	100	100.0%
Under $20,000	9.33	29	6.2
$20,000 to $39,999	14.80	47	10.5
$40,000 to $49,999	30.05	95	8.4
$50,000 to $69,999	28.96	92	13.2
$70,000 to $79,999	22.50	71	4.0
$80,000 to $99,999	27.98	88	7.8
$100,000 or more	84.18	266	49.8
HOUSEHOLD TYPE			
Average household	31.62	100	100.0
Married couples	43.31	137	66.5
Married couples, no children	37.77	119	24.9
Married couples with children	49.32	156	36.7
Oldest child under age 6	86.10	272	12.4
Oldest child aged 6 to 17	47.40	150	17.8
Oldest child aged 18 or older	28.78	91	6.4
Single parent with child under age 18	38.21	121	6.3
Single person	16.59	52	15.6
RACE AND HISPANIC ORIGIN			
Average household	31.62	100	100.0
Asian	42.24	134	5.8
Black	24.55	78	9.8
Hispanic	41.23	130	16.3
Non-Hispanic white and other	31.22	99	74.1
REGION			
Average household	31.62	100	100.0
Northeast	45.40	144	25.9
Midwest	34.32	109	24.1
South	26.28	83	31.0
West	26.76	85	19.1
EDUCATION			
Average household	31.62	100	100.0
Less than high school graduate	15.65	49	6.5
High school graduate	17.50	55	13.8
Some college	20.72	66	13.5
Associate's degree	26.01	82	8.1
Bachelor's degree or more	58.28	184	58.1
Bachelor's degree	48.55	154	30.6
Master's, professional, doctoral degree	74.99	237	27.5

Note: Market shares may not sum to 100.0 because of rounding and missing categories by household type. "Asian" and "black" include Hispanics and non-Hispanics who identify themselves as being of the respective race alone. "Hispanic" includes people of any race who identify themselves as Hispanic. "Other" includes people who identify themselves as non-Hispanic and as Alaska Native, American Indian, Asian (who are also included in the "Asian" row), or Native Hawaiian or other Pacific Islander, as well as non-Hispanics reporting more than one race.
Source: Calculations by New Strategist based on the Bureau of Labor Statistics' 2012 Consumer Expenditure Survey

Kitchen and Dining Room Linens

Best customers: **Householders aged 55 to 64**
Married couples without children at home
Married couples with preschoolers
Asians
Households in the Northeast and West

Customer trends: **Average household spending on kitchen and dining room linens is likely to stabilize as the economic recovery continues.**

The best customers of kitchen and dining room linens are older married couples. Householders aged 55 to 64 spend well over twice the average on kitchen and dining room linens. Married couples without children at home, most of them empty-nesters, spend 90 percent more than average on kitchen and dining room linens. Married couples with preschoolers spend 92 percent more than average on this item. Spending on kitchen and dining room linens by Asian householders is 39 percent above average. Households in the West, where many Asians reside, outspend the average by 35 percent, and those in the Northeast spend 39 percent more.

Average household spending on kitchen and dining room linens, already the second-smallest of the household furnishings categories, fell by an enormous 50 percent between 2000 and the overall trough spending year of 2010, after adjusting for inflation. Spending then rebounded strongly, rising 31 percent between 2010 and 2012. Behind the decline is the substitution of paper products for linens as well as the Great Recession, which reduced discretionary spending. The more recent growth is due to pent-up demand. Average household spending on kitchen and dining room linens is likely to stabilize as the economic recovery continues.

Table 7.14 Kitchen and dining room linens

Total household spending	$1,013,990,400.00
Average household spends	8.15

AGE OF HOUSEHOLDER	AVERAGE HOUSEHOLD SPENDING	BEST CUSTOMERS (index)	BIGGEST CUSTOMERS (market share)
Average household	**$8.15**	**100**	**100.0%**
Under age 25	5.99	73	4.8
Aged 25 to 34	5.78	71	11.5
Aged 35 to 44	6.77	83	14.4
Aged 45 to 54	5.66	69	13.7
Aged 55 to 64	18.84	231	42.3
Aged 65 to 74	6.07	74	9.0
Aged 75 or older	4.13	51	5.0

	AVERAGE HOUSEHOLD SPENDING	BEST CUSTOMERS (index)	BIGGEST CUSTOMERS (market share)
HOUSEHOLD INCOME			
Average household	**$8.15**	**100**	**100.0%**
Under $20,000	3.70	45	9.6
$20,000 to $39,999	4.51	55	12.5
$40,000 to $49,999	3.17	39	3.4
$50,000 to $69,999	5.05	62	9.0
$70,000 to $79,999	6.86	84	4.7
$80,000 to $99,999	13.61	167	14.7
$100,000 or more	20.86	256	47.9
HOUSEHOLD TYPE			
Average household	**8.15**	**100**	**100.0**
Married couples	12.42	152	74.0
Married couples, no children	15.51	190	39.7
Married couples with children	11.00	135	31.7
Oldest child under age 6	15.61	192	8.7
Oldest child aged 6 to 17	10.37	127	15.1
Oldest child aged 18 or older	9.16	112	7.9
Single parent with child under age 18	0.59	7	0.4
Single person	4.15	51	15.1
RACE AND HISPANIC ORIGIN			
Average household	**8.15**	**100**	**100.0**
Asian	14.80	182	7.9
Black	5.08	62	7.8
Hispanic	4.67	57	7.2
Non-Hispanic white and other	9.22	113	84.9
REGION			
Average household	**8.15**	**100**	**100.0**
Northeast	11.34	139	25.1
Midwest	8.37	103	22.8
South	4.76	58	21.8
West	10.97	135	30.3
EDUCATION			
Average household	**8.15**	**100**	**100.0**
Less than high school graduate	2.98	37	4.8
High school graduate	4.73	58	14.5
Some college	4.69	58	11.9
Associate's degree	9.97	122	12.1
Bachelor's degree or more	14.50	178	56.1
Bachelor's degree	10.55	129	25.8
Master's, professional, doctoral degree	21.17	260	30.1

Note: Market shares may not sum to 100.0 because of rounding and missing categories by household type. "Asian" and "black" include Hispanics and non-Hispanics who identify themselves as being of the respective race alone. "Hispanic" includes people of any race who identify themselves as Hispanic. "Other" includes people who identify themselves as non-Hispanic and as Alaska Native, American Indian, Asian (who are also included in the "Asian" row), or Native Hawaiian or other Pacific Islander, as well as non-Hispanics reporting more than one race.
Source: Calculations by New Strategist based on the Bureau of Labor Statistics' 2012 Consumer Expenditure Survey

Lamps and Lighting Fixtures

Best customers: Householders aged 45 to 74
                   Married couples without children at home
                   Married couples with school-aged children

Customer trends: Average household spending on lamps and lighting fixtures should stabilize in the years ahead
                   once light bulb replacement (of compact fluorescents for incandescents) is complete.

The best customers of lamps and lighting fixtures are older married couples without children at home. Householders aged 65 to 74 spend 72 percent more than average on lamps and lighting fixtures. Married couples without children at home spend 27 percent more than average on this item. Married couples with school-aged children spend 64 percent more than average on lamps and lighting fixtures. Householders aged 45 to 64 outspend the average on this item by 20 to 21 percent.

Average household spending on lamps and lighting fixtures climbed by an astonishing 86 percent between 2000 and 2012, after adjusting for inflation, despite the Great Recession. Behind the hefty increase was the switch to much more energy-efficient compact fluorescent light bulbs. Average household spending on lamps and lighting fixtures should stabilize in the years ahead once light bulb replacement is complete.

Table 7.15 Lamps and lighting fixtures

Total household spending $3,338,081,280.00
Average household spends   26.83

AGE OF HOUSEHOLDER	AVERAGE HOUSEHOLD SPENDING	BEST CUSTOMERS (index)	BIGGEST CUSTOMERS (market share)
Average household	$26.83	100	100.0%
Under age 25	12.19	45	3.0
Aged 25 to 34	18.03	67	10.9
Aged 35 to 44	16.80	63	10.9
Aged 45 to 54	32.29	120	23.8
Aged 55 to 64	32.55	121	22.2
Aged 65 to 74	46.17	172	20.7
Aged 75 or older	24.91	93	9.1

	AVERAGE HOUSEHOLD SPENDING	BEST CUSTOMERS (index)	BIGGEST CUSTOMERS (market share)
HOUSEHOLD INCOME			
Average household	**$26.83**	**100**	**100.0%**
Under $20,000	12.85	48	10.1
$20,000 to $39,999	12.30	46	10.3
$40,000 to $49,999	24.14	90	8.0
$50,000 to $69,999	17.13	64	9.2
$70,000 to $79,999	81.75	305	17.0
$80,000 to $99,999	43.50	162	14.3
$100,000 or more	44.31	165	30.9
HOUSEHOLD TYPE			
Average household	**26.83**	**100**	**100.0**
Married couples	34.74	129	62.9
Married couples, no children	34.03	127	26.4
Married couples with children	34.05	127	29.8
Oldest child under age 6	13.23	49	2.2
Oldest child aged 6 to 17	44.01	164	19.5
Oldest child aged 18 or older	30.42	113	8.0
Single parent with child under age 18	6.10	23	1.2
Single person	17.38	65	19.2
RACE AND HISPANIC ORIGIN			
Average household	**26.83**	**100**	**100.0**
Asian	14.64	55	2.4
Black	11.97	45	5.6
Hispanic	17.94	67	8.4
Non-Hispanic white and other	30.75	115	86.0
REGION			
Average household	**26.83**	**100**	**100.0**
Northeast	12.07	45	8.1
Midwest	31.92	119	26.4
South	28.37	106	39.4
West	31.15	116	26.2
EDUCATION			
Average household	**26.83**	**100**	**100.0**
Less than high school graduate	3.88	14	1.9
High school graduate	20.36	76	18.9
Some college	25.10	94	19.3
Associate's degree	25.14	94	9.3
Bachelor's degree or more	42.13	157	49.5
Bachelor's degree	39.20	146	29.1
Master's, professional, doctoral degree	47.08	175	20.4

Note: Market shares may not sum to 100.0 because of rounding and missing categories by household type. "Asian" and "black" include Hispanics and non-Hispanics who identify themselves as being of the respective race alone. "Hispanic" includes people of any race who identify themselves as Hispanic. "Other" includes people who identify themselves as non-Hispanic and as Alaska Native, American Indian, Asian (who are also included in the "Asian" row), or Native Hawaiian or other Pacific Islander, as well as non-Hispanics reporting more than one race.
Source: Calculations by New Strategist based on the Bureau of Labor Statistics' 2012 Consumer Expenditure Survey

Laundry and Cleaning Equipment

Best customers:
Householders aged 45 to 64
Married couples without children at home
Married couples with school-aged children

Customer trends:
Average household spending on laundry and cleaning equipment should stabilize in the years
ahead because the large baby-boom generation has entirely filled the best-customer age groups.

The best customers of laundry and cleaning equipment (such as dusters and mops) are older married couples and couples with school-aged children. Householders aged 45 to 64 spend 18 to 31 percent more than average on laundry and cleaning equipment. Married couples without children at home, most of them older, spend 48 percent more than average on this item, and couples with school-aged children spend 38 percent more.

Average household spending on laundry and cleaning equipment grew by 30 percent between 2000 and 2006 (the year overall household spending peaked), after adjusting for inflation, and then grew by another 12 percent between 2006 and 2012. Spending on laundry and cleaning equipment should stabilize in the years ahead because the large baby-boom generation has entirely filled the best-customer age groups.

Table 7.16 Laundry and cleaning equipment

| Total household spending | $2,437,309,440.00 |
| Average household spends | 19.59 |

	AVERAGE HOUSEHOLD SPENDING	BEST CUSTOMERS (index)	BIGGEST CUSTOMERS (market share)
AGE OF HOUSEHOLDER			
Average household	**$19.59**	**100**	**100.0%**
Under age 25	11.51	59	3.9
Aged 25 to 34	21.24	108	17.5
Aged 35 to 44	17.58	90	15.6
Aged 45 to 54	23.03	118	23.3
Aged 55 to 64	25.58	131	23.9
Aged 65 to 74	18.64	95	11.5
Aged 75 or older	9.04	46	4.5

	AVERAGE HOUSEHOLD SPENDING	BEST CUSTOMERS (index)	BIGGEST CUSTOMERS (market share)
HOUSEHOLD INCOME			
Average household	**$19.59**	**100**	**100.0%**
Under $20,000	9.05	46	9.7
$20,000 to $39,999	12.39	63	14.2
$40,000 to $49,999	22.00	112	9.9
$50,000 to $69,999	19.99	102	14.7
$70,000 to $79,999	25.90	132	7.4
$80,000 to $99,999	33.18	169	14.9
$100,000 or more	30.14	154	28.8
HOUSEHOLD TYPE			
Average household	**19.59**	**100**	**100.0**
Married couples	27.07	138	67.1
Married couples, no children	29.02	148	30.9
Married couples with children	24.58	125	29.5
Oldest child under age 6	23.29	119	5.4
Oldest child aged 6 to 17	27.00	138	16.4
Oldest child aged 18 or older	21.36	109	7.7
Single parent with child under age 18	15.72	80	4.2
Single person	8.91	45	13.5
RACE AND HISPANIC ORIGIN			
Average household	**19.59**	**100**	**100.0**
Asian	20.67	106	4.6
Black	11.02	56	7.1
Hispanic	21.95	112	14.0
Non-Hispanic white and other	20.61	105	79.0
REGION			
Average household	**19.59**	**100**	**100.0**
Northeast	14.78	75	13.6
Midwest	17.01	87	19.3
South	19.02	97	36.2
West	27.04	138	31.1
EDUCATION			
Average household	**19.59**	**100**	**100.0**
Less than high school graduate	13.95	71	9.3
High school graduate	15.11	77	19.2
Some college	22.34	114	23.5
Associate's degree	24.63	126	12.4
Bachelor's degree or more	21.75	111	35.0
Bachelor's degree	19.79	101	20.1
Master's, professional, doctoral degree	25.06	128	14.8

Note: Market shares may not sum to 100.0 because of rounding and missing categories by household type. "Asian" and "black" include Hispanics and non-Hispanics who identify themselves as being of the respective race alone. "Hispanic" includes people of any race who identify themselves as Hispanic. "Other" includes people who identify themselves as non-Hispanic and as Alaska Native, American Indian, Asian (who are also included in the "Asian" row), or Native Hawaiian or other Pacific Islander, as well as non-Hispanics reporting more than one race.
Source: Calculations by New Strategist based on the Bureau of Labor Statistics' 2012 Consumer Expenditure Survey

Lawn and Garden Equipment

Best customers:	Householders aged 25 to 34 and aged 75 or older
	High-income households
	Married couples without children at home
	Non-Hispanic whites
	Households in the South
Customer trends:	Average household spending on lawn and garden equipment is likely to stabilize until household formation picks up.

The best customers of lawn and garden equipment (such as lawnmowers, string trimmers, and blowers) are well-to-do non-Hispanic white empty-nest couples in the South. Householders aged 75 or older spend more than three times the average on lawn and garden equipment. Married couples without children at home—most of them older empty-nesters—spend nearly three times the average on this item. Households with incomes of $100,000 or more spend three-and-one-half times the average. Non-Hispanic whites outspend minorities by a wide margin on lawn and garden equipment and represent 94 percent of the market. Households in the South outspend the average on this item by 88 percent. Householders aged 25 to 34, many of them recent homebuyers, spend 36 percent more than average on this item.

Average household spending on lawn and garden equipment has been on a rollercoaster ride during the past 12 years. Spending fell 37 percent between 2000 and the overall trough spending year of 2010, after adjusting for inflation, then rebounded with an 82 percent increase in spending from 2010 to 2012. Behind the surge in spending was pent-up demand for these items. Spending on lawn and garden equipment is likely to stabilize until household formation picks up.

Table 7.17 Lawn and garden equipment

Total household spending	$8,847,221,760.00
Average household spends	71.11

	AVERAGE HOUSEHOLD SPENDING	BEST CUSTOMERS (index)	BIGGEST CUSTOMERS (market share)
AGE OF HOUSEHOLDER			
Average household	$71.11	100	100.0%
Under age 25	3.93	6	0.4
Aged 25 to 34	96.61	136	22.0
Aged 35 to 44	27.96	39	6.8
Aged 45 to 54	63.69	90	17.7
Aged 55 to 64	64.69	91	16.6
Aged 65 to 74	34.09	48	5.8
Aged 75 or older	228.97	322	31.5

	AVERAGE HOUSEHOLD SPENDING	BEST CUSTOMERS (index)	BIGGEST CUSTOMERS (market share)
HOUSEHOLD INCOME			
Average household	**$71.11**	**100**	**100.0%**
Under $20,000	6.69	9	2.0
$20,000 to $39,999	34.29	48	10.9
$40,000 to $49,999	64.35	90	8.0
$50,000 to $69,999	29.59	42	6.0
$70,000 to $79,999	39.73	56	3.1
$80,000 to $99,999	35.56	50	4.4
$100,000 or more	248.73	350	65.5
HOUSEHOLD TYPE			
Average household	**71.11**	**100**	**100.0**
Married couples	116.99	165	79.9
Married couples, no children	198.45	279	58.2
Married couples with children	53.20	75	17.6
Oldest child under age 6	23.51	33	1.5
Oldest child aged 6 to 17	60.15	85	10.1
Oldest child aged 18 or older	60.11	85	6.0
Single parent with child under age 18	1.86	3	0.1
Single person	23.73	33	9.9
RACE AND HISPANIC ORIGIN			
Average household	**71.11**	**100**	**100.0**
Asian	3.66	5	0.2
Black	23.92	34	4.2
Hispanic	12.50	18	2.2
Non-Hispanic white and other	88.66	125	93.6
REGION			
Average household	**71.11**	**100**	**100.0**
Northeast	29.61	42	7.5
Midwest	31.10	44	9.7
South	133.52	188	69.9
West	41.19	58	13.1
EDUCATION			
Average household	**71.11**	**100**	**100.0**
Less than high school graduate	12.81	18	2.4
High school graduate	64.14	90	22.5
Some college	61.88	87	17.9
Associate's degree	50.66	71	7.0
Bachelor's degree or more	111.00	156	49.2
Bachelor's degree	51.66	73	14.5
Master's, professional, doctoral degree	211.32	297	34.5

Note: Market shares may not sum to 100.0 because of rounding and missing categories by household type. "Asian" and "black" include Hispanics and non-Hispanics who identify themselves as being of the respective race alone. "Hispanic" includes people of any race who identify themselves as Hispanic. "Other" includes people who identify themselves as non-Hispanic and as Alaska Native, American Indian, Asian (who are also included in the "Asian" row), or Native Hawaiian or other Pacific Islander, as well as non-Hispanics reporting more than one race.
Source: Calculations by New Strategist based on the Bureau of Labor Statistics' 2012 Consumer Expenditure Survey

Living Room Chairs and Tables

Best customers: Householders aged 45 to 64
Married couples without children at home
Married couples with school-aged children
Households in the Midwest and South

Customer trends: Average household spending on living room chairs and tables is likely to continue to decline until household formation picks up speed and the housing market recovers.

The best customers of living room chairs and tables are older married couples, redecorating their home as their children establish independent households. Married couples without children at home (mostly older empty-nesters) spend 34 percent more than average on this item. Householders aged 45 to 64 spend 12 to 14 percent more than average on living room chairs and tables. Spending on this item by married couples with school-aged children is two-thirds higher than average. Households in the Midwest outspend the average on living room chairs and tables by 26 percent, and those in the South spend 15 percent more.

Average household spending on living room chairs and tables fell 42 percent between 2000 and 2012, after adjusting for inflation. This category suffered the fate of most types of furniture, with less spending as mortgages grew in size followed by less spending because of the Great Recession. Spending on living room chairs and tables is likely to continue to decline until household formation picks up speed and the housing market recovers.

Table 7.18 Living room chairs and tables

Total household spending $5,908,515,840.00
Average household spends 47.49

AGE OF HOUSEHOLDER	AVERAGE HOUSEHOLD SPENDING	BEST CUSTOMERS (index)	BIGGEST CUSTOMERS (market share)
Average household	$47.49	100	100.0%
Under age 25	22.22	47	3.1
Aged 25 to 34	50.96	107	17.3
Aged 35 to 44	49.96	105	18.3
Aged 45 to 54	53.06	112	22.1
Aged 55 to 64	54.31	114	20.9
Aged 65 to 74	43.63	92	11.1
Aged 75 or older	35.00	74	7.2

	AVERAGE HOUSEHOLD SPENDING	BEST CUSTOMERS (index)	BIGGEST CUSTOMERS (market share)
HOUSEHOLD INCOME			
Average household	$47.49	100	100.0%
Under $20,000	14.73	31	6.5
$20,000 to $39,999	35.90	76	17.0
$40,000 to $49,999	51.51	108	9.6
$50,000 to $69,999	34.54	73	10.5
$70,000 to $79,999	50.04	105	5.9
$80,000 to $99,999	64.37	136	12.0
$100,000 or more	97.61	206	38.5
HOUSEHOLD TYPE			
Average household	47.49	100	100.0
Married couples	61.64	130	63.0
Married couples, no children	63.66	134	27.9
Married couples with children	64.61	136	32.0
Oldest child under age 6	54.68	115	5.3
Oldest child aged 6 to 17	79.90	168	20.0
Oldest child aged 18 or older	45.27	95	6.7
Single parent with child under age 18	32.55	69	3.6
Single person	33.31	70	20.8
RACE AND HISPANIC ORIGIN			
Average household	47.49	100	100.0
Asian	23.17	49	2.1
Black	39.49	83	10.5
Hispanic	28.31	60	7.5
Non-Hispanic white and other	52.42	110	82.9
REGION			
Average household	47.49	100	100.0
Northeast	37.26	78	14.2
Midwest	59.60	126	27.8
South	54.51	115	42.7
West	32.16	68	15.3
EDUCATION			
Average household	47.49	100	100.0
Less than high school graduate	19.20	40	5.3
High school graduate	31.61	67	16.6
Some college	35.23	74	15.3
Associate's degree	60.90	128	12.7
Bachelor's degree or more	75.56	159	50.2
Bachelor's degree	66.18	139	27.8
Master's, professional, doctoral degree	91.65	193	22.4

Note: Market shares may not sum to 100.0 because of rounding and missing categories by household type. "Asian" and "black" include Hispanics and non-Hispanics who identify themselves as being of the respective race alone. "Hispanic" includes people of any race who identify themselves as Hispanic. "Other" includes people who identify themselves as non-Hispanic and as Alaska Native, American Indian, Asian (who are also included in the "Asian" row), or Native Hawaiian or other Pacific Islander, as well as non-Hispanics reporting more than one race.
Source: Calculations by New Strategist based on the Bureau of Labor Statistics' 2012 Consumer Expenditure Survey

Mattresses and Springs

Best customers: Householders aged 35 to 44
Married couples without children at home
Married couples with school-aged or older children at home
Asians

Customer trends: Average household spending on mattresses and springs should stabilize in the years ahead as the
large millennial generation enters the nest-building lifestage.

The best customers of mattresses and springs are married couples who purchase bedding for expanding families. Householders aged 35 to 44 spend 44 percent more than average on mattresses and springs. Married couples with school-aged or older children at home spend 53 to 72 percent more than average on this item. Married couples without children at home outspend the average on mattresses and springs by 21 percent. Asian households spend 44 percent more than average on mattresses and springs.

After climbing modestly from 2000 to 2006 (the year overall household spending peaked), average household spending on mattresses and springs fell 31 percent between 2006 and the overall trough spending year of 2010, after adjusting for inflation. In the two ensuing years, however, average household spending on mattresses and springs rebounded strongly, with a 49 percent gain. Behind the recent increase was pent-up demand for bedding. Average household spending on mattresses and springs should stabilize in the years ahead as the large millennial generation enters the nest-building lifestage.

Table 7.19 Mattresses and springs

Total household spending $9,509,114,880.00
Average household spends 76.43

AGE OF HOUSEHOLDER	AVERAGE HOUSEHOLD SPENDING	BEST CUSTOMERS (index)	BIGGEST CUSTOMERS (market share)
Average household	$76.43	100	100.0%
Under age 25	67.60	88	5.8
Aged 25 to 34	68.10	89	14.4
Aged 35 to 44	109.76	144	24.9
Aged 45 to 54	82.48	108	21.4
Aged 55 to 64	82.58	108	19.8
Aged 65 to 74	52.45	69	8.3
Aged 75 or older	42.76	56	5.5

	AVERAGE HOUSEHOLD SPENDING	BEST CUSTOMERS (index)	BIGGEST CUSTOMERS (market share)
HOUSEHOLD INCOME			
Average household	$76.43	100	100.0%
Under $20,000	23.03	30	6.3
$20,000 to $39,999	45.99	60	13.6
$40,000 to $49,999	67.96	89	7.9
$50,000 to $69,999	65.36	86	12.4
$70,000 to $79,999	68.23	89	5.0
$80,000 to $99,999	123.88	162	14.3
$100,000 or more	165.75	217	40.6
HOUSEHOLD TYPE			
Average household	76.43	100	100.0
Married couples	103.51	135	65.8
Married couples, no children	92.20	121	25.1
Married couples with children	113.25	148	34.8
Oldest child under age 6	75.52	99	4.5
Oldest child aged 6 to 17	117.14	153	18.2
Oldest child aged 18 or older	131.11	172	12.1
Single parent with child under age 18	60.31	79	4.1
Single person	37.63	49	14.6
RACE AND HISPANIC ORIGIN			
Average household	76.43	100	100.0
Asian	110.15	144	6.2
Black	59.00	77	9.7
Hispanic	50.11	66	8.2
Non-Hispanic white and other	83.84	110	82.3
REGION			
Average household	76.43	100	100.0
Northeast	86.91	114	20.5
Midwest	58.36	76	16.9
South	80.71	106	39.3
West	78.75	103	23.2
EDUCATION			
Average household	76.43	100	100.0
Less than high school graduate	35.53	46	6.1
High school graduate	57.74	76	18.8
Some college	61.63	81	16.6
Associate's degree	69.27	91	9.0
Bachelor's degree or more	120.06	157	49.5
Bachelor's degree	110.07	144	28.7
Master's, professional, doctoral degree	137.20	180	20.8

Note: Market shares may not sum to 100.0 because of rounding and missing categories by household type. "Asian" and "black" include Hispanics and non-Hispanics who identify themselves as being of the respective race alone. "Hispanic" includes people of any race who identify themselves as Hispanic. "Other" includes people who identify themselves as non-Hispanic and as Alaska Native, American Indian, Asian (who are also included in the "Asian" row), or Native Hawaiian or other Pacific Islander, as well as non-Hispanics reporting more than one race.
Source: Calculations by New Strategist based on the Bureau of Labor Statistics' 2012 Consumer Expenditure Survey

Outdoor Equipment

Best customers: Householders aged 35 to 44
Married couples with school-aged children
Households in the West

Customer trends: Average household spending on outdoor equipment is likely to decline in the years ahead
because the Great Recession has reduced household formation and homeownership.

The best customers of outdoor equipment (a broad category that includes grills, bird houses, and outdoor decorative items such as patio statues) are middle-aged couples with school-aged children. Householders aged 35 to 44 spend 29 percent more than average on outdoor equipment. Married couples with school-aged children spend two-and-three-quarter times the average on outdoor equipment. Households in the West spend 32 percent more than average on outdoor equipment.

Average household spending on outdoor equipment was the same in 2012 as it had been in 2000, after adjusting for inflation, but the apparent stability deceives. Spending on this item increased by a solid 33 percent between 2000 and the overall peak-spending year of 2006, then fell by 25 percent over the next six years to end up where it had started. The increase in homeownership during the early part of the 2000s is one factor behind the spending increase. Average household spending on outdoor equipment is likely to decline in the years ahead because the economic downturn has reduced household formation and homeownership.

Table 7.20 Outdoor equipment

Total household spending $3,049,436,160.00
Average household spends 24.51

AGE OF HOUSEHOLDER	AVERAGE HOUSEHOLD SPENDING	BEST CUSTOMERS (index)	BIGGEST CUSTOMERS (market share)
Average household	$24.51	100	100.0%
Under age 25	12.74	52	3.4
Aged 25 to 34	18.68	76	12.3
Aged 35 to 44	31.74	129	22.5
Aged 45 to 54	26.96	110	21.8
Aged 55 to 64	24.71	101	18.5
Aged 65 to 74	27.06	110	13.3
Aged 75 or older	20.95	85	8.4

	AVERAGE HOUSEHOLD SPENDING	BEST CUSTOMERS (index)	BIGGEST CUSTOMERS (market share)
HOUSEHOLD INCOME			
Average household	$24.51	100	100.0%
Under $20,000	3.21	13	2.8
$20,000 to $39,999	15.62	64	14.4
$40,000 to $49,999	31.27	128	11.3
$50,000 to $69,999	18.08	74	10.7
$70,000 to $79,999	17.71	72	4.0
$80,000 to $99,999	16.96	69	6.1
$100,000 or more	65.83	269	50.3
HOUSEHOLD TYPE			
Average household	24.51	100	100.0
Married couples	36.77	150	72.9
Married couples, no children	28.34	116	24.1
Married couples with children	47.94	196	46.0
Oldest child under age 6	24.96	102	4.6
Oldest child aged 6 to 17	68.12	278	33.1
Oldest child aged 18 or older	28.59	117	8.2
Single parent with child under age 18	1.93	8	0.4
Single person	11.84	48	14.3
RACE AND HISPANIC ORIGIN			
Average household	24.51	100	100.0
Asian	7.45	30	1.3
Black	6.28	26	3.2
Hispanic	25.75	105	13.2
Non-Hispanic white and other	27.33	112	83.7
REGION			
Average household	24.51	100	100.0
Northeast	9.58	39	7.1
Midwest	27.23	111	24.6
South	25.47	104	38.7
West	32.31	132	29.7
EDUCATION			
Average household	24.51	100	100.0
Less than high school graduate	8.25	34	4.4
High school graduate	14.88	61	15.1
Some college	19.65	80	16.5
Associate's degree	25.43	104	10.2
Bachelor's degree or more	41.04	167	52.8
Bachelor's degree	38.87	159	31.6
Master's, professional, doctoral degree	44.71	182	21.2

Note: Market shares may not sum to 100.0 because of rounding and missing categories by household type. "Asian" and "black" include Hispanics and non-Hispanics who identify themselves as being of the respective race alone. "Hispanic" includes people of any race who identify themselves as Hispanic. "Other" includes people who identify themselves as non-Hispanic and as Alaska Native, American Indian, Asian (who are also included in the "Asian" row), or Native Hawaiian or other Pacific Islander, as well as non-Hispanics reporting more than one race.
Source: Calculations by New Strategist based on the Bureau of Labor Statistics' 2012 Consumer Expenditure Survey

Outdoor Furniture

Best customers:	Householders aged 35 to 54
	High-income households
	Married couples
	Non-Hispanic whites and Asians
	Households in the West
	College graduates

Customer trends:	Average household spending on outdoor furniture may continue to decline because the small generation X is moving through the best-customer age groups.

The best customers of outdoor furniture are affluent, well-educated middle-aged married couples. Householders aged 35 to 54 spend 40 to 71 percent more than average on this item and control 58 percent of the market. Households with incomes of $100,000 or more spend three-and-one-quarter times the average on outdoor furniture and account for 61 percent of the market. College graduates, a wealthy demographic that spends twice the average on this item, control a similar 64 percent of the market for outdoor furniture. Married couples spend 64 percent more than the average household on outdoor furniture. Asians and non-Hispanic whites outspend the average on this item by 17 and 22 percent, respectively. Households in the West spend 82 percent more than average on outdoor furniture.

Average household spending on outdoor furniture seesawed between 2000 and 2012, falling 12 percent over the first six years of the period, after adjusting for inflation, then growing by 8 percent from 2006 to 2012. Spending on outdoor furniture may continue to decline because the small generation X is moving through the best-customer age groups.

Table 7.21 Outdoor furniture

Total household spending	$2,408,693,760.00
Average household spends	19.36

AGE OF HOUSEHOLDER	AVERAGE HOUSEHOLD SPENDING	BEST CUSTOMERS (index)	BIGGEST CUSTOMERS (market share)
Average household	$19.36	100	100.0%
Under age 25	5.18	27	1.8
Aged 25 to 34	12.60	65	10.5
Aged 35 to 44	27.03	140	24.2
Aged 45 to 54	33.01	171	33.7
Aged 55 to 64	17.71	91	16.7
Aged 65 to 74	17.02	88	10.6
Aged 75 or older	4.79	25	2.4

	AVERAGE HOUSEHOLD SPENDING	BEST CUSTOMERS (index)	BIGGEST CUSTOMERS (market share)
HOUSEHOLD INCOME			
Average household	$19.36	100	100.0%
Under $20,000	3.81	20	4.1
$20,000 to $39,999	7.68	40	8.9
$40,000 to $49,999	12.68	65	5.8
$50,000 to $69,999	11.95	62	8.9
$70,000 to $79,999	13.75	71	4.0
$80,000 to $99,999	16.63	86	7.6
$100,000 or more	62.73	324	60.7
HOUSEHOLD TYPE			
Average household	19.36	100	100.0
Married couples	32.05	166	80.4
Married couples, no children	27.90	144	30.0
Married couples with children	37.69	195	45.8
Oldest child under age 6	24.65	127	5.8
Oldest child aged 6 to 17	48.27	249	29.7
Oldest child aged 18 or older	28.30	146	10.3
Single parent with child under age 18	7.23	37	2.0
Single person	5.50	28	8.4
RACE AND HISPANIC ORIGIN			
Average household	19.36	100	100.0
Asian	22.73	117	5.1
Black	6.07	31	3.9
Hispanic	6.96	36	4.5
Non-Hispanic white and other	23.66	122	91.7
REGION			
Average household	19.36	100	100.0
Northeast	20.45	106	19.1
Midwest	18.79	97	21.5
South	15.84	82	30.5
West	24.87	128	28.9
EDUCATION			
Average household	19.36	100	100.0
Less than high school graduate	3.64	19	2.5
High school graduate	11.02	57	14.2
Some college	7.37	38	7.8
Associate's degree	21.77	112	11.1
Bachelor's degree or more	39.55	204	64.4
Bachelor's degree	33.69	174	34.7
Master's, professional, doctoral degree	49.60	256	29.7

Note: Market shares may not sum to 100.0 because of rounding and missing categories by household type. "Asian" and "black" include Hispanics and non-Hispanics who identify themselves as being of the respective race alone. "Hispanic" includes people of any race who identify themselves as Hispanic. "Other" includes people who identify themselves as non-Hispanic and as Alaska Native, American Indian, Asian (who are also included in the "Asian" row), or Native Hawaiian or other Pacific Islander, as well as non-Hispanics reporting more than one race.
Source: Calculations by New Strategist based on the Bureau of Labor Statistics' 2012 Consumer Expenditure Survey

Plants and Fresh Flowers, Indoor

Best customers: Householders aged 45 to 64
Married couples without children at home
Married couples with adult children at home
Asians and non-Hispanic whites
Households in the Northeast and West

Customer trends: Average household spending on indoor plants and fresh flowers should stabilize as the economic recovery continues.

The best customers of indoor plants and fresh flowers are older married couples. Many are buying flowers for anniversaries or for ailing friends and relatives. Married couples without children at home (most of them empty-nesters) spend 80 percent more than average on indoor plants and fresh flowers, while those with adult children at home spend 28 percent more. Householders aged 45 to 64 spend 22 to 49 percent more than average on this item and constitute just over half the market. Asians outspend the average by 23 percent, and non-Hispanic whites do so by 18 percent. Households in the Northeast outspend the average by 19 percent, and those in the West by 16 percent.

Average household spending on indoor plants and fresh flowers fell 41 percent between 2000 and 2010, after adjusting for inflation, but rebounded by a strong 19 percent in the ensuing two years. The lower prices offered by grocery stores and discounters such as Wal-Mart are behind the decline, as well as belt tightening in face of the Great Recession. Average household spending on indoor plants and fresh flowers should stabilize as the economic recovery continues.

Table 7.22 Plants and fresh flowers, indoor

Total household spending $6,664,965,120.00
Average household spends 53.57

AGE OF HOUSEHOLDER	AVERAGE HOUSEHOLD SPENDING	BEST CUSTOMERS (index)	BIGGEST CUSTOMERS (market share)
Average household	$53.57	100	100.0%
Under age 25	17.10	32	2.1
Aged 25 to 34	38.39	72	11.6
Aged 35 to 44	38.06	71	12.3
Aged 45 to 54	65.60	122	24.2
Aged 55 to 64	79.92	149	27.3
Aged 65 to 74	61.50	115	13.8
Aged 75 or older	47.22	88	8.6

	AVERAGE HOUSEHOLD SPENDING	BEST CUSTOMERS (index)	BIGGEST CUSTOMERS (market share)
HOUSEHOLD INCOME			
Average household	**$53.57**	**100**	**100.0%**
Under $20,000	16.72	31	6.6
$20,000 to $39,999	28.00	52	11.8
$40,000 to $49,999	42.19	79	7.0
$50,000 to $69,999	49.26	92	13.3
$70,000 to $79,999	66.33	124	6.9
$80,000 to $99,999	69.89	130	11.5
$100,000 or more	122.97	230	43.0
HOUSEHOLD TYPE			
Average household	**53.57**	**100**	**100.0**
Married couples	74.05	138	67.1
Married couples, no children	96.61	180	37.6
Married couples with children	58.71	110	25.8
Oldest child under age 6	47.26	88	4.0
Oldest child aged 6 to 17	57.20	107	12.7
Oldest child aged 18 or older	68.66	128	9.0
Single parent with child under age 18	26.24	49	2.6
Single person	32.91	61	18.2
RACE AND HISPANIC ORIGIN			
Average household	**53.57**	**100**	**100.0**
Asian	65.75	123	5.3
Black	19.81	37	4.6
Hispanic	29.76	56	7.0
Non-Hispanic white and other	63.11	118	88.4
REGION			
Average household	**53.57**	**100**	**100.0**
Northeast	63.60	119	21.4
Midwest	52.45	98	21.7
South	^4.04	82	30.6
West	62.38	116	26.2
EDUCATION			
Average household	**53.57**	**100**	**100.0**
Less than high school graduate	23.37	44	5.7
High school graduate	37.30	70	17.4
Some college	44.42	83	17.1
Associate's degree	48.91	91	9.0
Bachelor's degree or more	86.37	161	50.8
Bachelor's degree	78.21	146	29.1
Master's, professional, doctoral degree	100.39	187	21.8

Note: Market shares may not sum to 100.0 because of rounding and missing categories by household type. "Asian" and "black" include Hispanics and non-Hispanics who identify themselves as being of the respective race alone. "Hispanic" includes people of any race who identify themselves as Hispanic. "Other" includes people who identify themselves as non-Hispanic and as Alaska Native, American Indian, Asian (who are also included in the "Asian" row), or Native Hawaiian or other Pacific Islander, as well as non-Hispanics reporting more than one race.
Source: Calculations by New Strategist based on the Bureau of Labor Statistics' 2012 Consumer Expenditure Survey

Portable Heating and Cooling Equipment

Best customers:
Householders aged 45 to 64
Married couples without children at home
Married couples with preschoolers
Blacks
Households in the South

Customer trends:
Average household spending on portable heating and cooling equipment will continue to grow as global warming intensifies.

Older Americans are the biggest spenders on portable heating and cooling equipment, a category that includes window air conditioners. Householders aged 45 to 54 spend 51 percent more than average on this item, and those aged 55 to 64 spend 95 percent more than average. Many older householders live in homes without central air conditioning, necessitating the purchase of window air conditioners as average temperatures rise. Married couples without children at home (most of them older) spend 89 percent more than average on portable heating and cooling equipment. Couples with preschoolers spend nearly two-and-one-half times the average on such equipment. Black households spend 11 percent more than average on portable heating and cooling equipment. Households in the South, where many blacks reside, outspend the average by 33 percent and control 50 percent of the market.

Average household spending on portable heating and cooling equipment rose by 21 percent between 2000 and 2012, after adjusting for inflation. Behind the increase are rising temperatures, which drive the purchase of window air conditioners. Spending on portable heating and cooling equipment will continue to grow as global warming intensifies.

Table 7.23 Portable heating and cooling equipment

Total household spending $1,099,837,440.00
Average household spends   8.84

AGE OF HOUSEHOLDER	AVERAGE HOUSEHOLD SPENDING	BEST CUSTOMERS (index)	BIGGEST CUSTOMERS (market share)
Average household	$8.84	100	100.0%
Under age 25	4.95	56	3.7
Aged 25 to 34	2.43	27	4.4
Aged 35 to 44	6.90	78	13.5
Aged 45 to 54	13.36	151	29.9
Aged 55 to 64	17.20	195	35.6
Aged 65 to 74	8.83	100	12.0
Aged 75 or older	1.32	15	1.5

	AVERAGE HOUSEHOLD SPENDING	BEST CUSTOMERS (index)	BIGGEST CUSTOMERS (market share)
HOUSEHOLD INCOME			
Average household	**$8.84**	**100**	**100.0%**
Under $20,000	2.57	29	6.1
$20,000 to $39,999	10.32	117	26.3
$40,000 to $49,999	5.83	66	5.8
$50,000 to $69,999	8.32	94	13.6
$70,000 to $79,999	38.34	434	24.2
$80,000 to $99,999	3.43	39	3.4
$100,000 or more	10.36	117	21.9
HOUSEHOLD TYPE			
Average household	**8.84**	**100**	**100.0**
Married couples	10.89	123	59.8
Married couples, no children	16.73	189	39.5
Married couples with children	6.78	77	18.0
Oldest child under age 6	21.34	241	11.0
Oldest child aged 6 to 17	4.30	49	5.8
Oldest child aged 18 or older	1.86	21	1.5
Single parent with child under age 18	1.71	19	1.0
Single person	6.69	76	22.5
RACE AND HISPANIC ORIGIN			
Average household	**8.84**	**100**	**100.0**
Asian	2.33	26	1.1
Black	9.79	111	13.9
Hispanic	4.74	54	6.7
Non-Hispanic white and other	9.34	106	79.3
REGION			
Average household	**8.84**	**100**	**100.0**
Northeast	6.58	74	13.4
Midwest	6.09	69	15.3
South	11.79	133	49.7
West	8.56	97	21.8
EDUCATION			
Average household	**8.84**	**100**	**100.0**
Less than high school graduate	14.99	170	22.1
High school graduate	7.42	84	20.9
Some college	2.66	30	6.2
Associate's degree	6.60	75	7.4
Bachelor's degree or more	12.52	142	44.7
Bachelor's degree	15.64	177	35.3
Master's, professional, doctoral degree	7.23	82	9.5

Note: Market shares may not sum to 100.0 because of rounding and missing categories by household type. "Asian" and "black" include Hispanics and non-Hispanics who identify themselves as being of the respective race alone. "Hispanic" includes people of any race who identify themselves as Hispanic. "Other" includes people who identify themselves as non-Hispanic and as Alaska Native, American Indian, Asian (who are also included in the "Asian" row), or Native Hawaiian or other Pacific Islander, as well as non-Hispanics reporting more than one race.
Source: Calculations by New Strategist based on the Bureau of Labor Statistics' 2012 Consumer Expenditure Survey

Power and Hand Tools

Best customers: Householders aged 45 to 54
                         Married couples with adult children at home
                         Hispanics
                         Households in the South
                         Householders without a high school diploma

Customer trends: Average household spending on power and hand tools may continue to increase in the years
                         ahead as the large millennial generation enters the do-it-yourself lifestage.

The best customers of power and hand tools are homeowners tackling do-it-yourself projects. This explains why householders aged 45 to 54 spend 91 percent more than average on tools and control a sizeable 38 percent share of the market. Married couples with adult children at home spend more than three-and-one-half times the average on tools. Hispanics, many of whom have construction work experience, outspend the average for ths item by 20 percent. Households in the South spend 31 percent more than average on tools. Householders without a high school diploma, many of them Hispanics, spend over twice the average on power and hand tools.

Average household spending on power and hand tools fell 5 percent between 2000 and 2006, after adjusting for inflation, but grew by 41 percent between 2006 and 2012. Behind the increase was the Great Recession, spurring more homeowners to tackle projects themselves rather than hire someone. Spending on tools may continue to increase in the years ahead as the large millennial generation enters the do-it-yourself lifestage.

Table 7.24 Power and hand tools

Total household spending $6,361,390,080.00
Average household spends   51.13

AGE OF HOUSEHOLDER	AVERAGE HOUSEHOLD SPENDING	BEST CUSTOMERS (index)	BIGGEST CUSTOMERS (market share)
Average household	$51.13	100	100.0%
Under age 25	29.97	59	3.8
Aged 25 to 34	31.86	62	10.1
Aged 35 to 44	52.79	103	17.9
Aged 45 to 54	97.88	191	37.9
Aged 55 to 64	43.85	86	15.7
Aged 65 to 74	39.95	78	9.4
Aged 75 or older	26.75	52	5.1

	AVERAGE HOUSEHOLD SPENDING	BEST CUSTOMERS (index)	BIGGEST CUSTOMERS (market share)
HOUSEHOLD INCOME			
Average household	**$51.13**	**100**	**100.0%**
Under $20,000	21.25	42	8.7
$20,000 to $39,999	25.21	49	11.1
$40,000 to $49,999	41.03	80	7.1
$50,000 to $69,999	67.31	132	19.0
$70,000 to $79,999	37.91	74	4.1
$80,000 to $99,999	141.88	277	24.5
$100,000 or more	72.31	141	26.5
HOUSEHOLD TYPE			
Average household	**51.13**	**100**	**100.0**
Married couples	72.21	141	68.6
Married couples, no children	54.89	107	22.4
Married couples with children	85.91	168	39.5
Oldest child under age 6	26.17	51	2.3
Oldest child aged 6 to 17	48.59	95	11.3
Oldest child aged 18 or older	185.39	363	25.6
Single parent with child under age 18	19.60	38	2.0
Single person	32.34	63	18.8
RACE AND HISPANIC ORIGIN			
Average household	**51.13**	**100**	**100.0**
Asian	19.01	37	1.6
Black	28.06	55	6.9
Hispanic	61.43	120	15.1
Non-Hispanic white and other	53.22	104	78.1
REGION			
Average household	**51.13**	**100**	**100.0**
Northeast	28.94	57	10.2
Midwest	39.14	77	17.0
South	67.18	131	48.9
West	54.50	107	24.0
EDUCATION			
Average household	**51.13**	**100**	**100.0**
Less than high school graduate	108.03	211	27.6
High school graduate	38.47	75	18.8
Some college	40.60	79	16.4
Associate's degree	50.24	98	9.7
Bachelor's degree or more	46.96	92	29.0
Bachelor's degree	50.83	99	19.8
Master's, professional, doctoral degree	40.42	79	9.2

Note: Market shares may not sum to 100.0 because of rounding and missing categories by household type. "Asian" and "black" include Hispanics and non-Hispanics who identify themselves as being of the respective race alone. "Hispanic" includes people of any race who identify themselves as Hispanic. "Other" includes people who identify themselves as non-Hispanic and as Alaska Native, American Indian, Asian (who are also included in the "Asian" row), or Native Hawaiian or other Pacific Islander, as well as non-Hispanics reporting more than one race.
Source: Calculations by New Strategist based on the Bureau of Labor Statistics' 2012 Consumer Expenditure Survey

Sewing Materials for Household Items

Best customers: Householders aged 55 to 74
                        Married couples without children at home
                        Non-Hispanic whites
                        Households in the West

Customer trends: Average household spending on sewing materials for household items is likely to continue
                        to fall in the years ahead as younger generations with little skill in sewing fill the
                        best-customer age groups.

Sewing is becoming a lost art, and younger generations are much less knowledgeable about sewing than older women. The best customers of sewing materials for household items—such as quilts, slipcovers, and curtains—are householders aged 55 to 74. Those aged 55 to 64 spend 41 percent more than average on sewing materials, while householders aged 65 to 74 spend 84 percent more. Married couples without children at home (most of them older) outspend the average on sewing materials by 73 percent. Non-Hispanic whites dominate spending on this item and account for 95 percent of the market. Households in the West spend 67 percent more than average on sewing materials.

After climbing 6 percent from 2000 to 2006, average household spending on sewing materials for household items fell 38 percent between 2006 and 2012, after adjusting for inflation. Spending on sewing materials for household items is likely to continue to fall in the years ahead as younger generations with little skill in sewing fill the best-customer age groups.

Table 7.25 Sewing materials for household items

Total household spending $1,055,047,680.00
Average household spends   8.48

AGE OF HOUSEHOLDER	AVERAGE HOUSEHOLD SPENDING	BEST CUSTOMERS (index)	BIGGEST CUSTOMERS (market share)
Average household	$8.48	100	100.0%
Under age 25	2.13	25	1.6
Aged 25 to 34	5.44	64	10.4
Aged 35 to 44	3.73	44	7.6
Aged 45 to 54	9.46	112	22.1
Aged 55 to 64	11.92	141	25.7
Aged 65 to 74	15.57	184	22.1
Aged 75 or older	9.04	107	10.4

	AVERAGE HOUSEHOLD SPENDING	BEST CUSTOMERS (index)	BIGGEST CUSTOMERS (market share)
HOUSEHOLD INCOME			
Average household	**$8.48**	**100**	**100.0%**
Under $20,000	2.13	25	5.3
$20,000 to $39,999	5.40	64	14.3
$40,000 to $49,999	12.76	150	13.3
$50,000 to $69,999	6.89	81	11.7
$70,000 to $79,999	21.16	250	13.9
$80,000 to $99,999	13.68	161	14.2
$100,000 or more	12.29	145	27.1
HOUSEHOLD TYPE			
Average household	**8.48**	**100**	**100.0**
Married couples	11.88	140	68.0
Married couples, no children	14.66	173	36.0
Married couples with children	7.65	90	21.2
Oldest child under age 6	4.04	48	2.2
Oldest child aged 6 to 17	7.86	93	11.0
Oldest child aged 18 or older	9.62	113	8.0
Single parent with child under age 18	4.10	48	2.5
Single person	6.29	74	22.0
RACE AND HISPANIC ORIGIN			
Average household	**8.48**	**100**	**100.0**
Asian	2.18	26	1.1
Black	2.28	27	3.4
Hispanic	1.06	13	1.6
Non-Hispanic white and other	10.74	127	95.1
REGION			
Average household	**8.48**	**100**	**100.0**
Northeast	5.39	64	11.5
Midwest	8.54	101	22.3
South	6.50	77	28.5
West	14.17	167	37.7
EDUCATION			
Average household	**8.48**	**100**	**100.0**
Less than high school graduate	2.06	24	3.2
High school graduate	7.97	94	23.4
Some college	10.67	126	25.9
Associate's degree	8.82	104	10.3
Bachelor's degree or more	10.00	118	37.2
Bachelor's degree	9.82	116	23.1
Master's, professional, doctoral degree	10.31	122	14.1

Note: Market shares may not sum to 100.0 because of rounding and missing categories by household type. "Asian" and "black" include Hispanics and non-Hispanics who identify themselves as being of the respective race alone. "Hispanic" includes people of any race who identify themselves as Hispanic. "Other" includes people who identify themselves as non-Hispanic and as Alaska Native, American Indian, Asian (who are also included in the "Asian" row), or Native Hawaiian or other Pacific Islander, as well as non-Hispanics reporting more than one race.
Source: Calculations by New Strategist based on the Bureau of Labor Statistics' 2012 Consumer Expenditure Survey

Slipcovers and Decorative Pillows

Best customers: Householders aged 45 to 54
Married couples with adult children at home
Asians
Households in the Northeast

Customer trends: Average household spending on slipcovers and decorative pillows is likely to continue to fall as
the slow recovery from the Great Recession limits discretionary spending.

The biggest spenders on slipcovers and decorative pillows are married couples with grown children at home. Householders aged 45 to 54 spend 68 percent more than the average household on slipcovers and decorative pillows. Married couples with adult children at home spend close to four times the average on this item. Asians spend 26 percent more than average on slipcovers and decorative pillows, and households in the Northeast spend well over twice the average on this item.

After growing 52 percent between 2000 and 2006, average household spending on slipcovers and decorative pillows fell 29 percent between 2006 and 2012, after adjusting for inflation. Behind the decline was the end of the homeownership boom and belt tightening due to the Great Recession. Average household spending on slipcovers and decorative pillows is likely to continue to fall as the slow recovery from the economic downturn limits discretionary spending.

Table 7.26 **Slipcovers and decorative pillows**

Total household spending $490,199,040.00
Average household spends   3.94

	AVERAGE HOUSEHOLD SPENDING	BEST CUSTOMERS (index)	BIGGEST CUSTOMERS (market share)
AGE OF HOUSEHOLDER			
Average household	$3.94	100	100.0%
Under age 25	1.36	35	2.3
Aged 25 to 34	4.14	105	17.0
Aged 35 to 44	3.93	100	17.3
Aged 45 to 54	6.61	168	33.2
Aged 55 to 64	4.14	105	19.2
Aged 65 to 74	2.73	69	8.3
Aged 75 or older	1.12	28	2.8

	AVERAGE HOUSEHOLD SPENDING	BEST CUSTOMERS (index)	BIGGEST CUSTOMERS (market share)
HOUSEHOLD INCOME			
Average household	**$3.94**	**100**	**100.0%**
Under $20,000	1.64	42	8.8
$20,000 to $39,999	1.33	34	7.6
$40,000 to $49,999	1.57	40	3.5
$50,000 to $69,999	1.69	43	6.2
$70,000 to $79,999	3.33	85	4.7
$80,000 to $99,999	6.43	163	14.4
$100,000 or more	11.56	293	54.9
HOUSEHOLD TYPE			
Average household	**3.94**	**100**	**100.0**
Married couples	5.69	144	70.1
Married couples, no children	3.90	99	20.6
Married couples with children	7.44	189	44.4
Oldest child under age 6	3.27	83	3.8
Oldest child aged 6 to 17	4.56	116	13.8
Oldest child aged 18 or older	14.98	380	26.8
Single parent with child under age 18	2.13	54	2.8
Single person	1.87	47	14.1
RACE AND HISPANIC ORIGIN			
Average household	**3.94**	**100**	**100.0**
Asian	4.95	126	5.4
Black	3.43	87	10.9
Hispanic	1.57	40	5.0
Non-Hispanic white and other	4.42	112	84.2
REGION			
Average household	**3.94**	**100**	**100.0**
Northeast	9.34	237	42.8
Midwest	2.76	70	15.5
South	2.56	65	24.2
West	3.07	78	17.6
EDUCATION			
Average household	**3.94**	**100**	**100.0**
Less than high school graduate	1.00	25	3.3
High school graduate	1.88	48	11.9
Some college	3.25	82	17.0
Associate's degree	3.11	79	7.8
Bachelor's degree or more	7.51	191	60.1
Bachelor's degree	8.52	216	43.1
Master's, professional, doctoral degree	5.76	146	17.0

Note: Market shares may not sum to 100.0 because of rounding and missing categories by household type. "Asian" and "black" include Hispanics and non-Hispanics who identify themselves as being of the respective race alone. "Hispanic" includes people of any race who identify themselves as Hispanic. "Other" includes people who identify themselves as non-Hispanic and as Alaska Native, American Indian, Asian (who are also included in the "Asian" row), or Native Hawaiian or other Pacific Islander, as well as non-Hispanics reporting more than one race.
Source: Calculations by New Strategist based on the Bureau of Labor Statistics' 2012 Consumer Expenditure Survey

Sofas

Best customers:
Householders aged 35 to 54
Married couples with children at home
Asians

Customer trends:
Average household spending on sofas may resume its decline in the years ahead because of the slow recovery from the Great Recession and anemic household formation.

Sofas are the third-largest home furnishing expense for the average household and consume 6 percent of the average home furnishings budget. Householders aged 35 to 54 spend 18 to 34 percent more than average on sofas. Married couples with school-aged or older children at home spend 50 to 52 percent more than average on sofas, while couples with preschoolers outspend the average by 28 percent. Asian households spend 39 percent more than average on sofas.

After rising moderately between 2000 and 2006, average household spending on sofas declined 23 percent between 2006 and 2012, after adjusting for inflation. Behind the decline was the economic downturn and the collapse of the housing market. Spending on sofas grew by a solid 14 percent between 2010 and 2012, an increase likely due to pent-up demand for this item. Average household spending on sofas may resume its decline in the years ahead because of the slow recovery from the Great Recession and anemic household formation.

Table 7.27 Sofas

Total household spending $12,610,805,760.00
Average household spends 101.36

AGE OF HOUSEHOLDER	AVERAGE HOUSEHOLD SPENDING	BEST CUSTOMERS (index)	BIGGEST CUSTOMERS (market share)
Average household	$101.36	100	100.0%
Under age 25	107.62	106	7.0
Aged 25 to 34	112.62	111	18.0
Aged 35 to 44	136.20	134	23.3
Aged 45 to 54	119.60	118	23.4
Aged 55 to 64	100.63	99	18.2
Aged 65 to 74	58.65	58	7.0
Aged 75 or older	33.80	33	3.3

	AVERAGE HOUSEHOLD SPENDING	BEST CUSTOMERS (index)	BIGGEST CUSTOMERS (market share)
HOUSEHOLD INCOME			
Average household	$101.36	100	100.0%
Under $20,000	25.87	26	5.4
$20,000 to $39,999	65.88	65	14.6
$40,000 to $49,999	92.93	92	8.1
$50,000 to $69,999	99.74	98	14.2
$70,000 to $79,999	83.25	82	4.6
$80,000 to $99,999	110.99	110	9.7
$100,000 or more	235.04	232	43.4
HOUSEHOLD TYPE			
Average household	101.36	100	100.0
Married couples	126.25	125	60.5
Married couples, no children	106.95	106	22.0
Married couples with children	148.68	147	34.5
Oldest child under age 6	129.31	128	5.8
Oldest child aged 6 to 17	154.07	152	18.1
Oldest child aged 18 or older	152.11	150	10.6
Single parent with child under age 18	62.24	61	3.2
Single person	72.14	71	21.1
RACE AND HISPANIC ORIGIN			
Average household	101.36	100	100.0
Asian	140.40	139	6.0
Black	96.00	95	11.9
Hispanic	96.80	96	12.0
Non-Hispanic white and other	103.67	102	76.8
REGION			
Average household	101.36	100	100.0
Northeast	89.61	88	16.0
Midwest	111.66	110	24.4
South	105.35	104	38.7
West	94.06	93	20.9
EDUCATION			
Average household	101.36	100	100.0
Less than high school graduate	57.18	56	7.4
High school graduate	63.28	62	15.6
Some college	93.81	93	19.1
Associate's degree	106.13	105	10.3
Bachelor's degree or more	153.21	151	47.7
Bachelor's degree	131.98	130	26.0
Master's, professional, doctoral degree	189.66	187	21.7

Note: Market shares may not sum to 100.0 because of rounding and missing categories by household type. "Asian" and "black" include Hispanics and non-Hispanics who identify themselves as being of the respective race alone. "Hispanic" includes people of any race who identify themselves as Hispanic. "Other" includes people who identify themselves as non-Hispanic and as Alaska Native, American Indian, Asian (who are also included in the "Asian" row), or Native Hawaiian or other Pacific Islander, as well as non-Hispanics reporting more than one race.
Source: Calculations by New Strategist based on the Bureau of Labor Statistics' 2012 Consumer Expenditure Survey

Wall Units, Cabinets, and Other Furniture

Best customers: Householders aged 35 to 54
                         Married couples with school-aged children
                         Households in the West

Customer trends: Average household spending on wall units, cabinets, and other furniture may continue to decline
                         in the years ahead because of the slow recovery from the Great Recession and anemic
                         household formation.

The biggest spenders on wall units, cabinets, and other furniture are middle-aged married couples with children. Householders aged 35 to 54 spend 27 to 47 percent more than the average household on this item. Married couples with school-aged children spend more than two-and-one-half times the average. Households in the West outspend the average by 50 percent.

After growing by a moderate 7 percent from 2000 to 2006 (the year when overall household spending peaked), average household spending on wall units, cabinets, and other furniture plunged 41 percent between 2006 and 2012, after adjusting for inflation. Average household spending on wall units may continue to decline in the years ahead because of the slow recovery from the Great Recession and anemic household formation.

Table 7.28 Wall units, cabinets, and other furniture

Total household spending $5,273,994,240.00
Average household spends   42.39

	AVERAGE HOUSEHOLD SPENDING	BEST CUSTOMERS (index)	BIGGEST CUSTOMERS (market share)
AGE OF HOUSEHOLDER			
Average household	$42.39	100	100.0%
Under age 25	22.89	54	3.5
Aged 25 to 34	35.93	85	13.7
Aged 35 to 44	53.86	127	22.1
Aged 45 to 54	62.29	147	29.1
Aged 55 to 64	37.89	89	16.4
Aged 65 to 74	40.32	95	11.5
Aged 75 or older	16.42	39	3.8

	AVERAGE HOUSEHOLD SPENDING	BEST CUSTOMERS (index)	BIGGEST CUSTOMERS (market share)
HOUSEHOLD INCOME			
Average household	$42.39	100	100.0%
Under $20,000	14.83	35	7.4
$20,000 to $39,999	21.29	50	11.3
$40,000 to $49,999	34.40	81	7.2
$50,000 to $69,999	22.41	53	7.6
$70,000 to $79,999	30.53	72	4.0
$80,000 to $99,999	38.92	92	8.1
$100,000 or more	123.10	290	54.4
HOUSEHOLD TYPE			
Average household	42.39	100	100.0
Married couples	61.12	144	70.0
Married couples, no children	46.95	111	23.1
Married couples with children	75.06	177	41.6
Oldest child under age 6	35.74	84	3.8
Oldest child aged 6 to 17	111.54	263	31.3
Oldest child aged 18 or older	38.99	92	6.5
Single parent with child under age 18	17.57	41	2.2
Single person	26.73	63	18.7
RACE AND HISPANIC ORIGIN			
Average household	42.39	100	100.0
Asian	43.41	102	4.4
Black	21.49	51	6.4
Hispanic	21.87	52	6.5
Non-Hispanic white and other	49.26	116	87.2
REGION			
Average household	42.39	100	100.0
Northeast	37.24	88	15.9
Midwest	43.13	102	22.6
South	31.64	75	27.8
West	63.55	150	33.8
EDUCATION			
Average household	42.39	100	100.0
Less than high school graduate	10.94	26	3.4
High school graduate	19.98	47	11.8
Some college	26.02	61	12.6
Associate's degree	41.13	97	9.6
Bachelor's degree or more	84.20	199	62.6
Bachelor's degree	75.96	179	35.7
Master's, professional, doctoral degree	98.34	232	26.9

Note: Market shares may not sum to 100.0 because of rounding and missing categories by household type. "Asian" and "black" include Hispanics and non-Hispanics who identify themselves as being of the respective race alone. "Hispanic" includes people of any race who identify themselves as Hispanic. "Other" includes people who identify themselves as non-Hispanic and as Alaska Native, American Indian, Asian (who are also included in the "Asian" row), or Native Hawaiian or other Pacific Islander, as well as non-Hispanics reporting more than one race.
Source: Calculations by New Strategist based on the Bureau of Labor Statistics' 2012 Consumer Expenditure Survey

Window Coverings

Best customers:
Married couples without children at home
Married couples with school-aged children
Asians
Households in the West

Customer trends:
Average household spending on window coverings is likely to continue to fall because of the slow recovery from the Great Recession and anemic household formation.

The biggest spenders on window coverings—a category that includes blinds and shutters, but not curtains or draperies—are married couples with school-aged children, who spend twice the average on this item. Couples without children at home spend 54 percent more than average on window coverings. Asian households spend twice the average on window coverings. Households in the West, where many Asians reside, outspend the average by 48 percent.

After growing by 75 percent from 2000 to 2006, average household spending on window coverings fell 52 percent between 2006 and 2012, after adjusting for inflation. Behind the decline was the end of the homeownership boom and belt tightening due to the Great Recession. Average household spending on window coverings is likely to continue to fall because of the slow recovery from the Great Recession and anemic household formation.

Table 7.29 Window coverings

Total household spending $1,821,450,240.00
Average household spends 14.64

AGE OF HOUSEHOLDER	AVERAGE HOUSEHOLD SPENDING	BEST CUSTOMERS (index)	BIGGEST CUSTOMERS (market share)
Average household	$14.64	100	100.0%
Under age 25	2.65	18	1.2
Aged 25 to 34	6.88	47	7.6
Aged 35 to 44	18.58	127	22.0
Aged 45 to 54	13.67	93	18.5
Aged 55 to 64	20.31	139	25.4
Aged 65 to 74	13.22	90	10.9
Aged 75 or older	21.63	148	14.4

	AVERAGE HOUSEHOLD SPENDING	BEST CUSTOMERS (index)	BIGGEST CUSTOMERS (market share)
HOUSEHOLD INCOME			
Average household	**$14.64**	**100**	**100.0%**
Under $20,000	1.36	9	2.0
$20,000 to $39,999	4.88	33	7.5
$40,000 to $49,999	13.15	90	7.9
$50,000 to $69,999	10.79	74	10.6
$70,000 to $79,999	15.26	104	5.8
$80,000 to $99,999	25.61	175	15.4
$100,000 or more	39.63	271	50.7
HOUSEHOLD TYPE			
Average household	**14.64**	**100**	**100.0**
Married couples	20.97	143	69.6
Married couples, no children	22.57	154	32.1
Married couples with children	21.79	149	35.0
Oldest child under age 6	17.51	120	5.5
Oldest child aged 6 to 17	30.13	206	24.5
Oldest child aged 18 or older	10.51	72	5.1
Single parent with child under age 18	7.64	52	2.7
Single person	8.98	61	18.2
RACE AND HISPANIC ORIGIN			
Average household	**14.64**	**100**	**100.0**
Asian	29.46	201	8.7
Black	4.81	33	4.1
Hispanic	7.93	54	6.8
Non-Hispanic white and other	17.37	119	89.1
REGION			
Average household	**14.64**	**100**	**100.0**
Northeast	16.07	110	19.8
Midwest	15.69	107	23.8
South	9.09	62	23.1
West	21.65	148	33.3
EDUCATION			
Average household	**14.64**	**100**	**100.0**
Less than high school graduate	7.31	50	6.5
High school graduate	6.98	48	11.9
Some college	22.29	152	31.4
Associate's degree	7.84	54	5.3
Bachelor's degree or more	20.86	142	44.9
Bachelor's degree	11.87	81	16.2
Master's, professional, doctoral degree	36.31	248	28.8

Note: Market shares may not sum to 100.0 because of rounding and missing categories by household type. "Asian" and "black" include Hispanics and non-Hispanics who identify themselves as being of the respective race alone. "Hispanic" includes people of any race who identify themselves as Hispanic. "Other" includes people who identify themselves as non-Hispanic and as Alaska Native, American Indian, Asian (who are also included in the "Asian" row), or Native Hawaiian or other Pacific Islander, as well as non-Hispanics reporting more than one race.
Source: Calculations by New Strategist based on the Bureau of Labor Statistics' 2012 Consumer Expenditure Survey

Chapter 8.

Gifts for People in Other Households

Household Spending on Gifts for People in Other Households, 2000 to 2012

Average household spending on gifts for people in other households fell by one-quarter between 2000 and 2010, after adjusting for inflation. It then increased by 3 percent from 2010, the year overall household spending was at its lowest, to 2012. The most generous gift-givers are middle-aged and older Americans helping their children and grandchildren pay for college. Consequently, gifts of education expenses, which increased 29 percent between 2000 and 2012, account for the largest—and growing—share (23 percent) of gift giving. Spending on gifts of transportation, the second-largest gift category in 2012 with a 10 percent share, increased 39 percent from its low point in 2006 to 2012. Average household spending on gifts of food, the third-largest gift category, is on a rollercoaster ride, growing 43 percent from 2000 to 2006, declining 30 percent from 2006 to 2010, and growing 12 percent over the ensuing two-year period.

Average household spending on gifts of health care expenses, which had fallen a stark 56 percent from 2000 to 2010, more than doubled in the ensuing two years, after adjusting for inflation, for an unspectacular 4 percent cumulative gain. Gifts of women's and girls' clothing dropped 32 percent between 2000 and 2010 and then grew 12 percent from 2010 to 2012. Gifts of men's and boys' clothing declined an even steeper 42 percent during the 2000-to-2010 time period, but showed no sign of recovery in the following two-year period.

Spending on gifts for people in other households

(average annual spending of households on gifts for people in other households, 2000, 2006, 2010, and 2012; in 2012 dollars)

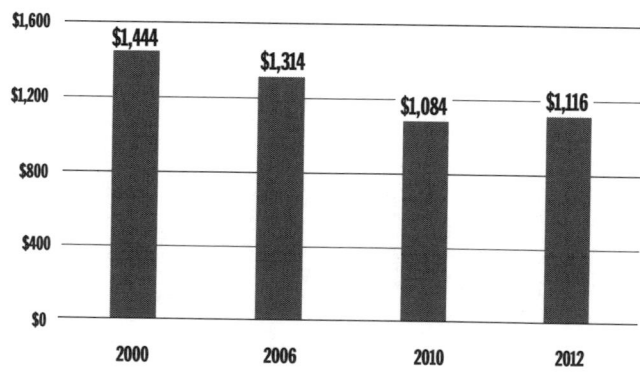

Table 8.1 Spending on gifts for people in other households, 2000 to 2012

(average annual household spending on gifts for people in other households and percent distribution, by category, 2000 to 2012; percent change and percentage point change in spending, 2000–06, 2006–12, and 2010–12; in 2012 dollars; ranked by amount spent)

	average annual household spending (in 2012$)				percent change		
	2012	2010	2006	2000	2010–12	2006–12	2000–06
Average household spending on gifts for people in other households	**$1,116.23**	**$1,083.93**	**$1,314.32**	**$1,444.15**	**3.0%**	**−15.1%**	**−9.0%**
Education expenses	260.19	232.64	239.10	201.33	11.8	8.8	18.8
Transportation	111.41	89.21	80.13	93.69	24.9	39.0	−14.5
Food	104.33	93.26	133.28	93.45	11.9	−21.7	42.6
Women's and girls' apparel	86.16	77.17	95.02	113.70	11.7	−9.3	−16.4
Entertainment	81.73	100.10	86.88	125.01	−18.4	−5.9	−30.5
Health care expenses	52.74	22.17	46.34	50.77	137.8	13.8	−8.7
Men's and boys' apparel	52.66	52.21	67.82	90.06	0.9	−22.4	−24.7
Household equipment	48.01	49.02	56.10	93.74	−2.1	−14.4	−40.2
Housekeeping supplies	28.52	26.46	31.61	52.13	7.8	−9.8	−39.4
Jewelry and watches	23.88	18.06	27.29	22.47	32.2	−12.5	21.5
Infants' apparel	20.03	49.43	59.28	54.28	−59.5	−66.2	9.2
Appliances and housewares	18.24	23.45	28.82	37.52	−22.2	−36.7	−23.2
Household textiles	9.88	8.83	13.01	17.60	11.8	−24.0	−26.1

					percentage point change		
PERCENT DISTRIBUTION OF SPENDING	2012	2010	2006	2000	2010–12	2006–12	2000–06
Average household spending on gifts for people in other households	**100.0%**	**100.0%**	**100.0%**	**100.0%**	**–**	**–**	**–**
Education expenses	23.3	21.5	18.2	13.9	1.8	5.1	4.3
Transportation	10.0	8.2	6.1	6.5	1.8	3.9	−0.4
Food	9.3	8.6	10.1	6.5	0.7	−0.8	3.7
Women's and girls' apparel	7.7	7.1	7.2	7.9	0.6	0.5	−0.6
Entertainment	7.3	9.2	6.6	8.7	−1.9	0.7	−2.0
Health care expenses	4.7	2.0	3.5	3.5	2.7	1.2	0.0
Men's and boys' apparel	4.7	4.8	5.2	6.2	−0.1	−0.4	−1.1
Household equipment	4.3	4.5	4.3	6.5	−0.2	0.0	−2.2
Housekeeping supplies	2.6	2.4	2.4	3.6	0.1	0.1	−1.2
Jewelry and watches	2.1	1.7	2.1	1.6	0.5	0.1	0.5
Infants' apparel	1.8	4.6	4.5	3.8	−2.8	−2.7	0.8
Appliances and housewares	1.6	2.2	2.2	2.6	−0.5	−0.6	−0.4
Household textiles	0.9	0.8	1.0	1.2	0.1	−0.1	−0.2

Note: Numbers do not add to total because not all categories are shown. Percentage point change calculations are based on unrounded figures. "–" means not applicable.
Source: Bureau of Labor Statistics, 2000, 2006, 2010, and 2012 Consumer Expenditure Surveys; calculations by New Strategist

Gifts of Appliances and Housewares

Best customers: Householders aged 55 to 74
Married couples without children at home
Asians and non-Hispanic whites
Households in the Northeast and Midwest

Customer trends: Average household spending on gifts of appliances and housewares may increase as more boomers help their adult children outfit their homes.

The biggest spenders on gifts of appliances and housewares for people in other households are older married couples, many of them empty-nesters. These households are buying appliances and housewares for grown children who live elsewhere. Householders aged 55 to 64 spend 90 percent more than average on this item and householders aged 64 to 75 spend 32 percent more. Married couples without children at home spend 89 percent more than average on appliances and housewares for people in other households. Asians spend one-quarter more than average on such gifts and non-Hispanic whites spend 24 percent more. Households in the Northeast and Midwest outspend the average by 22 to 23 percent.

Average household spending on gifts of appliances and housewares for people in other households fell a significant 51 percent between 2000 and 2012, after adjusting for inflation. Average household spending on this item may expand in the years ahead as boomers help their adult children outfit their homes.

Table 8.2 Gifts of appliances and housewares

Total household spending $2,269,347,840.00
Average household spends 18.24

AGE OF HOUSEHOLDER	AVERAGE HOUSEHOLD SPENDING	BEST CUSTOMERS (index)	BIGGEST CUSTOMERS (market share)
Average household	$18.24	100	100.0%
Under age 25	3.69	20	1.3
Aged 25 to 34	13.22	72	11.7
Aged 35 to 44	13.13	72	12.5
Aged 45 to 54	18.22	100	19.8
Aged 55 to 64	34.62	190	34.7
Aged 65 to 74	24.13	132	15.9
Aged 75 or older	8.06	44	4.3

	AVERAGE HOUSEHOLD SPENDING	BEST CUSTOMERS (index)	BIGGEST CUSTOMERS (market share)
HOUSEHOLD INCOME			
Average household	**$18.24**	**100**	**100.0%**
Under $20,000	7.47	41	8.6
$20,000 to $39,999	7.21	40	8.9
$40,000 to $49,999	3.48	19	1.7
$50,000 to $69,999	13.51	74	10.7
$70,000 to $79,999	13.76	75	4.2
$80,000 to $99,999	32.59	179	15.8
$100,000 or more	49.46	271	50.8
HOUSEHOLD TYPE			
Average household	**18.24**	**100**	**100.0**
Married couples	24.53	134	65.3
Married couples, no children	34.42	189	39.3
Married couples, with children	18.05	99	23.3
Oldest child under age 6	11.32	62	2.8
Oldest child aged 6 to 17	19.74	108	12.9
Oldest child aged 18 or older	19.49	107	7.5
Single parent with child under age 18	9.15	50	2.6
Single person	11.39	62	18.5
RACE AND HISPANIC ORIGIN			
Average household	**18.24**	**100**	**100.0**
Asian	22.76	125	5.4
Black	5.00	27	3.4
Hispanic	4.65	25	3.2
Non-Hispanic white and other	22.70	124	93.4
REGION			
Average household	**18.24**	**100**	**100.0**
Northeast	22.50	123	22.3
Midwest	22.33	122	27.1
South	14.70	81	30.0
West	16.63	91	20.5
EDUCATION			
Average household	**18.24**	**100**	**100.0**
Less than high school graduate	7.11	39	5.1
High school graduate	7.12	39	9.7
Some college	18.17	100	20.5
Associate's degree	14.97	82	8.1
Bachelor's degree or more	32.39	178	56.0
Bachelor's degree	31.59	173	34.5
Master's, professional, doctoral degree	33.72	185	21.5

Note: Market shares may not sum to 100.0 because of rounding and missing categories by household type. "Asian" and "black" include Hispanics and non-Hispanics who identify themselves as being of the respective race alone. "Hispanic" includes people of any race who identify themselves as Hispanic. "Other" includes people who identify themselves as non-Hispanic and as Alaska Native, American Indian, Asian (who are also included in the "Asian" row), or Native Hawaiian or other Pacific Islander, as well as non-Hispanics reporting more than one race.
Source: Calculations by New Strategist based on the Bureau of Labor Statistics' 2012 Consumer Expenditure Survey

Gifts of Education Expenses

Best customers: Householders aged 45 to 64
High-income households
Married couples without children at home
Married couples with school-aged or older children at home
Asians and non-Hispanic whites
Households in the Northeast
College graduates

Customer trends: Average household spending on gifts of education expenses should continue to rise in the years ahead as grandparents help their grandchildren pay college bills.

The biggest spenders on gifts of education expenses for people in other households are affluent, educated, middle-aged or older married couples likely to have children or grandchildren in college. Households with incomes of $100,000 or more spend almost four times the average on gifts of education expenses. Married couples without children at home, most of them empty-nesters, spend nearly twice the average on gifts of education expenses. Householders aged 45 to 54, married couples with adult children at home, and college graduates all spend about two-and-one-half times the average on this item. Married couples with school-aged children spend 49 percent more than average on this item. Asians spend 89 percent more than average on gifts of education expenses, and non-Hispanic whites spend 26 percent more. Households in the Northeast outspend the average by 43 percent.

Average household spending on gifts of education expenses for people in other households rose steadily as the children of boomers went to college, growing 29 percent between 2000 and 2012, after adjusting for inflation. This increase is in contrast to the 23 percent decline in overall gift spending during those years. Average household spending on gifts of college tuition should continue to rise in the years ahead as growing numbers of grandparents help their grandchildren pay college bills.

Table 8.3 Gifts of education expenses

Total household spending $32,371,799,040.00
Average household spends   260.19

	AVERAGE HOUSEHOLD SPENDING	BEST CUSTOMERS (index)	BIGGEST CUSTOMERS (market share)
AGE OF HOUSEHOLDER			
Average household	**$260.19**	**100**	**100.0%**
Under age 25	18.76	7	0.5
Aged 25 to 34	25.89	10	1.6
Aged 35 to 44	87.06	33	5.8
Aged 45 to 54	634.94	244	48.3
Aged 55 to 64	514.42	198	36.2
Aged 65 to 74	79.42	31	3.7
Aged 75 or older	105.46	41	4.0

	AVERAGE HOUSEHOLD SPENDING	BEST CUSTOMERS (index)	BIGGEST CUSTOMERS (market share)
HOUSEHOLD INCOME			
Average household	**$260.19**	**100**	**100.0%**
Under $20,000	36.03	14	2.9
$20,000 to $39,999	52.58	20	4.6
$40,000 to $49,999	83.06	32	2.8
$50,000 to $69,999	83.03	32	4.6
$70,000 to $79,999	151.21	58	3.2
$80,000 to $99,999	267.36	103	9.1
$100,000 or more	1,011.49	389	72.8
HOUSEHOLD TYPE			
Average household	**260.19**	**100**	**100.0**
Married couples	422.42	162	78.9
Married couples, no children	501.73	193	40.2
Married couples, with children	400.18	154	36.2
Oldest child under age 6	4.15	2	0.1
Oldest child aged 6 to 17	386.81	149	17.7
Oldest child aged 18 or older	678.80	261	18.4
Single parent with child under age 18	200.87	77	4.0
Single person	121.96	47	13.9
RACE AND HISPANIC ORIGIN			
Average household	**260.19**	**100**	**100.0**
Asian	492.70	189	8.2
Black	52.94	20	2.6
Hispanic	54.46	21	2.6
Non-Hispanic white and other	328.74	126	94.8
REGION			
Average household	**260.19**	**100**	**100.0**
Northeast	372.62	143	25.9
Midwest	293.35	113	25.0
South	185.51	71	26.6
West	260.93	100	22.6
EDUCATION			
Average household	**260.19**	**100**	**100.0**
Less than high school graduate	43.70	17	2.2
High school graduate	53.73	21	5.1
Some college	140.59	54	11.1
Associate's degree	221.44	85	8.4
Bachelor's degree or more	603.19	232	73.1
Bachelor's degree	475.39	183	36.4
Master's, professional, doctoral degree	822.58	316	36.7

Note: Market shares may not sum to 100.0 because of rounding and missing categories by household type. "Asian" and "black" include Hispanics and non-Hispanics who identify themselves as being of the respective race alone. "Hispanic" includes people of any race who identify themselves as Hispanic. "Other" includes people who identify themselves as non-Hispanic and as Alaska Native, American Indian, Asian (who are also included in the "Asian" row), or Native Hawaiian or other Pacific Islander, as well as non-Hispanics reporting more than one race.
Source: Calculations by New Strategist based on the Bureau of Labor Statistics' 2012 Consumer Expenditure Survey

Gifts of Entertainment

Best customers: Householders aged 45 to 74
                      Married couples without children at home
                      Married couples with adult children at home
                      Asians

Customer trends: Average household spending on gifts of entertainment may continue to decline as entertainment items become increasingly digital and more difficult to give as gifts.

The biggest spenders on gifts of entertainment (which includes items ranging from dance lessons to movie tickets, from iPods to video games) for people in other households are middle-aged and older married couples—most of them buying gifts for children and grandchildren who live elsewhere. Householders ranging in age from 45 to 74 spend 17 to 51 percent more than average on this item. Married couples without children at home (most of them empty-nesters) spend nearly twice the average on this item, while those with adult children at home spend 31 percent more. Asian households spend 44 percent more than average on gifts of entertainment for people in other households.

Average household spending on gifts of entertainment for people in other households shows an anticyclical trend. It fell a steep 30 percent between 2000 and 2006 (the year overall household spending peaked), after adjusting for inflation, but gained 15 percent from 2006 to 2010 (the year overall household spending reached a post–Great Recession low). Between 2010 and 2012, spending on gifts of entertainment declined again, by 18 percent, just as many other categories were showing signs of revival. Average household spending on gifts of entertainment may continue to decline as entertainment items become increasingly digital and more difficult to give as gifts.

Table 8.4 Gifts of entertainment

Total household spending $10,168,519,680.00
Average household spends   81.73

AGE OF HOUSEHOLDER	AVERAGE HOUSEHOLD SPENDING	BEST CUSTOMERS (index)	BIGGEST CUSTOMERS (market share)
Average household	$81.73	100	100.0%
Under age 25	20.88	26	1.7
Aged 25 to 34	67.65	83	13.4
Aged 35 to 44	65.13	80	13.8
Aged 45 to 54	95.26	117	23.1
Aged 55 to 64	123.43	151	27.6
Aged 65 to 74	101.95	125	15.0
Aged 75 or older	46.12	56	5.5

	AVERAGE HOUSEHOLD SPENDING	BEST CUSTOMERS (index)	BIGGEST CUSTOMERS (market share)
HOUSEHOLD INCOME			
Average household	**$81.73**	**100**	**100.0%**
Under $20,000	30.08	37	7.7
$20,000 to $39,999	43.81	54	12.1
$40,000 to $49,999	41.24	50	4.5
$50,000 to $69,999	58.71	72	10.4
$70,000 to $79,999	80.15	98	5.5
$80,000 to $99,999	116.41	142	12.6
$100,000 or more	208.78	255	47.8
HOUSEHOLD TYPE			
Average household	**81.73**	**100**	**100.0**
Married couples	113.80	139	67.6
Married couples, no children	160.33	196	40.9
Married couples, with children	83.72	102	24.1
Oldest child under age 6	54.91	67	3.1
Oldest child aged 6 to 17	80.97	99	11.8
Oldest child aged 18 or older	106.70	131	9.2
Single parent with child under age 18	37.23	46	2.4
Single person	46.51	57	16.9
RACE AND HISPANIC ORIGIN			
Average household	**81.73**	**100**	**100.0**
Asian	117.42	144	6.2
Black	36.94	45	5.7
Hispanic	37.08	45	5.7
Non-Hispanic white and other	96.56	118	88.7
REGION			
Average household	**81.73**	**100**	**100.0**
Northeast	76.29	93	16.9
Midwest	90.01	110	24.4
South	79.59	97	36.3
West	81.36	100	22.4
EDUCATION			
Average household	**81.73**	**100**	**100.0**
Less than high school graduate	23.01	28	3.7
High school graduate	63.40	78	19.3
Some college	75.92	93	19.1
Associate's degree	67.68	83	8.2
Bachelor's degree or more	127.42	156	49.2
Bachelor's degree	120.08	147	29.3
Master's, professional, doctoral degree	139.90	171	19.9

Note: Market shares may not sum to 100.0 because of rounding and missing categories by household type. "Asian" and "black" include Hispanics and non-Hispanics who identify themselves as being of the respective race alone. "Hispanic" includes people of any race who identify themselves as Hispanic. "Other" includes people who identify themselves as non-Hispanic and as Alaska Native, American Indian, Asian (who are also included in the "Asian" row), or Native Hawaiian or other Pacific Islander, as well as non-Hispanics reporting more than one race.
Source: Calculations by New Strategist based on the Bureau of Labor Statistics' 2012 Consumer Expenditure Survey

Gifts of Food

Best customers: Householders aged 45 to 64
High-income households
Married couples without children at home
Married couples with school-aged children
Asians

Customer trends: Average household spending on gifts of food should stabilize now that boomers have filled
the best customer age groups.

The biggest spenders on gifts of food for people in other households are older empty-nesters. Many gift givers are buying food for grown children who live elsewhere. Householders aged 45 to 64 spend more than average on gifts of food and control 65 percent of the market. Married couples without children at home (most of them empty-nesters) spend more than twice the average on gifts of food for people in other households, while those with school-aged children outspend the average by 64 percent. Householders with incomes of $100,000 or more spend three times the average on gifts of food. Asian households spend two-and-one-half times the average on this item.

Average household spending on gifts of food for people in other households grew 12 percent between 2010 (the spending trough year) and 2012, after adjusting for inflation. Spending on gifts of food had increased 43 percent between 2000 and the overall peak spending year of 2006, then declined 30 percent between 2006 and 2010 as the Great Recession set in. Behind the earlier growth was the entry of the baby-boom generation into the empty-nest lifestage. Average household spending on gifts of food should stabilize now that boomers have filled the best-customer age groups.

Table 8.5 Gifts of food

Total household spending $12,980,321,280.00
Average household spends   104.33

AGE OF HOUSEHOLDER	AVERAGE HOUSEHOLD SPENDING	BEST CUSTOMERS (index)	BIGGEST CUSTOMERS (market share)
Average household	$104.33	100	100.0%
Under age 25	16.31	16	1.0
Aged 25 to 34	43.34	42	6.7
Aged 35 to 44	79.55	76	13.2
Aged 45 to 54	140.04	134	26.6
Aged 55 to 64	218.90	210	38.4
Aged 65 to 74	72.15	69	8.3
Aged 75 or older	64.13	61	6.0

	AVERAGE HOUSEHOLD SPENDING	BEST CUSTOMERS (index)	BIGGEST CUSTOMERS (market share)
HOUSEHOLD INCOME			
Average household	**$104.33**	**100**	**100.0%**
Under $20,000	45.32	43	9.1
$20,000 to $39,999	37.77	36	8.2
$40,000 to $49,999	53.12	51	4.5
$50,000 to $69,999	50.47	48	7.0
$70,000 to $79,999	80.14	77	4.3
$80,000 to $99,999	131.23	126	11.1
$100,000 or more	313.93	301	56.3
HOUSEHOLD TYPE			
Average household	**104.33**	**100**	**100.0**
Married couples	162.02	155	75.4
Married couples, no children	217.73	209	43.5
Married couples, with children	126.69	121	28.6
Oldest child under age 6	27.21	26	1.2
Oldest child aged 6 to 17	171.34	164	19.5
Oldest child aged 18 or older	115.26	110	7.8
Single parent with child under age 18	46.10	44	2.3
Single person	56.23	54	16.0
RACE AND HISPANIC ORIGIN			
Average household	**104.33**	**100**	**100.0**
Asian	270.66	259	11.2
Black	26.91	26	3.2
Hispanic	28.07	27	3.4
Non-Hispanic white and other	129.83	124	93.4
REGION			
Average household	**104.33**	**100**	**100.0**
Northeast	101.72	97	17.6
Midwest	113.92	109	24.2
South	105.83	101	37.8
West	94.47	91	20.4
EDUCATION			
Average household	**104.33**	**100**	**100.0**
Less than high school graduate	12.34	12	1.5
High school graduate	49.28	47	11.8
Some college	84.34	81	16.6
Associate's degree	71.36	68	6.8
Bachelor's degree or more	207.15	199	62.6
Bachelor's degree	177.58	170	33.9
Master's, professional, doctoral degree	257.31	247	28.6

Note: Market shares may not sum to 100.0 because of rounding and missing categories by household type. "Asian" and "black" include Hispanics and non-Hispanics who identify themselves as being of the respective race alone. "Hispanic" includes people of any race who identify themselves as Hispanic. "Other" includes people who identify themselves as non-Hispanic and as Alaska Native, American Indian, Asian (who are also included in the "Asian" row), or Native Hawaiian or other Pacific Islander, as well as non-Hispanics reporting more than one race.
Source: Calculations by New Strategist based on the Bureau of Labor Statistics' 2012 Consumer Expenditure Survey

Gifts of Health Care Expenses

Best customers: Householders aged 55 or older
                        Married couples with school-aged children
                        People who live alone
                        Asians and non-Hispanic whites
                        Households in the Midwest and West

Customer trends: Average household spending on gifts of health care expenses will decline in the years ahead
                        as a growing proportion of the population has access to health insurance.

The biggest spenders on gifts of health care expenses for people in other households are middle-aged and older householders—many of them paying for the health care of their uninsured children or grandchildren. Householders aged 55 to 64 spend well more than twice the average on this item, and those aged 75 or older spend nearly three times the average. People who live alone, many of them elderly, spend 76 percent more than average on this item and account for 52 percent of the market although their share of consumer units is only 30 percent. Asian households spend 35 percent more than average, and non-Hispanics whites spend 25 percent more. Households in the West and Midwest outspend the average by 30 percent.

Average household spending on gifts of health care expenses fell 56 percent between 2000 and 2010, after adjusting for inflation, and then increased by a whopping 138 percent in the ensuing two-year period. Spending on gifts of health care expenses for people in other households is likely to decline again in the years ahead as health insurance reform results in a growing proportion of the population having access to health insurance.

Table 8.6 Gifts of health care expenses

Total household spending $6,561,699,840.00
Average household spends   52.74

AGE OF HOUSEHOLDER	AVERAGE HOUSEHOLD SPENDING	BEST CUSTOMERS (index)	BIGGEST CUSTOMERS (market share)
Average household	$52.74	100	100.0%
Under age 25	1.34	3	0.2
Aged 25 to 34	5.44	10	1.7
Aged 35 to 44	11.45	22	3.8
Aged 45 to 54	38.85	74	14.6
Aged 55 to 64	116.81	221	40.5
Aged 65 to 74	60.35	114	13.8
Aged 75 or older	140.03	266	26.0

	AVERAGE HOUSEHOLD SPENDING	BEST CUSTOMERS (index)	BIGGEST CUSTOMERS (market share)
HOUSEHOLD INCOME			
Average household	**$52.74**	**100**	**100.0%**
Under $20,000	42.20	80	16.8
$20,000 to $39,999	16.97	32	7.3
$40,000 to $49,999	33.53	64	5.6
$50,000 to $69,999	58.47	111	16.0
$70,000 to $79,999	43.51	82	4.6
$80,000 to $99,999	61.88	117	10.4
$100,000 or more	110.54	210	39.2
HOUSEHOLD TYPE			
Average household	**52.74**	**100**	**100.0**
Married couples	42.17	80	38.8
Married couples, no children	35.88	68	14.2
Married couples, with children	46.13	87	20.6
Oldest child under age 6	11.36	22	1.0
Oldest child aged 6 to 17	68.16	129	15.4
Oldest child aged 18 or older	31.23	59	4.2
Single parent with child under age 18	16.55	31	1.6
Single person	92.94	176	52.3
RACE AND HISPANIC ORIGIN			
Average household	**52.74**	**100**	**100.0**
Asian	71.46	135	5.9
Black	6.35	12	1.5
Hispanic	21.23	40	5.0
Non-Hispanic white and other	65.67	125	93.5
REGION			
Average household	**52.74**	**100**	**100.0**
Northeast	41.38	78	14.2
Midwest	68.61	130	28.8
South	39.54	75	27.9
West	68.33	130	29.2
EDUCATION			
Average household	**52.74**	**100**	**100.0**
Less than high school graduate	20.11	38	5.0
High school graduate	24.16	46	11.4
Some college	13.86	26	5.4
Associate's degree	135.42	257	25.4
Bachelor's degree or more	88.32	167	52.8
Bachelor's degree	95.20	181	36.0
Master's, professional, doctoral degree	76.49	145	16.8

Note: Market shares may not sum to 100.0 because of rounding and missing categories by household type. "Asian" and "black" include Hispanics and non-Hispanics who identify themselves as being of the respective race alone. "Hispanic" includes people of any race who identify themselves as Hispanic. "Other" includes people who identify themselves as non-Hispanic and as Alaska Native, American Indian, Asian (who are also included in the "Asian" row), or Native Hawaiian or other Pacific Islander, as well as non-Hispanics reporting more than one race.
Source: Calculations by New Strategist based on the Bureau of Labor Statistics' 2012 Consumer Expenditure Survey

Gifts of Household Equipment

Best customers: Householders aged 55 to 64
Married couples without children at home
Asians
Households in the Northeast

Customer trends: Average household spending on gifts of household equipment for people in other households should rise as millennials establish independent households.

The household equipment category includes many traditional gifts, such as infants' equipment, indoor plants and fresh flowers, and decorative household items. The biggest spenders on gifts of household equipment for people in other households are older married couples, many with grown children living elsewhere. Householders aged 55 to 64 spend three-quarters more than average on this item. Married couples without children at home (many of them empty-nesters) spend 53 percent more than average on gifts of household equipment. Asian households spend 40 percent more than average on this item. Households in the Northeast outspend the average by 45 percent.

Average household spending on gifts of household equipment fell by a significant 49 percent between 2000 and 2012. Behind the decline was the slow household formation of the millennial generation, a trend exacerbated by the Great Recession. Spending on gifts of household equipment should rise as millennials establish independent households.

Table 8.7 Gifts of household equipment

| Total household spending | $5,973,212,160.00 |
| Average household spends | 48.01 |

AGE OF HOUSEHOLDER	AVERAGE HOUSEHOLD SPENDING	BEST CUSTOMERS (index)	BIGGEST CUSTOMERS (market share)
Average household	$48.01	100	100.0%
Under age 25	12.66	26	1.7
Aged 25 to 34	40.51	84	13.6
Aged 35 to 44	48.50	101	17.5
Aged 45 to 54	46.26	96	19.1
Aged 55 to 64	84.73	176	32.3
Aged 65 to 74	48.97	102	12.3
Aged 75 or older	17.56	37	3.6

	AVERAGE HOUSEHOLD SPENDING	BEST CUSTOMERS (index)	BIGGEST CUSTOMERS (market share)
HOUSEHOLD INCOME			
Average household	**$48.01**	**100**	**100.0%**
Under $20,000	18.44	38	8.1
$20,000 to $39,999	25.20	52	11.8
$40,000 to $49,999	34.92	73	6.4
$50,000 to $69,999	33.80	70	10.2
$70,000 to $79,999	48.11	100	5.6
$80,000 to $99,999	53.46	111	9.8
$100,000 or more	122.75	256	47.9
HOUSEHOLD TYPE			
Average household	**48.01**	**100**	**100.0**
Married couples	55.41	115	56.1
Married couples, no children	73.42	153	31.9
Married couples, with children	45.03	94	22.1
Oldest child under age 6	40.32	84	3.8
Oldest child aged 6 to 17	54.24	113	13.4
Oldest child aged 18 or older	32.62	68	4.8
Single parent with child under age 18	15.30	32	1.7
Single person	31.30	65	19.4
RACE AND HISPANIC ORIGIN			
Average household	**48.01**	**100**	**100.0**
Asian	67.13	140	6.1
Black	16.04	33	4.2
Hispanic	24.88	52	6.5
Non-Hispanic white and other	57.18	119	89.4
REGION			
Average household	**48.01**	**100**	**100.0**
Northeast	69.85	145	26.3
Midwest	42.32	88	19.5
South	43.71	91	33.9
West	43.13	90	20.2
EDUCATION			
Average household	**48.01**	**100**	**100.0**
Less than high school graduate	17.30	36	4.7
High school graduate	37.44	78	19.4
Some college	46.42	97	19.9
Associate's degree	43.80	91	9.0
Bachelor's degree or more	70.63	147	46.4
Bachelor's degree	66.67	139	27.7
Master's, professional, doctoral degree	77.27	161	18.7

Note: Market shares may not sum to 100.0 because of rounding and missing categories by household type. "Asian" and "black" include Hispanics and non-Hispanics who identify themselves as being of the respective race alone. "Hispanic" includes people of any race who identify themselves as Hispanic. "Other" includes people who identify themselves as non-Hispanic and as Alaska Native, American Indian, Asian (who are also included in the "Asian" row), or Native Hawaiian or other Pacific Islander, as well as non-Hispanics reporting more than one race.
Source: Calculations by New Strategist based on the Bureau of Labor Statistics' 2012 Consumer Expenditure Survey

Gifts of Household Textiles

Best customers: Householders aged 45 to 64
Married couples without children at home
Married couples with preschoolers
Married couples with adult children at home
Asians

Customer trends: Average household spending on gifts of household textiles for people in other households may rise
as millions of older parents help their adult children outfit their homes.

The biggest spenders on gifts of household textiles (such as towels and bed linens) for people in other households are middle-aged and older married couples, many of them empty-nesters giving this traditional gift to adult children who live elsewhere. Householders aged 45 to 64 spend 29 to 94 percent more than the average household on this item. Married couples without children at home spend 47 percent more than average on this item. Couples with preschoolers or adult children at home spend over twice the average on gifts of household textiles. Asian households spend 57 percent more than average on this gift category.

Average household spending on gifts of household textiles for people in other households, already the smallest gift category, dropped by one-half between 2000 and 2010, but then showed a 12 percent rise in the ensuing two-year period. Spending on gifts of household textiles may grow further in the years ahead as millions of older parents help their adult children outfit their homes.

Table 8.8 Gifts of household textiles

Total household spending $1,229,230,080.00
Average household spends   9.88

AGE OF HOUSEHOLDER	AVERAGE HOUSEHOLD SPENDING	BEST CUSTOMERS (index)	BIGGEST CUSTOMERS (market share)
Average household	$9.88	100	100.0%
Under age 25	5.95	60	3.9
Aged 25 to 34	5.01	51	8.2
Aged 35 to 44	8.46	86	14.9
Aged 45 to 54	12.78	129	25.6
Aged 55 to 64	19.21	194	35.6
Aged 65 to 74	8.52	86	10.4
Aged 75 or older	1.91	19	1.9

	AVERAGE HOUSEHOLD SPENDING	BEST CUSTOMERS (index)	BIGGEST CUSTOMERS (market share)
HOUSEHOLD INCOME			
Average household	$9.88	100	100.0%
Under $20,000	3.02	31	6.4
$20,000 to $39,999	4.86	49	11.1
$40,000 to $49,999	7.72	78	6.9
$50,000 to $69,999	15.22	154	22.3
$70,000 to $79,999	22.16	224	12.5
$80,000 to $99,999	4.03	41	3.6
$100,000 or more	19.27	195	36.5
HOUSEHOLD TYPE			
Average household	9.88	100	100.0
Married couples	15.57	158	76.5
Married couples, no children	14.48	147	30.6
Married couples, with children	14.07	142	33.5
Oldest child under age 6	24.62	249	11.4
Oldest child aged 6 to 17	5.86	59	7.1
Oldest child aged 18 or older	21.19	214	15.1
Single parent with child under age 18	2.84	29	1.5
Single person	4.29	43	12.9
RACE AND HISPANIC ORIGIN			
Average household	9.88	100	100.0
Asian	15.51	157	6.8
Black	0.94	10	1.2
Hispanic	5.58	56	7.1
Non-Hispanic white and other	12.08	122	91.8
REGION			
Average household	9.88	100	100.0
Northeast	6.72	68	12.3
Midwest	9.14	93	20.5
South	11.32	115	42.7
West	10.78	109	24.6
EDUCATION			
Average household	9.88	100	100.0
Less than high school graduate	4.76	48	6.3
High school graduate	6.12	62	15.4
Some college	5.94	60	12.4
Associate's degree	7.55	76	7.5
Bachelor's degree or more	18.12	183	57.8
Bachelor's degree	15.70	159	31.7
Master's, professional, doctoral degree	22.22	225	26.1

Note: Market shares may not sum to 100.0 because of rounding and missing categories by household type. "Asian" and "black" include Hispanics and non-Hispanics who identify themselves as being of the respective race alone. "Hispanic" includes people of any race who identify themselves as Hispanic. "Other" includes people who identify themselves as non-Hispanic and as Alaska Native, American Indian, Asian (who are also included in the "Asian" row), or Native Hawaiian or other Pacific Islander, as well as non-Hispanics reporting more than one race.
Source: Calculations by New Strategist based on the Bureau of Labor Statistics' 2012 Consumer Expenditure Survey

Gifts of Housekeeping Supplies

Best customers:
Householders aged 55 to 74
Married couples without children at home
Married couples with school-aged children
Households in the Northeast and Midwest

Customer trends:
Average household spending on gifts of housekeeping supplies for people in other households may rise as older parents help their adult children outfit their homes.

The category gifts of housekeeping supplies (such as laundry and cleaning supplies, lawn and garden supplies, postage, and stationery) shows relatively little variation by demographic category. Householders aged 55 to 64 spend 26 percent more than average on this item, and those aged 65 to 74 spend 48 percent more. Married couples without children at home spend 73 percent more than average on gifts of housekeeping supplies, and those with school-aged children spend 22 percent more. Households in the Northeast and Midwest outspend the average by 20 to 23 percent.

Average household spending on gifts of housekeeping supplies for people in other households fell by an enormous 49 percent between 2000 and 2010, after adjusting for inflation, but increased 8 percent in the ensuing two years. A large part of the loss came before the peak spending year of 2006, but spending on gifts of housekeeping supplies decreased 16 percent between 2006 and 2010, the trough year for household spending. Average household spending on gifts of housekeeping supplies may rise in the years ahead as millions of older parents help their adult children outfit their homes.

Table 8.9 Gifts of housekeeping supplies

Total household spending $3,548,344,320.00
Average household spends   28.52

AGE OF HOUSEHOLDER	AVERAGE HOUSEHOLD SPENDING	BEST CUSTOMERS (index)	BIGGEST CUSTOMERS (market share)
Average household	$28.52	100	100.0%
Under age 25	31.90	112	7.3
Aged 25 to 34	16.33	57	9.3
Aged 35 to 44	26.41	93	16.1
Aged 45 to 54	26.05	91	18.1
Aged 55 to 64	35.99	126	23.1
Aged 65 to 74	42.35	148	17.9
Aged 75 or older	25.04	88	8.6

	AVERAGE HOUSEHOLD SPENDING	BEST CUSTOMERS (index)	BIGGEST CUSTOMERS (market share)
HOUSEHOLD INCOME			
Average household	$28.52	100	100.0%
Under $20,000	10.23	36	7.5
$20,000 to $39,999	15.61	55	12.3
$40,000 to $49,999	26.05	91	8.1
$50,000 to $69,999	27.16	95	13.8
$70,000 to $79,999	36.71	129	7.2
$80,000 to $99,999	40.07	140	12.4
$100,000 or more	58.62	206	38.5
HOUSEHOLD TYPE			
Average household	28.52	100	100.0
Married couples	37.40	131	63.7
Married couples, no children	49.21	173	36.0
Married couples, with children	29.72	104	24.5
Oldest child under age 6	30.97	109	5.0
Oldest child aged 6 to 17	34.70	122	14.5
Oldest child aged 18 or older	20.63	72	5.1
Single parent with child under age 18	21.60	76	4.0
Single person	17.52	61	18.2
RACE AND HISPANIC ORIGIN			
Average household	28.52	100	100.0
Asian	12.82	45	1.9
Black	8.57	30	3.8
Hispanic	15.22	53	6.7
Non-Hispanic white and other	34.04	119	89.6
REGION			
Average household	28.52	100	100.0
Northeast	34.98	123	22.1
Midwest	34.27	120	26.6
South	26.41	93	34.5
West	21.01	74	16.6
EDUCATION			
Average household	28.52	100	100.0
Less than high school graduate	5.08	18	2.3
High school graduate	24.58	86	21.5
Some college	26.66	93	19.3
Associate's degree	32.84	115	11.4
Bachelor's degree or more	40.26	141	44.5
Bachelor's degree	38.10	134	26.6
Master's, professional, doctoral degree	43.92	154	17.9

Note: Market shares may not sum to 100.0 because of rounding and missing categories by household type. "Asian" and "black" include Hispanics and non-Hispanics who identify themselves as being of the respective race alone. "Hispanic" includes people of any race who identify themselves as Hispanic. "Other" includes people who identify themselves as non-Hispanic and as Alaska Native, American Indian, Asian (who are also included in the "Asian" row), or Native Hawaiian or other Pacific Islander, as well as non-Hispanics reporting more than one race.
Source: Calculations by New Strategist based on the Bureau of Labor Statistics' 2012 Consumer Expenditure Survey

Gifts of Infants' Apparel

Best customers: Householders under age 25 and aged 55 to 64
Married couples with children at home
Single parents
Asians and Hispanics
Households in the Northeast

Customer trends: Average household spending on gifts of infants' apparel for people in other households should rise as the large millennial generation has children.

The biggest spenders on gifts of infants' apparel for people in other households are young people, many of whose friends are having children, and older people buying for grandchildren. Householders under age 25 spend 77 percent more than average on this item, while those aged 55 to 64 spend 39 percent more. Married couples with children at home spend 52 percent more than average on gifts of infant apparel, the figure peaking among couples with preschoolers at two-and-three-quarter times the average. Single parents, whose spending approaches average on only a few categories, spend one-third more than average on this gift category. Asians and Hispanics spend, respectively, 24 and 75 percent more than average on gifts of infants' apparel. Households in the Northeast outspend the average by 70 percent.

Average household spending on gifts of infants' apparel for people in other households declined by 9 percent between 2000 and 2010, after adjusting for inflation, then plummeted 59 percent in the ensuing two-year period. Behind the big decline since 2010 is the ongoing baby bust. Spending on gifts of infants' apparel should increase as the millennial generation has children.

Table 8.10 Gifts of infants' apparel

Total household spending $2,492,052,480.00
Average household spends   20.03

AGE OF HOUSEHOLDER	AVERAGE HOUSEHOLD SPENDING	BEST CUSTOMERS (index)	BIGGEST CUSTOMERS (market share)
Average household	$20.03	100	100.0%
Under age 25	35.41	177	11.6
Aged 25 to 34	18.31	91	14.8
Aged 35 to 44	20.56	103	17.8
Aged 45 to 54	15.73	79	15.5
Aged 55 to 64	27.82	139	25.4
Aged 65 to 74	21.80	109	13.1
Aged 75 or older	2.87	14	1.4

	AVERAGE HOUSEHOLD SPENDING	BEST CUSTOMERS (index)	BIGGEST CUSTOMERS (market share)
HOUSEHOLD INCOME			
Average household	**$20.03**	**100**	**100.0%**
Under $20,000	12.24	61	12.9
$20,000 to $39,999	14.25	71	16.0
$40,000 to $49,999	26.70	133	11.8
$50,000 to $69,999	14.43	72	10.4
$70,000 to $79,999	15.52	77	4.3
$80,000 to $99,999	27.70	138	12.2
$100,000 or more	35.53	177	33.2
HOUSEHOLD TYPE			
Average household	**20.03**	**100**	**100.0**
Married couples	26.24	131	63.6
Married couples, no children	23.99	120	25.0
Married couples, with children	30.50	152	35.8
Oldest child under age 6	55.27	276	12.6
Oldest child aged 6 to 17	26.32	131	15.6
Oldest child aged 18 or older	22.06	110	7.8
Single parent with child under age 18	26.69	133	7.0
Single person	8.19	41	12.1
RACE AND HISPANIC ORIGIN			
Average household	**20.03**	**100**	**100.0**
Asian	24.92	124	5.4
Black	19.07	95	12.0
Hispanic	35.02	175	21.9
Non-Hispanic white and other	17.67	88	66.2
REGION			
Average household	**20.03**	**100**	**100.0**
Northeast	34.08	170	30.7
Midwest	15.23	76	16.9
South	18.45	92	34.3
West	16.07	80	18.1
EDUCATION			
Average household	**20.03**	**100**	**100.0**
Less than high school graduate	26.84	134	17.5
High school graduate	20.45	102	25.5
Some college	16.03	80	16.5
Associate's degree	20.77	104	10.2
Bachelor's degree or more	19.73	99	31.1
Bachelor's degree	17.04	85	17.0
Master's, professional, doctoral degree	24.27	121	14.1

Note: Market shares may not sum to 100.0 because of rounding and missing categories by household type. "Asian" and "black" include Hispanics and non-Hispanics who identify themselves as being of the respective race alone. "Hispanic" includes people of any race who identify themselves as Hispanic. "Other" includes people who identify themselves as non-Hispanic and as Alaska Native, American Indian, Asian (who are also included in the "Asian" row), or Native Hawaiian or other Pacific Islander, as well as non-Hispanics reporting more than one race.
Source: Calculations by New Strategist based on the Bureau of Labor Statistics' 2012 Consumer Expenditure Survey

Gifts of Jewelry and Watches

Best customers: Householders aged 25 to 34
People who live alone
Asians
Households in the South

Customer trends: Average household spending on gifts of jewelry and watches for people in other households should continue to grow in the years ahead as the millennial generation, which has postponed marriage longer than any other, finally ties the knot.

The biggest spenders on gifts of jewelry and watches for people in other households are young adults, many buying engagement or wedding rings. Householders aged 25 to 34 spend nearly twice the average on gifts of jewelry and watches and account for 32 percent of the market. Single-person households—many headed by young adults—spend 78 percent more than average on this item. Asians spend four-and-one-half times the average on gifts of jewelry and watches. Households in the South outspend the average by 43 percent.

Average household spending on gifts of jewelry and watches for people in other households had grown by 21 percent between 2000 and the overall peak spending year of 2006, after adjusting for inflation. Then spending fell by an enormous 34 percent between 2006 and 2010, the trough year for household spending. Spending on gifts of jewelry and watches recovered by an equally impressive 32 percent in the ensuing two years. Average household spending on gifts of jewelry and watches for people in other households should continue to grow in the years ahead as the millennial generation, which has postponed marriage longer than any other, finally ties the knot.

Table 8.11 Gifts of jewelry and watches

Total household spending $2,971,054,080.00
Average household spends 23.88

AGE OF HOUSEHOLDER	AVERAGE HOUSEHOLD SPENDING	BEST CUSTOMERS (index)	BIGGEST CUSTOMERS (market share)
Average household	$23.88	100	100.0%
Under age 25	21.55	90	5.9
Aged 25 to 34	46.74	196	31.6
Aged 35 to 44	17.03	71	12.4
Aged 45 to 54	21.04	88	17.4
Aged 55 to 64	23.28	97	17.8
Aged 65 to 74	25.20	106	12.7
Aged 75 or older	5.05	21	2.1

	AVERAGE HOUSEHOLD SPENDING	BEST CUSTOMERS (index)	BIGGEST CUSTOMERS (market share)
HOUSEHOLD INCOME			
Average household	**$23.88**	**100**	**100.0%**
Under $20,000	9.86	41	8.7
$20,000 to $39,999	10.79	45	10.2
$40,000 to $49,999	12.72	53	4.7
$50,000 to $69,999	8.37	35	5.1
$70,000 to $79,999	40.01	168	9.4
$80,000 to $99,999	43.10	180	15.9
$100,000 or more	57.46	241	45.0
HOUSEHOLD TYPE			
Average household	**23.88**	**100**	**100.0**
Married couples	18.98	79	38.6
Married couples, no children	18.78	79	16.4
Married couples, with children	6.16	26	6.1
Oldest child under age 6	10.89	46	2.1
Oldest child aged 6 to 17	3.56	15	1.8
Oldest child aged 18 or older	7.55	32	2.2
Single parent with child under age 18	5.96	25	1.3
Single person	42.39	178	52.7
RACE AND HISPANIC ORIGIN			
Average household	**23.88**	**100**	**100.0**
Asian	107.97	452	19.6
Black	10.59	44	5.6
Hispanic	5.88	25	3.1
Non-Hispanic white and other	29.06	122	91.3
REGION			
Average household	**23.88**	**100**	**100.0**
Northeast	12.35	52	9.3
Midwest	23.18	97	21.5
South	34.05	143	53.1
West	17.00	71	16.0
EDUCATION			
Average household	**23.88**	**100**	**100.0**
Less than high school graduate	1.81	8	1.0
High school graduate	9.22	39	9.6
Some college	18.93	79	16.3
Associate's degree	38.71	162	16.0
Bachelor's degree or more	43.09	180	56.9
Bachelor's degree	40.08	168	33.5
Master's, professional, doctoral degree	48.25	202	23.5

Note: Market shares may not sum to 100.0 because of rounding and missing categories by household type. "Asian" and "black" include Hispanics and non-Hispanics who identify themselves as being of the respective race alone. "Hispanic" includes people of any race who identify themselves as Hispanic. "Other" includes people who identify themselves as non-Hispanic and as Alaska Native, American Indian, Asian (who are also included in the "Asian" row), or Native Hawaiian or other Pacific Islander, as well as non-Hispanics reporting more than one race.
Source: Calculations by New Strategist based on the Bureau of Labor Statistics' 2012 Consumer Expenditure Survey

Gifts of Men's and Boys' Apparel

Best customers: Householders aged 55 to 64
Married couples without children at home
Single parents
Asians

Customer trends: Average household spending on gifts of men's and boys' apparel for people in other households will continue to decline as electronics trump apparel as a gift for men and boys.

Apparel is one of the biggest gift-giving categories. In 2012, the average household spent a combined $159 on gifts of women's, men's, and children's apparel for people in other households. Older married couples dominate gifts of men's and boys' apparel, many of them buying clothes for adult children and grandchildren living elsewhere. Householders aged 55 to 64 spend 64 percent more than average on gifts of men's and boys' apparel. Married couples without children at home, most of them empty-nesters, spend 48 percent more than average on this item. Single parents, whose spending is below average on most items, spend nearly twice the average on gifts of clothing for males. Asian households outspend the average by 23 percent.

Average household spending on gifts of men's and boys' apparel for people in other households fell by a substantial 42 percent between 2000 and 2012, after adjusting for inflation. Spending in this category will continue to decline as electronics trump apparel as a gift for men and boys.

Table 8.12 Gifts of men's and boys' apparel

Total household spending $6,551,746,560.00
Average household spends   52.66

AGE OF HOUSEHOLDER	AVERAGE HOUSEHOLD SPENDING	BEST CUSTOMERS (index)	BIGGEST CUSTOMERS (market share)
Average household	$52.66	100	100.0%
Under age 25	28.19	54	3.5
Aged 25 to 34	32.20	61	9.9
Aged 35 to 44	38.90	74	12.8
Aged 45 to 54	61.56	117	23.1
Aged 55 to 64	86.26	164	30.0
Aged 65 to 74	59.11	112	13.5
Aged 75 or older	40.96	78	7.6

	AVERAGE HOUSEHOLD SPENDING	BEST CUSTOMERS (index)	BIGGEST CUSTOMERS (market share)
HOUSEHOLD INCOME			
Average household	$52.66	100	100.0%
Under $20,000	41.19	78	16.5
$20,000 to $39,999	37.28	71	16.0
$40,000 to $49,999	18.33	35	3.1
$50,000 to $69,999	54.41	103	14.9
$70,000 to $79,999	82.34	156	8.7
$80,000 to $99,999	85.82	163	14.4
$100,000 or more	79.01	150	28.1
HOUSEHOLD TYPE			
Average household	52.66	100	100.0
Married couples	55.96	106	51.6
Married couples, no children	77.73	148	30.8
Married couples, with children	31.97	61	14.3
Oldest child under age 6	24.13	46	2.1
Oldest child aged 6 to 17	21.31	40	4.8
Oldest child aged 18 or older	54.74	104	7.3
Single parent with child under age 18	102.17	194	10.2
Single person	44.06	84	24.8
RACE AND HISPANIC ORIGIN			
Average household	52.66	100	100.0
Asian	64.51	123	5.3
Black	42.18	80	10.1
Hispanic	36.75	70	8.7
Non-Hispanic white and other	56.96	108	81.2
REGION			
Average household	52.66	100	100.0
Northeast	55.88	106	19.2
Midwest	50.18	95	21.1
South	49.64	94	35.1
West	57.59	109	24.6
EDUCATION			
Average household	52.66	100	100.0
Less than high school graduate	38.65	73	9.6
High school graduate	53.59	102	25.4
Some college	40.23	76	15.7
Associate's degree	55.12	105	10.3
Bachelor's degree or more	64.91	123	38.9
Bachelor's degree	58.51	111	22.1
Master's, professional, doctoral degree	75.73	144	16.7

Note: Market shares may not sum to 100.0 because of rounding and missing categories by household type. "Asian" and "black" include Hispanics and non-Hispanics who identify themselves as being of the respective race alone. "Hispanic" includes people of any race who identify themselves as Hispanic. "Other" includes people who identify themselves as non-Hispanic and as Alaska Native, American Indian, Asian (who are also included in the "Asian" row), or Native Hawaiian or other Pacific Islander, as well as non-Hispanics reporting more than one race.
Source: Calculations by New Strategist based on the Bureau of Labor Statistics' 2012 Consumer Expenditure Survey

Gifts of Transportation

Best customers: Householders aged 55 to 64
Married couples without children at home
Married couples with adult children at home
Asians and non-Hispanic whites

Customer trends: Average household spending on gifts of transportation may continue to rise as growing numbers
of older parents help their adult children come home for a visit.

The biggest spenders on gifts of transportation for people in other households are older householders who buy airline tickets for adult children or help grown children buy a car. Householders aged 55 to 64, most having adult children who live elsewhere, spend twice the average amount on gifts of transportation. Married couples without children at home, most of them empty-nesters, spend 85 percent more than average on this item, while those with adult children at home spend 86 percent more. Asian households spend 27 percent more than average on this item.

Average household spending on gifts of transportation for people in other households fell 14 percent between 2000 and 2006, after adjusting for inflation, then increased 39 percent between 2006 and 2012. Average household spending on gifts of transportation may continue to rise as growing numbers of older parents help their adult children come home for a visit.

Table 8.13 Gifts of transportation

Total household spending $13,861,186,560.00
Average household spends   111.41

AGE AGE OF HOUSEHOLDER	AVERAGE HOUSEHOLD SPENDING	BEST CUSTOMERS (index)	BIGGEST CUSTOMERS (market share)
Average household	$111.41	100	100.0%
Under age 25	15.89	14	0.9
Aged 25 to 34	33.04	30	4.8
Aged 35 to 44	90.68	81	14.1
Aged 45 to 54	128.57	115	22.8
Aged 55 to 64	224.29	201	36.8
Aged 65 to 74	76.73	69	8.3
Aged 75 or older	138.89	125	12.2

	AVERAGE HOUSEHOLD SPENDING	BEST CUSTOMERS (index)	BIGGEST CUSTOMERS (market share)
HOUSEHOLD INCOME			
Average household	**$111.41**	**100**	**100.0%**
Under $20,000	73.34	66	13.8
$20,000 to $39,999	60.62	54	12.3
$40,000 to $49,999	33.41	30	2.7
$50,000 to $69,999	111.82	100	14.5
$70,000 to $79,999	107.86	97	5.4
$80,000 to $99,999	101.88	91	8.1
$100,000 or more	257.54	231	43.3
HOUSEHOLD TYPE			
Average household	**111.41**	**100**	**100.0**
Married couples	154.95	139	67.6
Married couples, no children	206.00	185	38.5
Married couples, with children	128.03	115	27.0
Oldest child under age 6	91.87	82	3.8
Oldest child aged 6 to 17	94.73	85	10.1
Oldest child aged 18 or older	207.45	186	13.1
Single parent with child under age 18	23.34	21	1.1
Single person	82.53	74	22.0
RACE AND HISPANIC ORIGIN			
Average household	**111.41**	**100**	**100.0**
Asian	141.49	127	5.5
Black	25.78	23	2.9
Hispanic	58.04	52	6.5
Non-Hispanic white and other	134.66	121	90.7
REGION			
Average household	**111.41**	**100**	**100.0**
Northeast	68.76	62	11.1
Midwest	96.59	87	19.2
South	124.73	112	41.7
West	138.18	124	27.9
EDUCATION			
Average household	**111.41**	**100**	**100.0**
Less than high school graduate	25.07	23	2.9
High school graduate	93.02	83	20.8
Some college	111.65	100	20.6
Associate's degree	95.14	85	8.4
Bachelor's degree or more	166.51	149	47.1
Bachelor's degree	145.39	130	26.0
Master's, professional, doctoral degree	202.80	182	21.1

Note: Market shares may not sum to 100.0 because of rounding and missing categories by household type. "Asian" and "black" include Hispanics and non-Hispanics who identify themselves as being of the respective race alone. "Hispanic" includes people of any race who identify themselves as Hispanic. "Other" includes people who identify themselves as non-Hispanic and as Alaska Native, American Indian, Asian (who are also included in the "Asian" row), or Native Hawaiian or other Pacific Islander, as well as non-Hispanics reporting more than one race.
Source: Calculations by New Strategist based on the Bureau of Labor Statistics' 2012 Consumer Expenditure Survey

Gifts of Women's and Girls' Apparel

Best customers: Householders aged 55 to 74
                       Married couples without children at home

Customer trends: Average household spending on gifts of women's and girls' apparel for people in other households may resume its decline in the years ahead as electronics increasingly replace apparel as gift items.

Older householders dominate spending on gifts of women's and girls' apparel for people in other households, many of them buying clothes for adult children and grandchildren. Householders aged 55 to 74 spend 52 to 53 percent more than average on this item and account for 46 percent of the market. Married couples without children at home, many of them empty-nesters, spend 85 percent more than average on gifts of women's and girls' apparel.

Average household spending on gifts of women's and girls' apparel for people in other households fell by nearly one-third between 2000 and 2010, after adjusting for inflation, and then grew 12 percent from 2010 to 2012. Price discounting is one factor behind the earlier decline, as is the substitution of electronics for apparel as gifts. Average household spending on gifts of women's and girls' apparel may resume its decline in the years ahead as this trend continues.

Table 8.14 Gifts of women's and girls' apparel

Total household spending $10,719,682,560.00
Average household spends   86.16

AGE OF HOUSEHOLDER	AVERAGE HOUSEHOLD SPENDING	BEST CUSTOMERS (index)	BIGGEST CUSTOMERS (market share)
Average household	$86.16	100	100.0%
Under age 25	40.62	47	3.1
Aged 25 to 34	50.53	59	9.5
Aged 35 to 44	61.32	71	12.4
Aged 45 to 54	80.83	94	18.6
Aged 55 to 64	130.68	152	27.8
Aged 65 to 74	132.03	153	18.5
Aged 75 or older	96.70	112	11.0

	AVERAGE HOUSEHOLD SPENDING	BEST CUSTOMERS (index)	BIGGEST CUSTOMERS (market share)
HOUSEHOLD INCOME			
Average household	**$86.16**	**100**	**100.0%**
Under $20,000	39.03	45	9.5
$20,000 to $39,999	66.61	77	17.4
$40,000 to $49,999	93.72	109	9.6
$50,000 to $69,999	71.79	83	12.0
$70,000 to $79,999	116.32	135	7.5
$80,000 to $99,999	103.37	120	10.6
$100,000 or more	151.56	176	32.9
HOUSEHOLD TYPE			
Average household	**86.16**	**100**	**100.0**
Married couples	111.00	129	62.6
Married couples, no children	159.70	185	38.6
Married couples, with children	70.03	81	19.1
Oldest child under age 6	26.06	30	1.4
Oldest child aged 6 to 17	62.47	73	8.6
Oldest child aged 18 or older	110.13	128	9.0
Single parent with child under age 18	42.35	49	2.6
Single person	68.13	79	23.5
RACE AND HISPANIC ORIGIN			
Average household	**86.16**	**100**	**100.0**
Asian	66.93	78	3.4
Black	71.05	82	10.4
Hispanic	85.78	100	12.5
Non-Hispanic white and other	88.62	103	77.2
REGION			
Average household	**86.16**	**100**	**100.0**
Northeast	80.62	94	16.9
Midwest	87.26	101	22.5
South	82.78	96	35.8
West	95.17	110	24.9
EDUCATION			
Average household	**86.16**	**100**	**100.0**
Less than high school graduate	65.23	76	9.9
High school graduate	72.50	84	21.0
Some college	81.49	95	19.5
Associate's degree	77.69	90	8.9
Bachelor's degree or more	110.57	128	40.5
Bachelor's degree	93.15	108	21.5
Master's, professional, doctoral degree	139.99	162	18.9

Note: Market shares may not sum to 100.0 because of rounding and missing categories by household type. "Asian" and "black" include Hispanics and non-Hispanics who identify themselves as being of the respective race alone. "Hispanic" includes people of any race who identify themselves as Hispanic. "Other" includes people who identify themselves as non-Hispanic and as Alaska Native, American Indian, Asian (who are also included in the "Asian" row), or Native Hawaiian or other Pacific Islander, as well as non-Hispanics reporting more than one race.
Source: Calculations by New Strategist based on the Bureau of Labor Statistics' 2012 Consumer Expenditure Survey

Chapter 9.
Groceries

Household Spending on Groceries, 2000 to 2012

Not surprisingly, groceries are one of the largest household expenses. In 2012, the average household spent $3,921 on groceries (or what the Consumer Expenditure Survey calls "food at home"). Average household spending on groceries fell 3 percent between 2000 and 2006 (the year household spending peaked; see Appendix D) because people were devoting more money to eating out. Grocery spending fell another 2 percent between 2006 and 2010, the year when overall household spending was at its lowest ebb. Grocery spending then recovered, rising 3 percent between 2010 and 2012.

Although many Americans cannot afford to eat out as frequently as they once did, they still want the convenience of prepared food. That explains why the grocery category "prepared foods (except salads, desserts, and frozen meals)," which did not crack the top-10 grocery spending categories in 2000, trailed only fresh fruit and fresh vegetables as the grocery category on which households spent the most in 2012. The average household devoted $148 to prepared foods in 2012, up 50 percent from the inflation-adjusted $99 in 2000. After fruit, vegetables, and prepared foods households spend the most on sodas, cheese, fresh milk, chicken, and potato chips and other snacks. They devoted $128 to fresh milk in 2012, 20 percent less than the inflation-adjusted $159 in 2000. Average household spending on carbonated beverages fell 22 percent during that time, but spending on cheese saw a 3 percent increase.

Average household spending on groceries is determined by household size, larger households spending more than smaller ones on most items. Average household spending on groceries may decline in the years ahead as the large baby-boom generation ages and household size drifts downward. But household demographic characteristics and nutritional claims will continue to affect spending patterns—patterns that will determine the future success of grocery retailers and food manufacturers.

Spending on groceries

(average annual spending of households on groceries, 2000, 2006, 2010, and 2012; in 2012 dollars)

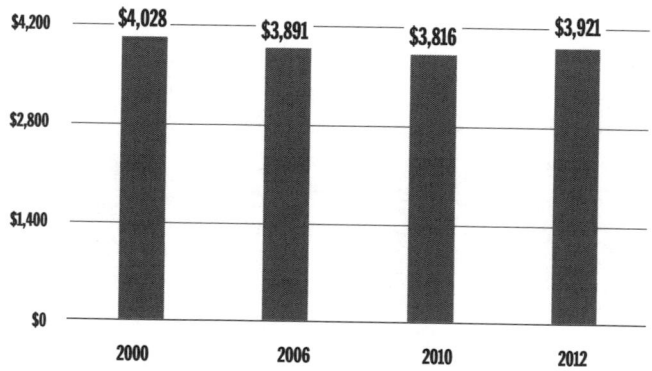

Table 9.1 Spending on groceries, 2000 to 2012

(average annual household spending on groceries and percent distribution, by category, 2000 to 2012; percent change in spending and percentage point change in distribution, 2000–06, 2006–12, and 2010–12; in 2012 dollars; ranked by amount spent)

	average annual household spending (in 2012$)				percent change		
	2012	2010	2006	2000	2010–12	2006–12	2000–06
Average household spending on groceries	**$3,920.65**	**$3,815.80**	**$3,891.32**	**$4,027.89**	**2.7%**	**0.8%**	**–3.4%**
Fruit, fresh (apples, bananas, and citrus also shown separately)	261.29	244.53	222.58	217.55	6.9	17.4	2.3
Vegetables, fresh (potatoes, tomatoes, and lettuce also shown separately)	226.14	221.61	220.10	211.62	2.0	2.7	4.0
Prepared food (except salads, desserts, and frozen meals)	147.81	154.53	151.10	98.54	–4.3	–2.2	53.3
Carbonated drinks	139.74	139.67	153.23	179.17	0.1	–8.8	–14.5
Cheese	131.47	121.54	126.13	127.94	8.2	4.2	–1.4
Milk, fresh	128.28	127.43	141.75	159.48	0.7	–9.5	–11.1
Chicken, fresh and frozen	126.52	116.08	127.68	152.57	9.0	–0.9	–16.3
Potato chips and other snacks	111.59	104.58	108.44	95.56	6.7	2.9	13.5
Cereal, ready-to-eat and cooked	94.82	87.21	96.50	115.84	8.7	–1.7	–16.7
Ground beef	93.50	89.15	102.73	117.01	4.9	–9.0	–12.2
Candy and chewing gum	87.86	81.43	90.12	101.73	7.9	–2.5	–11.4
Lunch meats (cold cuts)	87.23	86.13	86.12	90.65	1.3	1.3	–5.0
Coffee	86.50	63.44	56.82	55.80	36.4	52.2	1.8
Steak	79.44	86.62	96.47	126.02	–8.3	–17.7	–23.4
Prepared food, frozen (except meals)	70.22	74.94	76.92	82.26	–6.3	–8.7	–6.5
Fish and shellfish, fresh	63.29	58.17	70.99	89.09	8.8	–10.8	–20.3
Bread, other than white	61.60	62.88	61.76	63.22	–2.0	–0.3	–2.3
Prepared meals, frozen	60.61	64.18	78.63	38.00	–5.6	–22.9	106.9
Sauces and gravies	60.27	55.21	54.95	49.64	9.2	9.7	10.7
Ice cream and related products	57.37	57.13	70.18	75.41	0.4	–18.2	–6.9
Water, bottled	56.80	54.79	62.90	–	3.7	–9.7	–
Fruit juice, canned and bottled	54.92	54.72	62.97	74.94	0.4	–12.8	–16.0
Vegetables, canned	54.59	55.29	43.73	49.89	–1.3	24.8	–12.3
Eggs	53.08	48.74	41.76	45.95	8.9	27.1	–9.1
Dairy products (except butter, cheese, eggs, ice cream, and milk)	52.67	49.28	42.78	31.85	6.9	23.1	34.3
Biscuits and rolls	51.85	51.42	47.65	51.37	0.8	8.8	–7.2
Cookies	50.56	48.33	50.54	63.61	4.6	0.0	–20.5
Soup, canned and packaged	46.30	44.54	48.04	47.39	4.0	–3.6	1.4
Fish and shellfish, frozen	44.27	43.87	48.80	36.87	0.9	–9.3	32.4
Bananas	43.81	43.04	32.81	42.27	1.8	33.5	–22.4
Bread, white	43.52	41.94	36.18	48.83	3.8	20.3	–25.9
Nuts	42.35	35.43	36.99	27.77	19.5	14.5	33.2
Apples	41.61	39.27	38.64	39.32	5.9	7.7	–1.7
Pork (except bacon, frankfurters, ham, chops, and sausage)	39.99	37.48	44.62	51.76	6.7	–10.4	–13.8
Citrus fruit, fresh (other than oranges)	39.95	33.08	19.20	19.08	20.8	108.1	0.6
Tomatoes, fresh	39.35	41.36	41.75	39.37	–4.9	–5.7	6.0
Salt, spices, and other seasonings	38.72	34.21	28.86	27.53	13.2	34.2	4.8
Potatoes, fresh	38.44	38.02	35.60	37.43	1.1	8.0	–4.9
Cakes and cupcakes	37.94	37.17	39.88	51.23	2.1	–4.9	–22.1
Vegetables, frozen	37.50	38.07	34.78	35.23	–1.5	7.8	–1.3
Crackers	37.17	38.18	36.25	31.09	–2.6	2.5	16.6
Pasta, cornmeal, and other cereal products	36.98	35.71	27.59	38.19	3.5	34.0	–27.7
Fats and oils	36.79	33.16	32.30	31.13	11.0	13.9	3.7

	average annual household spending (in 2012$)				percent change		
	2012	2010	2006	2000	2010–12	2006–12	2000–06
Salads, prepared	$35.09	$37.30	$36.80	$24.73	−5.9%	−4.6%	48.8%
Roast beef	34.02	31.03	45.59	53.12	9.6	−25.4	−14.2
Ham	33.42	33.57	38.74	48.35	−0.4	−13.7	−19.9
Poultry (except chicken)	32.84	29.33	32.34	40.97	12.0	1.5	−21.1
Lettuce	32.33	31.66	28.86	27.67	2.1	12.0	4.3
Bacon	32.18	33.28	31.15	34.73	−3.3	3.3	−10.3
Sausage	32.14	27.51	29.37	33.65	16.8	9.4	−12.7
Salad dressings	31.29	30.29	29.76	36.24	3.3	5.1	−17.9
Tea	30.36	30.75	29.96	20.91	−1.3	1.3	43.3
Jams, preserves, other sweets	29.61	27.89	26.24	26.48	6.2	12.8	−0.9
Bakery products, frozen and refrigerated	28.77	26.52	29.15	32.71	8.5	−1.3	−10.9
Pork chops	28.04	25.03	35.18	54.09	12.0	−20.3	−35.0
Oranges	26.74	26.03	25.33	25.24	2.7	5.6	0.4
Fruit-flavored drinks, noncarbonated	25.83	25.53	20.21	25.89	1.2	27.8	−21.9
Butter	25.56	24.25	20.86	22.67	5.4	22.5	−8.0
Baby food	25.05	34.20	38.32	43.01	−26.8	−34.6	−10.9
Baking needs and miscellaneous products	24.95	27.57	26.15	22.61	−9.5	−4.6	15.6
Frankfurters	24.71	25.81	22.99	27.57	−4.3	7.5	−16.6
Rice	24.65	26.03	19.94	26.07	−5.3	23.6	−23.5
Sugar	24.38	23.96	18.84	22.40	1.7	29.4	−15.9
Sweetrolls, coffee cakes, and doughnuts	23.73	23.46	23.70	30.24	1.2	0.1	−21.6
Cream	23.58	20.93	17.89	15.48	12.7	31.8	15.6
Fruit, canned	20.35	21.62	20.98	20.64	−5.9	−3.0	1.6
Beef other than ground, roast, steak	19.35	21.35	24.26	21.44	−9.4	−20.2	13.1
Vegetable juice, fresh and canned	18.98	15.94	13.83	12.40	19.1	37.3	11.5
Peanut butter	18.68	16.28	12.81	15.75	14.8	45.8	−18.6
Nondairy cream and imitation milk	18.59	17.86	14.58	12.20	4.1	27.5	19.5
Vegetables, dried	18.22	19.22	13.43	14.00	−5.2	35.7	−4.1
Fish and seafood, canned	18.18	21.23	18.78	20.89	−14.4	−3.2	−10.1
Olives, pickles, and relishes	17.46	15.65	14.55	13.03	11.6	20.0	11.7
Fruit juice, fresh	17.06	20.17	19.85	31.25	−15.4	−14.1	−36.5
Flour, prepared mixes	16.18	16.06	12.85	17.80	0.8	26.0	−27.8
Other noncarbonated beverages and ice	15.36	15.92	–	–	−3.5	–	–
Sports drinks	15.12	20.12	–	–	−24.9	–	–
Desserts, prepared	14.29	17.40	13.69	12.41	−17.9	4.4	10.3
Pies, tarts, and turnovers	13.41	17.16	15.86	17.71	−21.9	−15.5	−10.4
Lamb, organ meats, and other meat	10.19	11.46	10.34	15.83	−11.0	−1.5	−34.7
Flour	9.36	8.31	5.64	10.64	12.7	66.0	−47.0
Margarine	8.74	10.44	8.31	15.48	−16.3	5.1	−46.3
Fruit, dried	8.71	8.63	10.20	7.33	0.9	−14.6	39.2
Bread and cracker products	7.31	7.88	4.95	5.88	−7.2	47.6	−15.7
Fruit, frozen	7.16	7.14	4.64	4.83	0.3	54.5	−4.0
Fruit juice, frozen	5.55	6.43	5.75	14.32	−13.7	−3.5	−59.8
Artificial sweeteners	4.91	5.69	6.61	5.59	−13.6	−25.7	18.2

PERCENT DISTRIBUTION OF SPENDING	average annual household spending (in 2012$)				percentage point change		
	2012	2010	2006	2000	2010–12	2006–12	2000–06
Average household spending on groceries	100.0%	100.0%	100.0%	100.0%	–	–	–
Fruit, fresh (apples, bananas, and citrus also shown separately)	6.7	6.4	5.7	5.4	0.3	0.9	0.3
Vegetables, fresh (potatoes, tomatoes, and lettuce also shown separately)	5.8	5.8	5.7	5.3	0.0	0.1	0.4
Prepared food (except salads, desserts, and frozen meals)	3.8	4.0	3.9	2.4	–0.3	–0.1	1.4
Carbonated drinks	3.6	3.7	3.9	4.4	–0.1	–0.4	–0.5
Cheese	3.4	3.2	3.2	3.2	0.2	0.1	0.1
Milk, fresh	3.3	3.3	3.6	4.0	–0.1	–0.4	–0.3
Chicken, fresh and frozen	3.2	3.0	3.3	3.8	0.2	–0.1	–0.5
Potato chips and other snacks	2.8	2.7	2.8	2.4	0.1	0.1	0.4
Cereal, ready-to-eat and cooked	2.4	2.3	2.5	2.9	0.1	–0.1	–0.4
Ground beef	2.4	2.3	2.6	2.9	0.0	–0.3	–0.3
Candy and chewing gum	2.2	2.1	2.3	2.5	0.1	–0.1	–0.2
Lunch meats (cold cuts)	2.2	2.3	2.2	2.3	0.0	0.0	0.0
Coffee	2.2	1.7	1.5	1.4	0.5	0.7	0.1
Steak	2.0	2.3	2.5	3.1	–0.2	–0.5	–0.6
Prepared food, frozen (except meals)	1.8	2.0	2.0	2.0	–0.2	–0.2	–0.1
Fish and shellfish, fresh	1.6	1.5	1.8	2.2	0.1	–0.2	–0.4
Bread, other than white	1.6	1.6	1.6	1.6	–0.1	0.0	0.0
Prepared meals, frozen	1.5	1.7	2.0	0.9	–0.1	–0.5	1.1
Sauces and gravies	1.5	1.4	1.4	1.2	0.1	0.1	0.2
Ice cream and related products	1.5	1.5	1.8	1.9	0.0	–0.3	–0.1
Water, bottled	1.4	1.4	1.6	–	0.0	–0.2	–
Fruit juice, canned and bottled	1.4	1.4	1.6	1.9	0.0	–0.2	–0.2
Vegetables, canned	1.4	1.4	1.1	1.2	–0.1	0.3	–0.1
Eggs	1.4	1.3	1.1	1.1	0.1	0.3	–0.1
Dairy products (except butter, cheese, eggs, ice cream, and milk)	1.3	1.3	1.1	0.8	0.1	0.2	0.3
Biscuits and rolls	1.3	1.3	1.2	1.3	0.0	0.1	–0.1
Cookies	1.3	1.3	1.3	1.6	0.0	0.0	–0.3
Soup, canned and packaged	1.2	1.2	1.2	1.2	0.0	–0.1	0.1
Fish and shellfish, frozen	1.1	1.1	1.3	0.9	0.0	–0.1	0.3
Bananas	1.1	1.1	0.8	1.0	0.0	0.3	–0.2
Bread, white	1.1	1.1	0.9	1.2	0.0	0.2	–0.3
Nuts	1.1	0.9	1.0	0.7	0.2	0.1	0.3
Apples	1.1	1.0	1.0	1.0	0.0	0.1	0.0
Pork (except bacon, frankfurters, ham, chops, and sausage)	1.0	1.0	1.1	1.3	0.0	–0.1	–0.1
Citrus fruit, fresh (other than oranges)	1.0	0.9	0.5	0.5	0.2	0.5	0.0
Tomatoes, fresh	1.0	1.1	1.1	1.0	–0.1	–0.1	0.1
Salt, spices, and other seasonings	1.0	0.9	0.7	0.7	0.1	0.2	0.1
Potatoes, fresh	1.0	1.0	0.9	0.9	0.0	0.1	0.0
Cakes and cupcakes	1.0	1.0	1.0	1.3	0.0	–0.1	–0.2
Vegetables, frozen	1.0	1.0	0.9	0.9	0.0	0.1	0.0
Crackers	0.9	1.0	0.9	0.8	–0.1	0.0	0.2
Pasta, cornmeal, and other cereal products	0.9	0.9	0.7	0.9	0.0	0.2	–0.2
Fats and oils	0.9	0.9	0.8	0.8	0.1	0.1	0.1
Salads, prepared	0.9	1.0	0.9	0.6	–0.1	–0.1	0.3
Roast beef	0.9	0.8	1.2	1.3	0.1	–0.3	–0.1
Ham	0.9	0.9	1.0	1.2	0.0	–0.1	–0.2
Poultry (except chicken)	0.8	0.8	0.8	1.0	0.1	0.0	–0.2
Lettuce	0.8	0.8	0.7	0.7	0.0	0.1	0.1

PERCENT DISTRIBUTION OF SPENDING	average annual household spending (in 2012$)				percentage point change		
	2012	2010	2006	2000	2010–12	2006–12	2000–06
Bacon	0.8%	0.9%	0.8%	0.9%	–0.1	0.0	–0.1
Sausage	0.8	0.7	0.8	0.8	0.1	0.1	–0.1
Salad dressings	0.8	0.8	0.8	0.9	0.0	0.0	–0.1
Tea	0.8	0.8	0.8	0.5	0.0	0.0	0.3
Jams, preserves, other sweets	0.8	0.7	0.7	0.7	0.0	0.1	0.0
Bakery products, frozen and refrigerated	0.7	0.7	0.7	0.8	0.0	0.0	–0.1
Pork chops	0.7	0.7	0.9	1.3	0.1	–0.2	–0.4
Oranges	0.7	0.7	0.7	0.6	0.0	0.0	0.0
Fruit-flavored drinks, noncarbonated	0.7	0.7	0.5	0.6	0.0	0.1	–0.1
Butter	0.7	0.6	0.5	0.6	0.0	0.1	0.0
Baby food	0.6	0.9	1.0	1.1	–0.3	–0.3	–0.1
Baking needs and miscellaneous products	0.6	0.7	0.7	0.6	–0.1	0.0	0.1
Frankfurters	0.6	0.7	0.6	0.7	0.0	0.0	–0.1
Rice	0.6	0.7	0.5	0.6	–0.1	0.1	–0.1
Sugar	0.6	0.6	0.5	0.6	0.0	0.1	–0.1
Sweetrolls, coffee cakes, and doughnuts	0.6	0.6	0.6	0.8	0.0	0.0	–0.1
Cream	0.6	0.5	0.5	0.4	0.1	0.1	0.1
Fruit, canned	0.5	0.6	0.5	0.5	0.0	0.0	0.0
Beef other than ground, roast, steak	0.5	0.6	0.6	0.5	–0.1	–0.1	0.1
Vegetable juice, fresh and canned	0.5	0.4	0.4	0.3	0.1	0.1	0.0
Peanut butter	0.5	0.4	0.3	0.4	0.0	0.1	–0.1
Nondairy cream and imitation milk	0.5	0.5	0.4	0.3	0.0	0.1	0.1
Vegetables, dried	0.5	0.5	0.3	0.3	0.0	0.1	0.0
Fish and seafood, canned	0.5	0.6	0.5	0.5	–0.1	0.0	0.0
Olives, pickles, and relishes	0.4	0.4	0.4	0.3	0.0	0.1	0.1
Fruit juice, fresh	0.4	0.5	0.5	0.8	–0.1	–0.1	–0.3
Flour, prepared mixes	0.4	0.4	0.3	0.4	0.0	0.1	–0.1
Other noncarbonated beverages and ice	0.4	0.4	–	–	0.0	–	–
Sports drinks	0.4	0.5	–	–	–0.1	–	–
Desserts, prepared	0.4	0.5	0.4	0.3	–0.1	0.0	0.0
Pies, tarts, and turnovers	0.3	0.4	0.4	0.4	–0.1	–0.1	0.0
Lamb, organ meats, and other meat	0.3	0.3	0.3	0.4	0.0	0.0	–0.1
Flour	0.2	0.2	0.1	0.3	0.0	0.1	–0.1
Margarine	0.2	0.3	0.2	0.4	–0.1	0.0	–0.2
Fruit, dried	0.2	0.2	0.3	0.2	0.0	0.0	0.1
Bread and cracker products	0.2	0.2	0.1	0.1	0.0	0.1	0.0
Fruit, frozen	0.2	0.2	0.1	0.1	0.0	0.1	0.0
Fruit juice, frozen	0.1	0.2	0.1	0.4	0.0	0.0	–0.2
Artificial sweeteners	0.1	0.1	0.2	0.1	0.0	0.0	0.0

Note: Numbers do not add to total because apples, bananas, and citrus fruit are shown separately and are included in the fresh fruit total; lettuce, potatoes, and tomatoes are shown separately and are included in the fresh vegetable total; and not all categories are shown. Percentage point change calculations are based on unrounded figures. "–" means not applicable or data are unavailable.
Source: Bureau of Labor Statistics, 2000, 2006, 2010, and 2012 Consumer Expenditure Surveys; calculations by New Strategist

Apples

Best customers: **Householders aged 35 to 54**
Married couples with children at home
Asians

Customer trends: **Average household spending on apples may fall as the population ages and household size shrinks.**

The largest households spend the most on apples. Married couples with children at home spend 61 percent more than the average household on apples. Householders aged 35 to 54, most with children at home, spend 16 to 25 percent more than average on apples and control 45 percent of the market. The spending on apples by Asian householders is 43 percent above average.

Average household spending on apples remained steady from 2000 to 2010, after adjusting for inflation, and then increased by 6 percent between 2010 and 2012. Behind these trends is the greater availability of conveniently packaged sliced apples, boosting household purchasing despite the baby-boom generation's exit from the best-customer lifestage. Average household spending on apples may fall as the population ages and household size shrinks.

Table 9.2 Apples

Total household spending $5,176,949,760.00
Average household spends   41.61

	AVERAGE HOUSEHOLD SPENDING	BEST CUSTOMERS (index)	BIGGEST CUSTOMERS (market share)
AGE OF HOUSEHOLDER			
Average household	**$41.61**	**100**	**100.0%**
Under age 25	32.09	77	5.1
Aged 25 to 34	40.38	97	15.7
Aged 35 to 44	52.08	125	21.7
Aged 45 to 54	48.45	116	23.0
Aged 55 to 64	38.33	92	16.9
Aged 65 to 74	35.26	85	10.2
Aged 75 or older	30.93	74	7.3

	AVERAGE HOUSEHOLD SPENDING	BEST CUSTOMERS (index)	BIGGEST CUSTOMERS (market share)
HOUSEHOLD INCOME			
Average household	**$41.61**	**100**	**100.0%**
Under $20,000	21.70	52	11.0
$20,000 to $39,999	27.89	67	15.1
$40,000 to $49,999	36.47	88	7.8
$50,000 to $69,999	41.39	99	14.4
$70,000 to $79,999	47.82	115	6.4
$80,000 to $99,999	52.27	126	11.1
$100,000 or more	76.07	183	34.2
HOUSEHOLD TYPE			
Average household	**41.61**	**100**	**100.0**
Married couples	56.27	135	65.7
Married couples, no children	47.18	113	23.6
Married couples with children	66.99	161	37.9
Oldest child under age 6	47.43	114	5.2
Oldest child aged 6 to 17	73.97	178	21.1
Oldest child aged 18 or older	67.52	162	11.4
Single parent with child under age 18	39.77	96	5.0
Single person	19.88	48	14.2
RACE AND HISPANIC ORIGIN			
Average household	**41.61**	**100**	**100.0**
Asian	59.54	143	6.2
Black	26.45	64	8.0
Hispanic	39.61	95	11.9
Non-Hispanic white and other	44.59	107	80.4
REGION			
Average household	**41.61**	**100**	**100.0**
Northeast	48.33	116	21.0
Midwest	44.46	107	23.7
South	33.44	80	29.9
West	46.87	113	25.4
EDUCATION			
Average household	**41.61**	**100**	**100.0**
Less than high school graduate	32.28	78	10.1
High school graduate	34.25	82	20.5
Some college	32.52	78	16.1
Associate's degree	43.16	104	10.2
Bachelor's degree or more	56.45	136	42.8
Bachelor's degree	55.99	135	26.8
Master's, professional, doctoral degree	57.22	138	16.0

Note: Market shares may not sum to 100.0 because of rounding and missing categories by household type. "Asian" and "black" include Hispanics and non-Hispanics who identify themselves as being of the respective race alone. "Hispanic" includes people of any race who identify themselves as Hispanic. "Other" includes people who identify themselves as non-Hispanic and as Alaska Native, American Indian, Asian (who are also included in the "Asian" row), or Native Hawaiian or other Pacific Islander, as well as non-Hispanics reporting more than one race.
Source: Calculations by New Strategist based on the Bureau of Labor Statistics' 2012 Consumer Expenditure Survey

Artificial Sweeteners

Best customers: Householders aged 55 or older
                      Married couples without children at home
                      Married couples with adult children at home
                      Households in the South

Customer trends: Average household spending on artificial sweeteners should stabilize now that the large baby-boom generation is in the best-customer age groups.

Older householders spend the most on artificial sweeteners. Householders aged 55 to 64 spend 70 percent more than the average household on artificial sweeteners. Those aged 65 or older spend 8 to 14 percent more than average on this item. Married couples without children at home (most of them older) spend one-half more than the average household on artificial sweeteners, while married couples with adult children at home outspend the average by 85 percent. Households in the South spend 32 percent more than average on this item.

Average household spending on artificial sweeteners grew 18 percent between 2000 and 2006, after adjusting for inflation, but fell 26 percent between 2006 and 2012. Spending on artificial sweeteners should stabilize now that the large baby-boom generation is in the best-customer age groups.

Table 9.3 Artificial sweeteners

Total household spending $610,882,560.00
Average household spends   4.91

AGE OF HOUSEHOLDER	AVERAGE HOUSEHOLD SPENDING	BEST CUSTOMERS (index)	BIGGEST CUSTOMERS (market share)
Average household	$4.91	100	100.0%
Under age 25	2.30	47	3.1
Aged 25 to 34	2.84	58	9.4
Aged 35 to 44	4.35	89	15.4
Aged 45 to 54	4.32	88	17.4
Aged 55 to 64	8.34	170	31.1
Aged 65 to 74	5.62	114	13.8
Aged 75 or older	5.31	108	10.6

	AVERAGE HOUSEHOLD SPENDING	BEST CUSTOMERS (index)	BIGGEST CUSTOMERS (market share)
HOUSEHOLD INCOME			
Average household	**$4.91**	**100**	**100.0%**
Under $20,000	4.28	87	18.4
$20,000 to $39,999	3.54	72	16.2
$40,000 to $49,999	5.06	103	9.1
$50,000 to $69,999	3.89	79	11.4
$70,000 to $79,999	7.87	160	8.9
$80,000 to $99,999	5.36	109	9.6
$100,000 or more	6.66	136	25.4
HOUSEHOLD TYPE			
Average household	**4.91**	**100**	**100.0**
Married couples	6.67	136	66.0
Married couples, no children	7.37	150	31.3
Married couples with children	5.64	115	27.0
Oldest child under age 6	1.14	23	1.1
Oldest child aged 6 to 17	5.26	107	12.7
Oldest child aged 18 or older	9.08	185	13.0
Single parent with child under age 18	3.01	61	3.2
Single person	2.66	54	16.1
RACE AND HISPANIC ORIGIN			
Average household	**4.91**	**100**	**100.0**
Asian	4.04	82	3.6
Black	3.78	77	9.7
Hispanic	4.56	93	11.6
Non-Hispanic white and other	5.14	105	78.6
REGION			
Average household	**4.91**	**100**	**100.0**
Northeast	4.35	89	16.0
Midwest	3.48	71	15.7
South	6.48	132	49.2
West	4.18	85	19.2
EDUCATION			
Average household	**4.91**	**100**	**100.0**
Less than high school graduate	5.16	105	13.7
High school graduate	4.27	87	21.7
Some college	4.71	96	19.8
Associate's degree	4.74	97	9.5
Bachelor's degree or more	5.49	112	35.3
Bachelor's degree	5.27	107	21.4
Master's, professional, doctoral degree	5.86	119	13.9

Note: Market shares may not sum to 100.0 because of rounding and missing categories by household type. "Asian" and "black" include Hispanics and non-Hispanics who identify themselves as being of the respective race alone. "Hispanic" includes people of any race who identify themselves as Hispanic. "Other" includes people who identify themselves as non-Hispanic and as Alaska Native, American Indian, Asian (who are also included in the "Asian" row), or Native Hawaiian or other Pacific Islander, as well as non-Hispanics reporting more than one race.
Source: Calculations by New Strategist based on the Bureau of Labor Statistics' 2012 Consumer Expenditure Survey

Baby Food

Best customers: Householders aged 25 to 34
                          Married couples with preschoolers
                          Single parents
                          Asians and Hispanics

Customer trends: Average household spending on baby food should stabilize when the baby bust comes to an end.

Not surprisingly, married couples with preschoolers spend much more on baby food than any other household type, almost eight times the average. Householders aged 25 to 34, many with infants, spend more than twice the average on baby food. Single parents, whose spending on most items is below average, spend well over twice the average on this item. Hispanics spend 21 percent more than average, and Asians spend 80 percent more.

Average household spending on baby food is in long-term decline. It fell 42 percent between 2000 and 2012, after adjusting for inflation. Behind the decline are price discounting, belt tightening during the economic downturn, and the ongoing baby bust. Average household spending on baby food should stabilize when the large millennial generation begins to have more children, although the low incomes of young adults may limit the increase.

Table 9.4 Baby food

Total household spending $3,116,620,800.00
Average household spends   25.05

	AVERAGE HOUSEHOLD SPENDING	BEST CUSTOMERS (index)	BIGGEST CUSTOMERS (market share)
AGE OF HOUSEHOLDER			
Average household	**$25.05**	**100**	**100.0%**
Under age 25	21.05	84	5.5
Aged 25 to 34	65.77	263	42.4
Aged 35 to 44	36.66	146	25.4
Aged 45 to 54	18.70	75	14.8
Aged 55 to 64	8.37	33	6.1
Aged 65 to 74	5.29	21	2.5
Aged 75 or older	4.78	19	1.9

	AVERAGE HOUSEHOLD SPENDING	BEST CUSTOMERS (index)	BIGGEST CUSTOMERS (market share)
HOUSEHOLD INCOME			
Average household	$25.05	100	100.0%
Under $20,000	14.72	59	12.4
$20,000 to $39,999	18.76	75	16.9
$40,000 to $49,999	38.02	152	13.4
$50,000 to $69,999	25.55	102	14.7
$70,000 to $79,999	28.68	114	6.4
$80,000 to $99,999	26.85	107	9.5
$100,000 or more	35.73	143	26.7
HOUSEHOLD TYPE			
Average household	25.05	100	100.0
Married couples	33.32	133	64.6
Married couples, no children	6.97	28	5.8
Married couples with children	55.70	222	52.3
Oldest child under age 6	196.42	784	35.8
Oldest child aged 6 to 17	32.04	128	15.2
Oldest child aged 18 or older	7.49	30	2.1
Single parent with child under age 18	59.87	239	12.5
Single person	3.69	15	4.4
RACE AND HISPANIC ORIGIN			
Average household	25.05	100	100.0
Asian	45.15	180	7.8
Black	12.26	49	6.2
Hispanic	30.28	121	15.2
Non-Hispanic white and other	26.37	105	79.0
REGION			
Average household	25.05	100	100.0
Northeast	24.52	98	17.7
Midwest	26.87	107	23.8
South	26.87	107	40.0
West	20.64	82	18.6
EDUCATION			
Average household	25.05	100	100.0
Less than high school graduate	23.05	92	12.0
High school graduate	18.24	73	18.2
Some college	26.71	107	22.0
Associate's degree	22.60	90	8.9
Bachelor's degree or more	30.73	123	38.7
Bachelor's degree	29.36	117	23.4
Master's, professional, doctoral degree	33.04	132	15.3

Note: Market shares may not sum to 100.0 because of rounding and missing categories by household type. "Asian" and "black" include Hispanics and non-Hispanics who identify themselves as being of the respective race alone. "Hispanic" includes people of any race who identify themselves as Hispanic. "Other" includes people who identify themselves as non-Hispanic and as Alaska Native, American Indian, Asian (who are also included in the "Asian" row), or Native Hawaiian or other Pacific Islander, as well as non-Hispanics reporting more than one race.
Source: Calculations by New Strategist based on the Bureau of Labor Statistics' 2012 Consumer Expenditure Survey

Bacon

Best customers: Householders aged 35 to 64
Married couples with children at home
Blacks and Hispanics

Customer trends: Average household spending on bacon may continue to decline as the large baby-boom generation ages and household size shrinks.

Married couples with children at home spend the most on bacon—36 percent more than the average household. Householders ranging in age from 35 to 64, many with children in the household, outspend the average by 7 to 20 percent. Black and Hispanic households spend slightly more than average on bacon.

Average household spending on bacon has been on a rollercoaster ride over the past 12 years. It declined 10 percent between 2000 and 2006, after adjusting for inflation, then rebounded between 2006 and 2010, only to decline again—by 3 percent—between 2010 and 2012. One factor behind the earlier spending decline was the growing propensity for households to eat fast-food breakfasts or no breakfast at all. More home-cooked meals in the aftermath of the Great Recession may be responsible for the 2006-to-2010 rise in spending on bacon. Average household spending on bacon may continue to decline in the years ahead as the large baby-boom generation ages and household size shrinks.

Table 9.5 Bacon

Total household spending $4,003,706,880.00
Average household spends   32.18

	AVERAGE HOUSEHOLD SPENDING	BEST CUSTOMERS (index)	BIGGEST CUSTOMERS (market share)
AGE OF HOUSEHOLDER			
Average household	**$32.18**	**100**	**100.0%**
Under age 25	21.70	67	4.4
Aged 25 to 34	29.13	91	14.6
Aged 35 to 44	34.40	107	18.6
Aged 45 to 54	38.76	120	23.8
Aged 55 to 64	36.79	114	20.9
Aged 65 to 74	29.31	91	11.0
Aged 75 or older	22.12	69	6.7

	AVERAGE HOUSEHOLD SPENDING	BEST CUSTOMERS (index)	BIGGEST CUSTOMERS (market share)
HOUSEHOLD INCOME			
Average household	**$32.18**	**100**	**100.0%**
Under $20,000	23.55	73	15.4
$20,000 to $39,999	24.29	75	17.0
$40,000 to $49,999	31.85	99	8.8
$50,000 to $69,999	31.40	98	14.1
$70,000 to $79,999	37.95	118	6.6
$80,000 to $99,999	45.65	142	12.5
$100,000 or more	44.17	137	25.7
HOUSEHOLD TYPE			
Average household	**32.18**	**100**	**100.0**
Married couples	39.17	122	59.1
Married couples, no children	32.90	102	21.3
Married couples with children	43.64	136	31.9
Oldest child under age 6	38.92	121	5.5
Oldest child aged 6 to 17	45.01	140	16.6
Oldest child aged 18 or older	44.29	138	9.7
Single parent with child under age 18	29.85	93	4.9
Single person	16.10	50	14.9
RACE AND HISPANIC ORIGIN			
Average household	**32.18**	**100**	**100.0**
Asian	31.38	98	4.2
Black	34.71	108	13.6
Hispanic	33.09	103	12.9
Non-Hispanic white and other	31.62	98	73.8
REGION			
Average household	**32.18**	**100**	**100.0**
Northeast	29.39	91	16.5
Midwest	32.84	102	22.6
South	33.77	105	39.1
West	31.16	97	21.8
EDUCATION			
Average household	**32.18**	**100**	**100.0**
Less than high school graduate	31.20	97	12.7
High school graduate	33.98	106	26.3
Some college	31.68	98	20.3
Associate's degree	37.28	116	11.4
Bachelor's degree or more	29.91	93	29.3
Bachelor's degree	29.83	93	18.5
Master's, professional, doctoral degree	30.04	93	10.8

Note: Market shares may not sum to 100.0 because of rounding and missing categories by household type. "Asian" and "black" include Hispanics and non-Hispanics who identify themselves as being of the respective race alone. "Hispanic" includes people of any race who identify themselves as Hispanic. "Other" includes people who identify themselves as non-Hispanic and as Alaska Native, American Indian, Asian (who are also included in the "Asian" row), or Native Hawaiian or other Pacific Islander, as well as non-Hispanics reporting more than one race.
Source: Calculations by New Strategist based on the Bureau of Labor Statistics' 2012 Consumer Expenditure Survey

Bakery Products, Frozen and Refrigerated

Best customers: Householders aged 35 to 44
Married couples with children at home
Single parents

Customer trends: Average household spending on frozen and refrigerated bakery products may rise as the large millennial generation begins to fill the best-customer age group.

Households with children spend the most on frozen and refrigerated bakery products. Married couples with children spend 71 percent more than the average household on this item. Many are busy two-earner couples trying to save time by buying heat-and-serve foods. Householders aged 35 to 44, most with children, spend 35 percent more than average on frozen and refrigerated bakery products. Single parents, whose spending on most items is below average, spend an average amount on frozen and refrigerated bakery products.

Average household spending on frozen and refrigerated bakery products fell 12 percent between 2000 and 2012, after adjusting for inflation. But the category made some gains at the end of the time period, rising 8 percent between 2010 and 2012. Behind the decline was the entry of the small generation X into the best-customer lifestage. Average household spending on frozen and refrigerated bakery products may rise in the years ahead as the large millennial generation fills the best-customer age group.

Table 9.6 Bakery products, frozen and refrigerated

Total household spending $3,579,448,320.00
Average household spends   28.77

AGE OF HOUSEHOLDER	AVERAGE HOUSEHOLD SPENDING	BEST CUSTOMERS (index)	BIGGEST CUSTOMERS (market share)
Average household	$28.77	100	100.0%
Under age 25	19.96	69	4.5
Aged 25 to 34	30.63	106	17.2
Aged 35 to 44	38.74	135	23.4
Aged 45 to 54	30.74	107	21.1
Aged 55 to 64	26.60	92	16.9
Aged 65 to 74	22.91	80	9.6
Aged 75 or older	20.66	72	7.0

	AVERAGE HOUSEHOLD SPENDING	BEST CUSTOMERS (index)	BIGGEST CUSTOMERS (market share)
HOUSEHOLD INCOME			
Average household	**$28.77**	**100**	**100.0%**
Under $20,000	17.02	59	12.4
$20,000 to $39,999	22.13	77	17.3
$40,000 to $49,999	24.90	87	7.7
$50,000 to $69,999	29.77	103	14.9
$70,000 to $79,999	42.11	146	8.2
$80,000 to $99,999	35.05	122	10.7
$100,000 or more	43.87	152	28.5
HOUSEHOLD TYPE			
Average household	**28.77**	**100**	**100.0**
Married couples	40.09	139	67.7
Married couples, no children	30.85	107	22.4
Married couples with children	49.10	171	40.1
Oldest child under age 6	41.84	145	6.6
Oldest child aged 6 to 17	55.02	191	22.7
Oldest child aged 18 or older	43.75	152	10.7
Single parent with child under age 18	29.02	101	5.3
Single person	12.50	43	12.9
RACE AND HISPANIC ORIGIN			
Average household	**28.77**	**100**	**100.0**
Asian	32.68	114	4.9
Black	18.95	66	8.3
Hispanic	20.48	71	8.9
Non-Hispanic white and other	31.83	111	83.0
REGION			
Average household	**28.77**	**100**	**100.0**
Northeast	27.91	97	17.5
Midwest	31.97	111	24.6
South	30.20	105	39.1
West	23.91	83	18.7
EDUCATION			
Average household	**28.77**	**100**	**100.0**
Less than high school graduate	22.87	79	10.4
High school graduate	28.58	99	24.8
Some college	25.35	88	18.1
Associate's degree	32.63	113	11.2
Bachelor's degree or more	32.24	112	35.3
Bachelor's degree	29.92	104	20.7
Master's, professional, doctoral degree	36.16	126	14.6

Note: Market shares may not sum to 100.0 because of rounding and missing categories by household type. "Asian" and "black" include Hispanics and non-Hispanics who identify themselves as being of the respective race alone. "Hispanic" includes people of any race who identify themselves as Hispanic. "Other" includes people who identify themselves as non-Hispanic and as Alaska Native, American Indian, Asian (who are also included in the "Asian" row), or Native Hawaiian or other Pacific Islander, as well as non-Hispanics reporting more than one race.
Source: Calculations by New Strategist based on the Bureau of Labor Statistics' 2012 Consumer Expenditure Survey

Baking Needs and Miscellaneous Products

Best customers: Married couples with children at home

Customer trends: Average household spending on baking needs and miscellaneous products is likely to fall
                        as cooking-challenged younger generations marry and have children.

Although cooking from scratch has become a lot less common than it once was, many people enjoy whipping up a home-cooked meal or dessert every now and then. Most are married couples, often with children at home. Married couples with children at home spend 65 percent more than the average household on products for baking, the figure peaking at 76 percent above average among couples with the largest households—those with adult children at home.

Average household spending on products for baking rose steadily over the entire decade of the 2000s, for a cumulative gain of 22 percent between 2000 and 2010, after adjusting for inflation. The trend then reversed and average household spending on baking products fell 9 percent between 2010 and 2012. The popularity of televised cooking programs may account for some of the increase. In the long term, however, average household spending on products for baking is likely to decline as cooking-challenged younger generations have children.

Table 9.7 Baking needs and miscellaneous products

Total household spending $3,104,179,200.00
Average household spends   24.95

AGE OF HOUSEHOLDER	AVERAGE HOUSEHOLD SPENDING	BEST CUSTOMERS (index)	BIGGEST CUSTOMERS (market share)
Average household	$24.95	100	100.0%
Under age 25	12.80	51	3.4
Aged 25 to 34	26.34	106	17.1
Aged 35 to 44	26.79	107	18.6
Aged 45 to 54	31.29	125	24.8
Aged 55 to 64	23.97	96	17.6
Aged 65 to 74	26.01	104	12.6
Aged 75 or older	15.07	60	5.9

	AVERAGE HOUSEHOLD SPENDING	BEST CUSTOMERS (index)	BIGGEST CUSTOMERS (market share)
HOUSEHOLD INCOME			
Average household	$24.95	100	100.0%
Under $20,000	13.52	54	11.4
$20,000 to $39,999	19.51	78	17.6
$40,000 to $49,999	24.92	100	8.8
$50,000 to $69,999	25.22	101	14.6
$70,000 to $79,999	27.54	110	6.2
$80,000 to $99,999	28.13	113	9.9
$100,000 or more	41.51	166	31.1
HOUSEHOLD TYPE			
Average household	24.95	100	100.0
Married couples	33.42	134	65.1
Married couples, no children	26.03	104	21.7
Married couples with children	41.05	165	38.7
Oldest child under age 6	29.66	119	5.4
Oldest child aged 6 to 17	43.62	175	20.8
Oldest child aged 18 or older	43.87	176	12.4
Single parent with child under age 18	22.96	92	4.8
Single person	11.89	48	14.1
RACE AND HISPANIC ORIGIN			
Average household	24.95	100	100.0
Asian	28.10	113	4.9
Black	15.18	61	7.6
Hispanic	18.06	72	9.1
Non-Hispanic white and other	27.81	111	83.7
REGION			
Average household	24.95	100	100.0
Northeast	26.67	107	19.3
Midwest	28.95	116	25.7
South	20.11	81	30.0
West	27.57	111	24.9
EDUCATION			
Average household	24.95	100	100.0
Less than high school graduate	19.01	76	9.9
High school graduate	21.21	85	21.2
Some college	23.27	93	19.2
Associate's degree	27.24	109	10.8
Bachelor's degree or more	30.49	122	38.5
Bachelor's degree	29.44	118	23.5
Master's, professional, doctoral degree	32.25	129	15.0

Note: Market shares may not sum to 100.0 because of rounding and missing categories by household type. "Asian" and "black" include Hispanics and non-Hispanics who identify themselves as being of the respective race alone. "Hispanic" includes people of any race who identify themselves as Hispanic. "Other" includes people who identify themselves as non-Hispanic and as Alaska Native, American Indian, Asian (who are also included in the "Asian" row), or Native Hawaiian or other Pacific Islander, as well as non-Hispanics reporting more than one race.
Source: Calculations by New Strategist based on the Bureau of Labor Statistics' 2012 Consumer Expenditure Survey

Bananas

Best customers:
Householders aged 35 to 54
Married couples with children at home
Single parents
Asians and Hispanics

Customer trends:
Average household spending on bananas may decline as the large baby-boom generation ages
and household size shrinks.

Households with children spend the most on bananas. Married couples with children at home spend 38 percent more than the average household on bananas. Householders aged 35 to 54, most with children at home, spend 11 to 22 percent more on bananas than the average household. Single parents, whose spending approaches average on only a few items, spend 18 percent more than average on bananas. Hispanics, who tend to have large families, spend 39 percent more than average and Asians spend 43 percent more.

Average household spending on bananas fell 22 percent between 2000 and 2006, after adjusting for inflation, but rebounded with a 34 percent gain between 2006 and 2012. The greater propensity to eat out and the exit of the baby-boom generation from the best-customer lifestage were factors in the earlier spending decline. The increased spending since 2006 is due to less eating out as households tightened their belts following the Great Recession. Average household spending on bananas may decline again in the years ahead as the large baby-boom generation ages and household size shrinks.

Table 9.8 Bananas

Total household spending $5,450,664,960.00
Average household spends   43.81

	AVERAGE HOUSEHOLD SPENDING	BEST CUSTOMERS (index)	BIGGEST CUSTOMERS (market share)
AGE OF HOUSEHOLDER			
Average household	**$43.81**	**100**	**100.0%**
Under age 25	27.94	64	4.2
Aged 25 to 34	39.98	91	14.8
Aged 35 to 44	48.55	111	19.2
Aged 45 to 54	53.35	122	24.1
Aged 55 to 64	43.12	98	18.0
Aged 65 to 74	39.00	89	10.7
Aged 75 or older	40.44	92	9.0

	AVERAGE HOUSEHOLD SPENDING	BEST CUSTOMERS (index)	BIGGEST CUSTOMERS (market share)
HOUSEHOLD INCOME			
Average household	**$43.81**	**100**	**100.0%**
Under $20,000	26.51	61	12.7
$20,000 to $39,999	34.35	78	17.7
$40,000 to $49,999	45.47	104	9.2
$50,000 to $69,999	47.47	108	15.7
$70,000 to $79,999	49.25	112	6.3
$80,000 to $99,999	56.11	128	11.3
$100,000 or more	63.14	144	27.0
HOUSEHOLD TYPE			
Average household	**43.81**	**100**	**100.0**
Married couples	54.68	125	60.6
Married couples, no children	45.56	104	21.7
Married couples with children	60.48	138	32.5
Oldest child under age 6	49.45	113	5.1
Oldest child aged 6 to 17	62.29	142	16.9
Oldest child aged 18 or older	64.34	147	10.4
Single parent with child under age 18	51.78	118	6.2
Single person	22.82	52	15.5
RACE AND HISPANIC ORIGIN			
Average household	**43.81**	**100**	**100.0**
Asian	62.66	143	6.2
Black	32.20	73	9.2
Hispanic	60.74	139	17.4
Non-Hispanic white and other	42.93	98	73.6
REGION			
Average household	**43.81**	**100**	**100.0**
Northeast	49.17	112	20.3
Midwest	44.91	103	22.7
South	36.86	84	31.3
West	49.91	114	25.7
EDUCATION			
Average household	**43.81**	**100**	**100.0**
Less than high school graduate	44.42	101	13.2
High school graduate	39.39	90	22.4
Some college	39.64	90	18.6
Associate's degree	44.67	102	10.1
Bachelor's degree or more	49.55	113	35.7
Bachelor's degree	48.26	110	22.0
Master's, professional, doctoral degree	51.74	118	13.7

Note: Market shares may not sum to 100.0 because of rounding and missing categories by household type. "Asian" and "black" include Hispanics and non-Hispanics who identify themselves as being of the respective race alone. "Hispanic" includes people of any race who identify themselves as Hispanic. "Other" includes people who identify themselves as non-Hispanic and as Alaska Native, American Indian, Asian (who are also included in the "Asian" row), or Native Hawaiian or other Pacific Islander, as well as non-Hispanics reporting more than one race.
Source: Calculations by New Strategist based on the Bureau of Labor Statistics' 2012 Consumer Expenditure Survey

Beef, Ground

Best customers: Householders aged 35 to 54
Married couples with school-aged or older children at home
Hispanics
Householders without a high school diploma

Customer trends: Average household spending on ground beef may decline as the small generation X passes
through the best-customer age groups and eating out claims more of the food dollar.

Households with children are the biggest spenders on ground beef. Married couples with school-aged or older children at home spend 56 to 58 percent more than average on this item. Householders aged 35 to 54, most with children at home, spend 16 to 21 percent more than average on ground beef and control 44 percent of the market. Hispanics, with their relatively large families, outspend the average by 14 percent. Householders with no more than a high school education, many of them Hispanic, spend 8 to 18 percent more on ground beef than the average household.

Average household spending on ground beef declined 24 percent between 2000 and 2010, after adjusting for inflation, but then grew 5 percent during the 2010-to-2012 time period. Behind the decline was the growing popularity of fast food as a substitute for home-cooked meals. The recent increase in spending on ground beef could be short-lived, a sign of economic recovery. Average household spending on ground beef is likely to resume its decline as the small generation X passes through the best-customer age groups and eating out claims more of the food dollar.

Table 9.9 Beef, ground

Total household spending $11,632,896,000.00
Average household spends   93.50

AGE OF HOUSEHOLDER	AVERAGE HOUSEHOLD SPENDING	BEST CUSTOMERS (index)	BIGGEST CUSTOMERS (market share)
Average household	$93.50	100	100.0%
Under age 25	64.24	69	4.5
Aged 25 to 34	90.01	96	15.6
Aged 35 to 44	108.48	116	20.1
Aged 45 to 54	112.67	121	23.8
Aged 55 to 64	101.04	108	19.8
Aged 65 to 74	80.44	86	10.4
Aged 75 or older	54.95	59	5.7

	AVERAGE HOUSEHOLD SPENDING	BEST CUSTOMERS (index)	BIGGEST CUSTOMERS (market share)
HOUSEHOLD INCOME			
Average household	**$93.50**	**100**	**100.0%**
Under $20,000	66.31	71	14.9
$20,000 to $39,999	83.23	89	20.1
$40,000 to $49,999	92.15	99	8.7
$50,000 to $69,999	97.80	105	15.1
$70,000 to $79,999	117.76	126	7.0
$80,000 to $99,999	119.62	128	11.3
$100,000 or more	114.03	122	22.8
HOUSEHOLD TYPE			
Average household	**93.50**	**100**	**100.0**
Married couples	118.02	126	61.3
Married couples, no children	90.36	97	20.1
Married couples with children	135.03	144	34.0
Oldest child under age 6	86.42	92	4.2
Oldest child aged 6 to 17	145.44	156	18.5
Oldest child aged 18 or older	147.95	158	11.2
Single parent with child under age 18	86.75	93	4.9
Single person	39.20	42	12.4
RACE AND HISPANIC ORIGIN			
Average household	**93.50**	**100**	**100.0**
Asian	61.81	66	2.9
Black	86.06	92	11.6
Hispanic	106.69	114	14.3
Non-Hispanic white and other	92.68	99	74.4
REGION			
Average household	**93.50**	**100**	**100.0**
Northeast	91.30	98	17.6
Midwest	100.76	108	23.9
South	97.39	104	38.8
West	81.56	87	19.7
EDUCATION			
Average household	**93.50**	**100**	**100.0**
Less than high school graduate	100.59	108	14.0
High school graduate	110.67	118	29.5
Some college	84.70	91	18.7
Associate's degree	109.91	118	11.6
Bachelor's degree or more	78.37	84	26.4
Bachelor's degree	80.54	86	17.2
Master's, professional, doctoral degree	74.70	80	9.3

Note: Market shares may not sum to 100.0 because of rounding and missing categories by household type. "Asian" and "black" include Hispanics and non-Hispanics who identify themselves as being of the respective race alone. "Hispanic" includes people of any race who identify themselves as Hispanic. "Other" includes people who identify themselves as non-Hispanic and as Alaska Native, American Indian, Asian (who are also included in the "Asian" row), or Native Hawaiian or other Pacific Islander, as well as non-Hispanics reporting more than one race.
Source: Calculations by New Strategist based on the Bureau of Labor Statistics' 2012 Consumer Expenditure Survey

Beef, Roast

Best customers:
Householders aged 45 to 54
Married couples with school-aged or older children at home
Hispanics and Asians
Households in the West

Customer trends:
Average household spending on roast beef may decline as the small generation X enters the best-customer age group and eating out claims more of the food dollar.

The largest households are the biggest spenders on roast beef. Married couples with adult children at home spend over twice the average on this item, and those with school-aged children spend 39 percent more. Householders aged 45 to 54, many with children at home, spend 34 percent more than average on roast beef. Hispanics, who have the largest families, spend 42 percent more than average on this item. Asians spend 34 percent more. Households in the West, where many Hispanics and Asians reside, outspend the average household by 27 percent.

Average household spending on roast beef fell a steep 42 percent between 2000 and 2010, after adjusting for inflation, but then increased 10 percent in the 2010-to-2012 time period. Behind the decline was the growing consumer preference for prepared foods and eating out as well as belt tightening in the aftermath of the Great Recession. The recent increase in spending on roast beef could be short-lived, a sign of economic recovery. Average household spending on roast beef is likely to resume its decline as the small generation X enters the best-customer age group and eating out claims more of the food dollar.

Table 9.10 Beef, roast

Total household spending $4,232,632,320.00
Average household spends   34.02

AGE OF HOUSEHOLDER	AVERAGE HOUSEHOLD SPENDING	BEST CUSTOMERS (index)	BIGGEST CUSTOMERS (market share)
Average household	$34.02	100	100.0%
Under age 25	25.04	74	4.8
Aged 25 to 34	23.42	69	11.1
Aged 35 to 44	35.62	105	18.2
Aged 45 to 54	45.64	134	26.6
Aged 55 to 64	37.18	109	20.0
Aged 65 to 74	33.02	97	11.7
Aged 75 or older	27.01	79	7.8

	AVERAGE HOUSEHOLD SPENDING	BEST CUSTOMERS (index)	BIGGEST CUSTOMERS (market share)
HOUSEHOLD INCOME			
Average household	**$34.02**	**100**	**100.0%**
Under $20,000	14.38	42	8.9
$20,000 to $39,999	25.32	74	16.8
$40,000 to $49,999	35.36	104	9.2
$50,000 to $69,999	29.95	88	12.7
$70,000 to $79,999	41.72	123	6.8
$80,000 to $99,999	41.24	121	10.7
$100,000 or more	62.99	185	34.7
HOUSEHOLD TYPE			
Average household	**34.02**	**100**	**100.0**
Married couples	45.41	133	64.8
Married couples, no children	37.09	109	22.7
Married couples with children	49.43	145	34.2
Oldest child under age 6	20.74	61	2.8
Oldest child aged 6 to 17	47.20	139	16.5
Oldest child aged 18 or older	71.01	209	14.7
Single parent with child under age 18	22.11	65	3.4
Single person	13.47	40	11.8
RACE AND HISPANIC ORIGIN			
Average household	**34.02**	**100**	**100.0**
Asian	45.58	134	5.8
Black	28.39	83	10.5
Hispanic	48.34	142	17.8
Non-Hispanic white and other	32.60	96	71.9
REGION			
Average household	**34.02**	**100**	**100.0**
Northeast	26.52	78	14.1
Midwest	30.19	89	19.7
South	34.43	101	37.7
West	43.29	127	28.7
EDUCATION			
Average household	**34.02**	**100**	**100.0**
Less than high school graduate	22.57	66	8.7
High school graduate	35.32	104	25.9
Some college	30.72	90	18.6
Associate's degree	46.30	136	13.4
Bachelor's degree or more	35.71	105	33.1
Bachelor's degree	29.65	87	17.4
Master's, professional, doctoral degree	45.95	135	15.7

Note: Market shares may not sum to 100.0 because of rounding and missing categories by household type. "Asian" and "black" include Hispanics and non-Hispanics who identify themselves as being of the respective race alone. "Hispanic" includes people of any race who identify themselves as Hispanic. "Other" includes people who identify themselves as non-Hispanic and as Alaska Native, American Indian, Asian (who are also included in the "Asian" row), or Native Hawaiian or other Pacific Islander, as well as non-Hispanics reporting more than one race.
Source: Calculations by New Strategist based on the Bureau of Labor Statistics' 2012 Consumer Expenditure Survey

Beef, Steak

Best customers:
Householders aged 35 to 54
Married couples with school-aged or older children at home
Hispanics

Customer trends:
Average household spending on steak should continue to decline as the small generation X passes
through the best-customer age groups and prepared meals claim more of the food dollar.

The best customers of steak are the largest households. Married couples with school-aged or older children at home spend 54 to 62 percent more than average on steak. Householders aged 35 to 54, most with children at home, spend 22 to 25 percent more than average on steak. Hispanics, who tend to have large families, spend 32 percent more than average on steak.

Average household spending on steak is in long-term decline. Spending on steak fell 23 percent between 2000 and 2006 and another 18 percent between 2006 and 2012, after adjusting for inflation. Average household spending on steak should continue to decline as the small generation X passes through the best-customer age groups and prepared meals claim more of the food dollar.

Table 9.11 Beef, steak

Total household spending $9,883,607,040.00
Average household spends   79.44

AGE OF HOUSEHOLDER	AVERAGE HOUSEHOLD SPENDING	BEST CUSTOMERS (index)	BIGGEST CUSTOMERS (market share)
Average household	$79.44	100	100.0%
Under age 25	59.84	75	4.9
Aged 25 to 34	64.13	81	13.0
Aged 35 to 44	97.02	122	21.2
Aged 45 to 54	99.24	125	24.7
Aged 55 to 64	85.36	107	19.7
Aged 65 to 74	71.22	90	10.8
Aged 75 or older	45.30	57	5.6

	AVERAGE HOUSEHOLD SPENDING	BEST CUSTOMERS (index)	BIGGEST CUSTOMERS (market share)
HOUSEHOLD INCOME			
Average household	$79.44	100	100.0%
Under $20,000	41.25	52	10.9
$20,000 to $39,999	55.01	69	15.6
$40,000 to $49,999	87.59	110	9.8
$50,000 to $69,999	75.30	95	13.7
$70,000 to $79,999	95.43	120	6.7
$80,000 to $99,999	87.30	110	9.7
$100,000 or more	141.19	178	33.3
HOUSEHOLD TYPE			
Average household	79.44	100	100.0
Married couples	104.63	132	64.0
Married couples, no children	89.47	113	23.5
Married couples with children	114.10	144	33.8
Oldest child under age 6	69.49	87	4.0
Oldest child aged 6 to 17	122.08	154	18.3
Oldest child aged 18 or older	128.59	162	11.4
Single parent with child under age 18	65.24	82	4.3
Single person	32.58	41	12.2
RACE AND HISPANIC ORIGIN			
Average household	79.44	100	100.0
Asian	71.52	90	3.9
Black	51.37	65	8.1
Hispanic	104.92	132	16.6
Non-Hispanic white and other	80.00	101	75.6
REGION			
Average household	79.44	100	100.0
Northeast	78.40	99	17.8
Midwest	78.43	99	21.9
South	76.89	97	36.0
West	85.51	108	24.3
EDUCATION			
Average household	79.44	100	100.0
Less than high school graduate	73.37	92	12.1
High school graduate	83.56	105	26.2
Some college	65.36	82	16.9
Associate's degree	79.66	100	9.9
Bachelor's degree or more	87.95	111	34.9
Bachelor's degree	85.50	108	21.5
Master's, professional, doctoral degree	92.09	116	13.5

Note: Market shares may not sum to 100.0 because of rounding and missing categories by household type. "Asian" and "black" include Hispanics and non-Hispanics who identify themselves as being of the respective race alone. "Hispanic" includes people of any race who identify themselves as Hispanic. "Other" includes people who identify themselves as non-Hispanic and as Alaska Native, American Indian, Asian (who are also included in the "Asian" row), or Native Hawaiian or other Pacific Islander, as well as non-Hispanics reporting more than one race.
Source: Calculations by New Strategist based on the Bureau of Labor Statistics' 2012 Consumer Expenditure Survey

Biscuits and Rolls

Best customers: Householders aged 35 to 64
Married couples with children at home
Households in the Northeast

Customer trends: Average household spending on biscuits and rolls may resume its decline as the large baby-boom generation ages and household size shrinks.

The largest households spend the most on biscuits and rolls. Married couples with school-aged children spend 73 percent more than the average household on this item, and those with adult children at home spend 45 percent more. Householders ranging in age from 35 to 64, many with children at home, spend 10 to 22 percent more than average on biscuits and rolls and control 63 percent of the market. Households in the Northeast spend 24 percent more than average on this item.

Average household spending on biscuits and rolls fell 7 percent between 2000 and 2006, then climbed 9 percent between 2006 and 2012, after adjusting for inflation. Behind the increase was the shift to homemade meals by financially strapped consumers. Average household spending on biscuits and rolls may resume its decline as the large baby-boom generation ages and household size shrinks.

Table 9.12 Biscuits and rolls

Total household spending $6,450,969,600.00
Average household spends   51.85

AGE OF HOUSEHOLDER	AVERAGE HOUSEHOLD SPENDING	BEST CUSTOMERS (index)	BIGGEST CUSTOMERS (market share)
Average household	$51.85	100	100.0%
Under age 25	27.14	52	3.4
Aged 25 to 34	44.52	86	13.9
Aged 35 to 44	63.28	122	21.2
Aged 45 to 54	57.59	111	22.0
Aged 55 to 64	57.18	110	20.2
Aged 65 to 74	50.52	97	11.7
Aged 75 or older	40.81	79	7.7

	AVERAGE HOUSEHOLD SPENDING	BEST CUSTOMERS (index)	BIGGEST CUSTOMERS (market share)
HOUSEHOLD INCOME			
Average household	**$51.85**	**100**	**100.0%**
Under $20,000	29.73	57	12.1
$20,000 to $39,999	38.23	74	16.6
$40,000 to $49,999	46.16	89	7.9
$50,000 to $69,999	51.65	100	14.4
$70,000 to $79,999	64.20	124	6.9
$80,000 to $99,999	62.26	120	10.6
$100,000 or more	86.94	168	31.4
HOUSEHOLD TYPE			
Average household	**51.85**	**100**	**100.0**
Married couples	69.57	134	65.2
Married couples, no children	56.64	109	22.8
Married couples with children	79.85	154	36.2
Oldest child under age 6	61.71	119	5.4
Oldest child aged 6 to 17	89.56	173	20.5
Oldest child aged 18 or older	74.97	145	10.2
Single parent with child under age 18	45.05	87	4.6
Single person	25.61	49	14.7
RACE AND HISPANIC ORIGIN			
Average household	**51.85**	**100**	**100.0**
Asian	47.57	92	4.0
Black	28.10	54	6.8
Hispanic	45.15	87	10.9
Non-Hispanic white and other	56.97	110	82.5
REGION			
Average household	**51.85**	**100**	**100.0**
Northeast	64.14	124	22.3
Midwest	56.15	108	24.0
South	43.80	84	31.5
West	50.95	98	22.1
EDUCATION			
Average household	**51.85**	**100**	**100.0**
Less than high school graduate	43.14	83	10.9
High school graduate	46.43	90	22.3
Some college	44.13	85	17.5
Associate's degree	54.53	105	10.4
Bachelor's degree or more	63.69	123	38.7
Bachelor's degree	63.52	123	24.4
Master's, professional, doctoral degree	63.97	123	14.3

Note: Market shares may not sum to 100.0 because of rounding and missing categories by household type. "Asian" and "black" include Hispanics and non-Hispanics who identify themselves as being of the respective race alone. "Hispanic" includes people of any race who identify themselves as Hispanic. "Other" includes people who identify themselves as non-Hispanic and as Alaska Native, American Indian, Asian (who are also included in the "Asian" row), or Native Hawaiian or other Pacific Islander, as well as non-Hispanics reporting more than one race.
Source: Calculations by New Strategist based on the Bureau of Labor Statistics' 2012 Consumer Expenditure Survey

Bread and Cracker Products

Best customers: Householders aged 35 to 54
Married couples with children at home
Households in the Northeast

Customer trends: Average household spending on bread and cracker products is likely to continue to decline as restaurant meals replace home cooking among younger generations.

The biggest spenders on bread and cracker products are the largest households. Married couples with children at home spend 59 percent more than average on this item. Householders aged 35 to 54, most with children at home, spend 11 to 20 percent more than average on bread and cracker products. Households in the Northeast spend 32 percent more.

Average household spending on bread and cracker products fell 16 percent between 2000 and 2006, after adjusting for inflation, then climbed 48 percent between 2006 and 2010 before falling again in the ensuing two years. Behind the 2006-to-2010 increase in spending was belt tightening in the face of the Great Recession as households opted for more meals at home rather than in restaurants. Average household spending on bread and cracker products is likely to continue to decline as restaurant meals replace home cooking among younger generations.

Table 9.13 Bread and cracker products

Total household spending $909,480,960.00
Average household spends   7.31

AGE OF HOUSEHOLDER	AVERAGE HOUSEHOLD SPENDING	BEST CUSTOMERS (index)	BIGGEST CUSTOMERS (market share)
Average household	**$7.31**	**100**	**100.0%**
Under age 25	6.03	82	5.4
Aged 25 to 34	7.31	100	16.2
Aged 35 to 44	8.09	111	19.2
Aged 45 to 54	8.78	120	23.8
Aged 55 to 64	6.55	90	16.4
Aged 65 to 74	7.03	96	11.6
Aged 75 or older	5.48	75	7.3

	AVERAGE HOUSEHOLD SPENDING	BEST CUSTOMERS (index)	BIGGEST CUSTOMERS (market share)
HOUSEHOLD INCOME			
Average household	**$7.31**	**100**	**100.0%**
Under $20,000	3.97	54	11.4
$20,000 to $39,999	5.75	79	17.7
$40,000 to $49,999	9.16	125	11.1
$50,000 to $69,999	7.74	106	15.3
$70,000 to $79,999	8.78	120	6.7
$80,000 to $99,999	8.77	120	10.6
$100,000 or more	10.51	144	26.9
HOUSEHOLD TYPE			
Average household	**7.31**	**100**	**100.0**
Married couples	9.75	133	64.8
Married couples, no children	7.58	104	21.6
Married couples with children	11.65	159	37.5
Oldest child under age 6	11.16	153	7.0
Oldest child aged 6 to 17	10.42	143	17.0
Oldest child aged 18 or older	14.00	192	13.5
Single parent with child under age 18	6.33	87	4.5
Single person	3.00	41	12.2
RACE AND HISPANIC ORIGIN			
Average household	**7.31**	**100**	**100.0**
Asian	7.84	107	4.6
Black	4.27	58	7.3
Hispanic	5.66	77	9.7
Non-Hispanic white and other	8.11	111	83.3
REGION			
Average household	**7.31**	**100**	**100.0**
Northeast	9.67	132	23.9
Midwest	8.36	114	25.4
South	5.83	80	29.7
West	6.80	93	21.0
EDUCATION			
Average household	**7.31**	**100**	**100.0**
Less than high school graduate	6.23	85	11.1
High school graduate	7.15	98	24.4
Some college	6.96	95	19.6
Associate's degree	8.26	113	11.2
Bachelor's degree or more	7.77	106	33.5
Bachelor's degree	8.01	110	21.8
Master's, professional, doctoral degree	7.36	101	11.7

Note: Market shares may not sum to 100.0 because of rounding and missing categories by household type. "Asian" and "black" include Hispanics and non-Hispanics who identify themselves as being of the respective race alone. "Hispanic" includes people of any race who identify themselves as Hispanic. "Other" includes people who identify themselves as non-Hispanic and as Alaska Native, American Indian, Asian (who are also included in the "Asian" row), or Native Hawaiian or other Pacific Islander, as well as non-Hispanics reporting more than one race.
Source: Calculations by New Strategist based on the Bureau of Labor Statistics' 2012 Consumer Expenditure Survey

Bread Other than White

Best customers: Householders aged 35 to 64
Married couples with school-aged or older children at home
Single parents

Customer trends: Average household spending on nonwhite bread should remain stable as households switch from white to other bread types, but shrinking household size may limit gains.

Bread took a beating a few years back as low-carb diets became popular. Nonwhite bread held its own, however. In 2000, nonwhite bread accounted for 56 percent of total household spending on bread. By 2012, the figure had grown to 59 percent of the total. The best customers of nonwhite bread are the largest households. Married couples with school-aged or older children at home spend 46 percent more than the average household on nonwhite bread. Householders aged 35 to 64, many with children at home, spend 8 to 18 percent more than average on this item. Nonwhite bread is one of the relatively few items on which single parents, with their lower incomes, spend an average amount.

Spending on nonwhite bread, in slow decline before the Great Recession, held steady between 2006 and 2012, after adjusting for inflation. Average household spending on nonwhite bread should remain stable in the years ahead because of the shift away from white bread, but shrinking household size may take a toll on all bread buying.

Table 9.14 Bread other than white

Total household spending $7,664,025,600.00
Average household spends 61.60

AGE OF HOUSEHOLDER	AVERAGE HOUSEHOLD SPENDING	BEST CUSTOMERS (index)	BIGGEST CUSTOMERS (market share)
Average household	$61.60	100	100.0%
Under age 25	32.37	53	3.4
Aged 25 to 34	54.36	88	14.3
Aged 35 to 44	66.54	108	18.8
Aged 45 to 54	72.53	118	23.3
Aged 55 to 64	68.43	111	20.3
Aged 65 to 74	61.73	100	12.1
Aged 75 or older	50.20	81	8.0

	AVERAGE HOUSEHOLD SPENDING	BEST CUSTOMERS (index)	BIGGEST CUSTOMERS (market share)
HOUSEHOLD INCOME			
Average household	**$61.60**	**100**	**100.0%**
Under $20,000	38.61	63	13.2
$20,000 to $39,999	50.45	82	18.5
$40,000 to $49,999	52.54	85	7.5
$50,000 to $69,999	63.26	103	14.8
$70,000 to $79,999	78.15	127	7.1
$80,000 to $99,999	76.49	124	11.0
$100,000 or more	91.67	149	27.9
HOUSEHOLD TYPE			
Average household	**61.60**	**100**	**100.0**
Married couples	79.77	129	62.9
Married couples, no children	70.92	115	24.0
Married couples with children	86.17	140	32.9
Oldest child under age 6	69.55	113	5.2
Oldest child aged 6 to 17	90.17	146	17.4
Oldest child aged 18 or older	89.86	146	10.3
Single parent with child under age 18	62.26	101	5.3
Single person	33.42	54	16.1
RACE AND HISPANIC ORIGIN			
Average household	**61.60**	**100**	**100.0**
Asian	57.63	94	4.1
Black	40.84	66	8.3
Hispanic	62.00	101	12.6
Non-Hispanic white and other	65.03	106	79.2
REGION			
Average household	**61.60**	**100**	**100.0**
Northeast	70.33	114	20.6
Midwest	57.54	93	20.7
South	53.55	87	32.4
West	71.97	117	26.3
EDUCATION			
Average household	**61.60**	**100**	**100.0**
Less than high school graduate	48.90	79	10.4
High school graduate	57.37	93	23.2
Some college	56.04	91	18.7
Associate's degree	65.79	107	10.5
Bachelor's degree or more	72.09	117	36.9
Bachelor's degree	66.92	109	21.7
Master's, professional, doctoral degree	80.83	131	15.2

Note: Market shares may not sum to 100.0 because of rounding and missing categories by household type. "Asian" and "black" include Hispanics and non-Hispanics who identify themselves as being of the respective race alone. "Hispanic" includes people of any race who identify themselves as Hispanic. "Other" includes people who identify themselves as non-Hispanic and as Alaska Native, American Indian, Asian (who are also included in the "Asian" row), or Native Hawaiian or other Pacific Islander, as well as non-Hispanics reporting more than one race.
Source: Calculations by New Strategist based on the Bureau of Labor Statistics' 2012 Consumer Expenditure Survey

Bread, White

Best customers: Householders aged 35 to 54
Married couples with school-aged or older children at home
Single parents

Customer trends: Average household spending on white bread is likely to resume its decline in the years ahead as consumers switch to nonwhite bread.

White bread accounts for 41 percent of the average household's bread spending, down from 44 percent in 2000. The best customers of white bread are the largest households. Married couples with school-aged or older children at home spend 44 to 50 percent more than the average household on this item. Householders aged 35 to 54, many with children at home, spend 14 to 19 percent more than average on white bread. Single parents, whose spending approaches average on only a few items, spend 18 percent more than average on white bread.

Average household spending on white bread declined by a substantial 26 percent between 2000 and 2006, after adjusting for inflation, but rebounded by 20 percent between 2006 and 2012. Behind the decline was the switch to nonwhite bread, and behind the more recent increase is the renewed popularity of brown-bag lunches as the Great Recession cut incomes and spending. Average household spending on white bread is likely to resume its decline in the years ahead as consumers continue to switch to more nutritious whole-grain bread.

Table 9.15 Bread, white

| Total household spending | $5,414,584,320.00 |
| Average household spends | 43.52 |

AGE OF HOUSEHOLDER	AVERAGE HOUSEHOLD SPENDING	BEST CUSTOMERS (index)	BIGGEST CUSTOMERS (market share)
Average household	$43.52	100	100.0%
Under age 25	26.38	61	4.0
Aged 25 to 34	42.02	97	15.6
Aged 35 to 44	51.89	119	20.7
Aged 45 to 54	49.56	114	22.5
Aged 55 to 64	45.14	104	19.0
Aged 65 to 74	38.46	88	10.6
Aged 75 or older	33.51	77	7.5

	AVERAGE HOUSEHOLD SPENDING	BEST CUSTOMERS (index)	BIGGEST CUSTOMERS (market share)
HOUSEHOLD INCOME			
Average household	**$43.52**	**100**	**100.0%**
Under $20,000	30.36	70	14.7
$20,000 to $39,999	37.75	87	19.5
$40,000 to $49,999	44.42	102	9.0
$50,000 to $69,999	43.81	101	14.5
$70,000 to $79,999	52.64	121	6.8
$80,000 to $99,999	52.62	121	10.7
$100,000 or more	57.07	131	24.6
HOUSEHOLD TYPE			
Average household	**43.52**	**100**	**100.0**
Married couples	53.77	124	60.0
Married couples, no children	45.20	104	21.7
Married couples with children	60.20	138	32.5
Oldest child under age 6	42.24	97	4.4
Oldest child aged 6 to 17	65.36	150	17.9
Oldest child aged 18 or older	62.79	144	10.2
Single parent with child under age 18	51.24	118	6.2
Single person	24.28	56	16.6
RACE AND HISPANIC ORIGIN			
Average household	**43.52**	**100**	**100.0**
Asian	43.57	100	4.3
Black	40.26	93	11.6
Hispanic	44.26	102	12.7
Non-Hispanic white and other	43.95	101	75.8
REGION			
Average household	**43.52**	**100**	**100.0**
Northeast	47.31	109	19.6
Midwest	43.40	100	22.1
South	41.37	95	35.4
West	44.12	101	22.8
EDUCATION			
Average household	**43.52**	**100**	**100.0**
Less than high school graduate	41.26	95	12.4
High school graduate	44.32	102	25.4
Some college	41.00	94	19.4
Associate's degree	47.09	108	10.7
Bachelor's degree or more	44.32	102	32.1
Bachelor's degree	42.00	97	19.2
Master's, professional, doctoral degree	48.25	111	12.9

Note: Market shares may not sum to 100.0 because of rounding and missing categories by household type. "Asian" and "black" include Hispanics and non-Hispanics who identify themselves as being of the respective race alone. "Hispanic" includes people of any race who identify themselves as Hispanic. "Other" includes people who identify themselves as non-Hispanic and as Alaska Native, American Indian, Asian (who are also included in the "Asian" row), or Native Hawaiian or other Pacific Islander, as well as non-Hispanics reporting more than one race.
Source: Calculations by New Strategist based on the Bureau of Labor Statistics' 2012 Consumer Expenditure Survey

Butter

Best customers: Householders aged 45 to 64
Married couples with school-aged or older children at home
Households in the Northeast

Customer trends: Average household spending on butter may continue to climb as butter's reputation improves, but shrinking household size due to the aging of the baby-boom generation may limit the increase.

The best customers of butter are households headed by baby boomers and the largest households—married couples with children at home. Householders aged 45 to 64, members of the baby-boom generation, spend 18 to 19 percent more than average on butter. Not only do these households have the income to afford butter, but unlike older adults they never made the switch to margarine. The largest households—married couples with school-aged or older children at home—spend 57 to 61 percent more than the average household on butter. Households in the Northeast spend 26 percent more.

After dropping by 8 percent between 2000 and 2006, average household spending on butter rebounded with a 23 percent rise between 2006 and 2012, after adjusting for inflation. Spending on butter may continue to climb in the years ahead as butter's reputation improves, but shrinking household size due to the aging of the baby-boom generation may limit the increase.

Table 9.16 Butter

Total household spending $3,180,072,960.00
Average household spends 25.56

AGE OF HOUSEHOLDER	AVERAGE HOUSEHOLD SPENDING	BEST CUSTOMERS (index)	BIGGEST CUSTOMERS (market share)
Average household	$25.56	100	100.0%
Under age 25	10.47	41	2.7
Aged 25 to 34	22.68	89	14.3
Aged 35 to 44	26.08	102	17.7
Aged 45 to 54	30.25	118	23.4
Aged 55 to 64	30.30	119	21.7
Aged 65 to 74	25.04	98	11.8
Aged 75 or older	22.35	87	8.5

	AVERAGE HOUSEHOLD SPENDING	BEST CUSTOMERS (index)	BIGGEST CUSTOMERS (market share)
HOUSEHOLD INCOME			
Average household	**$25.56**	**100**	**100.0%**
Under $20,000	13.58	53	11.2
$20,000 to $39,999	18.24	71	16.1
$40,000 to $49,999	24.65	96	8.5
$50,000 to $69,999	27.65	108	15.6
$70,000 to $79,999	33.06	129	7.2
$80,000 to $99,999	31.12	122	10.7
$100,000 or more	41.21	161	30.2
HOUSEHOLD TYPE			
Average household	**25.56**	**100**	**100.0**
Married couples	34.28	134	65.1
Married couples, no children	28.47	111	23.2
Married couples with children	38.78	152	35.7
Oldest child under age 6	30.00	117	5.4
Oldest child aged 6 to 17	41.22	161	19.2
Oldest child aged 18 or older	40.17	157	11.1
Single parent with child under age 18	20.47	80	4.2
Single person	12.72	50	14.8
RACE AND HISPANIC ORIGIN			
Average household	**25.56**	**100**	**100.0**
Asian	22.65	89	3.8
Black	17.95	70	8.8
Hispanic	15.76	62	7.7
Non-Hispanic white and other	28.47	111	83.6
REGION			
Average household	**25.56**	**100**	**100.0**
Northeast	32.31	126	22.8
Midwest	27.23	107	23.6
South	20.69	81	30.1
West	26.49	104	23.4
EDUCATION			
Average household	**25.56**	**100**	**100.0**
Less than high school graduate	18.11	71	9.3
High school graduate	23.77	93	23.2
Some college	23.51	92	18.9
Associate's degree	25.91	101	10.0
Bachelor's degree or more	31.00	121	38.3
Bachelor's degree	30.44	119	23.7
Master's, professional, doctoral degree	31.95	125	14.5

Note: Market shares may not sum to 100.0 because of rounding and missing categories by household type. "Asian" and "black" include Hispanics and non-Hispanics who identify themselves as being of the respective race alone. "Hispanic" includes people of any race who identify themselves as Hispanic. "Other" includes people who identify themselves as non-Hispanic and as Alaska Native, American Indian, Asian (who are also included in the "Asian" row), or Native Hawaiian or other Pacific Islander, as well as non-Hispanics reporting more than one race.
Source: Calculations by New Strategist based on the Bureau of Labor Statistics' 2012 Consumer Expenditure Survey

Cakes and Cupcakes

Best customers: Householders aged 35 to 54
Married couples with school-aged or older children at home
Households in the Midwest

Customer trends: Average household spending on cakes and cupcakes should continue to decline as the small generation X
passes through the best-customer age groups and household size shrinks.

The largest households—those with children—spend the most on cakes and cupcakes. Married couples with school-aged children spend 56 percent more than the average household on this item, and those with adult children at home spend 47 percent more. Householders aged 35 to 54, most with children, spend 8 to 11 percent more than average on cakes and cupcakes. Households in the Midwest spend 23 percent more than average on this item.

Average household spending on cakes and cupcakes fell 26 percent between 2000 and 2012, after adjusting for inflation. The baby-boom generation's exit from the best-customer lifestage is one factor behind the decline. Average household spending on cakes and cupcakes should continue to decline as the small generation X passes through the best-customer age groups and household size shrinks.

Table 9.17 **Cakes and cupcakes**

Total household spending $4,720,343,040.00
Average household spends   37.94

	AVERAGE HOUSEHOLD SPENDING	BEST CUSTOMERS (index)	BIGGEST CUSTOMERS (market share)
AGE OF HOUSEHOLDER			
Average household	$37.94	100	100.0%
Under age 25	21.02	55	3.6
Aged 25 to 34	38.61	102	16.5
Aged 35 to 44	41.93	111	19.2
Aged 45 to 54	40.92	108	21.3
Aged 55 to 64	37.60	99	18.1
Aged 65 to 74	35.39	93	11.2
Aged 75 or older	39.11	103	10.1

	AVERAGE HOUSEHOLD SPENDING	BEST CUSTOMERS (index)	BIGGEST CUSTOMERS (market share)
HOUSEHOLD INCOME			
Average household	**$37.94**	**100**	**100.0%**
Under $20,000	24.41	64	13.5
$20,000 to $39,999	22.68	60	13.5
$40,000 to $49,999	52.60	139	12.3
$50,000 to $69,999	36.58	96	13.9
$70,000 to $79,999	50.24	132	7.4
$80,000 to $99,999	49.28	130	11.5
$100,000 or more	55.98	148	27.6
HOUSEHOLD TYPE			
Average household	**37.94**	**100**	**100.0**
Married couples	49.11	129	62.9
Married couples, no children	40.09	106	22.0
Married couples with children	54.49	144	33.8
Oldest child under age 6	39.38	104	4.7
Oldest child aged 6 to 17	59.30	156	18.6
Oldest child aged 18 or older	55.89	147	10.4
Single parent with child under age 18	27.78	73	3.8
Single person	20.94	55	16.4
RACE AND HISPANIC ORIGIN			
Average household	**37.94**	**100**	**100.0**
Asian	40.21	106	4.6
Black	23.59	62	7.8
Hispanic	39.05	103	12.9
Non-Hispanic white and other	40.31	106	79.7
REGION			
Average household	**37.94**	**100**	**100.0**
Northeast	38.37	101	18.3
Midwest	46.49	123	27.2
South	35.79	94	35.1
West	32.60	86	19.4
EDUCATION			
Average household	**37.94**	**100**	**100.0**
Less than high school graduate	31.74	84	10.9
High school graduate	31.36	83	20.6
Some college	34.34	91	18.6
Associate's degree	35.37	93	9.2
Bachelor's degree or more	48.59	128	40.4
Bachelor's degree	39.32	104	20.7
Master's, professional, doctoral degree	64.27	169	19.7

Note: Market shares may not sum to 100.0 because of rounding and missing categories by household type. "Asian" and "black" include Hispanics and non-Hispanics who identify themselves as being of the respective race alone. "Hispanic" includes people of any race who identify themselves as Hispanic. "Other" includes people who identify themselves as non-Hispanic and as Alaska Native, American Indian, Asian (who are also included in the "Asian" row), or Native Hawaiian or other Pacific Islander, as well as non-Hispanics reporting more than one race.
Source: Calculations by New Strategist based on the Bureau of Labor Statistics' 2012 Consumer Expenditure Survey

Candy and Chewing Gum

Best customers: Householders aged 35 to 64
Married couples with school-aged or older children at home
Households in the West

Customer trends: Average household spending on candy and chewing gum should fall as the large baby-boom generation ages
and household size shrinks.

Households with children spend the most on candy and chewing gum. Married couples with school-aged children spend 78 percent more than the average household on this item, and those with adult children at home spend 34 percent more. Householders aged 35 to 64, many with children and grandchildren, spend 10 to 15 percent more than average on candy and chewing gum. Households in the West spend 23 percent more than average on this item.

Average household spending on candy and chewing gum fell 14 percent between 2000 and 2012, after adjusting for inflation, although spending climbed in the 2010-to-2012 time period. Average household spending on candy and chewing gum is likely to resume its decline as the large baby-boom generation ages and household size shrinks.

Table 9.18 Candy and chewing gum

Total household spending $10,931,189,760.00
Average household spends   87.86

AGE OF HOUSEHOLDER	AVERAGE HOUSEHOLD SPENDING	BEST CUSTOMERS (index)	BIGGEST CUSTOMERS (market share)
Average household	$87.86	100	100.0%
Under age 25	49.30	56	3.7
Aged 25 to 34	82.87	94	15.2
Aged 35 to 44	101.13	115	20.0
Aged 45 to 54	98.40	112	22.2
Aged 55 to 64	96.90	110	20.2
Aged 65 to 74	87.26	99	12.0
Aged 75 or older	61.37	70	6.8

	AVERAGE HOUSEHOLD SPENDING	BEST CUSTOMERS (index)	BIGGEST CUSTOMERS (market share)
HOUSEHOLD INCOME			
Average household	**$87.86**	**100**	**100.0%**
Under $20,000	46.60	53	11.2
$20,000 to $39,999	66.73	76	17.1
$40,000 to $49,999	74.22	84	7.5
$50,000 to $69,999	88.48	101	14.5
$70,000 to $79,999	128.02	146	8.1
$80,000 to $99,999	98.54	112	9.9
$100,000 or more	147.18	168	31.4
HOUSEHOLD TYPE			
Average household	**87.86**	**100**	**100.0**
Married couples	116.90	133	64.6
Married couples, no children	100.91	115	23.9
Married couples with children	129.44	147	34.6
Oldest child under age 6	75.99	86	3.9
Oldest child aged 6 to 17	156.60	178	21.2
Oldest child aged 18 or older	117.42	134	9.4
Single parent with child under age 18	79.01	90	4.7
Single person	46.24	53	15.6
RACE AND HISPANIC ORIGIN			
Average household	**87.86**	**100**	**100.0**
Asian	99.63	113	4.9
Black	50.62	58	7.2
Hispanic	66.61	76	9.5
Non-Hispanic white and other	97.69	111	83.5
REGION			
Average household	**87.86**	**100**	**100.0**
Northeast	80.05	91	16.4
Midwest	90.54	103	22.8
South	77.79	89	33.0
West	108.27	123	27.8
EDUCATION			
Average household	**87.86**	**100**	**100.0**
Less than high school graduate	66.27	75	9.8
High school graduate	71.02	81	20.2
Some college	75.47	86	17.7
Associate's degree	105.08	120	11.8
Bachelor's degree or more	111.97	127	40.2
Bachelor's degree	110.60	126	25.1
Master's, professional, doctoral degree	114.30	130	15.1

Note: Market shares may not sum to 100.0 because of rounding and missing categories by household type. "Asian" and "black" include Hispanics and non-Hispanics who identify themselves as being of the respective race alone. "Hispanic" includes people of any race who identify themselves as Hispanic. "Other" includes people who identify themselves as non-Hispanic and as Alaska Native, American Indian, Asian (who are also included in the "Asian" row), or Native Hawaiian or other Pacific Islander, as well as non-Hispanics reporting more than one race.
Source: Calculations by New Strategist based on the Bureau of Labor Statistics' 2012 Consumer Expenditure Survey

Carbonated Drinks

Best customers: Householders aged 35 to 54
Married couples with school-aged or older children at home
Hispanics

Customer trends: Average household spending on carbonated beverages may continue to fall as boomers age and
household size shrinks, but the substitution of colas for coffee among younger generations
may limit the decline.

The best customers of carbonated drinks are the largest households. Married couples with school-aged or older children at home spend 35 to 52 percent more than average on this item. Householders ranging in age from 35 to 54, many with children at home, spend 16 to 22 percent more than average on sodas and control 44 percent of the market. Hispanics, who have the largest households, outspend the average by 7 percent.

Average household spending on carbonated beverages purchased at grocery or convenience stores fell 22 percent between 2000 and 2012, after adjusting for inflation. Lower-priced private brands and discounters are one factor behind the decline. Average household spending on sodas may continue to fall as boomers age and household size shrinks. But younger generations, drinking cola rather than coffee, may limit the decline.

Table 9.19 Carbonated drinks

Total household spending $17,385,891,840.00
Average household spends   139.74

AGE OF HOUSEHOLDER	AVERAGE HOUSEHOLD SPENDING	BEST CUSTOMERS (index)	BIGGEST CUSTOMERS (market share)
Average household	**$139.74**	**100**	**100.0%**
Under age 25	112.25	80	5.3
Aged 25 to 34	130.56	93	15.1
Aged 35 to 44	161.92	116	20.1
Aged 45 to 54	171.16	122	24.2
Aged 55 to 64	148.37	106	19.4
Aged 65 to 74	122.32	88	10.5
Aged 75 or older	74.19	53	5.2

	AVERAGE HOUSEHOLD SPENDING	BEST CUSTOMERS (index)	BIGGEST CUSTOMERS (market share)
HOUSEHOLD INCOME			
Average household	**$139.74**	**100**	**100.0%**
Under $20,000	94.08	67	14.2
$20,000 to $39,999	123.52	88	19.9
$40,000 to $49,999	138.48	99	8.8
$50,000 to $69,999	145.14	104	15.0
$70,000 to $79,999	190.44	136	7.6
$80,000 to $99,999	151.96	109	9.6
$100,000 or more	184.03	132	24.7
HOUSEHOLD TYPE			
Average household	**139.74**	**100**	**100.0**
Married couples	173.24	124	60.2
Married couples, no children	144.39	103	21.5
Married couples with children	187.07	134	31.5
Oldest child under age 6	139.84	100	4.6
Oldest child aged 6 to 17	189.33	135	16.1
Oldest child aged 18 or older	212.76	152	10.7
Single parent with child under age 18	139.71	100	5.2
Single person	72.43	52	15.4
RACE AND HISPANIC ORIGIN			
Average household	**139.74**	**100**	**100.0**
Asian	83.55	60	2.6
Black	101.79	73	9.2
Hispanic	149.70	107	13.4
Non-Hispanic white and other	144.62	103	77.7
REGION			
Average household	**139.74**	**100**	**100.0**
Northeast	119.16	85	15.4
Midwest	145.73	104	23.1
South	149.95	107	40.0
West	133.47	96	21.5
EDUCATION			
Average household	**139.74**	**100**	**100.0**
Less than high school graduate	144.88	104	13.5
High school graduate	149.58	107	26.7
Some college	136.68	98	20.1
Associate's degree	159.16	114	11.2
Bachelor's degree or more	126.18	90	28.5
Bachelor's degree	121.35	87	17.3
Master's, professional, doctoral degree	134.35	96	11.2

Note: Market shares may not sum to 100.0 because of rounding and missing categories by household type. "Asian" and "black" include Hispanics and non-Hispanics who identify themselves as being of the respective race alone. "Hispanic" includes people of any race who identify themselves as Hispanic. "Other" includes people who identify themselves as non-Hispanic and as Alaska Native, American Indian, Asian (who are also included in the "Asian" row), or Native Hawaiian or other Pacific Islander, as well as non-Hispanics reporting more than one race.
Source: Calculations by New Strategist based on the Bureau of Labor Statistics' 2012 Consumer Expenditure Survey

Cereal, Ready-to-Eat and Cooked

Best customers: Householders aged 35 to 54
                         Married couples with children at home
                         Single parents

Customer trends: Average household spending on cereal should grow as the large millennial generation enters
                         the best-customer age groups, but the ongoing baby bust may limit the gains.

The biggest spenders on cereal are households with children. Married couples with children at home spend 56 percent more than the average household on cereal, the figure peaking at 77 percent among those with school-aged children. Householders aged 35 to 54, most of them parents, spend 22 to 23 percent more than average on cereal. Single parents, whose spending approaches the average on only a few items, spend just over an average amount on cereal.

Average household spending on cereal fell 25 percent between 2000 and 2010, after adjusting for inflation, then grew 9 percent in the ensuing two years. Behind the decline was the entry of the small generation X into the best-customer lifestage. Average household spending on cereal may grow as the large millennial generation enters the best-customer age groups, but the ongoing baby bust may limit the gains.

Table 9.20 Cereal, ready-to-eat and cooked

Total household spending	$11,797,125,120.00
Average household spends	94.82

	AVERAGE HOUSEHOLD SPENDING	BEST CUSTOMERS (index)	BIGGEST CUSTOMERS (market share)
AGE OF HOUSEHOLDER			
Average household	$94.82	100	100.0%
Under age 25	75.05	79	5.2
Aged 25 to 34	99.18	105	16.9
Aged 35 to 44	116.50	123	21.3
Aged 45 to 54	115.79	122	24.2
Aged 55 to 64	82.67	87	16.0
Aged 65 to 74	76.06	80	9.7
Aged 75 or older	63.54	67	6.5

	AVERAGE HOUSEHOLD SPENDING	BEST CUSTOMERS (index)	BIGGEST CUSTOMERS (market share)
HOUSEHOLD INCOME			
Average household	**$94.82**	**100**	**100.0%**
Under $20,000	57.41	61	12.7
$20,000 to $39,999	70.70	75	16.8
$40,000 to $49,999	92.91	98	8.7
$50,000 to $69,999	97.37	103	14.8
$70,000 to $79,999	123.96	131	7.3
$80,000 to $99,999	120.22	127	11.2
$100,000 or more	143.75	152	28.4
HOUSEHOLD TYPE			
Average household	**94.82**	**100**	**100.0**
Married couples	122.89	130	62.9
Married couples, no children	93.96	99	20.7
Married couples with children	147.53	156	36.6
Oldest child under age 6	112.48	119	5.4
Oldest child aged 6 to 17	168.24	177	21.1
Oldest child aged 18 or older	134.83	142	10.0
Single parent with child under age 18	97.55	103	5.4
Single person	43.12	45	13.5
RACE AND HISPANIC ORIGIN			
Average household	**94.82**	**100**	**100.0**
Asian	68.70	72	3.1
Black	79.75	84	10.6
Hispanic	103.76	109	13.7
Non-Hispanic white and other	95.95	101	76.0
REGION			
Average household	**94.82**	**100**	**100.0**
Northeast	95.38	101	18.2
Midwest	95.91	101	22.4
South	88.40	93	34.7
West	103.94	110	24.7
EDUCATION			
Average household	**94.82**	**100**	**100.0**
Less than high school graduate	73.65	78	10.1
High school graduate	85.77	90	22.6
Some college	89.11	94	19.4
Associate's degree	107.01	113	11.1
Bachelor's degree or more	109.80	116	36.5
Bachelor's degree	110.75	117	23.3
Master's, professional, doctoral degree	108.19	114	13.2

Note: Market shares may not sum to 100.0 because of rounding and missing categories by household type. "Asian" and "black" include Hispanics and non-Hispanics who identify themselves as being of the respective race alone. "Hispanic" includes people of any race who identify themselves as Hispanic. "Other" includes people who identify themselves as non-Hispanic and as Alaska Native, American Indian, Asian (who are also included in the "Asian" row), or Native Hawaiian or other Pacific Islander, as well as non-Hispanics reporting more than one race.
Source: Calculations by New Strategist based on the Bureau of Labor Statistics' 2012 Consumer Expenditure Survey

Cheese

Best customers: Householders aged 35 to 64
                              Married couples with children at home

Customer trends: Average household spending on cheese may decline in the years ahead as the large baby-boom generation ages and household size shrinks.

The largest households spend the most on cheese. Married couples with children at home spend 56 percent more than the average household on this item, the figure peaking at 63 percent among couples with school-aged children. Householders aged 35 to 64, many with children at home, spend 12 to 18 percent more than average on cheese.

Average household spending on cheese, the fifth-largest grocery item in dollar amount spent, declined 5 percent between 2000 and 2010, after adjusting for inflation. In the two years that followed, average spending on cheese rebounded by 8 percent. Spending on cheese may resume its decline in the years ahead as the large baby-boom generation ages and household size shrinks.

Table 9.21 Cheese

Total household spending $16,356,971,520.00
Average household spends   131.47

AGE OF HOUSEHOLDER	AVERAGE HOUSEHOLD SPENDING	BEST CUSTOMERS (index)	BIGGEST CUSTOMERS (market share)
Average household	$131.47	100	100.0%
Under age 25	67.10	51	3.3
Aged 25 to 34	123.26	94	15.2
Aged 35 to 44	154.60	118	20.4
Aged 45 to 54	152.14	116	22.9
Aged 55 to 64	146.85	112	20.4
Aged 65 to 74	128.43	98	11.8
Aged 75 or older	80.72	61	6.0

	AVERAGE HOUSEHOLD SPENDING	BEST CUSTOMERS (index)	BIGGEST CUSTOMERS (market share)
HOUSEHOLD INCOME			
Average household	**$131.47**	**100**	**100.0%**
Under $20,000	68.50	52	11.0
$20,000 to $39,999	93.61	71	16.0
$40,000 to $49,999	117.19	89	7.9
$50,000 to $69,999	125.86	96	13.8
$70,000 to $79,999	169.54	129	7.2
$80,000 to $99,999	167.23	127	11.2
$100,000 or more	230.47	175	32.8
HOUSEHOLD TYPE			
Average household	**131.47**	**100**	**100.0**
Married couples	180.88	138	66.8
Married couples, no children	154.46	117	24.5
Married couples with children	205.27	156	36.7
Oldest child under age 6	172.10	131	6.0
Oldest child aged 6 to 17	214.87	163	19.4
Oldest child aged 18 or older	209.93	160	11.3
Single parent with child under age 18	94.63	72	3.8
Single person	65.00	49	14.7
RACE AND HISPANIC ORIGIN			
Average household	**131.47**	**100**	**100.0**
Asian	63.20	48	2.1
Black	68.30	52	6.5
Hispanic	119.66	91	11.4
Non-Hispanic white and other	144.20	110	82.3
REGION			
Average household	**131.47**	**100**	**100.0**
Northeast	138.67	105	19.0
Midwest	133.79	102	22.6
South	117.32	89	33.2
West	146.80	112	25.2
EDUCATION			
Average household	**131.47**	**100**	**100.0**
Less than high school graduate	92.60	70	9.2
High school graduate	105.75	80	20.1
Some college	117.47	89	18.4
Associate's degree	134.97	103	10.1
Bachelor's degree or more	174.29	133	41.8
Bachelor's degree	168.30	128	25.5
Master's, professional, doctoral degree	184.40	140	16.3

Note: Market shares may not sum to 100.0 because of rounding and missing categories by household type. "Asian" and "black" include Hispanics and non-Hispanics who identify themselves as being of the respective race alone. "Hispanic" includes people of any race who identify themselves as Hispanic. "Other" includes people who identify themselves as non-Hispanic and as Alaska Native, American Indian, Asian (who are also included in the "Asian" row), or Native Hawaiian or other Pacific Islander, as well as non-Hispanics reporting more than one race.
Source: Calculations by New Strategist based on the Bureau of Labor Statistics' 2012 Consumer Expenditure Survey

Chicken, Fresh and Frozen

Best customers: Householders aged 35 to 54
                        Married couples with children at home
                        Single parents
                        Hispanics, blacks, and Asians

Customer trends: Average household spending on chicken may rise as minority populations grow and the large millennial
                        generation begins to fill the best-customer age groups.

Families with children are the best customers of chicken. Married couples with children at home spend 44 percent more than the average household on this item. Single parents, whose spending approaches average on only a few items, spend 5 percent more than average on chicken. Householders aged 35 to 54, most with children at home, spend 15 to 29 percent more than average on chicken. Asians spend 7 percent more, blacks spend 19 percent more, and Hispanics spend 46 percent more than average on chicken. Together, the minority groups, which represent 29 percent of the population, account for 38 percent of household spending on chicken.

Average household spending on chicken fell 24 percent between 2000 and 2010, after adjusting for inflation, then grew 9 percent in the ensuing two years. One factor behind the decline was the baby-boom generation's exit from the best-customer lifestage, as well as competition from fast-food restaurants. Spending on chicken may continue to rise in the years ahead as minority populations grow and the large millennial generation fills the best-customer age groups.

Table 9.22 Chicken, fresh and frozen

Total household spending $15,741,112,320.00
Average household spends   126.52

AGE OF HOUSEHOLDER	AVERAGE HOUSEHOLD SPENDING	BEST CUSTOMERS (index)	BIGGEST CUSTOMERS (market share)
Average household	**$126.52**	**100**	**100.0%**
Under age 25	95.41	75	4.9
Aged 25 to 34	133.05	105	17.0
Aged 35 to 44	145.33	115	19.9
Aged 45 to 54	163.66	129	25.6
Aged 55 to 64	122.15	97	17.7
Aged 65 to 74	97.45	77	9.3
Aged 75 or older	69.52	55	5.4

	AVERAGE HOUSEHOLD SPENDING	BEST CUSTOMERS (index)	BIGGEST CUSTOMERS (market share)
HOUSEHOLD INCOME			
Average household	**$126.52**	**100**	**100.0%**
Under $20,000	87.31	69	14.5
$20,000 to $39,999	108.10	85	19.3
$40,000 to $49,999	123.10	97	8.6
$50,000 to $69,999	119.74	95	13.7
$70,000 to $79,999	169.16	134	7.5
$80,000 to $99,999	154.48	122	10.8
$100,000 or more	173.54	137	25.7
HOUSEHOLD TYPE			
Average household	**126.52**	**100**	**100.0**
Married couples	157.92	125	60.6
Married couples, no children	121.14	96	20.0
Married couples with children	181.91	144	33.8
Oldest child under age 6	141.64	112	5.1
Oldest child aged 6 to 17	196.84	156	18.5
Oldest child aged 18 or older	182.10	144	10.2
Single parent with child under age 18	132.71	105	5.5
Single person	60.86	48	14.3
RACE AND HISPANIC ORIGIN			
Average household	**126.52**	**100**	**100.0**
Asian	135.04	107	4.6
Black	150.72	119	15.0
Hispanic	184.94	146	18.3
Non-Hispanic white and other	112.59	89	66.8
REGION			
Average household	**126.52**	**100**	**100.0**
Northeast	145.41	115	20.7
Midwest	109.04	86	19.1
South	120.41	95	35.4
West	138.84	110	24.7
EDUCATION			
Average household	**126.52**	**100**	**100.0**
Less than high school graduate	126.54	100	13.1
High school graduate	133.04	105	26.2
Some college	103.63	82	16.9
Associate's degree	148.35	117	11.6
Bachelor's degree or more	130.09	103	32.4
Bachelor's degree	133.14	105	21.0
Master's, professional, doctoral degree	124.95	99	11.5

Note: Market shares may not sum to 100.0 because of rounding and missing categories by household type. "Asian" and "black" include Hispanics and non-Hispanics who identify themselves as being of the respective race alone. "Hispanic" includes people of any race who identify themselves as Hispanic. "Other" includes people who identify themselves as non-Hispanic and as Alaska Native, American Indian, Asian (who are also included in the "Asian" row), or Native Hawaiian or other Pacific Islander, as well as non-Hispanics reporting more than one race.
Source: Calculations by New Strategist based on the Bureau of Labor Statistics' 2012 Consumer Expenditure Survey

Citrus Fruit Other than Oranges

Best customers: Householders aged 35 to 54
                        Married couples with children at home
                        Single parents
                        Asians and Hispanics
                        Households in the West

Customer trends: Average household spending on fresh citrus fruit other than oranges should rise as the Asian and Hispanic populations grow.

The largest households are the best customers of fresh citrus fruit other than oranges. Married couples with children at home spend 52 percent more than average on fresh citrus. Single parents, whose spending approaches average on only a few items, spend 5 percent more. Householders aged 35 to 54, most with children, spend 12 to 24 percent more than average on this item. Hispanics, whose families tend to be relatively large, spend 51 percent more than average and Asians spend twice the average. Together the two minority groups account for a sizeable 28 percent of the market. Households in the West, where many Asians and Hispanics reside and where fresh citrus fruit is widely available, spend 28 percent more than average on this item.

Average household spending on fresh citrus fruit other than oranges, which had stagnated between 2000 and 2006, more than doubled between 2006 and 2012, after adjusting for inflation. One factor behind the increase is the greater availability of a variety of citrus fruit in grocery stores. Average household spending on fresh citrus may continue to rise as the Asian and Hispanic populations grow.

Table 9.23 Citrus fruit other than oranges

Total household spending $4,970,419,200.00
Average household spends   39.95

	AVERAGE HOUSEHOLD SPENDING	BEST CUSTOMERS (index)	BIGGEST CUSTOMERS (market share)
AGE OF HOUSEHOLDER			
Average household	$39.95	100	100.0%
Under age 25	24.06	60	3.9
Aged 25 to 34	37.88	95	15.3
Aged 35 to 44	44.65	112	19.4
Aged 45 to 54	49.50	124	24.5
Aged 55 to 64	39.51	99	18.1
Aged 65 to 74	36.82	92	11.1
Aged 75 or older	30.97	78	7.6

	AVERAGE HOUSEHOLD SPENDING	BEST CUSTOMERS (index)	BIGGEST CUSTOMERS (market share)
HOUSEHOLD INCOME			
Average household	**$39.95**	**100**	**100.0%**
Under $20,000	22.06	55	11.6
$20,000 to $39,999	30.61	77	17.3
$40,000 to $49,999	34.30	86	7.6
$50,000 to $69,999	42.04	105	15.2
$70,000 to $79,999	44.43	111	6.2
$80,000 to $99,999	48.36	121	10.7
$100,000 or more	66.95	168	31.4
HOUSEHOLD TYPE			
Average household	**39.95**	**100**	**100.0**
Married couples	52.21	131	63.5
Married couples, no children	42.70	107	22.3
Married couples with children	60.90	152	35.8
Oldest child under age 6	50.42	126	5.8
Oldest child aged 6 to 17	58.78	147	17.5
Oldest child aged 18 or older	70.98	178	12.5
Single parent with child under age 18	41.84	105	5.5
Single person	20.24	51	15.0
RACE AND HISPANIC ORIGIN			
Average household	**39.95**	**100**	**100.0**
Asian	79.81	200	8.7
Black	21.62	54	6.8
Hispanic	60.13	151	18.9
Non-Hispanic white and other	39.76	100	74.7
REGION			
Average household	**39.95**	**100**	**100.0**
Northeast	44.66	112	20.2
Midwest	38.88	97	21.6
South	31.62	79	29.5
West	51.02	128	28.8
EDUCATION			
Average household	**39.95**	**100**	**100.0**
Less than high school graduate	43.13	108	14.1
High school graduate	31.32	78	19.5
Some college	30.44	76	15.7
Associate's degree	36.78	92	9.1
Bachelor's degree or more	52.82	132	41.7
Bachelor's degree	48.84	122	24.4
Master's, professional, doctoral degree	59.55	149	17.3

Note: Market shares may not sum to 100.0 because of rounding and missing categories by household type. "Asian" and "black" include Hispanics and non-Hispanics who identify themselves as being of the respective race alone. "Hispanic" includes people of any race who identify themselves as Hispanic. "Other" includes people who identify themselves as non-Hispanic and as Alaska Native, American Indian, Asian (who are also included in the "Asian" row), or Native Hawaiian or other Pacific Islander, as well as non-Hispanics reporting more than one race.
Source: Calculations by New Strategist based on the Bureau of Labor Statistics' 2012 Consumer Expenditure Survey

Coffee

Best customers: Householders aged 45 to 74
Married couples without children at home
Married couples with school-aged or older children at home

Customer trends: Average household spending on coffee may decline in the years ahead as the millennial generation—which prefers cola to coffee—enters middle age.

Starbucks has been successful in promoting coffee to the masses, and Keurig has made it easy to brew a cup of coffee at home. These factors may account for the much greater spending in the past few years on coffee purchased at grocery and convenience stores. The best customers of coffee are householders ranging in age from 45 to 74, who spend 15 to 25 percent more than average on coffee. Married couples without children at home (most of them middle aged or older) spend 36 percent more than average on this item, while those with adult children at home spend 54 percent more.

Average household spending on coffee purchased at grocery or convenience stores climbed slightly between 2000 and 2006 (up 2 percent after adjusting for inflation), then rose much more strongly between 2006 and 2012 (up 52 percent). Much of that growth occurred between 2010 and 2012. The surprising growth in spending on coffee purchased at groceries and convenience stores may be due to fewer trips to Starbucks and other coffee shops as the Great Recession reduced restaurant spending. Some of it is also due to the newfound convenience of single-cup coffee brewing. Average household spending on coffee could decline in the years ahead, however, as the millennial generation—which prefers cola to coffee—enters middle age.

Table 9.24 Coffee

Total household spending $10,761,984,000.00
Average household spends   86.50

	AVERAGE HOUSEHOLD SPENDING	BEST CUSTOMERS (index)	BIGGEST CUSTOMERS (market share)
AGE OF HOUSEHOLDER			
Average household	$86.50	100	100.0%
Under age 25	45.53	53	3.5
Aged 25 to 34	63.79	74	11.9
Aged 35 to 44	78.12	90	15.7
Aged 45 to 54	106.55	123	24.4
Aged 55 to 64	99.16	115	21.0
Aged 65 to 74	108.29	125	15.1
Aged 75 or older	78.06	90	8.8

	AVERAGE HOUSEHOLD SPENDING	BEST CUSTOMERS (index)	BIGGEST CUSTOMERS (market share)
HOUSEHOLD INCOME			
Average household	$86.50	100	100.0%
Under $20,000	50.50	58	12.3
$20,000 to $39,999	59.27	69	15.4
$40,000 to $49,999	73.50	85	7.5
$50,000 to $69,999	85.90	99	14.3
$70,000 to $79,999	118.64	137	7.7
$80,000 to $99,999	106.42	123	10.9
$100,000 or more	146.71	170	31.8
HOUSEHOLD TYPE			
Average household	86.50	100	100.0
Married couples	112.16	130	63.0
Married couples, no children	117.77	136	28.4
Married couples with children	108.06	125	29.4
Oldest child under age 6	72.41	84	3.8
Oldest child aged 6 to 17	106.36	123	14.6
Oldest child aged 18 or older	133.11	154	10.9
Single parent with child under age 18	59.60	69	3.6
Single person	49.93	58	17.1
RACE AND HISPANIC ORIGIN			
Average household	86.50	100	100.0
Asian	75.06	87	3.8
Black	40.47	47	5.9
Hispanic	61.78	71	9.0
Non-Hispanic white and other	98.41	114	85.4
REGION			
Average household	86.50	100	100.0
Northeast	99.85	115	20.8
Midwest	80.23	93	20.6
South	80.46	93	34.6
West	91.97	106	24.0
EDUCATION			
Average household	86.50	100	100.0
Less than high school graduate	65.40	76	9.9
High school graduate	79.04	91	22.8
Some college	85.57	99	20.4
Associate's degree	91.40	106	10.4
Bachelor's degree or more	99.28	115	36.2
Bachelor's degree	89.47	103	20.6
Master's, professional, doctoral degree	115.86	134	15.5

Note: Market shares may not sum to 100.0 because of rounding and missing categories by household type. "Asian" and "black" include Hispanics and non-Hispanics who identify themselves as being of the respective race alone. "Hispanic" includes people of any race who identify themselves as Hispanic. "Other" includes people who identify themselves as non-Hispanic and as Alaska Native, American Indian, Asian (who are also included in the "Asian" row), or Native Hawaiian or other Pacific Islander, as well as non-Hispanics reporting more than one race.
Source: Calculations by New Strategist based on the Bureau of Labor Statistics' 2012 Consumer Expenditure Survey

Cookies

Best customers: Householders aged 35 to 54
Married couples with school-aged or older children at home

Customer trends: Average household spending on cookies may resume its decline because of the ongoing baby bust.

The biggest spenders on cookies are households with children. Married couples with school-aged or older children at home spend 46 to 52 percent more than the average household on this item. Householders aged 35 to 54, many with children at home, spend 9 to 12 percent more than average on cookies.

Average household spending on cookies fell 24 percent between 2000 and 2010, after adjusting for inflation, then increased by 5 percent in the ensuing two years. Behind the decline was increased competition with other snack foods for the dollars of shoppers as well as the baby-boom generation's exit from the best-customer lifestage. The recent increase is a sign of economic recovery and may be short-lived. Average household spending on cookies may resume its decline because of the ongoing baby bust.

Table 9.25 Cookies

Total household spending $6,290,472,960.00
Average household spends   50.56

AGE OF HOUSEHOLDER	AVERAGE HOUSEHOLD SPENDING	BEST CUSTOMERS (index)	BIGGEST CUSTOMERS (market share)
Average household	**$50.56**	**100**	**100.0%**
Under age 25	34.75	69	4.5
Aged 25 to 34	45.30	90	14.5
Aged 35 to 44	54.98	109	18.9
Aged 45 to 54	56.65	112	22.2
Aged 55 to 64	52.60	104	19.0
Aged 65 to 74	52.56	104	12.5
Aged 75 or older	43.81	87	8.5

	AVERAGE HOUSEHOLD SPENDING	BEST CUSTOMERS (index)	BIGGEST CUSTOMERS (market share)
HOUSEHOLD INCOME			
Average household	**$50.56**	**100**	**100.0%**
Under $20,000	31.18	62	13.0
$20,000 to $39,999	37.88	75	16.9
$40,000 to $49,999	44.58	88	7.8
$50,000 to $69,999	56.01	111	16.0
$70,000 to $79,999	55.56	110	6.1
$80,000 to $99,999	60.72	120	10.6
$100,000 or more	79.30	157	29.4
HOUSEHOLD TYPE			
Average household	**50.56**	**100**	**100.0**
Married couples	64.94	128	62.4
Married couples, no children	54.51	108	22.5
Married couples with children	71.94	142	33.5
Oldest child under age 6	56.47	112	5.1
Oldest child aged 6 to 17	76.66	152	18.0
Oldest child aged 18 or older	73.72	146	10.3
Single parent with child under age 18	44.04	87	4.6
Single person	26.20	52	15.4
RACE AND HISPANIC ORIGIN			
Average household	**50.56**	**100**	**100.0**
Asian	51.90	103	4.4
Black	39.63	78	9.9
Hispanic	49.55	98	12.3
Non-Hispanic white and other	52.57	104	78.0
REGION			
Average household	**50.56**	**100**	**100.0**
Northeast	54.73	108	19.5
Midwest	51.20	101	22.5
South	46.89	93	34.5
West	52.65	104	23.5
EDUCATION			
Average household	**50.56**	**100**	**100.0**
Less than high school graduate	47.83	95	12.4
High school graduate	48.20	95	23.8
Some college	45.46	90	18.5
Associate's degree	52.73	104	10.3
Bachelor's degree or more	56.17	111	35.0
Bachelor's degree	53.39	106	21.0
Master's, professional, doctoral degree	60.88	120	14.0

Note: Market shares may not sum to 100.0 because of rounding and missing categories by household type. "Asian" and "black" include Hispanics and non-Hispanics who identify themselves as being of the respective race alone. "Hispanic" includes people of any race who identify themselves as Hispanic. "Other" includes people who identify themselves as non-Hispanic and as Alaska Native, American Indian, Asian (who are also included in the "Asian" row), or Native Hawaiian or other Pacific Islander, as well as non-Hispanics reporting more than one race.
Source: Calculations by New Strategist based on the Bureau of Labor Statistics' 2012 Consumer Expenditure Survey

Crackers

Best customers: Householders aged 35 to 54
Married couples with children at home

Customer trends: Average household spending on crackers is likely to stabilize as the small generation X passes
through the best-customer age groups.

Married couples with children at home are the biggest spenders on crackers. This household type spends 61 percent more than the average household on crackers. The figure peaks at 72 percent more than average among households with school-aged children. Householders aged 35 to 54, most with children, spend 12 to 22 percent more than average on this item and account for 43 percent of the market.

Average household spending on crackers grew 20 percent between 2000 and 2012, after adjusting for inflation. Several factors account for this increase, including the greater variety of crackers available and consumers' substitution of crackers for cookies in an attempt to cut calories. Average household spending on crackers is likely to stabilize as the small generation X passes through the best-customer age groups.

Table 9.26 Crackers

Total household spending $4,624,542,720.00
Average household spends   37.17

AGE OF HOUSEHOLDER	AVERAGE HOUSEHOLD SPENDING	BEST CUSTOMERS (index)	BIGGEST CUSTOMERS (market share)
Average household	$37.17	100	100.0%
Under age 25	23.14	62	4.1
Aged 25 to 34	35.33	95	15.4
Aged 35 to 44	41.52	112	19.4
Aged 45 to 54	45.17	122	24.1
Aged 55 to 64	36.42	98	17.9
Aged 65 to 74	36.62	99	11.9
Aged 75 or older	27.71	75	7.3

	AVERAGE HOUSEHOLD SPENDING	BEST CUSTOMERS (index)	BIGGEST CUSTOMERS (market share)
HOUSEHOLD INCOME			
Average household	**$37.17**	**100**	**100.0%**
Under $20,000	21.84	59	12.4
$20,000 to $39,999	26.46	71	16.0
$40,000 to $49,999	36.28	98	8.6
$50,000 to $69,999	34.82	94	13.5
$70,000 to $79,999	44.84	121	6.7
$80,000 to $99,999	47.21	127	11.2
$100,000 or more	62.51	168	31.5
HOUSEHOLD TYPE			
Average household	**37.17**	**100**	**100.0**
Married couples	49.80	134	65.1
Married couples, no children	39.36	106	22.1
Married couples with children	59.79	161	37.8
Oldest child under age 6	58.59	158	7.2
Oldest child aged 6 to 17	64.01	172	20.5
Oldest child aged 18 or older	53.51	144	10.2
Single parent with child under age 18	31.82	86	4.5
Single person	19.33	52	15.4
RACE AND HISPANIC ORIGIN			
Average household	**37.17**	**100**	**100.0**
Asian	27.20	73	3.2
Black	23.41	63	7.9
Hispanic	29.15	78	9.8
Non-Hispanic white and other	40.82	110	82.4
REGION			
Average household	**37.17**	**100**	**100.0**
Northeast	38.26	103	18.6
Midwest	40.13	108	23.9
South	33.27	90	33.3
West	39.78	107	24.1
EDUCATION			
Average household	**37.17**	**100**	**100.0**
Less than high school graduate	28.24	76	9.9
High school graduate	31.47	85	21.1
Some college	30.64	82	17.0
Associate's degree	39.28	106	10.4
Bachelor's degree or more	48.67	131	41.3
Bachelor's degree	47.78	129	25.6
Master's, professional, doctoral degree	50.17	135	15.7

Note: Market shares may not sum to 100.0 because of rounding and missing categories by household type. "Asian" and "black" include Hispanics and non-Hispanics who identify themselves as being of the respective race alone. "Hispanic" includes people of any race who identify themselves as Hispanic. "Other" includes people who identify themselves as non-Hispanic and as Alaska Native, American Indian, Asian (who are also included in the "Asian" row), or Native Hawaiian or other Pacific Islander, as well as non-Hispanics reporting more than one race.
Source: Calculations by New Strategist based on the Bureau of Labor Statistics' 2012 Consumer Expenditure Survey

Cream

Best customers: Householders aged 35 to 54
Married couples with school-aged or older children at home
Households in the Northeast and West

Customer trends: Average household spending on cream should stabilize as the large baby-boom generation ages
and household size shrinks.

Like butter, cream made a comeback when lower-carb diets became popular, especially among baby boomers. The biggest spenders on cream are the largest households—middle-aged married couples with children. Householders aged 35 to 54 spend 15 to 24 percent more than the average household on cream, and those aged 55 to 74 are also above-average spenders on this item. Married couples with school-aged or older children at home spend 52 to 96 percent more than average on this item. Households in the Northeast spend 27 percent more than average on cream, and those in the West spend 14 percent more.

Average household spending on cream rose 52 percent between 2000 and 2012, after adjusting for inflation. Behind the increase is the improved reputation of cream because of the popularity of low-carb diets. Spending on cream should stabilize as the large baby-boom generation ages and household size shrinks.

Table 9.27 Cream

Total household spending $2,933,729,280.00
Average household spends   23.58

AGE OF HOUSEHOLDER	AVERAGE HOUSEHOLD SPENDING	BEST CUSTOMERS (index)	BIGGEST CUSTOMERS (market share)
Average household	$23.58	100	100.0%
Under age 25	11.01	47	3.1
Aged 25 to 34	20.58	87	14.1
Aged 35 to 44	27.20	115	20.0
Aged 45 to 54	29.14	124	24.5
Aged 55 to 64	24.77	105	19.2
Aged 65 to 74	23.98	102	12.3
Aged 75 or older	16.76	71	6.9

	AVERAGE HOUSEHOLD SPENDING	BEST CUSTOMERS (index)	BIGGEST CUSTOMERS (market share)
HOUSEHOLD INCOME			
Average household	$23.58	100	100.0%
Under $20,000	13.19	56	11.8
$20,000 to $39,999	17.76	75	17.0
$40,000 to $49,999	23.45	99	8.8
$50,000 to $69,999	23.14	98	14.2
$70,000 to $79,999	28.33	120	6.7
$80,000 to $99,999	27.62	117	10.3
$100,000 or more	38.84	165	30.8
HOUSEHOLD TYPE			
Average household	23.58	100	100.0
Married couples	31.51	134	64.9
Married couples, no children	25.00	106	22.1
Married couples with children	37.32	158	37.2
Oldest child under age 6	26.78	114	5.2
Oldest child aged 6 to 17	35.91	152	18.1
Oldest child aged 18 or older	46.26	196	13.8
Single parent with child under age 18	20.77	88	4.6
Single person	10.07	43	12.7
RACE AND HISPANIC ORIGIN			
Average household	23.58	100	100.0
Asian	20.44	87	3.8
Black	11.08	47	5.9
Hispanic	22.47	95	11.9
Non-Hispanic white and other	25.86	110	82.3
REGION			
Average household	23.58	100	100.0
Northeast	30.03	127	23.0
Midwest	23.48	100	22.1
South	18.54	79	29.3
West	26.82	114	25.6
EDUCATION			
Average household	23.58	100	100.0
Less than high school graduate	21.68	92	12.0
High school graduate	21.84	93	23.1
Some college	19.39	82	16.9
Associate's degree	27.30	116	11.4
Bachelor's degree or more	27.31	116	36.5
Bachelor's degree	26.91	114	22.7
Master's, professional, doctoral degree	27.98	119	13.8

Note: Market shares may not sum to 100.0 because of rounding and missing categories by household type. "Asian" and "black" include Hispanics and non-Hispanics who identify themselves as being of the respective race alone. "Hispanic" includes people of any race who identify themselves as Hispanic. "Other" includes people who identify themselves as non-Hispanic and as Alaska Native, American Indian, Asian (who are also included in the "Asian" row), or Native Hawaiian or other Pacific Islander, as well as non-Hispanics reporting more than one race.
Source: Calculations by New Strategist based on the Bureau of Labor Statistics' 2012 Consumer Expenditure Survey

Dairy Products Other than Butter, Cheese, Cream, Ice Cream, and Milk

Best customers: Householders aged 35 to 54
Married couples with children at home
Households in the Northeast and West

Customer trends: Average household spending on dairy products other than butter, cheese, cream, ice cream, and milk
should continue to grow as more consumers seek the health benefits of yogurt.

Some dairy products, such as yogurt, are growing in popularity. The biggest spenders on dairy products other than butter, cheese, cream, ice cream, and milk—a category that includes yogurt—are the largest households. Married couples with children at home spend 60 percent more than the average household on such dairy products. Householders aged 35 to 54, many with children, spend 21 to 23 percent more than average and account for 45 percent of the market. Households in the Northeast spend 20 percent more than average on other dairy, and households in the West spend 12 percent more.

Average household spending on other dairy products rose by a substantial 65 percent between 2000 and 2012, after adjusting for inflation. Behind the increase is the growing popularity of yogurt and yogurt-based drinks. Average household spending on such dairy products may continue to rise as more consumers seek the health benefits of yogurt.

Table 9.28 Dairy products other than butter, cheese, cream, ice cream, and milk

Total household spending $6,552,990,720.00
Average household spends   52.67

AGE OF HOUSEHOLDER	AVERAGE HOUSEHOLD SPENDING	BEST CUSTOMERS (index)	BIGGEST CUSTOMERS (market share)
Average household	$52.67	100	100.0%
Under age 25	37.11	70	4.6
Aged 25 to 34	52.14	99	16.0
Aged 35 to 44	63.50	121	20.9
Aged 45 to 54	64.65	123	24.3
Aged 55 to 64	51.41	98	17.9
Aged 65 to 74	43.60	83	10.0
Aged 75 or older	33.35	63	6.2

	AVERAGE HOUSEHOLD SPENDING	BEST CUSTOMERS (index)	BIGGEST CUSTOMERS (market share)
HOUSEHOLD INCOME			
Average household	**$52.67**	**100**	**100.0%**
Under $20,000	24.17	46	9.7
$20,000 to $39,999	36.54	69	15.6
$40,000 to $49,999	43.53	83	7.3
$50,000 to $69,999	51.97	99	14.3
$70,000 to $79,999	70.86	135	7.5
$80,000 to $99,999	72.08	137	12.1
$100,000 or more	94.45	179	33.6
HOUSEHOLD TYPE			
Average household	**52.67**	**100**	**100.0**
Married couples	70.74	134	65.2
Married couples, no children	57.05	108	22.6
Married couples with children	84.18	160	37.6
Oldest child under age 6	80.89	154	7.0
Oldest child aged 6 to 17	91.65	174	20.7
Oldest child aged 18 or older	73.75	140	9.9
Single parent with child under age 18	42.63	81	4.2
Single person	26.43	50	14.9
RACE AND HISPANIC ORIGIN			
Average household	**52.67**	**100**	**100.0**
Asian	50.34	96	4.1
Black	32.07	61	7.7
Hispanic	53.44	101	12.7
Non-Hispanic white and other	56.01	106	79.8
REGION			
Average household	**52.67**	**100**	**100.0**
Northeast	63.21	120	21.7
Midwest	55.22	105	23.2
South	42.18	80	29.8
West	59.00	112	25.2
EDUCATION			
Average household	**52.67**	**100**	**100.0**
Less than high school graduate	37.86	72	9.4
High school graduate	38.20	73	18.1
Some college	43.47	83	17.0
Associate's degree	54.92	104	10.3
Bachelor's degree or more	74.93	142	44.9
Bachelor's degree	70.74	134	26.8
Master's, professional, doctoral degree	82.01	156	18.1

Note: Market shares may not sum to 100.0 because of rounding and missing categories by household type. "Asian" and "black" include Hispanics and non-Hispanics who identify themselves as being of the respective race alone. "Hispanic" includes people of any race who identify themselves as Hispanic. "Other" includes people who identify themselves as non-Hispanic and as Alaska Native, American Indian, Asian (who are also included in the "Asian" row), or Native Hawaiian or other Pacific Islander, as well as non-Hispanics reporting more than one race.
Source: Calculations by New Strategist based on the Bureau of Labor Statistics' 2012 Consumer Expenditure Survey

Desserts, Prepared

Best customers: Married couples with school-aged or older children at home
Single parents
Households in the Northeast and Midwest

Customer trends: Average household spending on prepared desserts may decline in the years ahead as the large baby-boom generation ages and household size shrinks.

The best customers of prepared desserts are the largest households. For convenience, they are buying prepared desserts rather than cooking from scratch. Couples with school-aged children spend 50 percent more than the average household on this item, and those with adult children at home spend 29 percent more. Prepared desserts are one of the relatively few items on which single parents, with their lower incomes, spend an average amount. Households in the Northeast spend 20 percent more than average on prepared desserts, and households in the Midwest spend 15 percent more.

Average household spending on prepared desserts climbed 40 percent between 2000 and 2010, after adjusting for inflation, then dropped by 18 percent in the ensuing two years. Behind the increase was the consumer preference for the convenience of prepared food. Average household spending on prepared desserts may continue to decline in the years ahead as the large baby-boom generation ages and household size shrinks.

Table 9.29 Desserts, prepared

Total household spending $1,777,904,640.00
Average household spends   14.29

AGE OF HOUSEHOLDER	AVERAGE HOUSEHOLD SPENDING	BEST CUSTOMERS (index)	BIGGEST CUSTOMERS (market share)
Average household	$14.29	100	100.0%
Under age 25	11.74	82	5.4
Aged 25 to 34	12.17	85	13.8
Aged 35 to 44	14.90	104	18.1
Aged 45 to 54	14.98	105	20.7
Aged 55 to 64	14.14	99	18.1
Aged 65 to 74	15.82	111	13.3
Aged 75 or older	15.64	109	10.7

	AVERAGE HOUSEHOLD SPENDING	BEST CUSTOMERS (index)	BIGGEST CUSTOMERS (market share)
HOUSEHOLD INCOME			
Average household	**$14.29**	**100**	**100.0%**
Under $20,000	8.49	59	12.5
$20,000 to $39,999	12.08	85	19.1
$40,000 to $49,999	12.01	84	7.4
$50,000 to $69,999	16.74	117	16.9
$70,000 to $79,999	14.92	104	5.8
$80,000 to $99,999	17.74	124	11.0
$100,000 or more	20.82	146	27.3
HOUSEHOLD TYPE			
Average household	**14.29**	**100**	**100.0**
Married couples	18.19	127	61.8
Married couples, no children	16.44	115	24.0
Married couples with children	19.32	135	31.8
Oldest child under age 6	15.25	107	4.9
Oldest child aged 6 to 17	21.41	150	17.8
Oldest child aged 18 or older	18.37	129	9.1
Single parent with child under age 18	14.92	104	5.5
Single person	8.23	58	17.1
RACE AND HISPANIC ORIGIN			
Average household	**14.29**	**100**	**100.0**
Asian	12.48	87	3.8
Black	9.02	63	7.9
Hispanic	12.57	88	11.0
Non-Hispanic white and other	15.48	108	81.3
REGION			
Average household	**14.29**	**100**	**100.0**
Northeast	17.15	120	21.7
Midwest	16.41	115	25.5
South	12.49	87	32.6
West	12.85	90	20.3
EDUCATION			
Average household	**14.29**	**100**	**100.0**
Less than high school graduate	13.24	93	12.1
High school graduate	12.80	90	22.3
Some college	14.14	99	20.4
Associate's degree	15.73	110	10.9
Bachelor's degree or more	15.50	108	34.2
Bachelor's degree	13.85	97	19.3
Master's, professional, doctoral degree	18.28	128	14.8

Note: Market shares may not sum to 100.0 because of rounding and missing categories by household type. "Asian" and "black" include Hispanics and non-Hispanics who identify themselves as being of the respective race alone. "Hispanic" includes people of any race who identify themselves as Hispanic. "Other" includes people who identify themselves as non-Hispanic and as Alaska Native, American Indian, Asian (who are also included in the "Asian" row), or Native Hawaiian or other Pacific Islander, as well as non-Hispanics reporting more than one race.
Source: Calculations by New Strategist based on the Bureau of Labor Statistics' 2012 Consumer Expenditure Survey

Eggs

Best customers: Householders aged 35 to 54
Married couples with school-aged or older children at home
Hispanics and Asians
Households in the West

Customer trends: Average household spending on eggs may stabilize or even decline as the small generation X passes
through the best-customer lifestage.

Household size is the most important factor in determining spending on eggs, the largest households spending the most. Married couples with school-aged children spend 43 percent more than the average household on eggs, and those with adult children at home spend 48 percent more. Householders aged 35 to 54, most with children, outspend the average by 13 to 14 percent. Hispanics, whose families are larger than average, spend 41 percent more than average on eggs, and Asians spend 31 percent more. Households in the West, where many Asians and Hispanics reside, spend 14 percent more than average on this item.

Average household spending on eggs declined 9 percent between 2000 and 2006, after adjusting for inflation, but rebounded by 27 percent between 2006 and 2012. Behind the rise was the improving reputation of eggs thanks to the popularity of low-carb diets, as well as consumers' increased propensity to eat at home as the Great Recession reduced incomes. Spending on eggs may stabilize or even decline as the small generation X passes through the best-customer lifestage.

Table 9.30 Eggs

Total household spending $6,604,001,280.00
Average household spends   53.08

AGE OF HOUSEHOLDER	AVERAGE HOUSEHOLD SPENDING	BEST CUSTOMERS (index)	BIGGEST CUSTOMERS (market share)
Average household	$53.08	100	100.0%
Under age 25	38.69	73	4.8
Aged 25 to 34	50.47	95	15.4
Aged 35 to 44	60.46	114	19.8
Aged 45 to 54	59.86	113	22.3
Aged 55 to 64	53.10	100	18.3
Aged 65 to 74	52.32	99	11.9
Aged 75 or older	41.01	77	7.6

	AVERAGE HOUSEHOLD SPENDING	BEST CUSTOMERS (index)	BIGGEST CUSTOMERS (market share)
HOUSEHOLD INCOME			
Average household	**$53.08**	**100**	**100.0%**
Under $20,000	39.83	75	15.8
$20,000 to $39,999	46.30	87	19.7
$40,000 to $49,999	49.58	93	8.3
$50,000 to $69,999	50.68	95	13.8
$70,000 to $79,999	63.96	120	6.7
$80,000 to $99,999	61.27	115	10.2
$100,000 or more	72.35	136	25.5
HOUSEHOLD TYPE			
Average household	**53.08**	**100**	**100.0**
Married couples	66.03	124	60.4
Married couples, no children	55.51	105	21.8
Married couples with children	72.17	136	32.0
Oldest child under age 6	52.36	99	4.5
Oldest child aged 6 to 17	75.71	143	17.0
Oldest child aged 18 or older	78.59	148	10.4
Single parent with child under age 18	50.64	95	5.0
Single person	29.31	55	16.4
RACE AND HISPANIC ORIGIN			
Average household	**53.08**	**100**	**100.0**
Asian	69.78	131	5.7
Black	45.03	85	10.7
Hispanic	74.62	141	17.6
Non-Hispanic white and other	50.85	96	71.9
REGION			
Average household	**53.08**	**100**	**100.0**
Northeast	55.30	104	18.8
Midwest	49.70	94	20.8
South	49.60	93	34.8
West	60.46	114	25.7
EDUCATION			
Average household	**53.08**	**100**	**100.0**
Less than high school graduate	54.21	102	13.3
High school graduate	54.60	103	25.6
Some college	47.26	89	18.3
Associate's degree	52.63	99	9.8
Bachelor's degree or more	55.55	105	33.0
Bachelor's degree	55.32	104	20.8
Master's, professional, doctoral degree	55.92	105	12.2

Note: Market shares may not sum to 100.0 because of rounding and missing categories by household type. "Asian" and "black" include Hispanics and non-Hispanics who identify themselves as being of the respective race alone. "Hispanic" includes people of any race who identify themselves as Hispanic. "Other" includes people who identify themselves as non-Hispanic and as Alaska Native, American Indian, Asian (who are also included in the "Asian" row), or Native Hawaiian or other Pacific Islander, as well as non-Hispanics reporting more than one race.
Source: Calculations by New Strategist based on the Bureau of Labor Statistics' 2012 Consumer Expenditure Survey

Fats and Oils

Best customers: Householders aged 35 to 54
Married couples with school-aged or older children at home
Hispanics, Asians, and blacks
Householders without a high school diploma

Customer trends: Average household spending on fats and oils may level out in the years ahead if eating out regains
its pre–Great Recession popularity.

The biggest spenders on fats and oils are Hispanics, Asians, and blacks. Hispanics spend 64 percent more than average on this item, Asians spend 54 percent more, and blacks spend 3 percent more. Together the three minorities, which represent 29 percent of the population, account for 40 percent of the market for fats and oils. Married couples with school-aged or older children at home spend 47 to 51 percent more than average on fats and oils. Householders aged 35 to 54, many with children, spend 20 to 23 percent more than average on this item. Householders who did not complete high school, many of them Hispanic, spend 43 percent above average on fats and oils.

Average household spending on fats and oils rose 18 percent between 2000 and 2012, after adjusting for inflation. Behind the increase was the popularity of high-priced specialty oils, as well as the growth of the Asian, black, and Hispanic populations. Average household spending on fats and oils may level out in the years ahead if eating out regains its pre–Great Recession popularity.

Table 9.31 Fats and oils

Total household spending $4,577,264,640.00
Average household spends   36.79

	AVERAGE HOUSEHOLD SPENDING	BEST CUSTOMERS (index)	BIGGEST CUSTOMERS (market share)
AGE OF HOUSEHOLDER			
Average household	**$36.79**	**100**	**100.0%**
Under age 25	31.44	85	5.6
Aged 25 to 34	32.70	89	14.4
Aged 35 to 44	45.27	123	21.4
Aged 45 to 54	44.33	120	23.8
Aged 55 to 64	33.40	91	16.6
Aged 65 to 74	31.56	86	10.3
Aged 75 or older	29.09	79	7.7

	AVERAGE HOUSEHOLD SPENDING	BEST CUSTOMERS (index)	BIGGEST CUSTOMERS (market share)
HOUSEHOLD INCOME			
Average household	**$36.79**	**100**	**100.0%**
Under $20,000	27.13	74	15.5
$20,000 to $39,999	32.88	89	20.1
$40,000 to $49,999	34.91	95	8.4
$50,000 to $69,999	31.23	85	12.3
$70,000 to $79,999	43.50	118	6.6
$80,000 to $99,999	44.50	121	10.7
$100,000 or more	51.86	141	26.4
HOUSEHOLD TYPE			
Average household	**36.79**	**100**	**100.0**
Married couples	45.33	123	59.8
Married couples, no children	37.04	101	21.0
Married couples with children	50.49	137	32.3
Oldest child under age 6	31.28	85	3.9
Oldest child aged 6 to 17	55.44	151	17.9
Oldest child aged 18 or older	54.22	147	10.4
Single parent with child under age 18	34.13	93	4.9
Single person	18.97	52	15.3
RACE AND HISPANIC ORIGIN			
Average household	**36.79**	**100**	**100.0**
Asian	56.61	154	6.7
Black	37.76	103	12.9
Hispanic	60.44	164	20.6
Non-Hispanic white and other	32.70	89	66.7
REGION			
Average household	**36.79**	**100**	**100.0**
Northeast	37.15	101	18.2
Midwest	31.57	86	19.0
South	35.61	97	36.0
West	43.67	119	26.7
EDUCATION			
Average household	**36.79**	**100**	**100.0**
Less than high school graduate	52.71	143	18.7
High school graduate	32.54	88	22.1
Some college	29.51	80	16.5
Associate's degree	38.03	103	10.2
Bachelor's degree or more	38.62	105	33.1
Bachelor's degree	37.21	101	20.2
Master's, professional, doctoral degree	41.00	111	12.9

Note: Market shares may not sum to 100.0 because of rounding and missing categories by household type. "Asian" and "black" include Hispanics and non-Hispanics who identify themselves as being of the respective race alone. "Hispanic" includes people of any race who identify themselves as Hispanic. "Other" includes people who identify themselves as non-Hispanic and as Alaska Native, American Indian, Asian (who are also included in the "Asian" row), or Native Hawaiian or other Pacific Islander, as well as non-Hispanics reporting more than one race.
Source: Calculations by New Strategist based on the Bureau of Labor Statistics' 2012 Consumer Expenditure Survey

Fish and Seafood, Canned

Best customers: Householders aged 35 to 74
Married couples with school-aged or older children at home
Asians
Households in the Northeast and West

Customer trends: Average household spending on canned fish and seafood may resume its slow decline as consumer preferences shift from canned to frozen fish.

The biggest spenders on canned fish and seafood are middle-aged and older householders. Householders ranging in age from 35 to 74 spend more than average on this item, the figure peaking at 24 percent more than average among householders aged 65 to 74. Couples with adult children at home spend 35 percent more than average on canned fish and seafood, and those with school-aged children spend 21 percent more. Asians outspend the average by 59 percent. Households in the Northeast spend 29 percent more than average on canned fish, and those in the West spend 17 percent more.

Average household spending on canned fish and seafood fell 10 percent between 2000 and 2006, grew 13 percent between 2006 and 2010, then fell 14 percent between 2010 and 2012, after adjusting for inflation. Behind the earlier decline was the shift from canned to frozen fish and the then-growing preference for eating out rather than preparing meals from scratch. The 2006-to-2010 growth was the result of more home cooking because of the Great Recession. The current decline is likely due to changing consumer preferences. Average household spending on canned fish and seafood may continue its decline as consumer preferences shift.

Table 9.32 Fish and seafood, canned

Total household spending $2,261,882,880.00
Average household spends 18.18

	AVERAGE HOUSEHOLD SPENDING	BEST CUSTOMERS (index)	BIGGEST CUSTOMERS (market share)
AGE OF HOUSEHOLDER			
Average household	$18.18	100	100.0%
Under age 25	7.79	43	2.8
Aged 25 to 34	13.49	74	12.0
Aged 35 to 44	20.22	111	19.3
Aged 45 to 54	18.55	102	20.2
Aged 55 to 64	21.34	117	21.5
Aged 65 to 74	22.46	124	14.9
Aged 75 or older	17.97	99	9.7

	AVERAGE HOUSEHOLD SPENDING	BEST CUSTOMERS (index)	BIGGEST CUSTOMERS (market share)
HOUSEHOLD INCOME			
Average household	$18.18	100	100.0%
Under $20,000	13.07	72	15.1
$20,000 to $39,999	15.03	83	18.6
$40,000 to $49,999	15.96	88	7.8
$50,000 to $69,999	18.65	103	14.8
$70,000 to $79,999	23.81	131	7.3
$80,000 to $99,999	25.14	138	12.2
$100,000 or more	23.50	129	24.2
HOUSEHOLD TYPE			
Average household	18.18	100	100.0
Married couples	21.58	119	57.7
Married couples, no children	20.92	115	24.0
Married couples with children	20.97	115	27.1
Oldest child under age 6	12.41	68	3.1
Oldest child aged 6 to 17	22.02	121	14.4
Oldest child aged 18 or older	24.57	135	9.5
Single parent with child under age 18	16.85	93	4.9
Single person	11.02	61	18.0
RACE AND HISPANIC ORIGIN			
Average household	18.18	100	100.0
Asian	28.87	159	6.9
Black	15.21	84	10.5
Hispanic	20.39	112	14.1
Non-Hispanic white and other	18.30	101	75.6
REGION			
Average household	18.18	100	100.0
Northeast	23.50	129	23.3
Midwest	15.68	86	19.1
South	15.23	84	31.2
West	21.26	117	26.4
EDUCATION			
Average household	18.18	100	100.0
Less than high school graduate	15.42	85	11.1
High school graduate	17.94	99	24.6
Some college	17.16	94	19.4
Associate's degree	17.97	99	9.8
Bachelor's degree or more	20.15	111	35.0
Bachelor's degree	18.38	101	20.2
Master's, professional, doctoral degree	23.16	127	14.8

Note: Market shares may not sum to 100.0 because of rounding and missing categories by household type. "Asian" and "black" include Hispanics and non-Hispanics who identify themselves as being of the respective race alone. "Hispanic" includes people of any race who identify themselves as Hispanic. "Other" includes people who identify themselves as non-Hispanic and as Alaska Native, American Indian, Asian (who are also included in the "Asian" row), or Native Hawaiian or other Pacific Islander, as well as non-Hispanics reporting more than one race.
Source: Calculations by New Strategist based on the Bureau of Labor Statistics' 2012 Consumer Expenditure Survey

Fish and Shellfish, Fresh

Best customers: Householders aged 35 to 64
Married couples without children at home
Married couples with school-aged or older children at home
Asians, blacks, and Hispanics
Households in the Northeast and West

Customer trends: Average household spending on fresh fish may resume its decline in the years ahead if consumers opt
for prepared meals rather than home cooking.

The best customers of fresh fish and shellfish are minorities and the largest households. Asians spend two-and-one-half times the average on fresh fish, while blacks and Hispanics spend, respectively, 25 and 20 percent more than average on this item. Together the three minority groups, which represent 29 percent of the population, account for 41 percent of the market for fresh fish. Householders ranging in age from 35 to 64 spend 15 to 26 percent more than average on fresh fish. Married couples with school-aged or older children at home spend 52 to 58 percent more than average on this item. Married couples without children at home, most of them older empty-nesters, spend 25 percent more than average on fresh fish. Households in the Northeast and West spend, respectively, 29 and 27 percent more than average on this item.

Average household spending on fresh fish fell 20 percent between 2000 and 2006, after adjusting for inflation, and fell another 18 percent between 2006 and 2010—the year in which overall household spending bottomed out. In the ensuing two years, however, spending on fresh fish grew by 9 percent. Behind the earlier decline was the shift from fresh to frozen fish, as well as the then-growing propensity of Americans to eat out rather than prepare a meal from scratch. The recent increase in spending on fresh fish may be a sign of economic recovery. Average household spending on fresh fish may resume its decline in the years ahead if consumers opt for prepared meals rather than home cooking.

Table 9.33 Fish and shellfish, fresh

Total household spending $7,874,288,640.00
Average household spends   63.29

	AVERAGE HOUSEHOLD SPENDING	BEST CUSTOMERS (index)	BIGGEST CUSTOMERS (market share)
AGE OF HOUSEHOLDER			
Average household	$63.29	100	100.0%
Under age 25	23.78	38	2.5
Aged 25 to 34	49.93	79	12.8
Aged 35 to 44	72.84	115	20.0
Aged 45 to 54	79.94	126	25.0
Aged 55 to 64	77.24	122	22.3
Aged 65 to 74	64.79	102	12.3
Aged 75 or older	34.34	54	5.3

	AVERAGE HOUSEHOLD SPENDING	BEST CUSTOMERS (index)	BIGGEST CUSTOMERS (market share)
HOUSEHOLD INCOME			
Average household	**$63.29**	**100**	**100.0%**
Under $20,000	41.39	65	13.8
$20,000 to $39,999	41.79	66	14.9
$40,000 to $49,999	48.04	76	6.7
$50,000 to $69,999	54.48	86	12.4
$70,000 to $79,999	78.67	124	6.9
$80,000 to $99,999	90.83	144	12.7
$100,000 or more	111.68	176	33.0
HOUSEHOLD TYPE			
Average household	**63.29**	**100**	**100.0**
Married couples	85.56	135	65.7
Married couples, no children	79.42	125	26.2
Married couples with children	88.73	140	33.0
Oldest child under age 6	46.86	74	3.4
Oldest child aged 6 to 17	99.96	158	18.8
Oldest child aged 18 or older	96.09	152	10.7
Single parent with child under age 18	57.45	91	4.8
Single person	27.21	43	12.8
RACE AND HISPANIC ORIGIN			
Average household	**63.29**	**100**	**100.0**
Asian	155.53	246	10.7
Black	79.02	125	15.7
Hispanic	75.70	120	15.0
Non-Hispanic white and other	58.48	92	69.4
REGION			
Average household	**63.29**	**100**	**100.0**
Northeast	81.36	129	23.2
Midwest	38.41	61	13.5
South	59.11	93	34.8
West	80.48	127	28.7
EDUCATION			
Average household	**63.29**	**100**	**100.0**
Less than high school graduate	54.72	86	11.3
High school graduate	58.35	92	23.0
Some college	45.46	72	14.8
Associate's degree	65.89	104	10.3
Bachelor's degree or more	81.54	129	40.6
Bachelor's degree	79.57	126	25.1
Master's, professional, doctoral degree	84.86	134	15.6

Note: Market shares may not sum to 100.0 because of rounding and missing categories by household type. "Asian" and "black" include Hispanics and non-Hispanics who identify themselves as being of the respective race alone. "Hispanic" includes people of any race who identify themselves as Hispanic. "Other" includes people who identify themselves as non-Hispanic and as Alaska Native, American Indian, Asian (who are also included in the "Asian" row), or Native Hawaiian or other Pacific Islander, as well as non-Hispanics reporting more than one race.
Source: Calculations by New Strategist based on the Bureau of Labor Statistics' 2012 Consumer Expenditure Survey

Fish and Shellfish, Frozen

Best customers: Householders aged 35 to 54 and 65 to 74
Married couples without children at home
Married couples with school-aged or older children at home
Asians and Hispanics

Customer trends: Average household spending on frozen fish may continue to decline because the small generation X
is in the best-customer lifestage, but the spending of aging boomers may limit the loss.

The largest households and older householders are the best customers of frozen fish. Married couples with school-aged or older children at home spend 24 to 72 percent more than average on frozen fish. Householders aged 35 to 54, most with children at home, spend 25 to 28 percent more. Couples without children at home, most of them older empty-nesters, spend 29 percent more than average on frozen fish, and householders aged 65 to 74 spend 13 percent more. Asian households spend more than twice the average on this item. Hispanics, who have the largest families, spend 35 percent above average on frozen fish. Frozen fish is one of the relatively few items on which blacks spend an average amount. Together the three minority groups, which represent 29 percent of the population, account for 39 percent of the market for frozen fish.

Average household spending on frozen fish rose by a healthy 32 percent between 2000 and 2006, after adjusting for inflation, but spending declined 9 percent between 2006 and 2012. Behind the earlier increase were nutritional claims regarding the benefits of fish consumption and the shift away from canned and fresh fish to the greater convenience of frozen fish. Average household spending on frozen fish may continue to decline because the small generation X is in the best-customer lifestage, but the spending of aging boomers may limit the loss.

Table 9.34 Fish and shellfish, frozen

Total household spending $5,507,896,320.00
Average household spends 44.27

AGE OF HOUSEHOLDER	AVERAGE HOUSEHOLD SPENDING	BEST CUSTOMERS (index)	BIGGEST CUSTOMERS (market share)
Average household	$44.27	100	100.0%
Under age 25	41.42	94	6.1
Aged 25 to 34	29.77	67	10.9
Aged 35 to 44	56.55	128	22.2
Aged 45 to 54	55.23	125	24.7
Aged 55 to 64	39.18	89	16.2
Aged 65 to 74	49.98	113	13.6
Aged 75 or older	28.24	64	6.2

	AVERAGE HOUSEHOLD SPENDING	BEST CUSTOMERS (index)	BIGGEST CUSTOMERS (market share)
HOUSEHOLD INCOME			
Average household	**$44.27**	**100**	**100.0%**
Under $20,000	28.03	63	13.3
$20,000 to $39,999	32.39	73	16.5
$40,000 to $49,999	35.26	80	7.0
$50,000 to $69,999	42.20	95	13.8
$70,000 to $79,999	54.23	122	6.8
$80,000 to $99,999	67.02	151	13.4
$100,000 or more	69.47	157	29.4
HOUSEHOLD TYPE			
Average household	**44.27**	**100**	**100.0**
Married couples	59.24	134	65.0
Married couples, no children	57.25	129	27.0
Married couples with children	62.86	142	33.4
Oldest child under age 6	40.92	92	4.2
Oldest child aged 6 to 17	75.96	172	20.4
Oldest child aged 18 or older	54.69	124	8.7
Single parent with child under age 18	25.85	58	3.1
Single person	18.22	41	12.2
RACE AND HISPANIC ORIGIN			
Average household	**44.27**	**100**	**100.0**
Asian	98.31	222	9.6
Black	43.34	98	12.3
Hispanic	59.88	135	17.0
Non-Hispanic white and other	41.74	94	70.8
REGION			
Average household	**44.27**	**100**	**100.0**
Northeast	38.91	88	15.9
Midwest	49.61	112	24.8
South	41.28	93	34.7
West	48.24	109	24.6
EDUCATION			
Average household	**44.27**	**100**	**100.0**
Less than high school graduate	38.69	87	11.4
High school graduate	43.55	98	24.5
Some college	41.80	94	19.4
Associate's degree	44.62	101	10.0
Bachelor's degree or more	48.48	110	34.5
Bachelor's degree	41.15	93	18.5
Master's, professional, doctoral degree	60.87	137	16.0

Note: Market shares may not sum to 100.0 because of rounding and missing categories by household type. "Asian" and "black" include Hispanics and non-Hispanics who identify themselves as being of the respective race alone. "Hispanic" includes people of any race who identify themselves as Hispanic. "Other" includes people who identify themselves as non-Hispanic and as Alaska Native, American Indian, Asian (who are also included in the "Asian" row), or Native Hawaiian or other Pacific Islander, as well as non-Hispanics reporting more than one race.
Source: Calculations by New Strategist based on the Bureau of Labor Statistics' 2012 Consumer Expenditure Survey

Flour

Best customers: Householders aged 25 to 64
Married couples with school-aged or older children at home
Hispanics
Householders without a high school diploma

Customer trends: Average household spending on flour should resume its decline as eating out regains its popularity.

The biggest spenders on flour are households most likely to cook from scratch—typically married couples with children at home. This household type spends 62 percent more than average on flour, the figure peaking at 80 percent above average among couples with adult children at home. Householders aged 25 to 64, many with children, spend more than average on this item. Hispanics, who have the largest households, spend 13 percent more. Households headed by people without a high school diploma, many of them Hispanic, spend 16 percent more than average on flour.

Average household spending on flour fell by a precipitous 47 percent between 2000 and 2006, after adjusting for inflation, then rebounded with a strong 66 percent increase between 2006 and 2012. Behind the earlier decline was the rise of eating out as busy families found less time to cook from scratch. The Great Recession then shifted restaurant dollars back to the grocery store as families endeavored to cut spending. Average household spending on flour should resume its decline as eating out regains its popularity.

Table 9.35 Flour

Total household spending $1,164,533,760.00
Average household spends   9.36

	AVERAGE HOUSEHOLD SPENDING	BEST CUSTOMERS (index)	BIGGEST CUSTOMERS (market share)
AGE OF HOUSEHOLDER			
Average household	**$9.36**	**100**	**100.0%**
Under age 25	6.15	66	4.3
Aged 25 to 34	9.95	106	17.2
Aged 35 to 44	9.82	105	18.2
Aged 45 to 54	11.47	123	24.3
Aged 55 to 64	10.01	107	19.6
Aged 65 to 74	7.24	77	9.3
Aged 75 or older	6.77	72	7.1

	AVERAGE HOUSEHOLD SPENDING	BEST CUSTOMERS (index)	BIGGEST CUSTOMERS (market share)
HOUSEHOLD INCOME			
Average household	**$9.36**	**100**	**100.0%**
Under $20,000	6.58	70	14.8
$20,000 to $39,999	7.04	75	16.9
$40,000 to $49,999	12.19	130	11.5
$50,000 to $69,999	8.96	96	13.8
$70,000 to $79,999	8.95	96	5.3
$80,000 to $99,999	10.01	107	9.4
$100,000 or more	13.77	147	27.5
HOUSEHOLD TYPE			
Average household	**9.36**	**100**	**100.0**
Married couples	12.76	136	66.2
Married couples, no children	10.90	116	24.3
Married couples with children	15.13	162	38.0
Oldest child under age 6	9.16	98	4.5
Oldest child aged 6 to 17	16.36	175	20.8
Oldest child aged 18 or older	16.81	180	12.7
Single parent with child under age 18	7.40	79	4.1
Single person	3.65	39	11.6
RACE AND HISPANIC ORIGIN			
Average household	**9.36**	**100**	**100.0**
Asian	9.17	98	4.2
Black	8.52	91	11.4
Hispanic	10.59	113	14.2
Non-Hispanic white and other	9.30	99	74.6
REGION			
Average household	**9.36**	**100**	**100.0**
Northeast	10.78	115	20.8
Midwest	9.37	100	22.2
South	8.99	96	35.8
West	8.80	94	21.2
EDUCATION			
Average household	**9.36**	**100**	**100.0**
Less than high school graduate	10.84	116	15.1
High school graduate	10.38	111	27.7
Some college	7.61	81	16.7
Associate's degree	8.60	92	9.1
Bachelor's degree or more	9.42	101	31.7
Bachelor's degree	8.25	88	17.6
Master's, professional, doctoral degree	11.40	122	14.1

Note: Market shares may not sum to 100.0 because of rounding and missing categories by household type. "Asian" and "black" include Hispanics and non-Hispanics who identify themselves as being of the respective race alone. "Hispanic" includes people of any race who identify themselves as Hispanic. "Other" includes people who identify themselves as non-Hispanic and as Alaska Native, American Indian, Asian (who are also included in the "Asian" row), or Native Hawaiian or other Pacific Islander, as well as non-Hispanics reporting more than one race.
Source: Calculations by New Strategist based on the Bureau of Labor Statistics' 2012 Consumer Expenditure Survey

Flour, Prepared Mixes

Best customers: Householders aged 35 to 54
                       Married couples with children at home

Customer trends: Average household spending on flour mixes should resume its decline as eating out regains its popularity.

The biggest spenders on prepared flour mixes—such as cake and biscuit mixes—are married couples with children at home. These households spend 70 percent more than average on flour mixes. Householders aged 35 to 54, most with children at home, spend 15 to 30 percent more than average on prepared flour mixes.

Average household spending on prepared flour mixes fell 28 percent between 2000 and 2006, after adjusting for inflation, then rebounded with a 26 percent increase between 2006 and 2012. Behind the earlier spending cut was the decline in home cooking. Behind the rebound is the Great Recession, leading more consumers to bake at home to save money. Average household spending on flour mixes should resume its decline as eating out regains its popularity.

Table 9.36 Flour, prepared mixes

Total household spending $2,013,050,880.00
Average household spends   16.18

AGE OF HOUSEHOLDER	AVERAGE HOUSEHOLD SPENDING	BEST CUSTOMERS (index)	BIGGEST CUSTOMERS (market share)
Average household	$16.18	100	100.0%
Under age 25	9.40	58	3.8
Aged 25 to 34	13.60	84	13.6
Aged 35 to 44	18.61	115	20.0
Aged 45 to 54	21.09	130	25.8
Aged 55 to 64	16.27	101	18.4
Aged 65 to 74	15.09	93	11.2
Aged 75 or older	11.93	74	7.2

	AVERAGE HOUSEHOLD SPENDING	BEST CUSTOMERS (index)	BIGGEST CUSTOMERS (market share)
HOUSEHOLD INCOME			
Average household	$16.18	100	100.0%
Under $20,000	9.55	59	12.4
$20,000 to $39,999	12.54	77	17.5
$40,000 to $49,999	18.11	112	9.9
$50,000 to $69,999	12.41	77	11.1
$70,000 to $79,999	20.54	127	7.1
$80,000 to $99,999	23.19	143	12.6
$100,000 or more	25.11	155	29.1
HOUSEHOLD TYPE			
Average household	16.18	100	100.0
Married couples	22.44	139	67.4
Married couples, no children	16.72	103	21.5
Married couples with children	27.50	170	40.0
Oldest child under age 6	22.04	136	6.2
Oldest child aged 6 to 17	30.09	186	22.1
Oldest child aged 18 or older	26.59	164	11.6
Single parent with child under age 18	13.92	86	4.5
Single person	6.35	39	11.7
RACE AND HISPANIC ORIGIN			
Average household	16.18	100	100.0
Asian	10.59	65	2.8
Black	12.58	78	9.8
Hispanic	12.80	79	9.9
Non-Hispanic white and other	17.34	107	80.4
REGION			
Average household	16.18	100	100.0
Northeast	14.57	90	16.3
Midwest	17.11	106	23.4
South	15.01	93	34.6
West	18.48	114	25.7
EDUCATION			
Average household	16.18	100	100.0
Less than high school graduate	11.99	74	9.7
High school graduate	14.64	90	22.6
Some college	15.16	94	19.3
Associate's degree	21.39	132	13.1
Bachelor's degree or more	17.99	111	35.1
Bachelor's degree	16.79	104	20.7
Master's, professional, doctoral degree	20.02	124	14.4

Note: Market shares may not sum to 100.0 because of rounding and missing categories by household type. "Asian" and "black" include Hispanics and non-Hispanics who identify themselves as being of the respective race alone. "Hispanic" includes people of any race who identify themselves as Hispanic. "Other" includes people who identify themselves as non-Hispanic and as Alaska Native, American Indian, Asian (who are also included in the "Asian" row), or Native Hawaiian or other Pacific Islander, as well as non-Hispanics reporting more than one race.
Source: Calculations by New Strategist based on the Bureau of Labor Statistics' 2012 Consumer Expenditure Survey

Frankfurters

Best customers:
Householders aged 35 to 54
Married couples with children at home
Single parents
Hispanics
Households in the Northeast
Householders with a high school diploma or less education

Customer trends:
Average household spending on frankfurters may resume its decline because the small generation X is in the best-customer lifestage.

Households with children are the biggest spenders on frankfurters. Married couples with children at home spend 47 percent more than average on this item. Householders aged 35 to 54, most with children, spend 11 to 31 percent more than average on hot dogs. Single parents, whose spending approaches the average on only a few items, spend 16 percent more than average on frankfurters. Hispanics, who have the largest families, spend 17 percent more. Households in the Northeast outspend the average on this item by 20 percent. Householders with no more than a high school education, many of them Hispanic, spend 18 to 19 percent more than average on frankfurters.

Average household spending on frankfurters fell 17 percent between 2000 and 2006, after adjusting for inflation, and then rebounded by 7 percent between 2006 and 2012. Average household spending on hot dogs may resume its decline because the small generation X is in the best-customer lifestage.

Table 9.37 Frankfurters

Total household spending $3,074,319,360.00
Average household spends   24.71

	AVERAGE HOUSEHOLD SPENDING	BEST CUSTOMERS (index)	BIGGEST CUSTOMERS (market share)
AGE OF HOUSEHOLDER			
Average household	$24.71	100	100.0%
Under age 25	19.14	77	5.1
Aged 25 to 34	23.50	95	15.4
Aged 35 to 44	32.33	131	22.7
Aged 45 to 54	27.55	111	22.1
Aged 55 to 64	26.11	106	19.3
Aged 65 to 74	19.86	80	9.7
Aged 75 or older	14.19	57	5.6

	AVERAGE HOUSEHOLD SPENDING	BEST CUSTOMERS (index)	BIGGEST CUSTOMERS (market share)
HOUSEHOLD INCOME			
Average household	**$24.71**	**100**	**100.0%**
Under $20,000	17.49	71	14.9
$20,000 to $39,999	23.46	95	21.4
$40,000 to $49,999	23.15	94	8.3
$50,000 to $69,999	22.16	90	13.0
$70,000 to $79,999	31.45	127	7.1
$80,000 to $99,999	29.14	118	10.4
$100,000 or more	32.52	132	24.6
HOUSEHOLD TYPE			
Average household	**24.71**	**100**	**100.0**
Married couples	31.16	126	61.2
Married couples, no children	21.99	89	18.6
Married couples with children	36.33	147	34.6
Oldest child under age 6	29.79	121	5.5
Oldest child aged 6 to 17	38.16	154	18.4
Oldest child aged 18 or older	37.34	151	10.7
Single parent with child under age 18	28.57	116	6.1
Single person	11.09	45	13.3
RACE AND HISPANIC ORIGIN			
Average household	**24.71**	**100**	**100.0**
Asian	18.32	74	3.2
Black	25.19	102	12.8
Hispanic	29.03	117	14.7
Non-Hispanic white and other	23.99	97	72.9
REGION			
Average household	**24.71**	**100**	**100.0**
Northeast	29.60	120	21.6
Midwest	25.28	102	22.7
South	23.34	94	35.2
West	22.46	91	20.5
EDUCATION			
Average household	**24.71**	**100**	**100.0**
Less than high school graduate	29.29	119	15.5
High school graduate	29.27	118	29.5
Some college	22.76	92	19.0
Associate's degree	23.19	94	9.3
Bachelor's degree or more	21.25	86	27.1
Bachelor's degree	21.71	88	17.5
Master's, professional, doctoral degree	20.48	83	9.6

Note: Market shares may not sum to 100.0 because of rounding and missing categories by household type. "Asian" and "black" include Hispanics and non-Hispanics who identify themselves as being of the respective race alone. "Hispanic" includes people of any race who identify themselves as Hispanic. "Other" includes people who identify themselves as non-Hispanic and as Alaska Native, American Indian, Asian (who are also included in the "Asian" row), or Native Hawaiian or other Pacific Islander, as well as non-Hispanics reporting more than one race.
Source: Calculations by New Strategist based on the Bureau of Labor Statistics' 2012 Consumer Expenditure Survey

Fruit-Flavored Drinks, Noncarbonated

Best customers: Householders aged 35 to 54
                       Married couples with school-aged or older children at home
                       Single parents
                       Hispanics and blacks

Customer trends: Average household spending on noncarbonated fruit-flavored drinks should continue to grow in the years
                       ahead as the millennial generation enters the best-customer lifestage.

The best customers of noncarbonated fruit-flavored drinks are parents with children. Married couples with school-aged or older children at home spend 53 to 60 percent more than the average household on this item. Single parents, whose spending approaches average on only a few items, spend 28 percent more than average on fruit-flavored drinks. Householders aged 35 to 54, most with children at home, spend 20 to 30 percent more than average on this item and account for 46 percent of the market. Hispanics spend 34 percent more than average on fruit-flavored drinks, and blacks spend 4 percent more.

Average household spending on noncarbonated fruit-flavored drinks purchased at grocery or convenience stores declined rapidly before the Great Recession, then rebounded strongly along with overall grocery spending. Behind the spending increase is the switch from fruit juice to less-expensive fruit-flavored drinks by some households. Average household spending on noncarbonated fruit-flavored drinks should continue to grow in the years ahead as the millennial generation enters the best-customer lifestage.

Table 9.38 Fruit-flavored drinks, noncarbonated

Total household spending $3,213,665,280.00
Average household spends   25.83

AGE OF HOUSEHOLDER	AVERAGE HOUSEHOLD SPENDING	BEST CUSTOMERS (index)	BIGGEST CUSTOMERS (market share)
Average household	$25.83	100	100.0%
Under age 25	29.14	113	7.4
Aged 25 to 34	23.60	91	14.8
Aged 35 to 44	33.70	130	22.6
Aged 45 to 54	31.11	120	23.8
Aged 55 to 64	19.62	76	13.9
Aged 65 to 74	20.92	81	9.8
Aged 75 or older	19.47	75	7.4

	AVERAGE HOUSEHOLD SPENDING	BEST CUSTOMERS (index)	BIGGEST CUSTOMERS (market share)
HOUSEHOLD INCOME			
Average household	**$25.83**	**100**	**100.0%**
Under $20,000	16.61	64	13.5
$20,000 to $39,999	23.66	92	20.6
$40,000 to $49,999	23.85	92	8.2
$50,000 to $69,999	32.09	124	17.9
$70,000 to $79,999	31.65	123	6.8
$80,000 to $99,999	31.01	120	10.6
$100,000 or more	30.63	119	22.2
HOUSEHOLD TYPE			
Average household	**25.83**	**100**	**100.0**
Married couples	31.27	121	58.8
Married couples, no children	21.97	85	17.7
Married couples with children	37.98	147	34.6
Oldest child under age 6	26.29	102	4.6
Oldest child aged 6 to 17	41.44	160	19.1
Oldest child aged 18 or older	39.50	153	10.8
Single parent with child under age 18	33.09	128	6.7
Single person	11.45	44	13.2
RACE AND HISPANIC ORIGIN			
Average household	**25.83**	**100**	**100.0**
Asian	23.52	91	3.9
Black	26.75	104	13.0
Hispanic	34.69	134	16.8
Non-Hispanic white and other	24.18	94	70.3
REGION			
Average household	**25.83**	**100**	**100.0**
Northeast	25.07	97	17.5
Midwest	24.62	95	21.1
South	25.90	100	37.3
West	27.54	107	24.0
EDUCATION			
Average household	**25.83**	**100**	**100.0**
Less than high school graduate	29.34	114	14.8
High school graduate	25.32	98	24.4
Some college	23.96	93	19.1
Associate's degree	22.87	89	8.7
Bachelor's degree or more	27.09	105	33.1
Bachelor's degree	28.76	111	22.2
Master's, professional, doctoral degree	24.26	94	10.9

Note: Market shares may not sum to 100.0 because of rounding and missing categories by household type. "Asian" and "black" include Hispanics and non-Hispanics who identify themselves as being of the respective race alone. "Hispanic" includes people of any race who identify themselves as Hispanic. "Other" includes people who identify themselves as non-Hispanic and as Alaska Native, American Indian, Asian (who are also included in the "Asian" row), or Native Hawaiian or other Pacific Islander, as well as non-Hispanics reporting more than one race.
Source: Calculations by New Strategist based on the Bureau of Labor Statistics' 2012 Consumer Expenditure Survey

Fruit, Canned

Best customers: Householders aged 35 to 54
Married couples with children at home
Households in the Northeast and Midwest

Customer trends: Average household spending on canned fruit is likely to continue to decline because the small generation X is in the best customer lifestage and packaged fresh fruit is becoming more widely available.

The biggest spenders on canned fruit are the largest households. Married couples with children at home spend 62 percent more than average on this item, the figure peaking at 70 percent among those with school-aged children. Householders aged 35 to 54, many with children, spend 11 to 19 percent more than average on canned fruit. Households in the Midwest spend 29 percent more than average on this item, and those in the Northeast spend 13 percent more.

Average household spending on canned fruit fell by 1 percent between 2000 and 2012, after adjusting for inflation. Behind the relative stability were two competing trends: the attempt by consumers to add more fruit to their diet, which boosted spending on canned fruit, and competition from sliced and conveniently packaged fresh fruit, which reduced spending on canned fruit. Average household spending on canned fruit is likely to continue to decline because the small generation X is in the best-customer lifestage and packaged fresh fruit is becoming more widely available.

Table 9.39 Fruit, canned

Total household spending $2,531,865,600.00
Average household spends 20.35

AGE OF HOUSEHOLDER	AVERAGE HOUSEHOLD SPENDING	BEST CUSTOMERS (index)	BIGGEST CUSTOMERS (market share)
Average household	$20.35	100	100.0%
Under age 25	10.34	51	3.3
Aged 25 to 34	19.21	94	15.3
Aged 35 to 44	22.41	110	19.1
Aged 45 to 54	24.12	119	23.5
Aged 55 to 64	18.78	92	16.9
Aged 65 to 74	19.96	98	11.8
Aged 75 or older	21.27	105	10.2

	AVERAGE HOUSEHOLD SPENDING	BEST CUSTOMERS (index)	BIGGEST CUSTOMERS (market share)
HOUSEHOLD INCOME			
Average household	$20.35	100	100.0%
Under $20,000	12.44	61	12.9
$20,000 to $39,999	19.16	94	21.2
$40,000 to $49,999	13.60	67	5.9
$50,000 to $69,999	21.43	105	15.2
$70,000 to $79,999	23.79	117	6.5
$80,000 to $99,999	27.38	135	11.9
$100,000 or more	29.10	143	26.8
HOUSEHOLD TYPE			
Average household	20.35	100	100.0
Married couples	27.27	134	65.1
Married couples, no children	21.39	105	21.9
Married couples with children	32.91	162	38.0
Oldest child under age 6	31.77	156	7.1
Oldest child aged 6 to 17	34.59	170	20.2
Oldest child aged 18 or older	30.81	151	10.7
Single parent with child under age 18	19.99	98	5.2
Single person	10.00	49	14.6
RACE AND HISPANIC ORIGIN			
Average household	20.35	100	100.0
Asian	16.55	81	3.5
Black	14.60	72	9.0
Hispanic	17.40	86	10.7
Non-Hispanic white and other	21.82	107	80.5
REGION			
Average household	20.35	100	100.0
Northeast	22.91	113	20.3
Midwest	26.22	129	28.6
South	17.73	87	32.4
West	16.75	82	18.5
EDUCATION			
Average household	20.35	100	100.0
Less than high school graduate	18.37	90	11.8
High school graduate	18.21	89	22.3
Some college	20.38	100	20.6
Associate's degree	17.45	86	8.5
Bachelor's degree or more	23.64	116	36.6
Bachelor's degree	24.17	119	23.7
Master's, professional, doctoral degree	22.74	112	13.0

Note: Market shares may not sum to 100.0 because of rounding and missing categories by household type. "Asian" and "black" include Hispanics and non-Hispanics who identify themselves as being of the respective race alone. "Hispanic" includes people of any race who identify themselves as Hispanic. "Other" includes people who identify themselves as non-Hispanic and as Alaska Native, American Indian, Asian (who are also included in the "Asian" row), or Native Hawaiian or other Pacific Islander, as well as non-Hispanics reporting more than one race.
Source: Calculations by New Strategist based on the Bureau of Labor Statistics' 2012 Consumer Expenditure Survey

Fruit, Dried

Best customers: Householders aged 25 to 34 and 65 or older
Married couples without children at home
Married couples with children under age 18

Customer trends: Average household spending on dried fruit should increase again as the population ages.

The biggest spenders on dried fruit are older householders and the largest households. Married couples with preschoolers spend twice the average on dried fruit, and those with school-aged children spend one-third more than average. Householders aged 25 to 34, many with children, spend 21 percent more than average on dried fruit, and those aged 65 or older spend 11 to 19 percent more. Married couples without children at home (most of them older empty-nesters) spend 35 percent more than average on this item.

Average household spending on dried fruit, which had grown strongly between 2000 and 2006, declined 15 percent between 2006 and 2012, after adjusting for inflation. Behind the earlier increase was the greater availability of dried fruit and its growing popularity as a snack food. Spending on dried fruit should increase again as the population ages.

Table 9.40 Fruit, dried

Total household spending $1,083,663,360.00
Average household spends   8.71

	AVERAGE HOUSEHOLD SPENDING	BEST CUSTOMERS (index)	BIGGEST CUSTOMERS (market share)
AGE OF HOUSEHOLDER			
Average household	**$8.71**	**100**	**100.0%**
Under age 25	3.29	38	2.5
Aged 25 to 34	10.52	121	19.5
Aged 35 to 44	7.53	86	15.0
Aged 45 to 54	8.52	98	19.4
Aged 55 to 64	8.86	102	18.6
Aged 65 to 74	10.39	119	14.4
Aged 75 or older	9.69	111	10.9

	AVERAGE HOUSEHOLD SPENDING	BEST CUSTOMERS (index)	BIGGEST CUSTOMERS (market share)
HOUSEHOLD INCOME			
Average household	**$8.71**	**100**	**100.0%**
Under $20,000	3.38	39	8.2
$20,000 to $39,999	7.32	84	18.9
$40,000 to $49,999	7.11	82	7.2
$50,000 to $69,999	9.83	113	16.3
$70,000 to $79,999	9.02	104	5.8
$80,000 to $99,999	10.12	116	10.3
$100,000 or more	15.37	176	33.0
HOUSEHOLD TYPE			
Average household	**8.71**	**100**	**100.0**
Married couples	12.18	140	67.9
Married couples, no children	11.78	135	28.2
Married couples with children	12.12	139	32.7
Oldest child under age 6	17.20	197	9.0
Oldest child aged 6 to 17	11.73	135	16.0
Oldest child aged 18 or older	9.62	110	7.8
Single parent with child under age 18	6.29	72	3.8
Single person	4.55	52	15.5
RACE AND HISPANIC ORIGIN			
Average household	**8.71**	**100**	**100.0**
Asian	6.78	78	3.4
Black	4.06	47	5.9
Hispanic	5.64	65	8.1
Non-Hispanic white and other	9.99	115	86.1
REGION			
Average household	**8.71**	**100**	**100.0**
Northeast	10.19	117	21.1
Midwest	9.60	110	24.4
South	6.55	75	28.0
West	10.21	117	26.4
EDUCATION			
Average household	**8.71**	**100**	**100.0**
Less than high school graduate	6.04	69	9.1
High school graduate	7.45	86	21.3
Some college	7.25	83	17.1
Associate's degree	9.62	110	10.9
Bachelor's degree or more	11.40	131	41.3
Bachelor's degree	10.61	122	24.3
Master's, professional, doctoral degree	12.73	146	17.0

Note: Market shares may not sum to 100.0 because of rounding and missing categories by household type. "Asian" and "black" include Hispanics and non-Hispanics who identify themselves as being of the respective race alone. "Hispanic" includes people of any race who identify themselves as Hispanic. "Other" includes people who identify themselves as non-Hispanic and as Alaska Native, American Indian, Asian (who are also included in the "Asian" row), or Native Hawaiian or other Pacific Islander, as well as non-Hispanics reporting more than one race.
Source: Calculations by New Strategist based on the Bureau of Labor Statistics' 2012 Consumer Expenditure Survey

Fruit, Fresh, Total

Best customers: Householders aged 35 to 54
Married couples with children at home
Asians and Hispanics
Households in the West

Customer trends: Average household spending on fresh fruit should continue to rise because of growing minority populations
and the interest in healthy eating.

The biggest spenders on fresh fruit are the largest households. Married couples with children at home spend 51 percent more than average on fresh fruit. Householders aged 35 to 54, most with children, spend 14 to 18 percent more than average on fresh fruit. Asians spend 57 percent more than average on this item. Hispanics, who have the largest households, spend 18 percent more. Households in the West, where many Asians and Hispanics live, spend 20 percent more than average on fresh fruit.

Fresh fruit is the grocery category on which the average household spends the most. Average household spending on fresh fruit climbed 20 percent between 2000 and 2012, after adjusting for inflation. Behind the increase was the growing variety of sliced and packaged fresh fruit available in grocery stores, boosting sales. Average household spending on fresh fruit should continue to rise because of growing minority populations and the interest in healthy eating.

Table 9.41 Fruit, fresh, total

| Total household spending | $32,508,656,640.00 |
| Average household spends | 261.29 |

	AVERAGE HOUSEHOLD SPENDING	BEST CUSTOMERS (index)	BIGGEST CUSTOMERS (market share)
AGE OF HOUSEHOLDER			
Average household	**$261.29**	**100**	**100.0%**
Under age 25	162.19	62	4.1
Aged 25 to 34	236.97	91	14.7
Aged 35 to 44	296.71	114	19.7
Aged 45 to 54	308.31	118	23.4
Aged 55 to 64	257.81	99	18.1
Aged 65 to 74	259.75	99	12.0
Aged 75 or older	219.11	84	8.2

	AVERAGE HOUSEHOLD SPENDING	BEST CUSTOMERS (index)	BIGGEST CUSTOMERS (market share)
HOUSEHOLD INCOME			
Average household	**$261.29**	**100**	**100.0%**
Under $20,000	141.93	54	11.4
$20,000 to $39,999	186.03	71	16.0
$40,000 to $49,999	232.87	89	7.9
$50,000 to $69,999	261.43	100	14.5
$70,000 to $79,999	306.16	117	6.5
$80,000 to $99,999	332.65	127	11.2
$100,000 or more	451.13	173	32.3
HOUSEHOLD TYPE			
Average household	**261.29**	**100**	**100.0**
Married couples	346.98	133	64.5
Married couples, no children	296.93	114	23.7
Married couples with children	394.92	151	35.5
Oldest child under age 6	326.03	125	5.7
Oldest child aged 6 to 17	408.84	156	18.6
Oldest child aged 18 or older	414.63	159	11.2
Single parent with child under age 18	251.61	96	5.0
Single person	133.79	51	15.2
RACE AND HISPANIC ORIGIN			
Average household	**261.29**	**100**	**100.0**
Asian	409.42	157	6.8
Black	165.90	63	8.0
Hispanic	307.27	118	14.7
Non-Hispanic white and other	269.89	103	77.5
REGION			
Average household	**261.29**	**100**	**100.0**
Northeast	285.29	109	19.7
Midwest	261.53	100	22.2
South	217.99	83	31.1
West	313.53	120	27.0
EDUCATION			
Average household	**261.29**	**100**	**100.0**
Less than high school graduate	226.81	87	11.3
High school graduate	209.78	80	20.0
Some college	213.16	82	16.8
Associate's degree	250.07	96	9.5
Bachelor's degree or more	350.04	134	42.2
Bachelor's degree	329.50	126	25.1
Master's, professional, doctoral degree	384.78	147	17.1

Note: Market shares may not sum to 100.0 because of rounding and missing categories by household type. "Asian" and "black" include Hispanics and non-Hispanics who identify themselves as being of the respective race alone. "Hispanic" includes people of any race who identify themselves as Hispanic. "Other" includes people who identify themselves as non-Hispanic and as Alaska Native, American Indian, Asian (who are also included in the "Asian" row), or Native Hawaiian or other Pacific Islander, as well as non-Hispanics reporting more than one race.
Source: Calculations by New Strategist based on the Bureau of Labor Statistics' 2012 Consumer Expenditure Survey

Fruit, Frozen

Best customers: Married couples without children at home
Married couples with school-aged or older children at home
Asians
Households in the Midwest and West

Customer trends: Average household spending on frozen fruit may continue to rise as consumers attempt to improve their diet.

The largest households are the best customers of frozen fruit. Married couples with school-aged children spend 86 percent more than average on frozen fruit, and those with adult children at home spend more than twice the average. Couples without children at home, most of them older empty-nesters, outspend the average by 60 percent. Asian households spend 51 percent more than average on frozen fruit. Households in the Midwest and West spend, respectively, 30 and 39 percent more than average on frozen fruit.

Average household spending on frozen fruit grew by a substantial 48 percent between 2000 and 2012, after adjusting for inflation. One factor behind the rise was growing health consciousness among consumers, who were adding more fruit to their diet. Average household spending on frozen fruit may continue to rise as consumers attempt to improve their diet.

Table 9.42 Fruit, frozen

Total household spending $890,818,560.00
Average household spends   7.16

AGE OF HOUSEHOLDER	AVERAGE HOUSEHOLD SPENDING	BEST CUSTOMERS (index)	BIGGEST CUSTOMERS (market share)
Average household	$7.16	100	100.0%
Under age 25	2.65	37	2.4
Aged 25 to 34	4.70	66	10.6
Aged 35 to 44	7.47	104	18.1
Aged 45 to 54	11.86	166	32.8
Aged 55 to 64	7.24	101	18.5
Aged 65 to 74	6.92	97	11.6
Aged 75 or older	4.44	62	6.1

	AVERAGE HOUSEHOLD SPENDING	BEST CUSTOMERS (index)	BIGGEST CUSTOMERS (market share)
HOUSEHOLD INCOME			
Average household	$7.16	100	100.0%
Under $20,000	2.87	40	8.4
$20,000 to $39,999	4.87	68	15.3
$40,000 to $49,999	4.40	61	5.4
$50,000 to $69,999	7.29	102	14.7
$70,000 to $79,999	11.97	167	9.3
$80,000 to $99,999	11.40	159	14.0
$100,000 or more	12.73	178	33.3
HOUSEHOLD TYPE			
Average household	7.16	100	100.0
Married couples	11.18	156	75.8
Married couples, no children	11.48	160	33.4
Married couples with children	11.96	167	39.3
Oldest child under age 6	2.06	29	1.3
Oldest child aged 6 to 17	13.34	186	22.2
Oldest child aged 18 or older	15.84	221	15.6
Single parent with child under age 18	4.11	57	3.0
Single person	3.41	48	14.1
RACE AND HISPANIC ORIGIN			
Average household	7.16	100	100.0
Asian	10.78	151	6.5
Black	2.53	35	4.4
Hispanic	5.20	73	9.1
Non-Hispanic white and other	8.33	116	87.3
REGION			
Average household	7.16	100	100.0
Northeast	6.53	91	16.5
Midwest	9.33	130	28.9
South	4.49	63	23.4
West	9.95	139	31.3
EDUCATION			
Average household	7.16	100	100.0
Less than high school graduate	3.30	46	6.0
High school graduate	4.40	61	15.3
Some college	5.36	75	15.4
Associate's degree	10.36	145	14.3
Bachelor's degree or more	10.97	153	48.3
Bachelor's degree	9.72	136	27.1
Master's, professional, doctoral degree	13.08	183	21.2

Note: Market shares may not sum to 100.0 because of rounding and missing categories by household type. "Asian" and "black" include Hispanics and non-Hispanics who identify themselves as being of the respective race alone. "Hispanic" includes people of any race who identify themselves as Hispanic. "Other" includes people who identify themselves as non-Hispanic and as Alaska Native, American Indian, Asian (who are also included in the "Asian" row), or Native Hawaiian or other Pacific Islander, as well as non-Hispanics reporting more than one race.
Source: Calculations by New Strategist based on the Bureau of Labor Statistics' 2012 Consumer Expenditure Survey

Fruit Juice, Canned and Bottled

Best customers: Householders aged 35 to 54
Married couples with children at home
Single parents
Hispanics, Asians, and blacks
Households in the West

Customer trends: Average household spending on canned and bottled fruit juice may begin to grow again
as the large millennial generation fills the best-customer lifestage.

Households with children are the biggest spenders on canned and bottled fruit juice, which dominates fruit juice sales. Married couples with children at home spend 40 percent more than average on canned and bottled fruit juice. Despite their low incomes single parents spend 10 percent more than the average household on this item. Householders aged 35 to 54, most with children at home, spend 8 to 14 percent more than average on canned and bottled fruit juice. Blacks, Asians, and Hispanics outspend the average by 3 to 28 percent and account for one-third of the market. Households in the West outspend the average household on this item by 16 percent.

Average household spending on canned and bottled fruit juice purchased at grocery or convenience stores fell 27 percent between 2000 and 2010, but has held steady since then. Behind the decline was the growing propensity of consumers to eat fast-food breakfasts or no breakfast at all, and the rise of fruit-flavored drinks as a substitute for juice. Spending on canned and bottled fruit juice may begin to grow again as the large millennial generation fills the best-customer lifestage.

Table 9.43 Fruit juice, canned and bottled

Total household spending $6,832,926,720.00
Average household spends 54.92

AGE OF HOUSEHOLDER	AVERAGE HOUSEHOLD SPENDING	BEST CUSTOMERS (index)	BIGGEST CUSTOMERS (market share)
Average household	$54.92	100	100.0%
Under age 25	45.51	83	5.4
Aged 25 to 34	56.60	103	16.7
Aged 35 to 44	59.27	108	18.7
Aged 45 to 54	62.55	114	22.5
Aged 55 to 64	54.46	99	18.1
Aged 65 to 74	44.56	81	9.8
Aged 75 or older	48.54	88	8.6

	AVERAGE HOUSEHOLD SPENDING	BEST CUSTOMERS (index)	BIGGEST CUSTOMERS (market share)
HOUSEHOLD INCOME			
Average household	**$54.92**	**100**	**100.0%**
Under $20,000	35.94	65	13.8
$20,000 to $39,999	45.64	83	18.7
$40,000 to $49,999	51.34	93	8.3
$50,000 to $69,999	51.34	93	13.5
$70,000 to $79,999	78.87	144	8.0
$80,000 to $99,999	63.16	115	10.1
$100,000 or more	80.91	147	27.6
HOUSEHOLD TYPE			
Average household	**54.92**	**100**	**100.0**
Married couples	67.54	123	59.7
Married couples, no children	53.97	98	20.5
Married couples with children	76.65	140	32.8
Oldest child under age 6	62.91	115	5.2
Oldest child aged 6 to 17	79.66	145	17.3
Oldest child aged 18 or older	80.18	146	10.3
Single parent with child under age 18	60.14	110	5.7
Single person	33.37	61	18.0
RACE AND HISPANIC ORIGIN			
Average household	**54.92**	**100**	**100.0**
Asian	57.64	105	4.5
Black	56.53	103	12.9
Hispanic	70.05	128	16.0
Non-Hispanic white and other	52.11	95	71.2
REGION			
Average household	**54.92**	**100**	**100.0**
Northeast	60.05	109	19.7
Midwest	48.91	89	19.7
South	50.64	92	34.3
West	63.89	116	26.2
EDUCATION			
Average household	**54.92**	**100**	**100.0**
Less than high school graduate	46.34	84	11.0
High school graduate	46.44	85	21.1
Some college	51.89	94	19.5
Associate's degree	51.41	94	9.2
Bachelor's degree or more	67.84	124	39.0
Bachelor's degree	63.57	116	23.1
Master's, professional, doctoral degree	75.07	137	15.9

Note: Market shares may not sum to 100.0 because of rounding and missing categories by household type. "Asian" and "black" include Hispanics and non-Hispanics who identify themselves as being of the respective race alone. "Hispanic" includes people of any race who identify themselves as Hispanic. "Other" includes people who identify themselves as non-Hispanic and as Alaska Native, American Indian, Asian (who are also included in the "Asian" row), or Native Hawaiian or other Pacific Islander, as well as non-Hispanics reporting more than one race.
Source: Calculations by New Strategist based on the Bureau of Labor Statistics' 2012 Consumer Expenditure Survey

Fruit Juice, Fresh

Best customers: Householders aged 35 to 54
Married couples with children at home
Households in the Northeast

Customer trends: Average household spending on fresh fruit juice may stabilize as the large millennial generation enters the best-customer lifestage.

Middle-aged married couples are the biggest spenders on fresh fruit juice. Householders aged 35 to 54 spend 25 to 27 percent more than average on this item. Married couples with children at home spend 48 percent more than average on fresh fruit juice, the figure peaking among those with school-aged children at 57 percent above average. Households in the Northeast outspend the average by 38 percent.

Average household spending on fresh fruit juice purchased at grocery or convenience stores fell by a substantial 36 percent between 2000 and 2006, after adjusting for inflation. Spending on this item fell another 14 percent between 2006 and 2012. Behind the long decline in spending on fresh fruit juice is the baby-boom generation's exit from the best-customer lifestage and the growing propensity of consumers to eat fast-food breakfasts or no breakfast at all. Average household spending on fresh fruit juice may stabilize as the large millennial generation enters the best-customer lifestage.

Table 9.44 Fruit juice, fresh

Total household spending $2,122,536,960.00
Average household spends 17.06

AGE OF HOUSEHOLDER	AVERAGE HOUSEHOLD SPENDING	BEST CUSTOMERS (index)	BIGGEST CUSTOMERS (market share)
Average household	$17.06	100	100.0%
Under age 25	10.35	61	4.0
Aged 25 to 34	14.40	84	13.6
Aged 35 to 44	21.68	127	22.1
Aged 45 to 54	21.28	125	24.7
Aged 55 to 64	17.69	104	19.0
Aged 65 to 74	13.28	78	9.4
Aged 75 or older	12.66	74	7.3

	AVERAGE HOUSEHOLD SPENDING	BEST CUSTOMERS (index)	BIGGEST CUSTOMERS (market share)
HOUSEHOLD INCOME			
Average household	$17.06	100	100.0%
Under $20,000	10.03	59	12.4
$20,000 to $39,999	13.67	80	18.1
$40,000 to $49,999	14.42	85	7.5
$50,000 to $69,999	16.19	95	13.7
$70,000 to $79,999	18.13	106	5.9
$80,000 to $99,999	22.68	133	11.7
$100,000 or more	28.12	165	30.9
HOUSEHOLD TYPE			
Average household	17.06	100	100.0
Married couples	21.31	125	60.7
Married couples, no children	16.66	98	20.4
Married couples with children	25.24	148	34.8
Oldest child under age 6	22.50	132	6.0
Oldest child aged 6 to 17	26.72	157	18.6
Oldest child aged 18 or older	24.47	143	10.1
Single parent with child under age 18	14.73	86	4.5
Single person	10.33	61	18.0
RACE AND HISPANIC ORIGIN			
Average household	17.06	100	100.0
Asian	18.52	109	4.7
Black	15.05	88	11.1
Hispanic	17.00	100	12.5
Non-Hispanic white and other	17.39	102	76.5
REGION			
Average household	17.06	100	100.0
Northeast	23.51	138	24.9
Midwest	18.56	109	24.1
South	13.63	80	29.8
West	16.01	94	21.1
EDUCATION			
Average household	17.06	100	100.0
Less than high school graduate	15.81	93	12.1
High school graduate	14.48	85	21.2
Some college	14.21	83	17.2
Associate's degree	18.09	106	10.5
Bachelor's degree or more	21.12	124	39.0
Bachelor's degree	18.79	110	22.0
Master's, professional, doctoral degree	25.07	147	17.1

Note: Market shares may not sum to 100.0 because of rounding and missing categories by household type. "Asian" and "black" include Hispanics and non-Hispanics who identify themselves as being of the respective race alone. "Hispanic" includes people of any race who identify themselves as Hispanic. "Other" includes people who identify themselves as non-Hispanic and as Alaska Native, American Indian, Asian (who are also included in the "Asian" row), or Native Hawaiian or other Pacific Islander, as well as non-Hispanics reporting more than one race.
Source: Calculations by New Strategist based on the Bureau of Labor Statistics' 2012 Consumer Expenditure Survey

Fruit Juice, Frozen

Best customers:	**Married couples without children at home**
	Married couples with school-aged children
	Hispanics and Asians
	Households in the Midwest and West
Customer trends:	**Average household spending on frozen fruit juice may continue its decline as consumer preferences shift.**

Households with school-aged children are the best customers of frozen fruit juice. Married couples with school-aged children spend 76 percent more than average on frozen fruit juice. Hispanic householders, who have the largest families, outspend the average by 29 percent. Asians spend 16 percent more. Married couples without children at home (most of them older empty-nesters) spend one-quarter more than average on frozen fruit juice. Households in the Midwest and West spend, respectively, 36 and 28 percent more than average on frozen fruit juice.

Average household spending on frozen fruit juice fell steeply between 2000 and 2006 (down 60 percent, after adjusting for inflation) and continued to decline—although more slowly—between 2006 and 2012. The declines occurred because consumers were looking for more convenience from fruit juice, and they were increasingly eating breakfast away from home—a trend slowed by household belt tightening in face of the Great Recession. Average household spending on frozen fruit juice is likely to continue its decline as consumer preferences shift.

Table 9.45 Fruit juice, frozen

Total household spending	$690,508,800.00
Average household spends	5.55

AGE OF HOUSEHOLDER	AVERAGE HOUSEHOLD SPENDING	BEST CUSTOMERS (index)	BIGGEST CUSTOMERS (market share)
Average household	$5.55	100	100.0%
Under age 25	4.65	84	5.5
Aged 25 to 34	6.49	117	18.9
Aged 35 to 44	5.70	103	17.8
Aged 45 to 54	6.58	119	23.5
Aged 55 to 64	3.88	70	12.8
Aged 65 to 74	4.45	80	9.7
Aged 75 or older	6.60	119	11.6

	AVERAGE HOUSEHOLD SPENDING	BEST CUSTOMERS (index)	BIGGEST CUSTOMERS (market share)
HOUSEHOLD INCOME			
Average household	**$5.55**	**100**	**100.0%**
Under $20,000	4.27	77	16.2
$20,000 to $39,999	4.69	85	19.0
$40,000 to $49,999	4.17	75	6.6
$50,000 to $69,999	7.21	130	18.8
$70,000 to $79,999	7.87	142	7.9
$80,000 to $99,999	5.88	106	9.3
$100,000 or more	6.52	117	22.0
HOUSEHOLD TYPE			
Average household	**5.55**	**100**	**100.0**
Married couples	7.25	131	63.4
Married couples, no children	6.95	125	26.1
Married couples with children	7.91	143	33.5
Oldest child under age 6	5.19	94	4.3
Oldest child aged 6 to 17	9.79	176	21.0
Oldest child aged 18 or older	6.48	117	8.2
Single parent with child under age 18	5.62	101	5.3
Single person	2.47	45	13.2
RACE AND HISPANIC ORIGIN			
Average household	**5.55**	**100**	**100.0**
Asian	6.43	116	5.0
Black	4.39	79	9.9
Hispanic	7.14	129	16.1
Non-Hispanic white and other	5.52	99	74.7
REGION			
Average household	**5.55**	**100**	**100.0**
Northeast	4.15	75	13.5
Midwest	7.53	136	30.1
South	4.11	74	27.6
West	7.09	128	28.8
EDUCATION			
Average household	**5.55**	**100**	**100.0**
Less than high school graduate	4.85	87	11.4
High school graduate	5.44	98	24.4
Some college	5.95	107	22.1
Associate's degree	6.20	112	11.0
Bachelor's degree or more	5.41	97	30.7
Bachelor's degree	4.62	83	16.6
Master's, professional, doctoral degree	6.77	122	14.2

Note: Market shares may not sum to 100.0 because of rounding and missing categories by household type. "Asian" and "black" include Hispanics and non-Hispanics who identify themselves as being of the respective race alone. "Hispanic" includes people of any race who identify themselves as Hispanic. "Other" includes people who identify themselves as non-Hispanic and as Alaska Native, American Indian, Asian (who are also included in the "Asian" row), or Native Hawaiian or other Pacific Islander, as well as non-Hispanics reporting more than one race.
Source: Calculations by New Strategist based on the Bureau of Labor Statistics' 2012 Consumer Expenditure Survey

Ham

Best customers: Householders aged 35 to 54
        Married couples with school-aged or older children at home
        Hispanics
        Householders without a high school diploma

Customer trends: Average household spending on ham may continue its decline as the small generation X passes through the best-customer lifestage.

Households with children are the biggest spenders on ham. Married couples with school-aged or older children at home spend 52 to 73 percent more than average on this item. Householders aged 35 to 54, most with children at home, spend one-fifth more than average on ham. Hispanics, who tend to have larger families, outspend the average by 35 percent. Householders without a high school diploma, many of them Hispanic, spend 14 percent more than average on ham.

Average household spending on ham declined 31 percent between 2000 and 2012, after adjusting for inflation. Average household spending on ham may continue its decline as the small generation X passes through the best-customer lifestage.

Table 9.46 Ham

Total household spending $4,157,982,720.00
Average household spends   33.42

AGE OF HOUSEHOLDER	AVERAGE HOUSEHOLD SPENDING	BEST CUSTOMERS (index)	BIGGEST CUSTOMERS (market share)
Average household	$33.42	100	100.0%
Under age 25	20.85	62	4.1
Aged 25 to 34	28.37	85	13.7
Aged 35 to 44	39.99	120	20.8
Aged 45 to 54	39.72	119	23.5
Aged 55 to 64	33.92	101	18.6
Aged 65 to 74	35.39	106	12.8
Aged 75 or older	22.45	67	6.6

	AVERAGE HOUSEHOLD SPENDING	BEST CUSTOMERS (index)	BIGGEST CUSTOMERS (market share)
HOUSEHOLD INCOME			
Average household	$33.42	100	100.0%
Under $20,000	24.94	75	15.7
$20,000 to $39,999	27.78	83	18.7
$40,000 to $49,999	27.06	81	7.2
$50,000 to $69,999	34.55	103	14.9
$70,000 to $79,999	50.17	150	8.4
$80,000 to $99,999	42.01	126	11.1
$100,000 or more	43.34	130	24.3
HOUSEHOLD TYPE			
Average household	33.42	100	100.0
Married couples	43.48	130	63.2
Married couples, no children	34.48	103	21.5
Married couples with children	49.67	149	34.9
Oldest child under age 6	26.10	78	3.6
Oldest child aged 6 to 17	57.78	173	20.6
Oldest child aged 18 or older	50.82	152	10.7
Single parent with child under age 18	28.70	86	4.5
Single person	16.67	50	14.8
RACE AND HISPANIC ORIGIN			
Average household	33.42	100	100.0
Asian	30.13	90	3.9
Black	22.98	69	8.6
Hispanic	45.28	135	17.0
Non-Hispanic white and other	33.20	99	74.6
REGION			
Average household	33.42	100	100.0
Northeast	33.23	99	17.9
Midwest	30.41	91	20.2
South	35.57	106	39.6
West	33.03	99	22.3
EDUCATION			
Average household	33.42	100	100.0
Less than high school graduate	38.24	114	14.9
High school graduate	33.41	100	24.9
Some college	32.22	96	19.9
Associate's degree	37.19	111	11.0
Bachelor's degree or more	31.25	94	29.5
Bachelor's degree	28.49	85	17.0
Master's, professional, doctoral degree	35.93	108	12.5

Note: Market shares may not sum to 100.0 because of rounding and missing categories by household type. "Asian" and "black" include Hispanics and non-Hispanics who identify themselves as being of the respective race alone. "Hispanic" includes people of any race who identify themselves as Hispanic. "Other" includes people who identify themselves as non-Hispanic and as Alaska Native, American Indian, Asian (who are also included in the "Asian" row), or Native Hawaiian or other Pacific Islander, as well as non-Hispanics reporting more than one race.
Source: Calculations by New Strategist based on the Bureau of Labor Statistics' 2012 Consumer Expenditure Survey

Ice Cream and Related Products

Best customers: Householders aged 35 to 74
Married couples with school-aged or older children at home

Customer trends: Average household spending on ice cream may continue to fall as the large baby-boom generation ages
and household size shrinks.

Households with children spend the most on ice cream and related products. Married couples with school-aged or older children at home spend 51 to 69 percent more than the average household on this item. Because ice cream is such a commonly purchased item, householders ranging in age from 35 to 75 spend more than average on ice cream.

Average household spending on ice cream and related products fell 24 percent between 2000 and 2012, after adjusting for inflation. Behind the decline was price discounting as private-label brands competed with premium brands in the grocery store. Average household spending on ice cream may continue to fall as the large baby-boom generation ages and household size shrinks.

Table 9.47 Ice cream and related products

Total household spending	$7,137,745,920.00
Average household spends	57.37

AGE OF HOUSEHOLDER	AVERAGE HOUSEHOLD SPENDING	BEST CUSTOMERS (index)	BIGGEST CUSTOMERS (market share)
Average household	$57.37	100	100.0%
Under age 25	36.91	64	4.2
Aged 25 to 34	46.19	81	13.0
Aged 35 to 44	62.96	110	19.1
Aged 45 to 54	69.27	121	23.9
Aged 55 to 64	62.34	109	19.9
Aged 65 to 74	61.75	108	13.0
Aged 75 or older	41.48	72	7.1

	AVERAGE HOUSEHOLD SPENDING	BEST CUSTOMERS (index)	BIGGEST CUSTOMERS (market share)
HOUSEHOLD INCOME			
Average household	$57.37	100	100.0%
Under $20,000	34.85	61	12.8
$20,000 to $39,999	42.28	74	16.6
$40,000 to $49,999	46.75	81	7.2
$50,000 to $69,999	57.06	99	14.4
$70,000 to $79,999	75.09	131	7.3
$80,000 to $99,999	77.64	135	11.9
$100,000 or more	91.07	159	29.7
HOUSEHOLD TYPE			
Average household	57.37	100	100.0
Married couples	76.44	133	64.7
Married couples, no children	62.46	109	22.7
Married couples with children	87.34	152	35.8
Oldest child under age 6	62.96	110	5.0
Oldest child aged 6 to 17	96.93	169	20.1
Oldest child aged 18 or older	86.54	151	10.6
Single parent with child under age 18	49.33	86	4.5
Single person	27.24	47	14.1
RACE AND HISPANIC ORIGIN			
Average household	57.37	100	100.0
Asian	55.05	96	4.2
Black	38.88	68	8.5
Hispanic	53.54	93	11.7
Non-Hispanic white and other	61.19	107	80.1
REGION			
Average household	57.37	100	100.0
Northeast	60.88	106	19.2
Midwest	60.91	106	23.5
South	54.59	95	35.4
West	55.59	97	21.8
EDUCATION			
Average household	57.37	100	100.0
Less than high school graduate	55.32	96	12.6
High school graduate	45.98	80	20.0
Some college	53.38	93	19.2
Associate's degree	65.08	113	11.2
Bachelor's degree or more	67.23	117	37.0
Bachelor's degree	62.46	109	21.7
Master's, professional, doctoral degree	75.29	131	15.2

Note: Market shares may not sum to 100.0 because of rounding and missing categories by household type. "Asian" and "black" include Hispanics and non-Hispanics who identify themselves as being of the respective race alone. "Hispanic" includes people of any race who identify themselves as Hispanic. "Other" includes people who identify themselves as non-Hispanic and as Alaska Native, American Indian, Asian (who are also included in the "Asian" row), or Native Hawaiian or other Pacific Islander, as well as non-Hispanics reporting more than one race.
Source: Calculations by New Strategist based on the Bureau of Labor Statistics' 2012 Consumer Expenditure Survey

Jams, Preserves, and Other Sweets

Best customers: Householders aged 35 to 54
Married couples

Customer trends: Average household spending on jams, preserves, and other sweets is likely to decline as the large baby-boom generation ages and household size shrinks.

Married couples with children at home spend the most on jams, preserves, and other sweets—52 percent more than the average household. Couples without children at home spend 22 percent more than average on this item. Householders aged 35 to 54, most with children at home, spend 13 to 17 percent more than average on jams.

Average household spending on jams, preserves, and other sweets held steady between 2000 and 2006, but increased 13 percent between 2006 and 2012, after adjusting for inflation. One factor behind the increase was more brown-bag lunches as the Great Recession reduced eating out. Average household spending on jams is likely to fall in the years ahead as the large baby-boom generation ages and household size shrinks.

Table 9.48 Jams, preserves, and other sweets

Total household spending	$3,683,957,760.00		
Average household spends	29.61		

AGE OF HOUSEHOLDER	AVERAGE HOUSEHOLD SPENDING	BEST CUSTOMERS (index)	BIGGEST CUSTOMERS (market share)
Average household	$29.61	100	100.0%
Under age 25	17.82	60	3.9
Aged 25 to 34	25.39	86	13.9
Aged 35 to 44	34.55	117	20.3
Aged 45 to 54	33.52	113	22.4
Aged 55 to 64	30.72	104	19.0
Aged 65 to 74	26.29	89	10.7
Aged 75 or older	30.17	102	10.0

	AVERAGE HOUSEHOLD SPENDING	BEST CUSTOMERS (index)	BIGGEST CUSTOMERS (market share)
HOUSEHOLD INCOME			
Average household	**$29.61**	**100**	**100.0%**
Under $20,000	18.06	61	12.8
$20,000 to $39,999	21.73	73	16.5
$40,000 to $49,999	25.57	86	7.6
$50,000 to $69,999	29.05	98	14.2
$70,000 to $79,999	32.50	110	6.1
$80,000 to $99,999	39.96	135	11.9
$100,000 or more	48.70	164	30.8
HOUSEHOLD TYPE			
Average household	**29.61**	**100**	**100.0**
Married couples	40.24	136	66.0
Married couples, no children	35.99	122	25.3
Married couples with children	45.11	152	35.8
Oldest child under age 6	38.09	129	5.9
Oldest child aged 6 to 17	49.56	167	19.9
Oldest child aged 18 or older	42.07	142	10.0
Single parent with child under age 18	22.71	77	4.0
Single person	14.09	48	14.1
RACE AND HISPANIC ORIGIN			
Average household	**29.61**	**100**	**100.0**
Asian	22.48	76	3.3
Black	19.83	67	8.4
Hispanic	22.85	77	9.7
Non-Hispanic white and other	32.40	109	82.1
REGION			
Average household	**29.61**	**100**	**100.0**
Northeast	27.36	92	16.7
Midwest	33.48	113	25.1
South	27.73	94	34.9
West	30.71	104	23.4
EDUCATION			
Average household	**29.61**	**100**	**100.0**
Less than high school graduate	22.83	77	10.1
High school graduate	25.21	85	21.2
Some college	25.52	86	17.7
Associate's degree	30.44	103	10.2
Bachelor's degree or more	38.07	129	40.5
Bachelor's degree	37.17	126	25.0
Master's, professional, doctoral degree	39.60	134	15.5

Note: Market shares may not sum to 100.0 because of rounding and missing categories by household type. "Asian" and "black" include Hispanics and non-Hispanics who identify themselves as being of the respective race alone. "Hispanic" includes people of any race who identify themselves as Hispanic. "Other" includes people who identify themselves as non-Hispanic and as Alaska Native, American Indian, Asian (who are also included in the "Asian" row), or Native Hawaiian or other Pacific Islander, as well as non-Hispanics reporting more than one race.
Source: Calculations by New Strategist based on the Bureau of Labor Statistics' 2012 Consumer Expenditure Survey

Lettuce

Best customers: Householders aged 35 to 74
                       Married couples
                       Asians

Customer trends: Average household spending on lettuce may continue to rise as Americans strive to improve their diet.

Because lettuce is a common purchase, there is little variation in spending on lettuce by household segment. The best customers of lettuce tend to be the largest households. Married couples with school-aged or older children at home spend 39 to 53 percent more than average on this item. Married couples without children at home spend 17 percent more. Householders aged 35 to 54, most with children, spend 12 to 16 percent more than average on lettuce. Spending is average or above average in the 55-to-74 age groups as well. Asians spend 30 percent more than average on lettuce.

Average household spending on lettuce climbed 17 percent between 2000 and 2012, after adjusting for inflation. Among factors behind the growth were the attempt by many Americans to eat a healthier diet and the convenience of bagged lettuce available in the grocery store. Average household spending on lettuce may continue to rise as Americans strive to improve their diet.

Table 9.49 **Lettuce**

Total household spending $4,022,369,280.00
Average household spends   32.33

AGE OF HOUSEHOLDER	AVERAGE HOUSEHOLD SPENDING	BEST CUSTOMERS (index)	BIGGEST CUSTOMERS (market share)
Average household	$32.33	100	100.0%
Under age 25	18.93	59	3.8
Aged 25 to 34	29.73	92	14.9
Aged 35 to 44	36.22	112	19.4
Aged 45 to 54	37.38	116	22.9
Aged 55 to 64	32.37	100	18.3
Aged 65 to 74	34.24	106	12.8
Aged 75 or older	26.24	81	7.9

	AVERAGE HOUSEHOLD SPENDING	BEST CUSTOMERS (index)	BIGGEST CUSTOMERS (market share)
HOUSEHOLD INCOME			
Average household	**$32.33**	**100**	**100.0%**
Under $20,000	19.16	59	12.5
$20,000 to $39,999	23.71	73	16.5
$40,000 to $49,999	28.46	88	7.8
$50,000 to $69,999	33.91	105	15.2
$70,000 to $79,999	45.37	140	7.8
$80,000 to $99,999	37.49	116	10.2
$100,000 or more	51.53	159	29.8
HOUSEHOLD TYPE			
Average household	**32.33**	**100**	**100.0**
Married couples	41.99	130	63.1
Married couples, no children	37.73	117	24.3
Married couples with children	44.94	139	32.7
Oldest child under age 6	37.67	117	5.3
Oldest child aged 6 to 17	44.85	139	16.5
Oldest child aged 18 or older	49.60	153	10.8
Single parent with child under age 18	24.25	75	3.9
Single person	17.54	54	16.1
RACE AND HISPANIC ORIGIN			
Average household	**32.33**	**100**	**100.0**
Asian	41.93	130	5.6
Black	20.89	65	8.1
Hispanic	34.02	105	13.2
Non-Hispanic white and other	34.05	105	79.1
REGION			
Average household	**32.33**	**100**	**100.0**
Northeast	37.28	115	20.8
Midwest	35.34	109	24.2
South	26.84	83	30.9
West	34.42	106	24.0
EDUCATION			
Average household	**32.33**	**100**	**100.0**
Less than high school graduate	27.94	86	11.3
High school graduate	30.36	94	23.4
Some college	28.25	87	18.0
Associate's degree	32.36	100	9.9
Bachelor's degree or more	38.25	118	37.3
Bachelor's degree	37.07	115	22.9
Master's, professional, doctoral degree	40.24	124	14.4

Note: Market shares may not sum to 100.0 because of rounding and missing categories by household type. "Asian" and "black" include Hispanics and non-Hispanics who identify themselves as being of the respective race alone. "Hispanic" includes people of any race who identify themselves as Hispanic. "Other" includes people who identify themselves as non-Hispanic and as Alaska Native, American Indian, Asian (who are also included in the "Asian" row), or Native Hawaiian or other Pacific Islander, as well as non-Hispanics reporting more than one race.
Source: Calculations by New Strategist based on the Bureau of Labor Statistics' 2012 Consumer Expenditure Survey

Lunch Meats (Cold Cuts)

Best customers: Householders aged 35 to 54
Married couples with school-aged or older children at home
Single parents

Customer trends: Average household spending on lunch meats will continue to decline as the small generation X passes through the best-customer lifestage.

The best customers of lunch meats are the largest households. Married couples with school-aged or older children at home spend 53 to 73 percent more than the average household on this item. Householders aged 35 to 54, most with children, spend 20 to 27 percent more than average on lunch meats. Cold cuts are one of the relatively few items on which single parents, with their lower incomes, spend an average amount.

Average household spending on lunch meats fell 5 percent between 2000 and 2006, after adjusting for inflation, then increased by 1 percent from 2006 to 2012. Behind the earlier decline was the substitution of fast food for brown-bag lunches, a pattern that reversed following the Great Recession. Average household spending on lunch meats will continue to decline as the small generation X passes through the best-customer lifestage.

Table 9.50 Lunch meats (cold cuts)

Total household spending $10,852,807,680.00
Average household spends 87.23

	AVERAGE HOUSEHOLD SPENDING	BEST CUSTOMERS (index)	BIGGEST CUSTOMERS (market share)
AGE OF HOUSEHOLDER			
Average household	$87.23	100	100.0%
Under age 25	49.46	57	3.7
Aged 25 to 34	79.71	91	14.8
Aged 35 to 44	110.73	127	22.0
Aged 45 to 54	104.25	120	23.7
Aged 55 to 64	86.42	99	18.1
Aged 65 to 74	80.49	92	11.1
Aged 75 or older	58.13	67	6.5

	AVERAGE HOUSEHOLD SPENDING	BEST CUSTOMERS (index)	BIGGEST CUSTOMERS (market share)
HOUSEHOLD INCOME			
Average household	**$87.23**	**100**	**100.0%**
Under $20,000	50.30	58	12.1
$20,000 to $39,999	68.36	78	17.7
$40,000 to $49,999	82.60	95	8.4
$50,000 to $69,999	86.92	100	14.4
$70,000 to $79,999	117.67	135	7.5
$80,000 to $99,999	107.16	123	10.8
$100,000 or more	134.29	154	28.8
HOUSEHOLD TYPE			
Average household	**87.23**	**100**	**100.0**
Married couples	115.42	132	64.3
Married couples, no children	92.69	106	22.2
Married couples with children	135.87	156	36.6
Oldest child under age 6	100.25	115	5.2
Oldest child aged 6 to 17	150.75	173	20.6
Oldest child aged 18 or older	133.22	153	10.8
Single parent with child under age 18	87.03	100	5.2
Single person	44.41	51	15.1
RACE AND HISPANIC ORIGIN			
Average household	**87.23**	**100**	**100.0**
Asian	61.82	71	3.1
Black	56.99	65	8.2
Hispanic	83.96	96	12.1
Non-Hispanic white and other	92.95	107	80.0
REGION			
Average household	**87.23**	**100**	**100.0**
Northeast	98.89	113	20.5
Midwest	94.43	108	24.0
South	78.70	90	33.6
West	84.71	97	21.9
EDUCATION			
Average household	**87.23**	**100**	**100.0**
Less than high school graduate	76.99	88	11.5
High school graduate	81.97	94	23.4
Some college	76.29	87	18.0
Associate's degree	93.54	107	10.6
Bachelor's degree or more	100.54	115	36.3
Bachelor's degree	106.93	123	24.4
Master's, professional, doctoral degree	89.72	103	11.9

Note: Market shares may not sum to 100.0 because of rounding and missing categories by household type. "Asian" and "black" include Hispanics and non-Hispanics who identify themselves as being of the respective race alone. "Hispanic" includes people of any race who identify themselves as Hispanic. "Other" includes people who identify themselves as non-Hispanic and as Alaska Native, American Indian, Asian (who are also included in the "Asian" row), or Native Hawaiian or other Pacific Islander, as well as non-Hispanics reporting more than one race.
Source: Calculations by New Strategist based on the Bureau of Labor Statistics' 2012 Consumer Expenditure Survey

Margarine

Best customers: **Householders aged 65 or older**
                        Married couples without children at home
                        Married couples with school-aged children
                        Single parents
                        Households in the Midwest

Customer trends: **Average household spending on margarine may depend more on marketing than demographics in the years ahead.**

Margarine's fortunes have been waning as the reputation of butter improved. In 2000, the average household spent 68 percent as much on margarine as on butter. By 2012, the figure had fallen to 34 percent. Some of the best customers of margarine are the oldest consumers. Householders aged 65 or older spend 15 to 25 percent more than average on margarine. Married couples without children at home (most of them older empty-nesters) spend 15 percent more than the average household on this item. Couples with school-aged children spend 47 percent more than average on margarine. Single parents, whose spending approaches average on only a few items, spend 29 percent more. Households in the Midwest spend 35 percent more than average on margarine.

Average household spending on margarine fell 44 percent between 2000 and 2012, after adjusting for inflation. Behind the downward slide were health warnings about transfats in margarine and the improving reputation of butter. Average household spending on margarine may depend more on marketing than demographics in the years ahead.

Table 9.51 Margarine

Total household spending	$1,087,395,840.00
Average household spends	8.74

AGE OF HOUSEHOLDER	AVERAGE HOUSEHOLD SPENDING	BEST CUSTOMERS (index)	BIGGEST CUSTOMERS (market share)
Average household	$8.74	100	100.0%
Under age 25	7.40	85	5.6
Aged 25 to 34	6.40	73	11.8
Aged 35 to 44	9.96	114	19.8
Aged 45 to 54	8.38	96	19.0
Aged 55 to 64	8.60	98	18.0
Aged 65 to 74	10.01	115	13.8
Aged 75 or older	10.95	125	12.2

	AVERAGE HOUSEHOLD SPENDING	BEST CUSTOMERS (index)	BIGGEST CUSTOMERS (market share)
HOUSEHOLD INCOME			
Average household	**$8.74**	**100**	**100.0%**
Under $20,000	7.35	84	17.7
$20,000 to $39,999	7.73	88	19.9
$40,000 to $49,999	6.28	72	6.4
$50,000 to $69,999	10.45	120	17.3
$70,000 to $79,999	11.54	132	7.4
$80,000 to $99,999	9.23	106	9.3
$100,000 or more	10.42	119	22.3
HOUSEHOLD TYPE			
Average household	**8.74**	**100**	**100.0**
Married couples	10.19	117	56.6
Married couples, no children	10.07	115	24.0
Married couples with children	10.07	115	27.1
Oldest child under age 6	5.99	69	3.1
Oldest child aged 6 to 17	12.88	147	17.5
Oldest child aged 18 or older	7.91	91	6.4
Single parent with child under age 18	11.24	129	6.7
Single person	4.41	50	15.0
RACE AND HISPANIC ORIGIN			
Average household	**8.74**	**100**	**100.0**
Asian	4.93	56	2.4
Black	8.61	99	12.4
Hispanic	7.17	82	10.3
Non-Hispanic white and other	9.01	103	77.4
REGION			
Average household	**8.74**	**100**	**100.0**
Northeast	10.06	115	20.8
Midwest	11.79	135	29.9
South	7.24	83	30.9
West	7.13	82	18.4
EDUCATION			
Average household	**8.74**	**100**	**100.0**
Less than high school graduate	9.18	105	13.7
High school graduate	8.87	101	25.3
Some college	8.37	96	19.7
Associate's degree	12.07	138	13.6
Bachelor's degree or more	7.69	88	27.7
Bachelor's degree	7.10	81	16.2
Master's, professional, doctoral degree	8.70	100	11.6

Note: Market shares may not sum to 100.0 because of rounding and missing categories by household type. "Asian" and "black" include Hispanics and non-Hispanics who identify themselves as being of the respective race alone. "Hispanic" includes people of any race who identify themselves as Hispanic. "Other" includes people who identify themselves as non-Hispanic and as Alaska Native, American Indian, Asian (who are also included in the "Asian" row), or Native Hawaiian or other Pacific Islander, as well as non-Hispanics reporting more than one race.
Source: Calculations by New Strategist based on the Bureau of Labor Statistics' 2012 Consumer Expenditure Survey

Milk, Fresh

Best customers: Householders aged 35 to 54
Married couples with children at home
Asians and Hispanics

Customer trends: Average household spending on milk is unlikely to grow much in the years ahead because the small generation X is in the best customer lifestage.

The best customers of milk are the largest households. Married couples with children at home spend 58 percent more than the average household on milk. Householders aged 35 to 54, most with children, spend 19 to 27 percent more than average on milk. Hispanics, who have the largest households, spend 27 percent more than average, while Asians spend 25 percent more.

Average household spending on milk purchased at grocery or convenience stores declined 20 percent between 2000 and 2010, after adjusting for inflation, as the large baby-boom generation exited the best-customer lifestage and was replaced by the small generation X. From 2010 to 2012, however, average household spending on fresh milk stabilized, rising 1 percent. Average household spending on milk is unlikely to grow much in the years ahead because the small generation X is in the best customer lifestage.

Table 9.52 Milk, fresh

Total household spending $15,960,084,480.00
Average household spends   128.28

	AVERAGE HOUSEHOLD SPENDING	BEST CUSTOMERS (index)	BIGGEST CUSTOMERS (market share)
AGE OF HOUSEHOLDER			
Average household	**$128.28**	**100**	**100.0%**
Under age 25	88.89	69	4.5
Aged 25 to 34	129.01	101	16.3
Aged 35 to 44	162.73	127	22.0
Aged 45 to 54	152.50	119	23.5
Aged 55 to 64	117.35	91	16.7
Aged 65 to 74	101.83	79	9.6
Aged 75 or older	94.21	73	7.2

	AVERAGE HOUSEHOLD SPENDING	BEST CUSTOMERS (index)	BIGGEST CUSTOMERS (market share)
HOUSEHOLD INCOME			
Average household	**$128.28**	**100**	**100.0%**
Under $20,000	87.93	69	14.4
$20,000 to $39,999	108.80	85	19.1
$40,000 to $49,999	118.36	92	8.2
$50,000 to $69,999	128.43	100	14.5
$70,000 to $79,999	164.55	128	7.2
$80,000 to $99,999	157.02	122	10.8
$100,000 or more	176.59	138	25.8
HOUSEHOLD TYPE			
Average household	**128.28**	**100**	**100.0**
Married couples	166.88	130	63.2
Married couples, no children	120.59	94	19.6
Married couples with children	203.11	158	37.2
Oldest child under age 6	197.74	154	7.0
Oldest child aged 6 to 17	212.58	166	19.7
Oldest child aged 18 or older	190.65	149	10.5
Single parent with child under age 18	124.72	97	5.1
Single person	65.23	51	15.1
RACE AND HISPANIC ORIGIN			
Average household	**128.28**	**100**	**100.0**
Asian	160.78	125	5.4
Black	85.31	67	8.4
Hispanic	162.35	127	15.9
Non-Hispanic white and other	129.85	101	76.0
REGION			
Average household	**128.28**	**100**	**100.0**
Northeast	122.68	96	17.3
Midwest	120.64	94	20.9
South	130.01	101	37.7
West	137.60	107	24.2
EDUCATION			
Average household	**128.28**	**100**	**100.0**
Less than high school graduate	120.85	94	12.3
High school graduate	125.99	98	24.5
Some college	114.52	89	18.4
Associate's degree	133.75	104	10.3
Bachelor's degree or more	140.40	109	34.5
Bachelor's degree	138.95	108	21.6
Master's, professional, doctoral degree	142.86	111	12.9

Note: Market shares may not sum to 100.0 because of rounding and missing categories by household type. "Asian" and "black" include Hispanics and non-Hispanics who identify themselves as being of the respective race alone. "Hispanic" includes people of any race who identify themselves as Hispanic. "Other" includes people who identify themselves as non-Hispanic and as Alaska Native, American Indian, Asian (who are also included in the "Asian" row), or Native Hawaiian or other Pacific Islander, as well as non-Hispanics reporting more than one race.
Source: Calculations by New Strategist based on the Bureau of Labor Statistics' 2012 Consumer Expenditure Survey

Nondairy Cream and Imitation Milk

Best customers: Householders aged 45 to 54
Married couples with children at home

Customer trends: Average household spending on nondairy cream and imitation milk may continue to rise in the years ahead as soy products become more commonly consumed.

Older householders and the largest households are the biggest spenders on nondairy cream and imitation milk. Married couples with children at home spend 42 percent more than average on this item, the figure peaking at 80 percent above average among couples with adult children at home. Householders aged 45 to 54, many with (adult) children at home, spend 33 percent more than average on nondairy cream and imitation milk.

Average household spending on nondairy cream and imitation milk grew by an enormous 52 percent between 2000 and 2012, after adjusting for inflation. Behind the increase was the growing popularity of soy products. Average household spending on nondairy cream and imitation milk may continue to rise in the years ahead as soy products become more commonly consumed.

Table 9.53 Nondairy cream and imitation milk

Total household spending $2,312,893,440.00
Average household spends   18.59

AGE OF HOUSEHOLDER	AVERAGE HOUSEHOLD SPENDING	BEST CUSTOMERS (index)	BIGGEST CUSTOMERS (market share)
Average household	$18.59	100	100.0%
Under age 25	12.06	65	4.3
Aged 25 to 34	15.84	85	13.8
Aged 35 to 44	19.98	107	18.7
Aged 45 to 54	24.73	133	26.3
Aged 55 to 64	19.43	105	19.1
Aged 65 to 74	16.82	90	10.9
Aged 75 or older	13.29	71	7.0

	AVERAGE HOUSEHOLD SPENDING	BEST CUSTOMERS (index)	BIGGEST CUSTOMERS (market share)
HOUSEHOLD INCOME			
Average household	**$18.59**	**100**	**100.0%**
Under $20,000	12.05	65	13.6
$20,000 to $39,999	14.57	78	17.7
$40,000 to $49,999	21.85	118	10.4
$50,000 to $69,999	20.34	109	15.8
$70,000 to $79,999	23.83	128	7.2
$80,000 to $99,999	18.27	98	8.7
$100,000 or more	26.10	140	26.3
HOUSEHOLD TYPE			
Average household	**18.59**	**100**	**100.0**
Married couples	23.03	124	60.2
Married couples, no children	19.07	103	21.4
Married couples with children	26.43	142	33.4
Oldest child under age 6	22.93	123	5.6
Oldest child aged 6 to 17	23.51	126	15.0
Oldest child aged 18 or older	33.48	180	12.7
Single parent with child under age 18	17.25	93	4.9
Single person	9.40	51	15.0
RACE AND HISPANIC ORIGIN			
Average household	**18.59**	**100**	**100.0**
Asian	15.23	82	3.6
Black	11.98	64	8.1
Hispanic	16.42	88	11.1
Non-Hispanic white and other	20.09	108	81.1
REGION			
Average household	**18.59**	**100**	**100.0**
Northeast	19.95	107	19.4
Midwest	18.17	98	21.7
South	16.92	91	33.9
West	20.68	111	25.1
EDUCATION			
Average household	**18.59**	**100**	**100.0**
Less than high school graduate	16.53	89	11.6
High school graduate	19.23	103	25.8
Some college	20.38	110	22.6
Associate's degree	19.57	105	10.4
Bachelor's degree or more	17.35	93	29.4
Bachelor's degree	17.75	95	19.0
Master's, professional, doctoral degree	16.68	90	10.4

Note: Market shares may not sum to 100.0 because of rounding and missing categories by household type. "Asian" and "black" include Hispanics and non-Hispanics who identify themselves as being of the respective race alone. "Hispanic" includes people of any race who identify themselves as Hispanic. "Other" includes people who identify themselves as non-Hispanic and as Alaska Native, American Indian, Asian (who are also included in the "Asian" row), or Native Hawaiian or other Pacific Islander, as well as non-Hispanics reporting more than one race.
Source: Calculations by New Strategist based on the Bureau of Labor Statistics' 2012 Consumer Expenditure Survey

Nuts

Older Americans are the biggest spenders on nuts. Householders ranging in age from 45 to 74 spend 16 to 43 percent more than the average household on nuts and control 62 percent of the market. Married couples without children at home (most of them older) spend 56 percent more than average on nuts, while those with school-aged or older children at home (the largest households) spend 32 to 43 percent more.

Average household spending on nuts increased 52 percent between 2000 and 2012, after adjusting for inflation. Behind the increase was the aging of the baby-boom generation into the best-customer age groups, as well as the increased attention to the health benefits of nut consumption. Average household spending on nuts should continue to climb as boomers age.

Table 9.54 **Nuts**

Total household spending	$5,269,017,600.00		
Average household spends	42.35		

AGE OF HOUSEHOLDER	AVERAGE HOUSEHOLD SPENDING	BEST CUSTOMERS (index)	BIGGEST CUSTOMERS (market share)
Average household	$42.35	100	100.0%
Under age 25	23.37	55	3.6
Aged 25 to 34	30.24	71	11.5
Aged 35 to 44	39.57	93	16.2
Aged 45 to 54	51.08	121	23.9
Aged 55 to 64	49.13	116	21.2
Aged 65 to 74	60.36	143	17.2
Aged 75 or older	28.69	68	6.6

	AVERAGE HOUSEHOLD SPENDING	BEST CUSTOMERS (index)	BIGGEST CUSTOMERS (market share)
HOUSEHOLD INCOME			
Average household	**$42.35**	**100**	**100.0%**
Under $20,000	19.28	46	9.6
$20,000 to $39,999	27.13	64	14.4
$40,000 to $49,999	39.90	94	8.3
$50,000 to $69,999	38.89	92	13.3
$70,000 to $79,999	58.24	138	7.7
$80,000 to $99,999	60.32	142	12.6
$100,000 or more	76.78	181	33.9
HOUSEHOLD TYPE			
Average household	**42.35**	**100**	**100.0**
Married couples	59.22	140	67.9
Married couples, no children	65.90	156	32.4
Married couples with children	54.77	129	30.4
Oldest child under age 6	42.91	101	4.6
Oldest child aged 6 to 17	55.85	132	15.7
Oldest child aged 18 or older	60.35	143	10.1
Single parent with child under age 18	23.03	54	2.9
Single person	23.04	54	16.2
RACE AND HISPANIC ORIGIN			
Average household	**42.35**	**100**	**100.0**
Asian	48.42	114	5.0
Black	19.11	45	5.7
Hispanic	29.10	69	8.6
Non-Hispanic white and other	48.49	114	85.9
REGION			
Average household	**42.35**	**100**	**100.0**
Northeast	47.19	111	20.1
Midwest	43.05	102	22.5
South	37.62	89	33.1
West	45.55	108	24.2
EDUCATION			
Average household	**42.35**	**100**	**100.0**
Less than high school graduate	25.72	61	7.9
High school graduate	28.19	67	16.6
Some college	33.63	79	16.4
Associate's degree	39.72	94	9.3
Bachelor's degree or more	66.24	156	49.3
Bachelor's degree	57.53	136	27.1
Master's, professional, doctoral degree	80.95	191	22.2

Note: Market shares may not sum to 100.0 because of rounding and missing categories by household type. "Asian" and "black" include Hispanics and non-Hispanics who identify themselves as being of the respective race alone. "Hispanic" includes people of any race who identify themselves as Hispanic. "Other" includes people who identify themselves as non-Hispanic and as Alaska Native, American Indian, Asian (who are also included in the "Asian" row), or Native Hawaiian or other Pacific Islander, as well as non-Hispanics reporting more than one race.
Source: Calculations by New Strategist based on the Bureau of Labor Statistics' 2012 Consumer Expenditure Survey

Olives, Pickles, and Relishes

Best customers: Householders aged 45 to 64
                       Married couples without children at home
                       Married couples with school-aged or older children at home
                       Households in the Midwest and West

Customer trends: Average household spending on olives, pickles, and relishes should stabilize now that boomers
                       have filled the best-customer age groups.

The best customers of olives, pickles, and relishes are the largest households and older householders. Married couples with school-aged children spend 39 percent more than the average household on this item, and those with adult children at home spend 68 percent more. Married couples without children at home, most of them older empty-nesters, outspend the average by one-quarter. Householders aged 45 to 64 spend 19 to 21 percent more than average on olives, pickles, and relishes. Households in the Midwest spend 16 percent more than average, and those in the West spend 12 percent more.

Average household spending on olives, pickles, and relishes increased 34 percent between 2000 and 2012, after adjusting for inflation. Behind the increase is the greater availability of fresh olives and relishes in grocery stores. Average household spending on olives, pickles, and relishes should stabilize now that boomers have filled the best-customer age groups.

Table 9.55 Olives, pickles, and relishes

Total household spending $2,172,303,360.00
Average household spends   17.46

AGE OF HOUSEHOLDER	AVERAGE HOUSEHOLD SPENDING	BEST CUSTOMERS (index)	BIGGEST CUSTOMERS (market share)
Average household	$17.46	100	100.0%
Under age 25	9.32	53	3.5
Aged 25 to 34	13.70	78	12.7
Aged 35 to 44	17.73	102	17.6
Aged 45 to 54	20.84	119	23.6
Aged 55 to 64	21.12	121	22.1
Aged 65 to 74	19.26	110	13.3
Aged 75 or older	13.11	75	7.3

	AVERAGE HOUSEHOLD SPENDING	BEST CUSTOMERS (index)	BIGGEST CUSTOMERS (market share)
HOUSEHOLD INCOME			
Average household	$17.46	100	100.0%
Under $20,000	9.55	55	11.5
$20,000 to $39,999	13.07	75	16.9
$40,000 to $49,999	13.67	78	6.9
$50,000 to $69,999	19.63	112	16.2
$70,000 to $79,999	24.52	140	7.8
$80,000 to $99,999	24.37	140	12.3
$100,000 or more	26.43	151	28.3
HOUSEHOLD TYPE			
Average household	17.46	100	100.0
Married couples	23.10	132	64.3
Married couples, no children	21.84	125	26.1
Married couples with children	24.64	141	33.2
Oldest child under age 6	18.39	105	4.8
Oldest child aged 6 to 17	24.19	139	16.5
Oldest child aged 18 or older	29.30	168	11.8
Single parent with child under age 18	12.36	71	3.7
Single person	9.57	55	16.3
RACE AND HISPANIC ORIGIN			
Average household	17.46	100	100.0
Asian	8.48	49	2.1
Black	10.94	63	7.9
Hispanic	11.77	67	8.5
Non-Hispanic white and other	19.49	112	83.8
REGION			
Average household	17.46	100	100.0
Northeast	15.57	89	16.1
Midwest	20.21	116	25.7
South	15.44	88	32.9
West	19.57	112	25.3
EDUCATION			
Average household	17.46	100	100.0
Less than high school graduate	10.53	60	7.9
High school graduate	14.52	83	20.7
Some college	17.60	101	20.8
Associate's degree	18.13	104	10.3
Bachelor's degree or more	22.01	126	39.8
Bachelor's degree	21.31	122	24.3
Master's, professional, doctoral degree	23.21	133	15.4

Note: Market shares may not sum to 100.0 because of rounding and missing categories by household type. "Asian" and "black" include Hispanics and non-Hispanics who identify themselves as being of the respective race alone. "Hispanic" includes people of any race who identify themselves as Hispanic. "Other" includes people who identify themselves as non-Hispanic and as Alaska Native, American Indian, Asian (who are also included in the "Asian" row), or Native Hawaiian or other Pacific Islander, as well as non-Hispanics reporting more than one race.
Source: Calculations by New Strategist based on the Bureau of Labor Statistics' 2012 Consumer Expenditure Survey

Oranges

Best customers: Householders aged 35 to 54
Married couples with school-aged or older children at home
Asians and Hispanics
Households in the Northeast and West

Customer trends: Average household spending on oranges may continue to rise due to the growth of the Asian and Hispanic populations, but the presence of the small generation X in the best-customer lifestage may limit gains.

The biggest spenders on oranges are the largest households. Married couples with school-aged or older children at home spend 70 to 74 percent more than average on oranges. Householders aged 35 to 54, many with children at home, spend 23 to 29 percent more than average on oranges. Asians spend 48 percent more than average. Hispanics, who have the largest families, spend 22 percent more. Households in the Northeast spend 14 percent more than average on oranges, and those in the West spend 11 percent more.

Average household spending on oranges grew 6 percent between 2000 and 2012, after adjusting for inflation. Behind the increase was the rapid growth in the Asian and Hispanic populations. Spending on oranges may continue to rise due to the ongoing increase in those populations, but the presence of the small generation X in the best-customer lifestage may limit gains.

Table 9.56 Oranges

Total household spending $3,326,883,840.00
Average household spends 26.74

AGE OF HOUSEHOLDER	AVERAGE HOUSEHOLD SPENDING	BEST CUSTOMERS (index)	BIGGEST CUSTOMERS (market share)
Average household	$26.74	100	100.0%
Under age 25	19.10	71	4.7
Aged 25 to 34	21.41	80	12.9
Aged 35 to 44	34.47	129	22.4
Aged 45 to 54	32.91	123	24.4
Aged 55 to 64	25.19	94	17.2
Aged 65 to 74	26.34	99	11.9
Aged 75 or older	17.61	66	6.4

	AVERAGE HOUSEHOLD SPENDING	BEST CUSTOMERS (index)	BIGGEST CUSTOMERS (market share)
HOUSEHOLD INCOME			
Average household	**$26.74**	**100**	**100.0%**
Under $20,000	12.93	48	10.2
$20,000 to $39,999	20.45	76	17.2
$40,000 to $49,999	21.82	82	7.2
$50,000 to $69,999	27.92	104	15.1
$70,000 to $79,999	30.32	113	6.3
$80,000 to $99,999	38.57	144	12.7
$100,000 or more	44.47	166	31.1
HOUSEHOLD TYPE			
Average household	**26.74**	**100**	**100.0**
Married couples	36.45	136	66.2
Married couples, no children	29.74	111	23.2
Married couples with children	42.44	159	37.3
Oldest child under age 6	26.93	101	4.6
Oldest child aged 6 to 17	46.43	174	20.7
Oldest child aged 18 or older	45.45	170	12.0
Single parent with child under age 18	22.48	84	4.4
Single person	12.06	45	13.4
RACE AND HISPANIC ORIGIN			
Average household	**26.74**	**100**	**100.0**
Asian	39.52	148	6.4
Black	21.07	79	9.9
Hispanic	32.72	122	15.3
Non-Hispanic white and other	26.66	100	74.8
REGION			
Average household	**26.74**	**100**	**100.0**
Northeast	30.55	114	20.6
Midwest	28.12	105	23.3
South	22.27	83	31.0
West	29.70	111	25.0
EDUCATION			
Average household	**26.74**	**100**	**100.0**
Less than high school graduate	24.55	92	12.0
High school graduate	23.78	89	22.2
Some college	23.66	88	18.2
Associate's degree	28.77	108	10.6
Bachelor's degree or more	31.28	117	36.9
Bachelor's degree	30.11	113	22.4
Master's, professional, doctoral degree	33.27	124	14.4

Note: Market shares may not sum to 100.0 because of rounding and missing categories by household type. "Asian" and "black" include Hispanics and non-Hispanics who identify themselves as being of the respective race alone. "Hispanic" includes people of any race who identify themselves as Hispanic. "Other" includes people who identify themselves as non-Hispanic and as Alaska Native, American Indian, Asian (who are also included in the "Asian" row), or Native Hawaiian or other Pacific Islander, as well as non-Hispanics reporting more than one race.
Source: Calculations by New Strategist based on the Bureau of Labor Statistics' 2012 Consumer Expenditure Survey

Pasta, Cornmeal, and Other Cereal Products

Best customers: Householders aged 35 to 54
                       Married couples with school-aged or older children at home
                       Asians
                       Households in the Northeast and West

Customer trends: Average household spending on pasta should resume its decline as the baby-boom generation
                        ages and household size shrinks.

The biggest spenders on pasta, cornmeal, and other cereal products are households with children. Married couples with children at home spend 47 percent more than the average household on this item. Householders aged 35 to 54, most with children at home, spend one-quarter more than average on pasta. Asians spend 50 percent more. Households in the Northeast spend 16 percent more than average on pasta, and those in the West spend 14 percent more.

Average household spending on pasta, cornmeal, and other cereal products fell 28 percent between 2000 and 2006, after adjusting for inflation, then grew 34 percent between 2006 and 2012. Behind the decline was the growing propensity of consumers to eat out rather than cook a meal at home. Efforts at belt tightening and a renewed surge of home cooking may have been responsible for the ensuing rise in average household spending on pasta. Average household spending on pasta should resume its decline as the baby-boom generation ages and household size shrinks.

Table 9.57 Pasta, cornmeal, and other cereal products

Total household spending $4,600,903,680.00
Average household spends   36.98

AGE OF HOUSEHOLDER	AVERAGE HOUSEHOLD SPENDING	BEST CUSTOMERS (index)	BIGGEST CUSTOMERS (market share)
Average household	$36.98	100	100.0%
Under age 25	27.23	74	4.8
Aged 25 to 34	37.07	100	16.2
Aged 35 to 44	46.21	125	21.7
Aged 45 to 54	46.48	126	24.9
Aged 55 to 64	32.02	87	15.8
Aged 65 to 74	29.04	79	9.5
Aged 75 or older	25.98	70	6.9

	AVERAGE HOUSEHOLD SPENDING	BEST CUSTOMERS (index)	BIGGEST CUSTOMERS (market share)
HOUSEHOLD INCOME			
Average household	**$36.98**	**100**	**100.0%**
Under $20,000	24.19	65	13.8
$20,000 to $39,999	28.20	76	17.2
$40,000 to $49,999	29.59	80	7.1
$50,000 to $69,999	33.85	92	13.2
$70,000 to $79,999	51.79	140	7.8
$80,000 to $99,999	48.17	130	11.5
$100,000 or more	58.45	158	29.6
HOUSEHOLD TYPE			
Average household	**36.98**	**100**	**100.0**
Married couples	47.11	127	61.9
Married couples, no children	35.63	96	20.1
Married couples with children	54.39	147	34.6
Oldest child under age 6	40.51	110	5.0
Oldest child aged 6 to 17	58.81	159	18.9
Oldest child aged 18 or older	55.69	151	10.6
Single parent with child under age 18	32.45	88	4.6
Single person	19.70	53	15.8
RACE AND HISPANIC ORIGIN			
Average household	**36.98**	**100**	**100.0**
Asian	55.51	150	6.5
Black	29.33	79	10.0
Hispanic	33.09	89	11.2
Non-Hispanic white and other	38.92	105	79.0
REGION			
Average household	**36.98**	**100**	**100.0**
Northeast	42.77	116	20.9
Midwest	38.25	103	22.9
South	30.22	82	30.4
West	42.22	114	25.7
EDUCATION			
Average household	**36.98**	**100**	**100.0**
Less than high school graduate	29.75	80	10.5
High school graduate	33.79	91	22.8
Some college	31.87	86	17.7
Associate's degree	39.17	106	10.5
Bachelor's degree or more	44.91	121	38.3
Bachelor's degree	43.34	117	23.4
Master's, professional, doctoral degree	47.56	129	14.9

Note: Market shares may not sum to 100.0 because of rounding and missing categories by household type. "Asian" and "black" include Hispanics and non-Hispanics who identify themselves as being of the respective race alone. "Hispanic" includes people of any race who identify themselves as Hispanic. "Other" includes people who identify themselves as non-Hispanic and as Alaska Native, American Indian, Asian (who are also included in the "Asian" row), or Native Hawaiian or other Pacific Islander, as well as non-Hispanics reporting more than one race.
Source: Calculations by New Strategist based on the Bureau of Labor Statistics' 2012 Consumer Expenditure Survey

Peanut Butter

Best customers: Householders aged 35 to 54
Married couples with children at home
Single parents
Households in the Midwest

Customer trends: Average household spending on peanut butter may decline because the small generation X
is in the best-customer lifestage.

Married couples with children at home spend the most on peanut butter, 75 percent more than average. The figure peaks among those with adult children at home at 93 percent above average. Householders aged 35 to 54, most with children, spend 26 to 34 percent more than the average household on peanut butter. Single parents, whose spending approaches average on only a few items, surpass the average on peanut butter by 17 percent. Households in the Midwest spend 15 percent more than average on this item.

Average household spending on peanut butter fell 19 percent between 2000 and 2006, after adjusting for inflation, then rebounded 46 percent between 2006 and 2012. Behind the rebound was belt tightening by parents who substituted homemade sandwiches for school-bought meals in an effort to cut costs. Average household spending on peanut butter may decline because the small generation X is in the best-customer lifestage.

Table 9.58 Peanut butter

Total household spending $2,324,090,880.00
Average household spends   18.68

	AVERAGE HOUSEHOLD SPENDING	BEST CUSTOMERS (index)	BIGGEST CUSTOMERS (market share)
AGE OF HOUSEHOLDER			
Average household	**$18.68**	**100**	**100.0%**
Under age 25	11.37	61	4.0
Aged 25 to 34	16.10	86	13.9
Aged 35 to 44	24.97	134	23.2
Aged 45 to 54	23.62	126	25.0
Aged 55 to 64	16.98	91	16.6
Aged 65 to 74	16.74	90	10.8
Aged 75 or older	12.04	64	6.3

	AVERAGE HOUSEHOLD SPENDING	BEST CUSTOMERS (index)	BIGGEST CUSTOMERS (market share)
HOUSEHOLD INCOME			
Average household	**$18.68**	**100**	**100.0%**
Under $20,000	9.87	53	11.1
$20,000 to $39,999	15.59	83	18.8
$40,000 to $49,999	18.32	98	8.7
$50,000 to $69,999	18.45	99	14.3
$70,000 to $79,999	24.56	131	7.3
$80,000 to $99,999	18.27	98	8.6
$100,000 or more	30.54	163	30.6
HOUSEHOLD TYPE			
Average household	**18.68**	**100**	**100.0**
Married couples	24.78	133	64.4
Married couples, no children	16.45	88	18.4
Married couples with children	32.68	175	41.1
Oldest child under age 6	25.46	136	6.2
Oldest child aged 6 to 17	33.33	178	21.2
Oldest child aged 18 or older	36.09	193	13.6
Single parent with child under age 18	21.77	117	6.1
Single person	9.71	52	15.4
RACE AND HISPANIC ORIGIN			
Average household	**18.68**	**100**	**100.0**
Asian	15.09	81	3.5
Black	11.54	62	7.8
Hispanic	15.50	83	10.4
Non-Hispanic white and other	20.46	110	82.2
REGION			
Average household	**18.68**	**100**	**100.0**
Northeast	18.65	100	18.0
Midwest	21.53	115	25.6
South	16.46	88	32.8
West	19.55	105	23.6
EDUCATION			
Average household	**18.68**	**100**	**100.0**
Less than high school graduate	13.18	71	9.2
High school graduate	14.71	79	19.6
Some college	16.21	87	17.9
Associate's degree	23.77	127	12.6
Bachelor's degree or more	23.89	128	40.3
Bachelor's degree	24.08	129	25.7
Master's, professional, doctoral degree	23.57	126	14.6

Note: Market shares may not sum to 100.0 because of rounding and missing categories by household type. "Asian" and "black" include Hispanics and non-Hispanics who identify themselves as being of the respective race alone. "Hispanic" includes people of any race who identify themselves as Hispanic. "Other" includes people who identify themselves as non-Hispanic and as Alaska Native, American Indian, Asian (who are also included in the "Asian" row), or Native Hawaiian or other Pacific Islander, as well as non-Hispanics reporting more than one race.
Source: Calculations by New Strategist based on the Bureau of Labor Statistics' 2012 Consumer Expenditure Survey

Pies, Tarts, and Turnovers

Best customers: Householders aged 35 to 54 and 65 to 74
Married couples with school-aged or older children at home
Households in the Northeast

Customer trends: Average household spending on pies, tarts, and turnovers is likely to continueto decline
because the small generation X is in the best-customer lifestage.

The best customers of pies, tarts, and turnovers are households with children. Married couples with school-aged or older children at home spend 39 to 65 percent more than average on pies. Householders aged 35 to 54, many with children, spend 21 to 23 percent more than average on this item and control 45 percent of the market. Householders aged 65 to 74 spend 25 percent more than average on pies, tarts, and turnovers. Households in the Northeast spend 16 percent more.

Average household spending on pies, tarts, and turnovers fell 25 percent between 2000 and 2012, after adjusting for inflation. Behind the decline is the substitution of other snack categories for this one and the propensity to buy snacks from restaurants rather than grocery stores. Spending on pies, tarts, and turnovers is likely to continue to decline because the small generation X is in the best-customer lifestage.

Table 9.59 Pies, tarts, and turnovers

Total household spending $1,668,418,560.00
Average household spends   13.41

AGE OF HOUSEHOLDER	AVERAGE HOUSEHOLD SPENDING	BEST CUSTOMERS (index)	BIGGEST CUSTOMERS (market share)
Average household	$13.41	100	100.0%
Under age 25	6.78	51	3.3
Aged 25 to 34	9.43	70	11.4
Aged 35 to 44	16.23	121	21.0
Aged 45 to 54	16.50	123	24.4
Aged 55 to 64	12.49	93	17.0
Aged 65 to 74	16.81	125	15.1
Aged 75 or older	10.87	81	7.9

	AVERAGE HOUSEHOLD SPENDING	BEST CUSTOMERS (index)	BIGGEST CUSTOMERS (market share)
HOUSEHOLD INCOME			
Average household	**$13.41**	**100**	**100.0%**
Under $20,000	8.38	62	13.1
$20,000 to $39,999	11.44	85	19.2
$40,000 to $49,999	9.95	74	6.6
$50,000 to $69,999	16.86	126	18.2
$70,000 to $79,999	17.52	131	7.3
$80,000 to $99,999	19.11	143	12.6
$100,000 or more	16.49	123	23.0
HOUSEHOLD TYPE			
Average household	**13.41**	**100**	**100.0**
Married couples	16.95	126	61.4
Married couples, no children	12.41	93	19.3
Married couples with children	19.55	146	34.3
Oldest child under age 6	14.27	106	4.9
Oldest child aged 6 to 17	22.10	165	19.6
Oldest child aged 18 or older	18.59	139	9.8
Single parent with child under age 18	13.01	97	5.1
Single person	7.95	59	17.6
RACE AND HISPANIC ORIGIN			
Average household	**13.41**	**100**	**100.0**
Asian	13.74	102	4.4
Black	9.92	74	9.3
Hispanic	9.42	70	8.8
Non-Hispanic white and other	14.64	109	81.9
REGION			
Average household	**13.41**	**100**	**100.0**
Northeast	15.61	116	21.0
Midwest	12.83	96	21.2
South	12.70	95	35.3
West	13.39	100	22.5
EDUCATION			
Average household	**13.41**	**100**	**100.0**
Less than high school graduate	7.07	53	6.9
High school graduate	15.30	114	28.4
Some college	11.11	83	17.1
Associate's degree	15.43	115	11.4
Bachelor's degree or more	15.25	114	35.9
Bachelor's degree	14.02	105	20.8
Master's, professional, doctoral degree	17.34	129	15.0

Note: Market shares may not sum to 100.0 because of rounding and missing categories by household type. "Asian" and "black" include Hispanics and non-Hispanics who identify themselves as being of the respective race alone. "Hispanic" includes people of any race who identify themselves as Hispanic. "Other" includes people who identify themselves as non-Hispanic and as Alaska Native, American Indian, Asian (who are also included in the "Asian" row), or Native Hawaiian or other Pacific Islander, as well as non-Hispanics reporting more than one race.
Source: Calculations by New Strategist based on the Bureau of Labor Statistics' 2012 Consumer Expenditure Survey

Pork Chops

Best customers: Householders aged 35 to 54

Married couples with school-aged or older children at home

Single parents

Blacks

Households in the South

Householders without a high school diploma

Customer trends: Average household spending on pork chops is likely to resume its decline as the baby-boom generation ages and household size shrinks.

Households with children and households headed by blacks are the biggest spenders on pork chops. Married couples with school-aged or older children at home spend 35 to 47 percent more than average on this item. Single parents, whose spending approaches average on only a few items, spend 28 percent more than average on pork chops. Householders aged 35 to 54, most with children, spend 12 to 23 percent more. Black households spend 39 percent more than average on pork chops. Households in the South, where many blacks reside, spend 23 percent more than average on this item. Householders with no more than a high school education spend 18 to 21 percent more than average on pork chops.

Average household spending on pork chops fell by a steep 54 percent between 2000 and 2010, after adjusting for inflation, then climbed 12 percent between 2010 and 2012. Spending on pork chops had been in decline as Americans substituted fast food and deli items for home-cooked meals. The recent rise could be a sign of economic recovery and may be short-lived. Average household spending on pork chops is likely to resume its decline as the baby-boom generation ages and household size shrinks.

Table 9.60 Pork chops

Total household spending $3,488,624,640.00
Average household spends   28.04

AGE OF HOUSEHOLDER	AVERAGE HOUSEHOLD SPENDING	BEST CUSTOMERS (index)	BIGGEST CUSTOMERS (market share)
Average household	$28.04	100	100.0%
Under age 25	17.04	61	4.0
Aged 25 to 34	26.29	94	15.2
Aged 35 to 44	34.46	123	21.3
Aged 45 to 54	31.32	112	22.1
Aged 55 to 64	29.11	104	19.0
Aged 65 to 74	28.65	102	12.3
Aged 75 or older	17.45	62	6.1

	AVERAGE HOUSEHOLD SPENDING	BEST CUSTOMERS (index)	BIGGEST CUSTOMERS (market share)
HOUSEHOLD INCOME			
Average household	**$28.04**	**100**	**100.0%**
Under $20,000	20.67	74	15.5
$20,000 to $39,999	27.26	97	21.9
$40,000 to $49,999	25.06	89	7.9
$50,000 to $69,999	29.23	104	15.1
$70,000 to $79,999	35.73	127	7.1
$80,000 to $99,999	33.64	120	10.6
$100,000 or more	32.34	115	21.6
HOUSEHOLD TYPE			
Average household	**28.04**	**100**	**100.0**
Married couples	33.54	120	58.1
Married couples, no children	28.29	101	21.0
Married couples with children	37.37	133	31.3
Oldest child under age 6	26.10	93	4.2
Oldest child aged 6 to 17	41.20	147	17.5
Oldest child aged 18 or older	37.98	135	9.6
Single parent with child under age 18	35.99	128	6.7
Single person	13.85	49	14.7
RACE AND HISPANIC ORIGIN			
Average household	**28.04**	**100**	**100.0**
Asian	26.53	95	4.1
Black	39.00	139	17.5
Hispanic	29.51	105	13.2
Non-Hispanic white and other	25.95	93	69.5
REGION			
Average household	**28.04**	**100**	**100.0**
Northeast	28.75	103	18.5
Midwest	22.39	80	17.7
South	34.57	123	45.9
West	22.27	79	17.9
EDUCATION			
Average household	**28.04**	**100**	**100.0**
Less than high school graduate	32.96	118	15.3
High school graduate	34.03	121	30.3
Some college	24.56	88	18.0
Associate's degree	27.08	97	9.5
Bachelor's degree or more	24.21	86	27.2
Bachelor's degree	22.67	81	16.1
Master's, professional, doctoral degree	26.82	96	11.1

Note: Market shares may not sum to 100.0 because of rounding and missing categories by household type. "Asian" and "black" include Hispanics and non-Hispanics who identify themselves as being of the respective race alone. "Hispanic" includes people of any race who identify themselves as Hispanic. "Other" includes people who identify themselves as non-Hispanic and as Alaska Native, American Indian, Asian (who are also included in the "Asian" row), or Native Hawaiian or other Pacific Islander, as well as non-Hispanics reporting more than one race.
Source: Calculations by New Strategist based on the Bureau of Labor Statistics' 2012 Consumer Expenditure Survey

Potato Chips and Other Snacks

Best customers: Householders aged 35 to 54
Married couples with children at home
Single parents

Customer trends: Average household spending on potato chips and other snacks may decline because the small generation X is in the best-customer lifestage.

The best customers of potato chips and other snacks are households with children. Married couples with children at home spend 72 percent more than the average household on this item, the figure peaking among those with school-aged children at 93 percent more. Single parents, whose spending approaches average on only a few items, spend 2 percent more than average on potato chips. Householders aged 35 to 54, most with children at home, spend 28 to 29 percent more than average on potato chips and other snacks and control 48 percent of the market.

Average household spending on potato chips and other snacks increased 17 percent between 2000 and 2012, after adjusting for inflation. Americans' penchant for snack food was behind the increase, as was the growing variety of snacks on grocery store shelves. Average household spending on potato chips and other snacks may decline in the years ahead because the small generation X is in the best-customer lifestage.

Table 9.61 Potato chips and other snacks

Total household spending $13,883,581,440.00
Average household spends   111.59

AGE OF HOUSEHOLDER	AVERAGE HOUSEHOLD SPENDING	BEST CUSTOMERS (index)	BIGGEST CUSTOMERS (market share)
Average household	$111.59	100	100.0%
Under age 25	71.79	64	4.2
Aged 25 to 34	116.07	104	16.8
Aged 35 to 44	144.29	129	22.4
Aged 45 to 54	142.52	128	25.3
Aged 55 to 64	107.56	96	17.6
Aged 65 to 74	84.13	75	9.1
Aged 75 or older	48.88	44	4.3

	AVERAGE HOUSEHOLD SPENDING	BEST CUSTOMERS (index)	BIGGEST CUSTOMERS (market share)
HOUSEHOLD INCOME			
Average household	**$111.59**	**100**	**100.0%**
Under $20,000	61.11	55	11.5
$20,000 to $39,999	78.84	71	15.9
$40,000 to $49,999	101.06	91	8.0
$50,000 to $69,999	115.60	104	15.0
$70,000 to $79,999	149.57	134	7.5
$80,000 to $99,999	147.79	132	11.7
$100,000 or more	181.87	163	30.5
HOUSEHOLD TYPE			
Average household	**111.59**	**100**	**100.0**
Married couples	150.71	135	65.6
Married couples, no children	106.62	96	19.9
Married couples with children	191.88	172	40.4
Oldest child under age 6	136.74	123	5.6
Oldest child aged 6 to 17	214.89	193	22.9
Oldest child aged 18 or older	187.84	168	11.9
Single parent with child under age 18	113.87	102	5.4
Single person	47.68	43	12.7
RACE AND HISPANIC ORIGIN			
Average household	**111.59**	**100**	**100.0**
Asian	92.40	83	3.6
Black	69.45	62	7.8
Hispanic	101.70	91	11.4
Non-Hispanic white and other	120.43	108	81.0
REGION			
Average household	**111.59**	**100**	**100.0**
Northeast	101.33	91	16.4
Midwest	120.20	108	23.9
South	105.94	95	35.4
West	120.67	108	24.4
EDUCATION			
Average household	**111.59**	**100**	**100.0**
Less than high school graduate	90.22	81	10.6
High school graduate	92.90	83	20.8
Some college	105.10	94	19.4
Associate's degree	126.05	113	11.2
Bachelor's degree or more	133.92	120	37.8
Bachelor's degree	129.20	116	23.1
Master's, professional, doctoral degree	141.88	127	14.8

Note: Market shares may not sum to 100.0 because of rounding and missing categories by household type. "Asian" and "black" include Hispanics and non-Hispanics who identify themselves as being of the respective race alone. "Hispanic" includes people of any race who identify themselves as Hispanic. "Other" includes people who identify themselves as non-Hispanic and as Alaska Native, American Indian, Asian (who are also included in the "Asian" row), or Native Hawaiian or other Pacific Islander, as well as non-Hispanics reporting more than one race.
Source: Calculations by New Strategist based on the Bureau of Labor Statistics' 2012 Consumer Expenditure Survey

Potatoes, Fresh

Best customers: Householders aged 35 to 74
Married couples with school-aged or older children at home
Asians
Households in the Northeast

Customer trends: Average household spending on fresh potatoes may resume its decline as home cooking
becomes less common, but only if discretionary income grows.

Families that cook meals from scratch are the best customers of fresh potatoes. Married couples with school-aged or older children at home spend 47 to 48 percent more than average on potatoes. Householders ranging in age from 35 to 74 spend 5 to 18 percent more than average on this item. Asian households spend 37 percent more than average on potatoes. Households in the Northeast outspend the average by 15 percent.

After declining 5 percent between 2000 and 2006, average household spending on fresh potatoes grew 8 percent between 2006 and 2012, after adjusting for inflation. Behind the increase is the renewed surge of home cooking in an effort to control spending. Average household spending on potatoes may resume its decline as home cooking becomes less common, but only if discretionary income grows.

Table 9.62 **Potatoes, fresh**

Total household spending $4,782,551,040.00
Average household spends   38.44

	AVERAGE HOUSEHOLD SPENDING	BEST CUSTOMERS (index)	BIGGEST CUSTOMERS (market share)
AGE OF HOUSEHOLDER			
Average household	$38.44	100	100.0%
Under age 25	25.57	67	4.4
Aged 25 to 34	33.70	88	14.2
Aged 35 to 44	41.84	109	18.9
Aged 45 to 54	45.52	118	23.4
Aged 55 to 64	40.69	106	19.4
Aged 65 to 74	40.33	105	12.6
Aged 75 or older	28.20	73	7.2

	AVERAGE HOUSEHOLD SPENDING	BEST CUSTOMERS (index)	BIGGEST CUSTOMERS (market share)
HOUSEHOLD INCOME			
Average household	**$38.44**	**100**	**100.0%**
Under $20,000	26.09	68	14.3
$20,000 to $39,999	31.23	81	18.3
$40,000 to $49,999	37.51	98	8.6
$50,000 to $69,999	39.93	104	15.0
$70,000 to $79,999	45.03	117	6.5
$80,000 to $99,999	45.66	119	10.5
$100,000 or more	54.66	142	26.6
HOUSEHOLD TYPE			
Average household	**38.44**	**100**	**100.0**
Married couples	48.85	127	61.7
Married couples, no children	41.94	109	22.7
Married couples with children	53.59	139	32.8
Oldest child under age 6	40.51	105	4.8
Oldest child aged 6 to 17	56.38	147	17.4
Oldest child aged 18 or older	57.06	148	10.5
Single parent with child under age 18	37.56	98	5.1
Single person	18.44	48	14.2
RACE AND HISPANIC ORIGIN			
Average household	**38.44**	**100**	**100.0**
Asian	52.68	137	5.9
Black	30.29	79	9.9
Hispanic	39.60	103	12.9
Non-Hispanic white and other	39.55	103	77.2
REGION			
Average household	**38.44**	**100**	**100.0**
Northeast	44.38	115	20.8
Midwest	37.54	98	21.7
South	36.75	96	35.6
West	37.32	97	21.9
EDUCATION			
Average household	**38.44**	**100**	**100.0**
Less than high school graduate	39.84	104	13.5
High school graduate	37.28	97	24.2
Some college	32.93	86	17.6
Associate's degree	43.57	113	11.2
Bachelor's degree or more	40.92	106	33.6
Bachelor's degree	40.15	104	20.8
Master's, professional, doctoral degree	42.22	110	12.7

Note: Market shares may not sum to 100.0 because of rounding and missing categories by household type. "Asian" and "black" include Hispanics and non-Hispanics who identify themselves as being of the respective race alone. "Hispanic" includes people of any race who identify themselves as Hispanic. "Other" includes people who identify themselves as non-Hispanic and as Alaska Native, American Indian, Asian (who are also included in the "Asian" row), or Native Hawaiian or other Pacific Islander, as well as non-Hispanics reporting more than one race.
Source: Calculations by New Strategist based on the Bureau of Labor Statistics' 2012 Consumer Expenditure Survey

Poultry Other than Chicken

Best customers: Householders aged 35 to 64
Married couples with children at home
Single parents
Blacks

Customer trends: Average household spending on poultry other than chicken is likely to resume its decline as home cooking becomes less common, but only if discretionary income grows.

Middle-aged married couples, many with children, spend the most on poultry other than chicken (primarily turkey). Married couples with children at home spend 41 percent more than the average household on this item. Couples without children at home, many of them empty-nesters, spend 19 percent more than average on this item. Poultry other than chicken is one of the relatively few items on which single parents, with their lower incomes, spend an average amount. Householders ranging in age from 35 to 64, many with children at home, spend more than average on this item. Blacks spend 17 percent more than the average household on other poultry.

Average household spending on poultry other than chicken tumbled 21 percent between 2000 and 2006, after adjusting for inflation, then climbed by a small 1 percent between 2006 and 2012. Behind the decline was Americans' waning interest in cooking from scratch, and behind the increase was the reluctant return to home cooking. Average household spending on poultry other than chicken is likely to resume its decline as home cooking becomes less common, but only if discretionary income grows.

Table 9.63 **Poultry other than chicken**

Total household spending $4,085,821,440.00
Average household spends 32.84

	AVERAGE HOUSEHOLD SPENDING	BEST CUSTOMERS (index)	BIGGEST CUSTOMERS (market share)
AGE OF HOUSEHOLDER			
Average household	$32.84	100	100.0%
Under age 25	18.97	58	3.8
Aged 25 to 34	30.32	92	14.9
Aged 35 to 44	34.29	104	18.1
Aged 45 to 54	43.69	133	26.3
Aged 55 to 64	37.26	113	20.8
Aged 65 to 74	25.30	77	9.3
Aged 75 or older	22.95	70	6.8

	AVERAGE HOUSEHOLD SPENDING	BEST CUSTOMERS (index)	BIGGEST CUSTOMERS (market share)
HOUSEHOLD INCOME			
Average household	**$32.84**	**100**	**100.0%**
Under $20,000	19.51	59	12.5
$20,000 to $39,999	21.07	64	14.5
$40,000 to $49,999	26.13	80	7.0
$50,000 to $69,999	32.73	100	14.4
$70,000 to $79,999	38.61	118	6.6
$80,000 to $99,999	45.96	140	12.3
$100,000 or more	57.42	175	32.7
HOUSEHOLD TYPE			
Average household	**32.84**	**100**	**100.0**
Married couples	41.97	128	62.1
Married couples, no children	39.24	119	24.9
Married couples with children	46.23	141	33.1
Oldest child under age 6	38.60	118	5.4
Oldest child aged 6 to 17	46.07	140	16.7
Oldest child aged 18 or older	51.26	156	11.0
Single parent with child under age 18	33.28	101	5.3
Single person	16.18	49	14.6
RACE AND HISPANIC ORIGIN			
Average household	**32.84**	**100**	**100.0**
Asian	24.54	75	3.2
Black	38.32	117	14.7
Hispanic	25.68	78	9.8
Non-Hispanic white and other	33.13	101	75.7
REGION			
Average household	**32.84**	**100**	**100.0**
Northeast	32.11	98	17.7
Midwest	28.77	88	19.4
South	33.84	103	38.4
West	35.84	109	24.6
EDUCATION			
Average household	**32.84**	**100**	**100.0**
Less than high school graduate	22.97	70	9.1
High school graduate	25.43	77	19.3
Some college	32.22	98	20.2
Associate's degree	30.36	92	9.1
Bachelor's degree or more	43.47	132	41.7
Bachelor's degree	38.36	117	23.3
Master's, professional, doctoral degree	52.11	159	18.4

Note: Market shares may not sum to 100.0 because of rounding and missing categories by household type. "Asian" and "black" include Hispanics and non-Hispanics who identify themselves as being of the respective race alone. "Hispanic" includes people of any race who identify themselves as Hispanic. "Other" includes people who identify themselves as non-Hispanic and as Alaska Native, American Indian, Asian (who are also included in the "Asian" row), or Native Hawaiian or other Pacific Islander, as well as non-Hispanics reporting more than one race.
Source: Calculations by New Strategist based on the Bureau of Labor Statistics' 2012 Consumer Expenditure Survey

Prepared Food (except Desserts, Frozen Meals, and Salads)

Best customers: Householders aged 35 to 64
Married couples with school-aged or older children at home
Asians and Hispanics
Households in the West

Customer trends: Average household spending on prepared foods should resume its growth in the years ahead as grocery stores compete with restaurants for customers.

Grocery stores increasingly offer fresh prepared foods as they compete with fast-food restaurants for customers. Americans have responded, the average household spending $148 on prepared foods (not including desserts, frozen meals, or salads) in 2012. The biggest spenders on prepared foods are the busiest—households with children. Married couples with school-aged or older children at home spend 63 to 81 percent more than average on this item. Householders aged 35 to 64, many with children at home, spend 11 to 15 percent more than average on prepared foods. Hispanic households, which tend to include more children than average, spend 16 percent more on prepared food. Asian households spend 19 percent more than average on this item. Households in the West, where many Hispanics and Asians reside, spend 40 percent more than average on prepared food.

Average household spending on prepared food from grocery stores rose by a substantial 53 percent between 2000 and 2006, after adjusting for inflation, then fell 2 percent between 2006 and 2012. Behind the earlier increase were consumers looking for eat-and-run convenience and the growing variety of prepared food offered by grocery store delis. Behind the more recent decline is the shift to more meals cooked from scratch following the Great Recession. Average household spending on prepared foods should resume its growth in the years ahead as grocery stores continue to compete with restaurants for customers.

Table 9.64 Prepared food (except desserts, frozen meals, and salads)

Total household spending $18,389,928,960.00
Average household spends   147.81

	AVERAGE HOUSEHOLD SPENDING	BEST CUSTOMERS (index)	BIGGEST CUSTOMERS (market share)
AGE OF HOUSEHOLDER			
Average household	**$147.81**	**100**	**100.0%**
Under age 25	82.31	56	3.7
Aged 25 to 34	152.41	103	16.7
Aged 35 to 44	163.54	111	19.2
Aged 45 to 54	163.81	111	21.9
Aged 55 to 64	170.26	115	21.1
Aged 65 to 74	142.81	97	11.6
Aged 75 or older	88.38	60	5.8

	AVERAGE HOUSEHOLD SPENDING	BEST CUSTOMERS (index)	BIGGEST CUSTOMERS (market share)
HOUSEHOLD INCOME			
Average household	$147.81	100	100.0%
Under $20,000	96.39	65	13.7
$20,000 to $39,999	107.96	73	16.5
$40,000 to $49,999	131.05	89	7.8
$50,000 to $69,999	137.25	93	13.4
$70,000 to $79,999	179.92	122	6.8
$80,000 to $99,999	188.87	128	11.3
$100,000 or more	241.24	163	30.6
HOUSEHOLD TYPE			
Average household	147.81	100	100.0
Married couples	192.16	130	63.1
Married couples, no children	149.81	101	21.1
Married couples with children	232.60	157	37.0
Oldest child under age 6	153.52	104	4.7
Oldest child aged 6 to 17	241.58	163	19.4
Oldest child aged 18 or older	266.89	181	12.7
Single parent with child under age 18	132.06	89	4.7
Single person	73.68	50	14.8
RACE AND HISPANIC ORIGIN			
Average household	147.81	100	100.0
Asian	175.55	119	5.1
Black	93.07	63	7.9
Hispanic	170.85	116	14.5
Non-Hispanic white and other	153.41	104	77.9
REGION			
Average household	147.81	100	100.0
Northeast	114.39	77	14.0
Midwest	130.55	88	19.6
South	138.57	94	34.9
West	207.62	140	31.7
EDUCATION			
Average household	147.81	100	100.0
Less than high school graduate	164.25	111	14.5
High school graduate	122.37	83	20.6
Some college	143.27	97	20.0
Associate's degree	139.20	94	9.3
Bachelor's degree or more	167.09	113	35.7
Bachelor's degree	171.23	116	23.1
Master's, professional, doctoral degree	160.08	108	12.6

Note: Market shares may not sum to 100.0 because of rounding and missing categories by household type. "Asian" and "black" include Hispanics and non-Hispanics who identify themselves as being of the respective race alone. "Hispanic" includes people of any race who identify themselves as Hispanic. "Other" includes people who identify themselves as non-Hispanic and as Alaska Native, American Indian, Asian (who are also included in the "Asian" row), or Native Hawaiian or other Pacific Islander, as well as non-Hispanics reporting more than one race.
Source: Calculations by New Strategist based on the Bureau of Labor Statistics' 2012 Consumer Expenditure Survey

Prepared Food, Frozen (Other than Meals)

Best customers: Householders aged 25 to 54
Married couples with school-aged or older children at home
Single parents
Households in the Midwest

Customer trends: Average household spending on frozen prepared food other than meals will continue to fall because of the growing preference for fresh food.

The biggest spenders on frozen prepared food other than meals are the busiest households—parents with children. Married couples with school-aged children spend 85 percent more than average on this item, and those with adult children at home spend 45 percent more. Single parents spend 17 percent more than average on frozen prepared food other than meals. Householders ranging in age from 25 to 54, most with children, spend 12 to 23 percent more than average on frozen prepared food. Households in the Midwest outspend the average by 17 percent.

Average household spending on frozen prepared food fell by 15 percent between 2000 and 2012, after adjusting for inflation. One factor behind the decline is the growing availability of fresh rather than frozen prepared food. Average household spending on frozen prepared food will continue to fall because of consumers' preference for fresh food.

Table 9.65 Prepared food, frozen (other than meals)

Total household spending $8,736,491,520.00
Average household spends   70.22

AGE OF HOUSEHOLDER	AVERAGE HOUSEHOLD SPENDING	BEST CUSTOMERS (index)	BIGGEST CUSTOMERS (market share)
Average household	$70.22	100	100.0%
Under age 25	61.76	88	5.8
Aged 25 to 34	86.04	123	19.8
Aged 35 to 44	78.80	112	19.5
Aged 45 to 54	86.02	123	24.2
Aged 55 to 64	65.28	93	17.0
Aged 65 to 74	48.77	69	8.4
Aged 75 or older	35.96	51	5.0

	AVERAGE HOUSEHOLD SPENDING	BEST CUSTOMERS (index)	BIGGEST CUSTOMERS (market share)
HOUSEHOLD INCOME			
Average household	$70.22	100	100.0%
Under $20,000	45.31	65	13.6
$20,000 to $39,999	58.69	84	18.8
$40,000 to $49,999	76.82	109	9.7
$50,000 to $69,999	81.13	116	16.7
$70,000 to $79,999	85.86	122	6.8
$80,000 to $99,999	78.03	111	9.8
$100,000 or more	90.28	129	24.1
HOUSEHOLD TYPE			
Average household	70.22	100	100.0
Married couples	85.41	122	59.1
Married couples, no children	58.76	84	17.4
Married couples with children	111.48	159	37.3
Oldest child under age 6	77.92	111	5.1
Oldest child aged 6 to 17	129.73	185	22.0
Oldest child aged 18 or older	101.94	145	10.2
Single parent with child under age 18	82.22	117	6.1
Single person	34.23	49	14.5
RACE AND HISPANIC ORIGIN			
Average household	70.22	100	100.0
Asian	51.52	73	3.2
Black	59.79	85	10.7
Hispanic	59.23	84	10.6
Non-Hispanic white and other	73.90	105	79.0
REGION			
Average household	70.22	100	100.0
Northeast	62.54	89	16.1
Midwest	82.07	117	25.9
South	68.96	98	36.6
West	66.69	95	21.4
EDUCATION			
Average household	70.22	100	100.0
Less than high school graduate	59.90	85	11.1
High school graduate	63.25	90	22.5
Some college	75.60	108	22.2
Associate's degree	75.90	108	10.7
Bachelor's degree or more	74.09	106	33.3
Bachelor's degree	77.24	110	21.9
Master's, professional, doctoral degree	68.76	98	11.4

Note: Market shares may not sum to 100.0 because of rounding and missing categories by household type. "Asian" and "black" include Hispanics and non-Hispanics who identify themselves as being of the respective race alone. "Hispanic" includes people of any race who identify themselves as Hispanic. "Other" includes people who identify themselves as non-Hispanic and as Alaska Native, American Indian, Asian (who are also included in the "Asian" row), or Native Hawaiian or other Pacific Islander, as well as non-Hispanics reporting more than one race.
Source: Calculations by New Strategist based on the Bureau of Labor Statistics' 2012 Consumer Expenditure Survey

Prepared Meals, Frozen

Best customers: Householders aged 45 to 54
Married couples with school-aged or older children at home
Single parents

Customer trends: Average household spending on frozen meals is likely to continue to decline as grocery stores offer
more of the fresh variety.

The biggest spenders on frozen meals are householders who want the least bother. Some are buying low-fat or low-carb frozen meals as part of a dietary regimen. Others are on the go and do not want to take the time to cook or stop at a restaurant. Married couples with school-aged or older children at home spend the most on frozen meals, 21 to 43 percent more than the average household. Even single parents, whose spending on most items is well below average, spend 23 percent more on this item. Spending on frozen prepared meals is 30 percent above average among householders aged 45 to 54.

Average household spending on frozen meals more than doubled between 2000 and 2006, after adjusting for inflation. It then fell 23 percent from 2006 to 2012. The earlier increase occurred as consumers demanded greater convenience in meal preparation and as the variety of frozen meals—including many ethnic options—expanded. The decline occurred in part because of budget cutting in face of the Great Recession and because grocery stores were offering more fresh prepared meals. Average household spending on frozen meals is likely to continue to decline as grocery stores offer more of the fresh variety.

Table 9.66 Prepared meals, frozen

Total household spending $7,540,853,760.00
Average household spends 60.61

AGE OF HOUSEHOLDER	AVERAGE HOUSEHOLD SPENDING	BEST CUSTOMERS (index)	BIGGEST CUSTOMERS (market share)
Average household	$60.61	100	100.0%
Under age 25	37.28	62	4.0
Aged 25 to 34	60.48	100	16.1
Aged 35 to 44	59.38	98	17.0
Aged 45 to 54	79.08	130	25.8
Aged 55 to 64	58.72	97	17.7
Aged 65 to 74	58.06	96	11.5
Aged 75 or older	47.97	79	7.7

	AVERAGE HOUSEHOLD SPENDING	BEST CUSTOMERS (index)	BIGGEST CUSTOMERS (market share)
HOUSEHOLD INCOME			
Average household	**$60.61**	**100**	**100.0%**
Under $20,000	46.02	76	16.0
$20,000 to $39,999	46.60	77	17.3
$40,000 to $49,999	52.37	86	7.6
$50,000 to $69,999	63.59	105	15.2
$70,000 to $79,999	75.42	124	6.9
$80,000 to $99,999	65.91	109	9.6
$100,000 or more	88.98	147	27.5
HOUSEHOLD TYPE			
Average household	**60.61**	**100**	**100.0**
Married couples	70.15	116	56.2
Married couples, no children	61.49	101	21.1
Married couples with children	75.65	125	29.3
Oldest child under age 6	63.62	105	4.8
Oldest child aged 6 to 17	73.57	121	14.4
Oldest child aged 18 or older	86.63	143	10.1
Single parent with child under age 18	74.39	123	6.4
Single person	44.23	73	21.7
RACE AND HISPANIC ORIGIN			
Average household	**60.61**	**100**	**100.0**
Asian	51.55	85	3.7
Black	46.52	77	9.6
Hispanic	41.95	69	8.7
Non-Hispanic white and other	66.03	109	81.8
REGION			
Average household	**60.61**	**100**	**100.0**
Northeast	60.56	100	18.0
Midwest	67.52	111	24.7
South	57.58	95	35.4
West	58.75	97	21.8
EDUCATION			
Average household	**60.61**	**100**	**100.0**
Less than high school graduate	43.38	72	9.3
High school graduate	49.20	81	20.2
Some college	64.92	107	22.1
Associate's degree	58.12	96	9.5
Bachelor's degree or more	73.77	122	38.4
Bachelor's degree	64.89	107	21.3
Master's, professional, doctoral degree	88.78	146	17.0

Note: Market shares may not sum to 100.0 because of rounding and missing categories by household type. "Asian" and "black" include Hispanics and non-Hispanics who identify themselves as being of the respective race alone. "Hispanic" includes people of any race who identify themselves as Hispanic. "Other" includes people who identify themselves as non-Hispanic and as Alaska Native, American Indian, Asian (who are also included in the "Asian" row), or Native Hawaiian or other Pacific Islander, as well as non-Hispanics reporting more than one race.
Source: Calculations by New Strategist based on the Bureau of Labor Statistics' 2012 Consumer Expenditure Survey

Rice

Best customers: Householders aged 35 to 54
Married couples with school-aged or older children at home
Single parents
Asians, Hispanics, and blacks
Households in the Northeast
Householders without a high school diploma

Customer trends: Average household spending on rice should decline as prepared food claims a bigger share of the food dollar, but growing minority populations may limit the drop.

Asian households are the biggest spenders on rice by far—they spend three-and-three-quarter times the average. Hispanics, who tend to have large families, spend 65 percent more than average, and blacks spend 18 percent more. Together the three groups, which represent 29 percent of the population, account for 52 percent of the market for rice. Married couples with school-aged or older children at home spend 41 to 50 percent more than the average household on this item. Single parents, whose spending approaches average on only a few items, outspend the average on rice by a solid 24 percent. Householders aged 35 to 54, most with children, spend 28 to 34 percent more than average on rice. Households in the Northeast outspend the average by 26 percent. Householders who did not complete high school, many of them Hispanic, spend 24 percent more than average on this item.

Average household spending on rice fell 23 percent between 2000 and 2006, then grew 31 percent between 2006 and 2010, after adjusting for inflation. Between 2010 and 2012, average household spending on rice declined 5 percent. Behind the 2006-to-2010 spending increase were growing Asian and Hispanic populations, a renewed surge of home cooking in an effort to rein in household spending because of the Great Recession, and soaring prices for rice. Spending on rice should continue its decline as prepared food claims a growing share of the food dollar, but growing minority populations may limit the drop.

Table 9.67 Rice

Total household spending $3,066,854,400.00
Average household spends   24.65

	AVERAGE HOUSEHOLD SPENDING	BEST CUSTOMERS (index)	BIGGEST CUSTOMERS (market share)
AGE OF HOUSEHOLDER			
Average household	$24.65	100	100.0%
Under age 25	25.33	103	6.7
Aged 25 to 34	27.06	110	17.7
Aged 35 to 44	31.53	128	22.2
Aged 45 to 54	33.08	134	26.6
Aged 55 to 64	17.86	72	13.3
Aged 65 to 74	15.39	62	7.5
Aged 75 or older	13.88	56	5.5

	AVERAGE HOUSEHOLD SPENDING	BEST CUSTOMERS (index)	BIGGEST CUSTOMERS (market share)
HOUSEHOLD INCOME			
Average household	**$24.65**	**100**	**100.0%**
Under $20,000	19.26	78	16.4
$20,000 to $39,999	20.54	83	18.8
$40,000 to $49,999	23.51	95	8.4
$50,000 to $69,999	24.41	99	14.3
$70,000 to $79,999	28.31	115	6.4
$80,000 to $99,999	26.39	107	9.4
$100,000 or more	34.54	140	26.2
HOUSEHOLD TYPE			
Average household	**24.65**	**100**	**100.0**
Married couples	28.68	116	56.5
Married couples, no children	18.18	74	15.4
Married couples with children	33.42	136	31.9
Oldest child under age 6	21.79	88	4.0
Oldest child aged 6 to 17	36.94	150	17.8
Oldest child aged 18 or older	34.81	141	10.0
Single parent with child under age 18	30.62	124	6.5
Single person	11.64	47	14.0
RACE AND HISPANIC ORIGIN			
Average household	**24.65**	**100**	**100.0**
Asian	91.55	371	16.1
Black	29.04	118	14.8
Hispanic	40.74	165	20.7
Non-Hispanic white and other	21.20	86	64.6
REGION			
Average household	**24.65**	**100**	**100.0**
Northeast	31.17	126	22.8
Midwest	22.48	91	20.2
South	21.95	89	33.2
West	26.02	106	23.8
EDUCATION			
Average household	**24.65**	**100**	**100.0**
Less than high school graduate	30.45	124	16.1
High school graduate	24.63	100	24.9
Some college	19.59	79	16.4
Associate's degree	21.44	87	8.6
Bachelor's degree or more	26.92	109	34.4
Bachelor's degree	24.70	100	20.0
Master's, professional, doctoral degree	30.66	124	14.4

Note: Market shares may not sum to 100.0 because of rounding and missing categories by household type. "Asian" and "black" include Hispanics and non-Hispanics who identify themselves as being of the respective race alone. "Hispanic" includes people of any race who identify themselves as Hispanic. "Other" includes people who identify themselves as non-Hispanic and as Alaska Native, American Indian, Asian (who are also included in the "Asian" row), or Native Hawaiian or other Pacific Islander, as well as non-Hispanics reporting more than one race.
Source: Calculations by New Strategist based on the Bureau of Labor Statistics' 2012 Consumer Expenditure Survey

Salad Dressing

Best customers:
Householders aged 35 to 74
Married couples without children at home
Married couples with school-aged or older children at home

Customer trends:
Average household spending on salad dressing may resume its decline as the economy continues to recover from the Great Recession and eating out and prepared food regain their popularity.

Older married couples spend the most on salad dressing. Householders ranging in age from 35 to 74 spend more than average on this item. Married couples without children at home (most empty-nesters) outspend the average on salad dressing by 23 percent. Married couples with school-aged children spend 34 percent more than the average household on salad dressing, and those with adult children at home spend 54 percent more.

Average household spending on salad dressing fell 18 percent between 2000 and 2006, after adjusting for inflation, but stabilized since then with a 5 percent gain between 2006 and 2012. The earlier spending decline was due to the growing popularity of fast food as well as prepared salads from grocery stores. The more recent gain reflects the return to home cooking in the wake of the Great Recession. Average household spending on salad dressing may resume its decline as the economy continues to recover and eating out and prepared food regain their popularity.

Table 9.68 Salad dressing

Total household spending $3,892,976,640.00
Average household spends   31.29

AGE OF HOUSEHOLDER	AVERAGE HOUSEHOLD SPENDING	BEST CUSTOMERS (index)	BIGGEST CUSTOMERS (market share)
Average household	$31.29	100	100.0%
Under age 25	19.27	62	4.0
Aged 25 to 34	26.81	86	13.9
Aged 35 to 44	32.90	105	18.3
Aged 45 to 54	36.28	116	22.9
Aged 55 to 64	34.81	111	20.4
Aged 65 to 74	33.97	109	13.1
Aged 75 or older	24.33	78	7.6

	AVERAGE HOUSEHOLD SPENDING	BEST CUSTOMERS (index)	BIGGEST CUSTOMERS (market share)
HOUSEHOLD INCOME			
Average household	**$31.29**	**100**	**100.0%**
Under $20,000	20.70	66	13.9
$20,000 to $39,999	23.65	76	17.0
$40,000 to $49,999	32.66	104	9.2
$50,000 to $69,999	34.15	109	15.8
$70,000 to $79,999	37.20	119	6.6
$80,000 to $99,999	37.97	121	10.7
$100,000 or more	44.53	142	26.6
HOUSEHOLD TYPE			
Average household	**31.29**	**100**	**100.0**
Married couples	41.85	134	65.0
Married couples, no children	38.34	123	25.5
Married couples with children	42.94	137	32.3
Oldest child under age 6	36.80	118	5.4
Oldest child aged 6 to 17	42.04	134	16.0
Oldest child aged 18 or older	48.26	154	10.9
Single parent with child under age 18	24.14	77	4.0
Single person	16.01	51	15.2
RACE AND HISPANIC ORIGIN			
Average household	**31.29**	**100**	**100.0**
Asian	15.93	51	2.2
Black	22.27	71	8.9
Hispanic	29.27	94	11.7
Non-Hispanic white and other	33.22	106	79.7
REGION			
Average household	**31.29**	**100**	**100.0**
Northeast	28.52	91	16.5
Midwest	34.24	109	24.3
South	30.09	96	35.8
West	32.58	104	23.5
EDUCATION			
Average household	**31.29**	**100**	**100.0**
Less than high school graduate	23.23	74	9.7
High school graduate	31.42	100	25.0
Some college	31.65	101	20.8
Associate's degree	33.50	107	10.6
Bachelor's degree or more	33.28	106	33.5
Bachelor's degree	32.63	104	20.8
Master's, professional, doctoral degree	34.37	110	12.7

Note: Market shares may not sum to 100.0 because of rounding and missing categories by household type. "Asian" and "black" include Hispanics and non-Hispanics who identify themselves as being of the respective race alone. "Hispanic" includes people of any race who identify themselves as Hispanic. "Other" includes people who identify themselves as non-Hispanic and as Alaska Native, American Indian, Asian (who are also included in the "Asian" row), or Native Hawaiian or other Pacific Islander, as well as non-Hispanics reporting more than one race.
Source: Calculations by New Strategist based on the Bureau of Labor Statistics' 2012 Consumer Expenditure Survey

Salads, Prepared

Best customers: Householders aged 35 to 74
Married couples without children at home
Married couples with school-aged or older children at home

Customer trends: Average household spending on prepared salads will continue to rise
as consumers look for healthy, convenient meal options.

The best customers of prepared salads are older married couples. Householders ranging in age from 35 to 74 spend 6 to 19 percent more than the average household on this item. Married couples with adult children at home spend 23 percent more than average on prepared salads. Those with school-aged children outspend the average by 28 percent. Couples without children at home (most of them empty-nesters) spend one-third more than average on prepared salads.

Average household spending on prepared salads rose by a stunning 49 percent between 2000 and 2006, after adjusting for inflation, then fell 5 percent between 2006 and 2012. Behind the gain was Americans' growing demand for the convenience and quality of fresh prepared food. Behind the more recent decline was the shift to more meals cooked from scratch at home in an attempt to save money. Average household spending on prepared salads may resume its rise in the years ahead as consumers look for healthy, convenient meal options.

Table 9.69 Salads, prepared

Total household spending $4,365,757,440.00
Average household spends   35.09

AGE OF HOUSEHOLDER	AVERAGE HOUSEHOLD SPENDING	BEST CUSTOMERS (index)	BIGGEST CUSTOMERS (market share)
Average household	$35.09	100	100.0%
Under age 25	15.95	45	3.0
Aged 25 to 34	30.86	88	14.2
Aged 35 to 44	37.07	106	18.3
Aged 45 to 54	41.07	117	23.2
Aged 55 to 64	38.02	108	19.8
Aged 65 to 74	41.87	119	14.4
Aged 75 or older	25.99	74	7.2

	AVERAGE HOUSEHOLD SPENDING	BEST CUSTOMERS (index)	BIGGEST CUSTOMERS (market share)
HOUSEHOLD INCOME			
Average household	**$35.09**	**100**	**100.0%**
Under $20,000	20.16	57	12.1
$20,000 to $39,999	27.13	77	17.4
$40,000 to $49,999	29.97	85	7.6
$50,000 to $69,999	34.45	98	14.2
$70,000 to $79,999	41.64	119	6.6
$80,000 to $99,999	40.44	115	10.2
$100,000 or more	59.95	171	32.0
HOUSEHOLD TYPE			
Average household	**35.09**	**100**	**100.0**
Married couples	43.86	125	60.7
Married couples, no children	46.82	133	27.8
Married couples with children	42.24	120	28.3
Oldest child under age 6	33.37	95	4.3
Oldest child aged 6 to 17	45.00	128	15.3
Oldest child aged 18 or older	43.14	123	8.7
Single parent with child under age 18	30.15	86	4.5
Single person	22.79	65	19.3
RACE AND HISPANIC ORIGIN			
Average household	**35.09**	**100**	**100.0**
Asian	32.48	93	4.0
Black	21.63	62	7.7
Hispanic	22.64	65	8.1
Non-Hispanic white and other	39.50	113	84.5
REGION			
Average household	**35.09**	**100**	**100.0**
Northeast	38.37	109	19.7
Midwest	38.48	110	24.3
South	28.72	82	30.5
West	39.60	113	25.4
EDUCATION			
Average household	**35.09**	**100**	**100.0**
Less than high school graduate	20.86	59	7.8
High school graduate	28.08	80	20.0
Some college	35.40	101	20.8
Associate's degree	36.91	105	10.4
Bachelor's degree or more	45.07	128	40.5
Bachelor's degree	40.55	116	23.0
Master's, professional, doctoral degree	52.72	150	17.4

Note: Market shares may not sum to 100.0 because of rounding and missing categories by household type. "Asian" and "black" include Hispanics and non-Hispanics who identify themselves as being of the respective race alone. "Hispanic" includes people of any race who identify themselves as Hispanic. "Other" includes people who identify themselves as non-Hispanic and as Alaska Native, American Indian, Asian (who are also included in the "Asian" row), or Native Hawaiian or other Pacific Islander, as well as non-Hispanics reporting more than one race.
Source: Calculations by New Strategist based on the Bureau of Labor Statistics' 2012 Consumer Expenditure Survey

Salt, Spices, and Other Seasonings

Best customers: Householders aged 35 to 54
                        Married couples with school-aged or older children at home
                        Asians

Customer trends: Average household spending on salt, spices, and other seasonings may decline as household size shrinks
                        with the aging of the population.

The biggest spenders on salt, spices, and other seasonings are households most likely to cook from scratch—married couples with children. Married couples with children at home spend 45 percent more than average on this item. Householders aged 35 to 54, many with children, spend 15 to 25 percent more than average on salt and spices. Asians outspend the average by 59 percent.

Average household spending on salt, spices, and other seasonings grew 41 percent between 2000 and 2012, after adjusting for inflation—despite the growing propensity of Americans to substitute prepared food for home-cooked meals. Behind the increase were changing tastes, with specialty flavorings growing in popularity. Spending on salt, spices, and other seasonings may decline in the years ahead as household size shrinks along with the aging of the population.

Table 9.70 Salt, spices, and other seasonings

Total household spending $4,817,387,520.00
Average household spends   38.72

AGE OF HOUSEHOLDER	AVERAGE HOUSEHOLD SPENDING	BEST CUSTOMERS (index)	BIGGEST CUSTOMERS (market share)
Average household	$38.72	100	100.0%
Under age 25	27.05	70	4.6
Aged 25 to 34	36.62	95	15.3
Aged 35 to 44	44.68	115	20.0
Aged 45 to 54	48.40	125	24.7
Aged 55 to 64	38.58	100	18.2
Aged 65 to 74	36.27	94	11.3
Aged 75 or older	22.77	59	5.7

	AVERAGE HOUSEHOLD SPENDING	BEST CUSTOMERS (index)	BIGGEST CUSTOMERS (market share)
HOUSEHOLD INCOME			
Average household	**$38.72**	**100**	**100.0%**
Under $20,000	24.53	63	13.3
$20,000 to $39,999	29.16	75	17.0
$40,000 to $49,999	35.40	91	8.1
$50,000 to $69,999	34.21	88	12.8
$70,000 to $79,999	47.04	121	6.8
$80,000 to $99,999	47.57	123	10.8
$100,000 or more	64.84	167	31.4
HOUSEHOLD TYPE			
Average household	**38.72**	**100**	**100.0**
Married couples	51.60	133	64.7
Married couples, no children	44.13	114	23.8
Married couples with children	56.32	145	34.2
Oldest child under age 6	42.82	111	5.0
Oldest child aged 6 to 17	58.74	152	18.0
Oldest child aged 18 or older	60.68	157	11.1
Single parent with child under age 18	36.66	95	5.0
Single person	16.06	41	12.3
RACE AND HISPANIC ORIGIN			
Average household	**38.72**	**100**	**100.0**
Asian	61.41	159	6.9
Black	34.18	88	11.1
Hispanic	42.01	108	13.6
Non-Hispanic white and other	38.97	101	75.5
REGION			
Average household	**38.72**	**100**	**100.0**
Northeast	38.78	100	18.1
Midwest	38.40	99	22.0
South	36.21	94	34.8
West	43.17	111	25.1
EDUCATION			
Average household	**38.72**	**100**	**100.0**
Less than high school graduate	38.18	99	12.9
High school graduate	33.70	87	21.7
Some college	34.58	89	18.4
Associate's degree	38.22	99	9.7
Bachelor's degree or more	45.76	118	37.3
Bachelor's degree	46.78	121	24.1
Master's, professional, doctoral degree	44.04	114	13.2

Note: Market shares may not sum to 100.0 because of rounding and missing categories by household type. "Asian" and "black" include Hispanics and non-Hispanics who identify themselves as being of the respective race alone. "Hispanic" includes people of any race who identify themselves as Hispanic. "Other" includes people who identify themselves as non-Hispanic and as Alaska Native, American Indian, Asian (who are also included in the "Asian" row), or Native Hawaiian or other Pacific Islander, as well as non-Hispanics reporting more than one race.
Source: Calculations by New Strategist based on the Bureau of Labor Statistics' 2012 Consumer Expenditure Survey

Sauces and Gravies

Best customers: Householders aged 35 to 54
                         Married couples with school-aged or older children at home

Customer trends: Average household spending on sauces and gravies is likely to decline as the small generation X passes
                         through the best-customer lifestage and prepared food claims a growing share of the food dollar.

Married couples with children at home, the householders most likely to cook from scratch, are the best customers of sauces and gravies. They spend 55 percent more than average on this item, the figure peaking among those with school-aged children at 69 percent more. Householders aged 35 to 54, most with children, spend 20 to 25 percent more than average on sauces and gravies.

Average household spending on sauces and gravies increased 21 percent between 2000 and 2012, after adjusting for inflation. Behind the increase are changing tastes, with specialty sauces growing in popularity. Average household spending on this item is likely to decline in the years ahead as the small generation X passes through the best-customer lifestage and prepared food claims a growing share of the food dollar.

Table 9.71 Sauces and gravies

Total household spending $7,498,552,320.00
Average household spends   60.27

AGE OF HOUSEHOLDER	AVERAGE HOUSEHOLD SPENDING	BEST CUSTOMERS (index)	BIGGEST CUSTOMERS (market share)
Average household	$60.27	100	100.0%
Under age 25	35.37	59	3.8
Aged 25 to 34	59.78	99	16.0
Aged 35 to 44	72.31	120	20.8
Aged 45 to 54	75.54	125	24.8
Aged 55 to 64	60.60	101	18.4
Aged 65 to 74	50.91	84	10.2
Aged 75 or older	35.78	59	5.8

	AVERAGE HOUSEHOLD SPENDING	BEST CUSTOMERS (index)	BIGGEST CUSTOMERS (market share)
HOUSEHOLD INCOME			
Average household	$60.27	100	100.0%
Under $20,000	33.43	55	11.7
$20,000 to $39,999	47.05	78	17.6
$40,000 to $49,999	51.82	86	7.6
$50,000 to $69,999	63.25	105	15.2
$70,000 to $79,999	80.16	133	7.4
$80,000 to $99,999	76.92	128	11.3
$100,000 or more	94.19	156	29.3
HOUSEHOLD TYPE			
Average household	60.27	100	100.0
Married couples	80.06	133	64.5
Married couples, no children	64.47	107	22.3
Married couples with children	93.37	155	36.4
Oldest child under age 6	69.58	115	5.3
Oldest child aged 6 to 17	101.97	169	20.1
Oldest child aged 18 or older	93.84	156	11.0
Single parent with child under age 18	56.56	94	4.9
Single person	27.60	46	13.6
RACE AND HISPANIC ORIGIN			
Average household	60.27	100	100.0
Asian	51.90	86	3.7
Black	48.38	80	10.1
Hispanic	50.76	84	10.6
Non-Hispanic white and other	63.85	106	79.5
REGION			
Average household	60.27	100	100.0
Northeast	62.62	104	18.8
Midwest	63.14	105	23.2
South	53.41	89	33.0
West	66.88	111	25.0
EDUCATION			
Average household	60.27	100	100.0
Less than high school graduate	45.47	75	9.9
High school graduate	53.39	89	22.1
Some college	56.75	94	19.4
Associate's degree	73.03	121	12.0
Bachelor's degree or more	69.53	115	36.4
Bachelor's degree	69.04	115	22.8
Master's, professional, doctoral degree	70.35	117	13.5

Note: Market shares may not sum to 100.0 because of rounding and missing categories by household type. "Asian" and "black" include Hispanics and non-Hispanics who identify themselves as being of the respective race alone. "Hispanic" includes people of any race who identify themselves as Hispanic. "Other" includes people who identify themselves as non-Hispanic and as Alaska Native, American Indian, Asian (who are also included in the "Asian" row), or Native Hawaiian or other Pacific Islander, as well as non-Hispanics reporting more than one race.
Source: Calculations by New Strategist based on the Bureau of Labor Statistics' 2012 Consumer Expenditure Survey

Sausage

Best customers:
Householders aged 35 to 54
Married couples with school-aged or older children at home
Single parents
Blacks

Customer trends:
Average household spending on sausage is likely to resume its decline in the years ahead because the small generation X is in the best-customer lifestage.

Households with children are the biggest spenders on sausage. Married couples with school-aged or older children at home spend 47 to 54 percent more than average on this item, and single parents, whose spending approaches average on only a few items, spend 8 percent more than average on sausage. Householders aged 35 to 54, many with children at home, spend 19 to 23 percent more than average on sausage. Blacks spend 20 percent more than average on this item.

Average household spending on sausage declined 13 percent between 2000 and 2006, after adjusting for inflation, and then climbed 9 percent between 2006 and 2012. The growing popularity of fast-food breakfasts rather than home-cooked meals during the period leading up to the Great Recession was one factor behind the earlier drop in spending. More home cooking in an attempt to save money is the reason for the recent increase. Average household spending on sausage is likely to resume its decline in the years ahead because the small generation X is in the best-customer lifestage.

Table 9.72 Sausage

Total household spending $3,998,730,240.00
Average household spends 32.14

	AVERAGE HOUSEHOLD SPENDING	BEST CUSTOMERS (index)	BIGGEST CUSTOMERS (market share)
AGE OF HOUSEHOLDER			
Average household	$32.14	100	100.0%
Under age 25	24.19	75	4.9
Aged 25 to 34	26.89	84	13.5
Aged 35 to 44	38.36	119	20.7
Aged 45 to 54	39.67	123	24.4
Aged 55 to 64	30.27	94	17.2
Aged 65 to 74	35.54	111	13.3
Aged 75 or older	18.91	59	5.8

	AVERAGE HOUSEHOLD SPENDING	BEST CUSTOMERS (index)	BIGGEST CUSTOMERS (market share)
HOUSEHOLD INCOME			
Average household	**$32.14**	**100**	**100.0%**
Under $20,000	23.69	74	15.5
$20,000 to $39,999	25.34	79	17.8
$40,000 to $49,999	26.28	82	7.2
$50,000 to $69,999	34.27	107	15.4
$70,000 to $79,999	41.48	129	7.2
$80,000 to $99,999	40.21	125	11.0
$100,000 or more	45.24	141	26.4
HOUSEHOLD TYPE			
Average household	**32.14**	**100**	**100.0**
Married couples	40.82	127	61.7
Married couples, no children	34.61	108	22.4
Married couples with children	45.91	143	33.6
Oldest child under age 6	35.99	112	5.1
Oldest child aged 6 to 17	47.40	147	17.5
Oldest child aged 18 or older	49.59	154	10.9
Single parent with child under age 18	34.86	108	5.7
Single person	15.01	47	13.9
RACE AND HISPANIC ORIGIN			
Average household	**32.14**	**100**	**100.0**
Asian	35.21	110	4.7
Black	38.45	120	15.0
Hispanic	33.48	104	13.1
Non-Hispanic white and other	30.85	96	72.0
REGION			
Average household	**32.14**	**100**	**100.0**
Northeast	34.18	106	19.2
Midwest	28.65	89	19.8
South	33.93	106	39.3
West	31.00	96	21.7
EDUCATION			
Average household	**32.14**	**100**	**100.0**
Less than high school graduate	37.31	116	15.2
High school graduate	33.67	105	26.1
Some college	28.19	88	18.1
Associate's degree	33.65	105	10.3
Bachelor's degree or more	31.21	97	30.6
Bachelor's degree	31.01	96	19.2
Master's, professional, doctoral degree	31.54	98	11.4

Note: Market shares may not sum to 100.0 because of rounding and missing categories by household type. "Asian" and "black" include Hispanics and non-Hispanics who identify themselves as being of the respective race alone. "Hispanic" includes people of any race who identify themselves as Hispanic. "Other" includes people who identify themselves as non-Hispanic and as Alaska Native, American Indian, Asian (who are also included in the "Asian" row), or Native Hawaiian or other Pacific Islander, as well as non-Hispanics reporting more than one race.
Source: Calculations by New Strategist based on the Bureau of Labor Statistics' 2012 Consumer Expenditure Survey

Soups, Canned and Packaged

Best customers: Married couples without children at home
Married couples with school-aged or older children at home
Households in the West

Customer trends: Average household spending on soup may rise if the product promotes itself
as an inexpensive convenience food.

Families with children are the best customers of soup. Couples with school-aged or older children at home spend 40 to 51 percent more than average on soup. Married couples without children at home, many of them older empty-nesters, spend 28 percent more than average on this item. Households in the West outspend the average by one-fifth.

Average household spending on canned and packaged soup has been fairly stable since 2000, rising 1 percent between 2000 and 2006 and falling 4 percent between 2006 and 2012, after adjusting for inflation. Spending on soup may rise if the product promotes itself as an inexpensive convenience food.

Table 9.73 Soups, canned and packaged

Total household spending $5,760,460,800.00
Average household spends 46.30

AGE OF HOUSEHOLDER	AVERAGE HOUSEHOLD SPENDING	BEST CUSTOMERS (index)	BIGGEST CUSTOMERS (market share)
Average household	$46.30	100	100.0%
Under age 25	29.63	64	4.2
Aged 25 to 34	38.40	83	13.4
Aged 35 to 44	47.59	103	17.8
Aged 45 to 54	56.21	121	24.0
Aged 55 to 64	45.27	98	17.9
Aged 65 to 74	54.07	117	14.1
Aged 75 or older	41.05	89	8.7

	AVERAGE HOUSEHOLD SPENDING	BEST CUSTOMERS (index)	BIGGEST CUSTOMERS (market share)
HOUSEHOLD INCOME			
Average household	$46.30	100	100.0%
Under $20,000	31.45	68	14.3
$20,000 to $39,999	38.13	82	18.6
$40,000 to $49,999	43.47	94	8.3
$50,000 to $69,999	46.27	100	14.4
$70,000 to $79,999	47.49	103	5.7
$80,000 to $99,999	58.13	126	11.1
$100,000 or more	68.17	147	27.6
HOUSEHOLD TYPE			
Average household	46.30	100	100.0
Married couples	60.48	131	63.4
Married couples, no children	59.16	128	26.6
Married couples with children	62.94	136	32.0
Oldest child under age 6	46.32	100	4.6
Oldest child aged 6 to 17	64.98	140	16.7
Oldest child aged 18 or older	69.89	151	10.7
Single parent with child under age 18	39.69	86	4.5
Single person	25.91	56	16.6
RACE AND HISPANIC ORIGIN			
Average household	46.30	100	100.0
Asian	46.13	100	4.3
Black	27.29	59	7.4
Hispanic	34.12	74	9.2
Non-Hispanic white and other	51.52	111	83.5
REGION			
Average household	46.30	100	100.0
Northeast	44.82	97	17.5
Midwest	47.31	102	22.7
South	40.72	88	32.8
West	55.75	120	27.1
EDUCATION			
Average household	46.30	100	100.0
Less than high school graduate	38.39	83	10.8
High school graduate	37.58	81	20.2
Some college	48.00	104	21.4
Associate's degree	48.53	105	10.4
Bachelor's degree or more	54.16	117	36.9
Bachelor's degree	53.71	116	23.1
Master's, professional, doctoral degree	54.94	119	13.8

Note: Market shares may not sum to 100.0 because of rounding and missing categories by household type. "Asian" and "black" include Hispanics and non-Hispanics who identify themselves as being of the respective race alone. "Hispanic" includes people of any race who identify themselves as Hispanic. "Other" includes people who identify themselves as non-Hispanic and as Alaska Native, American Indian, Asian (who are also included in the "Asian" row), or Native Hawaiian or other Pacific Islander, as well as non-Hispanics reporting more than one race.
Source: Calculations by New Strategist based on the Bureau of Labor Statistics' 2012 Consumer Expenditure Survey

Sports Drinks

Best customers: Householders aged 25 to 54
Married couples with school-aged or older children at home
Single parents
Hispanics
Households in the Midwest

Customer trends: Average household spending on sports drinks may stabilize in the years ahead because they are being marketed as a healthy alternative to sodas.

The biggest spenders on sports drinks are the largest households. Married couples with children at home spend 68 percent more than average on this item. Those with school-aged children spend nearly twice the average on this item. Householders aged 35 to 44, most of them parents, spend 57 percent more than average on sports drinks. Together with the adjacent younger and older age groups, which spend 11 to 12 percent more than average on sports drinks, they control two-thirds of the market. Single parents, whose spending approaches average on only a few items, spend 9 percent more than average on sports drinks. Hispanics, who have the largest families, outspend the average by 40 percent. Households in the Midwest spend 12 percent more than average on sports drinks.

Sports drinks is a recently added category in the Consumer Expenditure Survey, and there are no comparative spending data from 2000 or 2006. Between 2010 and 2012, however, average household spending on sports drinks declined by a substantial 25 percent. Spending on this item may stabilize in the years ahead because sports drinks are being marketed as a healthy alternative to sodas.

Table 9.74 Sports drinks

Total household spending $1,881,169,920.00
Average household spends   15.12

AGE OF HOUSEHOLDER	AVERAGE HOUSEHOLD SPENDING	BEST CUSTOMERS (index)	BIGGEST CUSTOMERS (market share)
Average household	$15.12	100	100.0%
Under age 25	11.13	74	4.8
Aged 25 to 34	16.96	112	18.1
Aged 35 to 44	23.78	157	27.3
Aged 45 to 54	16.84	111	22.0
Aged 55 to 64	12.35	82	14.9
Aged 65 to 74	10.00	66	8.0
Aged 75 or older	6.74	45	4.4

	AVERAGE HOUSEHOLD SPENDING	BEST CUSTOMERS (index)	BIGGEST CUSTOMERS (market share)
HOUSEHOLD INCOME			
Average household	$15.12	100	100.0%
Under $20,000	7.54	50	10.5
$20,000 to $39,999	10.92	72	16.3
$40,000 to $49,999	12.38	82	7.2
$50,000 to $69,999	16.81	111	16.1
$70,000 to $79,999	16.57	110	6.1
$80,000 to $99,999	16.46	109	9.6
$100,000 or more	27.65	183	34.2
HOUSEHOLD TYPE			
Average household	15.12	100	100.0
Married couples	19.12	126	61.4
Married couples, no children	11.64	77	16.0
Married couples with children	25.36	168	39.4
Oldest child under age 6	14.99	99	4.5
Oldest child aged 6 to 17	29.57	196	23.3
Oldest child aged 18 or older	24.79	164	11.6
Single parent with child under age 18	16.43	109	5.7
Single person	7.49	50	14.7
RACE AND HISPANIC ORIGIN			
Average household	15.12	100	100.0
Asian	7.18	47	2.1
Black	12.29	81	10.2
Hispanic	21.10	140	17.5
Non-Hispanic white and other	14.76	98	73.3
REGION			
Average household	15.12	100	100.0
Northeast	12.86	85	15.4
Midwest	16.96	112	24.9
South	14.81	98	36.5
West	15.64	103	23.3
EDUCATION			
Average household	15.12	100	100.0
Less than high school graduate	14.71	97	12.7
High school graduate	13.16	87	21.7
Some college	13.71	91	18.7
Associate's degree	21.46	142	14.0
Bachelor's degree or more	15.77	104	32.9
Bachelor's degree	17.01	113	22.4
Master's, professional, doctoral degree	13.67	90	10.5

Note: Market shares may not sum to 100.0 because of rounding and missing categories by household type. "Asian" and "black" include Hispanics and non-Hispanics who identify themselves as being of the respective race alone. "Hispanic" includes people of any race who identify themselves as Hispanic. "Other" includes people who identify themselves as non-Hispanic and as Alaska Native, American Indian, Asian (who are also included in the "Asian" row), or Native Hawaiian or other Pacific Islander, as well as non-Hispanics reporting more than one race.
Source: Calculations by New Strategist based on the Bureau of Labor Statistics' 2012 Consumer Expenditure Survey

Sugar

Best customers: Householders aged 35 to 54
Married couples with school-aged or older children at home
Single parents
Hispanics and blacks
Householders with no more than a high school diploma

Customer trends: Average household spending on sugar is likely to resume its decline as the small generation X passes
through the best-customer lifestage.

The biggest spenders on sugar are households that do the most cooking from scratch, typically families with children. Couples with school-aged or older children at home spend 35 to 62 percent more than average on sugar. Single parents spend 15 percent more. Householders aged 35 to 54, most with children, spend 9 to 24 percent more than average on this item. Hispanics, who tend to have large families, spend 30 percent more than average on sugar, and blacks spend 20 percent more. Householders with no more than a high school diploma, many of them Hispanic, spend 26 percent more than average on sugar.

Average household spending on sugar fell 16 percent between 2000 and 2006, after adjusting for inflation, then grew 29 percent between 2006 and 2012. Behind the earlier decline was the rise in popularity of prepared food as busy families found less time to cook from scratch. The rise since 2006 is due in part to more home cooking in the aftermath of the Great Recession. Average household spending on sugar is likely to resume its decline as the small generation X passes through the best-customer lifestage.

Table 9.75 Sugar

Total household spending $3,033,262,080.00
Average household spends 24.38

AGE OF HOUSEHOLDER	AVERAGE HOUSEHOLD SPENDING	BEST CUSTOMERS (index)	BIGGEST CUSTOMERS (market share)
Average household	$24.38	100	100.0%
Under age 25	21.22	87	5.7
Aged 25 to 34	23.80	98	15.8
Aged 35 to 44	30.30	124	21.6
Aged 45 to 54	26.51	109	21.5
Aged 55 to 64	23.60	97	17.7
Aged 65 to 74	21.72	89	10.7
Aged 75 or older	17.07	70	6.8

	AVERAGE HOUSEHOLD SPENDING	BEST CUSTOMERS (index)	BIGGEST CUSTOMERS (market share)
HOUSEHOLD INCOME			
Average household	$24.38	100	100.0%
Under $20,000	20.53	84	17.7
$20,000 to $39,999	21.26	87	19.7
$40,000 to $49,999	26.56	109	9.6
$50,000 to $69,999	30.66	126	18.2
$70,000 to $79,999	26.68	109	6.1
$80,000 to $99,999	22.45	92	8.1
$100,000 or more	26.28	108	20.2
HOUSEHOLD TYPE			
Average household	24.38	100	100.0
Married couples	29.41	121	58.6
Married couples, no children	23.33	96	19.9
Married couples with children	33.35	137	32.2
Oldest child under age 6	24.72	101	4.6
Oldest child aged 6 to 17	32.95	135	16.1
Oldest child aged 18 or older	39.42	162	11.4
Single parent with child under age 18	28.15	115	6.1
Single person	11.56	47	14.1
RACE AND HISPANIC ORIGIN			
Average household	24.38	100	100.0
Asian	23.53	97	4.2
Black	29.23	120	15.1
Hispanic	31.75	130	16.3
Non-Hispanic white and other	22.37	92	68.9
REGION			
Average household	24.38	100	100.0
Northeast	24.04	99	17.8
Midwest	25.33	104	23.0
South	26.11	107	39.9
West	20.84	85	19.3
EDUCATION			
Average household	24.38	100	100.0
Less than high school graduate	30.70	126	16.4
High school graduate	30.61	126	31.3
Some college	22.70	93	19.2
Associate's degree	23.85	98	9.7
Bachelor's degree or more	18.51	76	23.9
Bachelor's degree	18.53	76	15.1
Master's, professional, doctoral degree	18.47	76	8.8

Note: Market shares may not sum to 100.0 because of rounding and missing categories by household type. "Asian" and "black" include Hispanics and non-Hispanics who identify themselves as being of the respective race alone. "Hispanic" includes people of any race who identify themselves as Hispanic. "Other" includes people who identify themselves as non-Hispanic and as Alaska Native, American Indian, Asian (who are also included in the "Asian" row), or Native Hawaiian or other Pacific Islander, as well as non-Hispanics reporting more than one race.
Source: Calculations by New Strategist based on the Bureau of Labor Statistics' 2012 Consumer Expenditure Survey

Sweetrolls, Coffee Cakes, and Doughnuts

Best customers: Married couples with school-aged or older children at home
Hispanics and Asians
Households in the West

Customer trends: Average household spending on sweetrolls, coffee cakes, and doughnuts may decline in the years ahead because the small generation X is in the best-customer lifestage.

The biggest spenders on sweetrolls, coffee cakes, and doughnuts are households with children. Married couples with school-aged or older children at home spend 42 to 46 percent more than average on this item. Hispanics and Asians outspend the average by 18 and 12 percent, respectively. Households in the West, where many Asians and Hispanics reside, spend 19 percent more than average on sweetrolls, coffee cakes, and doughnuts.

Average household spending on sweetrolls, coffee cakes, and doughnuts fell 22 percent between 2000 and 2006, after adjusting for inflation, and was essentially flat between 2006 and 2012. Behind the spending decline was the growing propensity of Americans to grab snacks from restaurants rather than grocery stores. Average household spending on sweetrolls, coffee cakes, and doughnuts may decline in the years ahead because the small generation X is in the best-customer lifestage.

Table 9.76 Sweetrolls, coffee cakes, and doughnuts

Total household spending $2,952,391,680.00
Average household spends 23.73

AGE OF HOUSEHOLDER	AVERAGE HOUSEHOLD SPENDING	BEST CUSTOMERS (index)	BIGGEST CUSTOMERS (market share)
Average household	$23.73	100	100.0%
Under age 25	13.82	58	3.8
Aged 25 to 34	17.24	73	11.7
Aged 35 to 44	25.89	109	18.9
Aged 45 to 54	26.69	112	22.3
Aged 55 to 64	25.65	108	19.8
Aged 65 to 74	25.10	106	12.7
Aged 75 or older	26.62	112	11.0

	AVERAGE HOUSEHOLD SPENDING	BEST CUSTOMERS (index)	BIGGEST CUSTOMERS (market share)
HOUSEHOLD INCOME			
Average household	**$23.73**	**100**	**100.0%**
Under $20,000	15.33	65	13.6
$20,000 to $39,999	18.26	77	17.3
$40,000 to $49,999	24.09	102	9.0
$50,000 to $69,999	31.33	132	19.1
$70,000 to $79,999	21.12	89	5.0
$80,000 to $99,999	24.79	104	9.2
$100,000 or more	33.85	143	26.7
HOUSEHOLD TYPE			
Average household	**23.73**	**100**	**100.0**
Married couples	30.18	127	61.8
Married couples, no children	25.57	108	22.5
Married couples with children	31.89	134	31.6
Oldest child under age 6	21.69	91	4.2
Oldest child aged 6 to 17	34.66	146	17.4
Oldest child aged 18 or older	33.63	142	10.0
Single parent with child under age 18	22.58	95	5.0
Single person	12.51	53	15.7
RACE AND HISPANIC ORIGIN			
Average household	**23.73**	**100**	**100.0**
Asian	26.52	112	4.8
Black	16.04	68	8.5
Hispanic	28.07	118	14.8
Non-Hispanic white and other	24.35	103	77.0
REGION			
Average household	**23.73**	**100**	**100.0**
Northeast	24.51	103	18.6
Midwest	24.50	103	22.9
South	20.21	85	31.7
West	28.18	119	26.8
EDUCATION			
Average household	**23.73**	**100**	**100.0**
Less than high school graduate	24.74	104	13.6
High school graduate	23.91	101	25.1
Some college	23.75	100	20.6
Associate's degree	24.50	103	10.2
Bachelor's degree or more	22.96	97	30.5
Bachelor's degree	21.67	91	18.2
Master's, professional, doctoral degree	25.15	106	12.3

Note: Market shares may not sum to 100.0 because of rounding and missing categories by household type. "Asian" and "black" include Hispanics and non-Hispanics who identify themselves as being of the respective race alone. "Hispanic" includes people of any race who identify themselves as Hispanic. "Other" includes people who identify themselves as non-Hispanic and as Alaska Native, American Indian, Asian (who are also included in the "Asian" row), or Native Hawaiian or other Pacific Islander, as well as non-Hispanics reporting more than one race.
Source: Calculations by New Strategist based on the Bureau of Labor Statistics' 2012 Consumer Expenditure Survey

Tea

Best customers: Householders aged 35 to 64
                    Married couples with school-aged or older children at home
                    Single parents
                    Asians
                    Households in the Northeast

Customer trends: Average household spending on tea may rise because of the introduction of new products
                    and tea's touted health benefits.

Although the media frequently tout the nutritional benefits of tea, Americans still spend far less on tea than on coffee. For some years tea was closing in. In 2010, the average household spent 48 percent as much on tea as on coffee, up from 37 percent in 2000. With the recent surge in coffee spending, however, the ratio declined again, to 35 percent in 2012. The middle aged are the best customers of tea, with householders ranging in age from 35 to 64 spending 8 to 17 percent more than average on this item. Married couples with school-aged or older children at home spend 49 to 50 percent more than average on tea. Single parents, whose spending approaches average on only a few items, spend 13 percent more than average on tea. Asian householders outspend the average by 54 percent. Households in the Northeast spend 22 percent more than average on tea.

Average household spending on tea purchased at grocery or convenience stores rose by a substantial 47 percent between 2000 and 2010, after adjusting for inflation, but declined slightly (down 1 percent) from 2010 to 2012. Behind the rise in spending on tea are the health and nutritional claims for green and black tea, as well as the greater variety of tea available in grocery stores. Average household spending on tea may resume its rise because of the introduction of new products and tea's touted health benefits.

Table 9.77 Tea

Total household spending $3,777,269,760.00

Average household spends   30.36

AGE OF HOUSEHOLDER	AVERAGE HOUSEHOLD SPENDING	BEST CUSTOMERS (index)	BIGGEST CUSTOMERS (market share)
Average household	$30.36	100	100.0%
Under age 25	19.86	65	4.3
Aged 25 to 34	28.98	95	15.4
Aged 35 to 44	32.82	108	18.8
Aged 45 to 54	35.48	117	23.1
Aged 55 to 64	33.73	111	20.3
Aged 65 to 74	29.98	99	11.9
Aged 75 or older	19.21	63	6.2

	AVERAGE HOUSEHOLD SPENDING	BEST CUSTOMERS (index)	BIGGEST CUSTOMERS (market share)
HOUSEHOLD INCOME			
Average household	**$30.36**	**100**	**100.0%**
Under $20,000	19.06	63	13.2
$20,000 to $39,999	22.02	73	16.3
$40,000 to $49,999	31.96	105	9.3
$50,000 to $69,999	33.76	111	16.1
$70,000 to $79,999	52.19	172	9.6
$80,000 to $99,999	33.02	109	9.6
$100,000 or more	41.28	136	25.5
HOUSEHOLD TYPE			
Average household	**30.36**	**100**	**100.0**
Married couples	38.76	128	62.0
Married couples, no children	34.07	112	23.4
Married couples with children	41.42	136	32.1
Oldest child under age 6	24.79	82	3.7
Oldest child aged 6 to 17	45.15	149	17.7
Oldest child aged 18 or older	45.54	150	10.6
Single parent with child under age 18	34.43	113	5.9
Single person	14.49	48	14.2
RACE AND HISPANIC ORIGIN			
Average household	**30.36**	**100**	**100.0**
Asian	46.79	154	6.7
Black	20.00	66	8.3
Hispanic	30.07	99	12.4
Non-Hispanic white and other	32.15	106	79.5
REGION			
Average household	**30.36**	**100**	**100.0**
Northeast	36.99	122	22.0
Midwest	29.72	98	21.7
South	27.79	92	34.1
West	29.88	98	22.2
EDUCATION			
Average household	**30.36**	**100**	**100.0**
Less than high school graduate	26.90	89	11.6
High school graduate	28.36	93	23.3
Some college	27.98	92	19.0
Associate's degree	38.43	127	12.5
Bachelor's degree or more	32.29	106	33.5
Bachelor's degree	31.24	103	20.5
Master's, professional, doctoral degree	34.07	112	13.0

Note: Market shares may not sum to 100.0 because of rounding and missing categories by household type. "Asian" and "black" include Hispanics and non-Hispanics who identify themselves as being of the respective race alone. "Hispanic" includes people of any race who identify themselves as Hispanic. "Other" includes people who identify themselves as non-Hispanic and as Alaska Native, American Indian, Asian (who are also included in the "Asian" row), or Native Hawaiian or other Pacific Islander, as well as non-Hispanics reporting more than one race.
Source: Calculations by New Strategist based on the Bureau of Labor Statistics' 2012 Consumer Expenditure Survey

Tomatoes

Best customers: Householders aged 35 to 54
Married couples with children at home
Asians and Hispanics
Households in the Northeast and West

Customer trends: Average household spending on fresh tomatoes may grow along with the Asian and Hispanic populations.

The best customers of fresh tomatoes are the largest households. Married couples with children at home spend 40 percent more than average on tomatoes. Householders ranging in age from 35 to 54, many with children, spend 11 to 24 percent more than average on this item. Asians spend 48 percent more than average on tomatoes, and Hispanics—who have the largest families—spend 44 percent more. Households in the West, where many Asians and Hispanics live, spend 23 percent more than average on tomatoes. Households in the Northeast spend 10 percent more.

Average household spending on fresh tomatoes was essentially unchanged between 2000 and 2012, after adjusting for inflation. Although the small generation X is in the best-customer lifestage, average household spending on tomatoes may grow in the years ahead as the Asian and Hispanic populations grow.

Table 9.78 Tomatoes

Total household spending $4,895,769,600.00
Average household spends   39.35

AGE OF HOUSEHOLDER	AVERAGE HOUSEHOLD SPENDING	BEST CUSTOMERS (index)	BIGGEST CUSTOMERS (market share)
Average household	$39.35	100	100.0%
Under age 25	25.26	64	4.2
Aged 25 to 34	38.04	97	15.6
Aged 35 to 44	43.71	111	19.3
Aged 45 to 54	48.87	124	24.6
Aged 55 to 64	37.92	96	17.6
Aged 65 to 74	37.09	94	11.4
Aged 75 or older	29.30	74	7.3

	AVERAGE HOUSEHOLD SPENDING	BEST CUSTOMERS (index)	BIGGEST CUSTOMERS (market share)
HOUSEHOLD INCOME			
Average household	$39.35	100	100.0%
Under $20,000	24.11	61	12.9
$20,000 to $39,999	33.15	84	19.0
$40,000 to $49,999	38.41	98	8.6
$50,000 to $69,999	36.83	94	13.5
$70,000 to $79,999	45.89	117	6.5
$80,000 to $99,999	43.83	111	9.8
$100,000 or more	61.51	156	29.3
HOUSEHOLD TYPE			
Average household	39.35	100	100.0
Married couples	51.36	131	63.4
Married couples, no children	43.33	110	23.0
Married couples with children	55.27	140	33.0
Oldest child under age 6	44.65	113	5.2
Oldest child aged 6 to 17	54.81	139	16.6
Oldest child aged 18 or older	62.65	159	11.2
Single parent with child under age 18	30.66	78	4.1
Single person	21.58	55	16.3
RACE AND HISPANIC ORIGIN			
Average household	39.35	100	100.0
Asian	58.16	148	6.4
Black	24.92	63	8.0
Hispanic	56.70	144	18.1
Non-Hispanic white and other	38.89	99	74.2
REGION			
Average household	39.35	100	100.0
Northeast	43.37	110	19.9
Midwest	38.39	98	21.6
South	32.57	83	30.8
West	48.34	123	27.7
EDUCATION			
Average household	39.35	100	100.0
Less than high school graduate	42.72	109	14.2
High school graduate	34.83	89	22.1
Some college	32.92	84	17.2
Associate's degree	38.92	99	9.8
Bachelor's degree or more	46.07	117	36.9
Bachelor's degree	43.23	110	21.9
Master's, professional, doctoral degree	50.86	129	15.0

Note: Market shares may not sum to 100.0 because of rounding and missing categories by household type. "Asian" and "black" include Hispanics and non-Hispanics who identify themselves as being of the respective race alone. "Hispanic" includes people of any race who identify themselves as Hispanic. "Other" includes people who identify themselves as non-Hispanic and as Alaska Native, American Indian, Asian (who are also included in the "Asian" row), or Native Hawaiian or other Pacific Islander, as well as non-Hispanics reporting more than one race.
Source: Calculations by New Strategist based on the Bureau of Labor Statistics' 2012 Consumer Expenditure Survey

Vegetables, Canned

Best customers: Householders aged 35 to 64
　　　　　　　　　　Married couples with school-aged or older children at home
　　　　　　　　　　Households in the Midwest

Customer trends: Average household spending on canned vegetables is likely to decline in the years ahead
　　　　　　　　　　as the large baby-boom generation ages and household size shrinks.

The largest households spend the most on canned vegetables. Married couples with school-aged or older children at home spend 39 to 46 percent more than average on canned vegetables. Householders aged 35 to 64, many with children, spend 7 to 14 percent more than average on this item. Households in the Midwest outspend the average by 12 percent.

Average household spending on canned vegetables fell 12 percent between 2000 and 2006, after adjusting for inflation, then climbed 25 percent between 2006 and 2012. Behind the decline in the earlier part of the decade was the greater propensity to eat out. The increase in spending during the later part of the decade was due to more home cooking in the aftermath of the Great Recession. Average household spending on canned vegetables is likely to decline in the years ahead as the large baby-boom generation ages and household size shrinks.

Table 9.79 Vegetables, canned

Total household spending $6,791,869,440.00
Average household spends   54.59

AGE OF HOUSEHOLDER	AVERAGE HOUSEHOLD SPENDING	BEST CUSTOMERS (index)	BIGGEST CUSTOMERS (market share)
Average household	$54.59	100	100.0%
Under age 25	43.97	81	5.3
Aged 25 to 34	50.31	92	14.9
Aged 35 to 44	59.42	109	18.9
Aged 45 to 54	62.30	114	22.6
Aged 55 to 64	58.39	107	19.6
Aged 65 to 74	53.57	98	11.8
Aged 75 or older	38.78	71	6.9

	AVERAGE HOUSEHOLD SPENDING	BEST CUSTOMERS (index)	BIGGEST CUSTOMERS (market share)
HOUSEHOLD INCOME			
Average household	**$54.59**	**100**	**100.0%**
Under $20,000	36.02	66	13.9
$20,000 to $39,999	45.84	84	18.9
$40,000 to $49,999	51.82	95	8.4
$50,000 to $69,999	53.91	99	14.3
$70,000 to $79,999	63.31	116	6.5
$80,000 to $99,999	64.30	118	10.4
$100,000 or more	80.13	147	27.5
HOUSEHOLD TYPE			
Average household	**54.59**	**100**	**100.0**
Married couples	68.11	125	60.6
Married couples, no children	60.47	111	23.1
Married couples with children	73.08	134	31.5
Oldest child under age 6	55.65	102	4.7
Oldest child aged 6 to 17	75.67	139	16.5
Oldest child aged 18 or older	79.62	146	10.3
Single parent with child under age 18	52.86	97	5.1
Single person	28.68	53	15.6
RACE AND HISPANIC ORIGIN			
Average household	**54.59**	**100**	**100.0**
Asian	42.40	78	3.4
Black	45.91	84	10.6
Hispanic	55.14	101	12.7
Non-Hispanic white and other	56.00	103	77.0
REGION			
Average household	**54.59**	**100**	**100.0**
Northeast	54.28	99	17.9
Midwest	61.15	112	24.8
South	54.12	99	36.9
West	49.08	90	20.3
EDUCATION			
Average household	**54.59**	**100**	**100.0**
Less than high school graduate	50.56	93	12.1
High school graduate	54.77	100	25.0
Some college	52.49	96	19.8
Associate's degree	61.57	113	11.1
Bachelor's degree or more	55.20	101	31.9
Bachelor's degree	56.40	103	20.6
Master's, professional, doctoral degree	53.18	97	11.3

Note: Market shares may not sum to 100.0 because of rounding and missing categories by household type. "Asian" and "black" include Hispanics and non-Hispanics who identify themselves as being of the respective race alone. "Hispanic" includes people of any race who identify themselves as Hispanic. "Other" includes people who identify themselves as non-Hispanic and as Alaska Native, American Indian, Asian (who are also included in the "Asian" row), or Native Hawaiian or other Pacific Islander, as well as non-Hispanics reporting more than one race.
Source: Calculations by New Strategist based on the Bureau of Labor Statistics' 2012 Consumer Expenditure Survey

Vegetables, Dried

Best customers: Householders aged 45 to 54
Married couples with school-aged or older children at home
Single parents
Asians and Hispanics
Householders without a high school diploma

Customer trends: Average household spending on dried vegetables may continue to increase along with the Asian and Hispanic populations.

The biggest spenders on dried vegetables are Asian and Hispanic households, which spend 84 and 70 percent, respectively, more than the average household on this item and account for 29 percent of the market. Householders aged 45 to 54 outspend the average by 44 percent. Married couples with school-aged children spend 33 percent more than average on dried vegetables and those with adult children at home spend 63 percent more. Single parents, whose spending approaches average on only a few items, spend 4 percent more than average on dried vegetables. Householders without a high school diploma, many of them Hispanic, spend 37 percent more than average on dried vegetables.

Average household spending on dried vegetables increased 30 percent between 2000 and 2012, after adjusting for inflation. Behind this increase was growth of the Asian and Hispanic populations. Spending on dried vegetables may continue to increase along with the Asian and Hispanic populations.

Table 9.80 Vegetables, dried

Total household spending $2,266,859,520.00
Average household spends 18.22

AGE OF HOUSEHOLDER	AVERAGE HOUSEHOLD SPENDING	BEST CUSTOMERS (index)	BIGGEST CUSTOMERS (market share)
Average household	$18.22	100	100.0%
Under age 25	10.44	57	3.8
Aged 25 to 34	16.34	90	14.5
Aged 35 to 44	19.43	107	18.5
Aged 45 to 54	26.16	144	28.4
Aged 55 to 64	16.95	93	17.0
Aged 65 to 74	18.86	104	12.5
Aged 75 or older	9.88	54	5.3

	AVERAGE HOUSEHOLD SPENDING	BEST CUSTOMERS (index)	BIGGEST CUSTOMERS (market share)
HOUSEHOLD INCOME			
Average household	**$18.22**	**100**	**100.0%**
Under $20,000	–	–	–
$20,000 to $39,999	17.07	94	21.1
$40,000 to $49,999	16.86	93	8.2
$50,000 to $69,999	18.37	101	14.6
$70,000 to $79,999	21.11	116	6.5
$80,000 to $99,999	17.95	99	8.7
$100,000 or more	22.23	122	22.8
HOUSEHOLD TYPE			
Average household	**18.22**	**100**	**100.0**
Married couples	21.84	120	58.2
Married couples, no children	16.40	90	18.8
Married couples with children	24.27	133	31.3
Oldest child under age 6	15.53	85	3.9
Oldest child aged 6 to 17	24.31	133	15.9
Oldest child aged 18 or older	29.68	163	11.5
Single parent with child under age 18	18.86	104	5.4
Single person	8.79	48	14.3
RACE AND HISPANIC ORIGIN			
Average household	**18.22**	**100**	**100.0**
Asian	33.52	184	8.0
Black	16.92	93	11.7
Hispanic	31.00	170	21.3
Non-Hispanic white and other	16.30	89	67.1
REGION			
Average household	**18.22**	**100**	**100.0**
Northeast	15.29	84	15.1
Midwest	19.27	106	23.4
South	17.58	96	35.9
West	20.63	113	25.5
EDUCATION			
Average household	**18.22**	**100**	**100.0**
Less than high school graduate	24.89	137	17.8
High school graduate	19.48	107	26.7
Some college	17.64	97	19.9
Associate's degree	18.21	100	9.9
Bachelor's degree or more	15.16	83	26.2
Bachelor's degree	13.43	74	14.7
Master's, professional, doctoral degree	18.07	99	11.5

Note: Market shares may not sum to 100.0 because of rounding and missing categories by household type. "Asian" and "black" include Hispanics and non-Hispanics who identify themselves as being of the respective race alone. "Hispanic" includes people of any race who identify themselves as Hispanic. "Other" includes people who identify themselves as non-Hispanic and as Alaska Native, American Indian, Asian (who are also included in the "Asian" row), or Native Hawaiian or other Pacific Islander, as well as non-Hispanics reporting more than one race. "–" means sample is too small to make a reliable estimate.
Source: Calculations by New Strategist based on the Bureau of Labor Statistics' 2012 Consumer Expenditure Survey

Vegetables, Fresh, Total

Best customers: Householders aged 35 to 74
　　　　　　　　　　 Married couples
　　　　　　　　　　 Asians and Hispanics
　　　　　　　　　　 Households in the West

Customer trends: Average household spending on fresh vegetables may continue to rise as consumers opt for fresh vegetables
　　　　　　　　　　 over frozen and canned, but prepared meals may limit the increase.

Fresh vegetables are the second-largest grocery category in terms of household spending. The best customers of fresh vegetables are middle-aged and older married couples. Householders ranging in age from 35 to 74 spend more than average on this item. Married couples spend 32 percent more, the figure peaking at 47 percent among couples with adult children at home. Asians spend 71 percent more than average on fresh vegetables, and Hispanics spend 15 percent more. Households in the West, where many Asians and Hispanics reside and where high-quality fresh vegetables are available in abundance, spend 22 percent more than average on fresh vegetables.

Average household spending on fresh vegetables rose slowly but steadily over the entire 2000-to-2012 time period, after adjusting for inflation, gaining 7 percent overall. Average household spending on fresh vegetables may continue to rise as consumers opt for fresh vegetables over frozen and canned, but prepared meals may limit the increase.

Table 9.81 Vegetables, fresh, total

Total household spending	$28,135,434,240.00		
Average household spends	226.14		

	AVERAGE HOUSEHOLD SPENDING	BEST CUSTOMERS (index)	BIGGEST CUSTOMERS (market share)
AGE OF HOUSEHOLDER			
Average household	$226.14	100	100.0%
Under age 25	128.49	57	3.7
Aged 25 to 34	208.36	92	14.9
Aged 35 to 44	243.26	108	18.7
Aged 45 to 54	269.33	119	23.6
Aged 55 to 64	234.43	104	19.0
Aged 65 to 74	242.22	107	12.9
Aged 75 or older	169.44	75	7.3

	AVERAGE HOUSEHOLD SPENDING	BEST CUSTOMERS (index)	BIGGEST CUSTOMERS (market share)
HOUSEHOLD INCOME			
Average household	**$226.14**	**100**	**100.0%**
Under $20,000	135.71	60	12.6
$20,000 to $39,999	176.11	78	17.6
$40,000 to $49,999	209.28	93	8.2
$50,000 to $69,999	216.96	96	13.9
$70,000 to $79,999	267.51	118	6.6
$80,000 to $99,999	272.62	121	10.6
$100,000 or more	367.96	163	30.5
HOUSEHOLD TYPE			
Average household	**226.14**	**100**	**100.0**
Married couples	298.36	132	64.1
Married couples, no children	272.08	120	25.1
Married couples with children	317.32	140	33.0
Oldest child under age 6	260.26	115	5.3
Oldest child aged 6 to 17	329.64	146	17.3
Oldest child aged 18 or older	332.34	147	10.4
Single parent with child under age 18	176.69	78	4.1
Single person	118.25	52	15.5
RACE AND HISPANIC ORIGIN			
Average household	**226.14**	**100**	**100.0**
Asian	385.62	171	7.4
Black	148.65	66	8.3
Hispanic	259.06	115	14.4
Non-Hispanic white and other	233.73	103	77.6
REGION			
Average household	**226.14**	**100**	**100.0**
Northeast	249.49	110	19.9
Midwest	205.63	91	20.2
South	197.55	87	32.5
West	275.23	122	27.4
EDUCATION			
Average household	**226.14**	**100**	**100.0**
Less than high school graduate	212.98	94	12.3
High school graduate	191.57	85	21.1
Some college	185.27	82	16.9
Associate's degree	227.44	101	9.9
Bachelor's degree or more	284.97	126	39.7
Bachelor's degree	271.17	120	23.9
Master's, professional, doctoral degree	308.31	136	15.8

Note: Market shares may not sum to 100.0 because of rounding and missing categories by household type. "Asian" and "black" include Hispanics and non-Hispanics who identify themselves as being of the respective race alone. "Hispanic" includes people of any race who identify themselves as Hispanic. "Other" includes people who identify themselves as non-Hispanic and as Alaska Native, American Indian, Asian (who are also included in the "Asian" row), or Native Hawaiian or other Pacific Islander, as well as non-Hispanics reporting more than one race.
Source: Calculations by New Strategist based on the Bureau of Labor Statistics' 2012 Consumer Expenditure Survey

Vegetables, Frozen

Best customers: Householders aged 35 to 54
                         Married couples with school-aged or older children at home
                         Single parents
                         Households in the Northeast

Customer trends: Average household spending on frozen vegetables is likely to decline in the years ahead as Americans
                         opt for the fresh variety and prepared food claims a growing share of the food dollar.

The largest households are the best customers of frozen vegetables. Married couples with school-aged children spend 49 percent more than average on this item and those with adult children at home spend 73 percent more. Householders aged 35 to 54, most with children, spend 15 to 19 percent more than average on frozen vegetables. Single parents, whose spending approaches average on only a few items, spend 12 percent more than average on frozen vegetables. Households in the Northeast spend 18 percent more.

Average household spending on frozen vegetables fell by 1 percent between 2000 and 2006, after adjusting for inflation, as fewer households cooked meals at home. Then the trend reversed and spending on frozen vegetables grew 8 percent between 2006 and 2012 as household belt tightening caused a renewed interest in home cooking. Average household spending on frozen vegetables is likely to decline in the years ahead as Americans opt for the fresh variety and prepared food claims a growing share of the food dollar.

Table 9.82 Vegetables, frozen

Total household spending	$4,665,600,000.00
Average household spends	37.50

	AVERAGE HOUSEHOLD SPENDING	BEST CUSTOMERS (index)	BIGGEST CUSTOMERS (market share)
AGE OF HOUSEHOLDER			
Average household	**$37.50**	**100**	**100.0%**
Under age 25	18.91	50	3.3
Aged 25 to 34	39.02	104	16.8
Aged 35 to 44	43.03	115	19.9
Aged 45 to 54	44.50	119	23.5
Aged 55 to 64	37.42	100	18.3
Aged 65 to 74	35.27	94	11.3
Aged 75 or older	26.22	70	6.8

	AVERAGE HOUSEHOLD SPENDING	BEST CUSTOMERS (index)	BIGGEST CUSTOMERS (market share)
HOUSEHOLD INCOME			
Average household	**$37.50**	**100**	**100.0%**
Under $20,000	26.03	69	14.6
$20,000 to $39,999	28.85	77	17.3
$40,000 to $49,999	28.07	75	6.6
$50,000 to $69,999	38.32	102	14.8
$70,000 to $79,999	47.20	126	7.0
$80,000 to $99,999	53.59	143	12.6
$100,000 or more	54.59	146	27.3
HOUSEHOLD TYPE			
Average household	**37.50**	**100**	**100.0**
Married couples	47.95	128	62.1
Married couples, no children	39.99	107	22.2
Married couples with children	54.74	146	34.3
Oldest child under age 6	34.83	93	4.2
Oldest child aged 6 to 17	55.99	149	17.8
Oldest child aged 18 or older	65.06	173	12.2
Single parent with child under age 18	42.01	112	5.9
Single person	19.54	52	15.5
RACE AND HISPANIC ORIGIN			
Average household	**37.50**	**100**	**100.0**
Asian	26.13	70	3.0
Black	39.32	105	13.2
Hispanic	24.87	66	8.3
Non-Hispanic white and other	39.25	105	78.6
REGION			
Average household	**37.50**	**100**	**100.0**
Northeast	44.28	118	21.3
Midwest	38.50	103	22.8
South	37.68	100	37.4
West	30.70	82	18.4
EDUCATION			
Average household	**37.50**	**100**	**100.0**
Less than high school graduate	31.78	85	11.1
High school graduate	35.28	94	23.5
Some college	39.61	106	21.8
Associate's degree	38.19	102	10.1
Bachelor's degree or more	39.73	106	33.4
Bachelor's degree	39.86	106	21.2
Master's, professional, doctoral degree	39.51	105	12.2

Note: Market shares may not sum to 100.0 because of rounding and missing categories by household type. "Asian" and "black" include Hispanics and non-Hispanics who identify themselves as being of the respective race alone. "Hispanic" includes people of any race who identify themselves as Hispanic. "Other" includes people who identify themselves as non-Hispanic and as Alaska Native, American Indian, Asian (who are also included in the "Asian" row), or Native Hawaiian or other Pacific Islander, as well as non-Hispanics reporting more than one race.
Source: Calculations by New Strategist based on the Bureau of Labor Statistics' 2012 Consumer Expenditure Survey

Vegetable Juice, Fresh and Canned

Best customers: Householders aged 35 to 54
                         Married couples with children at home
                         Single parents
                         Asians

Customer trends: Average household spending on vegetable juice may continue to rise in the years ahead
                         as the large millennial generation has children.

The biggest spenders on vegetable juice are households with children. Married couples with school-aged children spend 53 percent more than average on vegetable juice, and those with adult children at home spend 52 percent more. Householders aged 35 to 54, most of them parents, spend 12 to 35 percent more than average on vegetable juice. Single parents, whose spending approaches average on only a few items, spend 21 percent more than the average household on vegetable juice. Asians outspend the average by 23 percent.

Average household spending on vegetable juice purchased at grocery or convenience stores has risen steadily. It grew 12 percent between 2000 and 2006, after adjusting for inflation, and 37 percent between 2006 and 2012. Spending on vegetable juice may continue to increase in the years ahead as the large millennial generation has children.

Table 9.83 Vegetable juice, fresh and canned

Total household spending $2,361,415,680.00
Average household spends   18.98

AGE OF HOUSEHOLDER	AVERAGE HOUSEHOLD SPENDING	BEST CUSTOMERS (index)	BIGGEST CUSTOMERS (market share)
Average household	$18.98	100	100.0%
Under age 25	15.50	82	5.4
Aged 25 to 34	19.99	105	17.0
Aged 35 to 44	21.26	112	19.4
Aged 45 to 54	25.58	135	26.7
Aged 55 to 64	16.47	87	15.9
Aged 65 to 74	13.40	71	8.5
Aged 75 or older	13.33	70	6.9

	AVERAGE HOUSEHOLD SPENDING	BEST CUSTOMERS (index)	BIGGEST CUSTOMERS (market share)
HOUSEHOLD INCOME			
Average household	**$18.98**	**100**	**100.0%**
Under $20,000	12.90	68	14.3
$20,000 to $39,999	16.36	86	19.4
$40,000 to $49,999	20.87	110	9.7
$50,000 to $69,999	16.46	87	12.5
$70,000 to $79,999	22.09	116	6.5
$80,000 to $99,999	23.72	125	11.0
$100,000 or more	26.72	141	26.4
HOUSEHOLD TYPE			
Average household	**18.98**	**100**	**100.0**
Married couples	22.84	120	58.4
Married couples, no children	16.09	85	17.7
Married couples with children	27.97	147	34.6
Oldest child under age 6	23.83	126	5.7
Oldest child aged 6 to 17	28.99	153	18.2
Oldest child aged 18 or older	28.84	152	10.7
Single parent with child under age 18	23.01	121	6.4
Single person	10.06	53	15.7
RACE AND HISPANIC ORIGIN			
Average household	**18.98**	**100**	**100.0**
Asian	23.29	123	5.3
Black	16.29	86	10.8
Hispanic	20.00	105	13.2
Non-Hispanic white and other	19.24	101	76.1
REGION			
Average household	**18.98**	**100**	**100.0**
Northeast	21.78	115	20.7
Midwest	20.78	109	24.3
South	14.65	77	28.7
West	22.08	116	26.2
EDUCATION			
Average household	**18.98**	**100**	**100.0**
Less than high school graduate	16.02	84	11.0
High school graduate	17.93	94	23.6
Some college	16.87	89	18.3
Associate's degree	25.61	135	13.3
Bachelor's degree or more	20.24	107	33.6
Bachelor's degree	19.63	103	20.6
Master's, professional, doctoral degree	21.26	112	13.0

Note: Market shares may not sum to 100.0 because of rounding and missing categories by household type. "Asian" and "black" include Hispanics and non-Hispanics who identify themselves as being of the respective race alone. "Hispanic" includes people of any race who identify themselves as Hispanic. "Other" includes people who identify themselves as non-Hispanic and as Alaska Native, American Indian, Asian (who are also included in the "Asian" row), or Native Hawaiian or other Pacific Islander, as well as non-Hispanics reporting more than one race.
Source: Calculations by New Strategist based on the Bureau of Labor Statistics' 2012 Consumer Expenditure Survey

Water, Bottled

Best customers: Householders aged 35 to 54
Married couples with school-aged or older children at home
Single parents
Hispanics and Asians

Customer trends: Average household spending on bottled water may climb in the years ahead as Americans question the quality of tap water and search for alternatives to calorie-laden colas and fruit drinks.

The biggest spenders on bottled water are the largest households. Householders aged 35 to 54, many with children, spend 19 to 29 percent more than average on bottled water and control 46 percent of spending on this item. Married couples with school-aged or older children at home spend one-half more than average on this item, and single parents, whose spending is below average on most items, spend 14 percent more than average on bottled water. Asians spend 22 percent more than average on bottled water, and Hispanics, who have the largest families, spend 33 percent more. Bottled water is one of the relatively few items in the Consumer Expenditure Survey on which non-Hispanic whites spend (slightly) less than average.

Bottled water is a relatively new category in the Consumer Expenditure Survey, and there are no comparative spending data from 2000. Between 2006 and 2010, spending on bottled water declined 13 percent, in part because less expensive alternatives entered the market. Spending rebounded with a 4 percent increase between 2010 and 2012. Average household spending on bottled water may climb in the years ahead as Americans question the quality of tap water and search for alternatives to calorie-laden colas and fruit drinks.

Table 9.84 **Water, bottled**

| Total household spending | $7,066,828,800.00 |
| Average household spends | 56.80 |

	AVERAGE HOUSEHOLD SPENDING	BEST CUSTOMERS (index)	BIGGEST CUSTOMERS (market share)
AGE OF HOUSEHOLDER			
Average household	$56.80	100	100.0%
Under age 25	42.01	74	4.9
Aged 25 to 34	54.25	96	15.4
Aged 35 to 44	67.82	119	20.7
Aged 45 to 54	73.49	129	25.6
Aged 55 to 64	55.05	97	17.7
Aged 65 to 74	49.54	87	10.5
Aged 75 or older	28.87	51	5.0

	AVERAGE HOUSEHOLD SPENDING	BEST CUSTOMERS (index)	BIGGEST CUSTOMERS (market share)
HOUSEHOLD INCOME			
Average household	**$56.80**	**100**	**100.0%**
Under $20,000	37.34	66	13.8
$20,000 to $39,999	44.69	79	17.7
$40,000 to $49,999	54.20	95	8.4
$50,000 to $69,999	56.22	99	14.3
$70,000 to $79,999	69.45	122	6.8
$80,000 to $99,999	75.20	132	11.7
$100,000 or more	82.32	145	27.1
HOUSEHOLD TYPE			
Average household	**56.80**	**100**	**100.0**
Married couples	67.37	119	57.6
Married couples, no children	52.49	92	19.3
Married couples with children	77.56	137	32.1
Oldest child under age 6	41.22	73	3.3
Oldest child aged 6 to 17	86.44	152	18.1
Oldest child aged 18 or older	85.38	150	10.6
Single parent with child under age 18	65.03	114	6.0
Single person	35.30	62	18.5
RACE AND HISPANIC ORIGIN			
Average household	**56.80**	**100**	**100.0**
Asian	69.52	122	5.3
Black	53.84	95	11.9
Hispanic	75.45	133	16.7
Non-Hispanic white and other	54.39	96	71.9
REGION			
Average household	**56.80**	**100**	**100.0**
Northeast	60.98	107	19.4
Midwest	49.99	88	19.5
South	58.06	102	38.1
West	58.14	102	23.1
EDUCATION			
Average household	**56.80**	**100**	**100.0**
Less than high school graduate	58.10	102	13.4
High school graduate	55.22	97	24.2
Some college	53.13	94	19.3
Associate's degree	62.15	109	10.8
Bachelor's degree or more	58.33	103	32.4
Bachelor's degree	55.61	98	19.5
Master's, professional, doctoral degree	62.92	111	12.9

Note: Market shares may not sum to 100.0 because of rounding and missing categories by household type. "Asian" and "black" include Hispanics and non-Hispanics who identify themselves as being of the respective race alone. "Hispanic" includes people of any race who identify themselves as Hispanic. "Other" includes people who identify themselves as non-Hispanic and as Alaska Native, American Indian, Asian (who are also included in the "Asian" row), or Native Hawaiian or other Pacific Islander, as well as non-Hispanics reporting more than one race.
Source: Calculations by New Strategist based on the Bureau of Labor Statistics' 2012 Consumer Expenditure Survey

Chapter 10.
Health Care

Household Spending on Health Care, 2000 to 2012

Out-of-pocket spending on health care by the average household has grown over the past few years as health care costs climbed and employers shifted more costs onto employees. Between 2000 and 2012, average household out-of-pocket spending on health care rose 29 percent, after adjusting for inflation. Out-of-pocket spending on health insurance ranks among the 10 biggest household expenses. It averaged $2,061 in 2012, 57 percent more than in 2000, after adjusting for inflation. Spending on Medicare premiums, the second-largest health care category, grew by an even larger 81 percent over the 12-year period.

Prescription drugs are the third-largest health care expense for the average household. Out-of-pocket spending on prescription drugs fell 10 percent between 2000 and 2012, thanks to the introduction of the Medicare prescription drug plan in 2006. Spending on nonprescription drugs increased 12 percent, while spending on vitamins fell 18 percent during those years.

Spending on a number of other health care categories also fell between 2000 and 2012. Households spent 10 percent less on eye care services, 15 percent less on eyeglasses and contact lenses, and 9 percent less on dental services, for example. Average household spending on commercial Medicare supplements declined 15 percent.

Older Americans are the biggest out-of-pocket spenders on health care. As the large baby-boom generation enters the older age groups, out-of-pocket spending on health care will soar.

Spending on health care

(average out-of-pocket spending by households on health care, 2000, 2006, 2010, and 2012; in 2012 dollars)

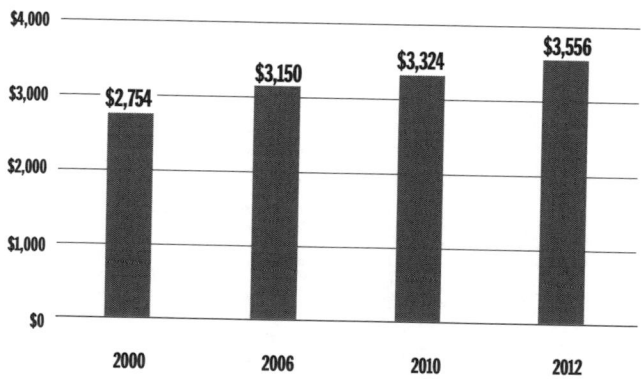

Table 10.1 Health care spending, 2000 to 2012

(average annual household spending on out-of-pocket health care costs and percent distribution, by category, 2000 to 2012; percent change in spending and percentage point change in distribution, 2000–06, 2006–12, and 2010–12; in 2012 dollars; ranked by amount spent)

	average annual household spending (in 2012$)				percent change		
	2012	2010	2006	2000	2010–12	2006–12	2000–06
Average household out-of-pocket spending on health care	$3,556.45	$3,323.92	$3,150.46	$2,754.15	7.0%	12.9%	14.4%
Health insurance, including Medicare, long-term care	2,060.78	1,927.39	1,668.41	1,310.17	6.9	23.5	27.3
Medicare premiums	396.60	372.05	346.89	218.71	6.6	14.3	58.6
Drugs, prescription	366.40	368.59	447.54	406.88	–0.6	–18.1	10.0
Dental services	268.32	276.52	272.14	294.38	–3.0	–1.4	–7.6
Physician services	204.16	192.86	191.21	179.21	5.9	6.8	6.7
Hospital room and services	161.48	121.59	106.84	102.77	32.8	51.1	4.0
Medicare supplements, commercial	149.34	162.16	156.05	175.98	–7.9	–4.3	–11.3
Drugs, nonprescription	97.49	94.30	91.77	86.78	3.4	6.2	5.7
Long-term care insurance	80.25	74.41	67.18	–	7.8	19.5	–
Eyeglasses and contact lenses	66.52	63.85	61.49	77.90	4.2	8.2	–21.1
Medicare prescription drug premiums	66.28	64.04	30.82	–	3.5	115.1	–
Nonphysician health care professional services	62.38	56.86	55.96	49.16	9.7	11.5	13.8
Vitamins, nonprescription	50.76	47.95	45.69	61.59	5.9	11.1	–25.8
Lab tests and X-rays	46.91	47.05	49.23	26.83	–0.3	–4.7	83.5
Eye care services	41.86	36.48	44.20	46.73	14.7	–5.3	–5.4
Topicals and dressings	40.99	38.08	36.55	27.99	7.6	12.2	30.6
Hearing aids	21.23	13.04	19.29	15.71	62.9	10.0	22.8

					percentage point change		
PERCENT DISTRIBUTION OF SPENDING	2012	2010	2006	2000	2010–12	2006–12	2000–06
Average household out-of-pocket spending on health care	100.0%	100.0%	100.0%	100.0%	–	–	–
Health insurance, including Medicare, long-term care	57.9	58.0	53.0	47.6	0.0	5.0	5.4
Medicare premiums	11.2	11.2	11.0	7.9	0.0	0.1	3.1
Drugs, prescription	10.3	11.1	14.2	14.8	–0.8	–3.9	–0.6
Dental services	7.5	8.3	8.6	10.7	–0.8	–1.1	–2.1
Physician services	5.7	5.8	6.1	6.5	–0.1	–0.3	–0.4
Hospital room and services	4.5	3.7	3.4	3.7	0.9	1.1	–0.3
Medicare supplements, commercial	4.2	4.9	5.0	6.4	–0.7	–0.8	–1.4
Drugs, nonprescription	2.7	2.8	2.9	3.2	–0.1	–0.2	–0.2
Long-term care insurance	2.3	2.2	2.1	–	0.0	0.1	–
Eyeglasses and contact lenses	1.9	1.9	2.0	2.8	–0.1	–0.1	–0.9
Medicare prescription drug premiums	1.9	1.9	1.0	–	–0.1	0.9	–
Nonphysician health care professional services	1.8	1.7	1.8	1.8	0.0	0.0	0.0
Vitamins, nonprescription	1.4	1.4	1.5	2.2	0.0	0.0	–0.8
Lab tests and X-rays	1.3	1.4	1.6	1.0	–0.1	–0.2	0.6
Eye care services	1.2	1.1	1.4	1.7	0.1	–0.2	–0.3
Topicals and dressings	1.2	1.1	1.2	1.0	0.0	0.0	0.1
Hearing aids	0.6	0.4	0.6	0.6	0.2	0.0	0.0

Note: Numbers sum to more than total because Medicare premiums and supplements and long-term care insurance are also included in health insurance total. Percentage point change calculations are based on unrounded figures. "–" means not applicable or data are unavailable.
Source: Bureau of Labor Statistics, 2000, 2006, 2010, and 2012 Consumer Expenditure Surveys; calculations by New Strategist

Dental Services (Out-of-Pocket Expenses)

Best customers: Householders aged 55 to 74
Married couples without children at home
Married couples with school-aged or older children at home
Non-Hispanic whites
Households in the West

Customer trends: Average household spending on dental services will increase as more boomers enter the age groups that spend the most.

The biggest out-of-pocket spenders on dental services are older Americans. Householders aged 55 to 74 spend 30 to 55 percent more than the average household on this item, in part because older Americans are less likely to have insurance coverage for dental care. Married couples without children at home (many of them older) spend 47 percent more than average on dental services. Couples with school-aged or older children at home spend 35 to 56 percent more than average on dental services because their households are larger than average and have more teeth that need fixing. Households in the West spend 27 percent more than average on this item. Non-Hispanic whites spend 19 percent more.

Average out-of-pocket spending on dental services declined by 9 percent between 2000 and 2012, after adjusting for inflation. One reason for the decline was greater health insurance coverage for dental care. Another factor was belt tightening as health care costs soared. It is likely that many Americans delayed dental visits as they were forced to pay more for health insurance. Out-of-pocket spending on dental services is likely to climb in the years ahead as boomers continue to age into the big-spending age groups.

Table 10.2 Dental services (out-of-pocket expenses)

Total household spending $33,383,301,120.00
Average household spends 268.32

AGE OF HOUSEHOLDER	AVERAGE HOUSEHOLD SPENDING	BEST CUSTOMERS (index)	BIGGEST CUSTOMERS (market share)
Average household	$268.32	100	100.0%
Under age 25	49.09	18	1.2
Aged 25 to 34	120.13	45	7.2
Aged 35 to 44	233.52	87	15.1
Aged 45 to 54	310.26	116	22.9
Aged 55 to 64	349.12	130	23.8
Aged 65 to 74	415.57	155	18.7
Aged 75 or older	304.55	114	11.1

	AVERAGE HOUSEHOLD SPENDING	BEST CUSTOMERS (index)	BIGGEST CUSTOMERS (market share)
HOUSEHOLD INCOME			
Average household	**$268.32**	**100**	**100.0%**
Under $20,000	124.87	47	9.8
$20,000 to $39,999	202.73	76	17.0
$40,000 to $49,999	189.81	71	6.3
$50,000 to $69,999	237.64	89	12.8
$70,000 to $79,999	279.97	104	5.8
$80,000 to $99,999	355.27	132	11.7
$100,000 or more	524.82	196	36.6
HOUSEHOLD TYPE			
Average household	**268.32**	**100**	**100.0**
Married couples	359.22	134	65.0
Married couples, no children	394.14	147	30.6
Married couples with children	337.62	126	29.6
Oldest child under age 6	151.34	56	2.6
Oldest child aged 6 to 17	361.09	135	16.0
Oldest child aged 18 or older	418.54	156	11.0
Single parent with child under age 18	121.41	45	2.4
Single person	203.81	76	22.6
RACE AND HISPANIC ORIGIN			
Average household	**268.32**	**100**	**100.0**
Asian	268.18	100	4.3
Black	96.00	36	4.5
Hispanic	134.71	50	6.3
Non-Hispanic white and other	318.91	119	89.2
REGION			
Average household	**268.32**	**100**	**100.0**
Northeast	298.88	111	20.1
Midwest	258.29	96	21.3
South	215.41	80	29.9
West	341.16	127	28.7
EDUCATION			
Average household	**268.32**	**100**	**100.0**
Less than high school graduate	89.93	34	4.4
High school graduate	161.67	60	15.0
Some college	308.76	115	23.7
Associate's degree	269.46	100	9.9
Bachelor's degree or more	399.73	149	47.0
Bachelor's degree	357.61	133	26.6
Master's, professional, doctoral degree	472.07	176	20.4

Note: Market shares may not sum to 100.0 because of rounding and missing categories by household type. "Asian" and "black" include Hispanics and non-Hispanics who identify themselves as being of the respective race alone. "Hispanic" includes people of any race who identify themselves as Hispanic. "Other" includes people who identify themselves as non-Hispanic and as Alaska Native, American Indian, Asian (who are also included in the "Asian" row), or Native Hawaiian or other Pacific Islander, as well as non-Hispanics reporting more than one race.
Source: Calculations by New Strategist based on the Bureau of Labor Statistics' 2012 Consumer Expenditure Survey

Drugs, Nonprescription

Best customers: Householders aged 55 to 74
                                 Married couples without children at home
                                 Married couples with school-aged or older children at home

Customer trends: Average household spending on nonprescription drugs should grow as boomers age.

The biggest spenders on nonprescription drugs are older Americans and the largest households. Householders aged 55 to 74 spend 25 to 51 percent more than the average household on over-the-counter drugs. Married couples without children at home (most of them older) spend 25 more than average on this item. Couples with school-aged or older children at home spend 28 to 42 percent more because their households are larger than average.

Average household spending on nonprescription drugs rose 12 percent between 2000 and 2012, after adjusting for inflation. Average household spending on nonprescription drugs is likely to continue to climb in the years ahead as the large baby-boom generation enters the 65-or-older age group.

Table 10.3 Drugs, nonprescription

Total household spending	$12,129,315,840.00
Average household spends	97.49

	AVERAGE HOUSEHOLD SPENDING	BEST CUSTOMERS (index)	BIGGEST CUSTOMERS (market share)
AGE OF HOUSEHOLDER			
Average household	**$97.49**	**100**	**100.0%**
Under age 25	28.02	29	1.9
Aged 25 to 34	63.33	65	10.5
Aged 35 to 44	85.41	88	15.2
Aged 45 to 54	104.75	107	21.3
Aged 55 to 64	147.15	151	27.6
Aged 65 to 74	121.55	125	15.0
Aged 75 or older	90.87	93	9.1

	AVERAGE HOUSEHOLD SPENDING	BEST CUSTOMERS (index)	BIGGEST CUSTOMERS (market share)
HOUSEHOLD INCOME			
Average household	**$97.49**	**100**	**100.0%**
Under $20,000	59.10	61	12.8
$20,000 to $39,999	76.62	79	17.7
$40,000 to $49,999	70.15	72	6.4
$50,000 to $69,999	89.10	91	13.2
$70,000 to $79,999	111.92	115	6.4
$80,000 to $99,999	135.18	139	12.2
$100,000 or more	166.09	170	31.9
HOUSEHOLD TYPE			
Average household	**97.49**	**100**	**100.0**
Married couples	125.13	128	62.3
Married couples, no children	122.33	125	26.2
Married couples with children	123.91	127	29.9
Oldest child under age 6	84.49	87	4.0
Oldest child aged 6 to 17	138.11	142	16.8
Oldest child aged 18 or older	124.77	128	9.0
Single parent with child under age 18	72.17	74	3.9
Single person	71.14	73	21.7
RACE AND HISPANIC ORIGIN			
Average household	**97.49**	**100**	**100.0**
Asian	72.60	74	3.2
Black	55.86	57	7.2
Hispanic	68.58	70	8.8
Non-Hispanic white and other	109.11	112	84.0
REGION			
Average household	**97.49**	**100**	**100.0**
Northeast	86.49	89	16.0
Midwest	102.39	105	23.3
South	93.52	96	35.7
West	108.12	111	25.0
EDUCATION			
Average household	**97.49**	**100**	**100.0**
Less than high school graduate	85.00	87	11.4
High school graduate	80.08	82	20.5
Some college	74.71	77	15.8
Associate's degree	133.93	137	13.6
Bachelor's degree or more	119.62	123	38.7
Bachelor's degree	97.89	100	20.0
Master's, professional, doctoral degree	156.35	160	18.6

Note: Market shares may not sum to 100.0 because of rounding and missing categories by household type. "Asian" and "black" include Hispanics and non-Hispanics who identify themselves as being of the respective race alone. "Hispanic" includes people of any race who identify themselves as Hispanic. "Other" includes people who identify themselves as non-Hispanic and as Alaska Native, American Indian, Asian (who are also included in the "Asian" row), or Native Hawaiian or other Pacific Islander, as well as non-Hispanics reporting more than one race.
Source: Calculations by New Strategist based on the Bureau of Labor Statistics' 2012 Consumer Expenditure Survey

Drugs, Prescription (Out-of-Pocket Expenses)

Best customers: Householders aged 55 or older
Married couples without children at home
Married couples with adult children at home
Non-Hispanic whites

Customer trends: Average household spending on prescription drugs should climb as boomers fill
the best-customer age groups.

Prescription drugs are the second-largest health care expense for the average household, trailing only health insurance spending. The biggest out-of-pocket spenders on prescription drugs are older Americans. Householders aged 55 or older spend 37 to 73 percent more than the average householder on this item and account for 62 percent of out-of-pocket spending in this market. Married couples without children at home (most of them older) spend 74 percent more than average on prescription drugs. Householders with adult children at home, whose households are larger than average, spend 42 percent more than average out-of-pocket on prescription drugs. Non-Hispanic whites outspend minorities by a wide margin on this item and control 87 percent of the market.

Average household spending on prescription drugs, which had risen 10 percent between 2000 and 2006, fell 18 percent between 2006 and 2012, after adjusting for inflation, largely because of the introduction of the Medicare prescription drug plan. As the pharmaceutical industry introduces new and improved drugs and as the baby-boom generation ages, average household spending on prescription drugs should rise.

Table 10.4 Drugs, prescription (out-of-pocket expenses)

Total household spending	$45,586,022,400.00
Average household spends	366.40

	AVERAGE HOUSEHOLD SPENDING	BEST CUSTOMERS (index)	BIGGEST CUSTOMERS (market share)
AGE OF HOUSEHOLDER			
Average household	$366.40	100	100.0%
Under age 25	73.62	20	1.3
Aged 25 to 34	116.70	32	5.1
Aged 35 to 44	242.44	66	11.5
Aged 45 to 54	370.95	101	20.0
Aged 55 to 64	501.19	137	25.0
Aged 65 to 74	609.25	166	20.0
Aged 75 or older	634.92	173	16.9

	AVERAGE HOUSEHOLD SPENDING	BEST CUSTOMERS (index)	BIGGEST CUSTOMERS (market share)
HOUSEHOLD INCOME			
Average household	**$366.40**	**100**	**100.0%**
Under $20,000	211.45	58	12.1
$20,000 to $39,999	366.72	100	22.6
$40,000 to $49,999	416.00	114	10.0
$50,000 to $69,999	371.49	101	14.6
$70,000 to $79,999	364.84	100	5.6
$80,000 to $99,999	391.13	107	9.4
$100,000 or more	501.58	137	25.6
HOUSEHOLD TYPE			
Average household	**366.40**	**100**	**100.0**
Married couples	488.20	133	64.7
Married couples, no children	636.23	174	36.2
Married couples with children	354.41	97	22.7
Oldest child under age 6	152.04	41	1.9
Oldest child aged 6 to 17	334.40	91	10.9
Oldest child aged 18 or older	519.01	142	10.0
Single parent with child under age 18	179.92	49	2.6
Single person	255.26	70	20.7
RACE AND HISPANIC ORIGIN			
Average household	**366.40**	**100**	**100.0**
Asian	206.75	56	2.4
Black	214.33	58	7.4
Hispanic	153.86	42	5.3
Non-Hispanic white and other	426.94	117	87.5
REGION			
Average household	**366.40**	**100**	**100.0**
Northeast	322.55	88	15.9
Midwest	391.71	107	23.7
South	374.95	102	38.1
West	362.49	99	22.3
EDUCATION			
Average household	**366.40**	**100**	**100.0**
Less than high school graduate	306.74	84	10.9
High school graduate	336.19	92	22.9
Some college	364.13	99	20.5
Associate's degree	403.42	110	10.9
Bachelor's degree or more	404.86	110	34.8
Bachelor's degree	383.29	105	20.9
Master's, professional, doctoral degree	441.91	121	14.0

Note: Market shares may not sum to 100.0 because of rounding and missing categories by household type. "Asian" and "black" include Hispanics and non-Hispanics who identify themselves as being of the respective race alone. "Hispanic" includes people of any race who identify themselves as Hispanic. "Other" includes people who identify themselves as non-Hispanic and as Alaska Native, American Indian, Asian (who are also included in the "Asian" row), or Native Hawaiian or other Pacific Islander, as well as non-Hispanics reporting more than one race.
Source: Calculations by New Strategist based on the Bureau of Labor Statistics' 2012 Consumer Expenditure Survey

Eye Care Services (Out-of-Pocket Expenses)

Best customers: Householders aged 55 to 74
Married couples without children at home
Married couples with adult children at home

Customer trends: Average household spending on eye care services is likely to continue to grow as boomers fill the best-customer age groups.

The biggest out-of-pocket spenders on eye care services are those who need bifocals and reading glasses as they enter the second half of their life. Householders aged 55 to 74 spend 42 to 49 percent more than average on this item. Married couples without children at home (most of them older) spend 63 percent more than average on eye care services. Married couples with adult children at home outspend the average on this item by two-thirds because of their larger households.

Average household spending on eye care services declined 22 percent between 2000 and 2010, after adjusting for inflation, but has seen a 15 percent increase in the two years since then. Behind the spending decline was increased health insurance coverage for this item, competition from discounters in the industry, and belt tightening as other health care costs increased. Average household spending on eye care services is likely to continue to grow as boomers fill the best-customer age groups.

Table 10.5 **Eye care services (out-of-pocket expenses)**

Total household spending $5,208,053,760.00
Average household spends   41.86

AGE OF HOUSEHOLDER	AVERAGE HOUSEHOLD SPENDING	BEST CUSTOMERS (index)	BIGGEST CUSTOMERS (market share)
Average household	**$41.86**	**100**	**100.0%**
Under age 25	23.13	55	3.6
Aged 25 to 34	20.75	50	8.0
Aged 35 to 44	27.02	65	11.2
Aged 45 to 54	49.00	117	23.2
Aged 55 to 64	62.25	149	27.2
Aged 65 to 74	59.63	142	17.2
Aged 75 or older	41.15	98	9.6

	AVERAGE HOUSEHOLD SPENDING	BEST CUSTOMERS (index)	BIGGEST CUSTOMERS (market share)
HOUSEHOLD INCOME			
Average household	**$41.86**	**100**	**100.0%**
Under $20,000	28.15	67	14.2
$20,000 to $39,999	32.34	77	17.4
$40,000 to $49,999	32.62	78	6.9
$50,000 to $69,999	32.13	77	11.1
$70,000 to $79,999	50.32	120	6.7
$80,000 to $99,999	53.75	128	11.3
$100,000 or more	72.46	173	32.4
HOUSEHOLD TYPE			
Average household	**41.86**	**100**	**100.0**
Married couples	57.52	137	66.7
Married couples, no children	68.33	163	34.0
Married couples with children	50.00	119	28.1
Oldest child under age 6	27.35	65	3.0
Oldest child aged 6 to 17	47.24	113	13.4
Oldest child aged 18 or older	69.30	166	11.7
Single parent with child under age 18	15.19	36	1.9
Single person	25.15	60	17.8
RACE AND HISPANIC ORIGIN			
Average household	**41.86**	**100**	**100.0**
Asian	28.48	68	2.9
Black	27.17	65	8.2
Hispanic	31.90	76	9.6
Non-Hispanic white and other	45.89	110	82.3
REGION			
Average household	**41.86**	**100**	**100.0**
Northeast	34.31	82	14.8
Midwest	46.60	111	24.7
South	40.44	97	36.0
West	45.59	109	24.5
EDUCATION			
Average household	**41.86**	**100**	**100.0**
Less than high school graduate	25.56	61	8.0
High school graduate	34.59	83	20.6
Some college	39.59	95	19.5
Associate's degree	40.19	96	9.5
Bachelor's degree or more	56.36	135	42.5
Bachelor's degree	60.52	145	28.8
Master's, professional, doctoral degree	49.22	118	13.6

Note: Market shares may not sum to 100.0 because of rounding and missing categories by household type. "Asian" and "black" include Hispanics and non-Hispanics who identify themselves as being of the respective race alone. "Hispanic" includes people of any race who identify themselves as Hispanic. "Other" includes people who identify themselves as non-Hispanic and as Alaska Native, American Indian, Asian (who are also included in the "Asian" row), or Native Hawaiian or other Pacific Islander, as well as non-Hispanics reporting more than one race.
Source: Calculations by New Strategist based on the Bureau of Labor Statistics' 2012 Consumer Expenditure Survey

Eyeglasses and Contact Lenses (Out-of-Pocket Expenses)

Best customers: Householders aged 45 to 64
Married couples without children at home
Married couples with school-aged or older children at home

Customer trends: Average household spending on eyeglasses and contact lenses should stabilize because the large baby-boom generation has filled the prime-spending age groups.

The biggest out-of-pocket spenders on eyeglasses and contact lenses are middle-aged and older Americans (who need bifocals) and households with children. Householders ranging in age from 45 to 64 spend 28 to 36 percent more than average on this item. Married couples with school-aged or older children at home spend 42 to 93 percent more than average because their households are relatively large. Couples without children at home (most of them older) spend 45 percent more than average out-of-pocket on eyeglasses and contact lenses.

Average household spending on eyeglasses and contact lenses fell 21 percent between 2000 and 2006, after adjusting for inflation, but has recovered some since then, rising 8 percent from 2006 to 2012. Behind the earlier decline was competition from discounters in the industry, as well as household belt tightening as other health care costs increased. Spending on eyeglasses and contact lenses should stabilize in the years ahead because the baby-boom generation has already filled the prime-spending age groups.

Table 10.6 Eyeglasses and contact lenses (out-of-pocket expenses)

Total household spending $8,276,152,320.00
Average household spends   66.52

AGE OF HOUSEHOLDER	AVERAGE HOUSEHOLD SPENDING	BEST CUSTOMERS (index)	BIGGEST CUSTOMERS (market share)
Average household	$66.52	100	100.0%
Under age 25	32.55	49	3.2
Aged 25 to 34	40.31	61	9.8
Aged 35 to 44	63.37	95	16.5
Aged 45 to 54	90.62	136	27.0
Aged 55 to 64	85.26	128	23.5
Aged 65 to 74	67.89	102	12.3
Aged 75 or older	52.69	79	7.7

	AVERAGE HOUSEHOLD SPENDING	BEST CUSTOMERS (index)	BIGGEST CUSTOMERS (market share)
HOUSEHOLD INCOME			
Average household	**$66.52**	**100**	**100.0%**
Under $20,000	21.58	32	6.8
$20,000 to $39,999	40.49	61	13.7
$40,000 to $49,999	50.45	76	6.7
$50,000 to $69,999	59.16	89	12.8
$70,000 to $79,999	81.34	122	6.8
$80,000 to $99,999	88.75	133	11.8
$100,000 or more	146.75	221	41.3
HOUSEHOLD TYPE			
Average household	**66.52**	**100**	**100.0**
Married couples	94.22	142	68.8
Married couples, no children	96.39	145	30.2
Married couples with children	95.41	143	33.7
Oldest child under age 6	47.15	71	3.2
Oldest child aged 6 to 17	94.34	142	16.9
Oldest child aged 18 or older	128.43	193	13.6
Single parent with child under age 18	40.33	61	3.2
Single person	35.64	54	15.9
RACE AND HISPANIC ORIGIN			
Average household	**66.52**	**100**	**100.0**
Asian	74.84	113	4.9
Black	30.91	46	5.8
Hispanic	42.45	64	8.0
Non-Hispanic white and other	76.38	115	86.2
REGION			
Average household	**66.52**	**100**	**100.0**
Northeast	66.95	101	18.2
Midwest	77.04	116	25.7
South	56.04	84	31.4
West	73.15	110	24.8
EDUCATION			
Average household	**66.52**	**100**	**100.0**
Less than high school graduate	28.69	43	5.6
High school graduate	49.42	74	18.5
Some college	57.88	87	17.9
Associate's degree	77.11	116	11.4
Bachelor's degree or more	98.03	147	46.5
Bachelor's degree	93.77	141	28.1
Master's, professional, doctoral degree	105.35	158	18.4

Note: Market shares may not sum to 100.0 because of rounding and missing categories by household type. "Asian" and "black" include Hispanics and non-Hispanics who identify themselves as being of the respective race alone. "Hispanic" includes people of any race who identify themselves as Hispanic. "Other" includes people who identify themselves as non-Hispanic and as Alaska Native, American Indian, Asian (who are also included in the "Asian" row), or Native Hawaiian or other Pacific Islander, as well as non-Hispanics reporting more than one race.
Source: Calculations by New Strategist based on the Bureau of Labor Statistics' 2012 Consumer Expenditure Survey

Health Insurance, Including Medicare and Supplements (Out-of-Pocket Payments)

Best customers: Householders aged 65 or older
Married couples without children at home
Married couples with adult children at home

Customer trends: Average household spending on health insurance will continue to climb steeply as health care costs rise faster than inflation and the population ages.

Not surprisingly, the only age group with universal health insurance coverage is the biggest out-of-pocket spender on health insurance. Americans aged 65 or older, covered by the federal government's Medicare program, spend 48 to 60 percent more than the average household out-of-pocket on health insurance. Married couples without children at home (most of them older) spend 58 percent more than average on this item. Those with adult children at home spend 41 percent more. Behind the higher average spending of older Americans is their nearly universal Medicare enrollment, the premiums being deducted from their Social Security checks. Also, many older Americans purchase commercial Medicare supplements for additional coverage.

The average household spent $2,061 out-of-pocket on health insurance in 2012, making it the seventh-largest household expense category. Average household spending on health insurance rose 57 percent between 2000 and 2012, after adjusting for inflation. Spending on health insurance will continue to grow rapidly as health care costs rise faster than inflation and the population ages.

Table 10.7 Health insurance, including Medicare and supplements (out-of-pocket payments)

Total household spending $256,394,004,480.00
Average household spends 2,060.78

AGE OF HOUSEHOLDER	AVERAGE HOUSEHOLD SPENDING	BEST CUSTOMERS (index)	BIGGEST CUSTOMERS (market share)
Average household	$2,060.78	100	100.0%
Under age 25	457.88	22	1.5
Aged 25 to 34	1,227.35	60	9.6
Aged 35 to 44	1,750.51	85	14.7
Aged 45 to 54	2,109.43	102	20.3
Aged 55 to 64	2,271.01	110	20.2
Aged 65 to 74	3,298.58	160	19.3
Aged 75 or older	3,047.42	148	14.5

	AVERAGE HOUSEHOLD SPENDING	BEST CUSTOMERS (index)	BIGGEST CUSTOMERS (market share)
HOUSEHOLD INCOME			
Average household	**$2,060.78**	**100**	**100.0%**
Under $20,000	1,004.51	49	10.3
$20,000 to $39,999	1,679.34	81	18.4
$40,000 to $49,999	1,926.08	93	8.3
$50,000 to $69,999	2,234.72	108	15.7
$70,000 to $79,999	2,476.27	120	6.7
$80,000 to $99,999	2,702.34	131	11.6
$100,000 or more	3,210.24	156	29.2
HOUSEHOLD TYPE			
Average household	**2,060.78**	**100**	**100.0**
Married couples	2,860.47	139	67.4
Married couples, no children	3,251.13	158	32.9
Married couples with children	2,517.80	122	28.7
Oldest child under age 6	2,118.94	103	4.7
Oldest child aged 6 to 17	2,438.70	118	14.1
Oldest child aged 18 or older	2,909.06	141	10.0
Single parent with child under age 18	923.51	45	2.3
Single person	1,269.01	62	18.3
RACE AND HISPANIC ORIGIN			
Average household	**2,060.78**	**100**	**100.0**
Asian	2,100.89	102	4.4
Black	1,349.27	65	8.2
Hispanic	1,018.79	49	6.2
Non-Hispanic white and other	2,351.39	114	85.6
REGION			
Average household	**2,060.78**	**100**	**100.0**
Northeast	2,161.63	105	18.9
Midwest	2,295.39	111	24.7
South	1,861.34	90	33.6
West	2,078.81	101	22.7
EDUCATION			
Average household	**2,060.78**	**100**	**100.0**
Less than high school graduate	1,318.35	64	8.4
High school graduate	1,900.68	92	23.0
Some college	1,823.46	88	18.2
Associate's degree	2,086.33	101	10.0
Bachelor's degree or more	2,641.73	128	40.4
Bachelor's degree	2,502.88	121	24.2
Master's, professional, doctoral degree	2,880.17	140	16.2

Note: Market shares may not sum to 100.0 because of rounding and missing categories by household type. "Asian" and "black" include Hispanics and non-Hispanics who identify themselves as being of the respective race alone. "Hispanic" includes people of any race who identify themselves as Hispanic. "Other" includes people who identify themselves as non-Hispanic and as Alaska Native, American Indian, Asian (who are also included in the "Asian" row), or Native Hawaiian or other Pacific Islander, as well as non-Hispanics reporting more than one race.
Source: Calculations by New Strategist based on the Bureau of Labor Statistics' 2012 Consumer Expenditure Survey

Hearing Aids

Best customers: Householders aged 65 or older
Married couples without children at home
Married couples with adult children at home
Non-Hispanic whites
Households in the Northeast

Customer trends: Average household spending on hearing aids is likely to grow as boomers enter the best-customer age group.

The biggest out-of-pocket spenders on hearing aids are households headed by older non-Hispanic whites. Householders aged 75 or older spend five-and-three-quarter times the average on hearing aids and account for 56 percent of the market. Householders aged 65 to 74 spend three-quarters more than average on hearing aids. Married couples without children at home (most of them older) spend 51 percent more than average on hearing aids. Married couples with adult children at home, which are older and have the largest households, spend two-and-one-half times the average on out-of-pocket hearing aid costs. Non-Hispanic whites outspend minorities by a huge margin and control 98 percent of the hearing aid market. Households in the Northeast spend 89 percent more than average on hearing aids.

Average household out-of-pocket spending on hearing aids increased 35 percent between 2000 and 2012, after adjusting for inflation. Average household spending on hearing aids is likely to grow as boomers enter the best-customer age group.

Table 10.8 Hearing aids

Total household spending $2,641,351,680.00
Average household spends   21.23

AGE OF HOUSEHOLDER	AVERAGE HOUSEHOLD SPENDING	BEST CUSTOMERS (index)	BIGGEST CUSTOMERS (market share)
Average household	$21.23	100	100.0%
Under age 25	–	–	–
Aged 25 to 34	2.01	9	1.5
Aged 35 to 44	0.52	2	0.4
Aged 45 to 54	10.30	49	9.6
Aged 55 to 64	12.92	61	11.1
Aged 65 to 74	37.47	176	21.3
Aged 75 or older	121.74	573	56.1

	AVERAGE HOUSEHOLD SPENDING	BEST CUSTOMERS (index)	BIGGEST CUSTOMERS (market share)
HOUSEHOLD INCOME			
Average household	**$21.23**	**100**	**100.0%**
Under $20,000	17.54	83	17.4
$20,000 to $39,999	15.63	74	16.6
$40,000 to $49,999	7.80	37	3.3
$50,000 to $69,999	33.66	159	22.9
$70,000 to $79,999	29.98	141	7.9
$80,000 to $99,999	11.28	53	4.7
$100,000 or more	30.99	146	27.3
HOUSEHOLD TYPE			
Average household	**21.23**	**100**	**100.0**
Married couples	24.18	114	55.3
Married couples, no children	32.10	151	31.5
Married couples with children	16.71	79	18.5
Oldest child under age 6	0.43	2	0.1
Oldest child aged 6 to 17	2.23	11	1.2
Oldest child aged 18 or older	51.63	243	17.2
Single parent with child under age 18	0.92	4	0.2
Single person	19.34	91	27.0
RACE AND HISPANIC ORIGIN			
Average household	**21.23**	**100**	**100.0**
Asian	0.20	1	0.0
Black	–	–	–
Hispanic	3.77	18	2.2
Non-Hispanic white and other	27.66	130	97.8
REGION			
Average household	**21.23**	**100**	**100.0**
Northeast	40.04	189	34.0
Midwest	14.91	70	15.6
South	14.20	67	24.9
West	24.01	113	25.5
EDUCATION			
Average household	**21.23**	**100**	**100.0**
Less than high school graduate	6.89	32	4.2
High school graduate	24.74	117	29.1
Some college	17.32	82	16.8
Associate's degree	20.52	97	9.5
Bachelor's degree or more	27.18	128	40.4
Bachelor's degree	9.13	43	8.6
Master's, professional, doctoral degree	58.17	274	31.8

Note: Market shares may not sum to 100.0 because of rounding and missing categories by household type. "Asian" and "black" include Hispanics and non-Hispanics who identify themselves as being of the respective race alone. "Hispanic" includes people of any race who identify themselves as Hispanic. "Other" includes people who identify themselves as non-Hispanic and as Alaska Native, American Indian, Asian (who are also included in the "Asian" row), or Native Hawaiian or other Pacific Islander, as well as non-Hispanics reporting more than one race. "–" means sample is too small to make a reliable estimate.
Source: Calculations by New Strategist based on the Bureau of Labor Statistics' 2012 Consumer Expenditure Survey

Hospital Room and Services (Out-of-Pocket Expenses)

Best customers: Householders under age 25 and aged 55 to 64
Married couples with children at home

Customer trends: Average household spending on hospital rooms and services should continue to rise as hospitals offer a greater variety of services and the population ages.

The biggest out-of-pocket spenders on hospital rooms and services are Americans aged 55 to 64, many of whom use outpatient facilities to monitor and manage their health. These householders spend 54 percent more than the average household on hospital rooms and services. Householders under age 25 spend 20 percent more than average on this item, primarily because of childbearing. Married couples with children at home outspend the average for hospital room and services by 55 percent, in part because of their larger families.

Average household out-of-pocket spending on hospital rooms and services increased by a modest 4 percent between 2000 and 2006, after adjusting for inflation, then increased by a much larger 51 percent in the next six-year period. Some of the factors behind the increase are larger deductibles and co-pays, as well as more services offered by hospitals such as diagnostic imaging, physical therapy, and wellness clinics. As the population ages, out-of-pocket spending on hospital services should continue to rise.

Table 10.9 Hospital room and services (out-of-pocket expenses)

Total household spending $20,090,695,680.00
Average household spends 161.48

AGE OF HOUSEHOLDER	AVERAGE HOUSEHOLD SPENDING	BEST CUSTOMERS (index)	BIGGEST CUSTOMERS (market share)
Average household	$161.48	100	100.0%
Under age 25	193.99	120	7.9
Aged 25 to 34	125.48	78	12.6
Aged 35 to 44	146.24	91	15.7
Aged 45 to 54	152.60	95	18.7
Aged 55 to 64	248.21	154	28.1
Aged 65 to 74	144.75	90	10.8
Aged 75 or older	102.46	63	6.2

	AVERAGE HOUSEHOLD SPENDING	BEST CUSTOMERS (index)	BIGGEST CUSTOMERS (market share)
HOUSEHOLD INCOME			
Average household	**$161.48**	**100**	**100.0%**
Under $20,000	61.11	38	8.0
$20,000 to $39,999	132.39	82	18.5
$40,000 to $49,999	182.56	113	10.0
$50,000 to $69,999	132.53	82	11.9
$70,000 to $79,999	203.08	126	7.0
$80,000 to $99,999	214.66	133	11.7
$100,000 or more	284.19	176	32.9
HOUSEHOLD TYPE			
Average household	**161.48**	**100**	**100.0**
Married couples	216.83	134	65.2
Married couples, no children	169.88	105	21.9
Married couples with children	250.78	155	36.5
Oldest child under age 6	293.01	181	8.3
Oldest child aged 6 to 17	193.22	120	14.2
Oldest child aged 18 or older	320.50	198	14.0
Single parent with child under age 18	119.87	74	3.9
Single person	106.00	66	19.5
RACE AND HISPANIC ORIGIN			
Average household	**161.48**	**100**	**100.0**
Asian	156.60	97	4.2
Black	60.33	37	4.7
Hispanic	134.13	83	10.4
Non-Hispanic white and other	182.65	113	84.9
REGION			
Average household	**161.48**	**100**	**100.0**
Northeast	111.74	69	12.5
Midwest	166.85	103	22.9
South	172.73	107	39.8
West	177.44	110	24.8
EDUCATION			
Average household	**161.48**	**100**	**100.0**
Less than high school graduate	87.53	54	7.1
High school graduate	183.18	113	28.3
Some college	172.13	107	22.0
Associate's degree	125.43	78	7.7
Bachelor's degree or more	179.27	111	35.0
Bachelor's degree	164.71	102	20.3
Master's, professional, doctoral degree	204.27	126	14.7

Note: Market shares may not sum to 100.0 because of rounding and missing categories by household type. "Asian" and "black" include Hispanics and non-Hispanics who identify themselves as being of the respective race alone. "Hispanic" includes people of any race who identify themselves as Hispanic. "Other" includes people who identify themselves as non-Hispanic and as Alaska Native, American Indian, Asian (who are also included in the "Asian" row), or Native Hawaiian or other Pacific Islander, as well as non-Hispanics reporting more than one race.
Source: Calculations by New Strategist based on the Bureau of Labor Statistics' 2012 Consumer Expenditure Survey

Lab Tests and X-Rays (Out-of-Pocket Expenses)

Best customers: Householders aged 55 to 64
Married couples without children at home
Married couples with school-aged or older children at home
Households in the Midwest

Customer trends: Average household spending on lab tests and X-rays is likely to resume growing as the population ages.

Householders aged 55 to 64 spend 63 percent more than the average on lab tests and X-rays. Married couples without children at home (most of them older) also spend 63 percent more than average on this item. Married couples with school-aged or adult children at home spend 24 to 34 percent more than average on lab tests and X-rays because they have some of the largest households.

Average household spending on lab tests and X-rays rose by a whopping 84 percent between 2000 and 2006, after adjusting for inflation, as medical centers and physician groups nationwide installed new kinds of imaging and testing equipment and insurance co-pays increased. From 2006 to 2012, spending on this item fell 5 percent as households reined in their spending. Average household spending in this category is likely to resume growing as the population ages.

Table 10.10 Lab tests and X-rays (out-of-pocket expenses)

Total household spending $5,836,354,560.00
Average household spends 46.91

AGE OF HOUSEHOLDER	AVERAGE HOUSEHOLD SPENDING	BEST CUSTOMERS (index)	BIGGEST CUSTOMERS (market share)
Average household	$46.91	100	100.0%
Under age 25	43.56	93	6.1
Aged 25 to 34	36.74	78	12.7
Aged 35 to 44	44.24	94	16.4
Aged 45 to 54	44.79	95	18.9
Aged 55 to 64	76.25	163	29.7
Aged 65 to 74	43.02	92	11.1
Aged 75 or older	24.85	53	5.2

	AVERAGE HOUSEHOLD SPENDING	BEST CUSTOMERS (index)	BIGGEST CUSTOMERS (market share)
HOUSEHOLD INCOME			
Average household	$46.91	100	100.0%
Under $20,000	16.81	36	7.5
$20,000 to $39,999	43.88	94	21.1
$40,000 to $49,999	36.40	78	6.9
$50,000 to $69,999	47.84	102	14.7
$70,000 to $79,999	52.87	113	6.3
$80,000 to $99,999	61.73	132	11.6
$100,000 or more	79.87	170	31.9
HOUSEHOLD TYPE			
Average household	46.91	100	100.0
Married couples	65.56	140	67.9
Married couples, no children	76.29	163	33.9
Married couples with children	58.25	124	29.2
Oldest child under age 6	51.23	109	5.0
Oldest child aged 6 to 17	58.22	124	14.8
Oldest child aged 18 or older	62.85	134	9.5
Single parent with child under age 18	15.72	34	1.8
Single person	22.84	49	14.5
RACE AND HISPANIC ORIGIN			
Average household	46.91	100	100.0
Asian	38.37	82	3.5
Black	18.61	40	5.0
Hispanic	45.68	97	12.2
Non-Hispanic white and other	51.80	110	82.9
REGION			
Average household	46.91	100	100.0
Northeast	46.13	98	17.8
Midwest	58.38	124	27.6
South	41.56	89	33.0
West	45.10	96	21.7
EDUCATION			
Average household	46.91	100	100.0
Less than high school graduate	33.67	72	9.4
High school graduate	40.90	87	21.7
Some college	43.01	92	18.9
Associate's degree	36.59	78	7.7
Bachelor's degree or more	62.92	134	42.3
Bachelor's degree	64.84	138	27.5
Master's, professional, doctoral degree	59.63	127	14.8

Note: Market shares may not sum to 100.0 because of rounding and missing categories by household type. "Asian" and "black" include Hispanics and non-Hispanics who identify themselves as being of the respective race alone. "Hispanic" includes people of any race who identify themselves as Hispanic. "Other" includes people who identify themselves as non-Hispanic and as Alaska Native, American Indian, Asian (who are also included in the "Asian" row), or Native Hawaiian or other Pacific Islander, as well as non-Hispanics reporting more than one race.
Source: Calculations by New Strategist based on the Bureau of Labor Statistics' 2012 Consumer Expenditure Survey

Long-Term Care Insurance

Best customers: Householders aged 55 and older
    Married couples without children at home
    Non-Hispanic whites
    Households in the West and Northeast

Customer trends: Average household spending on long-term care insurance will rise as boomers fill the prime-spending age groups.

The best customers of long-term care insurance are older householders worried they or a family member might require long-term care in an assisted living or nursing facility. Householders aged 55 to 64 spend 40 percent more than average on this item, while those aged 65 to 74 spend more than three times the average and those aged 75 or older spend almost two-and-one-half times the average on long-term care insurance. Married couples without children at home (most of them older) spend over two-and-one-half times the average on long-term care insurance and account for 56 percent of the market. Non-Hispanic whites, who account for 94 percent of spending on long-term care insurance, outspend the average by 25 percent. Households in the Midwest and Northeast spend, respectively, 33 and 28 percent more than average on long-term care insurance.

Average household spending on long-term care insurance rose 19 percent from 2006 to 2012. (Because the item is a relatively new category in the Consumer Expenditure Survey, there are no comparison data from 2000.) Average household spending on long-term care insurance is certain to continue to rise as boomers fill the prime-spending age groups.

Table 10.11 Long-term care insurance

Total household spending	$9,984,384,000.00
Average household spends	80.25

	AVERAGE HOUSEHOLD SPENDING	BEST CUSTOMERS (index)	BIGGEST CUSTOMERS (market share)
AGE OF HOUSEHOLDER			
Average household	$80.25	100	100.0%
Under age 25	4.03	5	0.3
Aged 25 to 34	9.63	12	1.9
Aged 35 to 44	13.45	17	2.9
Aged 45 to 54	31.42	39	7.7
Aged 55 to 64	112.45	140	25.6
Aged 65 to 74	253.00	315	38.0
Aged 75 or older	192.45	240	23.4

	AVERAGE HOUSEHOLD SPENDING	BEST CUSTOMERS (index)	BIGGEST CUSTOMERS (market share)
HOUSEHOLD INCOME			
Average household	**$80.25**	**100**	**100.0%**
Under $20,000	20.61	26	5.4
$20,000 to $39,999	53.24	66	15.0
$40,000 to $49,999	64.51	80	7.1
$50,000 to $69,999	64.39	80	11.6
$70,000 to $79,999	81.40	101	5.7
$80,000 to $99,999	175.63	219	19.3
$100,000 or more	154.19	192	36.0
HOUSEHOLD TYPE			
Average household	**80.25**	**100**	**100.0**
Married couples	113.37	141	68.6
Married couples, no children	214.75	268	55.8
Married couples with children	32.96	41	9.7
Oldest child under age 6	25.44	32	1.4
Oldest child aged 6 to 17	26.64	33	3.9
Oldest child aged 18 or older	48.46	60	4.3
Single parent with child under age 18	10.61	13	0.7
Single person	68.60	85	25.4
RACE AND HISPANIC ORIGIN			
Average household	**80.25**	**100**	**100.0**
Asian	52.55	65	2.8
Black	24.71	31	3.9
Hispanic	15.74	20	2.5
Non-Hispanic white and other	100.16	125	93.7
REGION			
Average household	**80.25**	**100**	**100.0**
Northeast	102.53	128	23.1
Midwest	75.00	93	20.7
South	56.33	70	26.1
West	107.13	133	30.1
EDUCATION			
Average household	**80.25**	**100**	**100.0**
Less than high school graduate	14.85	19	2.4
High school graduate	32.27	40	10.0
Some college	54.44	68	14.0
Associate's degree	61.06	76	7.5
Bachelor's degree or more	168.14	210	66.1
Bachelor's degree	155.48	194	38.6
Master's, professional, doctoral degree	189.89	237	27.5

Note: Market shares may not sum to 100.0 because of rounding and missing categories by household type. "Asian" and "black" include Hispanics and non-Hispanics who identify themselves as being of the respective race alone. "Hispanic" includes people of any race who identify themselves as Hispanic. "Other" includes people who identify themselves as non-Hispanic and as Alaska Native, American Indian, Asian (who are also included in the "Asian" row), or Native Hawaiian or other Pacific Islander, as well as non-Hispanics reporting more than one race.
Source: Calculations by New Strategist based on the Bureau of Labor Statistics' 2012 Consumer Expenditure Survey

Medicare Premiums

Best customers: Householders aged 65 or older
Households with incomes under $50,000
Married couples without children at home
Householders with no more than a high school education

Customer trends: Average household spending on Medicare premiums will rise steadily along with the aging of the population.

Naturally, the biggest spenders on Medicare premiums are people covered by Medicare—householders aged 65 or older. On average, householders aged 65 to 74 spend $1,368 per year on Medicare premiums, and those aged 75 or older spend $1,384. Married couples without children at home (most of them older) spend twice the average and account for 42 percent of spending on this item. Householders with no more than a high school education and those with incomes below $50,000 are also above-average spenders on Medicare premiums because older Americans make up large percentages of those groups.

Average household spending on Medicare premiums rose 81 percent between 2000 and 2012, after adjusting for inflation. Behind the increase was the aging of the population and the rise in premiums. Average household spending on Medicare premiums will grow even faster in the future as boomers enter the eligible age group.

Table 10.12 Medicare premiums

Total household spending $49,343,385,600.00
Average household spends 396.60

	AVERAGE HOUSEHOLD SPENDING	BEST CUSTOMERS (index)	BIGGEST CUSTOMERS (market share)
AGE OF HOUSEHOLDER			
Average household	$396.60	100	100.0%
Under age 25	50.26	13	0.8
Aged 25 to 34	41.52	10	1.7
Aged 35 to 44	93.06	23	4.1
Aged 45 to 54	142.72	36	7.1
Aged 55 to 64	229.96	58	10.6
Aged 65 to 74	1,368.03	345	41.6
Aged 75 or older	1,383.75	349	34.1

	AVERAGE HOUSEHOLD SPENDING	BEST CUSTOMERS (index)	BIGGEST CUSTOMERS (market share)
HOUSEHOLD INCOME			
Average household	**$396.60**	**100**	**100.0%**
Under $20,000	441.25	111	23.4
$20,000 to $39,999	558.65	141	31.7
$40,000 to $49,999	441.08	111	9.8
$50,000 to $69,999	356.70	90	13.0
$70,000 to $79,999	320.16	81	4.5
$80,000 to $99,999	295.98	75	6.6
$100,000 or more	231.33	58	10.9
HOUSEHOLD TYPE			
Average household	**396.60**	**100**	**100.0**
Married couples	451.17	114	55.3
Married couples, no children	805.06	203	42.3
Married couples with children	109.00	27	6.5
Oldest child under age 6	27.59	7	0.3
Oldest child aged 6 to 17	50.95	13	1.5
Oldest child aged 18 or older	259.50	65	4.6
Single parent with child under age 18	82.91	21	1.1
Single person	371.16	94	27.8
RACE AND HISPANIC ORIGIN			
Average household	**396.60**	**100**	**100.0**
Asian	211.39	53	2.3
Black	301.49	76	9.6
Hispanic	198.49	50	6.3
Non-Hispanic white and other	445.02	112	84.2
REGION			
Average household	**396.60**	**100**	**100.0**
Northeast	389.15	98	17.7
Midwest	404.93	102	22.6
South	410.22	103	38.5
West	371.87	94	21.1
EDUCATION			
Average household	**396.60**	**100**	**100.0**
Less than high school graduate	504.73	127	16.6
High school graduate	490.06	124	30.8
Some college	369.10	93	19.2
Associate's degree	325.11	82	8.1
Bachelor's degree or more	318.29	80	25.3
Bachelor's degree	274.74	69	13.8
Master's, professional, doctoral degree	393.09	99	11.5

Note: Market shares may not sum to 100.0 because of rounding and missing categories by household type. "Asian" and "black" include Hispanics and non-Hispanics who identify themselves as being of the respective race alone. "Hispanic" includes people of any race who identify themselves as Hispanic. "Other" includes people who identify themselves as non-Hispanic and as Alaska Native, American Indian, Asian (who are also included in the "Asian" row), or Native Hawaiian or other Pacific Islander, as well as non-Hispanics reporting more than one race.
Source: Calculations by New Strategist based on the Bureau of Labor Statistics' 2012 Consumer Expenditure Survey

Medicare Prescription Drug Premiums

Best customers: Householders aged 65 or older
Households with incomes under $50,000
Married couples without children at home
People who live alone
Householders with no more than a high school education

Customer trends: Average household spending on Medicare prescription drug premiums will rise steadily
along with the aging of the population.

Naturally, the biggest spenders on Medicare prescription drug premiums are people covered by Medicare—householders aged 65 or older. On average, householders aged 65 to 74 spend $229 per year on Medicare prescription drug premiums, and those aged 75 or older spend a similar $238. Married couples without children at home (most of them older) account for 42 percent of spending on this item. Households with incomes under $50,000 and householders with no more than a high school diploma are also above-average spenders on Medicare prescription drug premiums because older Americans make up large percentages of those groups. People who live alone, whose spending approaches average on only a few items, outspend the average on Medicare prescription drug premiums by 6 percent.

Average household spending on Medicare prescription drug premiums more than doubled between 2006 and 2012 as more consumers signed on. (There are no comparison data from 2000 because the Medicare prescription drug plan is a new program.) Average household spending on Medicare prescription drug premiums is certain to rise as boomers fill the prime-spending age groups.

Table 10.13 Medicare prescription drug premiums

Total household spending $8,246,292,480.00
Average household spends 66.28

AGE OF HOUSEHOLDER	AVERAGE HOUSEHOLD SPENDING	BEST CUSTOMERS (index)	BIGGEST CUSTOMERS (market share)
Average household	$66.28	100	100.0%
Under age 25	8.54	13	0.8
Aged 25 to 34	5.37	8	1.3
Aged 35 to 44	11.77	18	3.1
Aged 45 to 54	23.98	36	7.2
Aged 55 to 64	39.49	60	10.9
Aged 65 to 74	229.19	346	41.7
Aged 75 or older	237.55	358	35.0

	AVERAGE HOUSEHOLD SPENDING	BEST CUSTOMERS (index)	BIGGEST CUSTOMERS (market share)
HOUSEHOLD INCOME			
Average household	**$66.28**	**100**	**100.0%**
Under $20,000	79.82	120	25.3
$20,000 to $39,999	92.99	140	31.6
$40,000 to $49,999	76.42	115	10.2
$50,000 to $69,999	56.02	85	12.2
$70,000 to $79,999	45.95	69	3.9
$80,000 to $99,999	41.32	62	5.5
$100,000 or more	39.89	60	11.3
HOUSEHOLD TYPE			
Average household	**66.28**	**100**	**100.0**
Married couples	70.44	106	51.6
Married couples, no children	133.29	201	41.9
Married couples with children	12.79	19	4.5
Oldest child under age 6	1.70	3	0.1
Oldest child aged 6 to 17	2.95	4	0.5
Oldest child aged 18 or older	36.55	55	3.9
Single parent with child under age 18	5.04	8	0.4
Single person	69.93	106	31.3
RACE AND HISPANIC ORIGIN			
Average household	**66.28**	**100**	**100.0**
Asian	45.91	69	3.0
Black	50.37	76	9.6
Hispanic	36.38	55	6.9
Non-Hispanic white and other	73.94	112	83.7
REGION			
Average household	**66.28**	**100**	**100.0**
Northeast	63.81	96	17.4
Midwest	70.97	107	23.7
South	65.99	100	37.1
West	64.14	97	21.8
EDUCATION			
Average household	**66.28**	**100**	**100.0**
Less than high school graduate	86.25	130	17.0
High school graduate	80.21	121	30.2
Some college	59.03	89	18.3
Associate's degree	55.29	83	8.2
Bachelor's degree or more	55.18	83	26.3
Bachelor's degree	48.57	73	14.6
Master's, professional, doctoral degree	66.53	100	11.7

Note: Market shares may not sum to 100.0 because of rounding and missing categories by household type. "Asian" and "black" include Hispanics and non-Hispanics who identify themselves as being of the respective race alone. "Hispanic" includes people of any race who identify themselves as Hispanic. "Other" includes people who identify themselves as non-Hispanic and as Alaska Native, American Indian, Asian (who are also included in the "Asian" row), or Native Hawaiian or other Pacific Islander, as well as non-Hispanics reporting more than one race.
Source: Calculations by New Strategist based on the Bureau of Labor Statistics' 2012 Consumer Expenditure Survey

Medicare Supplements, Commercial

Best customers: Householders aged 65 or older
Married couples without children at home
Non-Hispanic whites
Households in the Midwest

Customer trends: Average household spending on commercial Medicare supplements should increase in the years ahead as the baby-boom generation enters the Medicare program.

As with Medicare premiums, the biggest spenders on commercial Medicare supplements are people covered by Medicare—householders aged 65 or older. On average, householders aged 65 to 74 spend $416 per year on Medicare supplements, which cover services not included in Medicare. Householders aged 75 or older spend $475 per year on this item. Married couples without children at home (most of them older) spend a little over twice the average on Medicare supplements and account for 43 percent of spending on this item. Non-Hispanic whites dominate spending on this item and control 90 percent of the market. Households in the Midwest outspend the average on commercial Medicare supplements by 26 percent.

Average household spending on commercial Medicare supplements fell 15 percent between 2000 and 2012, after adjusting for inflation. Behind the spending decline was the introduction of the Medicare prescription drug program, which alleviated the need for some of the spending in this category. Average household spending on this item is likely to increase as aging boomers enter the Medicare program.

Table 10.14 Medicare supplements, commercial

Total household spending $18,580,285,440.00
Average household spends   149.34

AGE OF HOUSEHOLDER	AVERAGE HOUSEHOLD SPENDING	BEST CUSTOMERS (index)	BIGGEST CUSTOMERS (market share)
Average household	$149.34	100	100.0%
Under age 25	39.35	26	1.7
Aged 25 to 34	49.09	33	5.3
Aged 35 to 44	58.98	39	6.9
Aged 45 to 54	76.55	51	10.1
Aged 55 to 64	91.74	61	11.2
Aged 65 to 74	416.45	279	33.6
Aged 75 or older	475.35	318	31.1

	AVERAGE HOUSEHOLD SPENDING	BEST CUSTOMERS (index)	BIGGEST CUSTOMERS (market share)
HOUSEHOLD INCOME			
Average household	**$149.34**	**100**	**100.0%**
Under $20,000	96.81	65	13.6
$20,000 to $39,999	173.48	116	26.2
$40,000 to $49,999	179.31	120	10.6
$50,000 to $69,999	194.48	130	18.8
$70,000 to $79,999	142.89	96	5.3
$80,000 to $99,999	141.35	95	8.4
$100,000 or more	136.02	91	17.1
HOUSEHOLD TYPE			
Average household	**149.34**	**100**	**100.0**
Married couples	191.02	128	62.1
Married couples, no children	307.70	206	43.0
Married couples with children	83.85	56	13.2
Oldest child under age 6	60.58	41	1.9
Oldest child aged 6 to 17	66.72	45	5.3
Oldest child aged 18 or older	127.75	86	6.0
Single parent with child under age 18	37.62	25	1.3
Single person	121.67	81	24.2
RACE AND HISPANIC ORIGIN			
Average household	**149.34**	**100**	**100.0**
Asian	110.52	74	3.2
Black	78.77	53	6.6
Hispanic	40.00	27	3.4
Non-Hispanic white and other	179.10	120	90.0
REGION			
Average household	**149.34**	**100**	**100.0**
Northeast	157.54	105	19.0
Midwest	187.94	126	27.9
South	125.23	84	31.2
West	144.65	97	21.8
EDUCATION			
Average household	**149.34**	**100**	**100.0**
Less than high school graduate	119.03	80	10.4
High school graduate	176.39	118	29.5
Some college	153.24	103	21.1
Associate's degree	106.39	71	7.0
Bachelor's degree or more	151.40	101	32.0
Bachelor's degree	131.07	88	17.5
Master's, professional, doctoral degree	186.31	125	14.5

Note: Market shares may not sum to 100.0 because of rounding and missing categories by household type. "Asian" and "black" include Hispanics and non-Hispanics who identify themselves as being of the respective race alone. "Hispanic" includes people of any race who identify themselves as Hispanic. "Other" includes people who identify themselves as non-Hispanic and as Alaska Native, American Indian, Asian (who are also included in the "Asian" row), or Native Hawaiian or other Pacific Islander, as well as non-Hispanics reporting more than one race.
Source: Calculations by New Strategist based on the Bureau of Labor Statistics' 2012 Consumer Expenditure Survey

Nonphysician Health Care Professional Services (Out-of-Pocket Expenses) (Acupuncturists, Chiropractors, Nurse Practitioners, Etc.)

Best customers: Householders aged 55 to 64
Married couples
Households in the West and Northeast

Customer trends: Average household spending on nonphysician health care professional services will rise as nonphysicians provide more health care services.

Alternative health care has become popular over the past few decades, and millions of Americans seek the medical advice of nonphysicians such as chiropractors, acupuncturists, and nurse practitioners. The best customers of these services are householders aged 55 to 64, who spend 66 percent more than average on this item. Married couples without children at home (most of them older) spend 26 percent more than average on nonphysician services, while those with children at home spend 21 percent more, in part because their households are relatively large. Households in the West spend 41 percent more than average on this item, and those in the Northeast spend 22 percent more.

Average household spending on nonphysician health care professional services rose 27 percent between 2000 and 2012, after adjusting for inflation. Behind the increase is the greater variety of services provided by these professionals, as well as millions of uninsured Americans seeking care outside established medical circles. Spending in this category is likely to continue to increase as nonphysicians provide more health care services.

Table 10.15 Nonphysician health care professional services (out-of-pocket expenses) (acupuncturists, chiropractors, nurse practitioners, etc.)

Total household spending $7,761,070,080.00
Average household spends   62.38

	AVERAGE HOUSEHOLD SPENDING	BEST CUSTOMERS (index)	BIGGEST CUSTOMERS (market share)
AGE OF HOUSEHOLDER			
Average household	**$62.38**	**100**	**100.0%**
Under age 25	8.66	14	0.9
Aged 25 to 34	40.56	65	10.5
Aged 35 to 44	58.97	95	16.4
Aged 45 to 54	74.51	119	23.6
Aged 55 to 64	103.71	166	30.4
Aged 65 to 74	53.78	86	10.4
Aged 75 or older	49.21	79	7.7

	AVERAGE HOUSEHOLD SPENDING	BEST CUSTOMERS (index)	BIGGEST CUSTOMERS (market share)
HOUSEHOLD INCOME			
Average household	**$62.38**	**100**	**100.0%**
Under $20,000	24.78	40	8.4
$20,000 to $39,999	33.26	53	12.0
$40,000 to $49,999	38.53	62	5.5
$50,000 to $69,999	66.70	107	15.4
$70,000 to $79,999	52.02	83	4.7
$80,000 to $99,999	77.74	125	11.0
$100,000 or more	143.49	230	43.1
HOUSEHOLD TYPE			
Average household	**62.38**	**100**	**100.0**
Married couples	79.54	128	61.9
Married couples, no children	78.55	126	26.2
Married couples with children	75.51	121	28.5
Oldest child under age 6	65.48	105	4.8
Oldest child aged 6 to 17	81.05	130	15.5
Oldest child aged 18 or older	72.63	116	8.2
Single parent with child under age 18	42.82	69	3.6
Single person	47.93	77	22.8
RACE AND HISPANIC ORIGIN			
Average household	**62.38**	**100**	**100.0**
Asian	35.51	57	2.5
Black	15.42	25	3.1
Hispanic	57.01	91	11.5
Non-Hispanic white and other	71.03	114	85.5
REGION			
Average household	**62.38**	**100**	**100.0**
Northeast	76.06	122	22.0
Midwest	53.91	86	19.2
South	45.28	73	27.0
West	88.02	141	31.8
EDUCATION			
Average household	**62.38**	**100**	**100.0**
Less than high school graduate	28.94	46	6.1
High school graduate	42.64	68	17.0
Some college	41.07	66	13.6
Associate's degree	45.95	74	7.3
Bachelor's degree or more	110.90	178	56.1
Bachelor's degree	99.75	160	31.9
Master's, professional, doctoral degree	130.05	208	24.2

Note: Market shares may not sum to 100.0 because of rounding and missing categories by household type. "Asian" and "black" include Hispanics and non-Hispanics who identify themselves as being of the respective race alone. "Hispanic" includes people of any race who identify themselves as Hispanic. "Other" includes people who identify themselves as non-Hispanic and as Alaska Native, American Indian, Asian (who are also included in the "Asian" row), or Native Hawaiian or other Pacific Islander, as well as non-Hispanics reporting more than one race.
Source: Calculations by New Strategist based on the Bureau of Labor Statistics' 2012 Consumer Expenditure Survey

Physician Services (Out-of-Pocket Expenses)

Best customers: Householders aged 55 to 64
                  Married couples
                  Households in the West

Customer trends: Average household out-of-pocket spending on physician services is unlikely to grow much in the years ahead
                  because boomers will be joining Medicare, which largely covers these costs.

The biggest out-of-pocket spenders on physician services are older married couples. Householders aged 55 to 64 spend 57 percent more than average out-of-pocket on this item. Married couples without children at home spend 46 percent more than average on physician services because most are older. Couples with children at home spend 30 percent more than average because they have the largest households. Households in the West outspend the average on physician's services by 28 percent.

Average household out-of-pocket spending on physician services grew by 14 percent between 2000 and 2012, after adjusting for inflation. Behind the increase were rising co-payments. Spending in this category is unlikely to grow much in the future because boomers are becoming eligible for Medicare, which covers most physician expenses.

Table 10.16 Physician services (out-of-pocket expenses)

Total household spending $25,400,770,560.00
Average household spends 204.16

	AVERAGE HOUSEHOLD SPENDING	BEST CUSTOMERS (index)	BIGGEST CUSTOMERS (market share)
AGE OF HOUSEHOLDER			
Average household	$204.16	100	100.0%
Under age 25	77.09	38	2.5
Aged 25 to 34	161.18	79	12.8
Aged 35 to 44	186.16	91	15.8
Aged 45 to 54	218.58	107	21.2
Aged 55 to 64	321.27	157	28.8
Aged 65 to 74	187.51	92	11.1
Aged 75 or older	164.51	81	7.9

	AVERAGE HOUSEHOLD SPENDING	BEST CUSTOMERS (index)	BIGGEST CUSTOMERS (market share)
HOUSEHOLD INCOME			
Average household	**$204.16**	**100**	**100.0%**
Under $20,000	78.51	38	8.1
$20,000 to $39,999	145.50	71	16.1
$40,000 to $49,999	186.75	91	8.1
$50,000 to $69,999	181.40	89	12.8
$70,000 to $79,999	256.96	126	7.0
$80,000 to $99,999	261.73	128	11.3
$100,000 or more	398.91	195	36.6
HOUSEHOLD TYPE			
Average household	**204.16**	**100**	**100.0**
Married couples	280.56	137	66.7
Married couples, no children	297.07	146	30.3
Married couples with children	265.47	130	30.6
Oldest child under age 6	257.20	126	5.7
Oldest child aged 6 to 17	238.55	117	13.9
Oldest child aged 18 or older	316.20	155	10.9
Single parent with child under age 18	108.76	53	2.8
Single person	130.89	64	19.0
RACE AND HISPANIC ORIGIN			
Average household	**204.16**	**100**	**100.0**
Asian	145.85	71	3.1
Black	82.83	41	5.1
Hispanic	108.61	53	6.7
Non-Hispanic white and other	240.07	118	88.3
REGION			
Average household	**204.16**	**100**	**100.0**
Northeast	192.09	94	17.0
Midwest	200.86	98	21.8
South	177.51	87	32.4
West	261.13	128	28.8
EDUCATION			
Average household	**204.16**	**100**	**100.0**
Less than high school graduate	105.65	52	6.8
High school graduate	133.92	66	16.4
Some college	205.70	101	20.7
Associate's degree	191.82	94	9.3
Bachelor's degree or more	303.33	149	46.9
Bachelor's degree	300.49	147	29.3
Master's, professional, doctoral degree	308.21	151	17.5

Note: Market shares may not sum to 100.0 because of rounding and missing categories by household type. "Asian" and "black" include Hispanics and non-Hispanics who identify themselves as being of the respective race alone. "Hispanic" includes people of any race who identify themselves as Hispanic. "Other" includes people who identify themselves as non-Hispanic and as Alaska Native, American Indian, Asian (who are also included in the "Asian" row), or Native Hawaiian or other Pacific Islander, as well as non-Hispanics reporting more than one race.
Source: Calculations by New Strategist based on the Bureau of Labor Statistics' 2012 Consumer Expenditure Survey

Topicals and Dressings

Best customers: Householders aged 45 to 74
Married couples with school-aged or older children at home
Households in the West

Customer trends: Average household spending on topicals and dressings may continue to grow as boomers fill one of the best-customer age groups.

The biggest spenders on topicals and dressings are married couples whose households include school-aged or adult children. Householders ranging in age from 45 to 74 spend 11 to 40 percent more than average on this item. Married couples with school-aged children at home spend twice the average on topicals and dressing, and those with adult children at home spend 58 percent more than average. Households in the West spend 28 percent more than average on this item.

Average household spending on topicals and dressings increased 46 percent between 2000 and 2012, after adjusting for inflation. Spending in this category is likely to keep growing as boomers fill one of the best-customer age groups.

Table 10.17 Topicals and dressings

Total household spending $5,099,811,840.00
Average household spends   40.99

AGE OF HOUSEHOLDER	AVERAGE HOUSEHOLD SPENDING	BEST CUSTOMERS (index)	BIGGEST CUSTOMERS (market share)
Average household	$40.99	100	100.0%
Under age 25	13.80	34	2.2
Aged 25 to 34	31.06	76	12.2
Aged 35 to 44	39.03	95	16.5
Aged 45 to 54	46.59	114	22.5
Aged 55 to 64	57.42	140	25.6
Aged 65 to 74	52.16	127	15.3
Aged 75 or older	24.94	61	5.9

	AVERAGE HOUSEHOLD SPENDING	BEST CUSTOMERS (index)	BIGGEST CUSTOMERS (market share)
HOUSEHOLD INCOME			
Average household	$40.99	100	100.0%
Under $20,000	16.44	40	8.4
$20,000 to $39,999	23.86	58	13.1
$40,000 to $49,999	31.55	77	6.8
$50,000 to $69,999	41.23	101	14.5
$70,000 to $79,999	58.08	142	7.9
$80,000 to $99,999	58.57	143	12.6
$100,000 or more	80.45	196	36.7
HOUSEHOLD TYPE			
Average household	40.99	100	100.0
Married couples	55.31	135	65.5
Married couples, no children	45.08	110	22.9
Married couples with children	67.78	165	38.9
Oldest child under age 6	36.12	88	4.0
Oldest child aged 6 to 17	81.51	199	23.6
Oldest child aged 18 or older	64.61	158	11.1
Single parent with child under age 18	28.47	69	3.6
Single person	25.19	61	18.2
RACE AND HISPANIC ORIGIN			
Average household	40.99	100	100.0
Asian	24.96	61	2.6
Black	20.64	50	6.3
Hispanic	30.43	74	9.3
Non-Hispanic white and other	46.11	112	84.4
REGION			
Average household	40.99	100	100.0
Northeast	34.54	84	15.2
Midwest	35.55	87	19.2
South	40.50	99	36.8
West	52.49	128	28.9
EDUCATION			
Average household	40.99	100	100.0
Less than high school graduate	21.40	52	6.8
High school graduate	33.93	83	20.6
Some college	34.96	85	17.6
Associate's degree	63.72	155	15.4
Bachelor's degree or more	50.76	124	39.1
Bachelor's degree	49.78	121	24.2
Master's, professional, doctoral degree	52.42	128	14.8

Note: Market shares may not sum to 100.0 because of rounding and missing categories by household type. "Asian" and "black" include Hispanics and non-Hispanics who identify themselves as being of the respective race alone. "Hispanic" includes people of any race who identify themselves as Hispanic. "Other" includes people who identify themselves as non-Hispanic and as Alaska Native, American Indian, Asian (who are also included in the "Asian" row), or Native Hawaiian or other Pacific Islander, as well as non-Hispanics reporting more than one race.
Source: Calculations by New Strategist based on the Bureau of Labor Statistics' 2012 Consumer Expenditure Survey

Vitamins, Nonprescription

Best customers: Householders aged 55 to 74
Married couples without children at home
Married couples with adult children at home
Asians
Households in the West

Customer trends: Average household spending on vitamins should increase as boomers age.

As people age they become more health conscious. Consequently, older people are the best customers of vitamins. Householders aged 55 to 74 spend 49 to 61 percent more than average on this item and control 47 percent of the market. Married couples without children at home (most of them older) spend 70 percent more than average on vitamins. The spending on vitamins by married couples with adult children at home is 34 percent above average. Asian householders outspend the average on vitamins by three-quarters, and households in the West, where many Asians reside, do so by 38 percent.

Average household spending on vitamins fell 26 percent between 2000 and 2006, after adjusting for inflation, but spending rebounded by 11 percent between 2006 and 2012. Behind the decline was price competition from discounters, as well as belt tightening as other health care costs increased. Average household spending on vitamins should climb as boomers age and seek to prevent ailments through better nutrition.

Table 10.18 Vitamins, nonprescription

Total household spending $6,315,356,160.00
Average household spends 50.76

AGE OF HOUSEHOLDER	AVERAGE HOUSEHOLD SPENDING	BEST CUSTOMERS (index)	BIGGEST CUSTOMERS (market share)
Average household	$50.76	100	100.0%
Under age 25	11.90	23	1.5
Aged 25 to 34	32.58	64	10.4
Aged 35 to 44	35.30	70	12.1
Aged 45 to 54	51.05	101	19.9
Aged 55 to 64	75.64	149	27.3
Aged 65 to 74	81.83	161	19.4
Aged 75 or older	52.92	104	10.2

	AVERAGE HOUSEHOLD SPENDING	BEST CUSTOMERS (index)	BIGGEST CUSTOMERS (market share)
HOUSEHOLD INCOME			
Average household	$50.76	100	100.0%
Under $20,000	26.07	51	10.8
$20,000 to $39,999	39.48	78	17.5
$40,000 to $49,999	40.27	79	7.0
$50,000 to $69,999	66.36	131	18.9
$70,000 to $79,999	63.41	125	7.0
$80,000 to $99,999	47.96	94	8.3
$100,000 or more	80.53	159	29.7
HOUSEHOLD TYPE			
Average household	50.76	100	100.0
Married couples	68.87	136	65.9
Married couples, no children	86.25	170	35.4
Married couples with children	47.25	93	21.9
Oldest child under age 6	33.00	65	3.0
Oldest child aged 6 to 17	40.07	79	9.4
Oldest child aged 18 or older	68.11	134	9.5
Single parent with child under age 18	25.94	51	2.7
Single person	32.42	64	19.0
RACE AND HISPANIC ORIGIN			
Average household	50.76	100	100.0
Asian	88.99	175	7.6
Black	29.74	59	7.4
Hispanic	38.73	76	9.6
Non-Hispanic white and other	56.20	111	83.1
REGION			
Average household	50.76	100	100.0
Northeast	43.26	85	15.4
Midwest	55.49	109	24.2
South	39.94	79	29.3
West	70.12	138	31.1
EDUCATION			
Average household	50.76	100	100.0
Less than high school graduate	55.50	109	14.3
High school graduate	37.69	74	18.5
Some college	34.50	68	14.0
Associate's degree	44.35	87	8.6
Bachelor's degree or more	72.07	142	44.8
Bachelor's degree	69.58	137	27.3
Master's, professional, doctoral degree	76.28	150	17.4

Note: Market shares may not sum to 100.0 because of rounding and missing categories by household type. "Asian" and "black" include Hispanics and non-Hispanics who identify themselves as being of the respective race alone. "Hispanic" includes people of any race who identify themselves as Hispanic. "Other" includes people who identify themselves as non-Hispanic and as Alaska Native, American Indian, Asian (who are also included in the "Asian" row), or Native Hawaiian or other Pacific Islander, as well as non-Hispanics reporting more than one race.
Source: Calculations by New Strategist based on the Bureau of Labor Statistics' 2012 Consumer Expenditure Survey

Chapter 11.

Household Services

Household Spending on Household Services, 2000 to 2012

Spending on household services is dominated by day care needs. Spending on day care centers and babysitting accounted for 43 percent of the $750 the average household spent on household services in 2012. While the $237 that the average household spent on day care centers seems low, this—like all spending figures here—is an average that includes both purchasers and nonpurchasers. The 4.4 percent of households that paid for day care services during the average quarter of 2012 spent an average of $1,335 (see Appendix B), for an estimated annual expense of $5,340—a much more realistic figure.

The average household spent just $5 less on household services in 2012 than in 2000, after adjusting for inflation. Average household spending on services in 2006, however, had been 8 percent higher than in 2000. Between the overall peak spending year of 2006 and 2012, spending on day care centers fell 22 percent as householders cut their expenses in face of the Great Recession. Only three household service categories saw an appreciable increase in average household spending over those years: termite and pest control services, which gained 17 percent; moving, storage, and freight express, which gained 20 percent; and security system service fee, which also increased by 20 percent.

Average household spending on household services should grow as the millennial generation enters the lifestage at which day care needs are greatest.

Spending on household services

(average spending by households on household services, 2000, 2006, 2010, and 2012; in 2012 dollars)

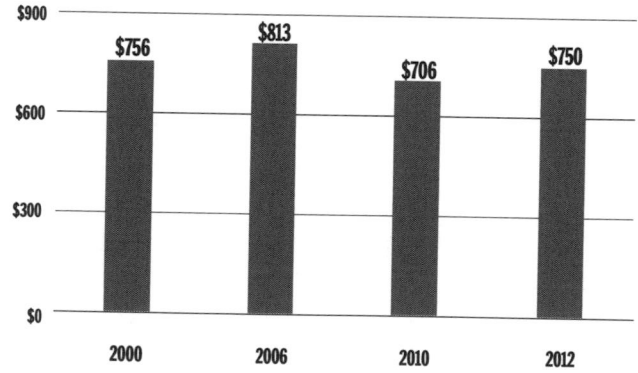

Table 11.1 Household services spending, 2000 to 2012

(average annual household spending on household services and percent distribution, by category, 2000 to 2012; percent change and percentage point change in spending, 2000–06, 2006–12, and 2010–12; in 2012 dollars; ranked by amount spent)

	average annual household spending (in 2012$)				percent change		
	2012	2010	2006	2000	2010–12	2006–12	2000–06
Average annual household spending on household services	$750.46	$705.59	$813.40	$755.79	6.4%	–7.7%	7.6%
Day care centers, nursery schools, and preschools	236.56	251.19	301.90	277.89	–5.8	–21.6	8.6
Housekeeping services	131.93	117.61	130.17	117.53	12.2	1.4	10.8
Gardening, lawn care service	125.40	113.36	124.28	104.34	10.6	0.9	19.1
Babysitting and childcare in own or other home	84.86	83.72	91.76	86.40	1.4	–7.5	6.2
Moving, storage, and freight express	56.88	47.11	47.34	43.24	20.7	20.1	9.5
Care for the elderly, invalids, handicapped	43.36	21.90	49.16	67.17	98.0	–11.8	–26.8
Security system service fee	27.23	24.87	22.70	24.89	9.5	20.0	–8.8
Termite and pest control products and services	24.58	22.08	21.00	13.41	11.3	17.0	56.6
Appliance repair, including service center	15.36	20.03	20.48	16.77	–23.3	–25.0	22.1
Water softening service	4.30	3.73	4.60	4.15	15.4	–6.5	11.0

					percentage point change		
PERCENT DISTRIBUTION OF SPENDING	2012	2010	2006	2000	2010–12	2006–12	2000–06
Average annual household spending on household services	100.0%	100.0%	100.0%	100.0%	–	–	–
Day care centers, nursery schools, and preschools	31.5	35.6	37.1	36.8	–4.1	–5.6	0.3
Housekeeping services	17.6	16.7	16.0	15.6	0.9	1.6	0.5
Gardening, lawn care service	16.7	16.1	15.3	13.8	0.6	1.4	1.5
Babysitting and childcare in own or other home	11.3	11.9	11.3	11.4	–0.6	0.0	–0.2
Moving, storage, and freight express	7.6	6.7	5.8	5.7	0.9	1.8	0.1
Care for the elderly, invalids, handicapped	5.8	3.1	6.0	8.9	2.7	–0.3	–2.8
Security system service fee	3.6	3.5	2.8	3.3	0.1	0.8	–0.5
Termite and pest control products and services	3.3	3.1	2.6	1.8	0.1	0.7	0.8
Appliance repair, including service center	2.0	2.8	2.5	2.2	–0.8	–0.5	0.3
Water softening service	0.6	0.5	0.6	0.5	0.0	0.0	0.0

Note: Percentage point change calculations are based on unrounded figures. "–" means not applicable.
Source: Bureau of Labor Statistics, 2000, 2006, 2010, and 2012 Consumer Expenditure Surveys; calculations by New Strategist

Appliance Repair, Including at Service Center

Best customers: Householders aged 55 to 74
Married couples without children at home
Married couples with school-aged or older children at home

Customer trends: Average household spending on appliance repair may recover as financially strapped boomers enter the older age groups.

The best customers of appliance repair are older householders. Not only do older householders have older appliances, but their appliances are often of higher quality, which makes it costlier to replace than to repair. Householders aged 55 to 74 spend 31 to 55 percent more than the average household on appliance repair. Married couples without children at home, most older empty-nesters, spend 46 percent more than average on appliance repair, while those with school-aged or older children at home spend 36 to 40 percent more than average on this item.

Average household spending on appliance repair grew 22 percent between 2000 and 2006 (the year overall household spending peaked), after adjusting for inflation, then declined by 25 percent over the next six-year period. Average household spending on appliance repair may recover as financially strapped boomers fill the older age groups.

Table 11.2 Appliance repair, including at service center

Total household spending $1,911,029,760.00
Average household spends 15.36

AGE OF HOUSEHOLDER	AVERAGE HOUSEHOLD SPENDING	BEST CUSTOMERS (index)	BIGGEST CUSTOMERS (market share)
Average household	$15.36	100	100.0%
Under age 25	2.70	18	1.2
Aged 25 to 34	10.60	69	11.2
Aged 35 to 44	13.44	88	15.2
Aged 45 to 54	15.50	101	20.0
Aged 55 to 64	23.87	155	28.4
Aged 65 to 74	20.19	131	15.8
Aged 75 or older	12.92	84	8.2

	AVERAGE HOUSEHOLD SPENDING	BEST CUSTOMERS (index)	BIGGEST CUSTOMERS (market share)
HOUSEHOLD INCOME			
Average household	**$15.36**	**100**	**100.0%**
Under $20,000	5.54	36	7.6
$20,000 to $39,999	12.90	84	18.9
$40,000 to $49,999	11.90	77	6.9
$50,000 to $69,999	15.51	101	14.6
$70,000 to $79,999	14.06	92	5.1
$80,000 to $99,999	18.34	119	10.5
$100,000 or more	29.84	194	36.4
HOUSEHOLD TYPE			
Average household	**15.36**	**100**	**100.0**
Married couples	20.93	136	66.2
Married couples, no children	22.42	146	30.4
Married couples with children	19.85	129	30.4
Oldest child under age 6	13.93	91	4.1
Oldest child aged 6 to 17	21.50	140	16.6
Oldest child aged 18 or older	20.90	136	9.6
Single parent with child under age 18	11.19	73	3.8
Single person	8.10	53	15.7
RACE AND HISPANIC ORIGIN			
Average household	**15.36**	**100**	**100.0**
Asian	8.99	59	2.5
Black	10.06	65	8.2
Hispanic	8.08	53	6.6
Non-Hispanic white and other	17.42	113	85.1
REGION			
Average household	**15.36**	**100**	**100.0**
Northeast	15.39	100	18.1
Midwest	15.97	104	23.1
South	14.75	96	35.8
West	15.73	102	23.1
EDUCATION			
Average household	**15.36**	**100**	**100.0**
Less than high school graduate	8.15	53	6.9
High school graduate	11.52	75	18.7
Some college	13.94	91	18.7
Associate's degree	15.21	99	9.8
Bachelor's degree or more	22.34	145	45.9
Bachelor's degree	23.53	153	30.5
Master's, professional, doctoral degree	20.30	132	15.3

Note: Market shares may not sum to 100.0 because of rounding and missing categories by household type. "Asian" and "black" include Hispanics and non-Hispanics who identify themselves as being of the respective race alone. "Hispanic" includes people of any race who identify themselves as Hispanic. "Other" includes people who identify themselves as non-Hispanic and as Alaska Native, American Indian, Asian (who are also included in the "Asian" row), or Native Hawaiian or other Pacific Islander, as well as non-Hispanics reporting more than one race.
Source: Calculations by New Strategist based on the Bureau of Labor Statistics' 2012 Consumer Expenditure Survey

Babysitting and Childcare in Own or Other Home

Best customers: Householders aged 25 to 44
High-income households
Married couples with children under age 18
Single parents
Hispanics

Customer trends: Average household spending on babysitting and childcare in own or other home should grow again as the large millennial generation has children.

Childcare is one of the largest expenses parents face. Those who spend the most on babysitting (which includes arrangements from hiring a teen to be with the kids on a Saturday night to a live-in nanny) are married couples with preschoolers. This household type spends over eight times the average on babysitting. Couples with school-aged children spend close to three times the average on this item, and single parents spend over twice the average. Householders aged 25 to 44, most with children, spend over twice the average on babysitting as well. High-income households spend nearly three times the average on this item. Hispanics, who tend to have the largest families, spend 57 percent more than average on babysitting.

Average household spending on babysitting rose 6 percent between 2000 and 2006, after adjusting for inflation. Then, between 2006 (the year overall household spending peaked) and 2010 (the year overall household spending bottomed out), average household spending on babysitting fell 9 percent as many families faced unemployment and had less need for babysitting services. In the two years since then, spending on babysitting rose by a tiny 1 percent. In the years ahead, spending on babysitting should grow again as the large millennial generation has children.

Table 11.3 Babysitting and childcare in own or other home

Total household spending $10,557,941,760.00
Average household spends 84.86

AGE OF HOUSEHOLDER	AVERAGE HOUSEHOLD SPENDING	BEST CUSTOMERS (index)	BIGGEST CUSTOMERS (market share)
Average household	$84.86	100	100.0%
Under age 25	81.53	96	6.3
Aged 25 to 34	186.71	220	35.6
Aged 35 to 44	184.30	217	37.7
Aged 45 to 54	72.64	86	16.9
Aged 55 to 64	13.50	16	2.9
Aged 65 to 74	3.58	4	0.5
Aged 75 or older	0.63	1	0.1

	AVERAGE HOUSEHOLD SPENDING	BEST CUSTOMERS (index)	BIGGEST CUSTOMERS (market share)
HOUSEHOLD INCOME			
Average household	**$84.86**	**100**	**100.0%**
Under $20,000	17.08	20	4.2
$20,000 to $39,999	39.06	46	10.4
$40,000 to $49,999	66.50	78	6.9
$50,000 to $69,999	48.22	57	8.2
$70,000 to $79,999	67.84	80	4.5
$80,000 to $99,999	99.35	117	10.3
$100,000 or more	251.36	296	55.5
HOUSEHOLD TYPE			
Average household	**84.86**	**100**	**100.0**
Married couples	140.76	166	80.6
Married couples, no children	2.35	3	0.6
Married couples with children	266.77	314	73.9
Oldest child under age 6	709.25	836	38.1
Oldest child aged 6 to 17	242.96	286	34.1
Oldest child aged 18 or older	20.79	24	1.7
Single parent with child under age 18	183.52	216	11.3
Single person	2.15	3	0.8
RACE AND HISPANIC ORIGIN			
Average household	**84.86**	**100**	**100.0**
Asian	95.43	112	4.9
Black	73.79	87	10.9
Hispanic	133.27	157	19.7
Non-Hispanic white and other	78.54	93	69.5
REGION			
Average household	**84.86**	**100**	**100.0**
Northeast	98.13	116	20.9
Midwest	70.46	83	18.4
South	82.77	98	36.3
West	91.83	108	24.4
EDUCATION			
Average household	**84.86**	**100**	**100.0**
Less than high school graduate	51.04	60	7.9
High school graduate	49.91	59	14.7
Some college	47.87	56	11.6
Associate's degree	68.98	81	8.0
Bachelor's degree or more	155.62	183	57.8
Bachelor's degree	142.45	168	33.5
Master's, professional, doctoral degree	178.24	210	24.4

Note: Market shares may not sum to 100.0 because of rounding and missing categories by household type. "Asian" and "black" include Hispanics and non-Hispanics who identify themselves as being of the respective race alone. "Hispanic" includes people of any race who identify themselves as Hispanic. "Other" includes people who identify themselves as non-Hispanic and as Alaska Native, American Indian, Asian (who are also included in the "Asian" row), or Native Hawaiian or other Pacific Islander, as well as non-Hispanics reporting more than one race.
Source: Calculations by New Strategist based on the Bureau of Labor Statistics' 2012 Consumer Expenditure Survey

Care for the Elderly, Invalids, Handicapped, Etc.

Best customers: Householders aged 75 or older
Married couples without children at home
People who live alone
Non-Hispanic whites

Customer trends: Average household spending on care for the elderly, invalids, and handicapped should rise as boomers age.

Older households spend the most out-of-pocket on care for the elderly, invalids, and the handicapped. Householders aged 75 or older spend seven-and-one-half times the average on elder care, many of them caring for ailing spouses. Married couples without children at home, most of them older, spend three-quarters more than average on this item. People who live alone (many of them older) spend 13 percent more than average. Non-Hispanic whites spend 28 percent more than average on this item and control 96 percent of the market.

Average household out-of-pocket spending on care for the elderly, invalids, and handicapped fell by 67 between 2000 and 2010 (the year when average household spending bottomed out), after adjusting for inflation. Average household spending on this item then doubled between 2010 and 2012. Average household spending on care for the elderly, invalids, and handicapped should continue to rise as boomers age.

Table 11.4 Care for the elderly, invalids, handicapped, etc.

Total household spending $5,394,677,760.00
Average household spends   43.36

AGE OF HOUSEHOLDER	AVERAGE HOUSEHOLD SPENDING	BEST CUSTOMERS (index)	BIGGEST CUSTOMERS (market share)
Average household	$43.36	100	100.0%
Under age 25	–	–	–
Aged 25 to 34	–	–	–
Aged 35 to 44	4.24	10	1.7
Aged 45 to 54	11.61	27	5.3
Aged 55 to 64	31.27	72	13.2
Aged 65 to 74	18.28	42	5.1
Aged 75 or older	331.52	765	74.7

	AVERAGE HOUSEHOLD SPENDING	BEST CUSTOMERS (index)	BIGGEST CUSTOMERS (market share)
HOUSEHOLD INCOME			
Average household	**$43.36**	**100**	**100.0%**
Under $20,000	29.90	69	14.5
$20,000 to $39,999	61.50	142	32.0
$40,000 to $49,999	29.89	69	6.1
$50,000 to $69,999	2.71	6	0.9
$70,000 to $79,999	67.50	156	8.7
$80,000 to $99,999	73.03	168	14.9
$100,000 or more	53.22	123	23.0
HOUSEHOLD TYPE			
Average household	**43.36**	**100**	**100.0**
Married couples	43.68	101	48.9
Married couples, no children	76.40	176	36.7
Married couples with children	6.09	14	3.3
Oldest child under age 6	–	–	–
Oldest child aged 6 to 17	4.98	11	1.4
Oldest child aged 18 or older	11.90	27	1.9
Single parent with child under age 18	5.86	14	0.7
Single person	48.96	113	33.5
RACE AND HISPANIC ORIGIN			
Average household	**43.36**	**100**	**100.0**
Asian	6.15	14	0.6
Black	11.81	27	3.4
Hispanic	1.39	3	0.4
Non-Hispanic white and other	55.56	128	96.2
REGION			
Average household	**43.36**	**100**	**100.0**
Northeast	136.96	316	57.0
Midwest	14.14	33	7.2
South	27.15	63	23.3
West	23.94	55	12.4
EDUCATION			
Average household	**43.36**	**100**	**100.0**
Less than high school graduate	26.04	60	7.8
High school graduate	76.16	176	43.8
Some college	34.27	79	16.3
Associate's degree	8.26	19	1.9
Bachelor's degree or more	41.53	96	30.2
Bachelor's degree	62.91	145	28.9
Master's, professional, doctoral degree	4.83	11	1.3

Note: Market shares may not sum to 100.0 because of rounding and missing categories by household type. "Asian" and "black" include Hispanics and non-Hispanics who identify themselves as being of the respective race alone. "Hispanic" includes people of any race who identify themselves as Hispanic. "Other" includes people who identify themselves as non-Hispanic and as Alaska Native, American Indian, Asian (who are also included in the "Asian" row), or Native Hawaiian or other Pacific Islander, as well as non-Hispanics reporting more than one race. "–" means sample is too small to make a reliable estimate.
Source: Calculations by New Strategist based on the Bureau of Labor Statistics' 2012 Consumer Expenditure Survey

Day Care Centers, Nursery Schools, and Preschools

Best customers: Householders aged 25 to 44
Married couples with children under age 18
Single parents
Asians
Households in the Northeast

Customer trends: Average household spending on day care centers, nursery schools, and preschools should rise again in the years ahead as the large millennial generation has children.

The best customers of day care centers are married couples with preschoolers. This household type spends almost 10 times the average on day care centers, nursery schools, and preschools. Married couples with school-aged children spend over twice the average on this item, as do single parents. Householders aged 25 to 44, most of them parents, also spend more than twice the average on day care centers and control 81 percent of the market. Another group that spends over twice the average on this item is Asian householders. Households in the Northeast spend 45 percent more than average on day care.

Average household spending on day care centers climbed 9 percent between 2000 and 2006 (the year overall household spending peaked), then fell 22 percent between 2006 and 2012, after adjusting for inflation. Behind the decline was high unemployment due to the Great Recession, which limited the need for day care. Average household spending on day care centers should rise again in the years ahead as the large millennial generation has children.

Table 11.5 Day care centers, nursery schools, and preschools

Total household spending $29,431,848,960.00
Average household spends 236.56

AGE OF HOUSEHOLDER	AVERAGE HOUSEHOLD SPENDING	BEST CUSTOMERS (index)	BIGGEST CUSTOMERS (market share)
Average household	$236.56	100	100.0%
Under age 25	113.61	48	3.1
Aged 25 to 34	541.67	229	37.0
Aged 35 to 44	603.26	255	44.3
Aged 45 to 54	121.48	51	10.2
Aged 55 to 64	32.53	14	2.5
Aged 65 to 74	54.68	23	2.8
Aged 75 or older	2.46	1	0.1

	AVERAGE HOUSEHOLD SPENDING	BEST CUSTOMERS (index)	BIGGEST CUSTOMERS (market share)
HOUSEHOLD INCOME			
Average household	**$236.56**	**100**	**100.0%**
Under $20,000	24.70	10	2.2
$20,000 to $39,999	89.75	38	8.6
$40,000 to $49,999	150.40	64	5.6
$50,000 to $69,999	159.82	68	9.8
$70,000 to $79,999	304.72	129	7.2
$80,000 to $99,999	345.51	146	12.9
$100,000 or more	679.65	287	53.8
HOUSEHOLD TYPE			
Average household	**236.56**	**100**	**100.0**
Married couples	380.97	161	78.2
Married couples, no children	11.41	5	1.0
Married couples with children	712.61	301	70.8
Oldest child under age 6	2,304.17	974	44.4
Oldest child aged 6 to 17	506.79	214	25.5
Oldest child aged 18 or older	30.38	13	0.9
Single parent with child under age 18	489.72	207	10.9
Single person	15.54	7	2.0
RACE AND HISPANIC ORIGIN			
Average household	**236.56**	**100**	**100.0**
Asian	561.91	238	10.3
Black	206.39	87	11.0
Hispanic	152.41	64	8.1
Non-Hispanic white and other	255.15	108	81.0
REGION			
Average household	**236.56**	**100**	**100.0**
Northeast	343.65	145	26.2
Midwest	238.55	101	22.4
South	194.68	82	30.7
West	218.05	92	20.8
EDUCATION			
Average household	**236.56**	**100**	**100.0**
Less than high school graduate	57.51	24	3.2
High school graduate	109.60	46	11.6
Some college	165.33	70	14.4
Associate's degree	230.82	98	9.6
Bachelor's degree or more	459.38	194	61.2
Bachelor's degree	406.60	172	34.3
Master's, professional, doctoral degree	550.01	233	27.0

Note: Market shares may not sum to 100.0 because of rounding and missing categories by household type. "Asian" and "black" include Hispanics and non-Hispanics who identify themselves as being of the respective race alone. "Hispanic" includes people of any race who identify themselves as Hispanic. "Other" includes people who identify themselves as non-Hispanic and as Alaska Native, American Indian, Asian (who are also included in the "Asian" row), or Native Hawaiian or other Pacific Islander, as well as non-Hispanics reporting more than one race.
Source: Calculations by New Strategist based on the Bureau of Labor Statistics' 2012 Consumer Expenditure Survey

Gardening and Lawn Care Services

Best customers: Householders aged 55 or older
Married couples without children at home
Married couples with adult children
Non-Hispanic whites
Households in the West

Customer trends: Average household spending on gardening and lawn care services should grow as the population ages.

Older householders are most likely to spend on gardening and lawn care services. Householders aged 55 or older, many of whom need help maintaining their lawns, spend 41 to 95 percent more than average on this item and control 64 percent of the market. Married couples without children at home (most of them older) spend 60 percent more than average on gardening and lawn care services, and those with adult children at home spend 32 percent more. Non-Hispanic whites spend 19 percent more than average on gardening and lawn care services because they are most likely to be homeowners. Households in the West spend 21 percent more than average on this service.

Average household spending on gardening and lawn care services climbed 19 percent between 2000 and 2006 (the year overall household spending peaked), after adjusting for inflation. Between 2006 and 2010, spending on gardening services fell 9 percent as households tightened their belts due to the Great Recession. In the two years since the overall trough spending year of 2010, average household spending on gardening and lawn care services rose 11 percent. This category should grow as the baby-boom generation fills the best-customer age groups.

Table 11.6 Gardening and lawn care services

Total household spending $15,601,766,400.00
Average household spends   125.40

	AVERAGE HOUSEHOLD SPENDING	BEST CUSTOMERS (index)	BIGGEST CUSTOMERS (market share)
AGE OF HOUSEHOLDER			
Average household	**$125.40**	**100**	**100.0%**
Under age 25	7.66	6	0.4
Aged 25 to 34	40.07	32	5.2
Aged 35 to 44	78.44	63	10.9
Aged 45 to 54	125.97	100	19.9
Aged 55 to 64	176.98	141	25.8
Aged 65 to 74	195.38	156	18.8
Aged 75 or older	244.92	195	19.1

	AVERAGE HOUSEHOLD SPENDING	BEST CUSTOMERS (index)	BIGGEST CUSTOMERS (market share)
HOUSEHOLD INCOME			
Average household	**$125.40**	**100**	**100.0%**
Under $20,000	54.97	44	9.2
$20,000 to $39,999	82.99	66	14.9
$40,000 to $49,999	92.50	74	6.5
$50,000 to $69,999	105.14	84	12.1
$70,000 to $79,999	104.94	84	4.7
$80,000 to $99,999	122.64	98	8.6
$100,000 or more	294.18	235	43.9
HOUSEHOLD TYPE			
Average household	**125.40**	**100**	**100.0**
Married couples	157.27	125	60.9
Married couples, no children	200.71	160	33.4
Married couples with children	130.43	104	24.5
Oldest child under age 6	89.91	72	3.3
Oldest child aged 6 to 17	124.87	100	11.8
Oldest child aged 18 or older	165.99	132	9.3
Single parent with child under age 18	46.59	37	1.9
Single person	118.74	95	28.1
RACE AND HISPANIC ORIGIN			
Average household	**125.40**	**100**	**100.0**
Asian	134.91	108	4.7
Black	69.29	55	6.9
Hispanic	36.86	29	3.7
Non-Hispanic white and other	149.31	119	89.4
REGION			
Average household	**125.40**	**100**	**100.0**
Northeast	134.57	107	19.4
Midwest	87.45	70	15.5
South	127.66	102	37.9
West	151.65	121	27.3
EDUCATION			
Average household	**125.40**	**100**	**100.0**
Less than high school graduate	42.89	34	4.5
High school graduate	76.09	61	15.1
Some college	103.41	82	17.0
Associate's degree	92.44	74	7.3
Bachelor's degree or more	223.24	178	56.1
Bachelor's degree	198.75	158	31.6
Master's, professional, doctoral degree	265.29	212	24.6

Note: Market shares may not sum to 100.0 because of rounding and missing categories by household type. "Asian" and "black" include Hispanics and non-Hispanics who identify themselves as being of the respective race alone. "Hispanic" includes people of any race who identify themselves as Hispanic. "Other" includes people who identify themselves as non-Hispanic and as Alaska Native, American Indian, Asian (who are also included in the "Asian" row), or Native Hawaiian or other Pacific Islander, as well as non-Hispanics reporting more than one race.
Source: Calculations by New Strategist based on the Bureau of Labor Statistics' 2012 Consumer Expenditure Survey

Housekeeping Services

Best customers: Householders aged 45 or older
High-income households
Married couples without children at home
Married couples with school-aged or older children at home
Non-Hispanic whites
Households in the West
College graduates

Customer trends: Average household spending on housekeeping services should rise as the population ages.

The best customers of housekeeping services are older couples and the affluent—the first group often needs such services, while the second group can afford them. Householders aged 45 or older spend at least 15 percent more than average on housekeeping services, the figure peaking at 92 percent above average among householders aged 75 or older. Households with incomes of $100,000 or more spend well over three times the average on this item. Married couples without children at home, most of them older, spend 29 percent more than average on housekeeping services, while those with school-aged children (the busiest households) spend 58 percent more. Non-Hispanic whites spend 26 percent more than average on housekeeping services. Western households spend 63 percent more than average on housekeeping services. College graduates, who dominate the nation's affluent, spend well more than twice the average on this item.

After rising 11 percent between 2000 and 2006 (the year overall household spending peaked), average household spending on housekeeping services fell 10 percent between 2006 and the overall trough spending year of 2010, after adjusting for inflation. In the ensuing two years, average household spending on housekeeping services rebounded by a solid 12 percent. Behind the recent increase is the aging of the baby-boom generation into the best-customer age groups. Spending on housekeeping services should continue its rise in the years ahead along with the aging of the population.

Table 11.7 Housekeeping services

| Total household spending | $16,414,202,880.00 |
| Average household spends | 131.93 |

AGE OF HOUSEHOLDER	AVERAGE HOUSEHOLD SPENDING	BEST CUSTOMERS (index)	BIGGEST CUSTOMERS (market share)
Average household	$131.93	100	100.0%
Under age 25	17.36	13	0.9
Aged 25 to 34	52.35	40	6.4
Aged 35 to 44	92.30	70	12.1
Aged 45 to 54	151.10	115	22.7
Aged 55 to 64	159.80	121	22.2
Aged 65 to 74	185.92	141	17.0
Aged 75 or older	253.23	192	18.8

	AVERAGE HOUSEHOLD SPENDING	BEST CUSTOMERS (index)	BIGGEST CUSTOMERS (market share)
HOUSEHOLD INCOME			
Average household	$131.93	100	100.0%
Under $20,000	42.11	32	6.7
$20,000 to $39,999	65.91	50	11.3
$40,000 to $49,999	82.20	62	5.5
$50,000 to $69,999	59.33	45	6.5
$70,000 to $79,999	66.41	50	2.8
$80,000 to $99,999	106.18	80	7.1
$100,000 or more	423.53	321	60.1
HOUSEHOLD TYPE			
Average household	131.93	100	100.0
Married couples	168.14	127	61.9
Married couples, no children	170.21	129	26.9
Married couples with children	185.55	141	33.1
Oldest child under age 6	146.79	111	5.1
Oldest child aged 6 to 17	208.35	158	18.8
Oldest child aged 18 or older	172.18	131	9.2
Single parent with child under age 18	88.98	67	3.5
Single person	113.53	86	25.6
RACE AND HISPANIC ORIGIN			
Average household	131.93	100	100.0
Asian	102.50	78	3.4
Black	21.28	16	2.0
Hispanic	38.89	29	3.7
Non-Hispanic white and other	165.71	126	94.3
REGION			
Average household	131.93	100	100.0
Northeast	152.17	115	20.8
Midwest	101.77	77	17.1
South	89.82	68	25.4
West	214.99	163	36.7
EDUCATION			
Average household	131.93	100	100.0
Less than high school graduate	24.06	18	2.4
High school graduate	37.42	28	7.1
Some college	88.45	67	13.8
Associate's degree	71.97	55	5.4
Bachelor's degree or more	298.48	226	71.4
Bachelor's degree	210.34	159	31.8
Master's, professional, doctoral degree	449.85	341	39.6

Note: Market shares may not sum to 100.0 because of rounding and missing categories by household type. "Asian" and "black" include Hispanics and non-Hispanics who identify themselves as being of the respective race alone. "Hispanic" includes people of any race who identify themselves as Hispanic. "Other" includes people who identify themselves as non-Hispanic and as Alaska Native, American Indian, Asian (who are also included in the "Asian" row), or Native Hawaiian or other Pacific Islander, as well as non-Hispanics reporting more than one race.
Source: Calculations by New Strategist based on the Bureau of Labor Statistics' 2012 Consumer Expenditure Survey

Moving, Storage, and Freight Express

Best customers: Householders aged 35 to 44 and 55 to 74
                    Married couples with children at home
                    Non-Hispanic whites
                    Households in the West

Customer trends: Average household spending on moving, storage, and freight express is likely to continue to grow
                    as boomers fill the best-customer age group.

The biggest spenders on moving, storage, and freight express are households that need storage space or can afford to pay for moving services. Householders aged 55 to 74 spend 22 to 24 percent more than average on moving and storage services. Married couples with children at home spend one-quarter more than average on this item as they move into larger homes for their expanding families. Householders aged 35 to 44, many of them parents, spend 20 percent more than average on moving, storage, and freight express. Non-Hispanic whites spend 21 percent more than average on this item and account for 91 percent of the market. Households in the West spend 60 percent above average on moving, storage, and freight express.

Average household spending on moving, storage, and freight express grew 32 percent between 2000 and 2012, after adjusting for inflation. Behind the solid growth in this category is the popularity of renting storage space for the accumulation of household goods. With no end in sight to this accumulation, and with boomers filling the best-customer age groups, average household spending on moving, storage, and freight express is likely to continue to grow.

Table 11.8 Moving, storage, and freight express

Total household spending $7,076,782,080.00
Average household spends   56.88

AGE OF HOUSEHOLDER	AVERAGE HOUSEHOLD SPENDING	BEST CUSTOMERS (index)	BIGGEST CUSTOMERS (market share)
Average household	$56.88	100	100.0%
Under age 25	50.56	89	5.8
Aged 25 to 34	50.81	89	14.4
Aged 35 to 44	68.01	120	20.8
Aged 45 to 54	42.36	74	14.7
Aged 55 to 64	70.52	124	22.7
Aged 65 to 74	69.64	122	14.8
Aged 75 or older	39.54	70	6.8

	AVERAGE HOUSEHOLD SPENDING	BEST CUSTOMERS (index)	BIGGEST CUSTOMERS (market share)
HOUSEHOLD INCOME			
Average household	**$56.88**	**100**	**100.0%**
Under $20,000	18.50	33	6.8
$20,000 to $39,999	43.61	77	17.3
$40,000 to $49,999	38.38	67	6.0
$50,000 to $69,999	43.46	76	11.0
$70,000 to $79,999	46.34	81	4.5
$80,000 to $99,999	66.12	116	10.3
$100,000 or more	133.87	235	44.1
HOUSEHOLD TYPE			
Average household	**56.88**	**100**	**100.0**
Married couples	66.11	116	56.5
Married couples, no children	63.91	112	23.4
Married couples with children	70.83	125	29.3
Oldest child under age 6	79.70	140	6.4
Oldest child aged 6 to 17	63.69	112	13.3
Oldest child aged 18 or older	77.14	136	9.6
Single parent with child under age 18	23.79	42	2.2
Single person	40.28	71	21.0
RACE AND HISPANIC ORIGIN			
Average household	**56.88**	**100**	**100.0**
Asian	59.42	104	4.5
Black	28.35	50	6.3
Hispanic	14.26	25	3.1
Non-Hispanic white and other	68.83	121	90.8
REGION			
Average household	**56.88**	**100**	**100.0**
Northeast	50.49	89	16.0
Midwest	30.08	53	11.7
South	55.20	97	36.1
West	91.14	160	36.1
EDUCATION			
Average household	**56.88**	**100**	**100.0**
Less than high school graduate	34.60	61	7.9
High school graduate	22.24	39	9.7
Some college	66.03	116	23.9
Associate's degree	54.26	95	9.4
Bachelor's degree or more	88.34	155	49.0
Bachelor's degree	85.78	151	30.1
Master's, professional, doctoral degree	92.74	163	18.9

Note: Market shares may not sum to 100.0 because of rounding and missing categories by household type. "Asian" and "black" include Hispanics and non-Hispanics who identify themselves as being of the respective race alone. "Hispanic" includes people of any race who identify themselves as Hispanic. "Other" includes people who identify themselves as non-Hispanic and as Alaska Native, American Indian, Asian (who are also included in the "Asian" row), or Native Hawaiian or other Pacific Islander, as well as non-Hispanics reporting more than one race.
Source: Calculations by New Strategist based on the Bureau of Labor Statistics' 2012 Consumer Expenditure Survey

Security System Service Fees

Best customers: **Married couples**
Blacks
Households in the South

Customer trends: **Average household spending on home security system service fees should continue to rise along with the aging of the population.**

The best customers of home security system service fees are older married couples. Married couples without children at home, most of them empty-nesters, spend 39 percent more than average on security system service fees, while those with children at home spend 41 percent more than average. Black households, whose spending surpasses average on relatively few items, outspend the average on home security system service fees by 37 percent. Households in the South, where many blacks reside, spend 33 percent more than average on home security.

Average household spending on home security system service fees fell 9 percent between 2000 and 2006, after adjusting for inflation, but then rebounded and climbed 20 percent between 2006 and 2012. Average household spending on home security system service fees should continue to rise in the years ahead along with the aging of the population.

Table 11.9 Security system service fees

| Total household spending | $3,387,847,680.00 |
| Average household spends | 27.23 |

AGE OF HOUSEHOLDER	AVERAGE HOUSEHOLD SPENDING	BEST CUSTOMERS (index)	BIGGEST CUSTOMERS (market share)
Average household	$27.23	100	100.0%
Under age 25	1.78	7	0.4
Aged 25 to 34	25.11	92	14.9
Aged 35 to 44	30.27	111	19.3
Aged 45 to 54	31.59	116	23.0
Aged 55 to 64	26.69	98	17.9
Aged 65 to 74	31.21	115	13.8
Aged 75 or older	29.67	109	10.7

	AVERAGE HOUSEHOLD SPENDING	BEST CUSTOMERS (index)	BIGGEST CUSTOMERS (market share)
HOUSEHOLD INCOME			
Average household	**$27.23**	**100**	**100.0%**
Under $20,000	7.63	28	5.9
$20,000 to $39,999	14.49	53	12.0
$40,000 to $49,999	18.28	67	5.9
$50,000 to $69,999	21.63	79	11.5
$70,000 to $79,999	26.94	99	5.5
$80,000 to $99,999	41.87	154	13.6
$100,000 or more	66.32	244	45.6
HOUSEHOLD TYPE			
Average household	**27.23**	**100**	**100.0**
Married couples	37.71	138	67.3
Married couples, no children	37.82	139	29.0
Married couples with children	38.40	141	33.2
Oldest child under age 6	44.10	162	7.4
Oldest child aged 6 to 17	39.04	143	17.1
Oldest child aged 18 or older	33.64	124	8.7
Single parent with child under age 18	19.98	73	3.8
Single person	16.55	61	18.0
RACE AND HISPANIC ORIGIN			
Average household	**27.23**	**100**	**100.0**
Asian	32.31	119	5.1
Black	37.27	137	17.2
Hispanic	16.04	59	7.4
Non-Hispanic white and other	27.36	100	75.4
REGION			
Average household	**27.23**	**100**	**100.0**
Northeast	21.87	80	14.5
Midwest	16.51	61	13.4
South	36.17	133	49.5
West	27.28	100	22.6
EDUCATION			
Average household	**27.23**	**100**	**100.0**
Less than high school graduate	11.27	41	5.4
High school graduate	17.00	62	15.6
Some college	19.97	73	15.1
Associate's degree	32.00	118	11.6
Bachelor's degree or more	45.16	166	52.3
Bachelor's degree	40.48	149	29.6
Master's, professional, doctoral degree	53.20	195	22.7

Note: Market shares may not sum to 100.0 because of rounding and missing categories by household type. "Asian" and "black" include Hispanics and non-Hispanics who identify themselves as being of the respective race alone. "Hispanic" includes people of any race who identify themselves as Hispanic. "Other" includes people who identify themselves as non-Hispanic and as Alaska Native, American Indian, Asian (who are also included in the "Asian" row), or Native Hawaiian or other Pacific Islander, as well as non-Hispanics reporting more than one race.
Source: Calculations by New Strategist based on the Bureau of Labor Statistics' 2012 Consumer Expenditure Survey

Termite and Pest Control Products and Services

Best customers: Householders aged 55 or older
                       Married couples
                       Households in the South

Customer trends: Average household spending on termite and pest control products and services should continue
                       to increase along with the population of the South.

The best customers of termite and pest control products and services are older married couples in the South, where insect problems are abundant because of the warm climate. Southern households spend 51 percent more than average on this item and control 56 percent of the market. Householders aged 55 or older spend 21 to 35 percent more than average on termite and pest control. Married couples without children at home, most of them older, spend 55 percent more than average on this item. Married couples with children outspend the average for this item by 49 percent.

Although the pace of growth has slowed since 2006, average household spending on termite and pest control products and services continued to rise throughout the years of economic downturn. Overall, spending on this item increased by a substantial 83 percent between 2000 and 2012, after adjusting for inflation. Behind the increase is the growing population of the South, where these services are often necessary. Spending on termite and pest control products and services should continue to increase along with the population of the South.

Table 11.10 Termite and pest control products and services

| Total household spending | $3,058,145,280.00 |
| Average household spends | 24.58 |

	AVERAGE HOUSEHOLD SPENDING	BEST CUSTOMERS (index)	BIGGEST CUSTOMERS (market share)
AGE OF HOUSEHOLDER			
Average household	**$24.58**	**100**	**100.0%**
Under age 25	3.86	16	1.0
Aged 25 to 34	13.01	53	8.6
Aged 35 to 44	25.85	105	18.3
Aged 45 to 54	26.04	106	21.0
Aged 55 to 64	31.50	128	23.5
Aged 65 to 74	29.62	121	14.5
Aged 75 or older	33.21	135	13.2

	AVERAGE HOUSEHOLD SPENDING	BEST CUSTOMERS (index)	BIGGEST CUSTOMERS (market share)
HOUSEHOLD INCOME			
Average household	**$24.58**	**100**	**100.0%**
Under $20,000	7.94	32	6.8
$20,000 to $39,999	14.32	58	13.1
$40,000 to $49,999	24.94	101	9.0
$50,000 to $69,999	20.67	84	12.1
$70,000 to $79,999	17.97	73	4.1
$80,000 to $99,999	34.74	141	12.5
$100,000 or more	55.65	226	42.4
HOUSEHOLD TYPE			
Average household	**24.58**	**100**	**100.0**
Married couples	36.63	149	72.4
Married couples, no children	38.10	155	32.3
Married couples with children	36.54	149	35.0
Oldest child under age 6	33.98	138	6.3
Oldest child aged 6 to 17	34.28	139	16.6
Oldest child aged 18 or older	42.02	171	12.1
Single parent with child under age 18	15.20	62	3.2
Single person	11.56	47	14.0
RACE AND HISPANIC ORIGIN			
Average household	**24.58**	**100**	**100.0**
Asian	16.92	69	3.0
Black	19.59	80	10.0
Hispanic	11.88	48	6.1
Non-Hispanic white and other	27.47	112	83.9
REGION			
Average household	**24.58**	**100**	**100.0**
Northeast	13.89	57	10.2
Midwest	9.72	40	8.8
South	37.12	151	56.2
West	27.01	110	24.8
EDUCATION			
Average household	**24.58**	**100**	**100.0**
Less than high school graduate	13.00	53	6.9
High school graduate	16.60	68	16.8
Some college	20.84	85	17.5
Associate's degree	27.12	110	10.9
Bachelor's degree or more	37.32	152	47.9
Bachelor's degree	34.72	141	28.2
Master's, professional, doctoral degree	41.79	170	19.7

Note: Market shares may not sum to 100.0 because of rounding and missing categories by household type. "Asian" and "black" include Hispanics and non-Hispanics who identify themselves as being of the respective race alone. "Hispanic" includes people of any race who identify themselves as Hispanic. "Other" includes people who identify themselves as non-Hispanic and as Alaska Native, American Indian, Asian (who are also included in the "Asian" row), or Native Hawaiian or other Pacific Islander, as well as non-Hispanics reporting more than one race.
Source: Calculations by New Strategist based on the Bureau of Labor Statistics' 2012 Consumer Expenditure Survey

Water Softening Service

Best customers:	Householders aged 65 to 74
	Married couples with school-aged children
	Households in the Northeast
Customer trends:	Average household spending on water softening service should stabilize in the years ahead because boomers are filling the best-customer age group.

The biggest spenders on water softening service are older married couples in the Northeast. Householders aged 65 to 74 spend 82 percent more than average on this item. Married couples with school-aged children spend 71 percent more. Households in the Northeast outspend the average on water softening service by 55 percent.

After rising 11 percent from 2000 to 2006, average household spending on water softening service declined 7 percent between 2006 and 2012, after adjusting for inflation. Average household spending on water softening service should stabilize in the years ahead because boomers are filling the best-customer age group.

Table 11.11 Water softening service

Total household spending	$534,988,800.00
Average household spends	4.30

	AVERAGE HOUSEHOLD SPENDING	BEST CUSTOMERS (index)	BIGGEST CUSTOMERS (market share)
AGE OF HOUSEHOLDER			
Average household	**$4.30**	**100**	**100.0%**
Under age 25	0.88	20	1.3
Aged 25 to 34	2.63	61	9.9
Aged 35 to 44	4.57	106	18.4
Aged 45 to 54	5.34	124	24.6
Aged 55 to 64	4.14	96	17.6
Aged 65 to 74	7.81	182	21.9
Aged 75 or older	2.77	64	6.3

	AVERAGE HOUSEHOLD SPENDING	BEST CUSTOMERS (index)	BIGGEST CUSTOMERS (market share)
HOUSEHOLD INCOME			
Average household	$4.30	100	100.0%
Under $20,000	3.12	72	15.3
$20,000 to $39,999	2.57	60	13.5
$40,000 to $49,999	5.99	139	12.3
$50,000 to $69,999	5.58	130	18.7
$70,000 to $79,999	6.02	140	7.8
$80,000 to $99,999	4.92	114	10.1
$100,000 or more	5.14	120	22.4
HOUSEHOLD TYPE			
Average household	4.30	100	100.0
Married couples	4.84	113	54.7
Married couples, no children	4.84	113	23.5
Married couples with children	5.08	118	27.8
Oldest child under age 6	0.60	14	0.6
Oldest child aged 6 to 17	7.34	171	20.3
Oldest child aged 18 or older	4.15	97	6.8
Single parent with child under age 18	1.37	32	1.7
Single person	3.69	86	25.5
RACE AND HISPANIC ORIGIN			
Average household	4.30	100	100.0
Asian	1.16	27	1.2
Black	4.30	100	12.6
Hispanic	1.63	38	4.8
Non-Hispanic white and other	4.74	110	82.7
REGION			
Average household	4.30	100	100.0
Northeast	6.66	155	28.0
Midwest	3.93	91	20.3
South	4.12	96	35.7
West	3.09	72	16.2
EDUCATION			
Average household	4.30	100	100.0
Less than high school graduate	2.81	65	8.5
High school graduate	3.71	86	21.5
Some college	4.77	111	22.8
Associate's degree	4.45	103	10.2
Bachelor's degree or more	5.03	117	36.9
Bachelor's degree	4.07	95	18.9
Master's, professional, doctoral degree	6.70	156	18.1

Note: Market shares may not sum to 100.0 because of rounding and missing categories by household type. "Asian" and "black" include Hispanics and non-Hispanics who identify themselves as being of the respective race alone. "Hispanic" includes people of any race who identify themselves as Hispanic. "Other" includes people who identify themselves as non-Hispanic and as Alaska Native, American Indian, Asian (who are also included in the "Asian" row), or Native Hawaiian or other Pacific Islander, as well as non-Hispanics reporting more than one race.
Source: Calculations by New Strategist based on the Bureau of Labor Statistics' 2012 Consumer Expenditure Survey

Chapter 12.

Housekeeping Supplies

Household Spending on Housekeeping Supplies, 2000 to 2012

Housekeeping supplies is a catchall category that includes a variety of products such as laundry detergent, toilet paper, paper towels, vegetable seeds, insecticides, postage, stationery, and giftwrap. In 2012, the average household spent $610 on these items, 5 percent less than in both 2010 and 2000, after adjusting for inflation. Spending in this category was highest in the overall peak spending year of 2006, at $728.

Laundry and cleaning supplies, the largest subcategory within housekeeping supplies, accounts for 25 percent of spending in the category. Between 2000 and 2012, average household spending on laundry and cleaning supplies fell 11 percent, after adjusting for inflation. The category of cleansing and toilet tissue, paper towels, and napkins saw the largest growth in average household spending during these years, a 29 percent increase. These paper products now account for 19 percent of spending on housekeeping supplies. Lawn and garden supplies spending increased by 24 percent between 2000 and 2006, after adjusting for inflation, but declined by 31 percent in the ensuing six-year period. Similarly, spending on stationery, stationery supplies, and giftwrap, which had grown by 15 percent from 2000 to 2006, decreased 23 percent between 2006 and 2012. Spending on postage plummeted 27 percent over the latter period despite multiple increases in the price of stamps.

Spending on housekeeping supplies

(average spending by households on housekeeping supplies, 2000, 2006, 2010, and 2012; in 2012 dollars)

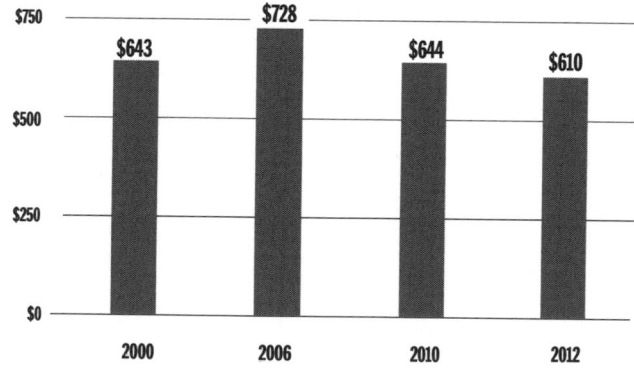

Table 12.1 Housekeeping supplies spending, 2000 to 2012

(average annual household spending on housekeeping supplies and percent distribution, by category, 2000 to 2012; percent change and percentage point change in spending, 2000–06, 2006–12, and 2010–12; in 2012 dollars; ranked by amount spent)

	average annual household spending (in 2012$)				percent change		
	2012	2010	2006	2000	2010–12	2006–12	2000–06
Average annual household spending on housekeeping supplies	**$609.86**	**$643.94**	**$728.38**	**$643.08**	**–5.3%**	**–16.3%**	**13.3%**
Laundry and cleaning supplies	155.39	158.21	172.22	174.34	–1.8	–9.8	–1.2
Cleansing and toilet tissue, paper towels, and napkins	117.50	108.88	113.73	91.26	7.9	3.3	24.6
Lawn and garden supplies	76.04	101.17	110.53	89.29	–24.8	–31.2	23.8
Stationery, stationery supplies, giftwrap	75.07	77.15	97.91	84.86	–2.7	–23.3	15.4
Postage	57.44	59.03	79.01	80.80	–2.7	–27.3	–2.2

					percentage point change		
PERCENT DISTRIBUTION OF SPENDING	2012	2010	2006	2000	2010–12	2006–12	2000–06
Average annual household spending on housekeeping supplies	**100.0%**	**100.0%**	**100.0%**	**100.0%**	–	–	–
Laundry and cleaning supplies	25.5	24.6	23.6	27.1	0.9	1.8	–3.5
Cleansing and toilet tissue, paper towels, and napkins	19.3	16.9	15.6	14.2	2.4	3.7	1.4
Lawn and garden supplies	12.5	15.7	15.2	13.9	–3.2	–2.7	1.3
Stationery, stationery supplies, giftwrap	12.3	12.0	13.4	13.2	0.3	–1.1	0.2
Postage	9.4	9.2	10.8	12.6	0.3	–1.4	–1.7

Note: Numbers do not add to total because not all categories are shown. Percentage point change calculations are based on unrounded figures. "–" means not applicable.
Source: Bureau of Labor Statistics, 2000, 2006, 2010, and 2012 Consumer Expenditure Surveys; calculations by New Strategist

Cleansing and Toilet Tissue, Paper Towels, and Napkins

Best customers: Householders aged 45 to 64
                       Married couples with school-aged or older children at home
                       Hispanics

Customer trends: Average household spending on cleansing and toilet tissue, paper towels, and napkins may fall
                       as household size declines with the aging of the baby-boom generation.

Because everyone buys cleansing and toilet tissue, paper towels, and napkins, there are few differences by demographic characteristic in spending on this item. Householders aged 45 to 64 spend 14 to 22 percent more than average on this item. Married couples with school-aged or older children at home spend 33 to 47 percent more because their households are larger. The spending on toilet tissue, paper towels, and napkins by Hispanics, who tend to have large families, is 16 percent higher than average.

Average household spending on cleansing and toilet tissue, paper towels, and napkins climbed 29 percent between 2000 and 2012, after adjusting for inflation. Average household spending on this item may fall in the years ahead as boomers age and average household size continues to decline.

Table 12.2 **Cleansing and toilet tissue, paper towels, and napkins**

Total household spending $14,618,880,000.00
Average household spends   117.50

AGE OF HOUSEHOLDER	AVERAGE HOUSEHOLD SPENDING	BEST CUSTOMERS (index)	BIGGEST CUSTOMERS (market share)
Average household	**$117.50**	**100**	**100.0%**
Under age 25	60.04	51	3.4
Aged 25 to 34	109.81	93	15.1
Aged 35 to 44	114.94	98	17.0
Aged 45 to 54	134.23	114	22.6
Aged 55 to 64	143.39	122	22.3
Aged 65 to 74	117.57	100	12.1
Aged 75 or older	93.26	79	7.8

	AVERAGE HOUSEHOLD SPENDING	BEST CUSTOMERS (index)	BIGGEST CUSTOMERS (market share)
HOUSEHOLD INCOME			
Average household	**$117.50**	**100**	**100.0%**
Under $20,000	73.98	63	13.2
$20,000 to $39,999	97.91	83	18.8
$40,000 to $49,999	120.47	103	9.1
$50,000 to $69,999	115.18	98	14.2
$70,000 to $79,999	171.02	146	8.1
$80,000 to $99,999	137.10	117	10.3
$100,000 or more	162.68	138	25.9
HOUSEHOLD TYPE			
Average household	**117.50**	**100**	**100.0**
Married couples	144.74	123	59.8
Married couples, no children	129.02	110	22.9
Married couples with children	153.90	131	30.8
Oldest child under age 6	118.42	101	4.6
Oldest child aged 6 to 17	156.04	133	15.8
Oldest child aged 18 or older	172.44	147	10.4
Single parent with child under age 18	97.50	83	4.4
Single person	67.75	58	17.1
RACE AND HISPANIC ORIGIN			
Average household	**117.50**	**100**	**100.0**
Asian	109.29	93	4.0
Black	109.91	94	11.8
Hispanic	135.98	116	14.5
Non-Hispanic white and other	115.69	98	73.9
REGION			
Average household	**117.50**	**100**	**100.0**
Northeast	113.09	96	17.4
Midwest	112.89	96	21.3
South	121.13	103	38.4
West	119.65	102	22.9
EDUCATION			
Average household	**117.50**	**100**	**100.0**
Less than high school graduate	96.57	82	10.7
High school graduate	119.51	102	25.4
Some college	109.92	94	19.3
Associate's degree	132.43	113	11.1
Bachelor's degree or more	124.23	106	33.3
Bachelor's degree	120.94	103	20.5
Master's, professional, doctoral degree	129.81	110	12.8

Note: Market shares may not sum to 100.0 because of rounding and missing categories by household type. "Asian" and "black" include Hispanics and non-Hispanics who identify themselves as being of the respective race alone. "Hispanic" includes people of any race who identify themselves as Hispanic. "Other" includes people who identify themselves as non-Hispanic and as Alaska Native, American Indian, Asian (who are also included in the "Asian" row), or Native Hawaiian or other Pacific Islander, as well as non-Hispanics reporting more than one race.
Source: Calculations by New Strategist based on the Bureau of Labor Statistics' 2012 Consumer Expenditure Survey

Laundry and Cleaning Supplies

Best customers: Householders aged 35 to 54
Married couples with school-aged or older children at home
Hispanics

Customer trends: Average household spending on laundry and cleaning supplies may stabilize as the large millennial generation moves into the best-customer lifestage.

Households with children spend the most on laundry and cleaning supplies—the second-most-costly household furnishings and supplies category. Householders aged 35 to 54, most with children at home, spend 13 percent more than average on laundry and cleaning supplies. Married couples with school-aged or older children at home spend 45 to 46 percent more than average on this item. Hispanics, who have the largest families, spend 27 percent more than average on laundry and cleaning supplies.

Average household spending on laundry and cleaning supplies fell by 11 percent between 2000 and 2012, after adjusting for inflation. Behind the decline was the baby-boom generation's exit from the crowded-nest lifestage. Average household spending on this item may stabilize as the large millennial generation moves into the best-customer lifestage.

Table 12.3 Laundry and cleaning supplies

Total household spending $19,333,002,240.00
Average household spends   155.39

AGE OF HOUSEHOLDER	AVERAGE HOUSEHOLD SPENDING	BEST CUSTOMERS (index)	BIGGEST CUSTOMERS (market share)
Average household	$155.39	100	100.0%
Under age 25	102.84	66	4.3
Aged 25 to 34	160.29	103	16.7
Aged 35 to 44	175.22	113	19.6
Aged 45 to 54	175.58	113	22.4
Aged 55 to 64	160.29	103	18.9
Aged 65 to 74	145.31	94	11.3
Aged 75 or older	109.01	70	6.9

	AVERAGE HOUSEHOLD SPENDING	BEST CUSTOMERS (index)	BIGGEST CUSTOMERS (market share)
HOUSEHOLD INCOME			
Average household	**$155.39**	**100**	**100.0%**
Under $20,000	87.11	56	11.8
$20,000 to $39,999	142.16	91	20.6
$40,000 to $49,999	142.73	92	8.1
$50,000 to $69,999	140.47	90	13.1
$70,000 to $79,999	228.71	147	8.2
$80,000 to $99,999	209.55	135	11.9
$100,000 or more	216.76	139	26.1
HOUSEHOLD TYPE			
Average household	**155.39**	**100**	**100.0**
Married couples	196.59	127	61.4
Married couples, no children	165.42	106	22.2
Married couples with children	217.71	140	32.9
Oldest child under age 6	182.13	117	5.3
Oldest child aged 6 to 17	225.96	145	17.3
Oldest child aged 18 or older	226.11	146	10.3
Single parent with child under age 18	149.55	96	5.0
Single person	80.82	52	15.4
RACE AND HISPANIC ORIGIN			
Average household	**155.39**	**100**	**100.0**
Asian	124.23	80	3.5
Black	148.76	96	12.0
Hispanic	198.07	127	16.0
Non-Hispanic white and other	149.19	96	72.1
REGION			
Average household	**155.39**	**100**	**100.0**
Northeast	151.40	97	17.6
Midwest	143.45	92	20.5
South	156.72	101	37.6
West	168.40	108	24.4
EDUCATION			
Average household	**155.39**	**100**	**100.0**
Less than high school graduate	141.72	91	11.9
High school graduate	155.24	100	24.9
Some college	152.75	98	20.2
Associate's degree	170.68	110	10.8
Bachelor's degree or more	157.64	101	32.0
Bachelor's degree	161.90	104	20.8
Master's, professional, doctoral degree	150.44	97	11.2

Note: Market shares may not sum to 100.0 because of rounding and missing categories by household type. "Asian" and "black" include Hispanics and non-Hispanics who identify themselves as being of the respective race alone. "Hispanic" includes people of any race who identify themselves as Hispanic. "Other" includes people who identify themselves as non-Hispanic and as Alaska Native, American Indian, Asian (who are also included in the "Asian" row), or Native Hawaiian or other Pacific Islander, as well as non-Hispanics reporting more than one race.
Source: Calculations by New Strategist based on the Bureau of Labor Statistics' 2012 Consumer Expenditure Survey

Lawn and Garden Supplies

Best customers: Householders aged 55 or older
Married couples without children at home
Married couples with school-aged children
Non-Hispanic whites

Customer trends: Average household spending on lawn and garden supplies should resume its growth as boomers
continue to fill the best-customer age groups.

The best customers of lawn and garden supplies are older married couples, most of whom are homeowners with lawns and gardens to tend. Householders aged 55 to 64 spend 53 percent more than average on lawn and garden supplies, while those aged 65 to 74 spend 35 percent more. The oldest householders spend 13 percent more than average on this item. Married couples without children at home (most of them older) spend 79 percent more than average on garden supplies, and those with school-aged children spend two-thirds more than average. Non-Hispanic whites account for 90 percent of the market for lawn and garden supplies.

Average household spending on lawn and garden supplies increased by 24 percent between 2000 and 2006, after adjusting for inflation, but declined 31 percent over the next six years in part because of the Great Recession. Spending on lawn and garden supplies should resume its growth as the baby-boom generation continues to fill the best-customer age groups.

Table 12.4 Lawn and garden supplies

Total household spending $9,460,592,640.00
Average household spends 76.04

AGE OF HOUSEHOLDER	AVERAGE HOUSEHOLD SPENDING	BEST CUSTOMERS (index)	BIGGEST CUSTOMERS (market share)
Average household	$76.04	100	100.0%
Under age 25	30.47	40	2.6
Aged 25 to 34	49.57	65	10.5
Aged 35 to 44	57.08	75	13.0
Aged 45 to 54	74.07	97	19.3
Aged 55 to 64	116.33	153	28.0
Aged 65 to 74	102.28	135	16.2
Aged 75 or older	85.78	113	11.0

	AVERAGE HOUSEHOLD SPENDING	BEST CUSTOMERS (index)	BIGGEST CUSTOMERS (market share)
HOUSEHOLD INCOME			
Average household	$76.04	100	100.0%
Under $20,000	26.39	35	7.3
$20,000 to $39,999	45.37	60	13.4
$40,000 to $49,999	45.23	59	5.3
$50,000 to $69,999	62.58	82	11.9
$70,000 to $79,999	96.95	127	7.1
$80,000 to $99,999	123.17	162	14.3
$100,000 or more	166.63	219	41.0
HOUSEHOLD TYPE			
Average household	76.04	100	100.0
Married couples	114.96	151	73.4
Married couples, no children	135.86	179	37.2
Married couples with children	105.74	139	32.7
Oldest child under age 6	75.87	100	4.6
Oldest child aged 6 to 17	126.43	166	19.8
Oldest child aged 18 or older	89.83	118	8.3
Single parent with child under age 18	15.99	21	1.1
Single person	39.55	52	15.4
RACE AND HISPANIC ORIGIN			
Average household	76.04	100	100.0
Asian	37.81	50	2.2
Black	19.71	26	3.3
Hispanic	40.28	53	6.6
Non-Hispanic white and other	91.37	120	90.2
REGION			
Average household	76.04	100	100.0
Northeast	65.72	86	15.6
Midwest	73.58	97	21.5
South	76.82	101	37.6
West	85.59	113	25.4
EDUCATION			
Average household	76.04	100	100.0
Less than high school graduate	31.24	41	5.4
High school graduate	53.83	71	17.7
Some college	61.66	81	16.7
Associate's degree	110.44	145	14.3
Bachelor's degree or more	108.97	143	45.2
Bachelor's degree	88.80	117	23.3
Master's, professional, doctoral degree	143.08	188	21.8

Note: Market shares may not sum to 100.0 because of rounding and missing categories by household type. "Asian" and "black" include Hispanics and non-Hispanics who identify themselves as being of the respective race alone. "Hispanic" includes people of any race who identify themselves as Hispanic. "Other" includes people who identify themselves as non-Hispanic and as Alaska Native, American Indian, Asian (who are also included in the "Asian" row), or Native Hawaiian or other Pacific Islander, as well as non-Hispanics reporting more than one race.
Source: Calculations by New Strategist based on the Bureau of Labor Statistics' 2012 Consumer Expenditure Survey

Postage

Best customers: Householders aged 65 or older
                         Married couples

Customer trends: Average household spending on postage will decline as younger, online Americans replace
                         older, offline generations.

Older Americans are the biggest spenders on postage. Householders aged 65 or older spend 30 to 46 percent more than average on this item. Married couples without children at home (most of them older) spend 45 percent more than average on postage. Couples with children at home outspend the average by 23 percent, the figure peaking among those with adult children at home—the largest households—at 34 percent above average.

Average household spending on postage declined 29 percent between 2000 and 2012, after adjusting for inflation. Postage spending would have fallen more precipitously, but was shored up by repeated hikes in the cost of postage as well as the popularity of the U.S. Postal Service's priority mail options. Average household spending on postage is likely to decline sharply in the years ahead as online generations move into the older age groups.

Table 12.5 Postage

Total household spending $7,146,455,040.00
Average household spends   57.44

AGE OF HOUSEHOLDER	AVERAGE HOUSEHOLD SPENDING	BEST CUSTOMERS (index)	BIGGEST CUSTOMERS (market share)
Average household	$57.44	100	100.0%
Under age 25	31.45	55	3.6
Aged 25 to 34	39.72	69	11.2
Aged 35 to 44	45.29	79	13.7
Aged 45 to 54	62.82	109	21.6
Aged 55 to 64	62.94	110	20.1
Aged 65 to 74	83.91	146	17.6
Aged 75 or older	74.84	130	12.7

	AVERAGE HOUSEHOLD SPENDING	BEST CUSTOMERS (index)	BIGGEST CUSTOMERS (market share)
HOUSEHOLD INCOME			
Average household	$57.44	100	100.0%
Under $20,000	33.68	59	12.3
$20,000 to $39,999	47.72	83	18.7
$40,000 to $49,999	60.39	105	9.3
$50,000 to $69,999	59.67	104	15.0
$70,000 to $79,999	71.76	125	7.0
$80,000 to $99,999	71.69	125	11.0
$100,000 or more	81.23	141	26.5
HOUSEHOLD TYPE			
Average household	57.44	100	100.0
Married couples	74.86	130	63.3
Married couples, no children	83.54	145	30.3
Married couples with children	70.55	123	28.9
Oldest child under age 6	63.86	111	5.1
Oldest child aged 6 to 17	69.35	121	14.4
Oldest child aged 18 or older	76.72	134	9.4
Single parent with child under age 18	50.39	88	4.6
Single person	33.73	59	17.4
RACE AND HISPANIC ORIGIN			
Average household	57.44	100	100.0
Asian	52.19	91	3.9
Black	52.41	91	11.5
Hispanic	43.10	75	9.4
Non-Hispanic white and other	60.62	106	79.2
REGION			
Average household	57.44	100	100.0
Northeast	57.43	100	18.0
Midwest	49.33	86	19.0
South	58.82	102	38.1
West	63.29	110	24.8
EDUCATION			
Average household	57.44	100	100.0
Less than high school graduate	37.55	65	8.5
High school graduate	48.68	85	21.1
Some college	51.82	90	18.6
Associate's degree	63.75	111	11.0
Bachelor's degree or more	73.50	128	40.4
Bachelor's degree	66.64	116	23.1
Master's, professional, doctoral degree	85.11	148	17.2

Note: Market shares may not sum to 100.0 because of rounding and missing categories by household type. "Asian" and "black" include Hispanics and non-Hispanics who identify themselves as being of the respective race alone. "Hispanic" includes people of any race who identify themselves as Hispanic. "Other" includes people who identify themselves as non-Hispanic and as Alaska Native, American Indian, Asian (who are also included in the "Asian" row), or Native Hawaiian or other Pacific Islander, as well as non-Hispanics reporting more than one race.
Source: Calculations by New Strategist based on the Bureau of Labor Statistics' 2012 Consumer Expenditure Survey

Stationery, Stationery Supplies, Giftwrap

Best customers: Householders aged 55 to 74
Married couples

Customer trends: Average household spending on stationery, stationery supplies, and giftwrap may continue to fall in the years ahead as households limit their discretionary spending.

The biggest spenders on the discretionary category of stationery, stationery supplies, and giftwrap are older married couples. They are best customers because of their extended families and large network of friends. Householders ranging in age from 55 to 74 spend 20 to 30 percent more than average on this item as they wrap gifts for their own and other children. Married couples without children at home, most of them older, spend 26 percent more than average on stationery, stationery supplies, and giftwrap, while those with children at home spend 56 percent more.

After growing by 15 percent from 2000 to 2006 (the year overall household spending peaked), average household spending on stationery, stationery supplies, and giftwrap shrank 23 percent over the ensuing six years, after adjusting for inflation. Behind the earlier increase was the baby-boom generation's entry into the grandparent lifestage, while the later decline owes to the Great Recession. Spending on stationery and giftwrap may continue to fall in the years ahead as households limit their discretionary spending.

Table 12.6 Stationery, stationery supplies, giftwrap

Total household spending $9,339,909,120.00
Average household spends 75.07

AGE OF HOUSEHOLDER	AVERAGE HOUSEHOLD SPENDING	BEST CUSTOMERS (index)	BIGGEST CUSTOMERS (market share)
Average household	$75.07	100	100.0%
Under age 25	27.48	37	2.4
Aged 25 to 34	63.52	85	13.7
Aged 35 to 44	81.20	108	18.8
Aged 45 to 54	73.70	98	19.4
Aged 55 to 64	97.24	130	23.7
Aged 65 to 74	90.32	120	14.5
Aged 75 or older	60.14	80	7.8

	AVERAGE HOUSEHOLD SPENDING	BEST CUSTOMERS (index)	BIGGEST CUSTOMERS (market share)
HOUSEHOLD INCOME			
Average household	**$75.07**	**100**	**100.0%**
Under $20,000	29.28	39	8.2
$20,000 to $39,999	53.12	71	15.9
$40,000 to $49,999	57.14	76	6.7
$50,000 to $69,999	64.12	85	12.3
$70,000 to $79,999	94.56	126	7.0
$80,000 to $99,999	95.36	127	11.2
$100,000 or more	154.18	205	38.5
HOUSEHOLD TYPE			
Average household	**75.07**	**100**	**100.0**
Married couples	104.19	139	67.4
Married couples, no children	94.69	126	26.3
Married couples with children	116.77	156	36.6
Oldest child under age 6	109.99	147	6.7
Oldest child aged 6 to 17	131.14	175	20.8
Oldest child aged 18 or older	97.01	129	9.1
Single parent with child under age 18	52.00	69	3.6
Single person	38.94	52	15.4
RACE AND HISPANIC ORIGIN			
Average household	**75.07**	**100**	**100.0**
Asian	66.48	89	3.8
Black	30.37	40	5.1
Hispanic	44.19	59	7.4
Non-Hispanic white and other	87.60	117	87.6
REGION			
Average household	**75.07**	**100**	**100.0**
Northeast	75.85	101	18.2
Midwest	81.38	108	24.0
South	69.42	92	34.4
West	77.49	103	23.3
EDUCATION			
Average household	**75.07**	**100**	**100.0**
Less than high school graduate	36.75	49	6.4
High school graduate	52.04	69	17.3
Some college	67.16	89	18.4
Associate's degree	84.42	112	11.1
Bachelor's degree or more	109.67	146	46.1
Bachelor's degree	97.83	130	26.0
Master's, professional, doctoral degree	129.67	173	20.0

Note: Market shares may not sum to 100.0 because of rounding and missing categories by household type. "Asian" and "black" include Hispanics and non-Hispanics who identify themselves as being of the respective race alone. "Hispanic" includes people of any race who identify themselves as Hispanic. "Other" includes people who identify themselves as non-Hispanic and as Alaska Native, American Indian, Asian (who are also included in the "Asian" row), or Native Hawaiian or other Pacific Islander, as well as non-Hispanics reporting more than one race.
Source: Calculations by New Strategist based on the Bureau of Labor Statistics' 2012 Consumer Expenditure Survey

Chapter 13.
Personal Care Products and Services

Household Spending on Personal Care Products and Services, 2000 to 2012

The average household spent $628 on personal care products and services in 2012. This category includes everything from haircuts, facials, and manicures to cosmetics, shampoo, and toothpaste. Spending on personal care products and services fell 16 percent between 2000 and 2012, after adjusting for inflation.

Personal care services (haircuts, manicures, etc.) account for the largest share of spending in the personal care category. Forty-seven percent of personal care spending was devoted to services in 2012. But spending on services fell by a substantial 29 percent between 2000 and 2012, after adjusting for inflation. Most of the decline occurred before the overall peak spending year of 2006, and average household spending on personal care services has remained relatively stable since then.

Spending on the second-largest personal care category—cosmetics, perfume, and bath products—also fell between 2000 and 2012 (down just 2 percent), but in this case a 9 percent rise between 2000 and 2006 was eclipsed by a 19 percent decline in spending between 2006 and the overall trough spending year of 2010, followed by an 11 percent increase in the ensuing two-year period to 2012. The only personal care categories to show spending increases between 2000 and 2012 are oral hygiene products (up 19 percent) and shaving products (up 9 percent).

One reason behind the decline in spending on personal care products and services was price discounting, which enabled consumers to buy more for less. Household belt tightening was another reason, as house-poor consumers stretched out their hair-care and manicure appointments. Because older householders are among the biggest spenders on personal care products and services, average household spending on these items should rise along with the aging of the population.

Spending on personal care products and services

(average spending by households on personal care products and services, 2000, 2006, 2010, and 2012; in 2012 dollars)

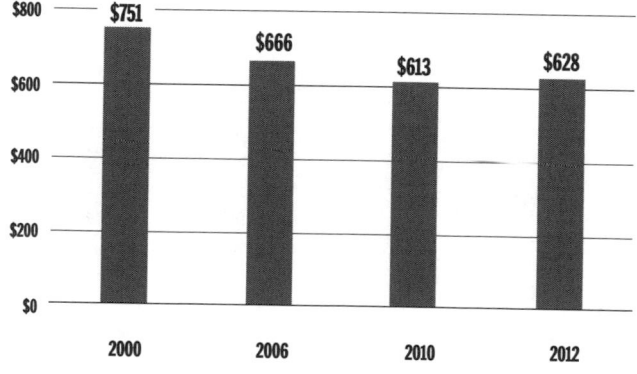

Table 13.1 Personal care spending, 2000 to 2012

(average annual household spending on personal care products and services and percent distribution, by category, 2000 to 2012; percent change and percentage point change in spending, 2000–06, 2006–12, and 2010–12; in 2012 dollars; ranked by amount spent)

	average annual household spending (in 2012$)				percent change		
	2012	2010	2006	2000	2010–12	2006–12	2000–06
Average household spending on personal care products and services	$628.20	$612.84	$665.96	$751.47	2.5%	–5.7%	–11.4%
Personal care services	292.83	291.93	312.09	409.74	0.3	–6.2	–23.8
Cosmetics, perfume, and bath products	157.04	141.30	173.69	159.88	11.1	–9.6	8.6
Hair care products	61.69	65.28	63.83	68.61	–5.5	–3.4	–7.0
Oral hygiene products	40.82	35.78	32.10	34.37	14.1	27.1	–6.6
Deodorants, feminine hygiene, miscellaneous products	34.51	37.10	39.95	38.95	–7.0	–13.6	2.6
Shaving products	19.18	18.90	19.18	17.59	1.5	0.0	9.1

					percentage point change		
PERCENT DISTRIBUTION OF SPENDING	2012	2010	2006	2000	2010–12	2006–12	2000–06
Average household spending on personal care products and services	100.0%	100.0%	100.0%	100.0%	–	–	–
Personal care services	46.6	47.6	46.9	54.5	–1.0	–0.2	–7.7
Cosmetics, perfume, and bath products	25.0	23.1	26.1	21.3	1.9	–1.1	4.8
Hair care products	9.8	10.7	9.6	9.1	–0.8	0.2	0.5
Oral hygiene products	6.5	5.8	4.8	4.6	0.7	1.7	0.2
Deodorants, feminine hygiene, miscellaneous products	5.5	6.1	6.0	5.2	–0.6	–0.5	0.8
Shaving products	3.1	3.1	2.9	2.3	0.0	0.2	0.5

Note: Numbers do not add to total because not all categories are shown. Percentage point change calculations are based on unrounded figures. "–" means not applicable.
Source: Bureau of Labor Statistics, 2000, 2006, 2010, and 2012 Consumer Expenditure Surveys; calculations by New Strategist

Cosmetics, Perfume, and Bath Products

Best customers: Householders aged 35 to 74
                       Married couples
                       Asians and Hispanics

Customer trends: Average household spending on cosmetics, perfume, and bath products may continue to grow
                       as the millennial generation enters the best-customer lifestage.

The best customers of cosmetics, perfume, and bath products are households with the most women. Married couples without children at home spend 22 percent more than average on this category. Those with children at home spend 27 percent more. Householders ranging in age from 35 to 74 spend more than average on cosmetics, perfume, and bath products. Asian households spend 16 percent more than average on this item. Hispanics, who have the largest households, spend 11 percent more.

Average household spending on cosmetics, perfume, and bath products climbed 9 percent between 2000 and 2006, after adjusting for inflation. The Great Recession led to a 19 percent decline in spending on this item between 2006 and 2010. Growth resumed in the 2010-to-2012 time period. The seesaw motion was the product of at least two factors—the expansion of the teen and young-adult population in the earlier part of the decade and the counteracting belt tightening of financially strapped households during the Great Recession. Average household spending on cosmetics, perfume, and bath products may continue to grow as the millennial generation enters the best-customer lifestage.

Table 13.2 Cosmetics, perfume, and bath products

Total household spending	$19,538,288,640.00
Average household spends	157.04

	AVERAGE HOUSEHOLD SPENDING	BEST CUSTOMERS (index)	BIGGEST CUSTOMERS (market share)
AGE OF HOUSEHOLDER			
Average household	$157.04	100	100.0%
Under age 25	97.39	62	4.1
Aged 25 to 34	148.83	95	15.3
Aged 35 to 44	167.90	107	18.6
Aged 45 to 54	168.23	107	21.2
Aged 55 to 64	190.38	121	22.2
Aged 65 to 74	178.79	114	13.7
Aged 75 or older	80.90	52	5.0

	AVERAGE HOUSEHOLD SPENDING	BEST CUSTOMERS (index)	BIGGEST CUSTOMERS (market share)
HOUSEHOLD INCOME			
Average household	**$157.04**	**100**	**100.0%**
Under $20,000	63.25	40	8.5
$20,000 to $39,999	107.16	68	15.4
$40,000 to $49,999	118.01	75	6.6
$50,000 to $69,999	159.19	101	14.6
$70,000 to $79,999	246.15	157	8.8
$80,000 to $99,999	209.38	133	11.8
$100,000 or more	287.87	183	34.3
HOUSEHOLD TYPE			
Average household	**157.04**	**100**	**100.0**
Married couples	196.82	125	60.9
Married couples, no children	192.27	122	25.5
Married couples, with children	199.46	127	29.9
Oldest child under age 6	186.43	119	5.4
Oldest child aged 6 to 17	213.63	136	16.2
Oldest child aged 18 or older	183.94	117	8.3
Single parent with child under age 18	125.81	80	4.2
Single person	91.11	58	17.2
RACE AND HISPANIC ORIGIN			
Average household	**157.04**	**100**	**100.0**
Asian	182.68	116	5.0
Black	123.43	79	9.9
Hispanic	175.06	111	14.0
Non-Hispanic white and other	159.81	102	76.4
REGION			
Average household	**157.04**	**100**	**100.0**
Northeast	132.30	84	15.2
Midwest	124.98	80	17.6
South	172.25	110	40.9
West	183.98	117	26.4
EDUCATION			
Average household	**157.04**	**100**	**100.0**
Less than high school graduate	110.94	71	9.2
High school graduate	116.86	74	18.6
Some college	128.33	82	16.8
Associate's degree	175.10	112	11.0
Bachelor's degree or more	219.14	140	44.0
Bachelor's degree	202.43	129	25.7
Master's, professional, doctoral degree	247.39	158	18.3

Note: Market shares may not sum to 100.0 because of rounding and missing categories by household type. "Asian" and "black" include Hispanics and non-Hispanics who identify themselves as being of the respective race alone. "Hispanic" includes people of any race who identify themselves as Hispanic. "Other" includes people who identify themselves as non-Hispanic and as Alaska Native, American Indian, Asian (who are also included in the "Asian" row), or Native Hawaiian or other Pacific Islander, as well as non-Hispanics reporting more than one race.
Source: Calculations by New Strategist based on the Bureau of Labor Statistics' 2012 Consumer Expenditure Survey

Deodorants, Feminine Hygiene, and Miscellaneous Personal Care Products

Best customers: Householders aged 35 to 54

Married couples with school-aged or older children at home

Customer trends: Average household spending on deodorants, feminine hygiene, and miscellaneous personal care products may continue to fall because the small generation X is in the best-customer lifestage.

The best customers of deodorants, feminine hygiene, and miscellaneous personal care products are households with the most women of childbearing age. Married couples with school-aged or older children at home spend 33 to 59 percent more than average on this item. Householders aged 35 to 54, many with teenage girls at home, spend 16 to 21 percent more than average on deodorants, feminine hygiene, and miscellaneous products.

Average household spending on deodorants, feminine hygiene, and miscellaneous personal care products fell 11 percent between 2000 and 2012, after adjusting for inflation. Behind the decline was price discounting, allowing consumers to buy more for less, as well as belt tightening in face of the Great Recession. Average household spending on this item may continue to fall because the small generation X is in the best-customer lifestage.

Table 13.3 Deodorants, feminine hygiene, and miscellaneous personal care products

Total household spending	$4,293,596,160.00		
Average household spends	34.51		

	AVERAGE HOUSEHOLD SPENDING	BEST CUSTOMERS (index)	BIGGEST CUSTOMERS (market share)
AGE OF HOUSEHOLDER			
Average household	$34.51	100	100.0%
Under age 25	34.59	100	6.6
Aged 25 to 34	34.98	101	16.4
Aged 35 to 44	41.80	121	21.0
Aged 45 to 54	40.13	116	23.0
Aged 55 to 64	33.14	96	17.6
Aged 65 to 74	19.55	57	6.8
Aged 75 or older	29.65	86	8.4

	AVERAGE HOUSEHOLD SPENDING	BEST CUSTOMERS (index)	BIGGEST CUSTOMERS (market share)
HOUSEHOLD INCOME			
Average household	**$34.51**	**100**	**100.0%**
Under $20,000	22.37	65	13.6
$20,000 to $39,999	23.50	68	15.3
$40,000 to $49,999	26.02	75	6.7
$50,000 to $69,999	35.94	104	15.0
$70,000 to $79,999	76.54	222	12.4
$80,000 to $99,999	37.74	109	9.6
$100,000 or more	49.07	142	26.6
HOUSEHOLD TYPE			
Average household	**34.51**	**100**	**100.0**
Married couples	39.72	115	55.9
Married couples, no children	28.60	83	17.3
Married couples, with children	48.28	140	32.9
Oldest child under age 6	33.83	98	4.5
Oldest child aged 6 to 17	55.03	159	19.0
Oldest child aged 18 or older	46.03	133	9.4
Single parent with child under age 18	27.81	81	4.2
Single person	24.64	71	21.2
RACE AND HISPANIC ORIGIN			
Average household	**34.51**	**100**	**100.0**
Asian	30.51	88	3.8
Black	32.21	93	11.7
Hispanic	34.61	100	12.6
Non-Hispanic white and other	34.88	101	75.9
REGION			
Average household	**34.51**	**100**	**100.0**
Northeast	30.66	89	16.0
Midwest	39.59	115	25.4
South	35.63	103	38.5
West	30.69	89	20.0
EDUCATION			
Average household	**34.51**	**100**	**100.0**
Less than high school graduate	29.48	85	11.2
High school graduate	31.89	92	23.0
Some college	30.29	88	18.1
Associate's degree	37.90	110	10.8
Bachelor's degree or more	40.22	117	36.8
Bachelor's degree	40.64	118	23.5
Master's, professional, doctoral degree	39.50	114	13.3

Note: Market shares may not sum to 100.0 because of rounding and missing categories by household type. "Asian" and "black" include Hispanics and non-Hispanics who identify themselves as being of the respective race alone. "Hispanic" includes people of any race who identify themselves as Hispanic. "Other" includes people who identify themselves as non-Hispanic and as Alaska Native, American Indian, Asian (who are also included in the "Asian" row), or Native Hawaiian or other Pacific Islander, as well as non-Hispanics reporting more than one race.
Source: Calculations by New Strategist based on the Bureau of Labor Statistics' 2012 Consumer Expenditure Survey

Hair Care Products

Best customers: Householders aged 35 to 54
Married couples with school-aged or older children at home
Hispanics
Households in the West

Customer trends: Average household spending on hair care products may continue to decline because the small generation X is now in the best-customer lifestage.

The best customers of hair care products are the largest households and households with the most women. Married couples with school-aged or older children at home spend 59 to 86 percent more than average on this item. Householders aged 35 to 54, many with children at home, spend 16 to 34 percent more than average on hair care products and control 46 percent of the market. Hispanics, who have the largest households, spend 17 percent more. Households in the West, where many Hispanics reside, spend 15 percent more than average on this item.

Average household spending on hair care products has been steadily declining, from inflation-adjusted $69 in 2000 to $62 in 2012, a 10 percent decrease. Average household spending on hair care products may continue to decline in the years ahead because the small generation X is in the best-customer lifestage.

Table 13.4 Hair care products

Total household spending $7,675,223,040.00
Average household spends 61.69

AGE OF HOUSEHOLDER	AVERAGE HOUSEHOLD SPENDING	BEST CUSTOMERS (index)	BIGGEST CUSTOMERS (market share)
Average household	**$61.69**	**100**	**100.0%**
Under age 25	46.59	76	5.0
Aged 25 to 34	59.65	97	15.6
Aged 35 to 44	82.41	134	23.2
Aged 45 to 54	71.48	116	22.9
Aged 55 to 64	64.19	104	19.0
Aged 65 to 74	54.29	88	10.6
Aged 75 or older	21.68	35	3.4

	AVERAGE HOUSEHOLD SPENDING	BEST CUSTOMERS (index)	BIGGEST CUSTOMERS (market share)
HOUSEHOLD INCOME			
Average household	**$61.69**	**100**	**100.0%**
Under $20,000	26.48	43	9.0
$20,000 to $39,999	49.95	81	18.2
$40,000 to $49,999	39.32	64	5.6
$50,000 to $69,999	61.48	100	14.4
$70,000 to $79,999	72.93	118	6.6
$80,000 to $99,999	70.12	114	10.0
$100,000 or more	118.38	192	35.9
HOUSEHOLD TYPE			
Average household	**61.69**	**100**	**100.0**
Married couples	80.87	131	63.7
Married couples, no children	61.85	100	20.9
Married couples, with children	98.97	160	37.7
Oldest child under age 6	58.16	94	4.3
Oldest child aged 6 to 17	114.87	186	22.1
Oldest child aged 18 or older	97.86	159	11.2
Single parent with child under age 18	53.30	86	4.5
Single person	33.97	55	16.4
RACE AND HISPANIC ORIGIN			
Average household	**61.69**	**100**	**100.0**
Asian	60.50	98	4.3
Black	34.43	56	7.0
Hispanic	72.12	117	14.7
Non-Hispanic white and other	64.51	105	78.5
REGION			
Average household	**61.69**	**100**	**100.0**
Northeast	46.57	75	13.6
Midwest	58.52	95	21.0
South	65.32	106	39.4
West	71.10	115	26.0
EDUCATION			
Average household	**61.69**	**100**	**100.0**
Less than high school graduate	46.21	75	9.8
High school graduate	49.50	80	20.0
Some college	53.64	87	17.9
Associate's degree	79.15	128	12.7
Bachelor's degree or more	76.89	125	39.3
Bachelor's degree	72.92	118	23.6
Master's, professional, doctoral degree	83.59	136	15.7

Note: Market shares may not sum to 100.0 because of rounding and missing categories by household type. "Asian" and "black" include Hispanics and non-Hispanics who identify themselves as being of the respective race alone. "Hispanic" includes people of any race who identify themselves as Hispanic. "Other" includes people who identify themselves as non-Hispanic and as Alaska Native, American Indian, Asian (who are also included in the "Asian" row), or Native Hawaiian or other Pacific Islander, as well as non-Hispanics reporting more than one race.
Source: Calculations by New Strategist based on the Bureau of Labor Statistics' 2012 Consumer Expenditure Survey

Oral Hygiene Products

Best customers: Householders aged 55 or older
Married couples without children at home
Households in the Midwest

Customer trends: Average household spending on oral hygiene products should rise as aging boomers try to maintain their teeth.

Older empty-nest couples are the best customers of oral hygiene products. Householders aged 55 or older spend 12 to 26 percent more than average on oral hygiene products. Married couples without children at home spend 45 percent more than average on this item. Households in the Midwest outspend the average by one-quarter.

Average household spending on oral hygiene products climbed 19 percent between 2000 and 2012, after adjusting for inflation, and was one of the few personal care product categories to see gains over the time period. Average household spending on oral hygiene products should continue to grow as boomers age and try to maintain the health of their teeth.

Table 13.5 Oral hygiene products

Total household spending $5,078,661,120.00
Average household spends 40.82

AGE OF HOUSEHOLDER	AVERAGE HOUSEHOLD SPENDING	BEST CUSTOMERS (index)	BIGGEST CUSTOMERS (market share)
Average household	$40.82	100	100.0%
Under age 25	23.15	57	3.7
Aged 25 to 34	39.48	97	15.6
Aged 35 to 44	35.96	88	15.3
Aged 45 to 54	37.37	92	18.1
Aged 55 to 64	48.63	119	21.8
Aged 65 to 74	45.76	112	13.5
Aged 75 or older	51.31	126	12.3

	AVERAGE HOUSEHOLD SPENDING	BEST CUSTOMERS (index)	BIGGEST CUSTOMERS (market share)
HOUSEHOLD INCOME			
Average household	**$40.82**	**100**	**100.0%**
Under $20,000	17.33	42	8.9
$20,000 to $39,999	27.73	68	15.3
$40,000 to $49,999	30.33	74	6.6
$50,000 to $69,999	40.15	98	14.2
$70,000 to $79,999	47.92	117	6.6
$80,000 to $99,999	79.03	194	17.1
$100,000 or more	69.25	170	31.8
HOUSEHOLD TYPE			
Average household	**40.82**	**100**	**100.0**
Married couples	52.35	128	62.3
Married couples, no children	59.33	145	30.3
Married couples, with children	45.49	111	26.2
Oldest child under age 6	45.13	111	5.0
Oldest child aged 6 to 17	46.91	115	13.7
Oldest child aged 18 or older	43.34	106	7.5
Single parent with child under age 18	33.96	83	4.4
Single person	23.47	57	17.1
RACE AND HISPANIC ORIGIN			
Average household	**40.82**	**100**	**100.0**
Asian	35.27	86	3.7
Black	30.16	74	9.3
Hispanic	32.10	79	9.9
Non-Hispanic white and other	44.00	108	80.9
REGION			
Average household	**40.82**	**100**	**100.0**
Northeast	31.57	77	14.0
Midwest	51.60	126	28.0
South	37.57	92	34.3
West	42.93	105	23.7
EDUCATION			
Average household	**40.82**	**100**	**100.0**
Less than high school graduate	26.06	64	8.3
High school graduate	28.17	69	17.2
Some college	33.02	81	16.7
Associate's degree	33.51	82	8.1
Bachelor's degree or more	63.70	156	49.2
Bachelor's degree	42.66	105	20.8
Master's, professional, doctoral degree	99.27	243	28.2

Note: Market shares may not sum to 100.0 because of rounding and missing categories by household type. "Asian" and "black" include Hispanics and non-Hispanics who identify themselves as being of the respective race alone. "Hispanic" includes people of any race who identify themselves as Hispanic. "Other" includes people who identify themselves as non-Hispanic and as Alaska Native, American Indian, Asian (who are also included in the "Asian" row), or Native Hawaiian or other Pacific Islander, as well as non-Hispanics reporting more than one race.
Source: Calculations by New Strategist based on the Bureau of Labor Statistics' 2012 Consumer Expenditure Survey

Personal Care Services

Best customers: Householders aged 35 to 74
                      Married couples
                      Households in the Northeast

Customer trends: Average household spending on personal care services will grow in the years ahead as aging boomers attempt to look their best, but only if discretionary income rebounds.

The largest households and older householders are the best customers of personal care services such as haircuts, massages, manicures, and facials. Householders ranging in age from 35 to 74 spend more than average on this item. Married couples without children at home (most of them empty-nesters) spend 32 percent more than average on personal care services, while those with school-aged or older children at home (the largest households) spend 33 to 35 percent more than average. Households in the Northeast outspend the average by 23 percent.

Average household spending on personal care services fell by a substantial 29 percent between 2000 and 2010, after adjusting for inflation, and has remained level since then. Price discounting was one factor behind the decline, as low-cost hair and nail salons became common throughout the country. Another factor was household belt tightening. Average household spending on personal care services may grow in the years ahead as aging boomers attempt to look their best, but only if discretionary income rebounds.

Table 13.6 Personal care services

Total household spending $36,432,737,280.00
Average household spends   292.83

AGE OF HOUSEHOLDER	AVERAGE HOUSEHOLD SPENDING	BEST CUSTOMERS (index)	BIGGEST CUSTOMERS (market share)
Average household	$292.83	100	100.0%
Under age 25	131.66	45	2.9
Aged 25 to 34	239.86	82	13.2
Aged 35 to 44	313.29	107	18.6
Aged 45 to 54	347.92	119	23.5
Aged 55 to 64	319.59	109	20.0
Aged 65 to 74	310.48	106	12.8
Aged 75 or older	268.79	92	9.0

	AVERAGE HOUSEHOLD SPENDING	BEST CUSTOMERS (index)	BIGGEST CUSTOMERS (market share)
HOUSEHOLD INCOME			
Average household	$292.83	100	100.0%
Under $20,000	112.08	38	8.1
$20,000 to $39,999	182.16	62	14.0
$40,000 to $49,999	228.96	78	6.9
$50,000 to $69,999	269.21	92	13.3
$70,000 to $79,999	365.02	125	7.0
$80,000 to $99,999	381.81	130	11.5
$100,000 or more	614.12	210	39.3
HOUSEHOLD TYPE			
Average household	292.83	100	100.0
Married couples	375.94	128	62.4
Married couples, no children	387.76	132	27.6
Married couples, with children	377.82	129	30.3
Oldest child under age 6	309.69	106	4.8
Oldest child aged 6 to 17	396.71	135	16.1
Oldest child aged 18 or older	390.01	133	9.4
Single parent with child under age 18	245.40	84	4.4
Single person	190.53	65	19.3
RACE AND HISPANIC ORIGIN			
Average household	292.83	100	100.0
Asian	253.77	87	3.8
Black	302.81	103	13.0
Hispanic	203.97	70	8.7
Non-Hispanic white and other	305.94	104	78.4
REGION			
Average household	292.83	100	100.0
Northeast	358.72	123	22.1
Midwest	259.92	89	19.7
South	269.74	92	34.3
West	310.58	106	23.9
EDUCATION			
Average household	292.83	100	100.0
Less than high school graduate	139.41	48	6.2
High school graduate	216.23	74	18.4
Some college	256.03	87	18.0
Associate's degree	290.78	99	9.8
Bachelor's degree or more	441.57	151	47.6
Bachelor's degree	404.37	138	27.5
Master's, professional, doctoral degree	505.47	173	20.0

Note: Market shares may not sum to 100.0 because of rounding and missing categories by household type. "Asian" and "black" include Hispanics and non-Hispanics who identify themselves as being of the respective race alone. "Hispanic" includes people of any race who identify themselves as Hispanic. "Other" includes people who identify themselves as non-Hispanic and as Alaska Native, American Indian, Asian (who are also included in the "Asian" row), or Native Hawaiian or other Pacific Islander, as well as non-Hispanics reporting more than one race.
Source: Calculations by New Strategist based on the Bureau of Labor Statistics' 2012 Consumer Expenditure Survey

Shaving Products

Best customers:	Householders aged 25 to 54
	Married couples

Customer trends:	Average household spending on shaving products should rise as the large millennial generation fills the best-customer age groups.

The best customers of shaving products are households with the most men. Households headed by people ranging in age from 25 to 64 spend more than average on this item. Married couples spend 40 percent more than average on shaving products.

Average household spending on shaving products grew 9 percent between 2000 and the overall peak pending year of 2006, after adjusting for inflation, and then held steady over the ensuing six-year period. Spending on shaving products should rise as the large millennial generation fills the best-customer age groups.

Table 13.7 Shaving products

Total household spending	$2,386,298,880.00
Average household spends	19.18

AGE OF HOUSEHOLDER	AVERAGE HOUSEHOLD SPENDING	BEST CUSTOMERS (index)	BIGGEST CUSTOMERS (market share)
Average household	$19.18	100	100.0%
Under age 25	14.67	76	5.0
Aged 25 to 34	24.02	125	20.2
Aged 35 to 44	21.63	113	19.6
Aged 45 to 54	21.05	110	21.7
Aged 55 to 64	20.27	106	19.3
Aged 65 to 74	17.57	92	11.0
Aged 75 or older	5.52	29	2.8

	AVERAGE HOUSEHOLD SPENDING	BEST CUSTOMERS (index)	BIGGEST CUSTOMERS (market share)
HOUSEHOLD INCOME			
Average household	**$19.18**	**100**	**100.0%**
Under $20,000	8.40	44	9.2
$20,000 to $39,999	9.39	49	11.0
$40,000 to $49,999	18.89	98	8.7
$50,000 to $69,999	20.69	108	15.6
$70,000 to $79,999	46.98	245	13.7
$80,000 to $99,999	25.94	135	11.9
$100,000 or more	29.89	156	29.2
HOUSEHOLD TYPE			
Average household	**19.18**	**100**	**100.0**
Married couples	26.88	140	68.1
Married couples, no children	25.19	131	27.4
Married couples, with children	29.15	152	35.7
Oldest child under age 6	25.12	131	6.0
Oldest child aged 6 to 17	32.76	171	20.3
Oldest child aged 18 or older	25.63	134	9.4
Single parent with child under age 18	16.37	85	4.5
Single person	7.21	38	11.2
RACE AND HISPANIC ORIGIN			
Average household	**19.18**	**100**	**100.0**
Asian	9.42	49	2.1
Black	10.55	55	6.9
Hispanic	15.36	80	10.0
Non-Hispanic white and other	21.23	111	83.1
REGION			
Average household	**19.18**	**100**	**100.0**
Northeast	16.51	86	15.5
Midwest	19.77	103	22.9
South	22.12	115	43.0
West	15.86	83	18.6
EDUCATION			
Average household	**19.18**	**100**	**100.0**
Less than high school graduate	15.72	82	10.7
High school graduate	16.55	86	21.5
Some college	17.38	91	18.7
Associate's degree	20.41	106	10.5
Bachelor's degree or more	23.34	122	38.4
Bachelor's degree	23.70	124	24.6
Master's, professional, doctoral degree	22.72	118	13.7

Note: Market shares may not sum to 100.0 because of rounding and missing categories by household type. "Asian" and "black" include Hispanics and non-Hispanics who identify themselves as being of the respective race alone. "Hispanic" includes people of any race who identify themselves as Hispanic. "Other" includes people who identify themselves as non-Hispanic and as Alaska Native, American Indian, Asian (who are also included in the "Asian" row), or Native Hawaiian or other Pacific Islander, as well as non-Hispanics reporting more than one race.
Source: Calculations by New Strategist based on the Bureau of Labor Statistics' 2012 Consumer Expenditure Survey

Chapter 14.
Reading Material

Household Spending on Reading Material, 2000 to 2012

The average American household spent just $109 on books, newspapers, and magazines in 2012. Spending on reading material fell by a precipitous 46 percent between 2000 and 2010, after adjusting for inflation. Between 2010 and 2012, however, spending on reading material increased 4 percent. Behind this increase was the introduction of digital book readers, which accounted for a substantial 12 percent of spending in the reading category in 2012. Behind the ongoing decline in spending on books, newspapers, and magazines is the rise of the Internet, with online news and features substituting for print magazines and newspapers among boomers and younger generations.

The best customers of periodicals are older Americans. Householders aged 55 or older are the biggest spenders on newspaper and magazine subscriptions. Books skew a bit younger, and average household spending on books fell by a smaller percentage than spending on newspapers and magazines—which suggests that printed books have a more stable future than printed newspapers and magazines. Paper-and-ink versions of newspapers and magazines face uncertainty in the years ahead as computer-savvy younger generations—who get their news and information online—replace older customers. These trends suggest that average household spending on reading material will continue to decline. But the purchase of digital book readers, especially by younger consumers, raises the possibility that spending on books may begin to grow in the years ahead.

Spending on reading material

(average spending by households on reading material, 2000, 2006, 2010, and 2012; in 2012 dollars)

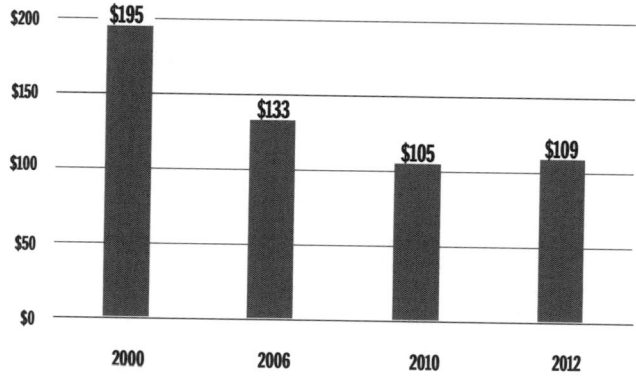

Table 14.1 Reading material spending, 2000 to 2012

(average annual household spending on reading material and percent distribution, by category, 2000 to 2012; percent change and percentage point change in spending, 2000–06, 2006–12, and 2010–12; in 2012 dollars; ranked by amount spent)

	average annual household spending (in 2012$)				percent change		
	2012	2010	2006	2000	2010–12	2006–12	2000–06
Average household spending on reading material	**$109.38**	**$104.90**	**$133.24**	**$195.29**	**4.3%**	**–17.9%**	**–31.8%**
Books	45.30	48.53	60.99	77.41	–6.7	–25.7	–21.2
Magazine and newspaper subscriptions	39.58	42.01	55.42	88.70	–5.8	–28.6	–37.5
Digital book readers	13.62	–	–	–	–	–	–
Magazines and newspapers, nonsubscription	10.88	13.30	16.57	29.01	–18.2	–34.3	–42.9

					percentage point change		
PERCENT DISTRIBUTION OF SPENDING	2012	2010	2006	2000	2010–12	2006–12	2000–06
Average household spending on reading material	**100.0%**	**100.0%**	**100.0%**	**100.0%**	**–**	**–**	**–**
Books	41.4	46.3	45.8	39.6	–4.8	–4.4	6.1
Magazine and newspaper subscriptions	36.2	40.0	41.6	45.4	–3.9	–5.4	–3.8
Digital book readers	12.5	–	–	–	–	–	–
Magazines and newspapers, nonsubscription	9.9	12.7	12.4	14.9	–2.7	–2.5	–2.4

Note: Numbers may not add to total because not all categories are shown. Percentage point change calculations are based on unrounded figures. "–" means not applicable or data unavailable.
Source: Bureau of Labor Statistics, 2000, 2006, 2010, and 2012 Consumer Expenditure Surveys; calculations by New Strategist

Books

Book buying is the province of older householders. Householders ranging in age from 45 to 74 spend 10 to 22 percent more than average on books. Many are retirees with time to read. Married couples without children at home spend 44 percent more than average on books, while couples with school-aged or older children at home spend 31 to 33 percent more than average on this item—buying books not only for themselves but also for their children. Non-Hispanic whites, who spend 21 percent more than average on books, control 91 percent of the market. The spending on books by households in the West is 40 percent above average.

Average household spending on books fell 37 percent between 2000 and 2010, after adjusting for inflation. Though this decline was smaller than the one experienced by newspapers and magazines, which may be good news for the book industry, it continues unabated. Spending on books declined by another 7 percent between 2010 and 2012. Books are likely to weather the Internet revolution better than other print media because there are no freely available electronic alternatives. Much of the decline in spending on books is due to price competition from discounters, used book sales, and the substitution of less expensive e-books for hardbacks. Average household spending on books may stabilize or even rise as a growing proportion of boomers retire and have more time to read.

Table 14.2 Books

Total household spending	$5,636,044,800.00
Average household spends	45.30

AGE OF HOUSEHOLDER	AVERAGE HOUSEHOLD SPENDING	BEST CUSTOMERS (index)	BIGGEST CUSTOMERS (market share)
Average household	$45.30	100	100.0%
Under age 25	24.66	54	3.6
Aged 25 to 34	35.50	78	12.7
Aged 35 to 44	45.53	101	17.4
Aged 45 to 54	53.45	118	23.4
Aged 55 to 64	55.10	122	22.3
Aged 65 to 74	50.04	110	13.3
Aged 75 or older	34.22	76	7.4

	AVERAGE HOUSEHOLD SPENDING	BEST CUSTOMERS (index)	BIGGEST CUSTOMERS (market share)
HOUSEHOLD INCOME			
Average household	**$45.30**	**100**	**100.0%**
Under $20,000	14.94	33	6.9
$20,000 to $39,999	23.76	52	11.8
$40,000 to $49,999	42.01	93	8.2
$50,000 to $69,999	38.93	86	12.4
$70,000 to $79,999	60.38	133	7.4
$80,000 to $99,999	60.56	134	11.8
$100,000 or more	100.12	221	41.4
HOUSEHOLD TYPE			
Average household	**45.30**	**100**	**100.0**
Married couples	59.09	130	63.4
Married couples, no children	65.33	144	30.1
Married couples with children	56.77	125	29.5
Oldest child under age 6	44.02	97	4.4
Oldest child aged 6 to 17	59.50	131	15.6
Oldest child aged 18 or older	60.43	133	9.4
Single parent with child under age 18	22.77	50	2.6
Single person	35.93	79	23.6
RACE AND HISPANIC ORIGIN			
Average household	**45.30**	**100**	**100.0**
Asian	46.87	103	4.5
Black	15.13	33	4.2
Hispanic	18.89	42	5.2
Non-Hispanic white and other	54.69	121	90.6
REGION			
Average household	**45.30**	**100**	**100.0**
Northeast	48.86	108	19.5
Midwest	42.11	93	20.6
South	34.49	76	28.4
West	63.45	140	31.6
EDUCATION			
Average household	**45.30**	**100**	**100.0**
Less than high school graduate	9.85	22	2.8
High school graduate	18.96	42	10.4
Some college	41.04	91	18.7
Associate's degree	43.89	97	9.6
Bachelor's degree or more	84.03	185	58.5
Bachelor's degree	66.28	146	29.2
Master's, professional, doctoral degree	114.50	253	29.3

Note: Market shares may not sum to 100.0 because of rounding and missing categories by household type. "Asian" and "black" include Hispanics and non-Hispanics who identify themselves as being of the respective race alone. "Hispanic" includes people of any race who identify themselves as Hispanic. "Other" includes people who identify themselves as non-Hispanic and as Alaska Native, American Indian, Asian (who are also included in the "Asian" row), or Native Hawaiian or other Pacific Islander, as well as non-Hispanics reporting more than one race.
Source: Calculations by New Strategist based on the Bureau of Labor Statistics' 2012 Consumer Expenditure Survey

Digital Book Readers

Best customers: Householders aged 35 to 54
Married couples with children at home
Single parents
Households in the West

Customer trends: Average household spending on digital book readers will increase as the technology wins widespread acceptance.

Middle-aged married couples with children are the best customers of digital book readers. Married couples with children at home spend 78 percent more than the average household on digital book readers, the figure peaking at 86 percent among those with adult children. Householders aged 35 to 54 (many with children) spend 39 to 46 percent more than average on digital book readers and control the majority of the market. Single parents, whose spending approaches average on only a few items, outspend the average on book readers by 4 percent. Households in the West spend 47 percent more than average on this item.

Because digital book readers are a recently added category in the Consumer Expenditure Survey, there are no comparative spending data for previous years. Average household spending on digital book readers will increase as the technology wins widespread acceptance.

Table 14.3 Digital book readers

Total household spending $1,694,545,920.00
Average household spends 13.62

AGE OF HOUSEHOLDER	AVERAGE HOUSEHOLD SPENDING	BEST CUSTOMERS (index)	BIGGEST CUSTOMERS (market share)
Average household	$13.62	100	100.0%
Under age 25	8.15	60	3.9
Aged 25 to 34	15.15	111	18.0
Aged 35 to 44	18.87	139	24.1
Aged 45 to 54	19.94	146	29.0
Aged 55 to 64	9.71	71	13.0
Aged 65 to 74	11.26	83	10.0
Aged 75 or older	2.90	21	2.1

	AVERAGE HOUSEHOLD SPENDING	BEST CUSTOMERS (index)	BIGGEST CUSTOMERS (market share)
HOUSEHOLD INCOME			
Average household	**$13.62**	**100**	**100.0%**
Under $20,000	4.65	34	7.2
$20,000 to $39,999	6.43	47	10.6
$40,000 to $49,999	6.55	48	4.3
$50,000 to $69,999	14.11	104	15.0
$70,000 to $79,999	16.37	120	6.7
$80,000 to $99,999	27.22	200	17.6
$100,000 or more	28.13	207	38.7
HOUSEHOLD TYPE			
Average household	**13.62**	**100**	**100.0**
Married couples	19.55	144	69.7
Married couples, no children	12.36	91	18.9
Married couples with children	24.19	178	41.8
Oldest child under age 6	20.77	152	7.0
Oldest child aged 6 to 17	24.85	182	21.7
Oldest child aged 18 or older	25.29	186	13.1
Single parent with child under age 18	14.10	104	5.4
Single person	6.12	45	13.3
RACE AND HISPANIC ORIGIN			
Average household	**13.62**	**100**	**100.0**
Asian	15.45	113	4.9
Black	9.33	69	8.6
Hispanic	6.52	48	6.0
Non-Hispanic white and other	15.50	114	85.4
REGION			
Average household	**13.62**	**100**	**100.0**
Northeast	12.96	95	17.2
Midwest	12.91	95	21.0
South	10.48	77	28.7
West	20.06	147	33.2
EDUCATION			
Average household	**13.62**	**100**	**100.0**
Less than high school graduate	3.17	23	3.0
High school graduate	8.14	60	14.9
Some college	15.34	113	23.2
Associate's degree	25.67	188	18.6
Bachelor's degree or more	17.40	128	40.3
Bachelor's degree	18.23	134	26.7
Master's, professional, doctoral degree	15.96	117	13.6

Note: Market shares may not sum to 100.0 because of rounding and missing categories by household type. "Asian" and "black" include Hispanics and non-Hispanics who identify themselves as being of the respective race alone. "Hispanic" includes people of any race who identify themselves as Hispanic. "Other" includes people who identify themselves as non-Hispanic and as Alaska Native, American Indian, Asian (who are also included in the "Asian" row), or Native Hawaiian or other Pacific Islander, as well as non-Hispanics reporting more than one race.
Source: Calculations by New Strategist based on the Bureau of Labor Statistics' 2012 Consumer Expenditure Survey

Magazine and Newspaper Subscriptions

Best customers: Householders aged 55 or older
                     Married couples without children at home
                     Married couples with adult children at home
                     Non-Hispanic whites
                     Households in the Northeast

Customer trends: Average household spending on newspaper and magazine subscriptions will continue to decline as Internet-savvy younger generations flock to electronic alternatives.

Older householders are by far the best customers of newspaper and magazine subscriptions. Householders aged 55 to 64 spend 35 percent more than average on this item, and those aged 65 to 74 spend 84 percent more. Householders aged 75 or older spend more than twice the average on subscriptions. Together the three age groups control over two-thirds of the market. Married couples without children at home (most of them older) spend 95 percent more than average on subscriptions. Couples with adult children at home spend 31 percent above normal on this item. Non-Hispanic white households spend 24 percent more than average on subscriptions. Households in the Northeast spend 32 percent more than average on this item.

Average household spending on newspaper and magazine subscriptions fell by a substantial 55 percent between 2000 and 2012, after adjusting for inflation. The downward trend is likely to continue as Internet-savvy younger generations flock to electronic alternatives.

Table 14.4 Magazine and newspaper subscriptions

Total household spending $4,924,385,280.00
Average household spends   39.58

AGE OF HOUSEHOLDER	AVERAGE HOUSEHOLD SPENDING	BEST CUSTOMERS (index)	BIGGEST CUSTOMERS (market share)
Average household	$39.58	100	100.0%
Under age 25	6.19	16	1.0
Aged 25 to 34	13.46	34	5.5
Aged 35 to 44	19.09	48	8.4
Aged 45 to 54	32.65	82	16.3
Aged 55 to 64	53.61	135	24.8
Aged 65 to 74	72.90	184	22.2
Aged 75 or older	88.30	223	21.8

	AVERAGE HOUSEHOLD SPENDING	BEST CUSTOMERS (index)	BIGGEST CUSTOMERS (market share)
HOUSEHOLD INCOME			
Average household	**$39.58**	**100**	**100.0%**
Under $20,000	20.10	51	10.7
$20,000 to $39,999	32.71	83	18.6
$40,000 to $49,999	29.47	74	6.6
$50,000 to $69,999	35.64	90	13.0
$70,000 to $79,999	50.83	128	7.2
$80,000 to $99,999	45.10	114	10.1
$100,000 or more	71.60	181	33.9
HOUSEHOLD TYPE			
Average household	**39.58**	**100**	**100.0**
Married couples	53.03	134	65.1
Married couples, no children	77.36	195	40.7
Married couples with children	35.45	90	21.1
Oldest child under age 6	23.70	60	2.7
Oldest child aged 6 to 17	30.15	76	9.1
Oldest child aged 18 or older	51.98	131	9.3
Single parent with child under age 18	7.98	20	1.1
Single person	32.60	82	24.5
RACE AND HISPANIC ORIGIN			
Average household	**39.58**	**100**	**100.0**
Asian	24.24	61	2.7
Black	13.48	34	4.3
Hispanic	8.04	20	2.5
Non-Hispanic white and other	49.14	124	93.2
REGION			
Average household	**39.58**	**100**	**100.0**
Northeast	52.38	132	23.9
Midwest	43.64	110	24.4
South	28.45	72	26.8
West	43.74	111	24.9
EDUCATION			
Average household	**39.58**	**100**	**100.0**
Less than high school graduate	16.60	42	5.5
High school graduate	27.03	68	17.0
Some college	32.13	81	16.7
Associate's degree	34.19	86	8.5
Bachelor's degree or more	65.58	166	52.3
Bachelor's degree	52.67	133	26.5
Master's, professional, doctoral degree	87.73	222	25.7

Note: Market shares may not sum to 100.0 because of rounding and missing categories by household type. "Asian" and "black" include Hispanics and non-Hispanics who identify themselves as being of the respective race alone. "Hispanic" includes people of any race who identify themselves as Hispanic. "Other" includes people who identify themselves as non-Hispanic and as Alaska Native, American Indian, Asian (who are also included in the "Asian" row), or Native Hawaiian or other Pacific Islander, as well as non-Hispanics reporting more than one race.
Source: Calculations by New Strategist based on the Bureau of Labor Statistics' 2012 Consumer Expenditure Survey

Magazines and Newspapers, Nonsubscription

Best customers: Householders aged 55 to 74
Married couples without children at home
Households in the Northeast

Customer trends: Average household spending on nonsubscription newspapers and magazines will continue to decline
as the availability of online news dampens impulse purchasing.

The best customers of nonsubscription magazines and newspapers are the mass transit–riding residents of the Northeast's commuter-friendly cities. Households in the Northeast spend 84 percent more than average on this item, many buying from newsstands or vending machines. Householders ranging in age from 55 to 74 spend 27 to 33 percent more than average on this item. Married couples without children at home spend 60 percent more than average on nonsubscription magazines and newspapers.

Average household spending on nonsubscription magazines and newspapers declined sharply between 2000 and 2012, falling by an enormous 62 percent after adjusting for inflation. The downward spiral is due in part to easy (and free) access to newspapers online, which dampens impulse purchasing. Unless newspapers and magazines can find a way to capture these lost dollars, the trend is likely to intensify as wireless Internet access becomes widely available to commuters and long-distance travelers.

Table 14.5 **Magazines and newspapers, nonsubscription**

Total household spending $1,353,646,080.00
Average household spends   10.88

	AVERAGE HOUSEHOLD SPENDING	BEST CUSTOMERS (index)	BIGGEST CUSTOMERS (market share)
AGE OF HOUSEHOLDER			
Average household	**$10.88**	**100**	**100.0%**
Under age 25	4.92	45	3.0
Aged 25 to 34	7.41	68	11.0
Aged 35 to 44	9.20	85	14.7
Aged 45 to 54	12.44	114	22.6
Aged 55 to 64	14.43	133	24.3
Aged 65 to 74	13.78	127	15.3
Aged 75 or older	10.17	93	9.1

	AVERAGE HOUSEHOLD SPENDING	BEST CUSTOMERS (index)	BIGGEST CUSTOMERS (market share)
HOUSEHOLD INCOME			
Average household	$10.88	100	100.0%
Under $20,000	5.19	48	10.0
$20,000 to $39,999	7.94	73	16.4
$40,000 to $49,999	8.54	78	6.9
$50,000 to $69,999	14.50	133	19.3
$70,000 to $79,999	13.55	125	7.0
$80,000 to $99,999	15.35	141	12.4
$100,000 or more	16.20	149	27.9
HOUSEHOLD TYPE			
Average household	10.88	100	100.0
Married couples	13.44	124	60.0
Married couples, no children	17.42	160	33.4
Married couples with children	9.57	88	20.7
Oldest child under age 6	7.32	67	3.1
Oldest child aged 6 to 17	10.27	94	11.2
Oldest child aged 18 or older	9.83	90	6.4
Single parent with child under age 18	5.37	49	2.6
Single person	8.02	74	21.9
RACE AND HISPANIC ORIGIN			
Average household	10.88	100	100.0
Asian	10.17	93	4.1
Black	6.80	63	7.9
Hispanic	6.67	61	7.7
Non-Hispanic white and other	12.24	113	84.4
REGION			
Average household	10.88	100	100.0
Northeast	19.99	184	33.2
Midwest	8.26	76	16.8
South	8.90	82	30.5
West	9.41	86	19.5
EDUCATION			
Average household	10.88	100	100.0
Less than high school graduate	6.51	60	7.8
High school graduate	9.82	90	22.5
Some college	9.93	91	18.8
Associate's degree	11.43	105	10.4
Bachelor's degree or more	13.97	128	40.5
Bachelor's degree	12.45	114	22.8
Master's, professional, doctoral degree	16.56	152	17.7

Note: Market shares may not sum to 100.0 because of rounding and missing categories by household type. "Asian" and "black" include Hispanics and non-Hispanics who identify themselves as being of the respective race alone. "Hispanic" includes people of any race who identify themselves as Hispanic. "Other" includes people who identify themselves as non-Hispanic and as Alaska Native, American Indian, Asian (who are also included in the "Asian" row), or Native Hawaiian or other Pacific Islander, as well as non-Hispanics reporting more than one race.
Source: Calculations by New Strategist based on the Bureau of Labor Statistics' 2012 Consumer Expenditure Survey

Chapter 15.
Restaurants and Carry-Outs

Household Spending at Restaurants and Carry-Outs, 2006 to 2012

In 2012, the average household spent a considerable $2,483 at restaurants and carry-outs—a figure that does not include alcoholic beverage spending (see Alcohol chapter for those figures). What once was a special occasion—eating out—has become a necessity as busy two-earner families try to save time. The Bureau of Labor Statistics reports that during the average week of 2012, 69 percent of households purchased food from restaurants and carry-outs and spent an average of $62. Average household spending at restaurants and carry-outs fell 15 percent from 2006 to 2010, after adjusting for inflation, and then increased 2 percent in the ensuing two-year period. (Comparisons with 2000 figures are invalid because of changes in methodology.) Behind the decline is price discounting, as well as belt tightening as the economic downturn took hold.

Households devote more of their restaurant dollars to dinners (44 percent) than to lunches (30 percent). Breakfasts account for another 9 percent of restaurant spending, snacks for 7 percent, and restaurant meals on trips (which are not broken down by type of restaurant) account for 10 percent.

The average household devotes less of the eating-out dollar to fast food than to full-service restaurants. Of the $2,483 the average household spent on eating out in 2012, fast-food restaurants captured a 38 percent share, and full-service restaurants took a larger 46 percent. The remainder is spent at employer and school cafeterias, vending machines, mobile vendors, and on trips.

Older Americans, particularly empty-nesters, are far more likely to choose full-service over fast-food restaurants. Consequently, as the population ages, expect to see faster growth in spending on the full-service category.

Restaurant spending

(average annual spending by households on restaurants by type of establishment, 2012)

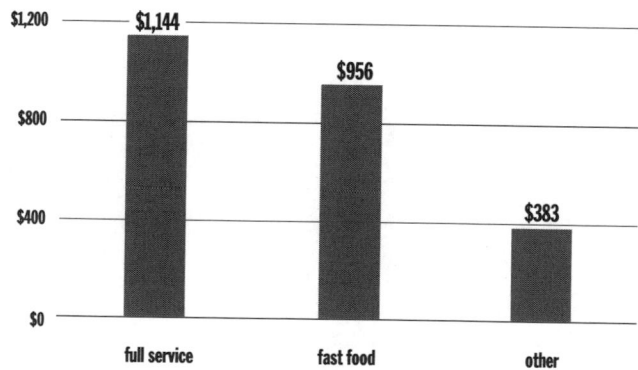

Table 15.1 Restaurant and carry-out spending, 2006 to 2012

(average annual household spending at restaurants and carry-outs and percent distribution, by category, 2006, 2010, and 2012; percent and percentage point change in spending, 2006–12 and 2010–12, in 2012 dollars; ranked by amount spent)

	average annual household spending (in 2012$)			percent change	
	2012	2010	2006	2010–12	2006–12
AVERAGE HOUSEHOLD SPENDING AT RESTAURANTS BY TYPE OF MEAL					
Total restaurant spending	**$2,482.65**	**$2,425.94**	**$2,838.39**	**2.3%**	**−12.5%**
Dinner	1,082.12	1,039.21	1,221.65	4.1	−11.4
Lunch	746.81	765.06	875.35	−2.4	−14.7
Restaurant meals on trips	257.15	234.88	276.66	9.5	−7.1
Breakfast and brunch	227.60	223.27	265.84	1.9	−14.4
Snacks and nonalcoholic beverages	168.97	163.51	198.88	3.3	−15.0
AVERAGE HOUSEHOLD SPENDING AT RESTAURANTS BY TYPE OF RESTAURANT					
Total restaurant spending	**2,482.65**	**2,425.94**	**2,838.39**	**2.3**	**−12.5**
Full service	1,144.08	1,099.17	1,327.26	4.1	−13.8
Fast food	955.55	943.05	1,051.85	1.3	−9.2
Other (trips, cafeterias, vendors)	383.02	383.72	459.28	−0.2	−16.6
AVERAGE HOUSEHOLD SPENDING BY TYPE OF MEAL AND RESTAURANT					
Total restaurant spending	**2,482.65**	**2,425.94**	**2,838.39**	**2.3**	**−12.5**
Dinner	1,082.12	1,039.21	1,221.65	4.1	−11.4
At full-service restaurants	721.27	679.59	825.18	6.1	−12.6
At fast-food restaurants*	350.68	348.96	384.82	0.5	−8.9
Lunch	746.81	765.06	875.35	−2.4	−14.7
At fast-food restaurants*	366.70	369.97	421.45	−0.9	−13.0
At full-service restaurants	300.91	300.24	342.90	0.2	−12.2
At employer and school cafeterias	71.63	86.49	98.11	−17.2	−27.0
Restaurant meals on trips	257.15	234.88	276.66	9.5	−7.1
Breakfast and brunch	227.60	223.27	265.84	1.9	−14.4
At fast-food restaurants*	123.87	116.46	123.21	6.4	0.5
At full-service restaurants	92.25	89.30	125.24	3.3	−26.3
Snacks and nonalcoholic beverages	168.97	163.51	198.88	3.3	−15.0
At fast-food restaurants*	114.30	107.66	122.37	6.2	−6.6
At full-service restaurants	29.65	30.04	33.94	−1.3	−12.6
At vending machines, mobile vendors	17.55	19.57	34.80	−10.3	−49.6
At employer and school cafeterias	7.47	6.24	7.77	19.6	−3.8

PERCENT DISTRIBUTION OF SPENDING	average annual household spending (in 2012$)			percentage point change	
	2012	2010	2006	2010–12	2006–12
AVERAGE HOUSEHOLD SPENDING AT RESTAURANTS BY TYPE OF MEAL					
Total restaurant spending	**100.0%**	**100.0%**	**100.0%**	–	–
Dinner	43.6	42.8	43.0	0.7	0.5
Lunch	30.1	31.5	30.8	–1.5	–0.8
Restaurant meals on trips	10.4	9.7	9.7	0.7	0.6
Breakfast and brunch	9.2	9.2	9.4	0.0	–0.2
Snacks and nonalcoholic beverages	6.8	6.7	7.0	0.1	–0.2
AVERAGE HOUSEHOLD SPENDING AT RESTAURANTS BY TYPE OF RESTAURANT					
Total restaurant spending	**100.0**	**100.0**	**100.0**	–	–
Full service	46.1	45.3	46.8	0.8	–0.7
Fast food	38.5	38.9	37.1	–0.4	1.4
Other (trips, cafeterias, vendors)	15.4	15.8	16.2	–0.4	–0.8
AVERAGE HOUSEHOLD SPENDING BY TYPE OF MEAL AND RESTAURANT					
Total restaurant spending	**100.0**	**100.0**	**100.0**	–	–
Dinner	43.6	42.8	43.0	0.7	0.5
At full-service restaurants	29.1	28.0	29.1	1.0	0.0
At fast-food restaurants*	14.1	14.4	13.6	–0.3	0.6
Lunch	30.1	31.5	30.8	–1.5	–0.8
At fast-food restaurants*	14.8	15.3	14.8	–0.5	–0.1
At full-service restaurants	12.1	12.4	12.1	–0.3	0.0
At employer and school cafeterias	2.9	3.6	3.5	–0.7	–0.6
Restaurant meals on trips	10.4	9.7	9.7	0.7	0.6
Breakfast and brunch	9.2	9.2	9.4	0.0	–0.2
At fast-food restaurants*	5.0	4.8	4.3	0.2	0.6
At full-service restaurants	3.7	3.7	4.4	0.0	–0.7
Snacks and nonalcoholic beverages	6.8	6.7	7.0	0.1	–0.2
At fast-food restaurants*	4.6	4.4	4.3	0.2	0.3
At full-service restaurants	1.2	1.2	1.2	0.0	0.0
At vending machines, mobile vendors	0.7	0.8	1.2	–0.1	–0.5
At employer and school cafeterias	0.3	0.3	0.3	0.0	0.0

*"At fast-food restaurants" also includes take-out and delivery as well as food from concession stands, buffets, and cafeterias other than employer and school.

Note: Subcategories do not add to total because not all types of restaurants or meals are shown. Percentage point change calculations are based on unrounded figures. "–" means not applicable.

Source: Bureau of Labor Statistics, 2006, 2010, and 2012 Consumer Expenditure Surveys; calculations by New Strategist

Breakfast and Brunch at Fast-Food Restaurants, Including Take-Outs, Deliveries, Concession Stands, Buffets, and Cafeterias (except Employer and School)

Best customers: Householders aged 25 to 54
Married couples with children at home
Hispanics and Asians
Households in the Northeast

Customer trends: Average household spending on breakfast at fast-food restaurants is likely to continue to grow
as the large millennial generation fills the best-customer age groups.

The busiest people are the biggest spenders on breakfast at fast-food restaurants—workers and parents. Householders of prime working age, 25 to 54, spend 19 to 25 percent more than average on this item. Married couples with children at home spend 23 percent more than average on breakfast at fast-food restaurants as they try to fit meals into their busy schedules. Hispanics spend 28 percent more than average on breakfast at fast-food restaurants, and Asians spend 19 percent more. Households in the Northeast outspend the average by 22 percent.

Among restaurant categories, fast-food breakfasts experienced the smallest decline in spending between 2006 and 2010, a 5 percent drop after adjusting for inflation. Average household spending on this category then increased 6 percent between 2010 and 2012. Spending on this item is likely to continue to grow as the large millennial generation fills the best-customer age groups.

Table 15.2 Breakfast and brunch at fast-food restaurants, including take-outs, deliveries, concession stands, buffets, and cafeterias (except employer and school)

Total household spending $15,411,409,920.00
Average household spends   123.87

AGE OF HOUSEHOLDER	AVERAGE HOUSEHOLD SPENDING	BEST CUSTOMERS (index)	BIGGEST CUSTOMERS (market share)
Average household	$123.87	100	100.0%
Under age 25	119.07	96	6.3
Aged 25 to 34	147.25	119	19.2
Aged 35 to 44	155.18	125	21.7
Aged 45 to 54	150.08	121	24.0
Aged 55 to 64	119.91	97	17.7
Aged 65 to 74	75.31	61	7.3
Aged 75 or older	41.90	34	3.3

	AVERAGE HOUSEHOLD SPENDING	BEST CUSTOMERS (index)	BIGGEST CUSTOMERS (market share)
HOUSEHOLD INCOME			
Average household	**$123.87**	**100**	**100.0%**
Under $20,000	53.29	43	9.1
$20,000 to $39,999	91.29	74	16.6
$40,000 to $49,999	96.54	78	6.9
$50,000 to $69,999	132.86	107	15.5
$70,000 to $79,999	190.96	154	8.6
$80,000 to $99,999	177.37	143	12.6
$100,000 or more	202.67	164	30.6
HOUSEHOLD TYPE			
Average household	**123.87**	**100**	**100.0**
Married couples	142.01	115	55.7
Married couples, no children	114.42	92	19.3
Married couples with children	152.92	123	29.0
Oldest child under age 6	153.91	124	5.7
Oldest child aged 6 to 17	161.01	130	15.5
Oldest child aged 18 or older	138.82	112	7.9
Single parent with child under age 18	121.63	98	5.1
Single person	82.70	67	19.8
RACE AND HISPANIC ORIGIN			
Average household	**123.87**	**100**	**100.0**
Asian	147.82	119	5.2
Black	110.11	89	11.2
Hispanic	158.51	128	16.0
Non-Hispanic white and other	120.48	97	73.0
REGION			
Average household	**123.87**	**100**	**100.0**
Northeast	150.68	122	22.0
Midwest	109.73	89	19.6
South	115.18	93	34.6
West	130.70	106	23.8
EDUCATION			
Average household	**123.87**	**100**	**100.0**
Less than high school graduate	93.89	76	9.9
High school graduate	118.13	95	23.8
Some college	112.42	91	18.7
Associate's degree	168.31	136	13.4
Bachelor's degree or more	133.39	108	34.0
Bachelor's degree	139.59	113	22.5
Master's, professional, doctoral degree	122.90	99	11.5

Note: Market shares may not sum to 100.0 because of rounding and missing categories by household type. "Asian" and "black" include Hispanics and non-Hispanics who identify themselves as being of the respective race alone. "Hispanic" includes people of any race who identify themselves as Hispanic. "Other" includes people who identify themselves as non-Hispanic and as Alaska Native, American Indian, Asian (who are also included in the "Asian" row), or Native Hawaiian or other Pacific Islander, as well as non-Hispanics reporting more than one race.
Source: Calculations by New Strategist based on the Bureau of Labor Statistics' 2012 Consumer Expenditure Survey

Breakfast and Brunch at Full-Service Restaurants

Best customers: Householders aged 55 to 74
                        Married couples without children at home
                        Married couples with school-aged or older children at home
                        Hispanics
                        Households in the West

Customer trends: Average household spending on breakfast and brunch at full-service restaurants may rise
                        as baby boomers fill the best-customer age groups.

The biggest spenders on breakfast and brunch at full-service restaurants are older married couples enjoying a leisurely meal. Householders aged 55 to 74 spend 25 percent more than average on this item. Married couples without children at home (many of them empty-nesters) spend 56 percent more than average on breakfast and brunch at full-service restaurants. Married couples with school-aged or older children at home, who have the largest households, spend 23 to 34 percent more than average on breakfast at full-service restaurants. Hispanics outspend the average by 17 percent. Households in the West, where many Hispanics reside, spend 27 percent more than average on this item.

Average household spending on breakfast at full-service restaurants declined by a substantial 29 percent between 2006 and 2010, after adjusting for inflation, then grew 3 percent over the ensuing two years. Behind the decline was the Great Recession and a reduction in spending on all types of restaurant meals. In the years ahead, spending on full-service breakfasts should rise as boomers fill the best-customer age groups.

Table 15.3 Breakfast and brunch at full-service restaurants

Total household spending $11,477,376,000.00
Average household spends   92.25

	AVERAGE HOUSEHOLD SPENDING	BEST CUSTOMERS (index)	BIGGEST CUSTOMERS (market share)
AGE OF HOUSEHOLDER			
Average household	$92.25	100	100.0%
Under age 25	31.54	34	2.2
Aged 25 to 34	69.89	76	12.2
Aged 35 to 44	95.17	103	17.9
Aged 45 to 54	94.49	102	20.3
Aged 55 to 64	115.17	125	22.8
Aged 65 to 74	115.09	125	15.0
Aged 75 or older	93.08	101	9.9

	AVERAGE HOUSEHOLD SPENDING	BEST CUSTOMERS (index)	BIGGEST CUSTOMERS (market share)
HOUSEHOLD INCOME			
Average household	**$92.25**	**100**	**100.0%**
Under $20,000	42.69	46	9.7
$20,000 to $39,999	59.28	64	14.5
$40,000 to $49,999	103.90	113	10.0
$50,000 to $69,999	83.84	91	13.1
$70,000 to $79,999	129.89	141	7.9
$80,000 to $99,999	127.53	138	12.2
$100,000 or more	159.99	173	32.5
HOUSEHOLD TYPE			
Average household	**92.25**	**100**	**100.0**
Married couples	123.69	134	65.1
Married couples, no children	144.02	156	32.5
Married couples with children	105.98	115	27.0
Oldest child under age 6	57.76	63	2.9
Oldest child aged 6 to 17	113.22	123	14.6
Oldest child aged 18 or older	123.96	134	9.5
Single parent with child under age 18	54.25	59	3.1
Single person	61.86	67	19.9
RACE AND HISPANIC ORIGIN			
Average household	**92.25**	**100**	**100.0**
Asian	82.21	89	3.9
Black	54.45	59	7.4
Hispanic	107.79	117	14.6
Non-Hispanic white and other	95.96	104	78.1
REGION			
Average household	**92.25**	**100**	**100.0**
Northeast	85.09	92	16.7
Midwest	90.27	98	21.7
South	81.86	89	33.0
West	117.32	127	28.7
EDUCATION			
Average household	**92.25**	**100**	**100.0**
Less than high school graduate	64.85	70	9.2
High school graduate	82.83	90	22.4
Some college	91.89	100	20.5
Associate's degree	90.81	98	9.7
Bachelor's degree or more	110.51	120	37.8
Bachelor's degree	104.12	113	22.5
Master's, professional, doctoral degree	121.32	132	15.3

Note: Market shares may not sum to 100.0 because of rounding and missing categories by household type. "Asian" and "black" include Hispanics and non-Hispanics who identify themselves as being of the respective race alone. "Hispanic" includes people of any race who identify themselves as Hispanic. "Other" includes people who identify themselves as non-Hispanic and as Alaska Native, American Indian, Asian (who are also included in the "Asian" row), or Native Hawaiian or other Pacific Islander, as well as non-Hispanics reporting more than one race.
Source: Calculations by New Strategist based on the Bureau of Labor Statistics' 2012 Consumer Expenditure Survey

Dinner at Fast-Food Restaurants, Including Take-Outs, Deliveries, Concession Stands, Buffets, and Cafeterias (except Employer and School)

Best customers: Householders aged 25 to 44
Married couples with children at home
Single parents
Hispanics

Customer trends: Average household spending on dinner at fast-food restaurants is likely to grow in the years ahead as the large millennial generation marries and has children.

Families with children are the biggest spenders on dinners at fast-food restaurants. Householders ranging in age from 25 to 44 spend 33 to 35 percent more than average on this item and account for 45 percent of the market. Married couples with children at home spend 52 percent more than average on dinner at fast-food restaurants as they try to fit meals into their busy schedules. Single parents, whose spending approaches average on only a few items, spend 15 percent more than average on fast-food dinners. Hispanics, who have the largest families, spend 20 percent more than average on fast-food dinners.

Average household spending on dinner at fast-food restaurants fell 9 percent between 2006 and 2012 as households cut their spending during the Great Recession. Unlike most other restaurant categories, dinner at fast-food restaurants experienced little recovery in the 2010 to 2012 time period because the millennial generation has postponed marriage and childbearing and delayed its entry into the best-customer lifestage. Average household spending on dinner at fast-food restaurants is likely to grow in the years ahead as the large millennial generation marries and has children.

Table 15.4 Dinner at fast-food restaurants, including take-outs, deliveries, concession stands, buffets, and cafeterias (except employer and school)

Total household spending $43,630,202,880.00
Average household spends 350.68

AGE OF HOUSEHOLDER	AVERAGE HOUSEHOLD SPENDING	BEST CUSTOMERS (index)	BIGGEST CUSTOMERS (market share)
Average household	**$350.68**	**100**	**100.0%**
Under age 25	348.75	99	6.5
Aged 25 to 34	473.71	135	21.8
Aged 35 to 44	465.06	133	23.0
Aged 45 to 54	416.48	119	23.5
Aged 55 to 64	280.76	80	14.7
Aged 65 to 74	198.91	57	6.8
Aged 75 or older	108.97	31	3.0

	AVERAGE HOUSEHOLD SPENDING	BEST CUSTOMERS (index)	BIGGEST CUSTOMERS (market share)
HOUSEHOLD INCOME			
Average household	**$350.68**	**100**	**100.0%**
Under $20,000	164.62	47	9.9
$20,000 to $39,999	253.33	72	16.3
$40,000 to $49,999	332.71	95	8.4
$50,000 to $69,999	394.07	112	16.2
$70,000 to $79,999	420.15	120	6.7
$80,000 to $99,999	517.06	147	13.0
$100,000 or more	552.72	158	29.5
HOUSEHOLD TYPE			
Average household	**350.68**	**100**	**100.0**
Married couples	422.19	120	58.5
Married couples, no children	299.48	85	17.8
Married couples with children	533.09	152	35.7
Oldest child under age 6	447.24	128	5.8
Oldest child aged 6 to 17	587.62	168	19.9
Oldest child aged 18 or older	495.63	141	10.0
Single parent with child under age 18	401.58	115	6.0
Single person	187.46	53	15.9
RACE AND HISPANIC ORIGIN			
Average household	**350.68**	**100**	**100.0**
Asian	335.64	96	4.1
Black	336.95	96	12.1
Hispanic	422.03	120	15.1
Non-Hispanic white and other	341.02	97	73.0
REGION			
Average household	**350.68**	**100**	**100.0**
Northeast	346.13	99	17.8
Midwest	337.45	96	21.3
South	349.74	100	37.1
West	369.18	105	23.7
EDUCATION			
Average household	**350.68**	**100**	**100.0**
Less than high school graduate	223.78	64	8.3
High school graduate	315.45	90	22.4
Some college	366.11	104	21.5
Associate's degree	358.43	102	10.1
Bachelor's degree or more	412.72	118	37.1
Bachelor's degree	431.07	123	24.5
Master's, professional, doctoral degree	381.71	109	12.6

Note: Market shares may not sum to 100.0 because of rounding and missing categories by household type. "Asian" and "black" include Hispanics and non-Hispanics who identify themselves as being of the respective race alone. "Hispanic" includes people of any race who identify themselves as Hispanic. "Other" includes people who identify themselves as non-Hispanic and as Alaska Native, American Indian, Asian (who are also included in the "Asian" row), or Native Hawaiian or other Pacific Islander, as well as non-Hispanics reporting more than one race.
Source: Calculations by New Strategist based on the Bureau of Labor Statistics' 2012 Consumer Expenditure Survey

Dinner at Full-Service Restaurants

Best customers: **Householders aged 35 to 54**
Married couples without children at home
Married couples with school-aged or older children at home
Asians
Households in the Northeast

Customer trends: **Average household spending on dinner at full-service restaurants should rise in the years ahead**
as growing numbers of baby boomers retire and gain more free time.

The biggest spenders on dinners at full-service restaurants are married couples with children at home as well as empty-nesters. Householders ranging in age from 35 to 54 spend 15 percent more than average on this item. Married couples with school-aged children spend 51 percent more than average on dinner at full-service restaurants, and those with adult children at home spend 20 percent more. Married couples without children at home (many of them empty-nesters) spend 39 percent more than average on full-service restaurant dinners. Asians spend 30 percent more than average on full-service dinners. Households in the Northeast lead those in other regions in spending on full-service dinners, their bill being 29 percent higher than average.

Average household spending on dinners in full-service restaurants fell by 18 percent between 2006 and 2010, after adjusting for inflation, as households cut their budgets in the midst of the Great Recession. Spending then rose 6 percent from 2010 to 2012. Average household spending in the category should continue to rise in the years ahead as baby boomers retire and gain more free time.

Table 15.5 Dinner at full-service restaurants

Total household spending $89,737,528,320.00
Average household spends   721.27

	AVERAGE HOUSEHOLD SPENDING	BEST CUSTOMERS (index)	BIGGEST CUSTOMERS (market share)
AGE OF HOUSEHOLDER			
Average household	$721.27	100	100.0%
Under age 25	380.17	53	3.5
Aged 25 to 34	739.18	102	16.6
Aged 35 to 44	832.72	115	20.0
Aged 45 to 54	827.52	115	22.7
Aged 55 to 64	753.78	105	19.1
Aged 65 to 74	677.87	94	11.3
Aged 75 or older	499.19	69	6.8

	AVERAGE HOUSEHOLD SPENDING	BEST CUSTOMERS (index)	BIGGEST CUSTOMERS (market share)
HOUSEHOLD INCOME			
Average household	**$721.27**	**100**	**100.0%**
Under $20,000	276.42	38	8.1
$20,000 to $39,999	401.13	56	12.5
$40,000 to $49,999	504.95	70	6.2
$50,000 to $69,999	689.40	96	13.8
$70,000 to $79,999	829.08	115	6.4
$80,000 to $99,999	1,026.93	142	12.6
$100,000 or more	1,571.64	218	40.8
HOUSEHOLD TYPE			
Average household	**721.27**	**100**	**100.0**
Married couples	967.54	134	65.2
Married couples, no children	1,005.09	139	29.0
Married couples with children	954.07	132	31.1
Oldest child under age 6	735.80	102	4.7
Oldest child aged 6 to 17	1,089.66	151	18.0
Oldest child aged 18 or older	863.90	120	8.5
Single parent with child under age 18	446.18	62	3.2
Single person	423.38	59	17.4
RACE AND HISPANIC ORIGIN			
Average household	**721.27**	**100**	**100.0**
Asian	938.11	130	5.6
Black	387.73	54	6.8
Hispanic	528.59	73	9.2
Non-Hispanic white and other	808.67	112	84.2
REGION			
Average household	**721.27**	**100**	**100.0**
Northeast	927.00	129	23.2
Midwest	635.49	88	19.5
South	649.89	90	33.6
West	758.73	105	23.7
EDUCATION			
Average household	**721.27**	**100**	**100.0**
Less than high school graduate	282.83	39	5.1
High school graduate	497.78	69	17.2
Some college	662.21	92	18.9
Associate's degree	809.40	112	11.1
Bachelor's degree or more	1,070.96	148	46.8
Bachelor's degree	977.23	135	27.0
Master's, professional, doctoral degree	1,229.41	170	19.8

Note: Market shares may not sum to 100.0 because of rounding and missing categories by household type. "Asian" and "black" include Hispanics and non-Hispanics who identify themselves as being of the respective race alone. "Hispanic" includes people of any race who identify themselves as Hispanic. "Other" includes people who identify themselves as non-Hispanic and as Alaska Native, American Indian, Asian (who are also included in the "Asian" row), or Native Hawaiian or other Pacific Islander, as well as non-Hispanics reporting more than one race.
Source: Calculations by New Strategist based on the Bureau of Labor Statistics' 2012 Consumer Expenditure Survey

Lunch at Employer and School Cafeterias

Best customers: Householders aged 35 to 54
Married couples with school-aged or older children at home
Single parents
Asians
Households in the Northeast and Midwest

Customer trends: Average household spending on lunch at employer and school cafeterias may continue to decline
as more children qualify for subsidized lunches and fewer employers offer cafeteria meals
in an attempt to cut costs.

Not surprisingly, parents and workers are the biggest spenders on lunch at employer and school cafeterias. Householders aged 35 to 44 spend more than twice the average on this item, and those aged 45 to 54 spend 47 percent more. Together, the two age groups account for 64 percent of the market. Married couples with school-aged children, many of them dual-income couples, spend well over three times the average on this item. Couples with adult children at home spend 78 percent more than average on employer and school cafeteria lunches. Single parents, whose spending approaches average on only a few items, spend 84 percent more than average. Asians spend nearly double the average on this item. Households in the Northeast and Midwest spend 18 and 14 percent more than average, respectively.

Average household spending on lunch at employer and school cafeterias fell 27 percent between 2006 and 2012, after adjusting for inflation. Behind the decline were fewer workers and household budget cutting in the midst of the economic downturn. This category may continue to decline as a growing percentage of children qualify for subsidized lunches and fewer employers offer cafeteria meals in an attempt to cut costs.

Table 15.6 Lunch at employer and school cafeterias

Total household spending $8,911,918,080.00
Average household spends 71.63

	AVERAGE HOUSEHOLD SPENDING	BEST CUSTOMERS (index)	BIGGEST CUSTOMERS (market share)
AGE OF HOUSEHOLDER			
Average household	**$71.63**	**100**	**100.0%**
Under age 25	53.51	75	4.9
Aged 25 to 34	52.38	73	11.8
Aged 35 to 44	143.86	201	34.9
Aged 45 to 54	105.03	147	29.0
Aged 55 to 64	53.73	75	13.7
Aged 65 to 74	17.30	24	2.9
Aged 75 or older	15.67	22	2.1

	AVERAGE HOUSEHOLD SPENDING	BEST CUSTOMERS (index)	BIGGEST CUSTOMERS (market share)
HOUSEHOLD INCOME			
Average household	**$71.63**	**100**	**100.0%**
Under $20,000	22.18	31	6.5
$20,000 to $39,999	31.54	44	9.9
$40,000 to $49,999	51.93	72	6.4
$50,000 to $69,999	66.53	93	13.4
$70,000 to $79,999	63.99	89	5.0
$80,000 to $99,999	91.48	128	11.3
$100,000 or more	184.02	257	48.1
HOUSEHOLD TYPE			
Average household	**71.63**	**100**	**100.0**
Married couples	102.89	144	69.8
Married couples, no children	35.90	50	10.4
Married couples with children	165.95	232	54.5
Oldest child under age 6	41.99	59	2.7
Oldest child aged 6 to 17	235.23	328	39.1
Oldest child aged 18 or older	127.62	178	12.6
Single parent with child under age 18	131.50	184	9.6
Single person	26.22	37	10.9
RACE AND HISPANIC ORIGIN			
Average household	**71.63**	**100**	**100.0**
Asian	139.93	195	8.5
Black	51.94	73	9.1
Hispanic	60.59	85	10.6
Non-Hispanic white and other	76.63	107	80.3
REGION			
Average household	**71.63**	**100**	**100.0**
Northeast	84.46	118	21.3
Midwest	81.75	114	25.3
South	62.04	87	32.3
West	67.01	94	21.1
EDUCATION			
Average household	**71.63**	**100**	**100.0**
Less than high school graduate	24.60	34	4.5
High school graduate	51.34	72	17.9
Some college	67.78	95	19.5
Associate's degree	90.64	127	12.5
Bachelor's degree or more	101.63	142	44.7
Bachelor's degree	93.60	131	26.0
Master's, professional, doctoral degree	115.20	161	18.7

Note: Market shares may not sum to 100.0 because of rounding and missing categories by household type. "Asian" and "black" include Hispanics and non-Hispanics who identify themselves as being of the respective race alone. "Hispanic" includes people of any race who identify themselves as Hispanic. "Other" includes people who identify themselves as non-Hispanic and as Alaska Native, American Indian, Asian (who are also included in the "Asian" row), or Native Hawaiian or other Pacific Islander, as well as non-Hispanics reporting more than one race.
Source: Calculations by New Strategist based on the Bureau of Labor Statistics' 2012 Consumer Expenditure Survey

Lunch at Fast-Food Restaurants, Including Take-Outs, Deliveries, Concession Stands, Buffets, and Cafeterias (except Employer and School)

Best customers: Householders aged 25 to 44
Married couples with children at home
Asians and Hispanics
Households in the West

Customer trends: Average household spending on lunch at fast-food restaurants may begin to grow in the years ahead as the large millennial generation marries and has children.

Workers and parents are the best customers of fast-food lunches. Householders of prime working age, 25 to 44, spend 23 to 26 percent more than average on this item and account for 42 percent of the market. Married couples with children at home spend 43 percent more than average on lunches at fast-food restaurants as they try to fit meals into their busy schedules. Asians spend 31 percent more than average on this item, and Hispanics spend 18 percent more. Households in the West, where many Asians and Hispanics reside, spend 16 percent more than average on fast-food lunches.

Average household spending on fast-food lunches fell by 13 percent between 2006 and 2012, after adjusting for inflation. Behind the decline was belt tightening as households cut their budget in the midst of the Great Recession. Unlike most other restaurant categories, spending on lunch at fast-food restaurants did not begin to recover in the 2010-to-2012 time period because the millennial generation has postponed marriage and childbearing and delayed its entry into the best-customer lifestage. Average household spending on dinner at fast-food restaurants may begin to grow in the years ahead as the large millennial generation marries and has children.

Table 15.7 Lunch at fast-food restaurants, including take-outs, deliveries, concession stands, buffets, and cafeterias (except employer and school)

Total household spending $45,623,347,200.00
Average household spends   366.70

	AVERAGE HOUSEHOLD SPENDING	BEST CUSTOMERS (index)	BIGGEST CUSTOMERS (market share)
AGE OF HOUSEHOLDER			
Average household	$366.70	100	100.0%
Under age 25	320.59	87	5.7
Aged 25 to 34	450.52	123	19.9
Aged 35 to 44	460.94	126	21.8
Aged 45 to 54	416.93	114	22.5
Aged 55 to 64	369.32	101	18.4
Aged 65 to 74	227.08	62	7.5
Aged 75 or older	143.78	39	3.8

	AVERAGE HOUSEHOLD SPENDING	BEST CUSTOMERS (index)	BIGGEST CUSTOMERS (market share)
HOUSEHOLD INCOME			
Average household	**$366.70**	**100**	**100.0%**
Under $20,000	180.84	49	10.4
$20,000 to $39,999	257.52	70	15.8
$40,000 to $49,999	342.15	93	8.3
$50,000 to $69,999	379.89	104	15.0
$70,000 to $79,999	472.35	129	7.2
$80,000 to $99,999	486.93	133	11.7
$100,000 or more	620.57	169	31.7
HOUSEHOLD TYPE			
Average household	**366.70**	**100**	**100.0**
Married couples	447.27	122	59.2
Married couples, no children	347.57	95	19.8
Married couples with children	524.60	143	33.6
Oldest child under age 6	540.26	147	6.7
Oldest child aged 6 to 17	552.87	151	17.9
Oldest child aged 18 or older	467.67	128	9.0
Single parent with child under age 18	338.35	92	4.8
Single person	226.42	62	18.3
RACE AND HISPANIC ORIGIN			
Average household	**366.70**	**100**	**100.0**
Asian	481.20	131	5.7
Black	308.58	84	10.6
Hispanic	434.04	118	14.8
Non-Hispanic white and other	365.88	100	74.9
REGION			
Average household	**366.70**	**100**	**100.0**
Northeast	350.32	96	17.2
Midwest	324.02	88	19.6
South	365.91	100	37.2
West	424.08	116	26.1
EDUCATION			
Average household	**366.70**	**100**	**100.0**
Less than high school graduate	235.01	64	8.4
High school graduate	322.92	88	22.0
Some college	357.35	97	20.1
Associate's degree	380.04	104	10.2
Bachelor's degree or more	452.12	123	38.9
Bachelor's degree	449.40	123	24.4
Master's, professional, doctoral degree	456.73	125	14.5

Note: Market shares may not sum to 100.0 because of rounding and missing categories by household type. "Asian" and "black" include Hispanics and non-Hispanics who identify themselves as being of the respective race alone. "Hispanic" includes people of any race who identify themselves as Hispanic. "Other" includes people who identify themselves as non-Hispanic and as Alaska Native, American Indian, Asian (who are also included in the "Asian" row), or Native Hawaiian or other Pacific Islander, as well as non-Hispanics reporting more than one race.
Source: Calculations by New Strategist based on the Bureau of Labor Statistics' 2012 Consumer Expenditure Survey

Lunch at Full-Service Restaurants

Best customers: Householders aged 45 to 64
Married couples without children at home
Married couples with school-aged or older children at home
Asians
Households in the West

Customer trends: Average household spending on lunch at full-service restaurants should rise as growing numbers
of aging boomers retire and have more free time.

The biggest spenders on lunch at full-service restaurants are older married couples enjoying a leisurely meal. Householders aged 45 to 64 spend 8 to 12 percent more than average on this item. Married couples without children at home (many of them empty-nesters) spend 40 percent more than average on lunch at full-service restaurants. Couples with school-aged or older children at home spend 36 to 38 percent more than average on full-service lunches, in part because their households are larger than average. Asians outspend the average on lunch at full-service restaurants by 62 percent. Households in the West, where many Asians reside, spend 18 percent more than average on this item.

Average household spending on full-service lunches declined by 12 percent between 2006 and 2010, after adjusting for inflation, then remained essentially unchanged over the ensuing two years. Behind the decline in spending was belt tightening during the Great Recession. Spending on full-service lunches may increase in the years ahead as aging boomers retire and have more free time to enjoy a leisurely meal.

Table 15.8 Lunch at full-service restaurants

Total household spending	$37,438,018,560.00
Average household spends	300.91

	AVERAGE HOUSEHOLD SPENDING	BEST CUSTOMERS (index)	BIGGEST CUSTOMERS (market share)
AGE OF HOUSEHOLDER			
Average household	**$300.91**	**100**	**100.0%**
Under age 25	155.91	52	3.4
Aged 25 to 34	277.31	92	14.9
Aged 35 to 44	309.73	103	17.9
Aged 45 to 54	337.51	112	22.2
Aged 55 to 64	324.89	108	19.8
Aged 65 to 74	308.31	102	12.3
Aged 75 or older	298.95	99	9.7

	AVERAGE HOUSEHOLD SPENDING	BEST CUSTOMERS (index)	BIGGEST CUSTOMERS (market share)
HOUSEHOLD INCOME			
Average household	**$300.91**	**100**	**100.0%**
Under $20,000	125.76	42	8.8
$20,000 to $39,999	175.28	58	13.1
$40,000 to $49,999	209.63	70	6.2
$50,000 to $69,999	294.43	98	14.1
$70,000 to $79,999	405.54	135	7.5
$80,000 to $99,999	430.72	143	12.6
$100,000 or more	607.61	202	37.8
HOUSEHOLD TYPE			
Average household	**300.91**	**100**	**100.0**
Married couples	402.66	134	65.0
Married couples, no children	421.28	140	29.2
Married couples with children	389.72	130	30.5
Oldest child under age 6	296.39	98	4.5
Oldest child aged 6 to 17	409.34	136	16.2
Oldest child aged 18 or older	415.14	138	9.7
Single parent with child under age 18	173.98	58	3.0
Single person	199.65	66	19.7
RACE AND HISPANIC ORIGIN			
Average household	**300.91**	**100**	**100.0**
Asian	486.45	162	7.0
Black	141.45	47	5.9
Hispanic	245.92	82	10.2
Non-Hispanic white and other	337.26	112	84.1
REGION			
Average household	**300.91**	**100**	**100.0**
Northeast	302.40	100	18.1
Midwest	235.93	78	17.4
South	306.18	102	37.9
West	356.05	118	26.7
EDUCATION			
Average household	**300.91**	**100**	**100.0**
Less than high school graduate	152.28	51	6.6
High school graduate	200.14	67	16.6
Some college	286.01	95	19.6
Associate's degree	299.12	99	9.8
Bachelor's degree or more	445.24	148	46.7
Bachelor's degree	418.52	139	27.7
Master's, professional, doctoral degree	490.42	163	18.9

Note: Market shares may not sum to 100.0 because of rounding and missing categories by household type. "Asian" and "black" include Hispanics and non-Hispanics who identify themselves as being of the respective race alone. "Hispanic" includes people of any race who identify themselves as Hispanic. "Other" includes people who identify themselves as non-Hispanic and as Alaska Native, American Indian, Asian (who are also included in the "Asian" row), or Native Hawaiian or other Pacific Islander, as well as non-Hispanics reporting more than one race.
Source: Calculations by New Strategist based on the Bureau of Labor Statistics' 2012 Consumer Expenditure Survey

Restaurant and Carry-Out Food on Trips

Best customers: Householders aged 45 to 74
                    Married couples without children at home
                    Married couples with school-aged or older children at home
                    Asians and non-Hispanic whites
                    Households in the West

Customer trends: Average household spending on restaurant and carry-out food on trips should grow as boomers retire
                    and devote more time and money to travel.

The biggest spenders on restaurant and carry-out meals on trips are the most avid travelers—older married couples. Householders ranging in age from 45 to 74 spend 18 to 30 percent more than average on this item. Married couples without children at home (most of them empty-nesters) spend 71 percent more than average on restaurant and carry-out meals on trips and control 36 percent of the market. Those with school-aged or older children at home spend 42 to 52 percent more. Asians, the most affluent racial and ethnic group, spend 49 percent more than average on eating out while traveling. Non-Hispanic whites spend 18 percent more. Households in the West outspend the average by 20 percent.

Average household spending on restaurant and carry-out food on trips fell 15 percent between 2006 and the overall trough-spending year of 2010, after adjusting for inflation. Behind the decline was household budget cutting in the midst of the Great Recession. Spending on restaurant meals rebounded with a 9 increase between 2010 and 2012. Spending on this item should grow in the years ahead as boomers retire and devote more time and money to travel.

Table 15.9 Restaurant and carry-out food on trips

Total household spending $31,993,574,400.00
Average household spends   257.15

	AVERAGE HOUSEHOLD SPENDING	BEST CUSTOMERS (index)	BIGGEST CUSTOMERS (market share)
AGE OF HOUSEHOLDER			
Average household	$257.15	100	100.0%
Under age 25	83.51	32	2.1
Aged 25 to 34	220.41	86	13.9
Aged 35 to 44	243.65	95	16.4
Aged 45 to 54	316.16	123	24.3
Aged 55 to 64	334.87	130	23.8
Aged 65 to 74	302.48	118	14.2
Aged 75 or older	137.46	53	5.2

	AVERAGE HOUSEHOLD SPENDING	BEST CUSTOMERS (index)	BIGGEST CUSTOMERS (market share)
HOUSEHOLD INCOME			
Average household	**$257.15**	**100**	**100.0%**
Under $20,000	64.47	25	5.3
$20,000 to $39,999	103.30	40	9.1
$40,000 to $49,999	157.93	61	5.4
$50,000 to $69,999	206.50	80	11.6
$70,000 to $79,999	312.12	121	6.8
$80,000 to $99,999	382.96	149	13.1
$100,000 or more	669.19	260	48.7
HOUSEHOLD TYPE			
Average household	**257.15**	**100**	**100.0**
Married couples	381.63	148	72.1
Married couples, no children	439.38	171	35.6
Married couples with children	358.93	140	32.8
Oldest child under age 6	267.92	104	4.8
Oldest child aged 6 to 17	390.44	152	18.1
Oldest child aged 18 or older	364.67	142	10.0
Single parent with child under age 18	114.33	44	2.3
Single person	135.77	53	15.7
RACE AND HISPANIC ORIGIN			
Average household	**257.15**	**100**	**100.0**
Asian	384.23	149	6.5
Black	106.44	41	5.2
Hispanic	132.11	51	6.4
Non-Hispanic white and other	302.84	118	88.4
REGION			
Average household	**257.15**	**100**	**100.0**
Northeast	273.45	106	19.2
Midwest	240.97	94	20.8
South	227.86	89	33.0
West	308.42	120	27.0
EDUCATION			
Average household	**257.15**	**100**	**100.0**
Less than high school graduate	58.94	23	3.0
High school graduate	135.57	53	13.1
Some college	186.36	72	14.9
Associate's degree	230.79	90	8.9
Bachelor's degree or more	489.81	190	60.1
Bachelor's degree	427.45	166	33.1
Master's, professional, doctoral degree	596.90	232	26.9

Note: Market shares may not sum to 100.0 because of rounding and missing categories by household type. "Asian" and "black" include Hispanics and non-Hispanics who identify themselves as being of the respective race alone. "Hispanic" includes people of any race who identify themselves as Hispanic. "Other" includes people who identify themselves as non-Hispanic and as Alaska Native, American Indian, Asian (who are also included in the "Asian" row), or Native Hawaiian or other Pacific Islander, as well as non-Hispanics reporting more than one race.
Source: Calculations by New Strategist based on the Bureau of Labor Statistics' 2012 Consumer Expenditure Survey

Snacks at Employer and School Cafeterias

Best customers: Householders under age 45
Married couples with adult children at home
Single parents
Asians and blacks

Customer trends: Average household spending on snacks at employer and school cafeterias may resume its decline as fewer employers provide cafeterias in an attempt to cut costs.

Not surprisingly, workers are the biggest spenders on snacks at employer and school cafeterias. Householders under age 25, most of them at school or in the workforce, spend two-and-one-half times the average on this item, and those aged 25 to 44 spend more than average. Married couples with adult children at home, the households with the most workers, spend 41 percent more than average on cafeteria snacks. Single parents, whose spending approaches average on only a few items, spend 45 percent more than average on this item. Asian households spend 70 percent more than average on snacks at employer and school cafeterias, and black households spend 17 percent more.

Average household spending on snacks at employer and school cafeterias fell a substantial 20 percent between 2006 and 2010, after adjusting for inflation, then grew by 20 percent between 2010 and 2012. Behind the spending downs and ups are the Great Recession and the economic recovery. Average household spending on snacks at employer and school cafeterias may resume its decline as employers cut costs by eliminating cafeterias.

Table 15.10 Snacks at employer and school cafeterias

Total household spending $929,387,520.00
Average household spends 7.47

AGE OF HOUSEHOLDER	AVERAGE HOUSEHOLD SPENDING	BEST CUSTOMERS (index)	BIGGEST CUSTOMERS (market share)
Average household	$7.47	100	100.0%
Under age 25	18.33	245	16.1
Aged 25 to 34	8.12	109	17.6
Aged 35 to 44	9.27	124	21.5
Aged 45 to 54	6.54	88	17.3
Aged 55 to 64	7.21	97	17.7
Aged 65 to 74	4.77	64	7.7
Aged 75 or older	0.98	13	1.3

	AVERAGE HOUSEHOLD SPENDING	BEST CUSTOMERS (index)	BIGGEST CUSTOMERS (market share)
HOUSEHOLD INCOME			
Average household	**$7.47**	**100**	**100.0%**
Under $20,000	6.04	81	17.0
$20,000 to $39,999	7.87	105	23.7
$40,000 to $49,999	5.23	70	6.2
$50,000 to $69,999	8.62	115	16.7
$70,000 to $79,999	7.64	102	5.7
$80,000 to $99,999	10.16	136	12.0
$100,000 or more	7.81	105	19.6
HOUSEHOLD TYPE			
Average household	**7.47**	**100**	**100.0**
Married couples	8.25	110	53.6
Married couples, no children	8.66	116	24.2
Married couples with children	7.89	106	24.8
Oldest child under age 6	6.16	82	3.8
Oldest child aged 6 to 17	6.96	93	11.1
Oldest child aged 18 or older	10.52	141	9.9
Single parent with child under age 18	10.82	145	7.6
Single person	6.59	88	26.2
RACE AND HISPANIC ORIGIN			
Average household	**7.47**	**100**	**100.0**
Asian	12.72	170	7.4
Black	8.76	117	14.7
Hispanic	6.56	88	11.0
Non-Hispanic white and other	7.39	99	74.3
REGION			
Average household	**7.47**	**100**	**100.0**
Northeast	8.12	109	19.6
Midwest	7.02	94	20.8
South	6.91	93	34.5
West	8.32	111	25.1
EDUCATION			
Average household	**7.47**	**100**	**100.0**
Less than high school graduate	6.41	86	11.2
High school graduate	7.65	102	25.5
Some college	8.16	109	22.5
Associate's degree	4.49	60	5.9
Bachelor's degree or more	8.18	110	34.5
Bachelor's degree	9.31	125	24.8
Master's, professional, doctoral degree	6.28	84	9.8

Note: Market shares may not sum to 100.0 because of rounding and missing categories by household type. "Asian" and "black" include Hispanics and non-Hispanics who identify themselves as being of the respective race alone. "Hispanic" includes people of any race who identify themselves as Hispanic. "Other" includes people who identify themselves as non-Hispanic and as Alaska Native, American Indian, Asian (who are also included in the "Asian" row), or Native Hawaiian or other Pacific Islander, as well as non-Hispanics reporting more than one race.
Source: Calculations by New Strategist based on the Bureau of Labor Statistics' 2012 Consumer Expenditure Survey

Snacks at Fast-Food Restaurants, Including Take-Outs, Deliveries, Concession Stands, Buffets, and Cafeterias (except Employer and School)

Best customers: Householders aged 25 to 54
Married couples with children at home
Single parents
Asians
Households in the West

Customer trends: Average household spending on snacks at fast-food restaurants should stabilize or even increase in the years ahead as the large millennial generation moves into the best-customer lifestage.

Parents are the best customers of snacks from fast-food restaurants. Householders ranging in age from 25 to 54, most with children, spend more than the average household on fast-food snacks. Married couples with children at home spend 66 percent more than average on this item. Single parents, whose spending approaches average on only a few items, spend 3 percent more than average on fast-food snacks. Asian households spend 26 percent more than average on this item, and households in the West outspend the average by 31 percent.

Average household spending on snacks from fast-food restaurants fell 12 percent between 2006 and 2010, after adjusting for inflation, then grew by 6 percent in the ensuing two years. Behind the decline was belt tightening due to the Great Recession. Spending on this item should stabilize or even increase in the years ahead as the large millennial generation moves into the best-customer lifestage.

Table 15.11 Snacks at fast-food restaurants, including take-outs, deliveries, concession stands, buffets, and cafeterias (except employer and school)

Total household spending	$14,220,748,800.00		
Average household spends	114.30		

	AVERAGE HOUSEHOLD SPENDING	BEST CUSTOMERS (index)	BIGGEST CUSTOMERS (market share)
AGE OF HOUSEHOLDER			
Average household	**$114.30**	**100**	**100.0%**
Under age 25	102.52	90	5.9
Aged 25 to 34	134.03	117	19.0
Aged 35 to 44	165.59	145	25.1
Aged 45 to 54	132.41	116	22.9
Aged 55 to 64	104.46	91	16.7
Aged 65 to 74	67.30	59	7.1
Aged 75 or older	32.58	29	2.8

	AVERAGE HOUSEHOLD SPENDING	BEST CUSTOMERS (index)	BIGGEST CUSTOMERS (market share)
HOUSEHOLD INCOME			
Average household	**$114.30**	**100**	**100.0%**
Under $20,000	41.74	37	7.7
$20,000 to $39,999	63.84	56	12.6
$40,000 to $49,999	101.45	89	7.9
$50,000 to $69,999	127.28	111	16.1
$70,000 to $79,999	139.90	122	6.8
$80,000 to $99,999	154.20	135	11.9
$100,000 or more	225.55	197	36.9
HOUSEHOLD TYPE			
Average household	**114.30**	**100**	**100.0**
Married couples	154.68	135	65.7
Married couples, no children	116.23	102	21.2
Married couples with children	190.17	166	39.1
Oldest child under age 6	162.37	142	6.5
Oldest child aged 6 to 17	223.66	196	23.3
Oldest child aged 18 or older	151.60	133	9.4
Single parent with child under age 18	117.87	103	5.4
Single person	49.41	43	12.8
RACE AND HISPANIC ORIGIN			
Average household	**114.30**	**100**	**100.0**
Asian	144.44	126	5.5
Black	63.67	56	7.0
Hispanic	111.97	98	12.3
Non-Hispanic white and other	123.65	108	81.2
REGION			
Average household	**114.30**	**100**	**100.0**
Northeast	111.95	98	17.7
Midwest	112.52	98	21.8
South	95.11	83	31.0
West	149.90	131	29.6
EDUCATION			
Average household	**114.30**	**100**	**100.0**
Less than high school graduate	56.00	49	6.4
High school graduate	81.74	72	17.8
Some college	109.59	96	19.7
Associate's degree	125.96	110	10.9
Bachelor's degree or more	160.90	141	44.4
Bachelor's degree	161.83	142	28.2
Master's, professional, doctoral degree	159.33	139	16.2

Note: Market shares may not sum to 100.0 because of rounding and missing categories by household type. "Asian" and "black" include Hispanics and non-Hispanics who identify themselves as being of the respective race alone. "Hispanic" includes people of any race who identify themselves as Hispanic. "Other" includes people who identify themselves as non-Hispanic and as Alaska Native, American Indian, Asian (who are also included in the "Asian" row), or Native Hawaiian or other Pacific Islander, as well as non-Hispanics reporting more than one race.
Source: Calculations by New Strategist based on the Bureau of Labor Statistics' 2012 Consumer Expenditure Survey

Snacks at Full-Service Restaurants

Best customers: Householders aged 25 to 34 and 45 to 54
Married couples with school-aged children
Households in the Midwest

Customer trends: Average household spending on snacks at full-service restaurants may rise in the years ahead
as casual sit-down restaurants compete with fast-food establishments for the dollars of snackers.

The biggest spenders on snacks at full-service restaurants are young adults and middle-aged married couples with children. Householders aged 25 to 34 spend 20 percent more than average on snacks at full-service restaurants, and those aged 45 to 54 spend 37 percent more. Married couples with school-aged children spend 87 percent more than average on this item. Households in the Midwest outspend the average by 27 percent.

Average household spending on snacks at full-service restaurants fell by 13 percent between 2006 and 2012, after adjusting for inflation. Behind the decline was belt tightening during the Great Recession. Spending on this item may grow in the years ahead as casual sit-down restaurants compete with fast-food establishments for the dollars of snackers.

Table 15.12 Snacks at full-service restaurants

Total household spending $3,688,934,400.00
Average household spends   29.65

AGE OF HOUSEHOLDER	AVERAGE HOUSEHOLD SPENDING	BEST CUSTOMERS (index)	BIGGEST CUSTOMERS (market share)
Average household	$29.65	100	100.0%
Under age 25	23.59	80	5.2
Aged 25 to 34	35.47	120	19.3
Aged 35 to 44	30.29	102	17.7
Aged 45 to 54	40.54	137	27.1
Aged 55 to 64	29.79	100	18.4
Aged 65 to 74	20.64	70	8.4
Aged 75 or older	10.91	37	3.6

	AVERAGE HOUSEHOLD SPENDING	BEST CUSTOMERS (index)	BIGGEST CUSTOMERS (market share)
HOUSEHOLD INCOME			
Average household	**$29.65**	**100**	**100.0%**
Under $20,000	18.68	63	13.3
$20,000 to $39,999	19.11	64	14.5
$40,000 to $49,999	21.51	73	6.4
$50,000 to $69,999	19.94	67	9.7
$70,000 to $79,999	38.15	129	7.2
$80,000 to $99,999	33.28	112	9.9
$100,000 or more	62.33	210	39.4
HOUSEHOLD TYPE			
Average household	**29.65**	**100**	**100.0**
Married couples	36.66	124	60.1
Married couples, no children	31.99	108	22.5
Married couples with children	42.15	142	33.4
Oldest child under age 6	21.34	72	3.3
Oldest child aged 6 to 17	55.52	187	22.3
Oldest child aged 18 or older	32.81	111	7.8
Single parent with child under age 18	27.69	93	4.9
Single person	18.70	63	18.7
RACE AND HISPANIC ORIGIN			
Average household	**29.65**	**100**	**100.0**
Asian	26.44	89	3.9
Black	17.22	58	7.3
Hispanic	26.72	90	11.3
Non-Hispanic white and other	32.17	108	81.4
REGION			
Average household	**29.65**	**100**	**100.0**
Northeast	28.41	96	17.3
Midwest	37.63	127	28.1
South	24.85	84	31.2
West	30.62	103	23.3
EDUCATION			
Average household	**29.65**	**100**	**100.0**
Less than high school graduate	23.33	79	10.3
High school graduate	31.14	105	26.2
Some college	22.60	76	15.7
Associate's degree	34.16	115	11.4
Bachelor's degree or more	34.20	115	36.4
Bachelor's degree	32.94	111	22.1
Master's, professional, doctoral degree	36.33	123	14.2

Note: Market shares may not sum to 100.0 because of rounding and missing categories by household type. "Asian" and "black" include Hispanics and non-Hispanics who identify themselves as being of the respective race alone. "Hispanic" includes people of any race who identify themselves as Hispanic. "Other" includes people who identify themselves as non-Hispanic and as Alaska Native, American Indian, Asian (who are also included in the "Asian" row), or Native Hawaiian or other Pacific Islander, as well as non-Hispanics reporting more than one race.
Source: Calculations by New Strategist based on the Bureau of Labor Statistics' 2012 Consumer Expenditure Survey

Snacks at Vending Machines and Mobile Vendors

Best customers: Householders under age 55
Married couples with children at home
Single parents
Hispanics and blacks
Households in the Midwest

Customer trends: Average household spending on snacks from vending machines and mobile vendors may continue
to decline as restaurants and supermarkets compete for snack dollars.

The biggest spenders on snacks from vending machines and mobile vendors are the youngest householders and parents with children. Householders under age 25 spend 57 percent more than average on this item. Householders ranging in age from 25 to 54, most of them parents, spend 21 to 33 percent more than average on snacks from vending machines and mobile vendors. Married couples with children at home spend 45 percent more than average on vending machine snacks. Single parents, whose spending approaches average on only a few items, spend 70 percent more than average on this item. Hispanic households spend 18 percent more than average on snacks from vending machines and street vendors, and black households spend 8 percent more. Households in the Midwest outspend the average by 26 percent.

Average household spending on snacks from vending machines and mobile vendors fell by 50 percent between 2006 and 2012, after adjusting for inflation. Spending on this category may continue to decline in the years ahead as fast-food and full-service restaurants, as well as grocery stores, compete for the snack dollar.

Table 15.13 Snacks at vending machines and mobile vendors

Total household spending $2,183,500,800.00
Average household spends   17.55

AGE OF HOUSEHOLDER	AVERAGE HOUSEHOLD SPENDING	BEST CUSTOMERS (index)	BIGGEST CUSTOMERS (market share)
Average household	$17.55	100	100.0%
Under age 25	27.57	157	10.3
Aged 25 to 34	23.28	133	21.4
Aged 35 to 44	21.19	121	21.0
Aged 45 to 54	21.40	122	24.1
Aged 55 to 64	15.71	90	16.4
Aged 65 to 74	5.13	29	3.5
Aged 75 or older	4.60	26	2.6

	AVERAGE HOUSEHOLD SPENDING	BEST CUSTOMERS (index)	BIGGEST CUSTOMERS (market share)
HOUSEHOLD INCOME			
Average household	**$17.55**	**100**	**100.0%**
Under $20,000	9.92	57	11.9
$20,000 to $39,999	11.57	66	14.9
$40,000 to $49,999	19.90	113	10.0
$50,000 to $69,999	22.12	126	18.2
$70,000 to $79,999	29.87	170	9.5
$80,000 to $99,999	19.72	112	9.9
$100,000 or more	23.58	134	25.2
HOUSEHOLD TYPE			
Average household	**17.55**	**100**	**100.0**
Married couples	19.09	109	52.8
Married couples, no children	12.39	71	14.7
Married couples with children	25.44	145	34.1
Oldest child under age 6	23.90	136	6.2
Oldest child aged 6 to 17	25.01	143	16.9
Oldest child aged 18 or older	27.10	154	10.9
Single parent with child under age 18	29.76	170	8.9
Single person	10.85	62	18.4
RACE AND HISPANIC ORIGIN			
Average household	**17.55**	**100**	**100.0**
Asian	18.02	103	4.5
Black	18.98	108	13.6
Hispanic	20.63	118	14.7
Non-Hispanic white and other	16.82	96	71.9
REGION			
Average household	**17.55**	**100**	**100.0**
Northeast	14.42	82	14.8
Midwest	22.04	126	27.8
South	18.67	106	39.6
West	13.74	78	17.6
EDUCATION			
Average household	**17.55**	**100**	**100.0**
Less than high school graduate	13.69	78	10.2
High school graduate	18.36	105	26.1
Some college	18.40	105	21.6
Associate's degree	15.23	87	8.6
Bachelor's degree or more	18.53	106	33.3
Bachelor's degree	19.46	111	22.1
Master's, professional, doctoral degree	16.95	97	11.2

Note: Market shares may not sum to 100.0 because of rounding and missing categories by household type. "Asian" and "black" include Hispanics and non-Hispanics who identify themselves as being of the respective race alone. "Hispanic" includes people of any race who identify themselves as Hispanic. "Other" includes people who identify themselves as non-Hispanic and as Alaska Native, American Indian, Asian (who are also included in the "Asian" row), or Native Hawaiian or other Pacific Islander, as well as non-Hispanics reporting more than one race.
Source: Calculations by New Strategist based on the Bureau of Labor Statistics' 2012 Consumer Expenditure Survey

Chapter 16.
Shelter

Household Spending on Shelter, 2000 to 2012

Americans spend more on shelter than on any other category, an average of $9,891 per household in 2012. Thirty-one percent of this total goes toward rent, which in 2012 surpassed mortgage interest as the most costly shelter subcategory. Rent is now a bigger cost than mortgage interest for the average household because fewer Americans own their home in the wake of the housing crisis and Great Recession. Mortgage interest devours 30 percent of average household spending on shelter, while 19 percent is devoted to property taxes. The average household in 2012 spent 4 percent more on shelter than in 2000, after adjusting for inflation, but 10 percent less than in 2006, the year when overall household spending peaked. Spending on mortgage interest was 11 percent lower in 2012 than in 2000, whereas spending on property taxes increased 21 percent. Spending on rent grew 16 percent over those 12 years.

The biggest spenders on shelter are the most affluent households, who tend to buy the most expensive homes. But the biggest spenders on many items, such as homeowner's insurance and property taxes, are older householders because they have the highest homeownership rate. Older homeowners are also the biggest spenders on maintenance and repair services since they are more likely than younger homeowners to hire others to do the work rather than do it themselves. Average household spending on shelter should continue to rise as the population ages

Spending on mortgage interest and rent

(average spending by households on mortgage interest and rent, 2000, 2006, 2010, and 2012; in 2012 dollars)

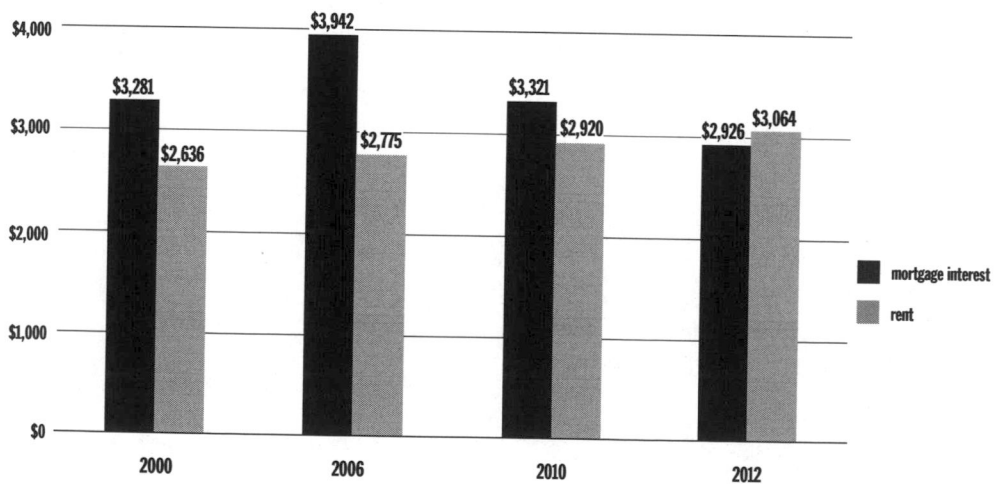

Table 16.1 Shelter spending, 2000 to 2012

(average annual household spending on shelter and percent distribution, by category, 2000 to 2012; percent change in spending and percentage point change in distribution, 2000–06, 2006–12, and 2010–12; in 2012 dollars; ranked by amount spent)

	average annual household spending (in 2012$)				percent change		
	2012	2010	2006	2000	2010–12	2006–12	2000–06
Average household spending on shelter	**$9,890.51**	**$10,330.95**	**$11,016.58**	**$9,485.43**	**–4.3%**	**–10.2%**	**16.1%**
Rent	3,064.09	2,919.98	2,775.27	2,636.37	4.9	10.4	5.3
Mortgage interest	2,926.47	3,321.38	3,941.55	3,280.55	–11.9	–25.8	20.1
Property taxes	1,835.60	1,909.82	1,877.67	1,518.03	–3.9	–2.2	23.7
Maintenance and repair services, owned home	578.78	606.61	637.31	585.21	–4.6	–9.2	8.9
Insurance, homeowner's	353.80	362.75	390.08	313.11	–2.5	–9.3	24.6
Vacation homes, owned	230.28	293.70	210.27	197.21	–21.6	9.5	6.6
Home equity loan/line of credit interest	140.37	207.15	332.19	237.30	–32.2	–57.7	40.0
Maintenance and repair materials, owned home	86.31	72.10	109.81	104.10	19.7	–21.4	5.5
Property management and security, owned home	66.84	65.67	67.40	41.32	1.8	–0.8	63.1
Maintenance and repair materials and services, rented home	22.83	35.13	84.72	24.91	–35.0	–73.1	240.2
Insurance, tenant's	14.74	12.93	10.84	11.81	14.0	36.0	–8.2

					percentage point change		
PERCENT DISTRIBUTION OF SPENDING	2012	2010	2006	2000	2010–12	2006–12	2000–06
Average household spending on shelter	**100.0%**	**100.0%**	**100.0%**	**100.0%**	–	–	–
Rent	31.0	28.3	25.2	27.8	2.7	5.8	–2.6
Mortgage interest	29.6	32.1	35.8	34.6	–2.6	–6.2	1.2
Property taxes	18.6	18.5	17.0	16.0	0.1	1.5	1.0
Maintenance and repair services, owned home	5.9	5.9	5.8	6.2	0.0	0.1	–0.4
Insurance, homeowner's	3.6	3.5	3.5	3.3	0.1	0.0	0.2
Vacation homes, owned	2.3	2.8	1.9	2.1	–0.5	0.4	–0.2
Home equity loan/line of credit interest	1.4	2.0	3.0	2.5	–0.6	–1.6	0.5
Maintenance and repair materials, owned home	0.9	0.7	1.0	1.1	0.2	–0.1	–0.1
Property management and security, owned home	0.7	0.6	0.6	0.4	0.0	0.1	0.2
Maintenance and repair services and materials, rented home	0.2	0.3	0.8	0.3	–0.1	–0.5	0.5
Insurance, tenant's	0.1	0.1	0.1	0.1	0.0	0.1	0.0

Note: The average household also spent $1,557 on mortgage principal payments and $809 on capital improvements to owned homes. These figures are not included in the shelter spending total because the Consumer Expenditure Survey considers them assets rather than expenditures. Numbers do not add to total because not all categories are shown. "–" means not applicable.
Source: Bureau of Labor Statistics, 2000, 2006, 2010, and 2012 Consumer Expenditure Surveys; calculations by New Strategist

Home Equity Loan and Line of Credit Interest

Best customers: Householders aged 45 to 74
Married couples without children at home
Married couples with school-aged or older children at home
Non-Hispanic whites

Customer trends: Average household spending on home equity loan and line of credit interest is likely to continue to decline as home values stabilize, households pay down their debt, and banks tighten lending standards.

Householders ranging in age from 45 to 74 spend more than the average household on interest for home equity loans and lines of credit. Married couples with school-aged children spend 83 percent more than average, while couples with adult children at home spend over twice the average. Married couples without children at home outspend the average by 48 percent. Non-Hispanic whites spend 20 percent more than average on interest for home equity loans and lines of credit. Households in the Northeast spend 49 percent more than average on this item, and those in the West spend 20 percent more.

Average household spending on interest for home equity loans and lines of credit increased by an enormous 40 percent between 2000 and the overall peak spending year of 2006, after adjusting for inflation. But when the housing bubble collapsed, so did spending on this item, plummeting 58 percent between 2006 and 2012 for an aggregate 41 percent decline since the beginning of the millennium. Spending on home equity interest is likely to continue to decline as home values stabilize, households pay down their debt, and banks tighten lending standards.

Table 16.2 Home equity loan and line of credit interest

Total household spending $17,464,273,920.00
Average household spends   140.37

AGE OF HOUSEHOLDER	AVERAGE HOUSEHOLD SPENDING	BEST CUSTOMERS (index)	BIGGEST CUSTOMERS (market share)
Average household	$140.37	100	100.0%
Under age 25	1.44	1	0.1
Aged 25 to 34	43.43	31	5.0
Aged 35 to 44	129.92	93	16.1
Aged 45 to 54	222.48	158	31.4
Aged 55 to 64	209.27	149	27.3
Aged 65 to 74	173.61	124	14.9
Aged 75 or older	76.14	54	5.3

	AVERAGE HOUSEHOLD SPENDING	BEST CUSTOMERS (index)	BIGGEST CUSTOMERS (market share)
HOUSEHOLD INCOME			
Average household	**$140.37**	**100**	**100.0%**
Under $20,000	33.11	24	5.0
$20,000 to $39,999	61.70	44	9.9
$40,000 to $49,999	99.56	71	6.3
$50,000 to $69,999	105.69	75	10.9
$70,000 to $79,999	179.11	128	7.1
$80,000 to $99,999	204.83	146	12.9
$100,000 or more	359.70	256	48.0
HOUSEHOLD TYPE			
Average household	**140.37**	**100**	**100.0**
Married couples	215.70	154	74.6
Married couples, no children	208.01	148	30.9
Married couples, with children	236.48	168	39.6
Oldest child under age 6	87.30	62	2.8
Oldest child aged 6 to 17	256.42	183	21.7
Oldest child aged 18 or older	299.36	213	15.0
Single parent with child under age 18	51.12	36	1.9
Single person	80.60	57	17.0
RACE AND HISPANIC ORIGIN			
Average household	**140.37**	**100**	**100.0**
Asian	149.75	107	4.6
Black	52.70	38	4.7
Hispanic	57.72	41	5.2
Non-Hispanic white and other	168.54	120	90.1
REGION			
Average household	**140.37**	**100**	**100.0**
Northeast	209.56	149	26.9
Midwest	122.45	87	19.3
South	100.50	72	26.7
West	168.44	120	27.0
EDUCATION			
Average household	**140.37**	**100**	**100.0**
Less than high school graduate	32.64	23	3.0
High school graduate	100.92	72	17.9
Some college	133.08	95	19.5
Associate's degree	135.83	97	9.6
Bachelor's degree or more	222.32	158	49.9
Bachelor's degree	189.19	135	26.9
Master's, professional, doctoral degree	279.21	199	23.1

Note: Market shares may not sum to 100.0 because of rounding and missing categories by household type. "Asian" and "black" include Hispanics and non-Hispanics who identify themselves as being of the respective race alone. "Hispanic" includes people of any race who identify themselves as Hispanic. "Other" includes people who identify themselves as non-Hispanic and as Alaska Native, American Indian, Asian (who are also included in the "Asian" row), or Native Hawaiian or other Pacific Islander, as well as non-Hispanics reporting more than one race.
Source: Calculations by New Strategist based on the Bureau of Labor Statistics' 2012 Consumer Expenditure Survey

Insurance, Homeowner's

Best customers: Householders aged 55 or older
Married couples without children at home
Married couples with school-aged or older children at home

Customer trends: Average household spending on homeowner's insurance may rise along with disaster-related insurance claims and the aging of the population.

Homeownership rises with age. This explains why householders aged 55 or older spend 28 to 34 percent more than average on homeowner's insurance. Married couples without children at home (most of them empty-nesters) spend 46 percent more than average on this item. Those with school-aged or older children at home spend 29 to 42 percent more than average on homeowner's insurance.

Average household spending on homeowner's insurance rose 25 percent between 2000 and the overall peak spending year of 2006, after adjusting for inflation, and then declined 9 percent in the ensuing six years as housing values and the homeownership rate declined. Average household spending on this item may increase as boomers age and disaster-related insurance claims boost rates.

Table 16.3 **Insurance, homeowner's**

Total household spending $44,018,380,800.00
Average household spends   353.80

AGE OF HOUSEHOLDER	AVERAGE HOUSEHOLD SPENDING	BEST CUSTOMERS (index)	BIGGEST CUSTOMERS (market share)
Average household	$353.80	100	100.0%
Under age 25	71.05	20	1.3
Aged 25 to 34	173.28	49	7.9
Aged 35 to 44	334.76	95	16.4
Aged 45 to 54	390.35	110	21.8
Aged 55 to 64	453.65	128	23.5
Aged 65 to 74	474.88	134	16.2
Aged 75 or older	465.62	132	12.9

	AVERAGE HOUSEHOLD SPENDING	BEST CUSTOMERS (index)	BIGGEST CUSTOMERS (market share)
HOUSEHOLD INCOME			
Average household	**$353.80**	**100**	**100.0%**
Under $20,000	156.43	44	9.3
$20,000 to $39,999	249.16	70	15.9
$40,000 to $49,999	325.47	92	8.1
$50,000 to $69,999	348.34	98	14.2
$70,000 to $79,999	392.62	111	6.2
$80,000 to $99,999	442.67	125	11.0
$100,000 or more	665.72	188	35.2
HOUSEHOLD TYPE			
Average household	**353.80**	**100**	**100.0**
Married couples	469.02	133	64.4
Married couples, no children	518.10	146	30.5
Married couples, with children	438.45	124	29.1
Oldest child under age 6	294.41	83	3.8
Oldest child aged 6 to 17	456.19	129	15.3
Oldest child aged 18 or older	501.69	142	10.0
Single parent with child under age 18	157.53	45	2.3
Single person	241.64	68	20.3
RACE AND HISPANIC ORIGIN			
Average household	**353.80**	**100**	**100.0**
Asian	369.89	105	4.5
Black	229.68	65	8.2
Hispanic	148.03	42	5.2
Non-Hispanic white and other	408.31	115	86.6
REGION			
Average household	**353.80**	**100**	**100.0**
Northeast	365.88	103	18.7
Midwest	364.41	103	22.8
South	376.09	106	39.6
West	296.84	84	18.9
EDUCATION			
Average household	**353.80**	**100**	**100.0**
Less than high school graduate	203.84	58	7.5
High school graduate	305.25	86	21.5
Some college	322.98	91	18.8
Associate's degree	308.37	87	8.6
Bachelor's degree or more	488.63	138	43.6
Bachelor's degree	451.73	128	25.4
Master's, professional, doctoral degree	551.99	156	18.1

Note: Market shares may not sum to 100.0 because of rounding and missing categories by household type. "Asian" and "black" include Hispanics and non-Hispanics who identify themselves as being of the respective race alone. "Hispanic" includes people of any race who identify themselves as Hispanic. "Other" includes people who identify themselves as non-Hispanic and as Alaska Native, American Indian, Asian (who are also included in the "Asian" row), or Native Hawaiian or other Pacific Islander, as well as non-Hispanics reporting more than one race.
Source: Calculations by New Strategist based on the Bureau of Labor Statistics' 2012 Consumer Expenditure Survey

Insurance, Tenant's

Best customers:
Householders under age 35
Married couples with preschoolers
Single parents
People who live alone
Blacks
Households in the West

Customer trends: Average household spending on tenant's insurance will continue to grow as renting becomes more common.

Young families and people who live alone are the best customers of tenant's insurance because they are most likely to be renters. Householders under age 35 spend 20 to 70 percent more than the average household on renter's insurance. Married couples with preschoolers spend 69 percent more than average on renter's insurance. Single parents, whose spending is below average on most items, spend 6 percent more than average on tenant's insurance, and people who live alone spend 14 percent more. Blacks outspend the average on renter's insurance by almost one-third. Households in the West spend 29 percent more than average on tenant's insurance.

Average household spending on tenant's insurance grew by a strong 36 percent between 2006 and 2012, after adjusting for inflation, after having fallen 8 percent from 2000 and 2006. Behind the increase since 2006 is the rise in the number of renters following the collapse of the housing market. Spending on this item will continue to grow as renting becomes more common.

Table 16.4 Insurance, tenant's

Total household spending $1,833,891,840.00
Average household spends   14.74

AGE OF HOUSEHOLDER	AVERAGE HOUSEHOLD SPENDING	BEST CUSTOMERS (index)	BIGGEST CUSTOMERS (market share)
Average household	$14.74	100	100.0%
Under age 25	17.71	120	7.9
Aged 25 to 34	25.00	170	27.4
Aged 35 to 44	13.36	91	15.7
Aged 45 to 54	15.29	104	20.5
Aged 55 to 64	9.89	67	12.3
Aged 65 to 74	12.38	84	10.1
Aged 75 or older	9.12	62	6.0

	AVERAGE HOUSEHOLD SPENDING	BEST CUSTOMERS (index)	BIGGEST CUSTOMERS (market share)
HOUSEHOLD INCOME			
Average household	**$14.74**	**100**	**100.0%**
Under $20,000	9.96	68	14.2
$20,000 to $39,999	16.17	110	24.7
$40,000 to $49,999	12.72	86	7.6
$50,000 to $69,999	20.82	141	20.4
$70,000 to $79,999	13.37	91	5.1
$80,000 to $99,999	16.51	112	9.9
$100,000 or more	14.23	97	18.1
HOUSEHOLD TYPE			
Average household	**14.74**	**100**	**100.0**
Married couples	12.68	86	41.8
Married couples, no children	11.82	80	16.7
Married couples, with children	15.11	103	24.1
Oldest child under age 6	24.94	169	7.7
Oldest child aged 6 to 17	15.43	105	12.4
Oldest child aged 18 or older	8.22	56	3.9
Single parent with child under age 18	15.68	106	5.6
Single person	16.87	114	34.0
RACE AND HISPANIC ORIGIN			
Average household	**14.74**	**100**	**100.0**
Asian	15.59	106	4.6
Black	19.28	131	16.4
Hispanic	9.30	63	7.9
Non-Hispanic white and other	14.93	101	76.0
REGION			
Average household	**14.74**	**100**	**100.0**
Northeast	14.34	97	17.6
Midwest	14.85	101	22.3
South	12.32	84	31.1
West	18.95	129	29.0
EDUCATION			
Average household	**14.74**	**100**	**100.0**
Less than high school graduate	8.40	57	7.4
High school graduate	11.46	78	19.4
Some college	18.28	124	25.5
Associate's degree	14.52	99	9.7
Bachelor's degree or more	17.72	120	37.9
Bachelor's degree	16.27	110	22.0
Master's, professional, doctoral degree	20.20	137	15.9

Note: Market shares may not sum to 100.0 because of rounding and missing categories by household type. "Asian" and "black" include Hispanics and non-Hispanics who identify themselves as being of the respective race alone. "Hispanic" includes people of any race who identify themselves as Hispanic. "Other" includes people who identify themselves as non-Hispanic and as Alaska Native, American Indian, Asian (who are also included in the "Asian" row), or Native Hawaiian or other Pacific Islander, as well as non-Hispanics reporting more than one race.
Source: Calculations by New Strategist based on the Bureau of Labor Statistics' 2012 Consumer Expenditure Survey

Maintenance and Repair Materials and Services, Rented Home

Best customers: Householders aged 25 to 34
Single parents
Hispanics
Households in the Northeast and West

Customer trends: Average household spending on maintenance and repair materials and services for rented homes may rise along with the number of renters.

Those most likely to rent—young adults and single parents—are the best customers of maintenance and repair materials and services for rented homes. Householders aged 25 to 34 spend 73 percent more than average on this item. Single parents spend 17 percent more than average on maintenance and repair services and materials for rented homes. Hispanic households outspend the average by 47 percent. Households in the Northeast and West spend 28 to 33 percent more than average on maintenance and repair materials and services for rented homes.

Average household spending on maintenance and repair materials and services for rented homes, which had grown sharply between 2000 and the overall peak spending year of 2006, fell by a significant 73 percent between 2006 and 2012, after adjusting for inflation. Behind the decline was the Great Recession and household belt tightening. Average household spending on maintenance and repair materials and services for rented homes may begin to rise again as renters increase in number.

Table 16.5 Maintenance and repair materials and services, rented home

Total household spending	$2,840,417,280.00
Average household spends	22.83

AGE OF HOUSEHOLDER	AVERAGE HOUSEHOLD SPENDING	BEST CUSTOMERS (index)	BIGGEST CUSTOMERS (market share)
Average household	$22.83	100	100.0%
Under age 25	17.82	78	5.1
Aged 25 to 34	39.48	173	28.0
Aged 35 to 44	24.11	106	18.3
Aged 45 to 54	20.29	89	17.6
Aged 55 to 64	17.27	76	13.8
Aged 65 to 74	26.18	115	13.8
Aged 75 or older	7.73	34	3.3

	AVERAGE HOUSEHOLD SPENDING	BEST CUSTOMERS (index)	BIGGEST CUSTOMERS (market share)
HOUSEHOLD INCOME			
Average household	**$22.83**	**100**	**100.0%**
Under $20,000	18.68	82	17.2
$20,000 to $39,999	22.25	97	22.0
$40,000 to $49,999	25.07	110	9.7
$50,000 to $69,999	29.68	130	18.8
$70,000 to $79,999	26.31	115	6.4
$80,000 to $99,999	30.34	133	11.7
$100,000 or more	17.24	76	14.1
HOUSEHOLD TYPE			
Average household	**22.83**	**100**	**100.0**
Married couples	19.52	86	41.5
Married couples, no children	22.49	99	20.5
Married couples, with children	17.88	78	18.4
Oldest child under age 6	3.80	17	0.8
Oldest child aged 6 to 17	22.29	98	11.6
Oldest child aged 18 or older	19.56	86	6.0
Single parent with child under age 18	26.76	117	6.1
Single person	20.41	89	26.5
RACE AND HISPANIC ORIGIN			
Average household	**22.83**	**100**	**100.0**
Asian	5.13	22	1.0
Black	14.15	62	7.8
Hispanic	33.49	147	18.4
Non-Hispanic white and other	22.74	100	74.8
REGION			
Average household	**22.83**	**100**	**100.0**
Northeast	30.44	133	24.1
Midwest	14.39	63	14.0
South	20.34	89	33.2
West	29.12	128	28.7
EDUCATION			
Average household	**22.83**	**100**	**100.0**
Less than high school graduate	23.45	103	13.4
High school graduate	22.62	99	24.7
Some college	28.51	125	25.7
Associate's degree	19.93	87	8.6
Bachelor's degree or more	19.91	87	27.5
Bachelor's degree	23.54	103	20.6
Master's, professional, doctoral degree	13.69	60	7.0

Note: Market shares may not sum to 100.0 because of rounding and missing categories by household type. "Asian" and "black" include Hispanics and non-Hispanics who identify themselves as being of the respective race alone. "Hispanic" includes people of any race who identify themselves as Hispanic. "Other" includes people who identify themselves as non-Hispanic and as Alaska Native, American Indian, Asian (who are also included in the "Asian" row), or Native Hawaiian or other Pacific Islander, as well as non-Hispanics reporting more than one race.
Source: Calculations by New Strategist based on the Bureau of Labor Statistics' 2012 Consumer Expenditure Survey

Maintenance and Repair Materials, Owned Home

Best customers: Householders aged 35 to 74

                              Married couples

                              Households in the Midwest

Customer trends: Average household spending on maintenance and repair materials for owned homes may rise as boomers fix up houses they are having a difficult time selling.

Middle-aged or older married couples are the best customers of maintenance and repair materials for owned homes. These do-it-yourselfers are likely to be homeowners, and they are still able to tackle home improvement tasks themselves. Householders ranging in age from 35 to 74 spend 11 to 22 percent more than average on this item. Married couples spend 50 percent more than average on maintenance and repair materials. Midwestern householders spend 19 percent more than average on maintenance and repair materials for owned homes.

Average household spending on maintenance and repair materials for owned homes, which had grown slowly between 2000 and the overall peak spending year of 2006, fell by a significant 34 percent between 2006 and 2010, after adjusting for inflation, but then climbed 20 percent over the next two years. Behind the decline was the Great Recession and household belt tightening, whereas the recent surge may signal pent-up demand for overdue repairs. Average household spending on maintenance and repair materials may continue to rise again as boomers fix up houses they are having a difficult time selling.

Table 16.6   Maintenance and repair materials, owned home

Total household spending $10,738,344,960.00

Average household spends   86.31

	AVERAGE HOUSEHOLD SPENDING	BEST CUSTOMERS (index)	BIGGEST CUSTOMERS (market share)
AGE OF HOUSEHOLDER			
Average household	$86.31	100	100.0%
Under age 25	24.78	29	1.9
Aged 25 to 34	74.50	86	14.0
Aged 35 to 44	100.65	117	20.2
Aged 45 to 54	95.60	111	21.9
Aged 55 to 64	105.04	122	22.3
Aged 65 to 74	101.70	118	14.2
Aged 75 or older	48.80	57	5.5

	AVERAGE HOUSEHOLD SPENDING	BEST CUSTOMERS (index)	BIGGEST CUSTOMERS (market share)
HOUSEHOLD INCOME			
Average household	**$86.31**	**100**	**100.0%**
Under $20,000	20.99	24	5.1
$20,000 to $39,999	58.25	67	15.2
$40,000 to $49,999	71.97	83	7.4
$50,000 to $69,999	77.45	90	13.0
$70,000 to $79,999	83.83	97	5.4
$80,000 to $99,999	184.21	213	18.8
$100,000 or more	161.73	187	35.1
HOUSEHOLD TYPE			
Average household	**86.31**	**100**	**100.0**
Married couples	129.41	150	72.8
Married couples, no children	129.02	149	31.2
Married couples, with children	127.75	148	34.8
Oldest child under age 6	120.26	139	6.4
Oldest child aged 6 to 17	130.65	151	18.0
Oldest child aged 18 or older	127.71	148	10.4
Single parent with child under age 18	40.79	47	2.5
Single person	37.03	43	12.7
RACE AND HISPANIC ORIGIN			
Average household	**86.31**	**100**	**100.0**
Asian	70.74	82	3.6
Black	28.50	33	4.2
Hispanic	52.58	61	7.6
Non-Hispanic white and other	101.44	118	88.2
REGION			
Average household	**86.31**	**100**	**100.0**
Northeast	88.30	102	18.5
Midwest	102.45	119	26.3
South	69.44	80	30.0
West	96.72	112	25.3
EDUCATION			
Average household	**86.31**	**100**	**100.0**
Less than high school graduate	45.02	52	6.8
High school graduate	83.40	97	24.1
Some college	65.62	76	15.7
Associate's degree	95.08	110	10.9
Bachelor's degree or more	116.48	135	42.6
Bachelor's degree	110.99	129	25.6
Master's, professional, doctoral degree	125.90	146	16.9

Note: Market shares may not sum to 100.0 because of rounding and missing categories by household type. "Asian" and "black" include Hispanics and non-Hispanics who identify themselves as being of the respective race alone. "Hispanic" includes people of any race who identify themselves as Hispanic. "Other" includes people who identify themselves as non-Hispanic and as Alaska Native, American Indian, Asian (who are also included in the "Asian" row), or Native Hawaiian or other Pacific Islander, as well as non-Hispanics reporting more than one race.
Source: Calculations by New Strategist based on the Bureau of Labor Statistics' 2012 Consumer Expenditure Survey

Maintenance and Repair Services, Owned Home

Best customers: Householders aged 55 or older
Married couples without children at home
Married couples with adult children at home
Non-Hispanic whites
Households in the Northeast

Customer trends: Average household spending on maintenance and repair services for owned homes is likely to resume growing as aging boomers hire others to maintain and improve their homes.

The best customers of maintenance and repair services for owned homes are householders aged 55 or older. Some are physically unable to do the work themselves, while others can better afford to hire help after the expenses of childrearing are over. Householders aged 55 or older spend 32 to 74 percent more than average on this item and control 59 percent of the market. Married couples without children at home (most of them empty-nesters) spend 47 percent more than average on maintenance and repair services for their homes, and those with adult children at home spend 42 percent more. Because they are most likely to be homeowners, non-Hispanic whites spend 15 percent more than average on this item. Households in the Northeast outspend the average by 32 percent.

Average household spending on maintenance and repair services for owned homes rose 9 percent between 2000 and 2006, after adjusting for inflation, then fell 9 percent over the ensuing six-year period. Behind the earlier increase was the aging of the baby-boom generation into the best-customer age groups. The spending decline was due to reduced homeownership and belt tightening in face of the Great Recession. Spending on home maintenance services is likely to resume growing as aging boomers continue to fill the best-customer age groups.

Table 16.7 Maintenance and repair services, owned home

Total household spending $72,009,492,480.00
Average household spends   578.78

	AVERAGE HOUSEHOLD SPENDING	BEST CUSTOMERS (index)	BIGGEST CUSTOMERS (market share)
AGE OF HOUSEHOLDER			
Average household	$578.78	100	100.0%
Under age 25	113.27	20	1.3
Aged 25 to 34	202.98	35	5.7
Aged 35 to 44	437.48	76	13.1
Aged 45 to 54	613.67	106	21.0
Aged 55 to 64	763.74	132	24.2
Aged 65 to 74	1,005.18	174	20.9
Aged 75 or older	820.95	142	13.9

	AVERAGE HOUSEHOLD SPENDING	BEST CUSTOMERS (index)	BIGGEST CUSTOMERS (market share)
HOUSEHOLD INCOME			
Average household	$578.78	100	100.0%
Under $20,000	207.28	36	7.5
$20,000 to $39,999	374.12	65	14.6
$40,000 to $49,999	501.31	87	7.7
$50,000 to $69,999	434.02	75	10.8
$70,000 to $79,999	485.31	84	4.7
$80,000 to $99,999	714.91	124	10.9
$100,000 or more	1,354.70	234	43.8
HOUSEHOLD TYPE			
Average household	578.78	100	100.0
Married couples	736.38	127	61.8
Married couples, no children	848.70	147	30.6
Married couples, with children	646.86	112	26.3
Oldest child under age 6	355.03	61	2.8
Oldest child aged 6 to 17	655.23	113	13.5
Oldest child aged 18 or older	821.46	142	10.0
Single parent with child under age 18	138.76	24	1.3
Single person	479.59	83	24.6
RACE AND HISPANIC ORIGIN			
Average household	578.78	100	100.0
Asian	531.02	92	4.0
Black	332.73	57	7.2
Hispanic	306.93	53	6.6
Non-Hispanic white and other	664.15	115	86.1
REGION			
Average household	578.78	100	100.0
Northeast	763.42	132	23.8
Midwest	521.57	90	20.0
South	508.81	88	32.7
West	602.81	104	23.5
EDUCATION			
Average household	578.78	100	100.0
Less than high school graduate	230.74	40	5.2
High school graduate	368.76	64	15.9
Some college	488.48	84	17.4
Associate's degree	533.16	92	9.1
Bachelor's degree or more	962.19	166	52.4
Bachelor's degree	878.95	152	30.3
Master's, professional, doctoral degree	1,105.13	191	22.2

Note: Market shares may not sum to 100.0 because of rounding and missing categories by household type. "Asian" and "black" include Hispanics and non-Hispanics who identify themselves as being of the respective race alone. "Hispanic" includes people of any race who identify themselves as Hispanic. "Other" includes people who identify themselves as non-Hispanic and as Alaska Native, American Indian, Asian (who are also included in the "Asian" row), or Native Hawaiian or other Pacific Islander, as well as non-Hispanics reporting more than one race.
Source: Calculations by New Strategist based on the Bureau of Labor Statistics' 2012 Consumer Expenditure Survey

Mortgage Interest

Best customers: Householders aged 35 to 54
Married couples with children at home
Asians
Households in the West

Customer trends: Average household spending on mortgage interest will continue to decline in the years ahead as a growing share of young adults rent rather than buy.

The longer people have owned their home, the less they spend on mortgage interest. This explains why older householders spend less than younger ones, and why empty-nesters spend less than couples with children. Householders aged 35 to 44 spend the most on mortgage interest—59 percent more than the average household. Householders aged 45 to 54 rank second, spending 32 percent more than average. Married couples with children under age 18 spend close to twice the average on mortgage interest, while those with adult children at home spend 60 percent more than average. Higher home prices in the West explain why households there spend 30 percent more than average on mortgage interest. Because many Asians live in the West, their spending on mortgage interest is 53 percent above average.

Average household spending on mortgage interest rose 20 percent between 2000 and the overall peak spending year of 2006, after adjusting for inflation, then dropped 26 percent over the six ensuing years as the rate of homeownership fell and both housing prices and mortgage interest rates declined. Average household spending on mortgage interest will continue to drop in the years ahead as a growing share of young adults rent rather than buy.

Table 16.8 Mortgage interest

Total household spending $364,099,691,520.00
Average household spends   2,926.47

AGE OF HOUSEHOLDER	AVERAGE HOUSEHOLD SPENDING	BEST CUSTOMERS (index)	BIGGEST CUSTOMERS (market share)
Average household	$2,926.47	100	100.0%
Under age 25	726.61	25	1.6
Aged 25 to 34	2,966.23	101	16.4
Aged 35 to 44	4,663.87	159	27.7
Aged 45 to 54	3,854.45	132	26.1
Aged 55 to 64	3,018.73	103	18.9
Aged 65 to 74	1,806.16	62	7.4
Aged 75 or older	580.45	20	1.9

	AVERAGE HOUSEHOLD SPENDING	BEST CUSTOMERS (index)	BIGGEST CUSTOMERS (market share)
HOUSEHOLD INCOME			
Average household	**$2,926.47**	**100**	**100.0%**
Under $20,000	582.80	20	4.2
$20,000 to $39,999	1,224.31	42	9.4
$40,000 to $49,999	2,026.19	69	6.1
$50,000 to $69,999	2,933.01	100	14.5
$70,000 to $79,999	3,438.47	117	6.6
$80,000 to $99,999	4,748.87	162	14.3
$100,000 or more	7,018.39	240	44.9
HOUSEHOLD TYPE			
Average household	**2,926.47**	**100**	**100.0**
Married couples	4,243.87	145	70.4
Married couples, no children	2,935.63	100	20.9
Married couples, with children	5,362.46	183	43.1
Oldest child under age 6	5,599.05	191	8.7
Oldest child aged 6 to 17	5,673.49	194	23.1
Oldest child aged 18 or older	4,685.17	160	11.3
Single parent with child under age 18	2,204.75	75	4.0
Single person	1,267.44	43	12.9
RACE AND HISPANIC ORIGIN			
Average household	**2,926.47**	**100**	**100.0**
Asian	4,477.61	153	6.6
Black	2,028.12	69	8.7
Hispanic	2,389.21	82	10.2
Non-Hispanic white and other	3,163.49	108	81.1
REGION			
Average household	**2,926.47**	**100**	**100.0**
Northeast	2,850.76	97	17.6
Midwest	2,493.67	85	18.9
South	2,692.68	92	34.3
West	3,799.39	130	29.3
EDUCATION			
Average household	**2,926.47**	**100**	**100.0**
Less than high school graduate	1,199.59	41	5.4
High school graduate	1,895.68	65	16.2
Some college	2,469.06	84	17.4
Associate's degree	3,017.04	103	10.2
Bachelor's degree or more	4,726.75	162	50.9
Bachelor's degree	4,267.78	146	29.1
Master's, professional, doctoral degree	5,514.93	188	21.9

Note: Market shares may not sum to 100.0 because of rounding and missing categories by household type. "Asian" and "black" include Hispanics and non-Hispanics who identify themselves as being of the respective race alone. "Hispanic" includes people of any race who identify themselves as Hispanic. "Other" includes people who identify themselves as non-Hispanic and as Alaska Native, American Indian, Asian (who are also included in the "Asian" row), or Native Hawaiian or other Pacific Islander, as well as non-Hispanics reporting more than one race.
Source: Calculations by New Strategist based on the Bureau of Labor Statistics' 2012 Consumer Expenditure Survey

Property Management and Security, Owned Home

Best customers: Householders aged 65 or older
Married couples without children at home
People who live alone
Asians
Households in the Northeast and West

Customer trends: Average household spending on property management and security will rise along with the aging of the population.

Older householders are the best customers of property management and security for owned homes. Householders aged 65 or older spend 87 to 96 percent more than average on this item. Married couples without children at home (most of them empty-nesters) spend 23 percent more than average on property management and security. Single-person households (many of them older) spend 41 percent more. Asians spend twice the average on these property services. Northeastern households spend 71 percent more than average on property management and security, and households in the West spend 40 percent more.

Average household spending on property management and security for owned homes increased by a substantial 63 percent between 2000 and the overall peak spending year of 2006, after adjusting for inflation, and then held essentially level over the next six years. Average household spending on this item may rise again along with the aging of the population.

Table 16.9 Property management and security, owned home

Total household spending $8,315,965,440.00
Average household spends   66.84

	AVERAGE HOUSEHOLD SPENDING	BEST CUSTOMERS (index)	BIGGEST CUSTOMERS (market share)
AGE OF HOUSEHOLDER			
Average household	$66.84	100	100.0%
Under age 25	18.19	27	1.8
Aged 25 to 34	35.88	54	8.7
Aged 35 to 44	47.33	71	12.3
Aged 45 to 54	60.09	90	17.8
Aged 55 to 64	64.32	96	17.6
Aged 65 to 74	130.68	196	23.6
Aged 75 or older	124.99	187	18.3

	AVERAGE HOUSEHOLD SPENDING	BEST CUSTOMERS (index)	BIGGEST CUSTOMERS (market share)
HOUSEHOLD INCOME			
Average household	**$66.84**	**100**	**100.0%**
Under $20,000	27.83	42	8.8
$20,000 to $39,999	50.76	76	17.1
$40,000 to $49,999	47.52	71	6.3
$50,000 to $69,999	82.22	123	17.8
$70,000 to $79,999	74.72	112	6.2
$80,000 to $99,999	71.62	107	9.5
$100,000 or more	122.69	184	34.4
HOUSEHOLD TYPE			
Average household	**66.84**	**100**	**100.0**
Married couples	63.86	96	46.4
Married couples, no children	82.45	123	25.7
Married couples, with children	54.79	82	19.3
Oldest child under age 6	74.09	111	5.1
Oldest child aged 6 to 17	46.80	70	8.3
Oldest child aged 18 or older	55.79	83	5.9
Single parent with child under age 18	12.11	18	1.0
Single person	94.07	141	41.8
RACE AND HISPANIC ORIGIN			
Average household	**66.84**	**100**	**100.0**
Asian	136.85	205	8.9
Black	41.37	62	7.8
Hispanic	35.76	54	6.7
Non-Hispanic white and other	76.32	114	85.7
REGION			
Average household	**66.84**	**100**	**100.0**
Northeast	114.04	171	30.8
Midwest	26.86	40	8.9
South	51.62	77	28.8
West	93.52	140	31.5
EDUCATION			
Average household	**66.84**	**100**	**100.0**
Less than high school graduate	14.09	21	2.8
High school graduate	42.04	63	15.7
Some college	58.09	87	17.9
Associate's degree	37.06	55	5.5
Bachelor's degree or more	123.32	185	58.2
Bachelor's degree	123.06	184	36.7
Master's, professional, doctoral degree	123.76	185	21.5

Note: Market shares may not sum to 100.0 because of rounding and missing categories by household type. "Asian" and "black" include Hispanics and non-Hispanics who identify themselves as being of the respective race alone. "Hispanic" includes people of any race who identify themselves as Hispanic. "Other" includes people who identify themselves as non-Hispanic and as Alaska Native, American Indian, Asian (who are also included in the "Asian" row), or Native Hawaiian or other Pacific Islander, as well as non-Hispanics reporting more than one race.
Source: Calculations by New Strategist based on the Bureau of Labor Statistics' 2012 Consumer Expenditure Survey

Property Taxes

Best customers: Householders aged 45 to 74
Married couples
Asians
Households in the Northeast

Customer trends: Average household spending on property taxes is likely to rise as local governments raise taxes
to pay for services.

Households in the Northeast spend 65 percent more than average on property taxes, while households in the South spend 29 percent less than average. Variations in state property tax law and rates are behind these regional differences. Married couples spend 41 percent more than average on property taxes because they are likely to be homeowners. This also explains the 17 to 27 percent greater spending of householders aged 45 to 74. Asian households, a relatively well-off demographic, spend 42 percent more on property taxes than the average household.

Average household spending on property taxes rose 26 percent between 2000 and 2010, after adjusting for inflation, but declined 4 percent in the following two years as renting became more common. Behind the earlier increase were the rise in homeownership earlier in the decade and tax hikes. Spending on property taxes is likely to rise as local governments raise taxes to pay for services.

Table 16.10 Property taxes

Total household spending $228,378,009,600.00
Average household spends   1,835.60

AGE OF HOUSEHOLDER	AVERAGE HOUSEHOLD SPENDING	BEST CUSTOMERS (index)	BIGGEST CUSTOMERS (market share)
Average household	$1,835.60	100	100.0%
Under age 25	317.96	17	1.1
Aged 25 to 34	1,024.07	56	9.0
Aged 35 to 44	1,909.53	104	18.1
Aged 45 to 54	2,331.81	127	25.1
Aged 55 to 64	2,310.18	126	23.0
Aged 65 to 74	2,147.72	117	14.1
Aged 75 or older	1,786.58	97	9.5

	AVERAGE HOUSEHOLD SPENDING	BEST CUSTOMERS (index)	BIGGEST CUSTOMERS (market share)
HOUSEHOLD INCOME			
Average household	$1,835.60	100	100.0%
Under $20,000	658.12	36	7.5
$20,000 to $39,999	1,063.31	58	13.1
$40,000 to $49,999	1,343.80	73	6.5
$50,000 to $69,999	1,560.33	85	12.3
$70,000 to $79,999	2,002.22	109	6.1
$80,000 to $99,999	2,470.88	135	11.9
$100,000 or more	4,184.37	228	42.7
HOUSEHOLD TYPE			
Average household	1,835.60	100	100.0
Married couples	2,583.12	141	68.3
Married couples, no children	2,503.92	136	28.4
Married couples, with children	2,724.67	148	34.9
Oldest child under age 6	2,269.64	124	5.6
Oldest child aged 6 to 17	2,765.16	151	17.9
Oldest child aged 18 or older	2,950.66	161	11.3
Single parent with child under age 18	840.46	46	2.4
Single person	1,122.60	61	18.2
RACE AND HISPANIC ORIGIN			
Average household	1,835.60	100	100.0
Asian	2,609.78	142	6.2
Black	911.83	50	6.2
Hispanic	1,106.77	60	7.6
Non-Hispanic white and other	2,109.28	115	86.2
REGION			
Average household	1,835.60	100	100.0
Northeast	3,033.24	165	29.8
Midwest	1,948.03	106	23.5
South	1,302.26	71	26.4
West	1,647.09	90	20.2
EDUCATION			
Average household	1,835.60	100	100.0
Less than high school graduate	871.34	47	6.2
High school graduate	1,301.71	71	17.7
Some college	1,457.59	79	16.4
Associate's degree	1,673.84	91	9.0
Bachelor's degree or more	2,954.45	161	50.8
Bachelor's degree	2,611.86	142	28.4
Master's, professional, doctoral degree	3,542.77	193	22.4

Note: Market shares may not sum to 100.0 because of rounding and missing categories by household type. "Asian" and "black" include Hispanics and non-Hispanics who identify themselves as being of the respective race alone. "Hispanic" includes people of any race who identify themselves as Hispanic. "Other" includes people who identify themselves as non-Hispanic and as Alaska Native, American Indian, Asian (who are also included in the "Asian" row), or Native Hawaiian or other Pacific Islander, as well as non-Hispanics reporting more than one race.
Source: Calculations by New Strategist based on the Bureau of Labor Statistics' 2012 Consumer Expenditure Survey

Rent

Best customers:
Householders under age 35
Married couples with preschoolers
Single parents
People who live alone
Asians, blacks, and Hispanics
Households in the Northeast and West

Customer trends:
Average household spending on rent will continue to rise as renting becomes more common.

Young adults are the best customers of rental housing. Householders under age 35 spend 77 to 83 percent more than average on this item. Married couples with preschoolers spend 19 percent more on rent than the average household. Single parents spend 50 percent more than average on rent, and single-person households (many of them young adults) spend 15 percent more. Asians and Hispanics spend 53 percent more than average on this item, and blacks spend 41 percent more. Together the minority groups account for 44 percent of the market. Households in the West, where many Asians and Hispanics reside, spend 40 percent more than average on rent. Households in the Northeast spend 23 percent more.

Average household spending on rent climbed 11 percent between 2000 and 2010, after adjusting for inflation, and another 5 percent in the ensuing two years. In fact, between 2010 and 2012, rent surpassed mortgage interest as the average household's largest shelter expense. As renting becomes more common, average household spending on rent will continue to rise.

Table 16.11 Rent

Total household spending $381,221,821,440.00
Average household spends 3,064.09

AGE OF HOUSEHOLDER	AVERAGE HOUSEHOLD SPENDING	BEST CUSTOMERS (index)	BIGGEST CUSTOMERS (market share)
Average household	$3,064.09	100	100.0%
Under age 25	5,608.42	183	12.0
Aged 25 to 34	5,430.20	177	28.6
Aged 35 to 44	3,589.59	117	20.3
Aged 45 to 54	2,594.98	85	16.8
Aged 55 to 64	1,691.61	55	10.1
Aged 65 to 74	1,430.17	47	5.6
Aged 75 or older	2,044.66	67	6.5

	AVERAGE HOUSEHOLD SPENDING	BEST CUSTOMERS (index)	BIGGEST CUSTOMERS (market share)
HOUSEHOLD INCOME			
Average household	**$3,064.09**	**100**	**100.0%**
Under $20,000	3,264.78	107	22.4
$20,000 to $39,999	3,663.36	120	26.9
$40,000 to $49,999	3,499.20	114	10.1
$50,000 to $69,999	3,442.09	112	16.2
$70,000 to $79,999	3,004.48	98	5.5
$80,000 to $99,999	2,645.99	86	7.6
$100,000 or more	1,834.61	60	11.2
HOUSEHOLD TYPE			
Average household	**3,064.09**	**100**	**100.0**
Married couples	2,156.43	70	34.2
Married couples, no children	1,649.87	54	11.2
Married couples, with children	2,500.03	82	19.2
Oldest child under age 6	3,632.53	119	5.4
Oldest child aged 6 to 17	2,563.02	84	9.9
Oldest child aged 18 or older	1,661.50	54	3.8
Single parent with child under age 18	4,598.56	150	7.9
Single person	3,536.04	115	34.3
RACE AND HISPANIC ORIGIN			
Average household	**3,064.09**	**100**	**100.0**
Asian	4,682.27	153	6.6
Black	4,308.52	141	17.7
Hispanic	4,700.68	153	19.2
Non-Hispanic white and other	2,588.16	84	63.4
REGION			
Average household	**3,064.09**	**100**	**100.0**
Northeast	3,775.72	123	22.2
Midwest	2,192.78	72	15.9
South	2,490.44	81	30.3
West	4,299.47	140	31.6
EDUCATION			
Average household	**3,064.09**	**100**	**100.0**
Less than high school graduate	3,238.61	106	13.8
High school graduate	2,809.33	92	22.9
Some college	3,150.26	103	21.2
Associate's degree	2,944.57	96	9.5
Bachelor's degree or more	3,174.39	104	32.7
Bachelor's degree	3,274.35	107	21.3
Master's, professional, doctoral degree	3,002.74	98	11.4

Note: Market shares may not sum to 100.0 because of rounding and missing categories by household type. "Asian" and "black" include Hispanics and non-Hispanics who identify themselves as being of the respective race alone. "Hispanic" includes people of any race who identify themselves as Hispanic. "Other" includes people who identify themselves as non-Hispanic and as Alaska Native, American Indian, Asian (who are also included in the "Asian" row), or Native Hawaiian or other Pacific Islander, as well as non-Hispanics reporting more than one race.
Source: Calculations by New Strategist based on the Bureau of Labor Statistics' 2012 Consumer Expenditure Survey

Vacation Homes, Owned

Best customers: Householders aged 45 to 74
High-income households
Married couples without children at home
Married couples with school-aged or older children at home
Non-Hispanic whites
Households in the Northeast

Customer trends: Average household spending on owned vacation homes may continue to fall because aging boomers have almost completely filled the best-customer lifestage and discretionary income is dwindling.

Not surprisingly, the affluent are the best customers of owned vacation homes. Households with incomes of $100,000 or more spend well over three times the average on vacation homes and control 61 percent of the market. Householders ranging in age from 45 to 74 spend 21 to 83 percent more than average on owned vacation homes. Married couples without children at home (most of them empty-nesters) spend over twice the average on this item. Married couples with school-aged children spend 38 percent more than average on vacation homes, and those with adult children at home spend 59 percent more. Non-Hispanic whites spend 22 percent more than average on this item. Households in the Northeast spend 57 percent more.

Average household spending on owned vacation homes grew by a small 7 percent between 2000 and the overall peak spending year of 2006, after adjusting for inflation, and then rose by an enormous 40 percent between 2006 and 2010, the year when overall household spending bottomed out. Spending on owned vacation homes declined a steep 22 percent between 2010 and 2012. Behind the earlier increase was the baby-boom generation's presence in the best-customer age groups. The ensuing rapid decline is in part a delayed reaction to the Great Recession. Average household spending on owned vacation homes is likely to continue to fall now that boomers have almost completely filled the best-customer age groups and the economic downturn diminishes discretionary income.

Table 16.12 Vacation homes, owned

Total household spending $28,650,516,480.00
Average household spends   230.28

AGE OF HOUSEHOLDER	AVERAGE HOUSEHOLD SPENDING	BEST CUSTOMERS (index)	BIGGEST CUSTOMERS (market share)
Average household	$230.28	100	100.0%
Under age 25	15.56	7	0.4
Aged 25 to 34	42.87	19	3.0
Aged 35 to 44	124.71	54	9.4
Aged 45 to 54	279.63	121	24.0
Aged 55 to 64	420.30	183	33.4
Aged 65 to 74	366.35	159	19.2
Aged 75 or older	248.34	108	10.5

	AVERAGE HOUSEHOLD SPENDING	BEST CUSTOMERS (index)	BIGGEST CUSTOMERS (market share)
HOUSEHOLD INCOME			
Average household	**$230.28**	**100**	**100.0%**
Under $20,000	61.70	27	5.6
$20,000 to $39,999	86.22	37	8.4
$40,000 to $49,999	116.45	51	4.5
$50,000 to $69,999	146.91	64	9.2
$70,000 to $79,999	199.40	87	4.8
$80,000 to $99,999	175.47	76	6.7
$100,000 or more	746.35	324	60.7
HOUSEHOLD TYPE			
Average household	**230.28**	**100**	**100.0**
Married couples	377.25	164	79.6
Married couples, no children	503.19	219	45.6
Married couples, with children	299.85	130	30.6
Oldest child under age 6	151.10	66	3.0
Oldest child aged 6 to 17	317.88	138	16.4
Oldest child aged 18 or older	365.65	159	11.2
Single parent with child under age 18	64.51	28	1.5
Single person	101.98	44	13.1
RACE AND HISPANIC ORIGIN			
Average household	**230.28**	**100**	**100.0**
Asian	140.24	61	2.6
Black	111.84	49	6.1
Hispanic	47.51	21	2.6
Non-Hispanic white and other	280.14	122	91.3
REGION			
Average household	**230.28**	**100**	**100.0**
Northeast	360.55	157	28.3
Midwest	193.84	84	18.7
South	192.03	83	31.1
West	225.02	98	22.0
EDUCATION			
Average household	**230.28**	**100**	**100.0**
Less than high school graduate	67.31	29	3.8
High school graduate	122.45	53	13.3
Some college	142.48	62	12.7
Associate's degree	201.96	88	8.7
Bachelor's degree or more	449.22	195	61.5
Bachelor's degree	354.84	154	30.7
Master's, professional, doctoral degree	611.32	265	30.8

Note: Market shares may not sum to 100.0 because of rounding and missing categories by household type. "Asian" and "black" include Hispanics and non-Hispanics who identify themselves as being of the respective race alone. "Hispanic" includes people of any race who identify themselves as Hispanic. "Other" includes people who identify themselves as non-Hispanic and as Alaska Native, American Indian, Asian (who are also included in the "Asian" row), or Native Hawaiian or other Pacific Islander, as well as non-Hispanics reporting more than one race.
Source: Calculations by New Strategist based on the Bureau of Labor Statistics' 2012 Consumer Expenditure Survey

Chapter 17.
Telephone

Household Spending on Telephone Service and Equipment, 2000 to 2012

American households spent an average of $1,267 on telephone service, equipment, and accessories in 2012, making the category one of the larger household expenses. Spending on this category rose 6 percent between 2000 and 2006, after adjusting for inflation, and then dropped about 1 percent over the ensuing six-year period.

Spending on residential phone service (a category that includes the miniscule amount of money households spend on pay phones) fell 64 percent between 2000 and 2012 as prices for long-distance service plummeted and a growing number of households abandoned landline service altogether. Not surprisingly, average household spending on cellular phone service surged, more than quintupling between 2000 and 2012 as cell phones became the norm. The average household now spends well more than twice as much on cell phone service as on landline service, but the sum of spending on these two services remained nearly identical over those years.

Spending on cell versus landline phone service

(average spending by households on cell and landline phone service, 2000, 2006, 2010, and 2012; in 2012 dollars)

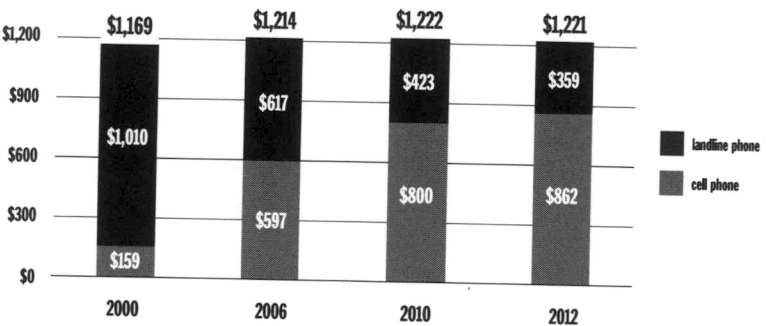

Table 17.1 Telephone spending, 2000 to 2012

(average annual household spending on telephone service and equipment and percent distribution, by category, 2000 to 2012; percent change and percentage point change in spending, 2000–06, 2006–12, and 2010–12; in 2012 dollars; ranked by amount spent)

	average annual household spending (in 2012$)				percent change		
	2012	2010	2006	2000	2010–12	2006–12	2000–06
Average household spending on telephone service and equipment	**$1,267.07**	**$1,274.75**	**$1,277.33**	**$1,210.51**	**–0.6%**	**–0.8%**	**5.5%**
Cellular phone service	861.97	799.88	596.51	159.32	7.8	44.5	274.4
Residential telephone service and pay phones	358.54	422.54	617.20	1,009.65	–15.1	–41.9	–38.9
Telephones and answering machines	27.92	34.68	39.52	41.55	–19.5	–29.3	–4.9
Voice over IP services	9.64	9.08	–	–	6.2	–	–
Phone cards	9.00	8.57	24.10	–	5.0	–62.7	–

					percentage point change		
PERCENT DISTRIBUTION OF SPENDING	2012	2010	2006	2000	2010–12	2006–12	2000–06
Average household spending on telephone service and equipment	**100.0%**	**100.0%**	**100.0%**	**100.0%**	**–**	**–**	**–**
Cellular phone service	68.0	62.7	46.7	13.2	5.3	21.3	33.5
Residential telephone service and pay phones	28.3	33.1	48.3	83.4	–4.9	–20.0	–35.1
Telephones and answering machines	2.2	2.7	3.1	3.4	–0.5	–0.9	–0.3
Voice over IP services	0.8	0.7	–	–	0.0	–	–
Phone cards	0.7	0.7	1.9	–	0.0	–1.2	–

Note: Percentage point change calculations are based on unrounded figures. "–" means not applicable or data are unavailable.
Source: Bureau of Labor Statistics, 2000, 2006, 2010, and 2012 Consumer Expenditure Surveys; calculations by New Strategist

Cellular Phone Service

Best customers:
Householders aged 25 to 54
Married couples with children at home
Single parents
Hispanics

Customer trends:
Average household spending on cell phone service should stabilize as cell phones become the norm and prices fall.

Parents are the biggest spenders on cell phone service. Couples with children at home spend 45 percent more than average on this item, the number peaking at 55 percent among those with adult children at home. Single parents, whose spending approaches average on only a few items, spend 4 percent more than average on cell phone service. Householders ranging in age from 25 to 54, most with children at home, spend 18 to 29 percent more than average on cell phone service and control 67 percent of the market. Hispanics spend 15 percent more than average on cellular phone service.

Average household spending on cell phone service soared between 2000 and 2012, rising from just $159 to $862 (in 2012 dollars). Behind the enormous increase is the growing share of households that spend on cell service, more than tripling from 21 percent during the average quarter of 2000 to 68 percent in 2012. The rapid growth in spending on cell service may soon lead to market saturation. Already the average annual rate of increase in average household spending on this item fell from 46 percent before the peak spending year of 2006 to just 7 percent since then. Not only is cell service becoming the norm, but cutthroat competition is lowering service prices.

Table 17.2 Cellular phone service

Total household spending	$107,242,859,520.00
Average household spends	861.97

	AVERAGE HOUSEHOLD SPENDING	BEST CUSTOMERS (index)	BIGGEST CUSTOMERS (market share)
AGE OF HOUSEHOLDER			
Average household	$861.97	100	100.0%
Under age 25	674.65	78	5.1
Aged 25 to 34	1,013.80	118	19.0
Aged 35 to 44	1,114.40	129	22.4
Aged 45 to 54	1,097.31	127	25.2
Aged 55 to 64	843.65	98	17.9
Aged 65 to 74	542.41	63	7.6
Aged 75 or older	239.98	28	2.7

	AVERAGE HOUSEHOLD SPENDING	BEST CUSTOMERS (index)	BIGGEST CUSTOMERS (market share)
HOUSEHOLD INCOME			
Average household	**$861.97**	**100**	**100.0%**
Under $20,000	381.98	44	9.3
$20,000 to $39,999	679.06	79	17.8
$40,000 to $49,999	842.40	98	8.6
$50,000 to $69,999	1,007.45	117	16.9
$70,000 to $79,999	1,078.50	125	7.0
$80,000 to $99,999	1,145.48	133	11.7
$100,000 or more	1,320.40	153	28.7
HOUSEHOLD TYPE			
Average household	**861.97**	**100**	**100.0**
Married couples	1,071.12	124	60.4
Married couples, no children	811.01	94	19.6
Married couples with children	1,249.25	145	34.1
Oldest child under age 6	1,099.41	128	5.8
Oldest child aged 6 to 17	1,255.28	146	17.3
Oldest child aged 18 or older	1,336.00	155	10.9
Single parent with child under age 18	894.97	104	5.4
Single person	448.05	52	15.4
RACE AND HISPANIC ORIGIN			
Average household	**861.97**	**100**	**100.0**
Asian	924.19	107	4.6
Black	822.64	95	12.0
Hispanic	988.31	115	14.4
Non-Hispanic white and other	847.20	98	73.8
REGION			
Average household	**861.97**	**100**	**100.0**
Northeast	836.91	97	17.5
Midwest	819.49	95	21.1
South	880.95	102	38.1
West	892.47	104	23.3
EDUCATION			
Average household	**861.97**	**100**	**100.0**
Less than high school graduate	616.22	71	9.3
High school graduate	790.58	92	22.9
Some college	841.51	98	20.1
Associate's degree	1,054.75	122	12.1
Bachelor's degree or more	973.15	113	35.6
Bachelor's degree	956.89	111	22.1
Master's, professional, doctoral degree	1,001.08	116	13.5

Note: Market shares may not sum to 100.0 because of rounding and missing categories by household type. "Asian" and "black" include Hispanics and non-Hispanics who identify themselves as being of the respective race alone. "Hispanic" includes people of any race who identify themselves as Hispanic. "Other" includes people who identify themselves as non-Hispanic and as Alaska Native, American Indian, Asian (who are also included in the "Asian" row), or Native Hawaiian or other Pacific Islander, as well as non-Hispanics reporting more than one race.
Source: Calculations by New Strategist based on the Bureau of Labor Statistics' 2012 Consumer Expenditure Survey

Phone Cards

Best customers:
   Householders under age 45
   Married couples with children at home
   Hispanics, Asians, and blacks
   Households in the Northeast
   Householders without a high school diploma

Customer trends:
   Average household spending on phone cards is unlikely to grow despite the increase in the Asian
   and Hispanic populations, as international rate plans and Internet telephony eat into
   the phone card business.

The biggest spenders on phone cards are households making international calls, many of them immigrants to the United States. Because immigrants tend to be younger adults, householders under age 45 spend more than others on this item—from 24 to 53 percent more than the average household. Black and Asian households spend, respectively, 40 and 81 percent more than average on phone cards, but Hispanic households spend three times the average. Minorities control 63 percent of the market. Households in the Northeast outspend the average by 57 percent. Householders without a high school diploma (many of them recent Hispanic immigrants) spend over twice the average on this item.

Phone cards were not included in the Consumer Expenditure Survey until recently, which limits the analysis of spending trends. A modest 5 percent gain in average household spending on phone cards between the overall spending trough year of 2010 and 2012 comes on the heels of a 64 percent decline between 2006 and 2010. Spending on phone cards is declining largely because international rate plans and Internet telephony are eating into the phone card business. Despite the growth of minority populations, average household spending on phone cards is unlikely to rise in the years ahead.

Table 17.3 Phone cards

Total household spending $1,119,744,000.00
Average household spends   9.00

AGE OF HOUSEHOLDER	AVERAGE HOUSEHOLD SPENDING	BEST CUSTOMERS (index)	BIGGEST CUSTOMERS (market share)
Average household	$9.00	100	100.0%
Under age 25	13.62	151	9.9
Aged 25 to 34	11.14	124	20.0
Aged 35 to 44	13.77	153	26.6
Aged 45 to 54	9.07	101	19.9
Aged 55 to 64	5.82	65	11.8
Aged 65 to 74	6.74	75	9.0
Aged 75 or older	2.46	27	2.7

	AVERAGE HOUSEHOLD SPENDING	BEST CUSTOMERS (index)	BIGGEST CUSTOMERS (market share)
HOUSEHOLD INCOME			
Average household	**$9.00**	**100**	**100.0%**
Under $20,000	9.90	110	23.1
$20,000 to $39,999	10.22	114	25.6
$40,000 to $49,999	9.93	110	9.8
$50,000 to $69,999	9.47	105	15.2
$70,000 to $79,999	6.69	74	4.1
$80,000 to $99,999	9.16	102	9.0
$100,000 or more	6.31	70	13.1
HOUSEHOLD TYPE			
Average household	**9.00**	**100**	**100.0**
Married couples	9.74	108	52.6
Married couples, no children	5.01	56	11.6
Married couples with children	12.88	143	33.6
Oldest child under age 6	18.76	208	9.5
Oldest child aged 6 to 17	11.01	122	14.5
Oldest child aged 18 or older	12.23	136	9.6
Single parent with child under age 18	6.62	74	3.9
Single person	6.06	67	20.0
RACE AND HISPANIC ORIGIN			
Average household	**9.00**	**100**	**100.0**
Asian	16.33	181	7.9
Black	12.63	140	17.6
Hispanic	26.75	297	37.3
Non-Hispanic white and other	5.53	61	46.1
REGION			
Average household	**9.00**	**100**	**100.0**
Northeast	14.12	157	28.3
Midwest	7.76	86	19.1
South	8.20	91	33.9
West	7.43	83	18.6
EDUCATION			
Average household	**9.00**	**100**	**100.0**
Less than high school graduate	20.63	229	29.9
High school graduate	8.27	92	22.9
Some college	7.44	83	17.0
Associate's degree	8.12	90	8.9
Bachelor's degree or more	6.05	67	21.2
Bachelor's degree	5.01	56	11.1
Master's, professional, doctoral degree	7.85	87	10.1

Note: Market shares may not sum to 100.0 because of rounding and missing categories by household type. "Asian" and "black" include Hispanics and non-Hispanics who identify themselves as being of the respective race alone. "Hispanic" includes people of any race who identify themselves as Hispanic. "Other" includes people who identify themselves as non-Hispanic and as Alaska Native, American Indian, Asian (who are also included in the "Asian" row), or Native Hawaiian or other Pacific Islander, as well as non-Hispanics reporting more than one race.
Source: Calculations by New Strategist based on the Bureau of Labor Statistics' 2012 Consumer Expenditure Survey

Residential Telephone Service

Best customers: Householders aged 55 or older
Married couples without children at home
Married couples with adult children at home
Households in the Northeast

Customer trends: Average household spending on residential telephone service will continue to decline as cell phones replace residential phones, especially among the younger generations.

Householder aged 55 or older spend far more than average on residential telephone service, while those under age 45 spend less because many use cell phones only. Householders aged 55 or older spend 28 to 46 percent more than average on residential phone service. Married couples without children at home, most of them older empty-nesters, spend 30 percent more than average on this item. Married couples with adult children at home are the biggest spenders on residential phone service because their households are larger than average. These households spend 43 percent more than average on this item. Households in the Northeast spend 18 percent more than average on residential phone service.

Average household spending on residential phone service fell by a stunning 64 percent between 2000 and 2012, after adjusting for inflation. Substitution of cell phones for residential phones is behind the decline. As a consequence of the drop in spending, residential phone service in 2007 relinquished its position as the number-one expenditure in the information and consumer electronics category, tumbling to third place behind cell phone service and cable and satellite television service. Average household spending on residential telephone service will continue to decline as cell phones replace residential phones, especially among the younger generations.

Table 17.4 Residential telephone service

Total household spending $44,608,112,640.00
Average household spends 358.54

AGE OF HOUSEHOLDER	AVERAGE HOUSEHOLD SPENDING	BEST CUSTOMERS (index)	BIGGEST CUSTOMERS (market share)
Average household	$358.54	100	100.0%
Under age 25	73.91	21	1.4
Aged 25 to 34	159.47	44	7.2
Aged 35 to 44	316.05	88	15.3
Aged 45 to 54	398.21	111	22.0
Aged 55 to 64	460.47	128	23.5
Aged 65 to 74	486.92	136	16.4
Aged 75 or older	524.68	146	14.3

	AVERAGE HOUSEHOLD SPENDING	BEST CUSTOMERS (index)	BIGGEST CUSTOMERS (market share)
HOUSEHOLD INCOME			
Average household	**$358.54**	**100**	**100.0%**
Under $20,000	268.11	75	15.7
$20,000 to $39,999	315.34	88	19.8
$40,000 to $49,999	345.63	96	8.5
$50,000 to $69,999	357.87	100	14.4
$70,000 to $79,999	358.61	100	5.6
$80,000 to $99,999	425.76	119	10.5
$100,000 or more	487.06	136	25.4
HOUSEHOLD TYPE			
Average household	**358.54**	**100**	**100.0**
Married couples	434.38	121	58.8
Married couples, no children	465.28	130	27.1
Married couples with children	409.38	114	26.8
Oldest child under age 6	244.73	68	3.1
Oldest child aged 6 to 17	410.78	115	13.6
Oldest child aged 18 or older	513.48	143	10.1
Single parent with child under age 18	243.61	68	3.6
Single person	276.13	77	22.9
RACE AND HISPANIC ORIGIN			
Average household	**358.54**	**100**	**100.0**
Asian	283.91	79	3.4
Black	369.20	103	12.9
Hispanic	249.34	70	8.7
Non-Hispanic white and other	374.81	105	78.5
REGION			
Average household	**358.54**	**100**	**100.0**
Northeast	429.99	120	21.6
Midwest	332.27	93	20.5
South	364.21	102	37.8
West	317.75	89	20.0
EDUCATION			
Average household	**358.54**	**100**	**100.0**
Less than high school graduate	323.53	90	11.8
High school graduate	354.02	99	24.6
Some college	329.46	92	18.9
Associate's degree	360.76	101	9.9
Bachelor's degree or more	394.89	110	34.7
Bachelor's degree	364.64	102	20.3
Master's, professional, doctoral degree	446.83	125	14.5

Note: Market shares may not sum to 100.0 because of rounding and missing categories by household type. "Asian" and "black" include Hispanics and non-Hispanics who identify themselves as being of the respective race alone. "Hispanic" includes people of any race who identify themselves as Hispanic. "Other" includes people who identify themselves as non-Hispanic and as Alaska Native, American Indian, Asian (who are also included in the "Asian" row), or Native Hawaiian or other Pacific Islander, as well as non-Hispanics reporting more than one race.
Source: Calculations by New Strategist based on the Bureau of Labor Statistics' 2012 Consumer Expenditure Survey

Telephones, Answering Machines, and Accessories

Best customers: Householders aged 25 to 34 and 45 to 54
Married couples with school-aged or older children at home
Hispanics and Asians
Households in the West

Customer trends: Average household spending on telephones, answering machines, and accessories may rise
in the years ahead if phone giveaways end.

Householders aged 25 to 34 spend 67 percent more than average on telephones, answering machines, and accessories, and those aged 45 to 54 spend 31 percent more. Married couples with school-aged children at home spend 40 percent more than average on these items. Asian households spend 22 percent more than average on telephones, answering machines, and accessories, and Hispanics spend three-quarters more than average. Households in the West outspend the average by 59 percent.

Average household spending on telephones, answering machines, and accessories fell 33 percent between 2000 and 2012, after adjusting for inflation. Average household spending on telephones may rise in the years ahead if phone giveaways end.

Table 17.5 Telephones, answering machines, and accessories

Total household spending $3,473,694,720.00
Average household spends 27.92

AGE OF HOUSEHOLDER	AVERAGE HOUSEHOLD SPENDING	BEST CUSTOMERS (index)	BIGGEST CUSTOMERS (market share)
Average household	$27.92	100	100.0%
Under age 25	26.60	95	6.2
Aged 25 to 34	46.56	167	27.0
Aged 35 to 44	29.26	105	18.2
Aged 45 to 54	36.68	131	26.0
Aged 55 to 64	20.40	73	13.4
Aged 65 to 74	14.86	53	6.4
Aged 75 or older	6.13	22	2.1

	AVERAGE HOUSEHOLD SPENDING	BEST CUSTOMERS (index)	BIGGEST CUSTOMERS (market share)
HOUSEHOLD INCOME			
Average household	$27.92	100	100.0%
Under $20,000	9.84	35	7.4
$20,000 to $39,999	12.26	44	9.9
$40,000 to $49,999	28.47	102	9.0
$50,000 to $69,999	23.33	84	12.1
$70,000 to $79,999	40.19	144	8.0
$80,000 to $99,999	49.63	178	15.7
$100,000 or more	56.77	203	38.1
HOUSEHOLD TYPE			
Average household	27.92	100	100.0
Married couples	30.57	109	53.2
Married couples, no children	24.07	86	18.0
Married couples with children	34.51	124	29.1
Oldest child under age 6	24.99	90	4.1
Oldest child aged 6 to 17	39.06	140	16.6
Oldest child aged 18 or older	32.85	118	8.3
Single parent with child under age 18	24.57	88	4.6
Single person	11.40	41	12.1
RACE AND HISPANIC ORIGIN			
Average household	27.92	100	100.0
Asian	34.16	122	5.3
Black	16.84	60	7.6
Hispanic	48.70	174	21.9
Non-Hispanic white and other	26.70	96	71.8
REGION			
Average household	27.92	100	100.0
Northeast	15.19	54	9.8
Midwest	22.47	80	17.8
South	27.45	98	36.6
West	44.52	159	35.9
EDUCATION			
Average household	27.92	100	100.0
Less than high school graduate	12.86	46	6.0
High school graduate	21.26	76	19.0
Some college	30.10	108	22.2
Associate's degree	18.95	68	6.7
Bachelor's degree or more	40.08	144	45.3
Bachelor's degree	37.65	135	26.9
Master's, professional, doctoral degree	44.21	158	18.4

Note: Market shares may not sum to 100.0 because of rounding and missing categories by household type. "Asian" and "black" include Hispanics and non-Hispanics who identify themselves as being of the respective race alone. "Hispanic" includes people of any race who identify themselves as Hispanic. "Other" includes people who identify themselves as non-Hispanic and as Alaska Native, American Indian, Asian (who are also included in the "Asian" row), or Native Hawaiian or other Pacific Islander, as well as non-Hispanics reporting more than one race.
Source: Calculations by New Strategist based on the Bureau of Labor Statistics' 2012 Consumer Expenditure Survey

Voice over IP Services

Best customers: Householders aged 45 to 54 and 65 to 74
Married couples with school-aged or older children at home
Asians
Households in the Northeast

Customer trends: Average household spending on voice over IP services will rise as computer-savvy younger generations replace older ones.

Asian households and parents are the best customers of voice over IP services. This explains why householders aged 45 to 54—many of whom are parents—spend 52 percent more than the average household on this item. Married couples with adult children at home spend 40 percent more than average on Internet telephony, whereas those with school-aged children spend 89 percent more than the average amount. Asian households spend over two-and-one-half times the average on Internet telephony. Northeastern households spend nearly three times the average on voice over IP services.

The category voice over IP services was added to the Consumer Expenditure Survey in 2007 and thus no comparable data exist from 2000. Average household spending on Internet telephony grew 6 percent from 2010 to 2012, after adjusting for inflation. Average household spending on this item is likely to rise in the years ahead as a broader demographic becomes comfortable with using their computers for voice (and video) communication.

Table 17.6 Voice over IP services

Total household spending $1,199,370,240.00
Average household spends   9.64

	AVERAGE HOUSEHOLD SPENDING	BEST CUSTOMERS (index)	BIGGEST CUSTOMERS (market share)
AGE OF HOUSEHOLDER			
Average household	**$9.64**	**100**	**100.0%**
Under age 25	1.73	18	1.2
Aged 25 to 34	5.31	55	8.9
Aged 35 to 44	10.88	113	19.6
Aged 45 to 54	14.70	152	30.2
Aged 55 to 64	8.64	90	16.4
Aged 65 to 74	12.42	129	15.5
Aged 75 or older	8.16	85	8.3

	AVERAGE HOUSEHOLD SPENDING	BEST CUSTOMERS (index)	BIGGEST CUSTOMERS (market share)
HOUSEHOLD INCOME			
Average household	**$9.64**	**100**	**100.0%**
Under $20,000	5.39	56	11.8
$20,000 to $39,999	5.95	62	13.9
$40,000 to $49,999	9.39	97	8.6
$50,000 to $69,999	8.26	86	12.4
$70,000 to $79,999	8.06	84	4.7
$80,000 to $99,999	11.75	122	10.8
$100,000 or more	19.54	203	37.9
HOUSEHOLD TYPE			
Average household	**9.64**	**100**	**100.0**
Married couples	13.21	137	66.6
Married couples, no children	10.02	104	21.7
Married couples with children	15.17	157	37.0
Oldest child under age 6	9.90	103	4.7
Oldest child aged 6 to 17	18.22	189	22.5
Oldest child aged 18 or older	13.45	140	9.8
Single parent with child under age 18	5.37	56	2.9
Single person	5.59	58	17.2
RACE AND HISPANIC ORIGIN			
Average household	**9.64**	**100**	**100.0**
Asian	25.52	265	11.5
Black	6.97	72	9.1
Hispanic	7.55	78	9.8
Non-Hispanic white and other	10.42	108	81.1
REGION			
Average household	**9.64**	**100**	**100.0**
Northeast	27.66	287	51.8
Midwest	1.93	20	4.4
South	7.50	78	29.0
West	6.35	66	14.8
EDUCATION			
Average household	**9.64**	**100**	**100.0**
Less than high school graduate	6.15	64	8.3
High school graduate	8.92	93	23.1
Some college	7.40	77	15.8
Associate's degree	6.76	70	6.9
Bachelor's degree or more	14.03	146	45.9
Bachelor's degree	12.90	134	26.7
Master's, professional, doctoral degree	15.98	166	19.2

Note: Market shares may not sum to 100.0 because of rounding and missing categories by household type. "Asian" and "black" include Hispanics and non-Hispanics who identify themselves as being of the respective race alone. "Hispanic" includes people of any race who identify themselves as Hispanic. "Other" includes people who identify themselves as non-Hispanic and as Alaska Native, American Indian, Asian (who are also included in the "Asian" row), or Native Hawaiian or other Pacific Islander, as well as non-Hispanics reporting more than one race.
Source: Calculations by New Strategist based on the Bureau of Labor Statistics' 2012 Consumer Expenditure Survey

Chapter 18.
Tobacco Products

Household Spending on Tobacco Products, 2000 to 2012

The average American household spent $332 on cigarettes, other tobacco products, and smoking accessories in 2012. Spending on this category declined 22 percent between 2000 and 2012 despite hefty price increases as consumers cut back on tobacco use.

Average household spending on cigarettes fell 24 percent between 2000 and 2012, after adjusting for inflation, despite rising prices. Behind the decline was the shrinking percentage of people who smoke cigarettes. Spending on other tobacco products (such as cigars and chewing tobacco) was essentially the same in 2012 as in 2000. Spending on smoking accessories was also essentially unchanged over the 12 years, despite ups and downs during the time period.

Spending on tobacco products

(average spending by households on tobacco products, 2000, 2006, 2010, and 2012; in 2012 dollars)

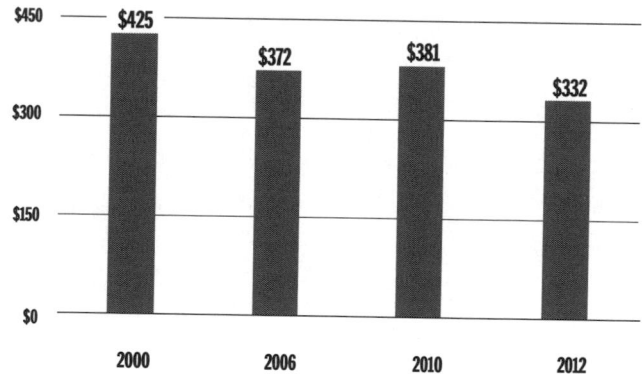

Table 18.1 Tobacco spending, 2000 to 2012

(average annual household spending on tobacco products and percent distribution, by category, 2000 to 2012; percent change in spending and percentage point change in distribution, 2000–06, 2006–12, and 2010–12; in 2012 dollars; ranked by amount spent)

	average annual household spending (in 2012$)				percent change		
	2012	2010	2006	2000	2010–12	2006–12	2000–06
Average annual household spending on tobacco products	$331.72	$381.21	$372.21	$424.82	–13.0%	–10.9%	–12.4%
Cigarettes	298.75	349.36	344.16	391.86	–14.5	–13.2	–12.2
Tobacco products other than cigarettes	30.30	27.92	25.64	30.03	8.5	18.2	–14.6
Smoking accessories	2.68	3.94	2.41	2.71	–31.9	11.0	–10.8

					percentage point change		
					2010–12	2006–12	2000–06
PERCENT DISTRIBUTION OF SPENDING							
Average annual household spending on tobacco products	100.0%	100.0%	100.0%	100.0%	–	–	–
Cigarettes	90.1	91.6	92.5	92.2	–1.6	–2.4	0.2
Tobacco products other than cigarettes	9.1	7.3	6.9	7.1	1.8	2.2	–0.2
Smoking accessories	0.8	1.0	0.6	0.6	–0.2	0.2	0.0

Note: Numbers may not add to total because not all categories are shown. Percentage point change calculations are based on unrounded figures. "–" means not applicable.
Source: Bureau of Labor Statistics, 2000, 2006, 2010, and 2012 Consumer Expenditure Surveys; calculations by New Strategist

Cigarettes

Best customers: Householders aged 45 to 54
Married couples with adult children at home
Non-Hispanic whites
High school graduate or less education

Customer trends: Average household spending on cigarettes should decline as smoking becomes less common.

Cigarettes account for 90 percent of household spending on tobacco products and smoking accessories. Householders aged 45 to 54 spend one-third more than average on cigarettes. Married couples with adult children at home spend 22 percent more than average on this item, in part because their households are the largest. Non-Hispanic whites spend 12 percent more than average. Householders with only a high school diploma or less education spend 36 to 42 percent more than average on cigarettes.

Average household spending on cigarettes fell 22 percent between 2000 and 2012, after adjusting for inflation. Behind the decline is the smaller proportion of smokers in the population as health warnings and higher prices drive consumers away. Spending on cigarettes is likely to continue to decline as smoking becomes less common.

Table 18.2 Cigarettes

Total household spending $37,169,280,000.00
Average household spends 298.75

AGE OF HOUSEHOLDER	AVERAGE HOUSEHOLD SPENDING	BEST CUSTOMERS (index)	BIGGEST CUSTOMERS (market share)
Average household	$298.75	100	100.0%
Under age 25	241.55	81	5.3
Aged 25 to 34	313.19	105	16.9
Aged 35 to 44	316.06	106	18.4
Aged 45 to 54	396.92	133	26.3
Aged 55 to 64	339.08	113	20.8
Aged 65 to 74	221.71	74	8.9
Aged 75 or older	103.16	35	3.4

	AVERAGE HOUSEHOLD SPENDING	BEST CUSTOMERS (index)	BIGGEST CUSTOMERS (market share)
HOUSEHOLD INCOME			
Average household	**$298.75**	**100**	**100.0%**
Under $20,000	276.42	93	19.5
$20,000 to $39,999	335.95	112	25.3
$40,000 to $49,999	327.83	110	9.7
$50,000 to $69,999	332.33	111	16.1
$70,000 to $79,999	340.29	114	6.4
$80,000 to $99,999	316.67	106	9.4
$100,000 or more	218.56	73	13.7
HOUSEHOLD TYPE			
Average household	**298.75**	**100**	**100.0**
Married couples	272.17	91	44.2
Married couples, no children	238.33	80	16.6
Married couples, with children	277.13	93	21.8
Oldest child under age 6	176.50	59	2.7
Oldest child aged 6 to 17	263.32	88	10.5
Oldest child aged 18 or older	365.49	122	8.6
Single parent with child under age 18	230.91	77	4.1
Single person	231.54	78	23.0
RACE AND HISPANIC ORIGIN			
Average household	**298.75**	**100**	**100.0**
Asian	153.95	52	2.2
Black	229.70	77	9.7
Hispanic	146.96	49	6.2
Non-Hispanic white and other	335.44	112	84.3
REGION			
Average household	**298.75**	**100**	**100.0**
Northeast	329.16	110	19.9
Midwest	309.23	104	22.9
South	325.77	109	40.6
West	219.41	73	16.5
EDUCATION			
Average household	**298.75**	**100**	**100.0**
Less than high school graduate	407.10	136	17.8
High school graduate	424.01	142	35.4
Some college	335.94	112	23.2
Associate's degree	293.03	98	9.7
Bachelor's degree or more	132.36	44	14.0
Bachelor's degree	153.61	51	10.2
Master's, professional, doctoral degree	95.87	32	3.7

Note: Market shares may not sum to 100.0 because of rounding and missing categories by household type. "Asian" and "black" include Hispanics and non-Hispanics who identify themselves as being of the respective race alone. "Hispanic" includes people of any race who identify themselves as Hispanic. "Other" includes people who identify themselves as non-Hispanic and as Alaska Native, American Indian, Asian (who are also included in the "Asian" row), or Native Hawaiian or other Pacific Islander, as well as non-Hispanics reporting more than one race.
Source: Calculations by New Strategist based on the Bureau of Labor Statistics' 2012 Consumer Expenditure Survey

Smoking Accessories

Smoking accessories include cigarette papers, pipes, lighters, and so on. Householders aged 25 to 44 spend 29 to 43 percent more than average on smoking accessories. Married couples with children at home spend 43 percent more than average on smoking accessories, the figure peaking among those with school-aged children at 64 percent. Single parents, whose spending approaches average on only a few items, spend 3 percent more than average on smoking accessories. Households in the Midwest outspend the average on this item by 29 percent.

Average household spending on smoking accessories grew 45 percent between 2000 and 2010, after adjusting for inflation, and then declined 32 percent in the ensuing two years, for an overall level performance. Spending on this item should decline as smoking becomes less common.

Table 18.3 Smoking accessories

Total household spending	$333,434,880.00
Average household spends	2.68

AGE OF HOUSEHOLDER	AVERAGE HOUSEHOLD SPENDING	BEST CUSTOMERS (index)	BIGGEST CUSTOMERS (market share)
Average household	$2.68	100	100.0%
Under age 25	0.63	24	1.5
Aged 25 to 34	3.82	143	23.0
Aged 35 to 44	3.46	129	22.4
Aged 45 to 54	2.57	96	19.0
Aged 55 to 64	3.15	118	21.5
Aged 65 to 74	1.75	65	7.9
Aged 75 or older	1.18	44	4.3

	AVERAGE HOUSEHOLD SPENDING	BEST CUSTOMERS (index)	BIGGEST CUSTOMERS (market share)
HOUSEHOLD INCOME			
Average household	**$2.68**	**100**	**100.0%**
Under $20,000	1.10	41	8.6
$20,000 to $39,999	3.28	122	27.6
$40,000 to $49,999	2.15	80	7.1
$50,000 to $69,999	1.83	68	9.9
$70,000 to $79,999	6.02	225	12.5
$80,000 to $99,999	2.61	97	8.6
$100,000 or more	3.53	132	24.7
HOUSEHOLD TYPE			
Average household	**2.68**	**100**	**100.0**
Married couples	3.25	121	58.9
Married couples, no children	2.41	90	18.7
Married couples, with children	3.82	143	33.5
Oldest child under age 6	3.22	120	5.5
Oldest child aged 6 to 17	4.40	164	19.5
Oldest child aged 18 or older	3.22	120	8.5
Single parent with child under age 18	2.76	103	5.4
Single person	1.24	46	13.7
RACE AND HISPANIC ORIGIN			
Average household	**2.68**	**100**	**100.0**
Asian	1.61	60	2.6
Black	1.40	52	6.6
Hispanic	1.77	66	8.3
Non-Hispanic white and other	3.04	113	85.1
REGION			
Average household	**2.68**	**100**	**100.0**
Northeast	2.27	85	15.3
Midwest	3.47	129	28.7
South	2.56	96	35.6
West	2.40	90	20.2
EDUCATION			
Average household	**2.68**	**100**	**100.0**
Less than high school graduate	2.97	111	14.5
High school graduate	2.08	78	19.4
Some college	3.40	127	26.1
Associate's degree	2.27	85	8.4
Bachelor's degree or more	2.66	99	31.3
Bachelor's degree	2.83	106	21.0
Master's, professional, doctoral degree	2.39	89	10.4

Note: Market shares may not sum to 100.0 because of rounding and missing categories by household type. "Asian" and "black" include Hispanics and non-Hispanics who identify themselves as being of the respective race alone. "Hispanic" includes people of any race who identify themselves as Hispanic. "Other" includes people who identify themselves as non-Hispanic and as Alaska Native, American Indian, Asian (who are also included in the "Asian" row), or Native Hawaiian or other Pacific Islander, as well as non-Hispanics reporting more than one race.
Source: Calculations by New Strategist based on the Bureau of Labor Statistics' 2012 Consumer Expenditure Survey

Tobacco Products Other than Cigarettes

Best customers: Householders aged 35 to 44
Married couples without children at home
Married couples with preschoolers
Non-Hispanic whites
Households in the South

Customer trends: Average household spending on tobacco products other than cigarettes should decline
as tobacco use becomes less common.

Cigars, chewing tobacco, and pipe tobacco are some of the products included in this category. Householders aged 35 to 44 spend 28 percent more than average on noncigarette tobacco products. Married couples without children at home spend 36 percent more than average on this item, while those with preschoolers spend 87 percent more. Non-Hispanic whites spend 21 percent more than average on tobacco products other than cigarettes. Southern households spend 19 percent more than average on this item.

Average household spending on noncigarette tobacco products declined 15 percent between 2000 and 2006, after adjusting for inflation, and then grew 18 percent during the ensuing six-year period, for an overall level performance. Spending on this item is likely to decline as tobacco use becomes less common.

Table 18.4 Tobacco products other than cigarettes

Total household spending $3,769,804,800.00
Average household spends   30.30

AGE OF HOUSEHOLDER	AVERAGE HOUSEHOLD SPENDING	BEST CUSTOMERS (index)	BIGGEST CUSTOMERS (market share)
Average household	$30.30	100	100.0%
Under age 25	19.46	64	4.2
Aged 25 to 34	33.94	112	18.1
Aged 35 to 44	38.93	128	22.3
Aged 45 to 54	31.40	104	20.5
Aged 55 to 64	29.95	99	18.1
Aged 65 to 74	25.84	85	10.3
Aged 75 or older	20.12	66	6.5

	AVERAGE HOUSEHOLD SPENDING	BEST CUSTOMERS (index)	BIGGEST CUSTOMERS (market share)
HOUSEHOLD INCOME			
Average household	$30.30	100	100.0%
Under $20,000	22.43	74	15.6
$20,000 to $39,999	19.57	65	14.6
$40,000 to $49,999	33.93	112	9.9
$50,000 to $69,999	40.32	133	19.2
$70,000 to $79,999	37.63	124	6.9
$80,000 to $99,999	37.60	124	10.9
$100,000 or more	36.97	122	22.8
HOUSEHOLD TYPE			
Average household	30.30	100	100.0
Married couples	38.90	128	62.4
Married couples, no children	41.35	136	28.4
Married couples, with children	36.41	120	28.3
Oldest child under age 6	56.74	187	8.5
Oldest child aged 6 to 17	30.91	102	12.1
Oldest child aged 18 or older	32.55	107	7.6
Single parent with child under age 18	13.87	46	2.4
Single person	18.36	61	18.0
RACE AND HISPANIC ORIGIN			
Average household	30.30	100	100.0
Asian	5.92	20	0.8
Black	14.11	47	5.9
Hispanic	8.64	29	3.6
Non-Hispanic white and other	36.58	121	90.6
REGION			
Average household	30.30	100	100.0
Northeast	22.93	76	13.7
Midwest	28.69	95	21.0
South	36.11	119	44.4
West	28.17	93	20.9
EDUCATION			
Average household	30.30	100	100.0
Less than high school graduate	31.57	104	13.6
High school graduate	33.56	111	27.6
Some college	34.17	113	23.2
Associate's degree	40.62	134	13.2
Bachelor's degree or more	21.43	71	22.3
Bachelor's degree	25.33	84	16.7
Master's, professional, doctoral degree	14.74	49	5.6

Note: Market shares may not sum to 100.0 because of rounding and missing categories by household type. "Asian" and "black" include Hispanics and non-Hispanics who identify themselves as being of the respective race alone. "Hispanic" includes people of any race who identify themselves as Hispanic. "Other" includes people who identify themselves as non-Hispanic and as Alaska Native, American Indian, Asian (who are also included in the "Asian" row), or Native Hawaiian or other Pacific Islander, as well as non-Hispanics reporting more than one race.
Source: Calculations by New Strategist based on the Bureau of Labor Statistics' 2012 Consumer Expenditure Survey

Chapter 19.
Transportation

Household Spending on Transportation, 2000 to 2012

Transportation is one of the biggest expenses of American households, second only to spending on shelter. In 2012, the average household spent $8,998 on transportation. This was 9 percent less than in 2000, after adjusting for inflation, but 11 percent more than in 2010—the year when overall household spending bottomed out. Almost one-third of transportation spending is devoted to gasoline, making it the largest transportation expense category.

Until 2010, when transportation spending reached its lowest ebb in recent memory, sharply reduced spending on new and used cars and trucks was behind the trend in spending on transportation. Even as car dealers pushed no-interest loans on new vehicles and the price of used vehicles fell, spending on car purchases slipped substantially, down 47 percent for new cars and 50 percent for used cars between 2000 and 2010. Spending on new trucks, a category that includes sport utility vehicles, fell 31 percent during those years, and spending on used trucks fell 29 percent. This downward trend came to an end, and between 2010 and 2012 all four of these categories posted spending gains.

Spending on leased vehicles showed no such turnaround, plummeting 63 (cars) to 71 percent (trucks) between 2000 and 2012, after adjusting for inflation. Spending on vehicle insurance and vehicle maintenance were stable in comparison, falling by a small 2 percent between 2000 and 2012. Spending on transportation may resume its decline in the next few years once households satisfy their pent-up demand for vehicles.

Spending on transportation

(average spending by households on transportation, 2000, 2006, 2010, and 2012; in 2012 dollars)

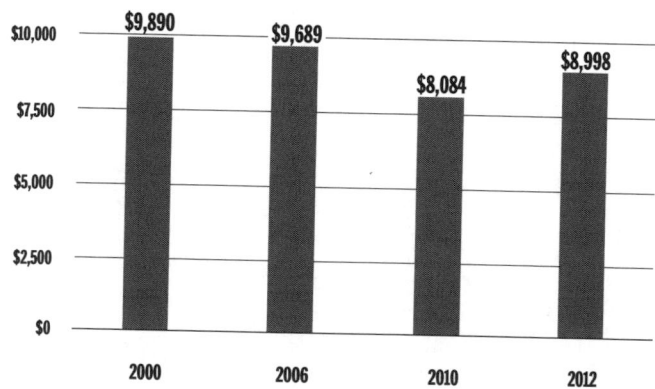

Table 19.1 Transportation spending, 2000 to 2012

(average annual household spending on transportation and percent change, by category, 2000 to 2012; percent and percentage point change in spending, 2000–06, 2006–12, and 2010–12; in 2012 dollars; ranked by amount spent)

	average annual household spending (in 2012$)				percent change		
	2012	2010	2006	2000	2010–12	2006–12	2000–06
Average household spending on transportation	**$8,998.12**	**$8,083.55**	**$9,689.30**	**$9,889.55**	**11.3%**	**−7.1%**	**−2.0%**
Gasoline and motor oil (including on trips)	2,755.78	2,245.14	2,536.76	1,721.62	22.7	8.6	47.3
Vehicle insurance	1,017.94	1,063.88	1,009.52	1,037.48	−4.3	0.8	−2.7
Trucks, new	937.38	636.40	1,065.10	917.23	47.3	−12.0	16.1
Vehicle maintenance and repair (including tires, oil changes)	814.27	828.94	784.04	831.66	−1.8	3.9	−5.7
Cars, used	763.60	668.22	857.49	1,348.30	14.3	−10.9	−36.4
Trucks, used	752.44	719.50	928.64	1,011.44	4.6	−19.0	−8.2
Cars, new	701.22	647.37	982.70	1,222.66	8.3	−28.6	−19.6
Airline fares*	352.53	342.52	381.06	365.35	2.9	−7.5	4.3
Vehicle finance charges	223.36	255.89	339.16	437.64	−12.7	−34.1	−22.5
Tires (purchased, replaced, installed)	146.53	146.78	117.68	116.30	−0.2	24.5	1.2
Vehicle registration, inspection, driver's license	134.74	138.22	126.45	135.26	−2.5	6.6	−6.5
Car lease payments	87.25	94.41	140.22	233.11	−7.6	−37.8	−39.9
Oil change, lube, and oil filters	80.21	76.74	76.16	78.33	4.5	5.3	−2.8
Parking fees and tolls, excluding residence	77.92	70.45	61.41	58.39	10.6	26.9	5.2
Mass transit, intracity fares	71.99	70.41	58.18	63.21	2.2	23.7	−8.0
Truck lease payments	57.41	63.22	124.33	197.93	−9.2	−53.8	−37.2
Ship fares*	56.53	41.42	62.66	48.77	36.5	−9.8	28.5
Motorcycles (new and used)	54.94	53.86	61.91	47.77	2.0	−11.3	29.6
Rented vehicles (including rentals on trips)	36.23	38.73	42.70	59.93	−6.4	−15.1	−28.8
Automobile service clubs	20.09	19.62	18.55	11.13	2.4	8.3	66.6
Train fares, intercity*	18.88	16.50	18.55	28.16	14.4	1.8	−34.1
Local transportation on trips*	17.81	17.75	14.95	22.56	0.3	19.1	−33.7
Bus fares, intercity*	11.96	10.89	12.90	21.47	9.9	−7.3	−39.9
Taxi fares and limousine service in home town	11.36	17.30	15.80	16.20	−34.3	−28.1	−2.5
Towing charges	4.37	4.20	5.82	6.24	4.0	−24.9	−6.7

PERCENT DISTRIBUTION OF SPENDING	average annual household spending (in 2012$)				percentage point change		
	2012	2010	2006	2000	2010–12	2006–12	2000–06
Average household spending on transportation	**100.0%**	**100.0%**	**100.0%**	**100.0%**	–	–	–
Gasoline and motor oil (including on trips)	30.6	27.8	26.2	17.4	2.9	4.4	8.8
Vehicle insurance	11.3	13.2	10.4	10.5	–1.8	0.9	–0.1
Trucks, new	10.4	7.9	11.0	9.3	2.5	–0.6	1.7
Vehicle maintenance and repair (including tires, oil changes)	9.0	10.3	8.1	8.4	–1.2	1.0	–0.3
Cars, used	8.5	8.3	8.8	13.6	0.2	–0.4	–4.8
Trucks, used	8.4	8.9	9.6	10.2	–0.5	–1.2	–0.6
Cars, new	7.8	8.0	10.1	12.4	–0.2	–2.3	–2.2
Airline fares	3.9	4.2	3.9	3.7	–0.3	0.0	0.2
Vehicle finance charges	2.5	3.2	3.5	4.4	–0.7	–1.0	–0.9
Tires (purchased, replaced, installed)	1.6	1.8	1.2	1.2	–0.2	0.4	0.0
Vehicle registration, inspection, driver's license	1.5	1.7	1.3	1.4	–0.2	0.2	–0.1
Car lease payments	1.0	1.2	1.4	2.4	–0.2	–0.5	–0.9
Oil change, lube, and oil filters	0.9	0.9	0.8	0.8	–0.1	0.1	0.0
Parking fees and tolls, excluding residence	0.9	0.9	0.6	0.6	0.0	0.2	0.0
Mass transit, intracity fares	0.8	0.9	0.6	0.6	–0.1	0.2	0.0
Truck lease payments	0.6	0.8	1.3	2.0	–0.1	–0.6	–0.7
Ship fares	0.6	0.5	0.6	0.5	0.1	0.0	0.2
Motorcycles (new and used)	0.6	0.7	0.6	0.5	–0.1	0.0	0.2
Rented vehicles (including rentals on trips)	0.4	0.5	0.4	0.6	–0.1	0.0	–0.2
Automobile service clubs	0.2	0.2	0.2	0.1	0.0	0.0	0.1
Train fares, intercity	0.2	0.2	0.2	0.3	0.0	0.0	–0.1
Local transportation on trips	0.2	0.2	0.2	0.2	0.0	0.0	–0.1
Bus fares, intercity	0.1	0.1	0.1	0.2	0.0	0.0	–0.1
Taxi fares and limousine service in home town	0.1	0.2	0.2	0.2	–0.1	0.0	0.0
Towing charges	0.0	0.1	0.1	0.1	0.0	0.0	0.0

* Detailed spending table for category appears in Chapter 20: Travel.

Note: Numbers do not add to total because spending on tires and oil changes is also included in vehicle maintenance and repairs and because some subcategories are not shown. Percentage point change calculations are based on unrounded figures. "–" means not applicable.

Source: Bureau of Labor Statistics, 2000, 2006, 2010, and 2012 Consumer Expenditure Surveys; calculations by New Strategist

Automobile Service Clubs

Best customers: Householders aged 55 or older
    Married couples without children at home
    Married couples with adult children at home
    Asians and non-Hispanic whites
    Households in the Northeast and West

Customer trends: Average household spending on automobile service clubs should continue to rise as the population ages.

Older householders are the best customers of automobile service club memberships. Householders aged 55 or older spend 30 to 60 percent more than average on this item and control 58 percent of the market. Married couples without children at home (most of them empty-nesters) spend 61 percent more than average, while those with adult children at home spend 57 percent more. Asians and non-Hispanic whites dominate spending in this category and control 87 percent of the market. Households in the Northeast and West spend, respectively, 56 and 27 percent more than the average household on automobile service club fees.

Average household spending on automobile service club memberships rose sharply between 2000 and 2006, after adjusting for inflation, and continued to rise between 2006 and 2012. It is one of the few items on which spending rose even through the overall household spending trough year of 2010. Spending on this item is likely to continue to rise along with the aging of the population.

Table 19.2 **Automobile service clubs**

Total household spending $2,499,517,440.00
Average household spends   20.09

	AVERAGE HOUSEHOLD SPENDING	BEST CUSTOMERS (index)	BIGGEST CUSTOMERS (market share)
AGE OF HOUSEHOLDER			
Average household	$20.09	100	100.0%
Under age 25	4.77	24	1.6
Aged 25 to 34	8.82	44	7.1
Aged 35 to 44	13.01	65	11.2
Aged 45 to 54	21.98	109	21.7
Aged 55 to 64	29.07	145	26.5
Aged 65 to 74	32.15	160	19.3
Aged 75 or older	26.04	130	12.7

	AVERAGE HOUSEHOLD SPENDING	BEST CUSTOMERS (index)	BIGGEST CUSTOMERS (market share)
HOUSEHOLD INCOME			
Average household	**$20.09**	**100**	**100.0%**
Under $20,000	9.34	46	9.8
$20,000 to $39,999	12.54	62	14.1
$40,000 to $49,999	15.50	77	6.8
$50,000 to $69,999	18.45	92	13.3
$70,000 to $79,999	27.20	135	7.6
$80,000 to $99,999	30.48	152	13.4
$100,000 or more	37.66	187	35.1
HOUSEHOLD TYPE			
Average household	**20.09**	**100**	**100.0**
Married couples	26.78	133	64.7
Married couples, no children	32.37	161	33.6
Married couples with children	21.92	109	25.7
Oldest child under age 6	15.18	76	3.4
Oldest child aged 6 to 17	18.85	94	11.2
Oldest child aged 18 or older	31.46	157	11.0
Single parent with child under age 18	8.91	44	2.3
Single person	13.94	69	20.6
RACE AND HISPANIC ORIGIN			
Average household	**20.09**	**100**	**100.0**
Asian	21.27	106	4.6
Black	9.80	49	6.1
Hispanic	11.32	56	7.1
Non-Hispanic white and other	23.27	116	86.9
REGION			
Average household	**20.09**	**100**	**100.0**
Northeast	31.37	156	28.2
Midwest	14.80	74	16.3
South	14.43	72	26.8
West	25.60	127	28.7
EDUCATION			
Average household	**20.09**	**100**	**100.0**
Less than high school graduate	11.01	55	7.2
High school graduate	14.53	72	18.0
Some college	17.32	86	17.8
Associate's degree	18.42	92	9.1
Bachelor's degree or more	30.58	152	48.0
Bachelor's degree	25.71	128	25.5
Master's, professional, doctoral degree	38.93	194	22.5

Note: Market shares may not sum to 100.0 because of rounding and missing categories by household type. "Asian" and "black" include Hispanics and non-Hispanics who identify themselves as being of the respective race alone. "Hispanic" includes people of any race who identify themselves as Hispanic. "Other" includes people who identify themselves as non-Hispanic and as Alaska Native, American Indian, Asian (who are also included in the "Asian" row), or Native Hawaiian or other Pacific Islander, as well as non-Hispanics reporting more than one race.
Source: Calculations by New Strategist based on the Bureau of Labor Statistics' 2012 Consumer Expenditure Survey

Car Lease Payments

Best customers: Householders aged 35 to 44
Married couples with school-aged or older children at home
Households in the Northeast

Customer trends: Average household spending on car lease payments will fluctuate depending on vehicle financing incentives.

The best customers of car leasing are married couples with adult children at home. These households spend 81 percent more than average on car lease payments. Married couples with school-aged children outspend the average on this item by 37 percent. Householders aged 35 to 44 spend 17 percent more than average on car lease payments. Households in the Northeast spend more than double the average.

Average household spending on car lease payments fell 63 percent between 2000 and 2012, after adjusting for inflation. Behind the spending drop was the shift to buying rather than leasing as car dealers offered no-interest loans and other purchasing incentives. Spending on leasing will fluctuate depending on dealer incentives.

Table 19.3 **Car lease payments**

Total household spending $10,855,296,000.00
Average household spends 87.25

AGE OF HOUSEHOLDER	AVERAGE HOUSEHOLD SPENDING	BEST CUSTOMERS (index)	BIGGEST CUSTOMERS (market share)
Average household	$87.25	100	100.0%
Under age 25	54.27	62	4.1
Aged 25 to 34	83.50	96	15.5
Aged 35 to 44	102.27	117	20.3
Aged 45 to 54	94.20	108	21.4
Aged 55 to 64	95.09	109	19.9
Aged 65 to 74	84.57	97	11.7
Aged 75 or older	63.48	73	7.1

	AVERAGE HOUSEHOLD SPENDING	BEST CUSTOMERS (index)	BIGGEST CUSTOMERS (market share)
HOUSEHOLD INCOME			
Average household	**$87.25**	**100**	**100.0%**
Under $20,000	23.70	27	5.7
$20,000 to $39,999	46.30	53	12.0
$40,000 to $49,999	51.00	58	5.2
$50,000 to $69,999	92.74	106	15.4
$70,000 to $79,999	56.97	65	3.6
$80,000 to $99,999	104.60	120	10.6
$100,000 or more	221.72	254	47.6
HOUSEHOLD TYPE			
Average household	**87.25**	**100**	**100.0**
Married couples	111.65	128	62.2
Married couples, no children	96.88	111	23.1
Married couples with children	125.58	144	33.8
Oldest child under age 6	90.89	104	4.8
Oldest child aged 6 to 17	119.69	137	16.3
Oldest child aged 18 or older	157.93	181	12.8
Single parent with child under age 18	81.37	93	4.9
Single person	57.09	65	19.4
RACE AND HISPANIC ORIGIN			
Average household	**87.25**	**100**	**100.0**
Asian	51.88	59	2.6
Black	70.33	81	10.1
Hispanic	82.76	95	11.9
Non-Hispanic white and other	91.00	104	78.3
REGION			
Average household	**87.25**	**100**	**100.0**
Northeast	178.78	205	37.0
Midwest	65.87	75	16.7
South	66.61	76	28.4
West	69.08	79	17.8
EDUCATION			
Average household	**87.25**	**100**	**100.0**
Less than high school graduate	37.39	43	5.6
High school graduate	67.99	78	19.4
Some college	60.31	69	14.2
Associate's degree	108.18	124	12.2
Bachelor's degree or more	134.17	154	48.5
Bachelor's degree	105.38	121	24.1
Master's, professional, doctoral degree	183.61	210	24.4

Note: Market shares may not sum to 100.0 because of rounding and missing categories by household type. "Asian" and "black" include Hispanics and non-Hispanics who identify themselves as being of the respective race alone. "Hispanic" includes people of any race who identify themselves as Hispanic. "Other" includes people who identify themselves as non-Hispanic and as Alaska Native, American Indian, Asian (who are also included in the "Asian" row), or Native Hawaiian or other Pacific Islander, as well as non-Hispanics reporting more than one race.
Source: Calculations by New Strategist based on the Bureau of Labor Statistics' 2012 Consumer Expenditure Survey

Cars, New

Best customers: Householders aged 65 to 74
Married couples without children at home
Married couples with preschoolers or adult children at home
Asians
Households in the West

Customer trends: Average household spending on new cars should rise as downsizing boomers replace
their gas-guzzling sport utility vehicles and minivans.

The best customers of new cars are older householders and married couples who are replacing minivans and SUVs (considered trucks). Householders aged 65 to 74 spend 24 percent more than average on new cars. Married couples without children at home, most of them older empty-nesters, spend 70 percent more than average. Couples with adult children at home, a demographic with more earners and drivers than average, spend 84 percent more than the average household on new cars. Couples with preschoolers outspend the average by 26 percent. Asians spend 33 percent more than average on new cars. Households in the West spend 24 percent more.

Average household spending on new cars fell 47 percent between 2000 and 2010, after adjusting for inflation, then increased 8 percent in the ensuing two years. Behind the decline was the growing popularity of sport utility vehicles (considered trucks) during the earlier part of the time period and the Great Recession in the latter part. Spending on new cars should rise as aging boomers downsize and search for greater fuel efficiency in their vehicles.

Table 19.4 Cars, new

| Total household spending | $87,242,987,520.00 |
| Average household spends | 701.22 |

AGE OF HOUSEHOLDER	AVERAGE HOUSEHOLD SPENDING	BEST CUSTOMERS (index)	BIGGEST CUSTOMERS (market share)
Average household	$701.22	100	100.0%
Under age 25	563.75	80	5.3
Aged 25 to 34	771.50	110	17.8
Aged 35 to 44	568.73	81	14.1
Aged 45 to 54	752.72	107	21.2
Aged 55 to 64	752.45	107	19.6
Aged 65 to 74	868.24	124	14.9
Aged 75 or older	506.35	72	7.1

	AVERAGE HOUSEHOLD SPENDING	BEST CUSTOMERS (index)	BIGGEST CUSTOMERS (market share)
HOUSEHOLD INCOME			
Average household	**$701.22**	**100**	**100.0%**
Under $20,000	211.97	30	6.4
$20,000 to $39,999	272.11	39	8.7
$40,000 to $49,999	448.33	64	5.7
$50,000 to $69,999	714.57	102	14.7
$70,000 to $79,999	1,056.18	151	8.4
$80,000 to $99,999	1,222.90	174	15.4
$100,000 or more	1,525.13	217	40.7
HOUSEHOLD TYPE			
Average household	**701.22**	**100**	**100.0**
Married couples	1,044.92	149	72.4
Married couples, no children	1,192.62	170	35.5
Married couples with children	936.90	134	31.4
Oldest child under age 6	880.53	126	5.7
Oldest child aged 6 to 17	748.81	107	12.7
Oldest child aged 18 or older	1,290.42	184	13.0
Single parent with child under age 18	377.17	54	2.8
Single person	337.28	48	14.3
RACE AND HISPANIC ORIGIN			
Average household	**701.22**	**100**	**100.0**
Asian	936.08	133	5.8
Black	515.17	73	9.2
Hispanic	419.49	60	7.5
Non-Hispanic white and other	777.89	111	83.3
REGION			
Average household	**701.22**	**100**	**100.0**
Northeast	643.78	92	16.6
Midwest	610.66	87	19.3
South	683.12	97	36.3
West	866.23	124	27.8
EDUCATION			
Average household	**701.22**	**100**	**100.0**
Less than high school graduate	304.55	43	5.7
High school graduate	524.70	75	18.7
Some college	699.69	100	20.5
Associate's degree	779.26	111	11.0
Bachelor's degree or more	981.56	140	44.1
Bachelor's degree	986.78	141	28.0
Master's, professional, doctoral degree	972.60	139	16.1

Note: Market shares may not sum to 100.0 because of rounding and missing categories by household type. "Asian" and "black" include Hispanics and non-Hispanics who identify themselves as being of the respective race alone. "Hispanic" includes people of any race who identify themselves as Hispanic. "Other" includes people who identify themselves as non-Hispanic and as Alaska Native, American Indian, Asian (who are also included in the "Asian" row), or Native Hawaiian or other Pacific Islander, as well as non-Hispanics reporting more than one race.
Source: Calculations by New Strategist based on the Bureau of Labor Statistics' 2012 Consumer Expenditure Survey

Cars, Used

Best customers: Householders under age 45
Married couples with children at home
Single parents
Asians, blacks, and Hispanics

Customer trends: Average household spending on used cars may climb as boomers downsize and the large millennial
generation fills the best-customer age group.

The best customers of used cars are young adults and married couples with children at home. Householders under age 45 spend 22 to 47 percent more than average on used cars. Married couples with children at home spend one-third more than average on this item, the figure peaking among those with adult children at two-thirds more than average. Single parents, whose spending approaches average on only a few items, spend 4 percent more than average on used cars. Asians, blacks, and Hispanics spend 4, 8, and 29 percent more than average on used cars, respectively. Together they account for 34 percent of the used-car market.

Average household spending on used cars fell 50 percent between 2000 and 2010, after adjusting for inflation, then climbed 14 percent in the ensuing two years. Behind the decline was the growing popularity of sport utility vehicles (considered trucks), as well as dealer incentives to buy new rather than used vehicles. Average household spending on used cars may climb as boomers downsize and the large millennial generation fills the best-customer age group.

Table 19.5 **Cars, used**

Total household spending $95,004,057,600.00
Average household spends 763.60

AGE OF HOUSEHOLDER	AVERAGE HOUSEHOLD SPENDING	BEST CUSTOMERS (index)	BIGGEST CUSTOMERS (market share)
Average household	$763.60	100	100.0%
Under age 25	933.38	122	8.0
Aged 25 to 34	1,124.98	147	23.8
Aged 35 to 44	948.46	124	21.6
Aged 45 to 54	880.28	115	22.8
Aged 55 to 64	540.54	71	13.0
Aged 65 to 74	446.79	59	7.1
Aged 75 or older	295.70	39	3.8

	AVERAGE HOUSEHOLD SPENDING	BEST CUSTOMERS (index)	BIGGEST CUSTOMERS (market share)
HOUSEHOLD INCOME			
Average household	**$763.60**	**100**	**100.0%**
Under $20,000	278.03	36	7.7
$20,000 to $39,999	504.95	66	14.9
$40,000 to $49,999	518.10	68	6.0
$50,000 to $69,999	897.09	117	17.0
$70,000 to $79,999	740.04	97	5.4
$80,000 to $99,999	1,305.99	171	15.1
$100,000 or more	1,385.12	181	34.0
HOUSEHOLD TYPE			
Average household	**763.60**	**100**	**100.0**
Married couples	937.97	123	59.7
Married couples, no children	666.54	87	18.2
Married couples with children	1,012.74	133	31.2
Oldest child under age 6	928.80	122	5.5
Oldest child aged 6 to 17	887.91	116	13.8
Oldest child aged 18 or older	1,277.45	167	11.8
Single parent with child under age 18	797.35	104	5.5
Single person	420.53	55	16.4
RACE AND HISPANIC ORIGIN			
Average household	**763.60**	**100**	**100.0**
Asian	796.33	104	4.5
Black	826.72	108	13.6
Hispanic	982.39	129	16.1
Non-Hispanic white and other	716.18	94	70.4
REGION			
Average household	**763.60**	**100**	**100.0**
Northeast	628.31	82	14.9
Midwest	830.81	109	24.1
South	734.54	96	35.8
West	853.88	112	25.2
EDUCATION			
Average household	**763.60**	**100**	**100.0**
Less than high school graduate	483.83	63	8.3
High school graduate	598.02	78	19.5
Some college	856.25	112	23.1
Associate's degree	933.33	122	12.1
Bachelor's degree or more	896.69	117	37.0
Bachelor's degree	819.64	107	21.4
Master's, professional, doctoral degree	1,029.02	135	15.6

Note: Market shares may not sum to 100.0 because of rounding and missing categories by household type. "Asian" and "black" include Hispanics and non-Hispanics who identify themselves as being of the respective race alone. "Hispanic" includes people of any race who identify themselves as Hispanic. "Other" includes people who identify themselves as non-Hispanic and as Alaska Native, American Indian, Asian (who are also included in the "Asian" row), or Native Hawaiian or other Pacific Islander, as well as non-Hispanics reporting more than one race.
Source: Calculations by New Strategist based on the Bureau of Labor Statistics' 2012 Consumer Expenditure Survey

Gasoline and Motor Oil (Including on Trips)

Best customers: Householders aged 35 to 54
Married couples with children at home

Customer trends: Average household spending on gasoline and motor oil will rise and fall along with the price of gas.

Gasoline and motor oil, the biggest transportation expense for the average household, accounts for 31 percent of transportation spending and is the fifth-largest household expense overall. The biggest spenders on gasoline and motor oil are middle-aged married couples because they have the largest households and the most vehicles. Householders aged 35 to 54 spend 21 to 24 percent more than average on gasoline and motor oil and account for 46 percent of the market. Married couples with school-aged children at home spend 47 percent more than average on this item, and those with adult children at home spend 60 percent more.

Average household spending on gasoline and motor oil rose by a substantial 47 percent between 2000 and 2006, after adjusting for inflation, fell 11 percent between 2006 and 2010, then climbed 23 percent between 2010 and 2012. Behind the increases were rises in the price of gasoline. The decline from 2006 to 2010 was due to lower prices and household belt tightening in the face of the Great Recession. Average household spending on gasoline and motor oil will fluctuate with gasoline prices.

Table 19.6 Gasoline and motor oil (including on trips)

Total household spending $342,863,124,480.00
Average household spends   2,755.78

AGE OF HOUSEHOLDER	AVERAGE HOUSEHOLD SPENDING	BEST CUSTOMERS (index)	BIGGEST CUSTOMERS (market share)
Average household	$2,755.78	100	100.0%
Under age 25	1,930.93	70	4.6
Aged 25 to 34	2,821.82	102	16.6
Aged 35 to 44	3,342.33	121	21.1
Aged 45 to 54	3,420.68	124	24.6
Aged 55 to 64	2,887.06	105	19.2
Aged 65 to 74	2,222.24	81	9.7
Aged 75 or older	1,223.90	44	4.3

	AVERAGE HOUSEHOLD SPENDING	BEST CUSTOMERS (index)	BIGGEST CUSTOMERS (market share)
HOUSEHOLD INCOME			
Average household	**$2,755.78**	**100**	**100.0%**
Under $20,000	1,249.95	45	9.5
$20,000 to $39,999	2,108.84	77	17.2
$40,000 to $49,999	2,650.97	96	8.5
$50,000 to $69,999	3,091.01	112	16.2
$70,000 to $79,999	3,432.21	125	7.0
$80,000 to $99,999	3,827.09	139	12.3
$100,000 or more	4,311.16	156	29.3
HOUSEHOLD TYPE			
Average household	**2,755.78**	**100**	**100.0**
Married couples	3,598.70	131	63.4
Married couples, no children	3,023.05	110	22.9
Married couples with children	3,999.17	145	34.1
Oldest child under age 6	3,283.05	119	5.4
Oldest child aged 6 to 17	4,037.71	147	17.4
Oldest child aged 18 or older	4,397.30	160	11.3
Single parent with child under age 18	2,231.37	81	4.2
Single person	1,419.96	52	15.3
RACE AND HISPANIC ORIGIN			
Average household	**2,755.78**	**100**	**100.0**
Asian	2,659.02	96	4.2
Black	2,329.08	85	10.6
Hispanic	2,727.22	99	12.4
Non-Hispanic white and other	2,831.29	103	77.1
REGION			
Average household	**2,755.78**	**100**	**100.0**
Northeast	2,502.71	91	16.4
Midwest	2,713.14	98	21.8
South	2,862.83	104	38.7
West	2,823.53	102	23.1
EDUCATION			
Average household	**2,755.78**	**100**	**100.0**
Less than high school graduate	2,080.33	75	9.9
High school graduate	2,596.02	94	23.5
Some college	2,675.07	97	20.0
Associate's degree	3,247.25	118	11.6
Bachelor's degree or more	3,060.55	111	35.0
Bachelor's degree	3,045.67	111	22.0
Master's, professional, doctoral degree	3,086.12	112	13.0

Note: Market shares may not sum to 100.0 because of rounding and missing categories by household type. "Asian" and "black" include Hispanics and non-Hispanics who identify themselves as being of the respective race alone. "Hispanic" includes people of any race who identify themselves as Hispanic. "Other" includes people who identify themselves as non-Hispanic and as Alaska Native, American Indian, Asian (who are also included in the "Asian" row), or Native Hawaiian or other Pacific Islander, as well as non-Hispanics reporting more than one race.
Source: Calculations by New Strategist based on the Bureau of Labor Statistics' 2012 Consumer Expenditure Survey

Mass Transit Fares, Intracity

Best customers: **Householders under age 35 and aged 45 to 54**
Married couples with school-aged or older children at home
Single parents
Asians, blacks, and Hispanics
Households in the Northeast

Customer trends: **Average household spending on mass transit may continue to increase as urban areas grow.**

Workers in the central cities of the Northeast are the best customers of mass transit. Households in the Northeast spend three times the average on intracity mass transit fares and account for 53 percent of the market. Householders aged 45 to 54, most at the peak of their career, spend 32 percent more than average on this item, and those under age 35 spend 31 to 37 percent more. Asians, blacks, and Hispanics spend much more than average on mass transit and account for 56 percent of the market. Married couples with adult children at home spend 38 percent more than average because they have the most workers in their households. Couples with school-aged children spend 18 percent more. Single parents, whose spending approaches average on only a few items, spend an average amount on mass transit fares.

Average household spending on intracity mass transit fares declined 8 percent between 2000 and 2006, after adjusting for inflation, but grew 24 percent between 2006 and 2012. Behind the increase was the rise in gasoline prices and the Great Recession, both of which encouraged greater mass transit use. Average household spending on mass transit may continue to increase as urban areas grow.

Table 19.7 Mass transit fares, intracity

Total household spending $8,956,707,840.00
Average household spends 71.99

AGE OF HOUSEHOLDER	AVERAGE HOUSEHOLD SPENDING	BEST CUSTOMERS (index)	BIGGEST CUSTOMERS (market share)
Average household	$71.99	100	100.0%
Under age 25	94.34	131	8.6
Aged 25 to 34	98.34	137	22.1
Aged 35 to 44	77.34	107	18.6
Aged 45 to 54	94.86	132	26.1
Aged 55 to 64	57.66	80	14.7
Aged 65 to 74	41.88	58	7.0
Aged 75 or older	21.54	30	2.9

	AVERAGE HOUSEHOLD SPENDING	BEST CUSTOMERS (index)	BIGGEST CUSTOMERS (market share)
HOUSEHOLD INCOME			
Average household	**$71.99**	**100**	**100.0%**
Under $20,000	55.28	77	16.2
$20,000 to $39,999	60.47	84	18.9
$40,000 to $49,999	54.73	76	6.7
$50,000 to $69,999	57.38	80	11.5
$70,000 to $79,999	69.76	97	5.4
$80,000 to $99,999	83.57	116	10.2
$100,000 or more	119.26	166	31.0
HOUSEHOLD TYPE			
Average household	**71.99**	**100**	**100.0**
Married couples	72.70	101	49.0
Married couples, no children	49.47	69	14.3
Married couples with children	86.64	120	28.3
Oldest child under age 6	71.16	99	4.5
Oldest child aged 6 to 17	84.97	118	14.0
Oldest child aged 18 or older	99.46	138	9.7
Single parent with child under age 18	72.67	101	5.3
Single person	53.53	74	22.1
RACE AND HISPANIC ORIGIN			
Average household	**71.99**	**100**	**100.0**
Asian	251.47	349	15.1
Black	120.07	167	21.0
Hispanic	117.01	163	20.4
Non-Hispanic white and other	56.64	79	59.1
REGION			
Average household	**71.99**	**100**	**100.0**
Northeast	212.71	295	53.3
Midwest	35.25	49	10.9
South	27.14	38	14.0
West	69.54	97	21.8
EDUCATION			
Average household	**71.99**	**100**	**100.0**
Less than high school graduate	72.98	101	13.2
High school graduate	46.45	65	16.1
Some college	55.64	77	15.9
Associate's degree	36.85	51	5.1
Bachelor's degree or more	113.45	158	49.7
Bachelor's degree	99.91	139	27.7
Master's, professional, doctoral degree	136.70	190	22.0

Note: Market shares may not sum to 100.0 because of rounding and missing categories by household type. "Asian" and "black" include Hispanics and non-Hispanics who identify themselves as being of the respective race alone. "Hispanic" includes people of any race who identify themselves as Hispanic. "Other" includes people who identify themselves as non-Hispanic and as Alaska Native, American Indian, Asian (who are also included in the "Asian" row), or Native Hawaiian or other Pacific Islander, as well as non-Hispanics reporting more than one race.
Source: Calculations by New Strategist based on the Bureau of Labor Statistics' 2012 Consumer Expenditure Survey

Motorcycles

Best customers: Householders under age 45
                           Households in the West

Customer trends: Average household spending on motorcycles may increase in the years ahead as Americans look for fuel-efficient transportation.

The biggest spenders on motorcycles are the youngest householders. Householders under age 25 spend almost four times the national average on motorcycles, and those aged 25 to 44 spend 27 to 32 percent more than average. Households in the West spend more than twice the average on motorcycles.

Average household spending on motorcycles grew 30 percent between 2000 and 2006, after adjusting for inflation. Spending then fell 13 percent between 2006 and 2010 before reversing course and climbing 2 percent between 2010 and 2012. Behind the decline was the Great Recession, which reduced spending on vehicles of all sorts. Average household spending on motorcycles may increase in the years ahead as Americans look for fuel-efficient transportation.

Table 19.8 Motorcycles

Total household spending	$6,835,415,040.00
Average household spends	54.94

AGE OF HOUSEHOLDER	AVERAGE HOUSEHOLD SPENDING	BEST CUSTOMERS (index)	BIGGEST CUSTOMERS (market share)
Average household	$54.94	100	100.0%
Under age 25	206.68	376	24.7
Aged 25 to 34	72.37	132	21.3
Aged 35 to 44	69.58	127	22.0
Aged 45 to 54	44.84	82	16.2
Aged 55 to 64	39.80	72	13.3
Aged 65 to 74	12.08	22	2.6
Aged 75 or older	0.00	0	0.0

	AVERAGE HOUSEHOLD SPENDING	BEST CUSTOMERS (index)	BIGGEST CUSTOMERS (market share)
HOUSEHOLD INCOME			
Average household	$54.94	100	100.0%
Under $20,000	8.80	16	3.4
$20,000 to $39,999	15.72	29	6.4
$40,000 to $49,999	21.45	39	3.5
$50,000 to $69,999	54.98	100	14.5
$70,000 to $79,999	129.47	236	13.2
$80,000 to $99,999	62.68	114	10.1
$100,000 or more	151.89	276	51.8
HOUSEHOLD TYPE			
Average household	54.94	100	100.0
Married couples	68.91	125	60.9
Married couples, no children	60.76	111	23.1
Married couples with children	72.71	132	31.1
Oldest child under age 6	8.98	16	0.7
Oldest child aged 6 to 17	105.84	193	22.9
Oldest child aged 18 or older	58.06	106	7.5
Single parent with child under age 18	21.06	38	2.0
Single person	10.34	19	5.6
RACE AND HISPANIC ORIGIN			
Average household	54.94	100	100.0
Asian	0.00	0	0.0
Black	49.01	89	11.2
Hispanic	32.53	59	7.4
Non-Hispanic white and other	59.57	108	81.4
REGION			
Average household	54.94	100	100.0
Northeast	22.18	40	7.3
Midwest	43.96	80	17.7
South	42.28	77	28.7
West	112.95	206	46.3
EDUCATION			
Average household	54.94	100	100.0
Less than high school graduate	5.04	9	1.2
High school graduate	92.41	168	41.9
Some college	49.91	91	18.7
Associate's degree	29.19	53	5.2
Bachelor's degree or more	57.34	104	32.9
Bachelor's degree	47.95	87	17.4
Master's, professional, doctoral degree	73.46	134	15.5

Note: Market shares may not sum to 100.0 because of rounding and missing categories by household type. "Asian" and "black" include Hispanics and non-Hispanics who identify themselves as being of the respective race alone. "Hispanic" includes people of any race who identify themselves as Hispanic. "Other" includes people who identify themselves as non-Hispanic and as Alaska Native, American Indian, Asian (who are also included in the "Asian" row), or Native Hawaiian or other Pacific Islander, as well as non-Hispanics reporting more than one race.
Source: Calculations by New Strategist based on the Bureau of Labor Statistics' 2012 Consumer Expenditure Survey

Oil Change, Lube, and Oil Filters

Best customers: Householders aged 35 to 64
Married couples with children at home

Customer trends: Average household spending on oil changes, lubes, and oil filters may decline in the years ahead as aging boomers downsize their fleets.

Middle-aged married couples with children at home are the biggest spenders on oil changes. Householders ranging in age from 35 to 64 spend 11 to 15 percent more than average on this item. Married couples with children at home, owning multiple cars, spend 41 percent more than average on oil changes.

Average household spending on oil changes, lubes, and oil filters fell 3 percent between 2000 and 2006, after adjusting for inflation, then climbed 5 percent between 2006 and 2012. Average household spending on this item may decline in the years ahead as aging boomers downsize their fleets.

Table 19.9 Oil change, lube, and oil filters

Total household spending	$9,979,407,360.00
Average household spends	80.21

AGE OF HOUSEHOLDER	AVERAGE HOUSEHOLD SPENDING	BEST CUSTOMERS (index)	BIGGEST CUSTOMERS (market share)
Average household	$80.21	100	100.0%
Under age 25	45.44	57	3.7
Aged 25 to 34	78.12	97	15.7
Aged 35 to 44	88.66	111	19.2
Aged 45 to 54	91.71	114	22.6
Aged 55 to 64	92.31	115	21.1
Aged 65 to 74	79.88	100	12.0
Aged 75 or older	46.48	58	5.7

	AVERAGE HOUSEHOLD SPENDING	BEST CUSTOMERS (index)	BIGGEST CUSTOMERS (market share)
HOUSEHOLD INCOME			
Average household	$80.21	100	100.0%
Under $20,000	35.30	44	9.3
$20,000 to $39,999	57.00	71	16.0
$40,000 to $49,999	72.06	90	8.0
$50,000 to $69,999	82.20	102	14.8
$70,000 to $79,999	102.95	128	7.2
$80,000 to $99,999	112.95	141	12.4
$100,000 or more	138.74	173	32.4
HOUSEHOLD TYPE			
Average household	80.21	100	100.0
Married couples	104.71	131	63.4
Married couples, no children	94.24	117	24.5
Married couples with children	112.76	141	33.1
Oldest child under age 6	105.27	131	6.0
Oldest child aged 6 to 17	113.38	141	16.8
Oldest child aged 18 or older	116.56	145	10.3
Single parent with child under age 18	59.96	75	3.9
Single person	49.81	62	18.4
RACE AND HISPANIC ORIGIN			
Average household	80.21	100	100.0
Asian	87.18	109	4.7
Black	66.14	82	10.4
Hispanic	68.41	85	10.7
Non-Hispanic white and other	84.49	105	79.1
REGION			
Average household	80.21	100	100.0
Northeast	71.43	89	16.1
Midwest	80.97	101	22.4
South	84.15	105	39.1
West	79.99	100	22.5
EDUCATION			
Average household	80.21	100	100.0
Less than high school graduate	45.59	57	7.4
High school graduate	67.00	84	20.8
Some college	76.07	95	19.5
Associate's degree	89.60	112	11.0
Bachelor's degree or more	104.76	131	41.2
Bachelor's degree	104.68	131	26.0
Master's, professional, doctoral degree	104.90	131	15.2

Note: Market shares may not sum to 100.0 because of rounding and missing categories by household type. "Asian" and "black" include Hispanics and non-Hispanics who identify themselves as being of the respective race alone. "Hispanic" includes people of any race who identify themselves as Hispanic. "Other" includes people who identify themselves as non-Hispanic and as Alaska Native, American Indian, Asian (who are also included in the "Asian" row), or Native Hawaiian or other Pacific Islander, as well as non-Hispanics reporting more than one race.
Source: Calculations by New Strategist based on the Bureau of Labor Statistics' 2012 Consumer Expenditure Survey

Parking Fees (Excluding at Residence) and Tolls

Best customers: Householders aged 25 to 64
                  Married couples with children at home
                  Asians
                  Households in the Northeast

Customer trends: Average household spending on parking fees and tolls should continue to rise as localities
                  recoup infrastructure costs by raising fees.

The biggest spenders on parking fees (excluding residential parking) and tolls are households with working-age adults (paying for parking while they work) and married couples with children (who have the most cars). Householders ranging in age from 25 to 64 spend more than average on parking and tolls. Married couples with children at home spend 51 percent more than average on this item. Asian households spend more than twice the average on parking and tolls. Households in the Northeast spend nearly double the average on this item.

Average household spending on parking fees and tolls rose 33 percent between 2000 and 2012, after adjusting for inflation. Spending on this item should continue to rise as localities recover infrastructure costs by raising parking fees and tolls.

Table 19.10 **Parking fees (excluding at residence) and tolls**

Total household spending $9,694,494,720.00
Average household spends   77.92

AGE OF HOUSEHOLDER	AVERAGE HOUSEHOLD SPENDING	BEST CUSTOMERS (index)	BIGGEST CUSTOMERS (market share)
Average household	$77.92	100	100.0%
Under age 25	45.37	58	3.8
Aged 25 to 34	88.97	114	18.5
Aged 35 to 44	90.85	117	20.2
Aged 45 to 54	102.32	131	26.0
Aged 55 to 64	84.44	108	19.8
Aged 65 to 74	54.46	70	8.4
Aged 75 or older	25.77	33	3.2

	AVERAGE HOUSEHOLD SPENDING	BEST CUSTOMERS (index)	BIGGEST CUSTOMERS (market share)
HOUSEHOLD INCOME			
Average household	**$77.92**	**100**	**100.0%**
Under $20,000	20.62	26	5.6
$20,000 to $39,999	35.69	46	10.3
$40,000 to $49,999	45.26	58	5.1
$50,000 to $69,999	62.15	80	11.5
$70,000 to $79,999	87.39	112	6.3
$80,000 to $99,999	104.37	134	11.8
$100,000 or more	205.42	264	49.4
HOUSEHOLD TYPE			
Average household	**77.92**	**100**	**100.0**
Married couples	104.54	134	65.2
Married couples, no children	92.78	119	24.8
Married couples with children	117.73	151	35.5
Oldest child under age 6	121.41	156	7.1
Oldest child aged 6 to 17	113.14	145	17.3
Oldest child aged 18 or older	123.07	158	11.1
Single parent with child under age 18	44.55	57	3.0
Single person	47.88	61	18.2
RACE AND HISPANIC ORIGIN			
Average household	**77.92**	**100**	**100.0**
Asian	161.15	207	9.0
Black	51.20	66	8.3
Hispanic	65.49	84	10.5
Non-Hispanic white and other	84.39	108	81.3
REGION			
Average household	**77.92**	**100**	**100.0**
Northeast	145.19	186	33.6
Midwest	61.16	78	17.4
South	56.66	73	27.1
West	75.63	97	21.9
EDUCATION			
Average household	**77.92**	**100**	**100.0**
Less than high school graduate	22.95	29	3.8
High school graduate	33.70	43	10.8
Some college	68.31	88	18.1
Associate's degree	69.94	90	8.9
Bachelor's degree or more	144.40	185	58.4
Bachelor's degree	121.58	156	31.1
Master's, professional, doctoral degree	183.56	236	27.3

Note: Market shares may not sum to 100.0 because of rounding and missing categories by household type. "Asian" and "black" include Hispanics and non-Hispanics who identify themselves as being of the respective race alone. "Hispanic" includes people of any race who identify themselves as Hispanic. "Other" includes people who identify themselves as non-Hispanic and as Alaska Native, American Indian, Asian (who are also included in the "Asian" row), or Native Hawaiian or other Pacific Islander, as well as non-Hispanics reporting more than one race.
Source: Calculations by New Strategist based on the Bureau of Labor Statistics' 2012 Consumer Expenditure Survey

Taxi Fares and Limousine Service in Home Town

Best customers: Householders aged 25 to 34
Married couples with preschoolers
People who live alone
Blacks
Households in the Northeast

Customer trends: Average household spending on taxi fares and limousine service may continue to decline as cash-strapped young adults increasingly depend on mass transit.

Households without cars are the best customers of taxi and limousine services. This explains why households in the Northeast spend over twice the average on this item and account for 39 percent of the market. Much of this spending probably occurs in New York City, where many households do not own cars. Householders aged 25 to 34, many of them without a vehicle, spend twice the average on this item. Married couples with preschoolers spend 47 percent more. People who live alone, whose spending is well below average on most items, spend an average amount on cabs. Black householders, who are less likely to own a vehicle, spend 57 percent more than average on taxis and limousines.

Average household spending on taxi fares and limousine service fell 30 percent between 2000 and 2012, after adjusting for inflation. One factor behind the decline was the increased use of mass transit rather than taxis as a budget-cutting measure by those without cars. Average household spending on taxi fares and limousine service may continue to decline as cash-strapped young adults increasingly depend on mass transit.

Table 19.11 Taxi fares and limousine service in home town

Total household spending $1,413,365,760.00
Average household spends   11.36

AGE OF HOUSEHOLDER	AVERAGE HOUSEHOLD SPENDING	BEST CUSTOMERS (index)	BIGGEST CUSTOMERS (market share)
Average household	$11.36	100	100.0%
Under age 25	5.65	50	3.3
Aged 25 to 34	23.32	205	33.2
Aged 35 to 44	15.11	133	23.1
Aged 45 to 54	7.59	67	13.2
Aged 55 to 64	7.60	67	12.2
Aged 65 to 74	7.88	69	8.4
Aged 75 or older	6.96	61	6.0

	AVERAGE HOUSEHOLD SPENDING	BEST CUSTOMERS (index)	BIGGEST CUSTOMERS (market share)
HOUSEHOLD INCOME			
Average household	**$11.36**	**100**	**100.0%**
Under $20,000	10.23	90	18.9
$20,000 to $39,999	6.01	53	11.9
$40,000 to $49,999	4.42	39	3.4
$50,000 to $69,999	13.03	115	16.6
$70,000 to $79,999	10.39	91	5.1
$80,000 to $99,999	9.91	87	7.7
$100,000 or more	22.70	200	37.4
HOUSEHOLD TYPE			
Average household	**11.36**	**100**	**100.0**
Married couples	11.12	98	47.5
Married couples, no children	13.19	116	24.2
Married couples with children	10.63	94	22.0
Oldest child under age 6	16.65	147	6.7
Oldest child aged 6 to 17	11.09	98	11.6
Oldest child aged 18 or older	6.12	54	3.8
Single parent with child under age 18	6.26	55	2.9
Single person	11.50	101	30.1
RACE AND HISPANIC ORIGIN			
Average household	**11.36**	**100**	**100.0**
Asian	8.75	77	3.3
Black	17.79	157	19.7
Hispanic	6.08	54	6.7
Non-Hispanic white and other	11.12	98	73.5
REGION			
Average household	**11.36**	**100**	**100.0**
Northeast	24.74	218	39.3
Midwest	9.92	87	19.4
South	6.53	57	21.4
West	9.96	88	19.8
EDUCATION			
Average household	**11.36**	**100**	**100.0**
Less than high school graduate	12.07	106	13.9
High school graduate	7.55	66	16.6
Some college	7.05	62	12.8
Associate's degree	5.71	50	5.0
Bachelor's degree or more	18.71	165	51.9
Bachelor's degree	17.39	153	30.5
Master's, professional, doctoral degree	20.95	184	21.4

Note: Market shares may not sum to 100.0 because of rounding and missing categories by household type. "Asian" and "black" include Hispanics and non-Hispanics who identify themselves as being of the respective race alone. "Hispanic" includes people of any race who identify themselves as Hispanic. "Other" includes people who identify themselves as non-Hispanic and as Alaska Native, American Indian, Asian (who are also included in the "Asian" row), or Native Hawaiian or other Pacific Islander, as well as non-Hispanics reporting more than one race.
Source: Calculations by New Strategist based on the Bureau of Labor Statistics' 2012 Consumer Expenditure Survey

Tires (Purchased, Replaced, Installed)

Best customers: Householders aged 35 to 64
Married couples with children at home

Customer trends: Average household spending on tires is likely to decline as aging boomers downsize their fleets.

The best customers of tires are households with the most cars—those headed by married couples, particularly households with teenage or adult children at home. Householders ranging in age from 35 to 64, many with teens and young adults at home, spend 11 to 31 percent more than the average household on tires and account for two-thirds of the market. Married couples with school-aged or older children at home spend 52 percent more than average on tires, and those with preschoolers spend 24 percent more.

Average household spending on tires held fairly steady between 2000 and 2006, the year overall household spending peaked, but then increased by a hefty 25 percent between 2006 and 2012, after adjusting for inflation. Behind the increase was the greater age of vehicles owned by the average household, boosting demand for replacement tires. Average household spending on tires is likely to decline in the years ahead as aging boomers downsize their fleets.

Table 19.12 Tires (purchased, replaced, installed)

Total household spending $18,230,676,480.00
Average household spends   146.53

AGE OF HOUSEHOLDER	AVERAGE HOUSEHOLD SPENDING	BEST CUSTOMERS (index)	BIGGEST CUSTOMERS (market share)
Average household	$146.53	100	100.0%
Under age 25	85.03	58	3.8
Aged 25 to 34	135.03	92	14.9
Aged 35 to 44	162.63	111	19.3
Aged 45 to 54	191.42	131	25.9
Aged 55 to 64	172.19	118	21.5
Aged 65 to 74	122.83	84	10.1
Aged 75 or older	68.51	47	4.6

	AVERAGE HOUSEHOLD SPENDING	BEST CUSTOMERS (index)	BIGGEST CUSTOMERS (market share)
HOUSEHOLD INCOME			
Average household	**$146.53**	**100**	**100.0%**
Under $20,000	67.32	46	9.7
$20,000 to $39,999	97.88	67	15.1
$40,000 to $49,999	144.49	99	8.7
$50,000 to $69,999	175.41	120	17.3
$70,000 to $79,999	169.34	116	6.5
$80,000 to $99,999	166.95	114	10.1
$100,000 or more	256.39	175	32.8
HOUSEHOLD TYPE			
Average household	**146.53**	**100**	**100.0**
Married couples	188.55	129	62.5
Married couples, no children	161.11	110	22.9
Married couples with children	214.20	146	34.4
Oldest child under age 6	181.02	124	5.6
Oldest child aged 6 to 17	222.23	152	18.0
Oldest child aged 18 or older	222.12	152	10.7
Single parent with child under age 18	102.25	70	3.7
Single person	91.32	62	18.5
RACE AND HISPANIC ORIGIN			
Average household	**146.53**	**100**	**100.0**
Asian	130.42	89	3.9
Black	90.60	62	7.8
Hispanic	124.20	85	10.6
Non-Hispanic white and other	159.46	109	81.7
REGION			
Average household	**146.53**	**100**	**100.0**
Northeast	133.76	91	16.5
Midwest	143.67	98	21.7
South	140.79	96	35.8
West	169.07	115	26.0
EDUCATION			
Average household	**146.53**	**100**	**100.0**
Less than high school graduate	80.04	55	7.1
High school graduate	132.90	91	22.6
Some college	140.36	96	19.7
Associate's degree	178.65	122	12.0
Bachelor's degree or more	178.81	122	38.5
Bachelor's degree	179.08	122	24.4
Master's, professional, doctoral degree	178.35	122	14.1

Note: Market shares may not sum to 100.0 because of rounding and missing categories by household type. "Asian" and "black" include Hispanics and non-Hispanics who identify themselves as being of the respective race alone. "Hispanic" includes people of any race who identify themselves as Hispanic. "Other" includes people who identify themselves as non-Hispanic and as Alaska Native, American Indian, Asian (who are also included in the "Asian" row), or Native Hawaiian or other Pacific Islander, as well as non-Hispanics reporting more than one race.
Source: Calculations by New Strategist based on the Bureau of Labor Statistics' 2012 Consumer Expenditure Survey

Towing Charges

Best customers: Householders aged 25 to 34 and 45 to 54
Married couples with school-aged or older children at home
Single parents
Hispanics
Households in the South

Customer trends: Average household spending on towing charges may rise as the economy recovers
and young adults buy more cars.

The biggest spenders on towing charges are households with unreliable vehicles who do not belong to automobile service clubs (which usually cover towing charges). They are also the heads of the largest households and most likely to own multiple and used vehicles, with frequent breakdowns. Householders aged 25 to 34 spend 55 percent more than average on towing charges. Those aged 45 to 54, many owning used cars driven by their children, spend 22 percent more. Married couples with school-aged or older children at home spend 47 to 56 percent more than average on towing charges. Single parents, whose spending is well below average on most items, spend 24 percent more than average on towing charges. Hispanics, who tend to have the largest families, spend 38 percent more than average. Households in the South spend 14 percent more than average on towing charges.

Average household spending on towing charges fell 30 percent between 2000 and 2012, after adjusting for inflation. On factor behind the decline was diminished car ownership among young adults. Also behind the decline was greater spending on automobile service clubs. Average household spending on towing charges may rise as the economy recovers and young adults buy more cars.

Table 19.13 Towing charges

Total household spending $543,697,920.00
Average household spends 4.37

AGE OF HOUSEHOLDER	AVERAGE HOUSEHOLD SPENDING	BEST CUSTOMERS (index)	BIGGEST CUSTOMERS (market share)
Average household	$4.37	100	100.0%
Under age 25	3.07	70	4.6
Aged 25 to 34	6.79	155	25.1
Aged 35 to 44	3.66	84	14.5
Aged 45 to 54	5.33	122	24.1
Aged 55 to 64	4.62	106	19.3
Aged 65 to 74	2.52	58	6.9
Aged 75 or older	2.35	54	5.3

	AVERAGE HOUSEHOLD SPENDING	BEST CUSTOMERS (index)	BIGGEST CUSTOMERS (market share)
HOUSEHOLD INCOME			
Average household	**$4.37**	**100**	**100.0%**
Under $20,000	3.65	83	17.6
$20,000 to $39,999	3.06	70	15.8
$40,000 to $49,999	5.13	117	10.4
$50,000 to $69,999	2.56	59	8.5
$70,000 to $79,999	4.81	110	6.1
$80,000 to $99,999	6.03	138	12.2
$100,000 or more	6.88	157	29.5
HOUSEHOLD TYPE			
Average household	**4.37**	**100**	**100.0**
Married couples	5.04	115	56.0
Married couples, no children	3.64	83	17.4
Married couples with children	6.07	139	32.7
Oldest child under age 6	3.97	91	4.1
Oldest child aged 6 to 17	6.44	147	17.5
Oldest child aged 18 or older	6.82	156	11.0
Single parent with child under age 18	5.40	124	6.5
Single person	2.90	66	19.7
RACE AND HISPANIC ORIGIN			
Average household	**4.37**	**100**	**100.0**
Asian	3.69	84	3.7
Black	3.95	90	11.4
Hispanic	6.05	138	17.4
Non-Hispanic white and other	4.20	96	72.1
REGION			
Average household	**4.37**	**100**	**100.0**
Northeast	4.27	98	17.6
Midwest	3.75	86	19.0
South	5.00	114	42.6
West	4.02	92	20.7
EDUCATION			
Average household	**4.37**	**100**	**100.0**
Less than high school graduate	5.90	135	17.6
High school graduate	4.32	99	24.6
Some college	4.03	92	19.0
Associate's degree	4.16	95	9.4
Bachelor's degree or more	4.07	93	29.4
Bachelor's degree	4.22	97	19.2
Master's, professional, doctoral degree	3.80	87	10.1

Note: Market shares may not sum to 100.0 because of rounding and missing categories by household type. "Asian" and "black" include Hispanics and non-Hispanics who identify themselves as being of the respective race alone. "Hispanic" includes people of any race who identify themselves as Hispanic. "Other" includes people who identify themselves as non-Hispanic and as Alaska Native, American Indian, Asian (who are also included in the "Asian" row), or Native Hawaiian or other Pacific Islander, as well as non-Hispanics reporting more than one race.
Source: Calculations by New Strategist based on the Bureau of Labor Statistics' 2012 Consumer Expenditure Survey

Truck Lease Payments

Best customers: Householders aged 25 to 44
                           Married couples
                           Households in the Northeast

Customer trends: Average household spending on truck lease payments is likely to continue to decline as the slow economic recovery drives consumers toward fuel-efficient cars.

The best customers of truck leasing are married couples with children at home, who lease a pickup, minivan, or sport utility vehicle (all are considered trucks). Householders aged 25 to 44 spend 20 to 45 percent more than average on truck lease payments. Married couples with children at home spend 72 percent more than average, the figure peaking among those with preschoolers at over two-and-one-half times the average. Married couples without children at home spend 45 percent more than average on this item. Households in the Northeast spend over twice the average on truck lease payments.

Average household spending on truck lease payments declined by a precipitous 71 percent between 2000 and 2012, after adjusting for inflation. Behind the spending decline was the shift to buying rather than leasing as automotive dealers offered no-interest loans and other purchasing incentives. Average household spending on truck leases is likely to continue to decline in the years ahead as the slow economic recovery drives consumers toward fuel-efficient cars.

Table 19.14 Truck lease payments

Total household spending	$7,142,722,560.00
Average household spends	57.41

	AVERAGE HOUSEHOLD SPENDING	BEST CUSTOMERS (index)	BIGGEST CUSTOMERS (market share)
AGE OF HOUSEHOLDER			
Average household	**$57.41**	**100**	**100.0%**
Under age 25	19.89	35	2.3
Aged 25 to 34	68.64	120	19.3
Aged 35 to 44	83.36	145	25.2
Aged 45 to 54	57.50	100	19.8
Aged 55 to 64	61.33	107	19.6
Aged 65 to 74	53.67	93	11.3
Aged 75 or older	15.00	26	2.6

	AVERAGE HOUSEHOLD SPENDING	BEST CUSTOMERS (index)	BIGGEST CUSTOMERS (market share)
HOUSEHOLD INCOME			
Average household	**$57.41**	**100**	**100.0%**
Under $20,000	7.21	13	2.6
$20,000 to $39,999	22.43	39	8.8
$40,000 to $49,999	43.77	76	6.7
$50,000 to $69,999	41.99	73	10.6
$70,000 to $79,999	67.73	118	6.6
$80,000 to $99,999	89.67	156	13.8
$100,000 or more	156.01	272	50.9
HOUSEHOLD TYPE			
Average household	**57.41**	**100**	**100.0**
Married couples	91.25	159	77.2
Married couples, no children	83.40	145	30.3
Married couples with children	98.60	172	40.4
Oldest child under age 6	146.04	254	11.6
Oldest child aged 6 to 17	93.27	162	19.3
Oldest child aged 18 or older	76.92	134	9.5
Single parent with child under age 18	31.47	55	2.9
Single person	15.77	27	8.2
RACE AND HISPANIC ORIGIN			
Average household	**57.41**	**100**	**100.0**
Asian	51.06	89	3.9
Black	16.52	29	3.6
Hispanic	59.26	103	12.9
Non-Hispanic white and other	63.82	111	83.4
REGION			
Average household	**57.41**	**100**	**100.0**
Northeast	120.71	210	38.0
Midwest	59.63	104	23.0
South	36.11	63	23.4
West	39.71	69	15.6
EDUCATION			
Average household	**57.41**	**100**	**100.0**
Less than high school graduate	16.80	29	3.8
High school graduate	40.41	70	17.6
Some college	51.42	90	18.4
Associate's degree	33.57	58	5.8
Bachelor's degree or more	99.04	173	54.4
Bachelor's degree	86.40	150	30.0
Master's, professional, doctoral degree	120.76	210	24.4

Note: Market shares may not sum to 100.0 because of rounding and missing categories by household type. "Asian" and "black" include Hispanics and non-Hispanics who identify themselves as being of the respective race alone. "Hispanic" includes people of any race who identify themselves as Hispanic. "Other" includes people who identify themselves as non-Hispanic and as Alaska Native, American Indian, Asian (who are also included in the "Asian" row), or Native Hawaiian or other Pacific Islander, as well as non-Hispanics reporting more than one race.
Source: Calculations by New Strategist based on the Bureau of Labor Statistics' 2012 Consumer Expenditure Survey

Trucks, New

Best customers: Householders aged 45 to 54
Married couples
Asians and non-Hispanic whites

Customer trends: Average household spending on new trucks is likely to decline because of higher gas prices and aging boomers.

The best customers of new trucks (a category that includes minivans, sport utility vehicles, and pickups) are middle-aged married couples, most with children. Householders aged 45 to 54 spend 30 percent more than average on new trucks. Married couples with children at home spend 58 percent more than average on new trucks. Those without children at home spend 72 percent more. Asian households spend 24 percent more than average on this item, and non-Hispanic whites spend 16 percent more. These two groups control 87 percent of the market for new trucks.

Average household spending on new trucks grew 16 percent between 2000 and the overall peak spending year of 2006, after adjusting for inflation. Then spending fell 40 percent between 2006 and 2010 as vehicle purchases plummeted during the Great Recession. Between 2010 and 2012, average household spending on new trucks rebounded, rising by a strong 47 percent. Spending on new trucks is likely to decline in the years ahead because of higher gas prices and aging boomers.

Table 19.15 Trucks, new

Total household spending	$116,625,070,080.00
Average household spends	937.38

AGE OF HOUSEHOLDER	AVERAGE HOUSEHOLD SPENDING	BEST CUSTOMERS (index)	BIGGEST CUSTOMERS (market share)
Average household	$937.38	100	100.0%
Under age 25	245.29	26	1.7
Aged 25 to 34	1,070.88	114	18.5
Aged 35 to 44	981.82	105	18.2
Aged 45 to 54	1,223.25	130	25.8
Aged 55 to 64	961.26	103	18.8
Aged 65 to 74	1,034.67	110	13.3
Aged 75 or older	358.49	38	3.7

	AVERAGE HOUSEHOLD SPENDING	BEST CUSTOMERS (index)	BIGGEST CUSTOMERS (market share)
HOUSEHOLD INCOME			
Average household	**$937.38**	**100**	**100.0%**
Under $20,000	337.26	36	7.6
$20,000 to $39,999	298.18	32	7.2
$40,000 to $49,999	653.00	70	6.2
$50,000 to $69,999	996.67	106	15.4
$70,000 to $79,999	1,204.90	129	7.2
$80,000 to $99,999	1,578.27	168	14.9
$100,000 or more	2,088.15	223	41.7
HOUSEHOLD TYPE			
Average household	**937.38**	**100**	**100.0**
Married couples	1,509.12	161	78.2
Married couples, no children	1,611.75	172	35.8
Married couples with children	1,476.59	158	37.0
Oldest child under age 6	1,441.63	154	7.0
Oldest child aged 6 to 17	1,399.76	149	17.8
Oldest child aged 18 or older	1,628.71	174	12.3
Single parent with child under age 18	427.24	46	2.4
Single person	315.89	34	10.0
RACE AND HISPANIC ORIGIN			
Average household	**937.38**	**100**	**100.0**
Asian	1,162.90	124	5.4
Black	300.24	32	4.0
Hispanic	682.90	73	9.1
Non-Hispanic white and other	1,084.53	116	86.8
REGION			
Average household	**937.38**	**100**	**100.0**
Northeast	954.62	102	18.4
Midwest	917.20	98	21.7
South	1,025.33	109	40.7
West	798.05	85	19.2
EDUCATION			
Average household	**937.38**	**100**	**100.0**
Less than high school graduate	217.65	23	3.0
High school graduate	734.52	78	19.5
Some college	1,002.88	107	22.0
Associate's degree	1,044.26	111	11.0
Bachelor's degree or more	1,319.51	141	44.4
Bachelor's degree	1,287.51	137	27.4
Master's, professional, doctoral degree	1,374.47	147	17.0

Note: Market shares may not sum to 100.0 because of rounding and missing categories by household type. "Asian" and "black" include Hispanics and non-Hispanics who identify themselves as being of the respective race alone. "Hispanic" includes people of any race who identify themselves as Hispanic. "Other" includes people who identify themselves as non-Hispanic and as Alaska Native, American Indian, Asian (who are also included in the "Asian" row), or Native Hawaiian or other Pacific Islander, as well as non-Hispanics reporting more than one race.
Source: Calculations by New Strategist based on the Bureau of Labor Statistics' 2012 Consumer Expenditure Survey

Trucks, Used

Best customers: Householders under age 45
        Married couples with children at home
        Households in the South

Customer trends: Average household spending on used trucks is likely to fall as higher gas prices and the slow economic recovery drive consumers toward fuel-efficient cars.

The best customers of used trucks (a category that includes minivans, sport utility vehicles, and pickups) are younger married couples with children. Householders under age 45, most with children, spend 22 to 51 percent more than average on used trucks and control 56 percent of the market. Married couples with children at home spend 64 percent more than the average on used trucks, the figure peaking among those with school-aged children at 83 percent above average. Households in the South spend 23 percent more than average on used trucks.

Average household spending on used trucks fell 29 percent between 2000 and 2010, after adjusting for inflation, then grew 5 percent in the ensuing two years. Most of the decline occurred between the overall peak spending year of 2006 and the overall trough spending year of 2010. Behind the spending decline were the generous incentives car dealers offered on new trucks as well as the Great Recession. Average household spending on used trucks is likely to fall as higher gas prices and the slow economic recovery drive consumers toward fuel-efficient cars.

Table 19.16 **Trucks, used**

Total household spending $93,615,575,040.00
Average household spends   752.44

AGE OF HOUSEHOLDER	AVERAGE HOUSEHOLD SPENDING	BEST CUSTOMERS (index)	BIGGEST CUSTOMERS (market share)
Average household	$752.44	100	100.0%
Under age 25	917.59	122	8.0
Aged 25 to 34	1,135.46	151	24.4
Aged 35 to 44	1,041.60	138	24.0
Aged 45 to 54	631.51	84	16.6
Aged 55 to 64	600.89	80	14.6
Aged 65 to 74	631.14	84	10.1
Aged 75 or older	172.82	23	2.2

	AVERAGE HOUSEHOLD SPENDING	BEST CUSTOMERS (index)	BIGGEST CUSTOMERS (market share)
HOUSEHOLD INCOME			
Average household	**$752.44**	**100**	**100.0%**
Under $20,000	171.97	23	4.8
$20,000 to $39,999	491.77	65	14.7
$40,000 to $49,999	556.44	74	6.5
$50,000 to $69,999	1,191.61	158	22.9
$70,000 to $79,999	1,136.19	151	8.4
$80,000 to $99,999	1,113.29	148	13.1
$100,000 or more	1,187.90	158	29.6
HOUSEHOLD TYPE			
Average household	**752.44**	**100**	**100.0**
Married couples	1,031.01	137	66.6
Married couples, no children	823.27	109	22.8
Married couples with children	1,233.32	164	38.5
Oldest child under age 6	1,097.08	146	6.7
Oldest child aged 6 to 17	1,380.20	183	21.8
Oldest child aged 18 or older	1,073.83	143	10.1
Single parent with child under age 18	481.18	64	3.4
Single person	292.64	39	11.5
RACE AND HISPANIC ORIGIN			
Average household	**752.44**	**100**	**100.0**
Asian	422.87	56	2.4
Black	464.00	62	7.8
Hispanic	772.76	103	12.9
Non-Hispanic white and other	799.29	106	79.7
REGION			
Average household	**752.44**	**100**	**100.0**
Northeast	656.99	87	15.8
Midwest	813.28	108	24.0
South	927.31	123	45.9
West	480.01	64	14.4
EDUCATION			
Average household	**752.44**	**100**	**100.0**
Less than high school graduate	586.26	78	10.2
High school graduate	710.95	94	23.6
Some college	803.93	107	22.0
Associate's degree	753.13	100	9.9
Bachelor's degree or more	820.21	109	34.4
Bachelor's degree	898.82	119	23.8
Master's, professional, doctoral degree	685.20	91	10.6

Note: Market shares may not sum to 100.0 because of rounding and missing categories by household type. "Asian" and "black" include Hispanics and non-Hispanics who identify themselves as being of the respective race alone. "Hispanic" includes people of any race who identify themselves as Hispanic. "Other" includes people who identify themselves as non-Hispanic and as Alaska Native, American Indian, Asian (who are also included in the "Asian" row), or Native Hawaiian or other Pacific Islander, as well as non-Hispanics reporting more than one race.
Source: Calculations by New Strategist based on the Bureau of Labor Statistics' 2012 Consumer Expenditure Survey

Vehicle Finance Charges

Best customers: Householders aged 25 to 54
Married couples with children at home
Households in the South

Customer trends: Average household spending on vehicle finance charges may continue to decline as aging boomers downsize their fleets.

The biggest spenders on vehicle finance charges are households with little savings and lots of vehicles—primarily young adults and couples with children. Householders ranging in age from 25 to 54 spend 26 to 35 percent more than average on vehicle finance charges and account for 70 percent of household spending on this item. Married couples with children at home spend 62 percent more than average on vehicle finance charges. Households in the South spend 10 percent more.

Average household spending on vehicle finance charges fell 49 percent between 2000 and 2012, after adjusting for inflation. Behind the decline were low-interest and no-interest loans on vehicles during the time period as well as diminished vehicle sales. Average household spending on vehicle finance charges may continue to decline as aging boomers downsize their fleets.

Table 19.17 Vehicle finance charges

Total household spending $27,789,557,760.00
Average household spends   223.36

AGE OF HOUSEHOLDER	AVERAGE HOUSEHOLD SPENDING	BEST CUSTOMERS (index)	BIGGEST CUSTOMERS (market share)
Average household	$223.36	100	100.0%
Under age 25	128.92	58	3.8
Aged 25 to 34	296.68	133	21.5
Aged 35 to 44	301.98	135	23.5
Aged 45 to 54	281.38	126	24.9
Aged 55 to 64	202.26	91	16.6
Aged 65 to 74	147.23	66	7.9
Aged 75 or older	41.67	19	1.8

	AVERAGE HOUSEHOLD SPENDING	BEST CUSTOMERS (index)	BIGGEST CUSTOMERS (market share)
HOUSEHOLD INCOME			
Average household	**$223.36**	**100**	**100.0%**
Under $20,000	47.51	21	4.5
$20,000 to $39,999	132.11	59	13.3
$40,000 to $49,999	197.25	88	7.8
$50,000 to $69,999	241.91	108	15.6
$70,000 to $79,999	335.46	150	8.4
$80,000 to $99,999	376.46	169	14.9
$100,000 or more	423.25	189	35.5
HOUSEHOLD TYPE			
Average household	**223.36**	**100**	**100.0**
Married couples	314.25	141	68.3
Married couples, no children	239.87	107	22.4
Married couples with children	362.21	162	38.1
Oldest child under age 6	401.59	180	8.2
Oldest child aged 6 to 17	361.82	162	19.3
Oldest child aged 18 or older	337.40	151	10.7
Single parent with child under age 18	166.18	74	3.9
Single person	92.12	41	12.2
RACE AND HISPANIC ORIGIN			
Average household	**223.36**	**100**	**100.0**
Asian	232.53	104	4.5
Black	206.95	93	11.6
Hispanic	192.91	86	10.8
Non-Hispanic white and other	231.20	104	77.7
REGION			
Average household	**223.36**	**100**	**100.0**
Northeast	205.70	92	16.6
Midwest	198.48	89	19.7
South	245.70	110	41.0
West	225.06	101	22.7
EDUCATION			
Average household	**223.36**	**100**	**100.0**
Less than high school graduate	103.94	47	6.1
High school graduate	198.23	89	22.1
Some college	221.60	99	20.4
Associate's degree	328.37	147	14.5
Bachelor's degree or more	260.92	117	36.8
Bachelor's degree	266.32	119	23.8
Master's, professional, doctoral degree	251.64	113	13.1

Note: Market shares may not sum to 100.0 because of rounding and missing categories by household type. "Asian" and "black" include Hispanics and non-Hispanics who identify themselves as being of the respective race alone. "Hispanic" includes people of any race who identify themselves as Hispanic. "Other" includes people who identify themselves as non-Hispanic and as Alaska Native, American Indian, Asian (who are also included in the "Asian" row), or Native Hawaiian or other Pacific Islander, as well as non-Hispanics reporting more than one race.
Source: Calculations by New Strategist based on the Bureau of Labor Statistics' 2012 Consumer Expenditure Survey

Vehicle Insurance

Best customers: Householders aged 45 to 64
Married couples without children at home
Married couples with adult children at home

Customer trends: Average household spending on vehicle insurance may continue to fall as aging boomers downsize their fleets.

The biggest spenders on vehicle insurance are households with multiple cars and drivers—particularly teens and young adults. Householders aged 45 to 54 (the age group likely to have young-adult children at home) spend 25 percent more than average on vehicle insurance, while those aged 55 to 64 spend 35 percent more. Together they account for 49 percent of the market for this item. Married couples with adult children at home spend 59 percent more than average on car insurance. Married couples without children at home spend 30 percent more than average.

Average household spending on vehicle insurance fell slightly between 2000 and 2012—down 2 percent, after adjusting for inflation. Behind the decline was the baby-boom generation's exit from the best-customer lifestage as well as the aging of household vehicles in the wake of the Great Recession. Average household spending on this item may continue to fall in the years ahead as aging boomers downsize their fleets.

Table 19.18 Vehicle insurance

Total household spending $126,648,023,040.00
Average household spends   1,017.94

AGE OF HOUSEHOLDER	AVERAGE HOUSEHOLD SPENDING	BEST CUSTOMERS (index)	BIGGEST CUSTOMERS (market share)
Average household	$1,017.94	100	100.0%
Under age 25	471.33	46	3.0
Aged 25 to 34	784.88	77	12.5
Aged 35 to 44	910.76	89	15.5
Aged 45 to 54	1,267.89	125	24.7
Aged 55 to 64	1,371.98	135	24.7
Aged 65 to 74	1,006.74	99	11.9
Aged 75 or older	843.26	83	8.1

	AVERAGE HOUSEHOLD SPENDING	BEST CUSTOMERS (index)	BIGGEST CUSTOMERS (market share)
HOUSEHOLD INCOME			
Average household	$1,017.94	100	100.0%
Under $20,000	474.95	47	9.8
$20,000 to $39,999	733.08	72	16.2
$40,000 to $49,999	1,135.54	112	9.9
$50,000 to $69,999	996.86	98	14.1
$70,000 to $79,999	1,675.89	165	9.2
$80,000 to $99,999	1,203.65	118	10.4
$100,000 or more	1,610.16	158	29.6
HOUSEHOLD TYPE			
Average household	1,017.94	100	100.0
Married couples	1,270.34	125	60.6
Married couples, no children	1,325.53	130	27.1
Married couples with children	1,200.84	118	27.7
Oldest child under age 6	840.84	83	3.8
Oldest child aged 6 to 17	1,085.64	107	12.7
Oldest child aged 18 or older	1,617.34	159	11.2
Single parent with child under age 18	743.96	73	3.8
Single person	599.97	59	17.5
RACE AND HISPANIC ORIGIN			
Average household	1,017.94	100	100.0
Asian	1,096.47	108	4.7
Black	863.30	85	10.7
Hispanic	1,082.69	106	13.3
Non-Hispanic white and other	1,031.54	101	76.1
REGION			
Average household	1,017.94	100	100.0
Northeast	942.46	93	16.7
Midwest	862.96	85	18.8
South	1,119.45	110	41.0
West	1,065.82	105	23.6
EDUCATION			
Average household	1,017.94	100	100.0
Less than high school graduate	861.34	85	11.0
High school graduate	1,003.73	99	24.6
Some college	942.47	93	19.1
Associate's degree	1,019.25	100	9.9
Bachelor's degree or more	1,138.18	112	35.3
Bachelor's degree	1,173.58	115	23.0
Master's, professional, doctoral degree	1,078.33	106	12.3

Note: Market shares may not sum to 100.0 because of rounding and missing categories by household type. "Asian" and "black" include Hispanics and non-Hispanics who identify themselves as being of the respective race alone. "Hispanic" includes people of any race who identify themselves as Hispanic. "Other" includes people who identify themselves as non-Hispanic and as Alaska Native, American Indian, Asian (who are also included in the "Asian" row), or Native Hawaiian or other Pacific Islander, as well as non-Hispanics reporting more than one race.
Source: Calculations by New Strategist based on the Bureau of Labor Statistics' 2012 Consumer Expenditure Survey

Vehicle Maintenance and Repair (Includes Oil Changes and Tires)

Best customers: Householders aged 45 to 64
                        Married couples with school-aged or older children at home

Customer trends: Average household spending on vehicle maintenance and repair may rise as the slow economic recovery forces more Americans to drive aging cars.

The biggest spenders on vehicle maintenance and repair are households with the most vehicles—married couples, particularly those with teenagers and young adults at home. Householders ranging in age from 45 to 64, many living with teens and young adults, spend 21 to 23 percent more than average on vehicle maintenance and repair. Married couples with school-aged or older children at home spend 42 to 54 percent more than average on this item.

Average household spending on vehicle maintenance and repair fell 6 percent between 2000 and 2006, after adjusting for inflation, then rose 4 percent between 2006 and 2012. Behind the earlier decline in spending was the increased ownership of new vehicles as dealers offered low-interest loans and other incentives. Average household spending on vehicle maintenance and repair may rise in the years ahead as the slow economic recovery forces more Americans to drive aging cars.

Table 19.19 Vehicle maintenance and repair (includes oil changes and tires)

Total household spending $101,308,216,320.00
Average household spends   814.27

AGE OF HOUSEHOLDER	AVERAGE HOUSEHOLD SPENDING	BEST CUSTOMERS (index)	BIGGEST CUSTOMERS (market share)
Average household	$814.27	100	100.0%
Under age 25	485.78	60	3.9
Aged 25 to 34	706.82	87	14.0
Aged 35 to 44	834.21	102	17.8
Aged 45 to 54	988.23	121	24.0
Aged 55 to 64	997.68	123	22.4
Aged 65 to 74	839.95	103	12.4
Aged 75 or older	452.50	56	5.4

	AVERAGE HOUSEHOLD SPENDING	BEST CUSTOMERS (index)	BIGGEST CUSTOMERS (market share)
HOUSEHOLD INCOME			
Average household	**$814.27**	**100**	**100.0%**
Under $20,000	359.79	44	9.3
$20,000 to $39,999	576.24	71	15.9
$40,000 to $49,999	722.12	89	7.8
$50,000 to $69,999	881.07	108	15.6
$70,000 to $79,999	913.59	112	6.3
$80,000 to $99,999	1,021.77	125	11.1
$100,000 or more	1,476.62	181	34.0
HOUSEHOLD TYPE			
Average household	**814.27**	**100**	**100.0**
Married couples	1,039.75	128	62.0
Married couples, no children	937.95	115	24.0
Married couples with children	1,136.42	140	32.8
Oldest child under age 6	899.86	111	5.0
Oldest child aged 6 to 17	1,156.00	142	16.9
Oldest child aged 18 or older	1,255.66	154	10.9
Single parent with child under age 18	587.30	72	3.8
Single person	525.49	65	19.2
RACE AND HISPANIC ORIGIN			
Average household	**814.27**	**100**	**100.0**
Asian	774.66	95	4.1
Black	582.73	72	9.0
Hispanic	641.51	79	9.9
Non-Hispanic white and other	881.62	108	81.3
REGION			
Average household	**814.27**	**100**	**100.0**
Northeast	814.86	100	18.1
Midwest	789.58	97	21.5
South	727.43	89	33.3
West	981.77	121	27.2
EDUCATION			
Average household	**814.27**	**100**	**100.0**
Less than high school graduate	451.79	55	7.2
High school graduate	669.64	82	20.5
Some college	732.68	90	18.5
Associate's degree	936.41	115	11.4
Bachelor's degree or more	1,091.88	134	42.3
Bachelor's degree	1,028.32	126	25.2
Master's, professional, doctoral degree	1,201.40	148	17.1

Note: Market shares may not sum to 100.0 because of rounding and missing categories by household type. "Asian" and "black" include Hispanics and non-Hispanics who identify themselves as being of the respective race alone. "Hispanic" includes people of any race who identify themselves as Hispanic. "Other" includes people who identify themselves as non-Hispanic and as Alaska Native, American Indian, Asian (who are also included in the "Asian" row), or Native Hawaiian or other Pacific Islander, as well as non-Hispanics reporting more than one race.
Source: Calculations by New Strategist based on the Bureau of Labor Statistics' 2012 Consumer Expenditure Survey

Vehicle Rentals (Including Rentals on Trips)

Best customers: Householders aged 45 to 64
　　　　　　　　　　　Married couples
　　　　　　　　　　　Asians
　　　　　　　　　　　Households in the Northeast and West

Customer trends: Average household spending on vehicle rentals should rise as boomers retire and begin to devote more money to travel.

The biggest spenders on vehicle rentals are travelers, since nearly three-quarters of spending on rented vehicles occurs on trips. Older married couples are the biggest travelers, which accounts for their above-average spending on rented vehicles. Householders aged 45 to 64 spend 16 to 39 percent more than average on rented vehicles. Married couples without children at home (most of them empty-nesters) spend 55 percent more than average on this item. Those with children at home spend 39 percent more than average, the figure peaking at 62 percent above average among those with school-aged children. Asian households outspend the average by 95 percent. Households in the West, where many Asians reside, spend 17 percent more than average on vehicle rentals. Households in the Northeast spend 11 percent more.

Average household spending on rented vehicles fell 40 percent between 2000 and 2012, after adjusting for inflation. Behind the decline was the Great Recession, which reduced spending on travel, as well as price discounting. Average household spending on vehicle rentals should rise as boomers retire and begin to devote more money to travel.

Table 19.20 **Vehicle rentals (including rentals on trips)**

Total household spending	$4,507,591,680.00
Average household spends	36.23

	AVERAGE HOUSEHOLD SPENDING	BEST CUSTOMERS (index)	BIGGEST CUSTOMERS (market share)
AGE OF HOUSEHOLDER			
Average household	**$36.23**	**100**	**100.0%**
Under age 25	15.07	42	2.7
Aged 25 to 34	36.37	100	16.2
Aged 35 to 44	36.30	100	17.4
Aged 45 to 54	42.03	116	23.0
Aged 55 to 64	50.33	139	25.4
Aged 65 to 74	31.39	87	10.4
Aged 75 or older	17.83	49	4.8

	AVERAGE HOUSEHOLD SPENDING	BEST CUSTOMERS (index)	BIGGEST CUSTOMERS (market share)
HOUSEHOLD INCOME			
Average household	$36.23	100	100.0%
Under $20,000	13.18	36	7.7
$20,000 to $39,999	16.29	45	10.1
$40,000 to $49,999	17.37	48	4.2
$50,000 to $69,999	31.73	88	12.7
$70,000 to $79,999	25.44	70	3.9
$80,000 to $99,999	48.92	135	11.9
$100,000 or more	95.74	264	49.5
HOUSEHOLD TYPE			
Average household	36.23	100	100.0
Married couples	51.17	141	68.6
Married couples, no children	56.17	155	32.3
Married couples with children	50.23	139	32.6
Oldest child under age 6	40.02	110	5.0
Oldest child aged 6 to 17	58.79	162	19.3
Oldest child aged 18 or older	42.41	117	8.3
Single parent with child under age 18	19.07	53	2.8
Single person	21.21	59	17.4
RACE AND HISPANIC ORIGIN			
Average household	36.23	100	100.0
Asian	70.57	195	8.4
Black	27.37	76	9.5
Hispanic	17.97	50	6.2
Non-Hispanic white and other	40.68	112	84.3
REGION			
Average household	36.23	100	100.0
Northeast	40.34	111	20.1
Midwest	33.65	93	20.6
South	32.12	89	33.0
West	42.24	117	26.3
EDUCATION			
Average household	36.23	100	100.0
Less than high school graduate	8.96	25	3.2
High school graduate	19.90	55	13.7
Some college	27.56	76	15.7
Associate's degree	27.04	75	7.4
Bachelor's degree or more	68.96	190	60.0
Bachelor's degree	52.16	144	28.7
Master's, professional, doctoral degree	97.81	270	31.3

Note: Market shares may not sum to 100.0 because of rounding and missing categories by household type. "Asian" and "black" include Hispanics and non-Hispanics who identify themselves as being of the respective race alone. "Hispanic" includes people of any race who identify themselves as Hispanic. "Other" includes people who identify themselves as non-Hispanic and as Alaska Native, American Indian, Asian (who are also included in the "Asian" row), or Native Hawaiian or other Pacific Islander, as well as non-Hispanics reporting more than one race.
Source: Calculations by New Strategist based on the Bureau of Labor Statistics' 2012 Consumer Expenditure Survey

Chapter 20.
Travel

Household Spending on Travel, 2000 to 2012

Travel is one of the most popular leisure-time activities of Americans. In 2012, the average household spent $1,478 on travel, including airfares, gasoline, lodging, luggage, food, and recreational expenses. The top-three travel expense categories—airline fares, lodging, and restaurant meals—account for nearly two-thirds of travel spending. Ranking fourth is gasoline and motor oil on trips, which accounts for 10 percent of the total.

After declining 14 percent from the overall peak spending year of 2006 to the overall trough spending year of 2010, average household spending on travel rose 7 percent during the ensuing two years, after adjusting for inflation. Behind the earlier drop in spending on travel was household belt tightening as the Great Recession took hold. The travel items that saw the largest increases in average household spending between 2010 and 2012 were ship fares (up 36 percent), gasoline and motor oil on trips (up 19 percent), intercity train fares (up 14 percent), and groceries on trips (up 10 percent). Spending on vehicle rentals, parking fees and tolls, and alcoholic beverages were the only travel categories to post spending losses between 2010 and 2012, dropping between 6 and 3 percent.

Because the best customers of travel are older Americans, average household spending on travel should rise in the future as the baby-boom generation ages—but only if discretionary income grows.

Spending on travel

(average spending by households on travel, 2000, 2006, 2010, and 2012; in 2012 dollars)

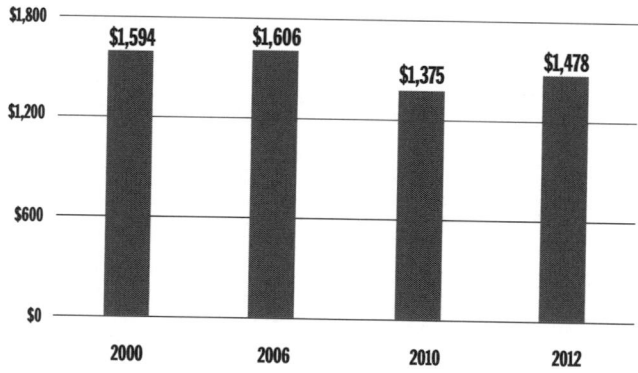

Table 20.1 Travel spending, 2000 to 2012

(average annual household spending on travel and percent distribution, by category, 2000 to 2012; percent and percentage point change in spending, 2000–06, 2006–12, and 2010–12; in 2012 dollars; ranked by amount spent)

	average annual household spending (in 2012$)				percent change		
	2012	2010	2006	2000	2010–12	2006–12	2000–06
Average household spending on travel	**$1,478.35**	**$1,375.23**	**$1,606.12**	**$1,593.93**	**7.5%**	**–8.0%**	**0.8%**
Airline fares	352.53	342.52	381.06	365.35	2.9	–7.5	4.3
Lodging on trips	341.61	314.85	365.16	335.48	8.5	–6.5	8.8
Restaurant and carry-out food on trips	257.15	234.88	276.66	288.07	9.5	–7.1	–4.0
Gasoline and motor oil on trips	148.97	125.49	146.81	123.62	18.7	1.5	18.8
Recreational expenses on trips	128.49	128.24	168.44	194.59	0.2	–23.7	–13.4
Ship fares	56.53	41.42	62.66	48.77	36.5	–9.8	28.5
Groceries on trips	50.23	45.65	48.85	53.25	10.0	2.8	–8.3
Alcoholic beverages on trips	43.80	44.97	49.38	45.65	–2.6	–11.3	8.2
Vehicle rentals on trips	25.38	26.95	31.42	45.77	–5.8	–19.2	–31.4
Train fares, intercity	18.88	16.50	18.55	28.16	14.4	1.8	–34.1
Local transportation on trips	17.81	17.75	23.73	22.56	0.3	–25.0	5.2
Luggage	13.79	13.31	8.92	11.09	3.6	54.6	–19.6
Bus fares, intercity	11.96	10.89	12.90	21.47	9.9	–7.3	–39.9
Parking fees and tolls on trips	11.22	11.79	11.57	10.08	–4.9	–3.0	14.8

					percentage point change		
PERCENT DISTRIBUTION OF SPENDING	2012	2010	2006	2000	2010–12	2006–12	2000–06
Average household spending on travel	**100.0%**	**100.0%**	**100.0%**	**100.0%**	–	–	–
Airline fares	23.8	24.9	23.7	22.9	–1.1	0.1	0.8
Lodging on trips	23.1	22.9	22.7	21.0	0.2	0.4	1.7
Restaurant and carry-out food on trips	17.4	17.1	17.2	18.1	0.3	0.2	–0.8
Gasoline and motor oil on trips	10.1	9.1	9.1	7.8	1.0	0.9	1.4
Recreational expenses on trips	8.7	9.3	10.5	12.2	–0.6	–1.8	–1.7
Ship fares	3.8	3.0	3.9	3.1	0.8	–0.1	0.8
Groceries on trips	3.4	3.3	3.0	3.3	0.1	0.4	–0.3
Alcoholic beverages on trips	3.0	3.3	3.1	2.9	–0.3	–0.1	0.2
Vehicle rentals on trips	1.7	2.0	2.0	2.9	–0.2	–0.2	–0.9
Train fares, intercity	1.3	1.2	1.2	1.8	0.1	0.1	–0.6
Local transportation on trips	1.2	1.3	1.5	1.4	–0.1	–0.3	0.1
Luggage	0.9	1.0	0.6	0.7	0.0	0.4	–0.1
Bus fares, intercity	0.8	0.8	0.8	1.3	0.0	0.0	–0.5
Parking fees and tolls on trips	0.8	0.9	0.7	0.6	–0.1	0.0	0.1

Note: Percentage point change calculations are based on unrounded figures. "–" means not applicable.
Source: Bureau of Labor Statistics, 2000, 2006, 2010, and 2012 Consumer Expenditure Surveys; calculations by New Strategist

Airline Fares

Best customers: Householders aged 45 to 64
                   Married couples without children at home
                   Married couples with school-aged or older children at home
                   Asians
                   Households in the West and Northeast
                   College graduates

Customer trends: Average household spending on airline fares may continue to grow as boomers
                   retire and devote more money to travel.

The biggest spenders on airline fares are college-educated middle-aged or older adults. Householders ranging in age from 45 to 64 spend 23 to 31 percent more than average on airfares and account for nearly half the market. College graduates spend over twice the average on airfares and account for two-thirds of the market. Married couples without children at home (most of them empty-nesters) spend 53 percent more than average on airfares, while those with school-aged or older children at home spend 52 to 55 percent more than average on this item. Asians spend almost three times the average on airfares. Households in the West and Northeast spend 38 and 27 percent more than average, respectively.

Average household spending on airline fares has been on a rollercoaster ride. Spending on airfares rose 4 percent from 2000 to the overall peak spending year of 2006, fell 10 percent between then and the overall trough spending year of 2010, and increased 3 percent between 2010 and 2012, after adjusting for inflation. Behind the decline was the Great Recession, which reduced spending on travel. Average household spending on airline fares may continue to grow as boomers retire and devote more money to travel.

Table 20.2 Airline fares

Total household spending $43,860,372,480.00
Average household spends   352.53

AGE OF HOUSEHOLDER	AVERAGE HOUSEHOLD SPENDING	BEST CUSTOMERS (index)	BIGGEST CUSTOMERS (market share)
Average household	$352.53	100	100.0%
Under age 25	157.82	45	2.9
Aged 25 to 34	299.42	85	13.7
Aged 35 to 44	328.25	93	16.2
Aged 45 to 54	433.37	123	24.3
Aged 55 to 64	463.30	131	24.1
Aged 65 to 74	386.59	110	13.2
Aged 75 or older	200.99	57	5.6

	AVERAGE HOUSEHOLD SPENDING	BEST CUSTOMERS (index)	BIGGEST CUSTOMERS (market share)
HOUSEHOLD INCOME			
Average household	**$352.53**	**100**	**100.0%**
Under $20,000	95.67	27	5.7
$20,000 to $39,999	140.67	40	9.0
$40,000 to $49,999	194.06	55	4.9
$50,000 to $69,999	305.61	87	12.5
$70,000 to $79,999	363.05	103	5.7
$80,000 to $99,999	426.10	121	10.7
$100,000 or more	969.51	275	51.5
HOUSEHOLD TYPE			
Average household	**352.53**	**100**	**100.0**
Married couples	510.99	145	70.4
Married couples, no children	540.00	153	31.9
Married couples with children	510.34	145	34.0
Oldest child under age 6	390.95	111	5.1
Oldest child aged 6 to 17	534.99	152	18.0
Oldest child aged 18 or older	546.01	155	10.9
Single parent with child under age 18	132.19	37	2.0
Single person	208.54	59	17.6
RACE AND HISPANIC ORIGIN			
Average household	**352.53**	**100**	**100.0**
Asian	986.90	280	12.1
Black	150.78	43	5.4
Hispanic	217.24	62	7.7
Non-Hispanic white and other	408.38	116	86.9
REGION			
Average household	**352.53**	**100**	**100.0**
Northeast	447.89	127	22.9
Midwest	304.40	86	19.1
South	253.02	72	26.7
West	487.96	138	31.2
EDUCATION			
Average household	**352.53**	**100**	**100.0**
Less than high school graduate	89.61	25	3.3
High school graduate	145.50	41	10.3
Some college	238.86	68	14.0
Associate's degree	221.63	63	6.2
Bachelor's degree or more	740.27	210	66.2
Bachelor's degree	628.98	178	35.6
Master's, professional, doctoral degree	931.39	264	30.7

Note: Market shares may not sum to 100.0 because of rounding and missing categories by household type. "Asian" and "black" include Hispanics and non-Hispanics who identify themselves as being of the respective race alone. "Hispanic" includes people of any race who identify themselves as Hispanic. "Other" includes people who identify themselves as non-Hispanic and as Alaska Native, American Indian, Asian (who are also included in the "Asian" row), or Native Hawaiian or other Pacific Islander, as well as non-Hispanics reporting more than one race.
Source: Calculations by New Strategist based on the Bureau of Labor Statistics' 2012 Consumer Expenditure Survey

Alcoholic Beverages Purchased on Trips

Best customers: Householders aged 55 to 64
Married couples without children at home
Non-Hispanic whites
Households in the West
College graduates

Customer trends: Average household spending on alcoholic beverages purchased on trips should begin to grow again as boomers retire and spend more time and money traveling.

The biggest spenders on alcoholic beverages purchased on trips can be found in a variety of demographic categories. Householders aged 55 to 64 spend 20 percent more than average on this item. Married couples without children at home (most of them older) spend 77 percent more than average on alcoholic beverages while on trips. These empty-nesters spend more than other household types on alcoholic beverages while traveling because they no longer need to devote their time and money to children's wants and needs. Non-Hispanic whites spend 19 percent more than average on alcoholic beverages while traveling and constitute 90 percent of the market. Households in the West spend 19 percent more than average on alcohol while traveling. College graduates spend twice the average on this item.

Average household spending on alcoholic beverages purchased on trips grew by 8 percent between 2000 and 2006, after adjusting for inflation, then fell 11 percent between 2006 and 2012. Behind the decline was the Great Recession, which reduced spending on travel. In the years ahead, spending on this item should rise again as boomers retire and spend more time and money traveling.

Table 20.3 Alcoholic beverages purchased on trips

Total household spending $5,449,420,800.00
Average household spends 43.80

	AVERAGE HOUSEHOLD SPENDING	BEST CUSTOMERS (index)	BIGGEST CUSTOMERS (market share)
AGE OF HOUSEHOLDER			
Average household	**$43.80**	**100**	**100.0%**
Under age 25	22.58	52	3.4
Aged 25 to 34	49.77	114	18.4
Aged 35 to 44	44.83	102	17.8
Aged 45 to 54	48.53	111	21.9
Aged 55 to 64	52.39	120	21.9
Aged 65 to 74	43.50	99	12.0
Aged 75 or older	21.08	48	4.7

	AVERAGE HOUSEHOLD SPENDING	BEST CUSTOMERS (index)	BIGGEST CUSTOMERS (market share)
HOUSEHOLD INCOME			
Average household	**$43.80**	**100**	**100.0%**
Under $20,000	10.62	24	5.1
$20,000 to $39,999	14.22	32	7.3
$40,000 to $49,999	27.11	62	5.5
$50,000 to $69,999	36.90	84	12.2
$70,000 to $79,999	42.62	97	5.4
$80,000 to $99,999	68.80	157	13.9
$100,000 or more	118.51	271	50.7
HOUSEHOLD TYPE			
Average household	**43.80**	**100**	**100.0**
Married couples	59.60	136	66.1
Married couples, no children	77.66	177	37.0
Married couples with children	48.43	111	26.0
Oldest child under age 6	49.77	114	5.2
Oldest child aged 6 to 17	49.47	113	13.4
Oldest child aged 18 or older	45.79	105	7.4
Single parent with child under age 18	14.50	33	1.7
Single person	29.67	68	20.1
RACE AND HISPANIC ORIGIN			
Average household	**43.80**	**100**	**100.0**
Asian	37.59	86	3.7
Black	14.51	33	4.2
Hispanic	21.94	50	6.3
Non-Hispanic white and other	52.29	119	89.6
REGION			
Average household	**43.80**	**100**	**100.0**
Northeast	47.75	109	19.7
Midwest	44.25	101	22.4
South	36.64	84	31.2
West	52.05	119	26.8
EDUCATION			
Average household	**43.80**	**100**	**100.0**
Less than high school graduate	8.20	19	2.4
High school graduate	17.72	40	10.1
Some college	35.62	81	16.7
Associate's degree	32.09	73	7.2
Bachelor's degree or more	88.17	201	63.5
Bachelor's degree	80.37	183	36.6
Master's, professional, doctoral degree	101.58	232	26.9

Note: Market shares may not sum to 100.0 because of rounding and missing categories by household type. "Asian" and "black" include Hispanics and non-Hispanics who identify themselves as being of the respective race alone. "Hispanic" includes people of any race who identify themselves as Hispanic. "Other" includes people who identify themselves as non-Hispanic and as Alaska Native, American Indian, Asian (who are also included in the "Asian" row), or Native Hawaiian or other Pacific Islander, as well as non-Hispanics reporting more than one race.
Source: Calculations by New Strategist based on the Bureau of Labor Statistics' 2012 Consumer Expenditure Survey

Bus Fares, Intercity

Best customers: Householders aged 55 to 74
Married couples without children at home
Married couples with adult children at home
Asians
Households in the Northeast and West

Customer trends: Average household spending on intercity bus fares should stabilize as travelers look for less expensive ways to get from point A to point B.

The best customers of intercity bus fares are older householders in the Northeast and West and households with adult children. Householders aged 55 to 74 spend 21 to 45 percent more than average on intercity bus fares. Married couples with adult children at home spend 48 percent more than average on this item, many of them paying for their college-aged children to go to and from school. Married couples without children at home spend 68 percent more than average on bus fares and control 35 percent of the market. Asian households spend twice the average on intercity bus travel. Households in the Northeast spend 17 percent more than average on this item, and households in the West spend 13 percent more.

Average household spending on intercity bus fares fell by a substantial 49 percent between 2000 and 2010, after adjusting for inflation, then rebounded by 10 percent between 2010 and 2012. Behind the decline were the Great Recession and the reduction in travel spending as well as discounters offering lower-cost bus travel along well-traveled routes. Average household spending on intercity bus fares should stabilize as travelers look for less expensive ways to get from point A to point B.

Table 20.4 Bus fares, intercity

Total household spending $1,488,015,360.00
Average household spends   11.96

	AVERAGE HOUSEHOLD SPENDING	BEST CUSTOMERS (index)	BIGGEST CUSTOMERS (market share)
AGE OF HOUSEHOLDER			
Average household	$11.96	100	100.0%
Under age 25	5.94	50	3.3
Aged 25 to 34	9.10	76	12.3
Aged 35 to 44	9.97	83	14.5
Aged 45 to 54	13.28	111	22.0
Aged 55 to 64	14.45	121	22.1
Aged 65 to 74	17.31	145	17.4
Aged 75 or older	10.37	87	8.5

	AVERAGE HOUSEHOLD SPENDING	BEST CUSTOMERS (index)	BIGGEST CUSTOMERS (market share)
HOUSEHOLD INCOME			
Average household	**$11.96**	**100**	**100.0%**
Under $20,000	6.29	53	11.1
$20,000 to $39,999	7.03	59	13.2
$40,000 to $49,999	6.91	58	5.1
$50,000 to $69,999	12.90	108	15.6
$70,000 to $79,999	13.80	115	6.4
$80,000 to $99,999	17.17	144	12.7
$100,000 or more	22.95	192	35.9
HOUSEHOLD TYPE			
Average household	**11.96**	**100**	**100.0**
Married couples	16.30	136	66.2
Married couples, no children	20.13	168	35.1
Married couples with children	12.83	107	25.2
Oldest child under age 6	9.04	76	3.4
Oldest child aged 6 to 17	11.38	95	11.3
Oldest child aged 18 or older	17.73	148	10.5
Single parent with child under age 18	4.74	40	2.1
Single person	7.92	66	19.7
RACE AND HISPANIC ORIGIN			
Average household	**11.96**	**100**	**100.0**
Asian	23.87	200	8.7
Black	8.73	73	9.2
Hispanic	11.51	96	12.1
Non-Hispanic white and other	12.60	105	79.1
REGION			
Average household	**11.96**	**100**	**100.0**
Northeast	13.94	117	21.0
Midwest	11.13	93	20.6
South	10.57	88	32.9
West	13.52	113	25.5
EDUCATION			
Average household	**11.96**	**100**	**100.0**
Less than high school graduate	9.90	83	10.8
High school graduate	6.62	55	13.8
Some college	9.25	77	15.9
Associate's degree	9.06	76	7.5
Bachelor's degree or more	19.73	165	52.0
Bachelor's degree	16.89	141	28.1
Master's, professional, doctoral degree	24.61	206	23.9

Note: Market shares may not sum to 100.0 because of rounding and missing categories by household type. "Asian" and "black" include Hispanics and non-Hispanics who identify themselves as being of the respective race alone. "Hispanic" includes people of any race who identify themselves as Hispanic. "Other" includes people who identify themselves as non-Hispanic and as Alaska Native, American Indian, Asian (who are also included in the "Asian" row), or Native Hawaiian or other Pacific Islander, as well as non-Hispanics reporting more than one race.
Source: Calculations by New Strategist based on the Bureau of Labor Statistics' 2012 Consumer Expenditure Survey

Gasoline and Motor Oil on Trips

Best customers: Householders aged 45 to 74
                    Married couples
                    Households in the Midwest and West

Customer trends: Average household spending on gasoline and motor oil on trips should rise in the next few years
                     as more boomers fill the peak traveling lifestage.

Because gasoline (and motor oil) are such commonly purchased items, variations in spending across most demographic categories are relatively small. The biggest spenders on gasoline purchased while traveling are the largest households as well as the most avid travelers—empty-nesters. Householders aged 45 to 74 spend 12 to 19 percent more than average on this item. Married couples without children at home (most of them empty-nesters) spend 67 percent more than average on gasoline and motor oil while traveling and account for over one-third of the market. Couples with children at home spend 37 percent more than average on this item, the figure peaking among those with school-aged children at 47 percent. Households in the Midwest and West outspend the average by 14 to 16 percent.

Average household spending on gasoline and motor oil on trips rose 19 percent between 2000 and the overall peak spending year of 2006, after adjusting for inflation, as gas prices increased. Spending then fell 15 percent between 2006 and 2010 as the Great Recession took hold and gas prices eased slightly, but rebounded strongly with a 19 percent rise between 2010 and 2012. Average household spending on gasoline and motor oil while traveling should rise in the next few years as more boomers fill the peak traveling lifestage.

Table 20.5 Gasoline and motor oil on trips

Total household spending $18,534,251,520.00
Average household spends   148.97

AGE OF HOUSEHOLDER	AVERAGE HOUSEHOLD SPENDING	BEST CUSTOMERS (index)	BIGGEST CUSTOMERS (market share)
Average household	$148.97	100	100.0%
Under age 25	74.71	50	3.3
Aged 25 to 34	146.97	99	15.9
Aged 35 to 44	155.27	104	18.1
Aged 45 to 54	167.28	112	22.2
Aged 55 to 64	176.77	119	21.7
Aged 65 to 74	170.19	114	13.8
Aged 75 or older	75.58	51	5.0

	AVERAGE HOUSEHOLD SPENDING	BEST CUSTOMERS (index)	BIGGEST CUSTOMERS (market share)
HOUSEHOLD INCOME			
Average household	**$148.97**	**100**	**100.0%**
Under $20,000	49.34	33	7.0
$20,000 to $39,999	93.53	63	14.2
$40,000 to $49,999	119.34	80	7.1
$50,000 to $69,999	152.37	102	14.8
$70,000 to $79,999	211.58	142	7.9
$80,000 to $99,999	243.86	164	14.4
$100,000 or more	275.65	185	34.6
HOUSEHOLD TYPE			
Average household	**148.97**	**100**	**100.0**
Married couples	219.03	147	71.4
Married couples, no children	248.26	167	34.7
Married couples with children	204.32	137	32.2
Oldest child under age 6	191.67	129	5.9
Oldest child aged 6 to 17	218.48	147	17.4
Oldest child aged 18 or older	188.62	127	8.9
Single parent with child under age 18	73.56	49	2.6
Single person	74.07	50	14.8
RACE AND HISPANIC ORIGIN			
Average household	**148.97**	**100**	**100.0**
Asian	111.56	75	3.2
Black	73.29	49	6.2
Hispanic	91.51	61	7.7
Non-Hispanic white and other	171.03	115	86.2
REGION			
Average household	**148.97**	**100**	**100.0**
Northeast	107.03	72	13.0
Midwest	169.99	114	25.3
South	141.98	95	35.5
West	173.43	116	26.2
EDUCATION			
Average household	**148.97**	**100**	**100.0**
Less than high school graduate	56.09	38	4.9
High school graduate	92.48	62	15.5
Some college	139.28	93	19.3
Associate's degree	171.42	115	11.4
Bachelor's degree or more	231.37	155	49.0
Bachelor's degree	222.88	150	29.8
Master's, professional, doctoral degree	245.96	165	19.2

Note: Market shares may not sum to 100.0 because of rounding and missing categories by household type. "Asian" and "black" include Hispanics and non-Hispanics who identify themselves as being of the respective race alone. "Hispanic" includes people of any race who identify themselves as Hispanic. "Other" includes people who identify themselves as non-Hispanic and as Alaska Native, American Indian, Asian (who are also included in the "Asian" row), or Native Hawaiian or other Pacific Islander, as well as non-Hispanics reporting more than one race.
Source: Calculations by New Strategist based on the Bureau of Labor Statistics' 2012 Consumer Expenditure Survey

Groceries on Trips

Best customers: Householders aged 45 to 74
Married couples without children at home
Married couples with school-aged children
Households in the West

Customer trends: Average household spending on groceries while traveling should rise in the next few years as boomers retire.

The biggest spenders on groceries purchased on trips are older married couples, the most avid travelers. These couples are stocking up on food and drink for their hotel rooms or RVs. Householders ranging in age from 45 to 74 spend 28 to 32 percent more than average on this item. Married couples without children at home (most of them empty-nesters) spend 78 percent more than average on groceries while traveling and account for 37 percent of the market. Couples with school-aged children spend 55 percent more. Households in the West spend 31 percent more than average on groceries while traveling.

Average household spending on groceries while traveling grew 10 percent between 2010 and 2012, after adjusting for inflation. It had fallen 14 percent in the 10 years before that time. One factor behind the decline was the reduction in travel spending because of the Great Recession. Average household spending on groceries while traveling should rise in the next few years as boomers retire.

Table 20.6 Groceries on trips

Total household spending $6,249,415,680.00
Average household spends   50.23

	AVERAGE HOUSEHOLD SPENDING	BEST CUSTOMERS (index)	BIGGEST CUSTOMERS (market share)
AGE OF HOUSEHOLDER			
Average household	$50.23	100	100.0%
Under age 25	8.36	17	1.1
Aged 25 to 34	39.51	79	12.7
Aged 35 to 44	47.04	94	16.3
Aged 45 to 54	66.42	132	26.2
Aged 55 to 64	64.15	128	23.4
Aged 65 to 74	65.21	130	15.6
Aged 75 or older	24.43	49	4.8

	AVERAGE HOUSEHOLD SPENDING	BEST CUSTOMERS (index)	BIGGEST CUSTOMERS (market share)
HOUSEHOLD INCOME			
Average household	$50.23	100	100.0%
Under $20,000	15.50	31	6.5
$20,000 to $39,999	27.90	56	12.5
$40,000 to $49,999	33.07	66	5.8
$50,000 to $69,999	43.13	86	12.4
$70,000 to $79,999	67.71	135	7.5
$80,000 to $99,999	79.43	158	14.0
$100,000 or more	110.76	221	41.3
HOUSEHOLD TYPE			
Average household	50.23	100	100.0
Married couples	74.10	148	71.7
Married couples, no children	89.21	178	37.0
Married couples with children	66.03	131	30.9
Oldest child under age 6	45.26	90	4.1
Oldest child aged 6 to 17	77.90	155	18.4
Oldest child aged 18 or older	59.45	118	8.4
Single parent with child under age 18	26.05	52	2.7
Single person	23.77	47	14.1
RACE AND HISPANIC ORIGIN			
Average household	50.23	100	100.0
Asian	53.06	106	4.6
Black	18.58	37	4.6
Hispanic	28.60	57	7.1
Non-Hispanic white and other	59.08	118	88.3
REGION			
Average household	50.23	100	100.0
Northeast	50.20	100	18.0
Midwest	44.88	89	19.8
South	44.01	88	32.6
West	65.81	131	29.5
EDUCATION			
Average household	50.23	100	100.0
Less than high school graduate	17.76	35	4.6
High school graduate	26.69	53	13.2
Some college	45.50	91	18.7
Associate's degree	51.76	103	10.2
Bachelor's degree or more	84.90	169	53.3
Bachelor's degree	72.82	145	28.9
Master's, professional, doctoral degree	105.63	210	24.4

Note: Market shares may not sum to 100.0 because of rounding and missing categories by household type. "Asian" and "black" include Hispanics and non-Hispanics who identify themselves as being of the respective race alone. "Hispanic" includes people of any race who identify themselves as Hispanic. "Other" includes people who identify themselves as non-Hispanic and as Alaska Native, American Indian, Asian (who are also included in the "Asian" row), or Native Hawaiian or other Pacific Islander, as well as non-Hispanics reporting more than one race.
Source: Calculations by New Strategist based on the Bureau of Labor Statistics' 2012 Consumer Expenditure Survey

Local Transportation on Trips

Best customers: Householders aged 55 to 74
High-income households
Married couples without children at home
Married couples with adult children at home
Asians and non-Hispanic whites
Households in the Northeast
College graduates

Customer trends: Average household spending on local transportation on trips should rise as more boomers retire and become avid travelers.

Older married couples and the affluent spend the most on local transportation on trips, a category that includes taxi fares and limousine service. Householders ranging in age from 55 to 74 spend 28 to 39 percent more than average on this item. Married couples without children at home (most of them empty-nesters) spend 73 percent more than average on local transportation on trips, and those with adult children at home spend 64 percent more. High-income households spend more than three times the average on this item, while college graduates and Asians (each an affluent demographic) spend twice the average. Non-Hispanic whites spend 15 percent more on this item. Households in the Northeast spend 46 percent more than average on local transportation on trips.

Average household spending on local transportation on trips rose slowly in the first part of the decade, after adjusting for inflation, then declined 25 percent between 2006 and 2010 and has stagnated since then. Average household spending on local transportation on trips should rise as more boomers retire and become avid travelers.

Table 20.7 Local transportation on trips

Total household spending $2,215,848,960.00
Average household spends 17.81

	AVERAGE HOUSEHOLD SPENDING	BEST CUSTOMERS (index)	BIGGEST CUSTOMERS (market share)
AGE OF HOUSEHOLDER			
Average household	$17.81	100	100.0%
Under age 25	6.94	39	2.6
Aged 25 to 34	14.84	83	13.5
Aged 35 to 44	15.02	84	14.6
Aged 45 to 54	20.40	115	22.7
Aged 55 to 64	24.81	139	25.5
Aged 65 to 74	22.72	128	15.4
Aged 75 or older	10.57	59	5.8

	AVERAGE HOUSEHOLD SPENDING	BEST CUSTOMERS (index)	BIGGEST CUSTOMERS (market share)
HOUSEHOLD INCOME			
Average household	$17.81	100	100.0%
Under $20,000	3.54	20	4.2
$20,000 to $39,999	5.55	31	7.0
$40,000 to $49,999	6.11	34	3.0
$50,000 to $69,999	16.08	90	13.0
$70,000 to $79,999	15.04	84	4.7
$80,000 to $99,999	18.24	102	9.0
$100,000 or more	56.11	315	59.0
HOUSEHOLD TYPE			
Average household	17.81	100	100.0
Married couples	25.51	143	69.6
Married couples, no children	30.83	173	36.1
Married couples with children	22.71	128	30.0
Oldest child under age 6	21.00	118	5.4
Oldest child aged 6 to 17	19.53	110	13.0
Oldest child aged 18 or older	29.19	164	11.6
Single parent with child under age 18	7.89	44	2.3
Single person	11.52	65	19.2
RACE AND HISPANIC ORIGIN			
Average household	17.81	100	100.0
Asian	36.27	204	8.8
Black	9.38	53	6.6
Hispanic	9.89	56	7.0
Non-Hispanic white and other	20.53	115	86.5
REGION			
Average household	17.81	100	100.0
Northeast	26.01	146	26.4
Midwest	15.03	84	18.7
South	13.54	76	28.3
West	21.03	118	26.6
EDUCATION			
Average household	17.81	100	100.0
Less than high school graduate	4.13	23	3.0
High school graduate	6.78	38	9.5
Some college	10.41	58	12.0
Associate's degree	11.85	67	6.6
Bachelor's degree or more	38.90	218	68.9
Bachelor's degree	34.59	194	38.7
Master's, professional, doctoral degree	46.32	260	30.2

Note: Market shares may not sum to 100.0 because of rounding and missing categories by household type. "Asian" and "black" include Hispanics and non-Hispanics who identify themselves as being of the respective race alone. "Hispanic" includes people of any race who identify themselves as Hispanic. "Other" includes people who identify themselves as non-Hispanic and as Alaska Native, American Indian, Asian (who are also included in the "Asian" row), or Native Hawaiian or other Pacific Islander, as well as non-Hispanics reporting more than one race.
Source: Calculations by New Strategist based on the Bureau of Labor Statistics' 2012 Consumer Expenditure Survey

Lodging on Trips

Best customers: Householders aged 45 to 74
Married couples without children at home
Married couples with school-aged or older children at home
Asians and non-Hispanic whites
College graduates

Customer trends: Average household spending on lodging should grow as boomers retire and spend more time and money traveling.

Lodging, the second-biggest travel expense after airline fares, accounts for 23 percent of all household travel spending. The biggest spenders on lodging are the most avid travelers—middle-aged and older empty-nesters. Householders ranging in age from 45 to 74 spend 25 to 35 percent more than average on this item and account for 65 percent of the market. Married couples without children at home (most of them empty-nesters) spend 78 percent more than average on lodging. Couples with school-aged or older children at home spend 44 to 56 percent more than the average household on lodging on trips. Non-Hispanic whites spend 21 percent more than average on lodging and Asians spend 16 percent more. College graduates spend twice the average on lodging while traveling.

Average household spending on lodging climbed by 9 percent between 2000 and the overall peak spending year of 2006, after adjusting for inflation. Spending on this item then declined 14 percent between 2006 and 2010 as the Great Recession took hold. Spending on lodging rebounded in the two years following the overall trough spending year of 2010, rising by 8 percent. Average household spending on lodging should grow as boomers retire and spend more time and money traveling.

Table 20.8 Lodging on trips

Total household spending $42,501,749,760.00
Average household spends 341.61

AGE OF HOUSEHOLDER	AVERAGE HOUSEHOLD SPENDING	BEST CUSTOMERS (index)	BIGGEST CUSTOMERS (market share)
Average household	$341.61	100	100.0%
Under age 25	83.10	24	1.6
Aged 25 to 34	246.44	72	11.7
Aged 35 to 44	317.22	93	16.1
Aged 45 to 54	427.72	125	24.8
Aged 55 to 64	438.71	128	23.5
Aged 65 to 74	460.65	135	16.2
Aged 75 or older	212.82	62	6.1

	AVERAGE HOUSEHOLD SPENDING	BEST CUSTOMERS (index)	BIGGEST CUSTOMERS (market share)
HOUSEHOLD INCOME			
Average household	$341.61	100	100.0%
Under $20,000	81.37	24	5.0
$20,000 to $39,999	126.48	37	8.3
$40,000 to $49,999	189.82	56	4.9
$50,000 to $69,999	243.26	71	10.3
$70,000 to $79,999	424.07	124	6.9
$80,000 to $99,999	450.83	132	11.6
$100,000 or more	964.61	282	52.9
HOUSEHOLD TYPE			
Average household	341.61	100	100.0
Married couples	523.87	153	74.5
Married couples, no children	609.63	178	37.2
Married couples with children	481.03	141	33.1
Oldest child under age 6	327.60	96	4.4
Oldest child aged 6 to 17	534.01	156	18.6
Oldest child aged 18 or older	490.94	144	10.1
Single parent with child under age 18	138.18	40	2.1
Single person	161.26	47	14.0
RACE AND HISPANIC ORIGIN			
Average household	341.61	100	100.0
Asian	397.20	116	5.0
Black	142.16	42	5.2
Hispanic	114.68	34	4.2
Non-Hispanic white and other	412.30	121	90.6
REGION			
Average household	341.61	100	100.0
Northeast	381.23	112	20.1
Midwest	328.23	96	21.3
South	294.30	86	32.1
West	401.22	117	26.5
EDUCATION			
Average household	341.61	100	100.0
Less than high school graduate	61.66	18	2.4
High school graduate	161.62	47	11.8
Some college	218.36	64	13.2
Associate's degree	310.87	91	9.0
Bachelor's degree or more	689.92	202	63.7
Bachelor's degree	572.12	167	33.4
Master's, professional, doctoral degree	892.23	261	30.3

Note: Market shares may not sum to 100.0 because of rounding and missing categories by household type. "Asian" and "black" include Hispanics and non-Hispanics who identify themselves as being of the respective race alone. "Hispanic" includes people of any race who identify themselves as Hispanic. "Other" includes people who identify themselves as non-Hispanic and as Alaska Native, American Indian, Asian (who are also included in the "Asian" row), or Native Hawaiian or other Pacific Islander, as well as non-Hispanics reporting more than one race.
Source: Calculations by New Strategist based on the Bureau of Labor Statistics' 2012 Consumer Expenditure Survey

Luggage

Best customers:
Householders aged 35 to 44 and 55 to 64
Married couples without children at home
Married couples with children under age 18
Single parents

Customer trends:
Average household spending on luggage is likely to stabilize along with college enrollment, although the growing number of boomer travelers may boost it a bit more.

The biggest spenders on luggage are middle-aged parents (with children going to college) and older householders (the most avid travelers). Householders aged 35 to 44, many with children, spend 48 percent more than average on this item. Married couples with children aged 6 to 17 spend twice the average on luggage. Single parents, whose spending approaches average on only a few items, spend 6 percent more than average on luggage. Householders aged 55 to 64 spend one-third more than average on luggage. Married couples without children at home (most older empty-nesters) outspend the average by 34 percent.

Average household spending on luggage grew 24 percent between 2000 and 2012, after adjusting for inflation, including a 4 percent increase from 2010 to 2012. One factor behind the increase in spending on luggage is the growing share of young adults who are going to college, requiring luggage for their travel to and from school. Average household spending on luggage is likely to stabilize along with college enrollment, although retiring boomers may boost it a bit more.

Table 20.9 Luggage

Total household spending $1,715,696,640.00
Average household spends 13.79

AGE OF HOUSEHOLDER	AVERAGE HOUSEHOLD SPENDING	BEST CUSTOMERS (index)	BIGGEST CUSTOMERS (market share)
Average household	$13.79	100	100.0%
Under age 25	6.95	50	3.3
Aged 25 to 34	16.36	119	19.2
Aged 35 to 44	20.35	148	25.6
Aged 45 to 54	14.51	105	20.8
Aged 55 to 64	18.36	133	24.4
Aged 65 to 74	4.02	29	3.5
Aged 75 or older	4.20	30	3.0

	AVERAGE HOUSEHOLD SPENDING	BEST CUSTOMERS (index)	BIGGEST CUSTOMERS (market share)
HOUSEHOLD INCOME			
Average household	**$13.79**	**100**	**100.0%**
Under $20,000	6.15	45	9.4
$20,000 to $39,999	13.67	99	22.3
$40,000 to $49,999	4.66	34	3.0
$50,000 to $69,999	12.42	90	13.0
$70,000 to $79,999	12.15	88	4.9
$80,000 to $99,999	10.35	75	6.6
$100,000 or more	31.67	230	43.0
HOUSEHOLD TYPE			
Average household	**13.79**	**100**	**100.0**
Married couples	18.40	133	64.8
Married couples, no children	18.51	134	28.0
Married couples with children	21.03	153	35.9
Oldest child under age 6	18.46	134	6.1
Oldest child aged 6 to 17	27.54	200	23.8
Oldest child aged 18 or older	11.77	85	6.0
Single parent with child under age 18	14.67	106	5.6
Single person	6.78	49	14.6
RACE AND HISPANIC ORIGIN			
Average household	**13.79**	**100**	**100.0**
Asian	9.90	72	3.1
Black	6.61	48	6.0
Hispanic	4.90	36	4.5
Non-Hispanic white and other	16.45	119	89.5
REGION			
Average household	**13.79**	**100**	**100.0**
Northeast	15.14	110	19.8
Midwest	13.29	96	21.4
South	13.51	98	36.5
West	13.67	99	22.3
EDUCATION			
Average household	**13.79**	**100**	**100.0**
Less than high school graduate	5.58	40	5.3
High school graduate	13.02	94	23.5
Some college	10.64	77	15.9
Associate's degree	12.16	88	8.7
Bachelor's degree or more	20.10	146	46.0
Bachelor's degree	21.26	154	30.7
Master's, professional, doctoral degree	18.15	132	15.3

Note: Market shares may not sum to 100.0 because of rounding and missing categories by household type. "Asian" and "black" include Hispanics and non-Hispanics who identify themselves as being of the respective race alone. "Hispanic" includes people of any race who identify themselves as Hispanic. "Other" includes people who identify themselves as non-Hispanic and as Alaska Native, American Indian, Asian (who are also included in the "Asian" row), or Native Hawaiian or other Pacific Islander, as well as non-Hispanics reporting more than one race.
Source: Calculations by New Strategist based on the Bureau of Labor Statistics' 2012 Consumer Expenditure Survey

Parking Fees and Tolls on Trips

Best customers: **Householders aged 55 to 64**
                        Married couples without children at home
                        Married couples with school-aged children
                        Asians
                        Households in the Northeast

Customer trends: **Average household spending on parking fees and tolls on trips should rise as more boomers retire**
                        and take up traveling.

The most avid travelers spend the most on parking fees and tolls on trips. Householders aged 55 to 64 spend 43 percent more than average on this item. Married couples without children at home, most of them empty-nesters, spend 57 percent more than average on parking fees and tolls on trips, and couples with school-aged children spend 55 percent more. Asians spend 31 percent more than average on this item. Households in the Northeast spend 56 percent more than average on parking and tolls on trips because of the many toll roads in the region and the relatively high parking fees in congested Northeastern cities.

Parking fees and tolls on trips is one of only three travel categories in which average household spending continued to decline since the overall trough spending year of 2010. (The others are vehicle rentals and alcoholic beverages.) Spending on parking and tolls had risen 17 percent between 2000 and 2010, after adjusting for inflation, but fell 5 percent between 2010 and 2012. Average household spending on parking fees and tolls on trips should rise as more boomers retire and take up traveling.

Table 20.10 Parking fees and tolls on trips

| Total household spending | $1,395,947,520.00 |
| Average household spends | 11.22 |

AGE OF HOUSEHOLDER	AVERAGE HOUSEHOLD SPENDING	BEST CUSTOMERS (index)	BIGGEST CUSTOMERS (market share)
Average household	$11.22	100	100.0%
Under age 25	4.44	40	2.6
Aged 25 to 34	9.97	89	14.4
Aged 35 to 44	11.22	100	17.4
Aged 45 to 54	12.73	113	22.5
Aged 55 to 64	16.00	143	26.1
Aged 65 to 74	12.41	111	13.3
Aged 75 or older	4.30	38	3.7

	AVERAGE HOUSEHOLD SPENDING	BEST CUSTOMERS (index)	BIGGEST CUSTOMERS (market share)
HOUSEHOLD INCOME			
Average household	$11.22	100	100.0%
Under $20,000	2.59	23	4.9
$20,000 to $39,999	4.60	41	9.2
$40,000 to $49,999	6.08	54	4.8
$50,000 to $69,999	11.63	104	15.0
$70,000 to $79,999	14.45	129	7.2
$80,000 to $99,999	17.00	152	13.4
$100,000 or more	27.27	243	45.5
HOUSEHOLD TYPE			
Average household	11.22	100	100.0
Married couples	16.13	144	69.8
Married couples, no children	17.59	157	32.7
Married couples with children	15.16	135	31.8
Oldest child under age 6	14.08	125	5.7
Oldest child aged 6 to 17	17.38	155	18.4
Oldest child aged 18 or older	12.12	108	7.6
Single parent with child under age 18	5.79	52	2.7
Single person	5.81	52	15.4
RACE AND HISPANIC ORIGIN			
Average household	11.22	100	100.0
Asian	14.68	131	5.7
Black	5.06	45	5.7
Hispanic	8.05	72	9.0
Non-Hispanic white and other	12.78	114	85.5
REGION			
Average household	11.22	100	100.0
Northeast	17.48	156	28.1
Midwest	10.48	93	20.7
South	8.85	79	29.4
West	10.84	97	21.8
EDUCATION			
Average household	11.22	100	100.0
Less than high school graduate	2.51	22	2.9
High school graduate	5.62	50	12.5
Some college	7.33	65	13.5
Associate's degree	13.17	117	11.6
Bachelor's degree or more	21.17	189	59.5
Bachelor's degree	18.56	165	33.0
Master's, professional, doctoral degree	25.64	229	26.5

Note: Market shares may not sum to 100.0 because of rounding and missing categories by household type. "Asian" and "black" include Hispanics and non-Hispanics who identify themselves as being of the respective race alone. "Hispanic" includes people of any race who identify themselves as Hispanic. "Other" includes people who identify themselves as non-Hispanic and as Alaska Native, American Indian, Asian (who are also included in the "Asian" row), or Native Hawaiian or other Pacific Islander, as well as non-Hispanics reporting more than one race.
Source: Calculations by New Strategist based on the Bureau of Labor Statistics' 2012 Consumer Expenditure Survey

Recreational Expenses on Trips

Best customers: Householders aged 45 to 64
Married couples without children at home
Married couples with school-aged or older children at home
Asians and non-Hispanic whites
Households in the West

Customer trends: Average household spending on recreational expenses on trips should grow as boomers retire
and spend more time and money on travel.

Recreational expenses on trips, the fifth-largest travel category, account for 9 percent of the average household's travel budget. The biggest spenders on recreational expenses on trips are older married couples. Householders ranging in age from 45 to 64 spend 29 to 33 percent more than average on this item. Married couples without children at home (most of them empty-nesters) spend 56 percent more than average on recreational expenses on trips, while those with school-aged children spend more than twice the average. Asians, who have the highest incomes among racial and ethnic groups, spend 42 percent more than average on recreational expenses on trips. Non-Hispanic whites spend 21 percent more. Households in the West outspend the average on this item by 32 percent.

Average household spending on recreational expenses on trips fell by a steep 34 percent between 2000 and the overall trough spending year of 2010, after adjusting for inflation. Behind the decline was the economic downturn, which reduced spending on travel. In contrast to many other travel categories, however, spending on this item so far has failed to recover. Average household spending on recreational expenses while traveling should grow as boomers retire and spend more time and money on travel.

Table 20.11 Recreational expenses on trips

Total household spending $15,986,211,840.00
Average household spends   128.49

AGE OF HOUSEHOLDER	AVERAGE HOUSEHOLD SPENDING	BEST CUSTOMERS (index)	BIGGEST CUSTOMERS (market share)
Average household	$128.49	100	100.0%
Under age 25	42.60	33	2.2
Aged 25 to 34	108.94	85	13.7
Aged 35 to 44	136.18	106	18.4
Aged 45 to 54	170.70	133	26.3
Aged 55 to 64	165.60	129	23.6
Aged 65 to 74	128.87	100	12.1
Aged 75 or older	49.31	38	3.8

	AVERAGE HOUSEHOLD SPENDING	BEST CUSTOMERS (index)	BIGGEST CUSTOMERS (market share)
HOUSEHOLD INCOME			
Average household	**$128.49**	**100**	**100.0%**
Under $20,000	31.45	24	5.1
$20,000 to $39,999	47.18	37	8.3
$40,000 to $49,999	64.96	51	4.5
$50,000 to $69,999	111.35	87	12.5
$70,000 to $79,999	130.54	102	5.7
$80,000 to $99,999	181.94	142	12.5
$100,000 or more	352.89	275	51.4
HOUSEHOLD TYPE			
Average household	**128.49**	**100**	**100.0**
Married couples	195.23	152	73.8
Married couples, no children	200.57	156	32.5
Married couples with children	209.27	163	38.3
Oldest child under age 6	116.10	90	4.1
Oldest child aged 6 to 17	266.00	207	24.6
Oldest child aged 18 or older	173.90	135	9.5
Single parent with child under age 18	57.12	44	2.3
Single person	66.59	52	15.4
RACE AND HISPANIC ORIGIN			
Average household	**128.49**	**100**	**100.0**
Asian	182.80	142	6.2
Black	43.78	34	4.3
Hispanic	52.79	41	5.2
Non-Hispanic white and other	155.17	121	90.6
REGION			
Average household	**128.49**	**100**	**100.0**
Northeast	139.47	109	19.6
Midwest	115.25	90	19.9
South	106.51	83	30.9
West	169.06	132	29.6
EDUCATION			
Average household	**128.49**	**100**	**100.0**
Less than high school graduate	31.80	25	3.2
High school graduate	64.22	50	12.5
Some college	89.74	70	14.4
Associate's degree	119.43	93	9.2
Bachelor's degree or more	247.48	193	60.7
Bachelor's degree	228.64	178	35.5
Master's, professional, doctoral degree	279.85	218	25.3

Note: Market shares may not sum to 100.0 because of rounding and missing categories by household type. "Asian" and "black" include Hispanics and non-Hispanics who identify themselves as being of the respective race alone. "Hispanic" includes people of any race who identify themselves as Hispanic. "Other" includes people who identify themselves as non-Hispanic and as Alaska Native, American Indian, Asian (who are also included in the "Asian" row), or Native Hawaiian or other Pacific Islander, as well as non-Hispanics reporting more than one race.
Source: Calculations by New Strategist based on the Bureau of Labor Statistics' 2012 Consumer Expenditure Survey

Restaurant and Carry-Out Food on Trips

Best customers: Householders aged 45 to 74
                   Married couples without children at home
                   Married couples with school-aged or older children at home
                   Asians and non-Hispanic whites
                   Households in the West

Customer trends: Average household spending on restaurant and carry-out food on trips should grow as boomers retire
                   and devote more time and money to travel.

The biggest spenders on restaurant and carry-out meals on trips are the most avid travelers—older married couples. Householders ranging in age from 45 to 74 spend 18 to 30 percent more than average on this item. Married couples without children at home (most of them empty-nesters) spend 71 percent more than average on restaurant and carry-out meals on trips and control 36 percent of the market. Those with school-aged or older children at home spend 42 to 52 percent more. Asians, the most affluent racial and ethnic group, spend 49 percent more than average on eating out while traveling. Non-Hispanic whites spend 18 percent more. Households in the West outspend the average by 20 percent.

Average household spending on restaurant and carry-out food on trips, the third-largest travel spending category, fell 15 percent between 2006 and the overall trough spending year of 2010, after adjusting for inflation. Behind the decline was household budget cutting in the midst of the Great Recession. Spending on restaurant meals rebounded with a 9 increase between 2010 and 2012. Spending on this item should grow in the years ahead as boomers retire and devote more time and money to travel.

Table 20.12 Restaurant and carry-out food on trips

Total household spending $31,993,574,400.00
Average household spends   257.15

AGE OF HOUSEHOLDER	AVERAGE HOUSEHOLD SPENDING	BEST CUSTOMERS (index)	BIGGEST CUSTOMERS (market share)
Average household	$257.15	100	100.0%
Under age 25	83.51	32	2.1
Aged 25 to 34	220.41	86	13.9
Aged 35 to 44	243.65	95	16.4
Aged 45 to 54	316.16	123	24.3
Aged 55 to 64	334.87	130	23.8
Aged 65 to 74	302.48	118	14.2
Aged 75 or older	137.46	53	5.2

	AVERAGE HOUSEHOLD SPENDING	BEST CUSTOMERS (index)	BIGGEST CUSTOMERS (market share)
HOUSEHOLD INCOME			
Average household	**$257.15**	**100**	**100.0%**
Under $20,000	64.47	25	5.3
$20,000 to $39,999	103.30	40	9.1
$40,000 to $49,999	157.93	61	5.4
$50,000 to $69,999	206.50	80	11.6
$70,000 to $79,999	312.12	121	6.8
$80,000 to $99,999	382.96	149	13.1
$100,000 or more	669.19	260	48.7
HOUSEHOLD TYPE			
Average household	**257.15**	**100**	**100.0**
Married couples	381.63	148	72.1
Married couples, no children	439.38	171	35.6
Married couples with children	358.93	140	32.8
Oldest child under age 6	267.92	104	4.8
Oldest child aged 6 to 17	390.44	152	18.1
Oldest child aged 18 or older	364.67	142	10.0
Single parent with child under age 18	114.33	44	2.3
Single person	135.77	53	15.7
RACE AND HISPANIC ORIGIN			
Average household	**257.15**	**100**	**100.0**
Asian	384.23	149	6.5
Black	106.44	41	5.2
Hispanic	132.11	51	6.4
Non-Hispanic white and other	302.84	118	88.4
REGION			
Average household	**257.15**	**100**	**100.0**
Northeast	273.45	106	19.2
Midwest	240.97	94	20.8
South	227.86	89	33.0
West	308.42	120	27.0
EDUCATION			
Average household	**257.15**	**100**	**100.0**
Less than high school graduate	58.94	23	3.0
High school graduate	135.57	53	13.1
Some college	186.36	72	14.9
Associate's degree	230.79	90	8.9
Bachelor's degree or more	489.81	190	60.1
Bachelor's degree	427.45	166	33.1
Master's, professional, doctoral degree	596.90	232	26.9

Note: Market shares may not sum to 100.0 because of rounding and missing categories by household type. "Asian" and "black" include Hispanics and non-Hispanics who identify themselves as being of the respective race alone. "Hispanic" includes people of any race who identify themselves as Hispanic. "Other" includes people who identify themselves as non-Hispanic and as Alaska Native, American Indian, Asian (who are also included in the "Asian" row), or Native Hawaiian or other Pacific Islander, as well as non-Hispanics reporting more than one race.
Source: Calculations by New Strategist based on the Bureau of Labor Statistics' 2012 Consumer Expenditure Survey

Ship Fares

Best customers: Householders aged 55 and older
High-income households
Married couples without children at home
Asians and non-Hispanic whites
Households in the Northeast and West

Customer trends: Average household spending on ship fares should increase in the years ahead as boomers
fill the older age groups.

The biggest spenders on ship fares are well-to-do older Americans. Householders aged 55 to 64 spend 73 percent more than average on this item, and those aged 65 to 74 spend 37 percent more. Even householders aged 75 or older are above-average spenders on ship fares. Together these three age groups account for more than half the market. Households with incomes of $100,000 or more spend almost three-and-one-half times the average on ship fares and control 64 percent of household spending on this item. Married couples without children at home (most of them empty-nesters) spend well more than twice the average on cruises. Non-Hispanic whites spend 20 percent more than average on ship fares, and Asians spend more than twice the average. Households in the Northeast outspend the average by 54 percent, and those in the West spend 24 percent more.

Average household spending on ship fares, which had grown by 28 percent from 2000 to 2006, declined 34 percent between 2006 and the overall trough spending year of 2010, after adjusting for inflation. Behind the decline was the economic downturn, which reduced spending on travel. Spending on this item strongly rebounded between 2010 and 2012, rising 36 percent. Average household spending on ship fares should increase in the years ahead as boomers fill the older age groups.

Table 20.13 Ship fares

Total household spending	$7,033,236,480.00		
Average household spends	56.53		

AGE OF HOUSEHOLDER	AVERAGE HOUSEHOLD SPENDING	BEST CUSTOMERS (index)	BIGGEST CUSTOMERS (market share)
Average household	$56.53	100	100.0%
Under age 25	13.45	24	1.6
Aged 25 to 34	29.30	52	8.4
Aged 35 to 44	44.98	80	13.8
Aged 45 to 54	49.37	87	17.3
Aged 55 to 64	97.58	173	31.6
Aged 65 to 74	77.27	137	16.5
Aged 75 or older	63.03	111	10.9

	AVERAGE HOUSEHOLD SPENDING	BEST CUSTOMERS (index)	BIGGEST CUSTOMERS (market share)
HOUSEHOLD INCOME			
Average household	**$56.53**	**100**	**100.0%**
Under $20,000	4.90	9	1.8
$20,000 to $39,999	21.78	39	8.7
$40,000 to $49,999	33.72	60	5.3
$50,000 to $69,999	28.15	50	7.2
$70,000 to $79,999	20.43	36	2.0
$80,000 to $99,999	69.73	123	10.9
$100,000 or more	193.60	342	64.1
HOUSEHOLD TYPE			
Average household	**56.53**	**100**	**100.0**
Married couples	92.07	163	79.1
Married couples, no children	127.16	225	46.9
Married couples with children	68.10	120	28.3
Oldest child under age 6	46.73	83	3.8
Oldest child aged 6 to 17	70.64	125	14.9
Oldest child aged 18 or older	77.64	137	9.7
Single parent with child under age 18	16.40	29	1.5
Single person	21.64	38	11.4
RACE AND HISPANIC ORIGIN			
Average household	**56.53**	**100**	**100.0**
Asian	119.70	212	9.2
Black	22.08	39	4.9
Hispanic	23.53	42	5.2
Non-Hispanic white and other	67.81	120	90.0
REGION			
Average household	**56.53**	**100**	**100.0**
Northeast	87.16	154	27.8
Midwest	37.10	66	14.6
South	45.02	80	29.7
West	70.14	124	28.0
EDUCATION			
Average household	**56.53**	**100**	**100.0**
Less than high school graduate	23.46	42	5.4
High school graduate	30.25	54	13.3
Some college	31.04	55	11.3
Associate's degree	58.06	103	10.1
Bachelor's degree or more	107.16	190	59.8
Bachelor's degree	91.14	161	32.1
Master's, professional, doctoral degree	134.67	238	27.6

Note: Market shares may not sum to 100.0 because of rounding and missing categories by household type. "Asian" and "black" include Hispanics and non-Hispanics who identify themselves as being of the respective race alone. "Hispanic" includes people of any race who identify themselves as Hispanic. "Other" includes people who identify themselves as non-Hispanic and as Alaska Native, American Indian, Asian (who are also included in the "Asian" row), or Native Hawaiian or other Pacific Islander, as well as non-Hispanics reporting more than one race.
Source: Calculations by New Strategist based on the Bureau of Labor Statistics' 2012 Consumer Expenditure Survey

Train Fares, Intercity

Best customers: Householders aged 55 to 74
Married couples without children at home
Asians and non-Hispanic whites
Households in the West and Northeast
College graduates

Customer trends: Average household spending on train fares will resume its decline unless train service improves.

Older Americans are the best customers of intercity train fares. Householders aged 55 to 64 spend 33 percent more than average on intercity train tickets, and those aged 65 to 74 spend 66 percent more. Married couples without children at home (most of them empty-nesters) spend nearly twice the average on intercity train fares. Asians outspend the average by 76 percent, and non-Hispanic whites spend 19 percent more. Households in the West and Northeast spend, respectively, 28 and 16 percent more than average on train fares. Households headed by people with a bachelor's degree spend more than twice the average on intercity train fares.

Average household spending on intercity train fares had been in a decade-long decline, but it recovered nicely in the last two years. Spending on train fares fell 34 percent between 2000 and 2006, after adjusting for inflation, and by another 11 percent between 2006 and 2010. Then came a big upswing, and average household spending on train fares climbed by a solid 14 percent between 2010 and 2012. Behind the earlier decline is increasingly limited train service in the United States and belt tightening because of the Great Recession. Unless train service improves, the recent upswing in average household spending on train fares will be short-lived.

Table 20.14 Train fares, intercity

Total household spending $2,348,974,080.00
Average household spends   18.88

AGE OF HOUSEHOLDER	AVERAGE HOUSEHOLD SPENDING	BEST CUSTOMERS (index)	BIGGEST CUSTOMERS (market share)
Average household	$18.88	100	100.0%
Under age 25	6.32	33	2.2
Aged 25 to 34	13.05	69	11.2
Aged 35 to 44	15.08	80	13.9
Aged 45 to 54	18.04	96	18.9
Aged 55 to 64	25.04	133	24.3
Aged 65 to 74	31.29	166	20.0
Aged 75 or older	18.55	98	9.6

	AVERAGE HOUSEHOLD SPENDING	BEST CUSTOMERS (index)	BIGGEST CUSTOMERS (market share)
HOUSEHOLD INCOME			
Average household	**$18.88**	**100**	**100.0%**
Under $20,000	10.32	55	11.5
$20,000 to $39,999	7.41	39	8.8
$40,000 to $49,999	14.44	76	6.8
$50,000 to $69,999	13.89	74	10.6
$70,000 to $79,999	15.72	83	4.6
$80,000 to $99,999	13.81	73	6.5
$100,000 or more	51.59	273	51.2
HOUSEHOLD TYPE			
Average household	**18.88**	**100**	**100.0**
Married couples	26.19	139	67.4
Married couples, no children	36.99	196	40.8
Married couples with children	18.20	96	22.7
Oldest child under age 6	15.11	80	3.7
Oldest child aged 6 to 17	18.59	98	11.7
Oldest child aged 18 or older	19.55	104	7.3
Single parent with child under age 18	7.97	42	2.2
Single person	15.54	82	24.4
RACE AND HISPANIC ORIGIN			
Average household	**18.88**	**100**	**100.0**
Asian	33.30	176	7.6
Black	8.31	44	5.5
Hispanic	7.40	39	4.9
Non-Hispanic white and other	22.54	119	89.6
REGION			
Average household	**18.88**	**100**	**100.0**
Northeast	21.95	116	21.0
Midwest	19.01	101	22.3
South	14.10	75	27.8
West	24.19	128	28.9
EDUCATION			
Average household	**18.88**	**100**	**100.0**
Less than high school graduate	1.72	9	1.2
High school graduate	7.24	38	9.6
Some college	11.42	60	12.5
Associate's degree	10.71	57	5.6
Bachelor's degree or more	42.62	226	71.2
Bachelor's degree	30.59	162	32.3
Master's, professional, doctoral degree	63.27	335	38.9

Note: Market shares may not sum to 100.0 because of rounding and missing categories by household type. "Asian" and "black" include Hispanics and non-Hispanics who identify themselves as being of the respective race alone. "Hispanic" includes people of any race who identify themselves as Hispanic. "Other" includes people who identify themselves as non-Hispanic and as Alaska Native, American Indian, Asian (who are also included in the "Asian" row), or Native Hawaiian or other Pacific Islander, as well as non-Hispanics reporting more than one race.
Source: Calculations by New Strategist based on the Bureau of Labor Statistics' 2012 Consumer Expenditure Survey

Vehicle Rentals on Trips

Best customers:
    Householders aged 45 to 64
    High-income households
    Married couples without children at home
    Married couples with school-aged or older children at home
    Asians and non-Hispanic whites
    Households in the West
    College graduates

Customer trends:
    Average household spending on vehicle rentals on trips should grow in the years ahead
    as more boomers retire and become avid travelers.

The biggest spenders on rented vehicles while traveling are middle-aged and older married couples. Householders ranging in age from 45 to 64 spend 24 to 57 percent more than average on this item. Married couples without children at home (most of them empty-nesters) spend 75 percent more than average on vehicle rentals while traveling. Couples with school-aged children spend 45 percent more than average on this item, and those with adult children at home spend 34 percent more. High-income households spend three times the average on vehicle rentals on trips, and college graduates spend two times the average. Asians spend 41 percent more than average and non-Hispanic whites spend 16 percent more. Households in the West spend 27 percent more than average on vehicle rentals while traveling.

Average household spending on vehicle rentals while traveling declined by a steep 41 percent between 2000 and 2010, after adjusting for inflation, and fell by another 6 percent in the two years since then. Price discounting was one factor behind the decline, as was the economic downturn. Average household spending on vehicle rentals while traveling should grow in the years ahead as more boomers retire and become avid travelers.

Table 20.15 Vehicle rentals on trips

Total household spending $3,157,678,080.00
Average household spends   25.38

AGE OF HOUSEHOLDER	AVERAGE HOUSEHOLD SPENDING	BEST CUSTOMERS (index)	BIGGEST CUSTOMERS (market share)
Average household	$25.38	100	100.0%
Under age 25	6.21	24	1.6
Aged 25 to 34	17.87	70	11.4
Aged 35 to 44	25.80	102	17.6
Aged 45 to 54	31.46	124	24.5
Aged 55 to 64	39.83	157	28.7
Aged 65 to 74	23.98	94	11.4
Aged 75 or older	12.24	48	4.7

	AVERAGE HOUSEHOLD SPENDING	BEST CUSTOMERS (index)	BIGGEST CUSTOMERS (market share)
HOUSEHOLD INCOME			
Average household	$25.38	100	100.0%
Under $20,000	3.68	15	3.1
$20,000 to $39,999	9.76	38	8.7
$40,000 to $49,999	11.56	46	4.0
$50,000 to $69,999	19.21	76	10.9
$70,000 to $79,999	18.53	73	4.1
$80,000 to $99,999	32.73	129	11.4
$100,000 or more	78.60	310	58.0
HOUSEHOLD TYPE			
Average household	25.38	100	100.0
Married couples	37.44	148	71.6
Married couples, no children	44.32	175	36.4
Married couples with children	33.67	133	31.2
Oldest child under age 6	25.16	99	4.5
Oldest child aged 6 to 17	36.81	145	17.2
Oldest child aged 18 or older	33.91	134	9.4
Single parent with child under age 18	10.62	42	2.2
Single person	12.84	51	15.0
RACE AND HISPANIC ORIGIN			
Average household	25.38	100	100.0
Asian	35.77	141	6.1
Black	17.94	71	8.9
Hispanic	7.62	30	3.8
Non-Hispanic white and other	29.53	116	87.3
REGION			
Average household	25.38	100	100.0
Northeast	23.04	91	16.4
Midwest	23.03	91	20.1
South	23.76	94	34.9
West	32.24	127	28.6
EDUCATION			
Average household	25.38	100	100.0
Less than high school graduate	2.36	9	1.2
High school graduate	10.95	43	10.8
Some college	19.09	75	15.5
Associate's degree	19.47	77	7.6
Bachelor's degree or more	52.27	206	65.0
Bachelor's degree	41.93	165	32.9
Master's, professional, doctoral degree	70.02	276	32.0

Note: Market shares may not sum to 100.0 because of rounding and missing categories by household type. "Asian" and "black" include Hispanics and non-Hispanics who identify themselves as being of the respective race alone. "Hispanic" includes people of any race who identify themselves as Hispanic. "Other" includes people who identify themselves as non-Hispanic and as Alaska Native, American Indian, Asian (who are also included in the "Asian" row), or Native Hawaiian or other Pacific Islander, as well as non-Hispanics reporting more than one race.
Source: Calculations by New Strategist based on the Bureau of Labor Statistics' 2012 Consumer Expenditure Survey

Chapter 21.
Utilities

Household Spending on Utilities, 2000 to 2012

Utilities—such as electricity and water—are one of the larger expenditure categories for American households. Electricity, in fact, ranks 10th among household expenditures. Overall, the average household spent $2,406 on utilities in 2012, 12 percent more than the inflation-adjusted $2,147 spent in 2000, but 8 percent less than the $2,610 spent in 2010, the year overall household spending bottomed out. Falling prices for natural gas were one factor behind the diminished spending.

Natural gas saw a 38 percent decline in average household spending between the overall peak spending year of 2006 and 2012, after having increased 41 percent in the earlier part of the decade. The average household now spends less on natural gas than on water and sewer. Spending on the latter item increased 41 percent between 2000 and 2012, and water and sewer is the only utility to post a spending increase from 2010 to 2012, all the others showing reductions.

By far the biggest utilities expense is electricity, which accounted for 58 percent of the average household's utilities bill. Spending on electricity was 7 percent lower in 2012 than in 2010 after rising 22 percent between 2000 and 2010. Spending on fuel oil rose 28 percent between 2000 and 2006 and then fell by 14 percent in the ensuing six-year period. Average household spending on bottled gas and on coal, wood, and other fuels was essentially the same in 2012 as in 2000, although both categories experienced intermediate upswings of around 20 percent.

Oil prices being volatile, it is likely that average household spending on utilities will increase substantially in the years ahead. Only if consumers switch to more energy-efficient appliances and attempt to conserve resources will spending remain stable or decline.

Spending on utilities

(average spending by households on utilities, 2000, 2006, 2010, and 2012; in 2012 dollars)

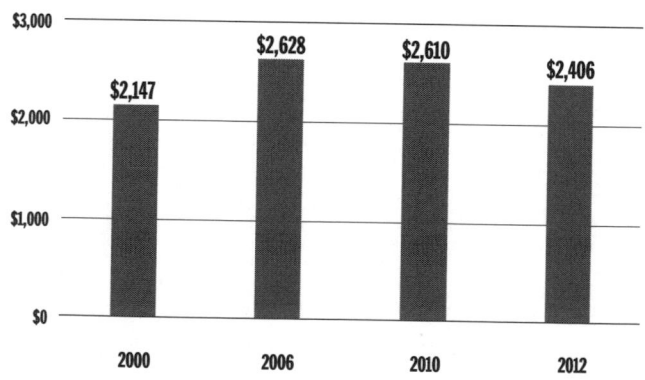

Table 21.1 Utilities spending, 2000 to 2012

(average annual household spending on utilities and percent distribution, by category, 2000 to 2012; percent change and percentage point change in spending, 2000–06, 2006–12, and 2010–12; in 2012 dollars; ranked by amount spent)

	average annual household spending (in 2012$)				percent change		
	2012	2010	2006	2000	2010–12	2006–12	2000–06
Average household spending on utlities	**$2,406.11**	**$2,609.87**	**$2,628.07**	**$2,146.86**	**−7.8%**	**−8.4%**	**22.4%**
Electricity	1,387.83	1,487.28	1,441.66	1,215.22	−6.7	−3.7	18.6
Water and sewer	398.56	379.47	326.27	283.62	5.0	22.2	15.0
Natural gas	359.35	463.25	579.38	409.79	−22.4	−38.0	41.4
Trash collection	123.44	132.13	123.58	108.98	−6.6	−0.1	13.4
Fuel oil	80.77	81.57	94.13	73.44	−1.0	−14.2	28.2
Bottled gas	47.44	56.73	56.09	47.01	−16.4	−15.4	19.3
Coal, wood, and other fuels	8.72	9.43	6.96	8.80	−7.6	25.3	−20.9

					percentage point change		
PERCENT DISTRIBUTION OF SPENDING	2012	2010	2006	2000	2010–12	2006–12	2000–06
Average household spending on utlities	**100.0%**	**100.0%**	**100.0%**	**100.0%**	–	–	–
Electricity	57.7	57.0	54.9	56.6	0.7	2.8	−1.7
Water and sewer	16.6	14.5	12.4	13.2	2.0	4.1	−0.8
Natural gas	14.9	17.7	22.0	19.1	−2.8	−7.1	3.0
Trash collection	5.1	5.1	4.7	5.1	0.1	0.4	−0.4
Fuel oil	3.4	3.1	3.6	3.4	0.2	−0.2	0.2
Bottled gas	2.0	2.2	2.1	2.2	−0.2	−0.2	−0.1
Coal, wood, and other fuels	0.4	0.4	0.3	0.4	0.0	0.1	−0.1

Note: Percentage point change calculations are based on unrounded figures. "–" means not applicable.
Source: Bureau of Labor Statistics, 2000, 2006, 2010, and 2012 Consumer Expenditure Surveys; calculations by New Strategist

Bottled Gas

Best customers:

Householders aged 55 to 74
Married couples without children at home
Married couples with preschoolers
Married couples with adult children at home
Non-Hispanic whites
Households in the Northeast and Midwest

Customer trends: Average household spending on bottled gas should decline as rural areas lose population.

Older, white householders in the Midwest and rural Northeast are the best customers of bottled gas. The average household in the Midwest, where bottled gas is most popular, spends 49 percent more than the national average on this item, and householders in the Northeast spend 23 percent more. Householders aged 55 to 74 spend 31 to 87 percent more than average on bottled gas. Married couples without children at home, most of them empty-nesters, spend 62 percent more than average on bottled gas, while couples with preschoolers or adult children at home spend 44 to 45 percent more. Non-Hispanic white households spend 23 percent more than average on bottled gas.

Average household spending on bottled gas fell 16 percent between 2010 to 2012, but despite the ongoing shift from bottled gas to other fuels it had risen 21 percent between 2000 and 2010, after adjusting for inflation. Average household spending on bottled gas should decline as rural areas lose population.

Table 21.2 Bottled gas

Total household spending $5,902,295,040.00
Average household spends   47.44

AGE OF HOUSEHOLDER	AVERAGE HOUSEHOLD SPENDING	BEST CUSTOMERS (index)	BIGGEST CUSTOMERS (market share)
Average household	$47.44	100	100.0%
Under age 25	5.94	13	0.8
Aged 25 to 34	32.76	69	11.2
Aged 35 to 44	41.46	87	15.2
Aged 45 to 54	44.50	94	18.6
Aged 55 to 64	62.09	131	24.0
Aged 65 to 74	88.56	187	22.5
Aged 75 or older	38.03	80	7.8

	AVERAGE HOUSEHOLD SPENDING	BEST CUSTOMERS (index)	BIGGEST CUSTOMERS (market share)
HOUSEHOLD INCOME			
Average household	$47.44	100	100.0%
Under $20,000	21.84	46	9.7
$20,000 to $39,999	41.62	88	19.8
$40,000 to $49,999	50.01	105	9.3
$50,000 to $69,999	48.49	102	14.8
$70,000 to $79,999	39.79	84	4.7
$80,000 to $99,999	64.46	136	12.0
$100,000 or more	75.46	159	29.8
HOUSEHOLD TYPE			
Average household	47.44	100	100.0
Married couples	68.63	145	70.3
Married couples, no children	76.65	162	33.7
Married couples, with children	59.52	125	29.5
Oldest child under age 6	68.92	145	6.6
Oldest child aged 6 to 17	50.80	107	12.7
Oldest child aged 18 or older	68.14	144	10.1
Single parent with child under age 18	14.10	30	1.6
Single person	28.83	61	18.0
RACE AND HISPANIC ORIGIN			
Average household	47.44	100	100.0
Asian	5.49	12	0.5
Black	13.77	29	3.6
Hispanic	16.50	35	4.4
Non-Hispanic white and other	58.15	123	92.0
REGION			
Average household	47.44	100	100.0
Northeast	58.48	123	22.3
Midwest	70.66	149	33.0
South	36.83	78	28.9
West	33.30	70	15.8
EDUCATION			
Average household	47.44	100	100.0
Less than high school graduate	31.79	67	8.8
High school graduate	56.26	119	29.6
Some college	40.99	86	17.8
Associate's degree	57.57	121	12.0
Bachelor's degree or more	48.00	101	31.9
Bachelor's degree	47.15	99	19.8
Master's, professional, doctoral degree	49.46	104	12.1

Note: Market shares may not sum to 100.0 because of rounding and missing categories by household type. "Asian" and "black" include Hispanics and non-Hispanics who identify themselves as being of the respective race alone. "Hispanic" includes people of any race who identify themselves as Hispanic. "Other" includes people who identify themselves as non-Hispanic and as Alaska Native, American Indian, Asian (who are also included in the "Asian" row), or Native Hawaiian or other Pacific Islander, as well as non-Hispanics reporting more than one race.
Source: Calculations by New Strategist based on the Bureau of Labor Statistics' 2012 Consumer Expenditure Survey

Electricity

Best customers: Householders aged 35 to 64

Married couples with school-aged or older children at home

Households in the South

Customer trends: Average household spending on electricity will increase as energy prices rise.

Electricity is one of the biggest expenses for the average household, ranking 10th in 2012. Because almost every household buys electricity, there are few differences in spending by demographic characteristic. Household and dwelling sizes are the biggest factors in determining electricity consumption. Consequently, middle-aged married couples with children spend the most on this item. Householders ranging in age from 35 to 64 spend 9 to 15 percent more than average on electricity. Married couples with school-aged or older children at home spend 28 to 35 percent more than average. Households in the South spend 17 percent more than average on electricity because most homes in the region are cooled (and heated) by electricity.

Average household spending on electricity rose 22 percent between 2000 and 2010, after adjusting for inflation, and then dropped 7 percent in the ensuing two years. Average household spending on electricity is certain to rise in the years ahead as energy prices climb.

Table 21.3 **Electricity**

Total household spending $172,668,257,280.00

Average household spends   1,387.83

	AVERAGE HOUSEHOLD SPENDING	BEST CUSTOMERS (index)	BIGGEST CUSTOMERS (market share)
AGE OF HOUSEHOLDER			
Average household	**$1,387.83**	**100**	**100.0%**
Under age 25	737.13	53	3.5
Aged 25 to 34	1,190.71	86	13.9
Aged 35 to 44	1,521.53	110	19.0
Aged 45 to 54	1,593.10	115	22.7
Aged 55 to 64	1,516.48	109	20.0
Aged 65 to 74	1,429.13	103	12.4
Aged 75 or older	1,205.57	87	8.5

	AVERAGE HOUSEHOLD SPENDING	BEST CUSTOMERS (index)	BIGGEST CUSTOMERS (market share)
HOUSEHOLD INCOME			
Average household	**$1,387.83**	**100**	**100.0%**
Under $20,000	964.45	69	14.6
$20,000 to $39,999	1,241.50	89	20.2
$40,000 to $49,999	1,367.25	99	8.7
$50,000 to $69,999	1,416.99	102	14.7
$70,000 to $79,999	1,538.39	111	6.2
$80,000 to $99,999	1,580.40	114	10.0
$100,000 or more	1,891.38	136	25.5
HOUSEHOLD TYPE			
Average household	**1,387.83**	**100**	**100.0**
Married couples	1,676.36	121	58.7
Married couples, no children	1,520.56	110	22.8
Married couples, with children	1,738.19	125	29.4
Oldest child under age 6	1,449.25	104	4.8
Oldest child aged 6 to 17	1,772.39	128	15.2
Oldest child aged 18 or older	1,867.38	135	9.5
Single parent with child under age 18	1,345.06	97	5.1
Single person	902.91	65	19.3
RACE AND HISPANIC ORIGIN			
Average household	**1,387.83**	**100**	**100.0**
Asian	1,145.12	83	3.6
Black	1,436.98	104	13.0
Hispanic	1,217.97	88	11.0
Non-Hispanic white and other	1,407.01	101	76.1
REGION			
Average household	**1,387.83**	**100**	**100.0**
Northeast	1,279.54	92	16.6
Midwest	1,262.77	91	20.2
South	1,624.99	117	43.6
West	1,205.64	87	19.6
EDUCATION			
Average household	**1,387.83**	**100**	**100.0**
Less than high school graduate	1,232.37	89	11.6
High school graduate	1,409.80	102	25.3
Some college	1,312.76	95	19.5
Associate's degree	1,523.03	110	10.8
Bachelor's degree or more	1,441.52	104	32.8
Bachelor's degree	1,409.88	102	20.2
Master's, professional, doctoral degree	1,495.86	108	12.5

Note: Market shares may not sum to 100.0 because of rounding and missing categories by household type. "Asian" and "black" include Hispanics and non-Hispanics who identify themselves as being of the respective race alone. "Hispanic" includes people of any race who identify themselves as Hispanic. "Other" includes people who identify themselves as non-Hispanic and as Alaska Native, American Indian, Asian (who are also included in the "Asian" row), or Native Hawaiian or other Pacific Islander, as well as non-Hispanics reporting more than one race.
Source: Calculations by New Strategist based on the Bureau of Labor Statistics' 2012 Consumer Expenditure Survey

Fuel Oil

Best customers: **Householders aged 75 or older**
                        Households in the Northeast

Customer trends: **Average household spending on fuel oil may decline as a growing proportion of households heat with natural gas or electricity.**

Older householders living in the Northeast are the biggest spenders on fuel oil. Households in the Northeast, where fuel oil heating systems are most common, spend almost five times the average on fuel oil and account for 87 percent of the market. Householders aged 45 to 74 spend 10 to 12 percent more than average on this item, in large part because they are most likely to live in older homes with fuel oil heating systems. For the same reason, householders aged 75 or older spend more than twice the average on fuel oil. Non-Hispanic whites spend 20 percent more than average on this item.

Average household spending on fuel oil rose 28 percent between 2000 and 2006, after adjusting for inflation, then fell 14 percent in the ensuing six years. Average household spending on fuel oil may continue to decline as it is replaced by other energy sources.

Table 21.4 Fuel oil

Total household spending	$10,049,080,320.00
Average household spends	80.77

	AVERAGE HOUSEHOLD SPENDING	BEST CUSTOMERS (index)	BIGGEST CUSTOMERS (market share)
AGE OF HOUSEHOLDER			
Average household	**$80.77**	**100**	**100.0%**
Under age 25	15.56	19	1.3
Aged 25 to 34	33.27	41	6.7
Aged 35 to 44	76.89	95	16.5
Aged 45 to 54	89.15	110	21.8
Aged 55 to 64	89.98	111	20.4
Aged 65 to 74	90.20	112	13.5
Aged 75 or older	164.19	203	19.9

	AVERAGE HOUSEHOLD SPENDING	BEST CUSTOMERS (index)	BIGGEST CUSTOMERS (market share)
HOUSEHOLD INCOME			
Average household	$80.77	100	100.0%
Under $20,000	44.69	55	11.6
$20,000 to $39,999	56.79	70	15.8
$40,000 to $49,999	57.56	71	6.3
$50,000 to $69,999	73.46	91	13.1
$70,000 to $79,999	74.59	92	5.2
$80,000 to $99,999	105.52	131	11.5
$100,000 or more	156.98	194	36.4
HOUSEHOLD TYPE			
Average household	80.77	100	100.0
Married couples	95.43	118	57.4
Married couples, no children	95.20	118	24.6
Married couples, with children	89.87	111	26.2
Oldest child under age 6	63.91	79	3.6
Oldest child aged 6 to 17	93.01	115	13.7
Oldest child aged 18 or older	101.35	125	8.9
Single parent with child under age 18	61.64	76	4.0
Single person	65.61	81	24.1
RACE AND HISPANIC ORIGIN			
Average household	80.77	100	100.0
Asian	70.42	87	3.8
Black	31.95	40	5.0
Hispanic	30.21	37	4.7
Non-Hispanic white and other	97.22	120	90.3
REGION			
Average household	80.77	100	100.0
Northeast	387.22	479	86.5
Midwest	13.27	16	3.6
South	17.47	22	8.1
West	6.32	8	1.8
EDUCATION			
Average household	80.77	100	100.0
Less than high school graduate	46.18	57	7.5
High school graduate	77.79	96	24.0
Some college	55.13	68	14.1
Associate's degree	72.74	90	8.9
Bachelor's degree or more	116.72	145	45.6
Bachelor's degree	104.08	129	25.7
Master's, professional, doctoral degree	138.42	171	19.9

Note: Market shares may not sum to 100.0 because of rounding and missing categories by household type. "Asian" and "black" include Hispanics and non-Hispanics who identify themselves as being of the respective race alone. "Hispanic" includes people of any race who identify themselves as Hispanic. "Other" includes people who identify themselves as non-Hispanic and as Alaska Native, American Indian, Asian (who are also included in the "Asian" row), or Native Hawaiian or other Pacific Islander, as well as non-Hispanics reporting more than one race.
Source: Calculations by New Strategist based on the Bureau of Labor Statistics' 2012 Consumer Expenditure Survey

Natural Gas

Best customers: Householders aged 35 to 64
Married couples with school-aged or older children at home
Households in the Northeast and Midwest

Customer trends: Average household spending on natural gas will increase as energy prices rise.

Because so many households heat with natural gas, there are few differences in spending on this item by demographic characteristic. Household and housing sizes are the biggest factors in determining natural gas consumption. Householders ranging in age from 35 to 64 spend 9 to 20 percent more than average on natural gas. Married couples with school-aged or older children at home spend 36 to 51 percent more than average on natural gas. Households in the Northeast and Midwest, the colder parts of the country, spend 40 percent more than average on natural gas.

Average household spending on natural gas rose 41 percent between 2000 and 2006, after adjusting for inflation, then dropped 38 percent over the next six years owing to reduced prices. Average household spending on natural gas is likely to rise in the years ahead as energy prices increase.

Table 21.5 Natural gas

Total household spending $44,708,889,600.00
Average household spends   359.35

	AVERAGE HOUSEHOLD SPENDING	BEST CUSTOMERS (index)	BIGGEST CUSTOMERS (market share)
AGE OF HOUSEHOLDER			
Average household	$359.35	100	100.0%
Under age 25	162.39	45	3.0
Aged 25 to 34	279.22	78	12.6
Aged 35 to 44	402.37	112	19.4
Aged 45 to 54	431.65	120	23.8
Aged 55 to 64	390.09	109	19.9
Aged 65 to 74	365.06	102	12.2
Aged 75 or older	336.64	94	9.2

	AVERAGE HOUSEHOLD SPENDING	BEST CUSTOMERS (index)	BIGGEST CUSTOMERS (market share)
HOUSEHOLD INCOME			
Average household	$359.35	100	100.0%
Under $20,000	206.03	57	12.1
$20,000 to $39,999	282.20	79	17.7
$40,000 to $49,999	351.14	98	8.6
$50,000 to $69,999	344.27	96	13.8
$70,000 to $79,999	421.31	117	6.5
$80,000 to $99,999	435.16	121	10.7
$100,000 or more	585.85	163	30.5
HOUSEHOLD TYPE			
Average household	359.35	100	100.0
Married couples	442.84	123	59.9
Married couples, no children	386.97	108	22.4
Married couples, with children	483.57	135	31.6
Oldest child under age 6	385.66	107	4.9
Oldest child aged 6 to 17	487.13	136	16.1
Oldest child aged 18 or older	540.88	151	10.6
Single parent with child under age 18	308.69	86	4.5
Single person	228.84	64	18.9
RACE AND HISPANIC ORIGIN			
Average household	359.35	100	100.0
Asian	414.43	115	5.0
Black	368.92	103	12.9
Hispanic	291.55	81	10.2
Non-Hispanic white and other	368.84	103	77.0
REGION			
Average household	359.35	100	100.0
Northeast	503.90	140	25.3
Midwest	502.80	140	31.0
South	211.20	59	21.9
West	347.29	97	21.8
EDUCATION			
Average household	359.35	100	100.0
Less than high school graduate	290.53	81	10.6
High school graduate	305.74	85	21.2
Some college	331.09	92	19.0
Associate's degree	346.31	96	9.5
Bachelor's degree or more	452.77	126	39.7
Bachelor's degree	430.28	120	23.9
Master's, professional, doctoral degree	491.38	137	15.9

Note: Market shares may not sum to 100.0 because of rounding and missing categories by household type. "Asian" and "black" include Hispanics and non-Hispanics who identify themselves as being of the respective race alone. "Hispanic" includes people of any race who identify themselves as Hispanic. "Other" includes people who identify themselves as non-Hispanic and as Alaska Native, American Indian, Asian (who are also included in the "Asian" row), or Native Hawaiian or other Pacific Islander, as well as non-Hispanics reporting more than one race.
Source: Calculations by New Strategist based on the Bureau of Labor Statistics' 2012 Consumer Expenditure Survey

Trash Collection

Best customers:
Householders aged 45 to 64
Married couples without children at home
Married couples with school-aged or older children at home
Households in the West

Customer trends:
Average household spending on trash collection should rise as local communities and private companies charge more for waste disposal, unless expanded recycling programs reduce the amount of trash discarded.

The biggest spenders on trash collection are homeowners, who are most likely to be older householders and married couples. Householders aged 45 to 64 spend 18 percent more than average on trash collection. Married couples without children at home spend 22 percent more than average on trash collection. Those with school-aged or older children at home, the largest households, spend 28 to 46 percent more than average. Households in the West spend 49 percent more than average on this category.

Average household spending on trash collection grew by 13 percent between 2000 and 2012, after adjusting for inflation. Although governments strengthened recycling laws nationwide over the period, rising disposal fees counteracted the cost savings. Average household spending on trash collection should continue its long-term rise as it becomes more expensive to dispose of waste.

Table 21.6 Trash collection

Total household spending $15,357,911,040.00
Average household spends 123.44

AGE OF HOUSEHOLDER	AVERAGE HOUSEHOLD SPENDING	BEST CUSTOMERS (index)	BIGGEST CUSTOMERS (market share)
Average household	$123.44	100	100.0%
Under age 25	37.95	31	2.0
Aged 25 to 34	88.38	72	11.6
Aged 35 to 44	126.80	103	17.8
Aged 45 to 54	145.22	118	23.3
Aged 55 to 64	145.57	118	21.6
Aged 65 to 74	137.05	111	13.4
Aged 75 or older	130.47	106	10.3

	AVERAGE HOUSEHOLD SPENDING	BEST CUSTOMERS (index)	BIGGEST CUSTOMERS (market share)
HOUSEHOLD INCOME			
Average household	$123.44	100	100.0%
Under $20,000	63.29	51	10.8
$20,000 to $39,999	95.18	77	17.4
$40,000 to $49,999	116.71	95	8.4
$50,000 to $69,999	124.54	101	14.6
$70,000 to $79,999	155.89	126	7.1
$80,000 to $99,999	157.14	127	11.2
$100,000 or more	201.83	164	30.6
HOUSEHOLD TYPE			
Average household	123.44	100	100.0
Married couples	155.30	126	61.1
Married couples, no children	150.40	122	25.4
Married couples, with children	157.21	127	29.9
Oldest child under age 6	118.57	96	4.4
Oldest child aged 6 to 17	158.20	128	15.2
Oldest child aged 18 or older	180.51	146	10.3
Single parent with child under age 18	80.74	65	3.4
Single person	84.95	69	20.4
RACE AND HISPANIC ORIGIN			
Average household	123.44	100	100.0
Asian	137.05	111	4.8
Black	72.98	59	7.4
Hispanic	115.97	94	11.8
Non-Hispanic white and other	133.05	108	80.9
REGION			
Average household	123.44	100	100.0
Northeast	97.27	79	14.2
Midwest	107.99	87	19.4
South	108.74	88	32.8
West	183.90	149	33.6
EDUCATION			
Average household	123.44	100	100.0
Less than high school graduate	90.29	73	9.6
High school graduate	108.46	88	21.9
Some college	114.53	93	19.1
Associate's degree	119.77	97	9.6
Bachelor's degree or more	155.98	126	39.9
Bachelor's degree	147.95	120	23.9
Master's, professional, doctoral degree	169.76	138	16.0

Note: Market shares may not sum to 100.0 because of rounding and missing categories by household type. "Asian" and "black" include Hispanics and non-Hispanics who identify themselves as being of the respective race alone. "Hispanic" includes people of any race who identify themselves as Hispanic. "Other" includes people who identify themselves as non-Hispanic and as Alaska Native, American Indian, Asian (who are also included in the "Asian" row), or Native Hawaiian or other Pacific Islander, as well as non-Hispanics reporting more than one race.
Source: Calculations by New Strategist based on the Bureau of Labor Statistics' 2012 Consumer Expenditure Survey

Water and Sewer

Best customers: Householders aged 35 to 64
Married couples with school-aged or older children at home
Households in the South and West

Customer trends: Average household spending on water and sewer will rise as clean water becomes increasingly
scarce and expensive.

Every household needs water and sewer service, but the category accounts for only 17 percent of household utility spending. Because most households consume water, there are few differences in spending on this item by demographic characteristic. Household and housing sizes are the biggest factors in determining spending on water and sewer. Householders ranging in age from 35 to 64, many with children, spend 11 to 17 percent more than average on this item. Married couples with school-aged or older children at home, the largest households, spend 33 to 50 percent more than average on this item. Households in the South and West, where water can be scarce, spend 10 to 18 percent more than average on water and sewer.

Average household spending on water and sewer rose 41 percent between 2000 and 2012, after adjusting for inflation. By 2012, it had become the average household's second-largest utility expense. Higher fees charged by local communities were behind the increases. Average household spending on water and sewer is certain to rise in the years ahead as clean water becomes increasingly scarce and expensive.

Table 21.7 Water and sewer

Total household spending $49,587,240,960.00
Average household spends   398.56

AGE OF HOUSEHOLDER	AVERAGE HOUSEHOLD SPENDING	BEST CUSTOMERS (index)	BIGGEST CUSTOMERS (market share)
Average household	$398.56	100	100.0%
Under age 25	155.25	39	2.6
Aged 25 to 34	310.91	78	12.6
Aged 35 to 44	441.59	111	19.2
Aged 45 to 54	467.88	117	23.2
Aged 55 to 64	453.05	114	20.8
Aged 65 to 74	415.33	104	12.6
Aged 75 or older	367.30	92	9.0

	AVERAGE HOUSEHOLD SPENDING	BEST CUSTOMERS (index)	BIGGEST CUSTOMERS (market share)
HOUSEHOLD INCOME			
Average household	**$398.56**	**100**	**100.0%**
Under $20,000	236.77	59	12.5
$20,000 to $39,999	318.34	80	18.0
$40,000 to $49,999	394.88	99	8.8
$50,000 to $69,999	413.51	104	15.0
$70,000 to $79,999	451.63	113	6.3
$80,000 to $99,999	487.16	122	10.8
$100,000 or more	609.59	153	28.6
HOUSEHOLD TYPE			
Average household	**398.56**	**100**	**100.0**
Married couples	503.02	126	61.3
Married couples, no children	455.32	114	23.8
Married couples, with children	524.27	132	30.9
Oldest child under age 6	400.19	100	4.6
Oldest child aged 6 to 17	528.36	133	15.8
Oldest child aged 18 or older	597.63	150	10.6
Single parent with child under age 18	333.77	84	4.4
Single person	239.95	60	17.9
RACE AND HISPANIC ORIGIN			
Average household	**398.56**	**100**	**100.0**
Asian	432.96	109	4.7
Black	387.34	97	12.2
Hispanic	377.39	95	11.9
Non-Hispanic white and other	403.89	101	76.1
REGION			
Average household	**398.56**	**100**	**100.0**
Northeast	321.80	81	14.6
Midwest	321.41	81	17.9
South	438.73	110	41.0
West	469.58	118	26.5
EDUCATION			
Average household	**398.56**	**100**	**100.0**
Less than high school graduate	317.22	80	10.4
High school graduate	378.97	95	23.7
Some college	365.69	92	18.9
Associate's degree	417.46	105	10.3
Bachelor's degree or more	463.28	116	36.7
Bachelor's degree	446.69	112	22.3
Master's, professional, doctoral degree	491.77	123	14.3

Note: Market shares may not sum to 100.0 because of rounding and missing categories by household type. "Asian" and "black" include Hispanics and non-Hispanics who identify themselves as being of the respective race alone. "Hispanic" includes people of any race who identify themselves as Hispanic. "Other" includes people who identify themselves as non-Hispanic and as Alaska Native, American Indian, Asian (who are also included in the "Asian" row), or Native Hawaiian or other Pacific Islander, as well as non-Hispanics reporting more than one race.
Source: Calculations by New Strategist based on the Bureau of Labor Statistics' 2012 Consumer Expenditure Survey

Appendix A
About the Consumer Expenditure Survey

History

The Consumer Expenditure Survey is an ongoing study of the day-to-day spending of American households. In taking the survey, government interviewers collect spending data on products and services as well as the amount and sources of household income, changes in saving and debt, and demographic and economic characteristics of household members. The Bureau of the Census collects data for the Consumer Expenditure Survey under contract with the Bureau of Labor Statistics, which is responsible for analysis and release of the survey data.

Since the late 19th century, the federal government has conducted expenditure surveys about every 10 years. Although the results have been used for a variety of purposes, their primary application is to track consumer prices. Beginning in 1980, the Consumer Expenditure Survey became a continuous survey with annual release of data. The survey is used to update prices for the market basket of products and services used in calculating the Consumer Price Index.

Components of the Consumer Expenditure Survey

The Consumer Expenditure Survey consists of two separate surveys: an interview survey and a diary survey. In the interview portion of the survey, respondents are asked each quarter for five consecutive quarters to report their expenditures for the previous three months. The interview survey records purchases of big-ticket items such as houses, cars, and major appliances as well as recurring expenses such as insurance premiums, utility payments, and rent. It covers about 95 percent of all expenditures.

The diary survey records expenditures on small, frequently purchased items during a two-week period. These detailed records include expenses for food and beverages purchased in grocery stores and at restaurants as well as other items such as tobacco, housekeeping supplies, nonprescription drugs, and personal care products and services. The diary survey is intended to capture expenditures respondents are likely to forget or recall incorrectly over longer periods of time.

The average spending figures shown in this report are the integrated data from both the diary and interview components of the survey. Integrated data provide a more complete accounting of consumer expenditures than either component of the survey is designed to do alone.

Data Collection and Processing

For the interview survey, about 7,100 consumer units are interviewed on a rotating panel basis each quarter for five consecutive quarters. Another 7,100 consumer units keep weekly diaries of spending for two consecutive weeks. Data collection is carried out in 91 areas of the country.

The Bureau of Labor Statistics reviews, audits, and cleanses the data, then weights them to reflect the number and characteristics of all U.S. consumer units. Like any sample survey, the Consumer Expenditure Survey is subject to two major types of error. Nonsampling error occurs when respondents misinterpret questions or interviewers are inconsistent in the way they ask questions or record answers. Respondents may forget items, recall expenses incorrectly, or deliberately give wrong answers. A respondent may remember how much he or she spent at the grocery store but forget the items picked up at a local convenience store. Most surveys of alcohol consumption or spending on alcohol, for example, suffer from underreporting. Mistakes during the various stages of data processing and refinement can also cause nonsampling error.

Sampling error occurs when a sample does not accurately represent the population it is supposed to represent. This kind of error is present in every sample-based survey and is minimized by using a proper sampling procedure. Standard error tables documenting the extent of sampling error in the Consumer Expenditure Survey are available from the Bureau of Labor Statistics at http://www.bls.gov/cex/csxcombined .htm.

Although the Consumer Expenditure Survey is the best source of information about the spending behavior of American households, it should be treated with caution because of the above problems. Comparisons with consumption data from other sources show that Consumer Expenditure Survey data tend to underestimate expenditures except for rent, fuel, telephone service, furniture, transportation, and personal care services. Despite these problems, the data reveal important spending patterns by demographic segment that can be used to better understand consumer behavior.

Definition of Consumer Unit

The Consumer Expenditure Survey uses the consumer unit as the sampling unit rather than the household, which is the sampling unit used by the Census Bureau. The term "household" is used interchangeably with the term "consumer unit" in this book for convenience, although they are not exactly the same. Some households contain more than one consumer unit.

The Bureau of Labor Statistics defines consumer unit as (1) members of a household who are related by blood, marriage, adoption, or other legal arrangements; (2) a person living alone or sharing a household with others or living as a roomer in a private home or lodging house or in permanent living quarters in a hotel or motel, but who is financially independent; or (3) two or more persons living together who pool their income to make joint expenditure decisions. The bureau defines financial independence in terms of "the three major expenses categories: housing, food, and other living expenses. To be considered financially independent, at least two of the three major expense categories have to be provided by the respondent."

The Census Bureau uses the household as its sampling unit in the decennial census and in the monthly Current Population Survey. The Census Bureau's household "consists of all persons who occupy a housing unit. A house, an apartment or other group of rooms, or a single room is regarded as a housing unit when it is occupied or intended for occupancy as separate living quarters; that is, when the occupants do not live and eat with any other persons in the structure and there is direct access from the outside or through a common hall."

The definition goes on to specify that "a household includes the related family members and all the unrelated persons, if any, such as lodgers, foster children, wards, or employees who share the housing unit. A person living alone in a housing unit or a group of unrelated persons sharing a housing unit as partners is also counted as a household. The count of households excludes group quarters."

Because there can be more than one consumer unit in a household, consumer units outnumber households by several million. Young adults under age 25 head most of the additional consumer units.

For More Information

To find out more about the Consumer Expenditure Survey, contact the specialists at the Bureau of Labor Statistics at (202) 691-6900, or visit the Consumer Expenditure Survey home page at http://www.bls.gov/cex/. The web site includes news releases, technical documentation, and current and historical summary-level data.

Appendix B
Percent Reporting Expenditure and Amount Spent, Average Quarter 2012

(percent of consumer units reporting expenditure and amount spent by purchasers during the average quarter, 2012)

	percent reporting expenditure during quarter	average amount spent by purchasers per quarter
ALCOHOLIC BEVERAGES	**38.4%**	**$237.34**
Consumed at home	**33.1**	**156.88**
Consumed away from home	**24.3**	**160.73**
Alcoholic beverages at restaurants, taverns	17.8	158.72
Alcoholic beverages purchased on trips	12.7	86.15
APPAREL AND SERVICES	**74.6**	**383.97**
Men's apparel	**31.4**	**170.51**
Suits	1.4	420.47
Sportcoats and tailored jackets	0.9	208.87
Coats and jackets	4.3	105.25
Underwear	5.6	35.85
Hosiery	4.4	22.23
Nightwear	1.1	43.58
Accessories	3.7	52.79
Sweaters and vests	3.2	91.20
Active sportswear	1.6	57.93
Shirts	17.2	78.42
Pants and shorts	19.5	89.67
Uniforms	0.6	154.91
Costumes	0.3	60.71
Boys' (aged 2 to 15) apparel	**11.7**	**133.99**
Coats and jackets	1.9	65.27
Sweaters	0.9	61.93
Shirts	6.6	64.88
Underwear	2.2	30.65
Nightwear	1.0	31.05
Hosiery	1.4	19.12
Accessories	0.9	28.89
Suits, sportcoats, and vests	0.3	115.00
Pants and shorts	8.4	80.65
Uniforms	0.5	109.13
Active sportswear	0.9	38.32
Costumes	0.6	39.29
Women's apparel	**42.3**	**203.89**
Coats and jackets	6.3	98.10
Dresses	9.0	141.40
Sportcoats and tailored jackets	0.6	93.97
Sweaters and vests	7.1	73.59
Shirts, blouses, and tops	24.3	79.87
Skirts	3.4	68.45
Pants and shorts	23.4	89.97
Active sportswear	3.4	59.46
Nightwear	4.1	42.55
Undergarments	9.3	51.89
Hosiery	5.4	20.50

	percent reporting expenditure during quarter	average amount spent by purchasers per quarter
Suits	0.9%	$265.23
Accessories	7.2	78.38
Uniforms	1.0	92.60
Costumes	0.4	49.42
Girls' (aged 2 to 15) apparel	**12.3**	**148.84**
Coats and jackets	2.0	63.65
Dresses and suits	2.4	70.76
Shirts, blouses, and sweaters	7.6	71.71
Skirts, pants, and shorts	8.2	80.09
Active sportswear	1.2	40.50
Underwear and nightwear	3.2	37.38
Hosiery	1.2	19.35
Accessories	1.4	30.62
Uniforms	0.5	120.28
Costumes	0.7	49.66
Children's (under age 2) apparel	**9.2**	**153.36**
Coats, jackets, and snowsuits	0.5	61.57
Outerwear including dresses	2.7	81.71
Underwear	7.9	132.37
Nightwear and loungewear	0.5	50.00
Accessories	1.8	42.60
Footwear	**34.5**	**125.26**
Men's	14.6	100.00
Boys'	6.5	83.49
Women's	20.4	89.61
Girls'	6.6	75.04
Other apparel products and services	**35.7**	**155.17**
Material for making clothes	0.9	97.16
Sewing patterns and notions	0.9	30.97
Watches	3.2	121.35
Jewelry	8.1	290.58
Shoe repair and other shoe services	1.1	34.86
Coin-operated apparel laundry and dry cleaning	13.1	76.68
Apparel alteration, repair, and tailoring services	2.9	51.98
Clothing rental	0.3	140.83
Watch and jewelry repair	1.8	65.56
Professional laundry, dry cleaning	14.3	91.26
Clothing storage	0.1	134.62
COMPUTERS		
Computer accessories	5.2	76.79
Computer information services	61.8	136.00
Computer software	2.4	154.73
Computers and computer hardware, nonbusiness use	7.2	568.12
Installation of computer	0.1	110.00
Portable memory	2.6	35.61
Repair of computer systems for nonbusiness use	1.0	135.29
EDUCATION	**15.3**	**1,886.82**
College tuition	5.7	3,599.43
Elementary and high school tuition	1.7	2,500.59
Vocational and technical school tuition	0.3	580.30
Test preparation, tutoring services	0.9	440.56
Other school tuition	0.3	955.36
Other school expenses including rentals	3.5	310.29
Books and supplies for college	4.8	340.81

	percent reporting expenditure during quarter	average amount spent by purchasers per quarter
Books and supplies for elementary and high school	3.3%	$124.62
Books and supplies for vocational and technical schools	0.1	147.92
Books and supplies for day care and nursery	0.1	67.86
Books and supplies for other schools	0.2	247.22
ENTERTAINMENT	**89.9**	**635.52**
Fees and admissions	**46.7**	**326.31**
Recreation expenses on trips	7.6	69.32
Social, recreation, health club memberships	13.5	236.35
Fees for participant sports	12.2	178.10
Participant sports on trips	3.5	191.35
Movie, theater, opera, ballet admissions	29.9	103.49
Movie, other admissions on trips	8.3	135.29
Admission to sports events	6.4	196.23
Admission to sports events on trips	8.3	45.07
Fees for recreational lessons	5.9	394.17
Other entertainment services on trips	7.6	69.32
Audio and visual equipment and services	**82.6**	**287.16**
Television sets	4.4	582.23
Cable and satellite television services	71.5	231.38
Satellite radio service	3.2	115.50
Online gaming services	2.1	41.79
Video cassette recorders and video disc players	1.8	102.08
Video cassettes, tapes, and discs	10.5	54.27
Video game software	4.8	96.39
Video game hardware and accessories	2.0	176.50
Streamed, downloaded video	4.5	29.92
Applications, games, ringtones for handheld devices	3.9	24.62
Repair of TV, radio, and sound equipment	0.4	188.41
Rental of television sets	0.1	315.00
Radios	0.6	79.10
Tape recorders and players	0.1	61.36
Personal digital audio players	1.1	168.41
Sound components and component systems	0.9	520.35
Compact discs, records, audio tapes	6.5	45.17
Streamed, downloaded audio	7.9	32.71
Rental of VCR, radio, sound equipment	0.0	175.00
Musical instruments and accessories	1.5	281.88
Rental and repair of musical instruments	0.3	128.79
Rental of video cassettes, tapes, discs, films	16.5	23.88
Sound equipment accessories	1.3	80.08
Satellite dishes	0.2	140.91
Installation of television sets	0.1	168.18
Pets, toys, hobbies, and playground equipment	**38.4**	**252.39**
Pets	29.2	253.73
Pet purchase, supplies, and medicines	22.6	150.30
Pet services	6.1	169.79
Veterinary services	10.0	298.47
Toys, games, arts and crafts, and tricycles	13.9	142.73
Stamp and coin collecting	0.9	244.44
Playground equipment	0.4	169.05
Other entertainment supplies, equipment, services	**21.2**	**400.65**
Unmotored recreational vehicles	0.2	6,581.25
Boat without motor and boat trailers	0.1	1,221.43
Trailer and other attachable campers	0.1	10,750.00

	percent reporting expenditure during quarter	average amount spent by purchasers per quarter
Motorized recreational vehicles	0.2%	$7,816.67
Rental of recreational vehicles	0.6	254.58
Docking and landing fees	0.3	642.24
Sports, recreation, and exercise equipment	13.6	240.26
Athletic gear, game tables, exercise equipment	6.9	173.26
Bicycles	2.3	235.76
Camping equipment	1.5	137.93
Hunting and fishing equipment	3.1	294.11
Winter sports equipment	0.5	222.87
Water sports equipment	0.6	198.66
Other sports equipment	1.1	133.88
Rental and repair of miscellaneous sports equipment	0.4	129.17
Photographic equipment and supplies	9.5	165.32
Photo processing	5.6	40.56
Repair and rental of photographic equipment	0.1	139.29
Photographic equipment	2.2	362.44
Photographer fees	2.2	242.20
Live entertainment for catered affairs	0.3	522.58
Rental of party supplies for catered affairs	0.7	478.41
FINANCIAL PRODUCTS AND SERVICES		
Miscellaneous financial products and services	**40.9**	**478.00**
Lotteries and parimutuel losses	13.1	107.40
Legal fees	2.5	1,376.09
Funeral expenses	1.0	1,804.25
Safe deposit box rental	2.1	39.44
Checking accounts, other bank service charges	11.5	50.35
Cemetery lots, vaults, and maintenance fees	0.5	731.11
Accounting fees	5.5	339.81
Finance charges, except mortgage and vehicles	5.7	803.23
Dating services	0.1	96.15
Vacation clubs	0.3	683.33
Expenses for other properties	5.6	668.14
Occupational expenses	5.7	212.70
Interest paid, home equity line of credit (other property)	0.0	200.00
Credit card memberships	0.8	89.02
Shopping club membership fees	4.1	62.41
Cash contributions	**51.8**	**922.68**
Support for college students	3.2	824.06
Alimony expenditures	0.3	7,679.46
Child support expenditures	3.2	1,628.59
Gifts of stocks, bonds, and mutual funds to people in other households	0.2	2,257.89
Cash contributions to charities	18.2	320.92
Cash contributions to religious organizations	27.7	662.01
Cash contributions to educational organizations	2.5	392.41
Cash contributions to political organizations	2.6	244.12
Other cash gifts to people in other households	19.3	602.31
Personal insurance and pensions	**82.0**	**1,704.13**
Life and other personal insurance	27.6	319.28
Life, endowment, annuity, other personal insurance	26.4	311.74
Other nonhealth insurance	2.8	215.18
Pensions and Social Security	77.6	1,686.95
Deductions for government retirement	2.8	910.69
Deductions for railroad retirement	0.1	1,204.17
Deductions for private pensions	9.0	1,415.38

	percent reporting expenditure during quarter	average amount spent by purchasers per quarter
Nonpayroll deposit to retirement plans	7.6%	$1,910.96
Deductions for Social Security	77.4	1,305.28
Personal taxes	**54.4**	**1,022.77**
Federal income taxes	48.3	811.09
Federal income tax deducted	21.8	2,377.99
Additional federal income tax paid	7.8	1,732.36
Federal income tax refunds	35.8	−729.17
State and local income taxes	33.2	396.03
State and local income tax deducted	15.9	851.79
Additional state and local income tax paid	6.2	492.68
State and local income tax refunds	22.1	−155.71
Other taxes	13.8	239.40
FURNISHINGS AND EQUIPMENT FOR THE HOME	**56.6**	**539.13**
Household textiles	**18.8**	**96.54**
Bathroom linens	5.8	42.75
Bedroom linens	10.2	93.14
Kitchen and dining room linens	1.8	23.49
Curtains and draperies	2.4	101.65
Slipcovers and decorative pillows	1.3	76.36
Sewing materials for household items	2.4	86.89
Other linens	0.4	59.29
Furniture	**12.2**	**804.21**
Mattresses and springs	2.3	834.39
Other bedroom furniture	2.5	645.31
Sofas	2.5	1,005.56
Living room chairs	1.8	474.86
Living room tables	1.3	244.70
Kitchen and dining room furniture	1.4	572.83
Infants' furniture	1.0	235.05
Outdoor furniture	1.7	288.10
Wall units, cabinets, and other furniture	2.9	367.97
Floor coverings	**3.0**	**136.07**
Major appliances	**8.9**	**541.79**
Dishwashers (built-in), garbage disposals, range hoods (renter)	0.0	318.75
Dishwashers (built-in), garbage disposals, range hoods (owner)	0.8	496.91
Refrigerators and freezers (renter)	0.4	411.81
Refrigerators and freezers (owner)	1.3	1,035.96
Washing machines (renter)	0.4	320.73
Washing machines (owner)	1.1	661.93
Clothes dryers (renter)	0.3	283.09
Clothes dryers (owner)	0.9	552.20
Cooking stoves, ovens (renter)	0.2	336.67
Cooking stoves, ovens (owner)	0.6	859.13
Microwave ovens (renter)	0.8	76.49
Microwave ovens (owner)	1.0	191.83
Window air conditioners (renter)	0.2	176.25
Window air conditioners (owner)	0.3	276.56
Electric floor-cleaning equipment	2.5	158.17
Sewing machines	0.3	204.84
Small appliances and miscellaneous housewares	**17.0**	**84.43**
Housewares	9.2	65.26
Plastic dinnerware	2.5	26.38
China and other dinnerware	1.9	79.41
Flatware	1.3	54.66

	percent reporting expenditure during quarter	average amount spent by purchasers per quarter
Glassware	1.8%	$36.01
Silver serving pieces	0.1	60.00
Other serving pieces	0.7	38.24
Nonelectric cookware	3.3	65.33
Small appliances	9.9	84.33
Small electric kitchen appliances	8.8	74.00
Portable heating and cooling equipment	1.5	126.34
Miscellaneous household equipment	**41.7**	**294.02**
Window coverings	1.5	244.00
Infants' equipment	1.1	138.74
Outdoor equipment	1.9	182.45
Lamps and lighting fixtures	3.4	79.30
Clocks and household decorative items	6.4	122.29
Telephones and accessories	6.5	157.59
Lawn and garden equipment	2.9	417.97
Power tools	2.4	205.54
Office furniture for home use	0.7	221.32
Hand tools	2.1	86.59
Indoor plants and fresh flowers	16.5	80.97
Closet and storage items	1.2	57.79
Rental of furniture	0.3	444.00
Luggage	1.5	112.16
Computers and computer hardware, nonbusiness use	7.2	568.12
Portable memory	2.6	35.61
Computer software	2.4	154.73
Computer accessories	5.2	76.79
Personal digital assistants	0.4	326.39
Internet services away from home	1.9	111.49
Telephone answering devices	0.2	81.94
Business equipment for home use	0.7	122.64
Smoke alarms (owner)	0.8	48.77
Smoke alarms (renter)	0.1	35.42
Other household appliances (owner)	1.2	155.37
Other household appliances (renter)	0.4	61.88
GIFTS FOR PEOPLE IN OTHER HOUSEHOLDS	**23.2**	**882.20**
Food	**1.4**	**834.63**
Housing	**9.0**	**357.50**
Household textiles	1.1	95.50
Appliances and miscellaneous housewares	1.8	167.56
Major appliances	0.4	439.19
Small appliances and miscellaneous housewares	1.5	91.11
Miscellaneous household equipment	4.6	147.92
Other housing	3.2	669.63
Apparel and services	**10.1**	**267.14**
Males aged 2 or older	4.3	147.78
Females aged 2 or older	5.5	182.91
Children under age 2	2.3	96.04
Other apparel products and services	4.0	213.06
Jewelry and watches	1.9	300.95
All other apparel products and services	2.6	115.88
Transportation	**4.5**	**608.84**
Health care	**1.0**	**1,007.04**
Entertainment	**7.5**	**204.14**
Toys, games, hobbies, and tricycles	4.1	126.17

	percent reporting expenditure during quarter	average amount spent by purchasers per quarter
Other entertainment	4.2%	$241.39
Education	**1.8**	**3,497.13**
All other gifts	**4.6**	**372.72**
GROCERIES	**99.1**	**1,268.52**
Purchased on trips	10.4	120.86
HEALTH CARE	**79.3**	**1,061.54**
Health insurance	**64.4**	**799.74**
Commercial health insurance	14.2	675.95
Traditional fee-for-service health plan (not BCBS)	4.5	593.88
Preferred-provider health plan (not BCBS)	9.9	697.50
Blue Cross, Blue Shield	22.5	711.67
Traditional fee-for-service health plan	3.5	842.96
Preferred-provider health plan	9.1	714.39
Health maintenance organization	7.7	654.91
Commercial Medicare supplement	2.1	579.81
Other BCBS health insurance	1.1	305.66
Health maintenance plans (HMOs)	13.1	626.00
Medicare payments	25.2	394.08
Medicare prescription drug premium	8.8	189.37
Commercial Medicare supplements/other health insurance	12.1	346.39
Commercial Medicare supplement (not BCBS)	4.7	528.22
Other health insurance (not BCBS)	7.9	212.09
Long-term care insurance	3.4	591.81
Medical services	**43.4**	**482.93**
Physician's services	25.7	198.60
Dental services	15.3	437.29
Eye care services	7.7	136.26
Service by professionals other than physician	6.1	257.34
Lab tests, X-rays	6.5	180.98
Hospital room and services	4.9	830.66
Care in convalescent or nursing home	0.2	3,756.52
Other medical services	1.8	258.06
Prescription drugs	**44.9**	**204.19**
Medical supplies	**10.3**	**247.03**
Eyeglasses and contact lenses	7.6	219.68
Hearing aids	0.4	1,263.69
Adult diapers	0.9	84.41
Medical equipment for general use	1.0	126.47
Supportive or convalescent medical equipment	0.7	127.94
Rental of medical equipment	0.4	98.08
Rental of supportive, convalescent medical equipment	0.2	89.47
HOUSEHOLD SERVICES	**72.2**	**393.84**
Personal services	**6.8**	**1,364.11**
Babysitting and child care in own home	1.8	765.11
Babysitting and child care in someone else's home	1.0	775.00
Care for elderly, invalids, handicapped, etc.	0.3	3,737.93
Day care centers, nurseries, and preschools	4.4	1,334.99
Other household services	71.0	270.98
Housekeeping services	6.3	526.88
Gardening and lawn care service	15.0	208.72
Water softening service	1.3	84.65
Nonclothing laundry and dry cleaning, sent out	0.7	44.29
Nonclothing laundry and dry cleaning, coin-operated	3.8	31.93
Termite and pest control services	4.3	120.49

	percent reporting expenditure during quarter	average amount spent by purchasers per quarter
Home security system service fee	5.1%	$133.74
Other home services	2.0	272.52
Termite and pest control products	3.4	27.57
Moving, storage, and freight express	2.7	520.88
Appliance repair, including at service center	2.6	150.59
Reupholstering and furniture repair	0.5	174.46
Repairs/rentals of lawn/garden equipment, hand/power tools, etc.	1.5	133.45
Appliance rental	0.3	138.89
Rental of office equipment for nonbusiness use	0.1	212.50
Repair of computer systems for nonbusiness use	1.0	135.29
Computer information services	61.8	136.00
Installation of computer	0.1	110.00
PERSONAL CARE PRODUCTS AND SERVICES	**60.3**	**126.19**
Wigs and hairpieces	0.7	103.68
Electric personal care appliances	3.9	54.41
Personal care services	59.0	124.10
READING	**35.3**	**77.49**
Newspaper and magazine subscriptions	15.9	62.08
Newspapers and magazines, nonsubscription	10.6	25.78
Books purchased through book clubs	1.1	62.62
Books not purchased through book clubs	17.5	59.71
Digital book readers	1.7	195.69
RESTAURANTS AND CARRY-OUTS	**78.0**	**615.31**
Restaurant food on trips	24.6	260.91
SHELTER	**97.8**	**2,528.77**
Owned dwellings	**64.6**	**2,342.82**
Mortgage interest and charges	39.6	1,937.60
Mortgage interest	37.0	1,975.21
Interest paid, home equity loan	2.1	588.79
Interest paid, home equity line of credit	4.2	539.39
Property taxes	63.5	722.90
Maintenance, repairs, insurance, other expenses	34.8	828.75
Homeowner's insurance	22.7	389.13
Ground rent	1.5	1,011.72
Maintenance and repair services	13.4	1,080.62
Painting and papering	1.1	1,439.96
Plumbing and water heating	3.9	382.75
Heat, air conditioning, electrical work	5.2	553.21
Roofing and gutters	1.1	2,743.24
Other repair and maintenance services	4.0	1,079.10
Repair/replacement of hard-surface flooring	0.6	1,764.58
Repair of built-in appliances	0.4	129.38
Maintenance and repair materials	4.9	441.26
Paints, wallpaper, and supplies	1.8	184.14
Tools/equipment for painting, wallpapering	1.8	19.71
Plumbing supplies and equipment	0.7	227.78
Electrical supplies, heating/cooling equipment	0.4	449.32
Hard-surface flooring repair and replacement	0.4	791.67
Roofing and gutters	0.3	1,117.31
Plaster, paneling, siding, windows, doors, screens, awnings	0.6	493.75
Patio, walk, fence, driveway, masonry, brick, and stucco work	0.3	40.52
Miscellaneous supplies and equipment	1.6	389.10
Insulation, other maintenance/repair	1.6	389.10

	percent reporting expenditure during quarter	average amount spent by purchasers per quarter
Property management and security	6.2%	$271.27
Property management	5.8	229.26
Management and upkeep services for security	1.7	194.83
Parking	1.8	122.51
Rented dwellings	**34.3**	**2,321.66**
Rent	33.2	2,306.60
Rent as pay	1.4	1,489.44
Maintenance, insurance, and other expenses	5.9	158.66
Tenant's insurance	4.7	77.74
Maintenance and repair services	0.6	677.16
Maintenance and repair materials	0.9	204.60
Other lodging	**18.9**	**858.78**
Owned vacation homes	4.5	1,279.33
Mortgage interest and charges	1.1	1,598.25
Property taxes	4.3	552.71
Maintenance, insurance, and other expenses	1.7	923.20
Housing while attending school	1.0	1,955.36
Lodging on trips	15.1	565.21
TELEPHONE	**91.2**	**339.68**
Residential phone service and pay phones	54.5	164.35
Cellular phone service	67.5	319.20
Telephone answering devices	0.2	81.94
Phone cards	3.8	59.68
Voice over IP service	1.8	131.69
TOBACCO PRODUCTS AND SMOKING SUPPLIES	**19.5**	**421.20**
Cigarettes	16.9	443.25
Other tobacco products	3.7	206.97
TRANSPORTATION	**94.8**	**2,321.18**
Vehicle purchases	**5.5**	**14,619.72**
Cars and trucks, new	1.5	26,950.66
New cars	0.8	22,766.88
New trucks	0.8	30,434.42
Cars and trucks, used	3.8	10,026.72
Used cars	2.2	8,797.24
Used trucks	1.7	11,264.07
Other vehicles	0.3	4,814.66
Gasoline and motor oil	**90.3**	**762.87**
Gasoline	89.7	710.67
Diesel fuel	2.2	540.74
Gasoline on trips	21.1	174.91
Motor oil	8.2	34.44
Motor oil on trips	21.1	1.77
Other vehicle expenses	**82.0**	**695.84**
Vehicle finance charges	28.3	197.66
Automobile finance charges	15.1	159.13
Truck finance charges	14.8	190.71
Motorcycle and plane finance charges	0.6	101.19
Other vehicle finance charges	1.1	273.11
Maintenance and repairs	55.2	331.11
Coolant, additives, brake and transmission fluids	5.5	21.97
Tires	8.7	421.06
Vehicle products and cleaning services	5.8	45.13
Parts, equipment, and accessories	9.1	130.07

	percent reporting expenditure during quarter	average amount spent by purchasers per quarter
Vechicle audio equipment	0.3%	$194.64
Vehicle video equipment	0.1	290.00
Body work and painting	1.1	628.74
Clutch, transmission repair	1.0	792.82
Drive shaft and rear-end repair	0.4	411.81
Brake work	5.2	287.06
Repair to steering or front-end	1.4	444.50
Repair to engine cooling system	1.7	277.35
Motor tune-up	4.5	290.67
Lube, oil change, and oil filters	35.4	56.58
Front-end alignment, wheel balance, rotation	3.3	144.10
Shock absorber replacement	0.4	417.31
Repair tires and other repair work	6.1	205.94
Exhaust system repair	0.8	371.20
Electrical system repair	2.3	278.21
Motor repair, replacement	2.6	676.80
Auto repair service policy	0.4	800.00
Vehicle accessories, including labor	0.4	150.00
Vehicle air conditioning repair	1.3	326.91
Vehicle insurance	54.5	410.42
Vehicle rental, leases, licenses, other charges	46.4	234.13
Leased and rented vehicles	5.6	868.54
Rented vehicles	2.9	316.70
Auto rental	0.6	328.45
Auto rental on trips	1.9	306.06
Truck rental	0.3	260.00
Truck rental on trips	0.1	291.07
Leased vehicles	2.9	1,358.56
Car lease payments	1.9	1,124.36
Truck lease payments	1.2	1,248.04
Vehicle registration, state	18.8	135.74
Vehicle registration, local	1.9	125.53
Driver's license	6.0	48.34
Vehicle inspection	7.2	41.09
Parking fees	13.5	78.55
Parking fees in home city, excluding residence	11.0	80.66
Parking fees on trips	3.5	49.28
Tolls or electronic toll passes	11.3	68.99
Tolls on trips	6.7	16.62
Towing charges	0.9	120.05
Global positioning services	0.6	81.75
Automobile service clubs	5.5	90.66
Public transportation	**19.5**	**702.32**
Airline fares	10.7	825.98
Intercity bus fares	4.4	67.49
Intracity mass transit fares	7.4	243.21
Local transportation on trips	5.3	53.33
Taxi fares and limousine service on trips	5.3	31.32
Taxi fares and limousine service	3.7	115.53
Intercity train fares	4.3	109.01
Ship fares	2.1	666.63
School bus	0.1	261.36
TRAVEL		
Admission to sports events on trips	8.3	45.07

	percent reporting expenditure during quarter	average amount spent by purchasers per quarter
Airline fares	10.7%	$825.98
Alcoholic beverages purchased on trips	12.7	86.15
Auto rental on trips	1.9	306.06
Bus fares, intercity	4.4	67.49
Gasoline on trips	21.1	174.91
Groceries purchased on trips	10.4	120.86
Local transportation on trips	5.3	53.33
Lodging on trips	15.1	565.21
Luggage	1.5	112.16
Motor oil on trips	21.1	1.77
Movie, other admissions on trips	8.3	135.29
Parking fees on trips	3.5	49.28
Participant sports on trips	3.5	191.35
Recreation expenses on trips	7.6	69.32
Restaurant food on trips	24.6	260.91
Ship fares	2.1	666.63
Taxi fares and limousine service on trips	5.3	31.32
Tolls on trips	6.7	16.62
Train fares, intercity	4.3	109.01
Truck rental on trips	0.1	291.07
UTILITIES	**97.6**	**934.20**
Natural gas	47.7	188.26
Electricity	91.8	378.03
Fuel oil and other fuels	7.8	441.17
Fuel oil	2.7	739.65
Coal, wood, and other fuels	0.7	298.63
Bottled gas	4.7	254.51
Water and other public services	64.6	203.09
Water and sewerage maintenance	57.9	172.03
Trash and garbage collection	40.8	75.64
Septic tank cleaning	0.3	230.47

Note: The categories shown here may be different from those analyzed in the book because these are from only the interview portion of the Consumer Expenditure Survey. Some categories shown here are not analyzed in the book because the sample size was too small to make reliable estimates.

Source: Calculations by New Strategist based on the 2012 Consumer Expenditure Survey

Appendix C
Spending by Product and Service Ranked by Amount Spent, 2012

(average annual spending of consumer units on products and services, ranked by amount spent, 2012)

1.	Deductions for Social Security	$4,040.62
2.	Groceries (also shown by individual category)	3,920.65
3.	Vehicle purchases (net outlay)	3,210.49
4.	Mortgage interest (or rent, $3,064.09)	2,926.47
5.	Gasoline and motor oil	2,755.78
6.	Restaurants (also shown by meal category)	2,225.50
7.	Health insurance	2,060.78
8.	Property taxes	1,835.60
9.	Federal income taxes	1,568.33
10.	Electricity	1,387.83
11.	Dinner at restaurants	1,082.12
12.	Vehicle insurance	1,017.94
13.	Cellular phone service	861.97
14.	College tuition	824.99
15.	Vehicle maintenance and repairs	814.27
16.	Lunch at restaurants	746.81
17.	Cash contributions to church, religious organizations	734.30
18.	Cable and satellite television services	661.76
19.	Nonpayroll deposit to retirement plans	582.46
20.	Maintenance and repair services, owner	578.78
21.	Women's apparel	572.53
22.	State and local income taxes	526.08
23.	Deductions for private pensions	511.80
24.	Cash gifts to members of other households	464.50
25.	Alcoholic beverages	451.16
26.	Water and sewerage maintenance	398.56
27.	Prescription drugs	366.40
28.	Natural gas	359.35
29.	Residential telephone service and pay phones	358.54
30.	Homeowner's insurance	353.80
31.	Life and other personal insurance	352.61
32.	Airline fares	352.53
33.	Lodging on trips	341.61
34.	Computer information services	336.30
35.	Men's apparel	319.73
36.	Cigarettes	298.75
37.	Personal care services	292.83
38.	Dental services	268.32
39.	Fresh fruits	261.29
40.	Restaurant meals on trips	257.15
41.	Day care centers, nurseries, and preschools	236.56
42.	Cash contributions to charities	233.63
43.	Owned vacation homes	230.28
44.	Breakfast at restaurants	227.60
45.	Beef	226.32
46.	Fresh vegetables	226.14
47.	Vehicle finance charges	223.36
48.	Child support expenditures	208.46
49.	Physician's services	204.16
50.	Pet food	194.70

51.	Finance charges, except mortgage and vehicles	$181.53
52.	Elementary and high school tuition	169.04
53.	Snacks at restaurants	168.97
54.	Movie, theater, amusement park, and other admissions	168.75
55.	Pork	165.77
56.	Computers and computer hardware for nonbusiness use	162.71
57.	Hospital room and services	161.48
58.	Poultry	159.36
59.	Women's footwear	158.87
60.	Leased vehicles	158.68
61.	Cosmetics, perfume, and bath products	157.04
62.	Laundry and cleaning supplies	155.39
63.	Veterinarian services	149.95
64.	Expenses for other properties	149.93
65.	Prepared foods except frozen, salads, and desserts	147.81
66.	Interest paid, home equity loan/line of credit	140.37
67.	Carbonated drinks	139.74
68.	Legal fees	138.71
69.	Pet purchase, supplies, and medicines	135.69
70.	Other taxes	131.96
71.	Housekeeping services	131.93
72.	Cheese	131.47
73.	Fresh milk, all types	128.28
74.	Social, recreation, health club membership	127.44
75.	Household decorative items	126.84
76.	Fish and seafood	125.74
77.	Gardening, lawn care service	125.40
78.	Miscellaneous household products	125.00
79.	Trash and garbage collection	123.44
80.	Fees for participant sports	118.19
81.	Cleansing and toilet tissue, paper towels, and napkins	117.50
82.	Girls' (aged 2 to 15) apparel	115.92
83.	Toys, games, hobbies, and tricycles	114.59
84.	Beer and ale at home	112.49
85.	Men's footwear	111.75
86.	Potato chips and other snacks	111.59
87.	Vehicle registration	111.25
88.	Support for college students	104.82
89.	Wine at home	102.62
90.	Television sets	102.24
91.	Sofas	101.36
92.	Deductions for government retirement	100.54
93.	Nonprescription drugs	97.49
94.	Ready-to-eat and cooked cereals	94.82
95.	Jewelry	94.38
96.	Fees for recreational lessons	92.55
97.	Boys' (aged 2 to 15) apparel	87.96
98.	Candy and chewing gum	87.86
99.	Lunch meats (cold cuts)	87.23
100.	Coffee	86.50
101.	Maintenance and repair materials, owner	86.31
102.	Alimony expenditures	86.01
103.	Babysitting and child care	84.86
104.	Rent as pay	84.60
105.	Fuel oil	80.77
106.	Housing while attending school	76.65
107.	Mattresses and springs	76.43

108.	Lawn and garden supplies	$76.04
109.	Beer and ale at bars, restaurants	75.94
110.	Stationery, stationery supplies, giftwrap	75.07
111.	Accounting fees	75.03
112.	Funeral expenses	72.17
113.	Intracity mass transit fares	71.99
114.	Lawn and garden equipment	71.11
115.	Frozen prepared foods, except meals	70.22
116.	Bedroom linens	67.43
117.	Eyeglasses and contact lenses	66.52
118.	Motorized recreational vehicles	65.66
119.	Admission to sports events	65.45
120.	Books and supplies for college	65.30
121.	Children's (under age 2) apparel	63.31
122.	Bedroom furniture except mattresses and springs	63.24
123.	Service by professionals other than physician	62.38
124.	Hair care products	61.69
125.	Bread, other than white	61.60
126.	Athletic gear, game tables, exercise equipment	60.99
127.	Frozen meals	60.61
128.	Sauces and gravies	60.27
129.	Catered affairs	60.19
130.	Refrigerators and freezers	59.80
131.	School lunches	59.56
132.	Ground rent	58.68
133.	Lottery and gambling losses	57.93
134.	Postage	57.44
135.	Ice cream and related products	57.37
136.	Moving, storage, and freight express	56.88
137.	Bottled water	56.80
138.	Ship fares	56.53
139.	School tuition, books, and supplies other than college, vocational/technical, elementary, high school	55.30
140.	Canned and bottled fruit juice	54.92
141.	Canned vegetables	54.59
142.	Indoor plants and fresh flowers	53.57
143.	Property management, owner	53.28
144.	Eggs	53.08
145.	Other dairy (yogurt, etc.)	52.67
146.	Professional laundry, dry cleaning	52.24
147.	Biscuits and rolls	51.85
148.	Nonprescription vitamins	50.76
149.	Cookies	50.56
150.	Food prepared by consumer unit on trips	50.23
151.	Occupational expenses	48.41
152.	Bottled gas	47.44
153.	Other alcoholic beverages at bars, restaurants	47.43
154.	Lab tests, X-rays	46.91
155.	Canned and packaged soups	46.30
156.	Books	45.30
157.	Board (including at school)	44.93
158.	Alcoholic beverages purchased on trips	43.80
159.	White bread	43.52
160.	Care for elderly, invalids, handicapped, etc.	43.36
161.	Wall units, cabinets, and other furniture	42.39
162.	Nuts	42.35
163.	Parking fees	42.29

164.	Unmotored recreational vehicles	$42.12
165.	Eye care services	41.86
166.	Pet services	41.70
167.	Topicals and dressings	40.99
168.	Oral hygiene products	40.82
169.	Coin-operated apparel laundry and dry cleaning	40.21
170.	Newspaper and magazine subscriptions	39.58
171.	Power tools	39.34
172.	Boys' footwear	39.09
173.	Miscellaneous personal services	38.97
174.	Cash contributions to educational institutions	38.77
175.	Salt, spices, and other seasonings	38.72
176.	Cakes and cupcakes	37.94
177.	Frozen vegetables	37.50
178.	Crackers	37.17
179.	Girls' footwear	37.12
180.	Video game hardware and accessories	37.03
181.	Pasta, cornmeal, and other cereal products	36.98
182.	Fats and oils	36.79
183.	Rented vehicles	36.23
184.	Tolls	35.63
185.	Prepared salads	35.09
186.	Living room chairs	34.57
187.	Care in convalescent or nursing home	34.56
188.	Wine at bars, restaurants	34.54
189.	Deodorants, feminine hygiene, miscellaneous products	34.51
190.	Washing machines	34.12
191.	Sound components, equipment, and accessories	32.07
192.	Kitchen and dining room furniture	31.62
193.	Salad dressings	31.29
194.	Photographic equipment	31.17
195.	Meals as pay	30.79
196.	Tea	30.36
197.	Tobacco products other than cigarettes	30.30
198.	Video cassettes, tapes, and discs	29.70
199.	Jams, preserves, other sweets	29.61
200.	Hunting and fishing equipment	29.06
201.	Frozen and refrigerated bakery products	28.77
202.	Telephones and accessories	27.33
203.	Home security system service fee	27.23
204.	Lamps and lighting fixtures	26.83
205.	Small electric kitchen appliances	25.90
206.	Noncarbonated fruit-flavored drinks	25.83
207.	Butter	25.56
208.	Baby food	25.05
209.	Baking needs	24.95
210.	Cash contributions to political organizations	24.90
211.	Frankfurters	24.71
212.	Rice	24.65
213.	Termite and pest control products and services	24.58
214.	Outdoor equipment	24.51
215.	Sugar	24.38
216.	Clothes dryers	23.95
217.	Bathroom linens	23.90
218.	Sweetrolls, coffee cakes, doughnuts	23.73
219.	Cooking stoves, ovens	23.67
220.	Cream	23.58

221.	Checking accounts, other bank service charges	$23.10
222.	Bicycles	21.69
223.	Other alcoholic beverages at home	21.40
224.	Hearing aids	21.23
225.	Photographer fees	21.12
226.	Nonclothing laundry and dry cleaning, sent out	21.09
227.	Recreation expenses on trips	20.99
228.	Canned fruits	20.35
229.	Automobile service clubs	20.09
230.	Laundry and cleaning equipment	19.59
231.	Outdoor furniture	19.36
232.	Shaving products	19.18
233.	Vegetable juices	18.98
234.	Tableware, nonelectric kitchenware	18.89
235.	Intercity train fares	18.88
236.	Nonelectric cookware	18.86
237.	Peanut butter	18.68
238.	Nondairy cream and imitation milk	18.59
239.	Dried vegetables	18.22
240.	Local transportation on trips	17.81
241.	Olives, pickles, relishes	17.46
242.	Gifts of stocks, bonds, and mutual funds to members of other households	17.16
243.	Fresh fruit juice	17.06
244.	Musical instruments and accessories	16.80
245.	Dishwashers (built-in), garbage disposals, range hoods	16.61
246.	Books and supplies for elementary and high school	16.25
247.	Floor coverings	16.22
248.	Prepared flour mixes	16.18
249.	Electric floor-cleaning equipment	16.07
250.	Test preparation, tutoring services	15.86
251.	Computer accessories	15.85
252.	Rental of video cassettes, tapes, discs, films	15.72
253.	Maintenance and repair services, renter	15.71
254.	Nonalcoholic beverages (except carbonated, coffee, fruit-flavored drinks, and tea) and ice	15.36
255.	Appliance repair, including at service center	15.36
256.	Sports drinks	15.12
257.	Watches	15.09
258.	Computer software	15.04
259.	Satellite radio service	14.83
260.	Tenant's insurance	14.74
261.	Window coverings	14.64
262.	Prepared desserts	14.29
263.	Luggage	13.79
264.	Digital book readers	13.62
265.	Security services, owner	13.56
266.	Infants' equipment	13.42
267.	Pies, tarts, turnovers	13.41
268.	Cemetery lots, vaults, and maintenance fees	13.16
269.	Whiskey at home	12.93
270.	Living room tables	12.92
271.	Rental of party supplies for catered affairs	12.63
272.	Closet and storage items	12.60
273.	Intercity bus fares	11.96
274.	Vehicle inspection	11.85
275.	Hand tools	11.79
276.	Compact discs, records, and audio tapes	11.78

277.	Driver's license	$11.64
278.	Taxi fares and limousine service	11.36
279.	Camping equipment	11.06
280.	Newspapers and magazines, nonsubscription	10.88
281.	Microwave ovens	10.55
282.	Streamed and downloaded audio	10.39
283.	Electric personal care appliances	10.39
284.	Lamb, organ meats, and others	10.19
285.	Shopping club membership fees	10.16
286.	Curtains and draperies	9.88
287.	Voice over IP	9.64
288.	Infants' furniture	9.59
289.	Flour	9.36
290.	Photo processing	9.15
291.	Phone cards	9.00
292.	Hair accessories	8.92
293.	Parking at owned home	8.87
294.	Portable heating and cooling equipment	8.84
295.	Stamp and coin collecting	8.80
296.	China and other dinnerware	8.76
297.	Margarine	8.74
298.	Material for making clothes	8.74
299.	Coal, wood, and other fuels	8.72
300.	Dried fruits	8.71
301.	Sewing materials for household items	8.48
302.	Internet services away from home	8.25
303.	Kitchen and dining room linens	8.15
304.	Miscellaneous video equipment	8.08
305.	Glassware	7.94
306.	Repairs and rentals of lawn and garden equipment, hand and power tools, etc.	7.90
307.	Vocational and technical school tuition	7.66
308.	Docking and landing fees	7.45
309.	Personal digital audio players	7.41
310.	Vacation clubs	7.38
311.	VCRs and video disc players	7.35
312.	Bread and cracker products	7.31
313.	Frozen fruits	7.16
314.	Maintenance and repair materials, renter	7.12
315.	Live entertainment for catered affairs	6.48
316.	Rental of recreational vehicles	6.11
317.	Apparel alteration, repair, and tailoring services	6.03
318.	Office furniture for home use	6.02
319.	Global positioning system devices	5.66
320.	Frozen fruit juices	5.55
321.	Repair of computer systems for nonbusiness use	5.52
322.	Streamed and downloaded video	5.35
323.	Medical equipment for general use	5.16
324.	Window air conditioners	4.95
325.	Artificial sweeteners	4.91
326.	Nonclothing laundry and dry cleaning, coin-operated	4.79
327.	Watch and jewelry repair	4.72
328.	Personal digital assistants	4.70
329.	Water sports equipment	4.45
330.	Rental of furniture	4.44
331.	Towing charges	4.37
332.	Water-softening service	4.30
333.	Sewing patterns and notions	4.20

334.	Winter sports equipment	$4.19
335.	Slipcovers and decorative pillows	3.94
336.	Applications, games, ringtones for handheld devices	3.86
337.	Portable memory	3.76
338.	Business equipment for home use	3.63
339.	Online gaming services	3.51
340.	Supportive and convalescent medical equipment	3.48
341.	Delivery services	3.43
342.	Safe deposit box rental	3.36
343.	Video game software	3.26
344.	Reupholstering and furniture repair	3.21
345.	Repair of TV, radio, and sound equipment	3.09
346.	Septic tank cleaning	2.95
347.	Flatware	2.93
348.	Credit card memberships	2.92
349.	Deductions for railroad retirement	2.89
350.	Adult diapers	2.86
351.	Playground equipment	2.84
352.	Wigs and hairpieces	2.82
353.	Plastic dinnerware	2.68
354.	Smoking accessories	2.68
355.	Sewing machines	2.54
356.	Fireworks	2.46
357.	Global positioning services	2.06
358.	Silver serving pieces	2.04
359.	Rental and repair of miscellaneous sports equipment	1.86
360.	Pinball, electronic video games	1.78
361.	Smoke alarms	1.75
362.	Rental and repair of musical instruments	1.70
363.	Clothing rental	1.69
364.	Rental of medical equipment	1.53
365.	Shoe repair and other shoe services	1.52
366.	Appliance rental	1.50
367.	Satellite dishes	1.24
368.	School bus	1.15
369.	Other serving pieces	1.04
370.	Installation of television sets	0.74
371.	Books and supplies for vocational and technical schools	0.71
372.	Clothing storage	0.70
373.	Rental of office equipment for nonbusiness use	0.68
374.	Rental of supportive and convalescent medical equipment	0.68
375.	Telephone answering devices	0.59
376.	Dating services	0.50
377.	Installation of computer	0.44
378.	Repair and rental of photographic equipment	0.39
379.	Books and supplies for day care and nursery	0.38

Source: Calculations by New Strategist based on the 2012 Consumer Expenditure Survey

Appendix D
Household Spending Trends, 2000 to 2012

(average annual spending of total consumer units, 2000, 2006, 2010, and 2012; percent change, 2000–06, 2006–12, and 2010–12; in 2012 dollars)

	average annual household spending (in 2012$)				percent change		
	2012	2010	2006	2000	2010–12	2006–12	2000–06
Number of consumer units (in 000s)	124,416	121,107	118,843	109,367	2.7%	4.7%	8.7%
Average annual spending of consumer units	$51,442	$50,655	$55,118	$50,725	1.6	–6.7	8.7
FOOD	6,599	6,453	6,960	6,877	2.3	–5.2	1.2
Food at home	3,921	3,816	3,891	4,028	2.8	0.8	–3.4
Cereals and bakery products	538	529	508	604	1.8	5.9	–15.9
Cereals and cereal products	182	174	163	208	4.8	11.8	–21.7
Bakery products	356	355	346	396	0.3	2.8	–12.6
Meats, poultry, fish, and eggs	852	825	908	1,060	3.2	–6.1	–14.4
Beef	226	228	269	317	–1.1	–15.9	–15.3
Pork	166	157	179	223	5.8	–7.2	–19.7
Other meats	122	123	120	135	–1.0	2.0	–11.2
Poultry	159	145	161	193	9.4	–1.0	–16.9
Fish and seafood	126	123	139	147	2.3	–9.3	–5.3
Eggs	53	48	42	45	9.4	25.8	–7.0
Dairy products	419	400	419	433	4.7	0.0	–3.3
Fresh milk and cream	152	148	159	175	2.4	–4.7	–8.7
Other dairy products	267	253	260	257	5.7	2.8	0.9
Fruits and vegetables	731	715	674	695	2.2	8.4	–2.9
Fresh fruits	261	244	222	217	6.8	17.5	2.2
Fresh vegetables	226	221	220	212	2.2	2.8	3.7
Processed fruits	114	119	124	153	–4.2	–8.2	–19.0
Processed vegetables	130	131	108	112	–0.4	20.2	–3.4
Other food at home	1,380	1,346	1,380	1,236	2.6	0.0	11.7
Sugar and other sweets	147	139	142	156	5.8	3.3	–8.7
Fats and oils	114	108	98	111	5.1	16.4	–11.5
Miscellaneous foods	699	702	714	583	–0.5	–2.1	22.6
Nonalcoholic beverages	370	351	378	333	5.5	–2.1	13.4
Food prepared by consumer unit on trips	50	45	49	53	10.4	2.1	–8.2
Food away from home	2,678	2,638	3,068	2,849	1.5	–12.7	7.7
ALCOHOLIC BEVERAGES	451	434	566	496	4.0	–20.3	14.1
HOUSING	16,887	17,433	18,639	16,425	–3.1	–9.4	13.5
Shelter	9,891	10,331	11,016	9,485	–4.3	–10.2	16.1
Owned dwellings	6,056	6,609	7,421	6,136	–8.4	–18.4	20.9
Mortgage interest and charges	3,067	3,528	4,274	3,519	–13.1	–28.2	21.5
Property taxes	1,836	1,910	1,878	1,519	–3.9	–2.2	23.7
Maintenance, repair, insurance, other expenses	1,153	1,171	1,270	1,100	–1.5	–9.2	15.4
Rented dwellings	3,186	3,053	2,950	2,712	4.3	8.0	8.8
Other lodging	649	669	646	637	–2.9	0.5	1.3
Utilities, fuels, and public services	3,648	3,854	3,869	3,319	–5.3	–5.7	16.6
Natural gas	359	463	580	409	–22.5	–38.1	41.6
Electricity	1,388	1,488	1,442	1,215	–6.7	–3.7	18.7
Fuel oil and other fuels	137	147	157	129	–7.1	–12.8	21.5
Telephone services	1,239	1,240	1,238	1,169	–0.1	0.1	5.9
Water and other public services	525	515	452	395	2.0	16.1	14.6
Household services	1,159	1,060	1,080	912	9.3	7.4	18.4
Personal services	368	358	448	435	2.8	–17.8	3.0
Other household services	791	702	632	477	12.6	25.1	32.4
Housekeeping supplies	610	644	729	643	–5.3	–16.3	13.4
Laundry and cleaning supplies	155	158	172	175	–1.9	–9.9	–1.5
Other household products	319	346	376	301	–7.9	–15.1	24.7
Postage and stationery	136	139	181	168	–2.1	–24.9	7.8
Household furnishings and equipment	1,580	1,545	1,945	2,065	2.3	–18.8	–5.8
Household textiles	123	107	175	141	14.5	–29.9	24.1
Furniture	391	374	527	521	4.6	–25.8	1.1
Floor coverings	16	38	55	59	–57.8	–70.7	–6.8

	average annual household spending (in 2012$)				percent change		
	2012	2010	2006	2000	2010–12	2006–12	2000–06
Major appliances	$197	$220	$274	$252	−10.5%	−28.2%	8.9%
Small appliances and miscellaneous housewares	98	113	124	116	−13.0	−21.1	7.0
Miscellaneous household equipment	754	692	789	975	9.0	−4.5	−19.0
APPAREL AND RELATED SERVICES	**1,736**	**1,790**	**2,134**	**2,475**	**−3.0**	**−18.7**	**−13.8**
Men and boys	**408**	**402**	**506**	**587**	**1.4**	**−19.3**	**−13.8**
Men, aged 16 or older	320	320	402	459	0.0	−20.4	−12.3
Boys, aged 2 to 15	88	82	104	128	7.1	−15.1	−19.0
Women and girls	**688**	**698**	**855**	**967**	**−1.4**	**−19.6**	**−11.5**
Women, aged 16 or older	573	592	716	809	−3.2	−20.0	−11.5
Girls, aged 2 to 15	116	106	139	157	9.1	−16.5	−11.7
Children under age 2	**63**	**96**	**109**	**109**	**−34.2**	**−42.4**	**0.0**
Footwear	**347**	**319**	**346**	**457**	**8.8**	**0.2**	**−24.3**
Other apparel products and services	**230**	**275**	**319**	**355**	**−16.3**	**−27.9**	**−10.1**
TRANSPORTATION	**8,998**	**8,083**	**9,689**	**9,889**	**11.3**	**−7.1**	**−2.0**
Vehicle purchases	**3,210**	**2,725**	**3,896**	**4,557**	**17.8**	**−17.6**	**−14.5**
Cars and trucks, new	1,639	1,284	2,048	2,140	27.7	−20.0	−4.3
Cars and trucks, used	1,516	1,388	1,786	2,360	9.2	−15.1	−24.3
Gasoline and motor oil	**2,756**	**2,245**	**2,536**	**1,721**	**22.8**	**8.7**	**47.3**
Other vehicle expenses	**2,490**	**2,594**	**2,682**	**3,041**	**−4.0**	**−7.2**	**−11.8**
Vehicle finance charges	223	256	339	437	−12.8	−34.3	−22.4
Maintenance and repairs	814	829	784	832	−1.8	3.9	−5.8
Vehicle insurance	1,018	1,063	1,009	1,037	−4.3	0.9	−2.7
Vehicle rentals, leases, licenses, other charges	434	445	549	735	−2.6	−20.9	−25.3
Public transportation	**542**	**519**	**575**	**569**	**4.4**	**−5.8**	**1.0**
HEALTH CARE	**3,556**	**3,324**	**3,150**	**2,755**	**7.0**	**12.9**	**14.4**
Health insurance	2,061	1,928	1,668	1,311	6.9	23.5	27.3
Medical services	839	760	763	757	10.4	10.0	0.8
Drugs	515	511	585	555	0.8	−12.0	5.5
Medical supplies	142	125	133	132	13.3	6.6	0.9
ENTERTAINMENT	**2,605**	**2,637**	**2,706**	**2,484**	**−1.2**	**−3.7**	**8.9**
Fees and admissions	614	612	690	687	0.4	−11.0	0.5
Audio and visual equipment and services	979	1,004	1,032	829	−2.5	−5.1	24.4
Pets, toys, and playground equipment	648	638	469	445	1.6	38.1	5.4
Other entertainment products and services	363	383	514	524	−5.3	−29.3	−2.0
PERSONAL CARE PRODUCTS AND SERVICES	**628**	**613**	**666**	**752**	**2.5**	**−5.7**	**−11.4**
READING	**109**	**105**	**133**	**195**	**3.5**	**−18.2**	**−31.5**
EDUCATION	**1,207**	**1,131**	**1,011**	**843**	**6.7**	**19.4**	**20.0**
TOBACCO PRODUCTS AND SMOKING SUPPLIES	**332**	**381**	**372**	**425**	**−12.9**	**−10.9**	**−12.4**
MISCELLANEOUS	**829**	**894**	**963**	**1,035**	**−7.3**	**−14.0**	**−6.9**
CASH CONTRIBUTIONS	**1,913**	**1,719**	**2,129**	**1,589**	**11.3**	**−10.1**	**33.9**
PERSONAL INSURANCE AND PENSIONS	**5,591**	**5,657**	**6,002**	**4,487**	**−1.2**	**−6.8**	**33.8**
Life and other personal insurance	353	335	367	532	5.4	−3.7	−31.1
Pensions and Social Security*	5,238	5,321	5,635	3,955	−1.6	−7.0	*
PERSONAL TAXES	**2,226**	**1,863**	**2,770**	**4,156**	**19.5**	**−19.6**	**−33.4**
Federal income taxes	1,568	1,196	1,949	3,212	31.1	−19.5	−39.3
State and local income taxes	526	508	591	749	3.6	−11.0	−21.1
Other taxes	132	159	230	195	−17.0	−42.6	18.2
GIFTS FOR PEOPLE IN OTHER HOUSEHOLDS	**1,116**	**1,083**	**1,314**	**1,444**	**3.0**	**−15.1**	**−9.0**

*Recent spending on pensions and Social Security is not comparable with 2000 because of changes in methodology.

Note: Spending by category does not add to total spending because gift spending is also included in the preceding product and service categories and personal taxes are not included in the total.

Source: Bureau of Labor Statistics, 2000, 2006, 2010, and 2012 Consumer Expenditure Surveys, Internet site http://www.bls.gov/cex/; calculations by New Strategist

Glossary

age The age of the reference person.

alcoholic beverages Includes beer and ale, wine, whiskey, gin, vodka, rum, and other alcoholic beverages.

annual spending The annual amount spent per household. The Bureau of Labor Statistics calculates the annual average for all households in a segment, not just for those that purchased an item. The averages are calculated by integrating the results of the diary (weekly) and interview (quarterly) portions of the Consumer Expenditure Survey. For items purchased by most households—such as bread— average annual spending figures are a fairly accurate account of actual spending. For products and services purchased by few households during a year's time—such as cars—the average annual amount spent is much less than what purchasers spend.

apparel, accessories, and related services Includes the following:

• *men's and boys' apparel* Includes coats, jackets, sweaters, vests, sport coats, tailored jackets, slacks, shorts and short sets, sportswear, shirts, underwear, nightwear, hosiery, uniforms, and other accessories.

• *women's and girls' apparel* Includes coats, jackets, furs, sport coats, tailored jackets, sweaters, vests, blouses, shirts, dresses, dungarees, culottes, slacks, shorts, sportswear, underwear, nightwear, uniforms, hosiery, and other accessories.

• *infants' apparel* Includes coats, jackets, snowsuits, underwear, diapers, dresses, crawlers, sleeping garments, hosiery, footwear, and other accessories for children.

• *footwear* Includes articles such as shoes, slippers, boots, and other similar items. It excludes footwear for babies and footwear used for sports such as bowling or golf shoes.

• *other apparel products and services* Includes material for making clothes, shoe repair, alterations and sewing patterns and notions, clothing rental, clothing storage, dry cleaning, sent-out laundry, watches, jewelry, and repairs to watches and jewelry.

baby boom Americans born between 1946 and 1964.

cash contributions Includes cash contributed to persons or organizations outside the consumer unit including court-ordered alimony, child support payments, support for college students, and contributions to religious, educational, charitable, or political organizations.

consumer unit (1) All members of a household who are related by blood, marriage, adoption, or other legal arrangements; (2) a person living alone or sharing a household with others or living as a roomer in a private home or lodging house or in permanent living quarters in a hotel or motel, but who is financially independent, or (3) two or more persons living together who pool their income to make joint expenditure decisions. Financial independence is determined by the three major expense categories: housing, food, and other living expenses. To be considered financially independent, at least two of the three major expense categories have to be provided by the respondent. For convenience, called household in the text of this report.

consumer unit, composition of The classification of interview households by type according to (1) relationship of other household members to the reference person; (2) age of the children of the reference person; and (3) combination of relationship to the reference person and age of the children. Stepchildren and adopted children are included with the reference person's own children.

earner A consumer unit member aged 14 or older who worked at least one week during the 12 months prior to the interview date.

education Includes tuition, fees, books, supplies, and equipment for public and private nursery schools, elementary and high schools, colleges and universities, and other schools.

entertainment Includes the following:

• *fees and admissions* Includes fees for participant sports; admissions to sporting events, movies, concerts, plays; health, swimming, tennis, and country club memberships, and other social recreational and fraternal organizations; recreational lessons or instructions; and recreational expenses on trips.

• *audio and visual equipment and services* Includes television sets; radios; cable TV; tape recorders and players; video cassettes, tapes, and discs; video cassette recorders and video disc players; video game hardware and software; personal digital audio players; streaming and downloading audio and video; sound components; CDs, records, and tapes; musical instruments; and rental and repair of TV and sound equipment.

• *pets, toys, hobbies, and playground equipment* Includes pet food, pet services, veterinary expenses, toys, games, hobbies, and playground equipment.

• *other entertainment equipment and services* Includes indoor exercise equipment, athletic shoes, bicycles, trailers, campers, camping equipment, rental of campers and trailers, hunting and fishing equipment, sports equipment, winter sports equipment, water sports equipment, boats, boat motors and boat trailers, rental of boats, landing and docking fees, rental and repair of sports equipment, photographic equipment, film, photo processing, photographer fees, repair and rental of photo equipment, fireworks, pinball and electronic video games.

expenditure The transaction cost including excise and sales taxes of goods and services acquired during the survey period. The full cost of each purchase is recorded even though full payment may not have been made at the date of purchase. Expenditure estimates include gifts. Excluded from expenditures are purchases or portions of purchases directly assignable to business purposes and periodic credit or installment payments on goods and services already acquired.

federal income tax Includes federal income tax withheld in the survey year to pay for income earned in survey year plus additional tax paid in survey year to cover any underpayment or underwithholding of tax in the year prior to the survey.

financial products and services Includes accounting fees, legal fees, union dues, professional dues and fees, other occupational expenses, funerals, cemetery lots, dating services, shopping club memberships, and unclassified fees and personal services.

food Includes the following:

• *food at home* Refers to the total expenditures for food at grocery stores or other food stores during the interview period. It is calculated by multiplying the number of visits to a grocery or other food store by the average amount spent per visit. It excludes the purchase of nonfood items.

• *food away from home* Includes all meals (breakfast, lunch, brunch, and dinner) at restaurants, carry-outs, and vending machines, including tips, plus meals as pay, special catered affairs such as weddings, bar mitzvahs, and confirmations, and meals away from home on trips.

generation X Americans born between 1965 and 1976. Also known as the baby-bust generation.

gifts for people in other households Includes gift expenditures for people living in other consumer units. The amount spent on gifts is also included in individual product and service categories.

health care Includes the following:

• *health insurance* Includes health maintenance plans (HMOs), Blue Cross/Blue Shield, commercial health insurance, Medicare, Medicare supplemental insurance, long-term care insurance, and other health insurance.

• *medical services* Includes hospital room and services, physicians' services, services of a practitioner other than a physician, eye and dental care, lab tests, X-rays, nursing, therapy services, care in convalescent or nursing home, and other medical care.

• *drugs* Includes prescription and nonprescription drugs, internal and respiratory over-the-counter drugs.

• *medical supplies* Includes eyeglasses and contact lenses, topicals and dressings, antiseptics, bandages, cotton, first aid kits, contraceptives; medical equipment for general use such as syringes, ice bags, thermometers, vaporizers, heating pads; supportive or convalescent medical equipment such as hearing aids, braces, canes, crutches, and walkers.

Hispanic origin The self-identified Hispanic origin of the consumer unit reference person. All consumer units are included in one of two Hispanic origin groups based on the reference person's Hispanic origin: Hispanic or non-Hispanic. Hispanics may be of any race.

household According to the Census Bureau, all the people who occupy a household. A group of unrelated people who share a housing unit as roommates or unmarried partners is also counted as a household. Households do not include group quarters such as college dormitories, prisons, or nursing homes. A household may contain more than one consumer unit. The terms "household" and "consumer unit" are used interchangeably in this report.

household furnishings and equipment Includes the following:

• *household textiles* Includes bathroom, kitchen, dining room, and other linens, curtains and drapes, slipcovers and decorative pillows, and sewing materials.

• *furniture* Includes living room, dining room, kitchen, bedroom, nursery, porch, lawn, and other outdoor furniture.

• *carpet, rugs, and other floor coverings* Includes installation and replacement of wall-to-wall carpets, room-size rugs, and other soft floor coverings.

• *major appliances* Includes refrigerators, freezers, dishwashers, stoves, ovens, garbage disposals, vacuum cleaners, microwave ovens, air-conditioners, sewing machines, washing machines, clothes dryers, and floor-cleaning equipment.

• *small appliances and miscellaneous housewares* Includes small electrical kitchen appliances, portable heating and cooling equipment, china and other dinnerware, flatware, glassware, silver and other serving pieces, nonelectric cookware, and plastic dinnerware. Excludes personal care appliances.

• *miscellaneous household equipment* Includes computer hardware and software, luggage, lamps and other lighting fixtures, window coverings, clocks, lawn mowers and gardening equipment, hand and power tools, telephone answering devices, personal digital assistants, Internet services away from home, office equipment for home use, fresh flowers and house plants, rental of furniture, closet and storage items, household decorative items, infants' equipment, outdoor equipment, smoke alarms, other household appliances, and small miscellaneous furnishing.

household services Includes the following:

• *personal services* Includes baby sitting, day care, and care of elderly and handicapped persons.

• *other household services* Includes computer information services; housekeeping services; gardening and lawn care services; coin-operated laundry and dry-cleaning of household textiles; termite and pest control products; moving, storage, and freight expenses; repair of household appliances and other household equipment; reupholstering and furniture repair; rental and repair of lawn and gardening tools; and rental of other household equipment.

housekeeping supplies Includes soaps, detergents, other laundry cleaning products, cleansing and toilet tissue, paper towels, napkins, and miscellaneous household products; lawn and garden supplies, postage, stationery, stationery supplies, and gift wrap.

housing tenure "Owner" includes households living in their own homes, cooperatives, condominiums, or townhouses. "Renter" includes households paying rent as well as families living rent free in lieu of wages.

income before taxes The total money earnings and selected money receipts accruing to a consumer unit during the 12 months prior to the interview date. Income includes the following components:

• *wages and salaries* Includes total money earnings for all members of the consumer unit aged 14 or older from all jobs, including civilian wages and salaries, Armed Forces pay and allowances, piece-rate payments, commissions, tips, National Guard or Reserve pay (received for training periods), and cash bonuses before deductions for taxes, pensions, union dues, etc.

• *self-employment income* Includes net business and farm income, which consists of net income (gross receipts minus operating expenses) from a profession or unincorporated business or from the operation of a farm by an owner, tenant, or sharecropper. If the business or farm is a partnership, only an appropriate share of net income is recorded. Losses are also recorded.

• *Social Security, private and government retirement* Includes payments by the federal government made under retirement, survivor, and disability insurance programs to retired persons, dependents of deceased insured workers, or to disabled workers; and private pensions or retirement benefits received by retired persons or their survivors, either directly or through an insurance company.

• *interest, dividends, rental income, and other property income* Includes interest income on savings or bonds; payments made by a corporation to its stockholders, periodic receipts from estates or trust funds; net income or loss from the rental of property, real estate, or farms, and net income or loss from roomers or boarders.

• *unemployment and workers' compensation and veterans' benefits* Includes income from unemployment compensation and workers' compensation, and veterans' payments including educational benefits, but excluding military retirement.

• *public assistance, supplemental security income, and food stamps* Includes public assistance or welfare, including money received from job training grants; supplemental security income paid by federal, state, and local welfare agencies to low-income persons who are aged 65 or older, blind, or disabled; and the value of food stamps obtained.

• *regular contributions for support* Includes alimony and child support as well as any regular contributions from persons outside the consumer unit.

• *other income* Includes money income from care of foster children, cash scholarships, fellowships, or stipends not based on working; and meals and rent as pay.

indexed spending Indexed spending figures compare the spending of particular demographic segments with that of the average household. To compute an index, the amount spent on an item by a demographic segment is divided by the amount spent on the item by the average household. That figure is then multiplied by 100. An index of 100 is the average for all households. An index of 125 means average spending by households in a segment is 25 percent above average (100 plus 25). An index of 75 means average spending by households in a segment is 25 percent below average (100 minus 25). Indexed spending figures identify the consumer units that spend the most on a product or service.

life and other personal insurance Includes premiums from whole life and term insurance; endowments; income and other life insurance; mortgage guarantee insurance; mortgage life insurance; premiums for personal life liability, accident and disability; and other non–health insurance other than homes and vehicles.

market share The market share is the percentage of total household spending on an item that is accounted for by a demographic segment. Market shares are calculated by dividing a demographic segment's total spending on an item by the total spending of all households on the item. Total spending on an item for all households is calculated by multiplying average spending by the total number of households. Total spending on an item for each demographic segment is calculated by multiplying the segment's average spending by the number of households in the segment. Market shares reveal the demographic segments that account for the largest share of spending on a product or service.

millennial generation Americans born between 1977 and 1994.

owner *See* housing tenure.

pensions and Social Security Includes all Social Security contributions paid by employees; employees' contributions to railroad retirement, government retirement and private pensions programs; retirement programs for self-employed.

personal care Includes products for the hair, oral hygiene products, shaving needs, cosmetics, bath products, suntan lotions, hand creams, electric personal care appliances, incontinence products, other personal care products, personal care services such as hair care services (haircuts, bleaching, tinting, coloring, conditioning treatments, permanents, press, and curls), styling and other services for wigs and hairpieces, body massages or slenderizing treatments, facials, manicures, pedicures, shaves, electrolysis.

quarterly spending Quarterly spending data are collected in the interview portion of the Consumer Expenditure Survey. Quarterly spending tables show the percentage of households that purchased an item during an average quarter, and the amount spent during the quarter on the item by purchasers. Not all items are included in the interview portion of the Consumer Expenditure Survey.

reading Includes subscriptions for newspapers, magazines, and books through book clubs; purchase of single-copy newspapers and magazines, books, and encyclopedias and other reference books.

reference person The first member mentioned by the respondent when asked to "Start with the name of the person or one of the persons who owns or rents the home." It is with respect to this person that the relationship of other consumer unit members is determined. Also called the householder or head of household.

region Consumer units are classified according to their address at the time of their participation in the survey. The four major census regions of the United States are the following state groupings:

• *Northeast* Connecticut, Maine, Massachusetts, New Hampshire, New Jersey, New York, Pennsylvania, Rhode Island, and Vermont.

• *Midwest* Illinois, Indiana, Iowa, Kansas, Michigan, Minnesota, Mississippi, Nebraska, North Dakota, Ohio, South Dakota, and Wisconsin.

• *South* Alabama, Arkansas, Delaware, District of Columbia, Florida, Georgia, Kentucky, Louisiana, Maryland, Mississippi, North Carolina, Oklahoma, South Carolina, Tennessee, Texas, Virginia, and West Virginia.

• *West* Alaska, Arizona, California, Colorado, Hawaii, Idaho, Minnesota, Nevada, New Mexico, Oregon, Utah, Washington, and Wyoming.

renter *See* housing tenure.

shelter Includes the following:

• *owned dwellings* Includes interest on mortgages, property taxes and insurance, refinancing and prepayment charges, ground rent, expenses for property management and security, homeowner's insurance, fire insurance and extended coverage, landscaping expenses for repairs and maintenance contracted out (including periodic maintenance and service contracts), and expenses of materials for owner-performed repairs and maintenance for dwellings used or maintained by the consumer unit, but not dwellings maintained for business or rent.

• *rented dwellings* Includes rent paid for dwellings, rent received as pay, parking fees, maintenance, and other expenses.

• *other lodging* Includes all expenses for vacation homes, school, college, hotels, motels, cottages, trailer camps, and other lodging while out of town.

• *utilities, fuels, and public services* Includes natural gas, electricity, fuel oil, coal, bottled gas, wood, other fuels; residential telephone service, cell phone service, phone cards; water, garbage, trash collection; sewerage maintenance, septic tank cleaning; and other public services.

size of consumer unit The number of people whose usual place of residence at the time of the interview is in the consumer unit.

state and local income taxes Includes state and local income taxes withheld in the survey year to pay for income earned in survey year plus additional taxes paid in the survey year to cover any underpayment or underwithholding of taxes in the year prior to the survey.

tobacco and smoking supplies Includes cigarettes, cigars, snuff, loose smoking tobacco, chewing tobacco, and smoking accessories such as cigarette or cigar holders, pipes, flints, lighters, pipe cleaners, and other smoking products and accessories.

transportation Includes the following:

• *vehicle purchases* (net outlay) Includes the net outlay (purchase price minus trade-in value) on new and used domestic and imported cars and trucks and other vehicles, including motorcycles and private planes.

• *gasoline and motor oil* Includes gasoline, diesel fuel, and motor oil.

• *other vehicle expenses* Includes vehicle finance charges, maintenance and repairs, vehicle insurance, and vehicle rental licenses and other charges.

• *vehicle finance charges* Includes the dollar amount of interest paid for a loan contracted for the purchase of vehicles described above.

• *maintenance and repairs* Includes tires, batteries,

tubes, lubrication, filters, coolant, additives, brake and transmission fluids, oil change, brake adjustment and repair, front-end alignment, wheel balancing, steering repair, shock absorber replacement, clutch and transmission repair, electrical system repair, repair to cooling system, drive train repair, drive shaft and rear-end repair, tire repair, vehicle video equipment, other maintenance and services, and auto repair policies.

• *vehicle insurance* Includes the premium paid for insuring cars, trucks, and other vehicles.

• *vehicle rental, licenses, and other charges* Includes leased and rented cars, trucks, motorcycles, and aircraft, inspection fees, state and local registration, drivers' license fees, parking fees, towing charges, tolls on trips, and global positioning services.

• *public transportation* Includes fares for mass transit, buses, trains, airlines, taxis, private school buses, and fares paid on trips for trains, boats, taxis, buses, and trains.

weekly spending Weekly spending data are collected in the diary portion of the Consumer Expenditure Survey. The data show the percentage of households that purchased an item during the average week, and the amount spent per week on the item by purchasers. Not all items are included in the diary portion of the Consumer Expenditure Survey.

Index